# My Story, My Journey

*From Silesia to Scotland*

# My Story, My Journey

*From Silesia to Scotland*

Paul Lippok

Copyright © 2015 by Paul Lippok.

Library of Congress Control Number: 2015903771
ISBN:      Hardcover    978-1-4990-9408-4
           Softcover    978-1-4990-9409-1
           eBook        978-1-4990-9410-7

All rights reserved. No part of this book may be reproduced or transmitted in any form or by any means, electronic or mechanical, including photocopying, recording, or by any information storage and retrieval system, without permission in writing from the copyright owner.

Any people depicted in stock imagery provided by Thinkstock are models, and such images are being used for illustrative purposes only.
Certain stock imagery © Thinkstock.

Print information available on the last page.

Rev. date: 10/09/2015

**To order additional copies of this book, contact:**
Xlibris
800-056-3182
www.Xlibrispublishing.co.uk
Orders@Xlibrispublishing.co.uk
516813

# CONTENTS

Dedication ......................................................................................... ix
Prologue ............................................................................................ xi
My Story, My Journey – from Silesia to Scotland ......................... xiii
'Silesia', the place of my birth ......................................................... xv
Chapter 1   The Lippok Family ....................................................... 1
Chapter 2   My life began in earnest! ............................................ 32
Chapter 3   Our first Christmas in war time ................................ 84
Chapter 4   1940 My adult life began .......................................... 89
Chapter 5   My Career at the Post Office ................................... 100
Chapter 6   My Military Service, at age 17 ................................. 138
Chapter 7   'Captured', my life as a POW .................................. 171
Chapter 8   My home at Viewfield .............................................. 228
Chapter 9   Demobilised and content to be in Tain, Scotland .... 251
Chapter 10  The Authentic Advert ............................................... 316
Chapter 11  Correspondence Courtship - Abridged .................... 323
Chapter 12  First visit to Hameln and my Love .......................... 348
Chapter 13  Ehrentraut's first visit to Tain and our Engagement ..... 399
Chapter 14  Preparation for our Wedding, Viewfield, Scotland ..... 476
Chapter 15  Our Wedding day! ..................................................... 487
Chapter 16  Our Honeymoon ........................................................ 494
Chapter 17  Home at last --- our life together has begun ............ 503
Epilogue .......................................................................................... 527
Acknowledgements and Thanks .................................................... 529

'Lower Silesia – looking towards the Sudeten Mountains'

# Dedication

*To Ehrentraut.*
*My Love, and Mother to our family,*
*for your lifelong unrestrained devotion in trials,*
*sickness and in health.*

# Prologue

"SILESIA"

LOVED AND NEVER FORGOTTEN

MOUNTAINS AND WOODLANDS

WAVING CORNFIELDS

FLOWERING MEADOWS

SPARKLING BROOKS AND RIVERS

WHERE HEARTH AND CRADLE STOOD

THE ENCOUNTER WITH OUR CREATOR

WHERE IT ALL BEGAN

\*\*\*\*\*\*\*\*\*\*\*\*\*\*\*\*\*\*\*\*\*\*\*\*\*\*\*\*\*\*\*\*\*\*\*\*\*\*

# My Story, My Journey – from Silesia to Scotland

This is a frank account of my life. It was not so different from that of our ancestors, until the folly of one man Mr Hitler, who acquired and abused power. Dictatorship and vanity caused him and his cohorts to disregard all human conventions and he left his country and others in ruin. To satisfy his ego, millions had to die at home and in foreign countries. They were forced from their homes leaving everything behind: the earth they had cultivated, sown and harvested; the land they had loved and sung about; where the cradle stood and the final resting place of loved ones for countless generations.

Now, half a century on, I am reminded of a chance meeting with a local resident, who found our conversation sufficiently interesting, to urge me to write my story down and publish it, if possible. As he was about to leave, he remarked "Do not apologise for your 'funny' accent, it comes from the land of your birth. My own ancestors had to leave everything and find a new home". As he departed, his finger pointed to the hills across the blue firth. Had he meant the forced clearances a century ago? Encouraged by our children and friends, here I am about to tell 'My Story'.

A story yes, but in reality it was my journey that made it 'My Story', for which I claim no uniqueness. It was a journey not of my choosing. Who am I then? I am of German origin, born in Gross Strehlitz, a rural town in the Province of 'Silesia' in South Eastern Germany; that is until 1945 when the peace treaty demanded the annexation of 'Silesia and North Eastern Germany' to Poland. Therefore, an atlas of pre-1945 would be helpful. One further guide to finding 'Silesia' in an atlas is between longitude 15-19 and latitude

52-50. Towns are now in the Polish language, although a good atlas or map does print their names in German and Polish.

War and military service brought me to the UK and finally to Scotland. My English vocabulary is not the result of academic teaching, but by listening attentively, reading and a willingness to converse regardless of mistakes, often hilarious, which would have any 'Hippodrome' audience rolling with laughter. You had to be more careful in female company, if you tried to impress with your new limited vocabulary. Now, more than fifty years on, it is possible that you may still find a word which may not be perfect to the learned ear. If that happens, pardon me, have a good laugh and read on.

# 'Silesia',
## THE PLACE OF MY BIRTH

There are many historical books on Silesia, if one is interested in more detail. For the purpose of 'My Story', a conversational aspect will suffice. For that reason and for the benefit of my readers, it is only right, that I should introduce some background history, recalling from my still vivid school history lesson on Silesia. Wherever Silesians meet nowadays, it is inevitable that in familiar gatherings, the subject of our unequalled love for our lost homeland will be mentioned, remembered in Silesian rich poetry and song, with a possible tear or two. More than two thousand years ago, a tribe of Teutonic and Celtic origin from Western and Central Europe, migrated east, to find new pastures. Some 250 miles on, they reached the River Elbe, which rises south in the Sudeten Mountains, flowing north to the North Sea. Water being the lifeblood, some may have settled there and possibly laid the foundations for the modern city of Dresden. Others carried on, until after some 100 miles further east, they came to another river, which at some time was given the name 'Oder'. It flows from south to north, where it joins the Baltic Sea. Finding the land fertile with large areas of fine timber, they decided to settle there. It was the Silingers who made it their home and gave the land its name: 'SILESIA'. There it all began and somewhere there our ancestors were born. The climate too, must have suited them. The reason for it being fertile was the composted layers of fallen trees for many centuries. East of the River Oder were the flat lands, undulating in parts to provide variety. West of the river the land too was fertile with some parts rising towards the Sudeten mountain ridge which stretches from north to south. The mountain ridge rises to 4,500 feet at its highest peak. During Silesia's history the Sudeten became the natural border between Silesia and 'Bohemia' until 1918, when Bohemia became 'Czechoslovakia'. All settlers during Silesia's history made good use of the natural available material. The timber for building purposes and the discovery of sand and limestone added to the advance in their ability to shape their new settlements. As the centuries passed, it was inevitable that the word got round and further migration continued. With it the establishing of some order had begun, helped by experienced administrators among the migrants.

From the east, the first trickle of Slavonic speaking migrants began to appear in Silesia, settling on the east of the River Oder. They were probably the first migrant workers seeking employment. As it became more difficult to acquire land and property in Western Europe, it was no surprise to see greater migration of young aristocrats from Western Europe into Silesia. Their wealth began to stimulate the economy of Silesia. By the 8th century, Silesia had organised itself into four regional administrations with the dominant office in the city of Breslau.

Already by the year 1040, the Bohemian king used Silesia as a bulwark against threats from eastern kings. One could say it was the beginning of using Silesia, with its increasing rising economy, as a ping-pong ball between the different kingdoms. The Bohemian king felt threatened and offered Silesia protection. A further 'boost' to the development of Silesia was the late entry of Christianity by the 9th century. Western Christianity and the skilled migrants played a major part in the development of Silesia. By the 12th century, the number of churches and monasteries built was surprising. Many grand Baroque, later Gothic churches employing Italian artists, created grandeur resulting in competition among town halls, stately homes and universities. Grand monasteries throughout Silesia were not left behind. Some were for the education of clergy and other students, while others were primarily closed cloisters for monks. Building schools to educate boys and girls helped to stimulate the Silesian economy, not forgetting the hospitals and schools, staffed by nuns providing employment and training.

It was the century of Silesia's most famous lady: 'Hedwig', born 1174, the daughter of Count Berthold VI of Andechs, in Thuringia, central Germany. Hedwig, who was a highly educated princess, married Heinrich I of Silesia, a talented administrator. She was an able assistant to her husband. Both lived a devout Christian life, often concerned for the poor in their land. Her husband died at a young age. Her son and heir died at the last battle defeating the Mongols. Leaving the running of the state to able and trusted administrators, she devoted the rest of her life to the care of the poor. She built a church and convent with a hospital at her home in Trebnitz, a small town some ten miles north-east of Silesia's capital Breslau. The beautiful church and hospital built by Hedwig is still operational to this day. Digressing for a moment, it is Trebnitz that will again play a part in my story at a later stage. On the death of her husband, she gave away all her fine dresses, keeping only simple ones for herself. Hedwig is buried in the convent church of Trebnitz. She was later declared a saint, becoming the patron saint of Silesia. It was she who played a major part in bringing weavers from Western Europe to Silesia, settling at the foot of the Sudeten, the melting snow providing the water needed for weaving.

Time to introduce the River Oder, Silesia's lifeblood, {see sketch of Silesia inside back cover} Silesia is likened to a beech leaf, the central vein being the River Oder, which rises in the south of Silesia, meandering north, spilling into the Baltic Sea. Eight tributaries from the Sudeten Mountains feed the Oder from the west, while four major tributaries feed the Oder from the east, draining the flat lands after heavy rainfall. Eighty per cent of the Oder is navigable, a ready-made highway delivering Silesia's goods and products as far as the Baltic Sea and beyond.

A satisfactory supply of water was necessary for the migrant weavers' trade. Among the foothills of the Sudeten Mountains they built their traditional timber houses, side by side in villages. They brought with them their own colourful traditional costumes. During the next centuries the picture of Silesia began to show 'Deutsche Ordnung' {German order} not only in administration, but also in schools and industry. At that time the discovery of iron, pewter and coal called for more tradesmen. As the centuries moved on, so the towns and villages increased. Official statistics recorded that by 1320 AD, 83 towns and 1,715 villages were established in Silesia.

This is a suitable place to mention the 'Magdeburg Town Charter' which Heinrich IV introduced to Silesia. Towns were to be constructed in chessboard fashion, with the Town House in the centre, surrounded by houses built in a square, the church close by, watch towers if affordable, and gateways only from the main roads. In villages, houses had to be built on either side of the roadway, the gables facing the road, and stables and other buildings attached to the end of the house. It is still a familiar pattern in many villages in Germany today.

Another important event occurred at that time, the birth of Johannes Gutenberg in the town of Mainz. His invention of the mechanical printing press was the first advance regarding speed in printing in the world. Books and stationery could now be produced, seen and read as never before by anyone. School books and hymnals, useful tools for poets and music sheets were available. Silesia and its advance in many fields at that time were due to Corvinus, King of Hungary. He wasted no time in calling an assembly of princes and administrators and presented them with a new constitution. He strenuously encouraged the Province's export trade. The early death of Corvinus was mourned by all.

Time does not stand still, due to Silesia's close proximity to Saxony, it was inevitable that the Lutheran Reformation would enter Silesia. It was not welcomed at first and there were skirmishes. The dreadful Thirty Years War was wrongly presented as a war between Catholics and the Lutherans, when in fact it was a war between the crowns under cover of religion. There were no winners, only a weary long-suffering population. With peace at last after thirty years, people were able to start to build life anew. History records the resilience of folk losing no time to rebuild what had been destroyed. From 1650 onwards, there was an awakening of poetry and creative writing. Silesia began almost in explosive fashion to bring poets and writers to the surface. Many of those poems have been set to music and most of them are still sung to most beautiful melodies today.

There was increasing interest by aristocrats with capital to invest in the south of the Province in the growing industrial areas. They invested in building great elaborate mansions and offices. As towns and villages grew, so did the demand for churches, schools and cultural buildings. Sadly, in Silesia, a counter reformation had begun to the detriment of the Reformers, not always in a Christian manner. Many Protestant reformers left Silesia to cross the border into Prussia where they were welcomed. Through time the Silesian population became disenchanted with the Austrian Habsburg as absentee landlords were pocketing the rent. A growing interest was shown by the 'Prince Elector' Friedrich Wilhelm of Prussia & Brandenburg to have the Province of Silesia as a neighbour. That made sense since the same language was spoken. Peace ensued and many reformers came back to Silesia, with both religious faiths living and working together amicably. Worth mentioning is that six churches, called the 'Friedenskirchen' {Churches of Peace} were given to the reformers, a true act of reconciliation, Lutheran and Catholics at last living in peace.

An interesting period followed for Silesia, although still unnoticed, the favoured association with the Prussian kingdom. In 1713, Friedrich Wilhelm I inherited from his grandfather a fair measure of ability to reign as King of Prussia. He saw his role as a family educator and schoolmaster of his subjects and introduced compulsory school attendance. His disciplinary tendency extended over a wide spectrum, including the state and those close to the court. He is credited that by typical Prussian discipline, he swiftly brought his land along the road to recovery. To ensure some sort of security for his kingdom from predators, he required an army. He looked for and engaged commanders who drew from experience and studies of mistakes made by others. He became known as the Soldier King. Though not of great physical height himself, he favoured tall men for his Regiment of Guards, recruiting far and wide, yes even in Scotland. {I was not to know that Scotland would play a part in my life one day}. Wilhelm turned his near bankrupt kingdom into a prosperous country. A stroke of luck came his way to increase the population when the 'Habsburgs' made 20,000 Salzburg Lutherans homeless. The Protestants welcomed the King's invitation to settle in East Prussia {1731-32}.

The Prussian Crown Prince Friedrich discovered he possessed a musical talent with a degree of proficiency playing the flute. He enjoyed playing with musician friends entertaining guests at royal parties. Added to it, there was of course the music of Bach, Beethoven and Mozart, and the literary work of Goethe and Schiller. His friendship with Voltaire had influenced Prince Friedrich's attitude concerning injustice and intolerance. Sadly, his father died in 1740, leaving a young king facing the burden of ruling a country. The young King Friedrich recalled his father's wish to see Silesia released from the Habsburgs, whose interests lay in the earnings from it. He also feared a close alliance between the Habsburg Maria Theresia and the Russian Tsarina Elisabeth. Showing a flair for statesmanship, having his father's well-trained army, and determined not to be intimidated by a 'pair of petticoats', he mobilised his army. It took three bruising battles to send the Austrians home. In short, Silesia became a part of the Prussian kingdom, but was left to continue to govern herself. It meant the severing of the umbilical cord that had linked Silesia to Bohemia.

More schools were built and freedom of worship for both religious faiths. His keen interest in Silesia and its rich potential in feeding his people are recorded in a well-known painting, of which there was one in our home. It shows Friedrich seeing men and women in a field of potatoes, pointing out to them not to pick the small green tubers on top of the plant, but to dig out the many large tubers hidden in the ground. It was a new imported 'fruit' from overseas. All Silesians remember old Father Fritz with affection. He died in 1786 and was succeeded by Wilhelm II.

At last, at the beginning of the 18$^{th}$ century, the city of Breslau had its own university, an impressive architectural building. Some say it is out-stripped by the extraordinary beauty of the 'Aula', the Graduation Hall. Further, it was the first university that had both the Catholic and Lutheran Theological Faculties under one roof, which did Breslau proud. The first Ecumenical establishment perhaps? At the turn of the 17$^{th}$ century, there had been an increase of Jewish migration into Germany from Eastern Europe. In due time the government of the day afforded full citizenship to its Jewish population. Many settled in Silesian towns, establishing shops etc. Sadly, at the same time, the defeated French army on their way home from Russia, battle weary and hungry, caused vandalism and misery in Silesian towns and villages.

'Silesian traditional Costume',

'One of Silesia's beautiful churches',

'Townhall in Silesia's capital Breslau'

Leaving aside the destructive short period of defeated French troops passing through part of Silesia on their way home, there is more to say about Silesia. Already at the beginning of 19$^{th}$ century medicinal springs were being discovered all along the Sudeten Mountains and the establishment of spas had begun in earnest. Small villages grew around them which in German is known as 'Bad', meaning spa. To name just three; Bad Aldheide, Bad Reinerz, where in 1826 Frederic Chopin, with his mother and two sisters, took the 'waters' and Bad Salzbrunn where Kaiser Wilhelm sent his wife to take the 'baths' with excellent results in regard to her weak lungs. I am proud that Sir Winston Churchill came in early 1900 to test the spas of my homeland. With some eight worldwide known spas well patronised by the wealthy and the working population, it is good to know that today those spas are thriving in their glory. The trim walks and colourful display of flowerbeds and borders is a 'Mecca' to see. Spas and flowerbeds alone though are not sufficient to keep a country alive.

Even more exciting for me is to bring to the reader's notice, the fact that Count Pükler-Burhaus called the British engineer John Baildon (1772-1846) to Silesia. Baildon built a coke blast furnace in 1796, the first in Silesia and outside Britain. He also constructed the first iron bridge across the 'Striegau' waters. It was the time when it became necessary to take a closer look at Silesia's administration. It is believed that it was in Old Fritz's head to ease the burden on Breslau. It was decided to give the southern large industrial heartland its own administration, which included our home and would be known as Upper Silesia. The city of Breslau would remain the capital of all Silesia. The sub-administration for Upper Silesia was in the town of Oppeln, with a population over 30,000 and some 60 miles south of Breslau. Twenty miles south of Oppeln was our home, Gross Strehlitz with a population of 12,000 at the end of 1800.

Silesia continued its industrial expansion at a greater rate with investments by the aristocracy and increasingly by the industrial elite who began to realise the potential wealth of coal and minerals. The start of a regulated apprenticeship in the various trades soon paid dividends. Inventing and producing tools and equipment for a rapidly modernising industry was paramount. While the horse was still the predominant form of transportation for man and commerce, it seemed everywhere was excitement with the arrival of iron wheels. It occupied the minds of engineers to dream and decide for what they might be useful. The answer was obvious, fix them to anything you wish to move, as heavy as you like. Just think of the British engineer James Watt and his steam engine, how it hastened progress in the development of coal-fired engines. Silesia had plenty of coal and rich deposits of iron ore. It was on 7th December 1835 that the first German railway engine with four small carriages travelled on steel rails from the town of Fürth to Nuremberg, a distance of 4.8 miles {6.04 km.} in nine minutes. The race to build railways in Europe had taken off. Silesian steel manufacturing capacity was well placed to supply all requirements. The rise in demand for shipping the goods on the River Oder was welcomed.

Progress there was, but all was not well regarding the weavers in their homes. Suddenly they found themselves at odds with the new mechanical inventions to weave cloth which they had woven for centuries. It did not take long for the weavers to start rioting, entering factories and damaging the new looms that robbed them of their livelihood. It was a sign of the times to come in other trades. If you were to ask miners, their story was different. With the advance of mechanical aids to extract coal, it was a blessing. Coal was the 'gold' to fire melting pots to manufacture steel. Coal was what Upper Silesia had in abundance. The benefit of it was soon felt widely. Having had miners in our family, I feel a sense of pride. I wish to record that mines and factories were often owned by aristocrats who were serious in the business of caring for their employees. Already at the turn of the century, miners had hot showers at the pithead and their own changing locker. Miners left their workplace in clean clothes, as they commuted by ordinary passenger trains, some up to fifteen miles. With railway lines being laid mile after mile, it must have seemed astonishing the number of bridges that had to be built. No less amazing was the building of gasworks in towns and cities. I remember well in my early youth seeing the 'gas-lighter' on his bicycle with a pole, to pull the little chain on the lamp to light it. It must have been some century. From the horse to the railway and to the car, the century of speed had begun. Agriculture too began to feel the benefit of steel with the manufacture of steel ploughs etc. It was possible to plough deeper and was less strenuous on the horse. The multi-plough to be driven by a steam engine was a reality on the design board.

Before looking into our family, let me take you on an imaginary journey by train, to introduce you to my homeland Silesia and its countryside prior to 1945. My sketch drawing on the inside back cover may help. We enter Silesia from the west {Dresden}, travelling east for a short distance, gradually turning in a southerly direction towards the city and ministerial capital of Silesia, Breslau. Looking into the distance on our right, you can see the outline of the Sudeten Mountains. Between us and the mountains the country is undulating with towns and villages and their inspiring church steeples and town houses. Looking left towards the east the land is a vast mass of green fields in spring, yellow ripening grain in summer. All would be white in winter with frost and snow a foot or more deep. The outline of the city of Breslau would now be begging you to watch through the window, tall factory chimney-stacks, impressive mansions, numerous steeples and towers and bridges over the many arms of the River Oder as it passes through the town on account of the flat and sandy soil. Little wonder Breslau is called the 'Venice' of Silesia.

Travelling on south you can still see the outline of the Sudeten and the beautiful scenery of lush meadows and well-managed forests - on either side beautiful, colourful villages and churches, more towns and their magnificent Baroque or Gothic churches with steeples reaching towards heaven. It does not take much imagination to hear their mighty bells echo across the countryside. Continuing south there are flat lands, meadows, cornfields and forests, with the Polish border on average only 50 miles away. The scenery changes little as we travel towards the invisible borderline of Lower and Upper Silesia. Some 65 miles from Breslau the train comes to a halt in the town of Oppeln. With its 45,000 population, it was the administrative city for Upper Silesia. Only 20 miles on we have reached my hometown, Gross Strehlitz, where we disembark. The train will reach its final destination 30 miles on, in the town of Beuthen, right in the heartland of the industrial and mining area, the city boundary being part of the Polish border.

Gross Strehlitz is first mentioned in the year 1271 in connection with a timber-constructed hunting castle surrounded by forests and agriculture. A fire destroyed the timber castle and parts of the small town. A larger stone built castle is officially mentioned in 1303 as 'CASTRUM STRELECENSE', with it also the town. The castle in its lifetime has been enlarged and modernised during the centuries. At a much later stage around 1700, a clock tower and flag pole had been added with a walkway just below the four clocks giving access to the flag pole. At this stage more important than the castle is the town itself since it was our home. The building of the town followed the formal 'Magdeburg' construction. The town square contained two- and three-storey buildings with a road leading in and out at each corner. The Town House with its offices was at the east end of the square. At the front stood a lead sculpture of a huntsman blowing his horn and holding his dog on a lead. The large area in front of the Town House provided space for the weekly open air market and public functions of all kinds.

Around the square or 'Ring' as it is called, are tall houses on all four sides with shops on the ground floor and living quarters and offices on the upper floors. The town expanded from the square on three sides. On the south side a short street of some fifty yards led to the back entrance of the castle, therefore called Castle Street. In my time, on one side of the short street stood the three-storey building of the town's Savings Bank, with the bank itself on the ground floor and offices on the other two floors. On the other side stood an equally large building with a doctor's practice on the ground floor and living quarters on the upper floors. This particular area will eventually become familiar in the life of my family.

In some areas of Germany the owner's farmland is around his individual house, as are the stables and barns. Not in Silesia, where the house and farm buildings are next to each other, separated by a fence or wall, thus forming villages. Next to the living quarters are the animals' quarters. Horses were mostly stabled opposite the house with other useful small buildings to form a yard. The barns stood away from the habitable buildings for safety reasons as they were vulnerable to lightning strikes. The fields stretched beyond the buildings.

This is the time to close my attempt to provide the background to my homeland which our ancestors created by their sweat and determination.

# Chapter 1

## The Lippok Family

The era of 'My Story' is the moment when the dormant world of our family ancestors comes alive. It was always regretted that our ancestors could not be traced further back than the 18$^{th}$ century. Attempts were even made to look into records outside our own Parish.

I am quoting from my brother's records of the short space of time preparing to escape the Russian front only hours away, "……end of January 1945 a foot of snow and frost, it was by the grace of God that our Dad's presence of mind made him gather a small collection of ancestral and family documents and photographs to take with us, as we hastily gathered warm clothing and food, before locking the door, to flee the Russian front which was expected to sweep into our town Gross Strehlitz by the morning…." {I myself at that time was in a comfortable POW camp.}

The genealogy of the Lippok male members leading to our grandfather Johann Lippok:

Great-great-grandfather Bernhard Lippok, born 1773/2?, married Marianne Panek on 20 November 1798.

Great-grandfather Matheus Lippok, born 18 February 1816, married Marianne Gromotka on 21 July 1839.

Grandfather Johann Lippok, born 13 May 1853, married Thekla Pyka, born 23 September 1862, on 13 February 1886.

All three marriages had taken place in the Catholic Parish Church of Gross Strehlitz.

Little is known about Great-great-grandfather Bernhard. Having been baptised in the parish church means his family would have been living within the town boundary and found employment there. Thus

Gross Strehlitz became the focal place for our branch of the Lippok family, a town in every sense of the word within the periphery of rural countryside.

When counties were introduced Gross Strehlitz became a county town with its boundary stretching some fifteen miles east to the Polish border, and west to the River Oder. Since limestone was found ages ago, it seemed natural that limestone quarrying took place on the eastern boundary of the town. Its success led to a significant number of employees. One other important aspect for the town was the relative nearness of some 30 miles to the aforementioned industrial area of coal mines and the manufacturing of steel etc. As a market town it offered a variety of opportunities in addition to shops. Think of all the trades; bakers, grocers, tailors, shoemakers, etc., schools and offices, not forgetting a large brewery, and there was also the castle, the Castle of Gross Strehlitz.

It was a decisive moment in our family when Great-grandfather Matheus applied in 1834 at the castle office to be apprenticed in the castle gardens. With his acceptance followed the 110 year employment of the Lippok family at the castle. The national well-thought-out state approved apprenticeship for most trades was already in place, requiring a signed agreement between employer and employee. On completion of apprenticeship a State Certificate was given. There are family records of Matheus having been accepted as an apprentice and a completion certificate was handed to him at the end of his successful apprenticeship. To the delight of his parents and himself he was taken into full time employment as a gardener. Other family members found other employment in town.

The following is an abridged history of Gross Strehlitz Castle for anyone interested, especially the future Lippok family wherever their home may be one day. Recalling that the original timber castle had been destroyed by fire there is proof that it had been rebuilt in stone and extended from its original design.

One of the early owners of the newly rebuilt castle was Duke Albert 1320-1370, who in 1347 married Agnes the daughter of the then count of Magdeburg. She too apparently added to the interior décor. Borders at that time were not always a hindrance to travel and communication among the aristocracy. Therefore owners were not always of western Germanic origin. With Slavonic aristocracy in close proximity, mixed marriages were not uncommon. One other known benefactor of Gross Strehlitz Castle was Count von Redern {1560-1600} who refurbished the castle exterior and interior. Others were Georg Hohenzollern von Ansbach, also Lady Margareth of Schnellendorf of the Colonna line. All played their part in the continuity of Gross Strehlitz Castle. What also has to be remembered is the fact that much of the town grounds were the property of the castle owner. Every citizen had to pay his tithe to the castle, which was common in every land.

The expansion of the town itself began after 1750, with the old town walls beginning to be used for other projects in the town. During the 1800s the town truly expanded and the population of the town increased. On the right of the castle a new wing was added consisting of 20 comfortable rooms on the upper floor - all for the benefit of shooting guests during the season, of which there were a number during the year. On the ground floor a new laundry was installed with a drying room and a full-size hand operated mangle. From the above mentioned guest wing a horse-shoe shaped brick extension was added to match the existing wing. It provided accommodation for two families, one for the housemaster, and the other for the head butler. Attached to the housemaster's house was the attractive stone built back-gate façade of the castle. The central twelve foot wide opening was fitted with a pair of eight foot high cast iron gates. On either side of the central opening a three foot wide, seven foot high cast iron pedestrian gate was fitted. From there you walked past the town's Saving Bank and you were in the town square. Adjoining the back gate façade on its left side were two villas. Attached to those was a ten foot high and a three hundred foot long stone wall, separating the castle from the town.

Returning to the castle family history, with the death of Count Philipp Colonna an inheritance problem arose. The hereditary commission in such matters approved Count Andreas Maria Renard as the next heritor. It proved to be a fortunate decision, the year 1815.

Count Andreas' parental home was at the foothills of the southern Sudeten, where his father had an extensive arable and woodland estate. In addition, he also had large interests in the coal and steel industry relatively close to his property. Andreas shared his father's interests, but showed a preferred interest in land and woodlands management.

The estate of Gross Strehlitz Castle included some four or five separate farming units within the county border. Apart from fertile cropping it had large well-managed woodlands, with timber always in great demand. A determined young man, Count Renard installed the first steam-driven sawmill on his estate near the town. It proved a great success. As regards the farming units, all managers had attended an agriculture college. Those units would have many pairs of heavy horses to pull the four-wheel wagons customary in Silesia. Always there would be a number of cottages for the employees and their family. A monthly inspection by the Chief Inspector was the norm.

The estate paymaster was driven by coach once a month round the out-of-town farmsteads to pay the customary monthly wages. An imposing large Estate Office stood at the edge of town within castle grounds.

The large garden was a mile east from the castle itself but still within the town boundary, and only half a mile from the town centre. How did one get to the castle garden? From the castle you walk a mile through the small park and you come to the main highway from north to south which passes through the town centre. Crossing the road you are in the one square mile castle garden. The garden is walled-in and surrounded by town houses on all sides. Carts and horses must follow the road north for half a mile before they can enter the garden. Count Renard loved his garden and its produce. He added a number of glass houses to allow exotic plants and trees to grow and to be used at the castle to good and useful effect.

The young Count Renard had been on several visits to England for the purpose of education. Among other interests, he discovered a real love for horses and horse racing, thus becoming an expert on horses. On other visits to Britain he also took a good look at parks and lawn management. In fact he sent his head gardener to England on a lengthy appraisal of fine gardens and parks. Soon a complete 'refurbishing' of the front of the castle was begun.

Count Renard invested much money and labour redesigning and beautifying the front of his home. A fine gravel drive from the stables, widened several yards as it approached the castle. A hundred yards past the castle it narrowed and crossed a major public road into the large park. To the front of the castle, beyond the wide drive, a splendid lawn led to a hundred square yard lake with water plants, etc.

There was no doubt; his visit to England really whetted his appetite for classic horses. On more than one occasion he would bring a pair of them to his castle to cross breed. His next ambition soon followed, to build a new and enlarged exercise hall which impressed friends and visitors. A new coach hall was added for larger well-upholstered coaches. Stabling too was enlarged and above a number of comfortable single rooms was provided for stable boys from out of town and visiting drivers.

One more important item to mention, the Count completely renovated the large park which is divided from the castle grounds by the main road I mentioned before. The park had a few miles of walkways which were wide enough to allow castle coaches to be driven on. The variety of trees and other woodlands was huge. The park was open to the public at all times, apart from one half-mile private driveway. At a certain place the walkway gradually rises to a height providing excellent sledging in winter. The large pond in the park was private for the owners to row small boats. Silesian winters lasted from Christmas until mid-March. The pond would freeze to a depth of some 18 inches. A third of the pond was for the cutting and moving of 18-inch ice blocks to the castle's thick-walled ice house to store venison and other game for the winter and beyond. Two thirds of the ice blocks would be sold to the brewery. The other two thirds of the lake during the deep frost period was available to the townsfolk to skate on.

True, Gross Strehlitz Castle has never been one of architectural grandeur. It has always been a hunting castle with its famous hunting potential. Looking at the front of it there are four pillars supporting a ten yard long balcony. The balcony allows coaches to drive under it, thus allowing guests to disembark dry in inclement weather. The main entrance under the balcony is an eight foot wide double door which opens into a spacious corridor to allow muddy boots to be removed. On each side of the entrance hall the walls display antlers of various sizes, and if exceptional the name of the one who shot it is recorded. The fifteen yards long hallway leads into the large inner entrance hall. Briefly, to the right are the owner's private rooms and to the left the children's playroom with the children's maid's room next to it and family guest rooms including the Countess' personal maid's room. Returning to the entrance hall, a few more paces take you into the main hall. Turning round facing the entrance hall, on each side are the wide stairs to the upper floor. There, the large dining room is in the centre with the three full-height glass doors leading on to the balcony. On the right of the dining room is the 'Blue' Salon, and the 'Yellow' Salon. On the left of the dining room is the 'Mirror' Salon. Other private rooms are on the right and family guestrooms to the left. Continuing along the right corridor is the great ballroom. At the end of the ballroom is the corridor where on the left is the large and beautiful chapel, which since 1500 has served the owners, Catholic or Lutherans. At the back of the altar is the door to the clock tower. At the left end of the castle are several rooms for female staff who live-in. A stair leads down to the store rooms and bathrooms for the staff, and an exit door.

Facing the castle from the town is the back entrance for tradesmen and deliveries. On the left are the two-storey wings of the housemaster's and butler's living apartments, attached to the left wing of the castle with stores and the large washroom and the old large functional ironing box. At the horse-shoe bend on the upper floor are the hunting guests' rooms. In the centre is a ten foot wide arched opening under the guest rooms into an inner courtyard. Once inside the twenty five yards square area, on the left is the butler's domain. Also here is the main room where the most valuable porcelain and all silver cutlery is washed, polished and stored by the butler and his assistant. Those items are never washed or polished in the main kitchen. There is a room for the butler to rest. Straight ahead of the square is the double door entrance into the main hall, used only occasionally. A door on the right of the square leads into the corridor where the linen store and the large kitchen are located.

It has taken me only one page to describe the castle within its walls. Yet, it had taken centuries to build and furnish it. So what is it all about the Gross Strehlitz Castle, one may ask? For the Lippok family it became a place of reality, providing employment, sustenance and a home. Evidently Matheus Lippok did well in the castle garden, which pleased the head gardener, who occasionally sent Matheus to the castle delivering produce from the garden. If one was willing, there were always opportunities to do honest favours to earn pocket money around the castle.

Great-grandfather Matheus at age 23 married Marianne Gromotka on 21 July 1839 in the old Roman Catholic Parish Church in Gross Strehlitz. It is only a guess, that after the birth of their first child they would have found accommodation in one of the castle's cottages, at the edge of town. Family history speaks of a contented great-grandfather. We have no record of the number or gender of children born. Important is the fact that one, our Granddad Johann {John} was born 13 May 1853 and baptised in the old parish church and attended the town public school. With Granddad Johann's arrival family records became authentic. He grew up in a family where church and faith meant a great deal. It was no surprise that he wanted to be a young altar server at church. Among his siblings he was the one that showed an early interest in the castle's gardens. He spent time after school and lessons helping his father and getting rides on the wagon, and no doubt an occasional grip of the reins.

When the time came to leave school at age 14, he made his formal appearance at the castle office and arrived home with an apprenticeship paper in his hand. As the first few months went by the head gardener seemed to be pleased with his enthusiasm. It was understood that Granddad would have met Count Renard on his regular visit to the garden, inspecting his exotic trees and shrubs in the large greenhouses. He completed his apprenticeship with recommendations in the year 1873. The estate manager was happy for Granddad Johann to be given full employment. Like everyone before him he still had much to learn in such a large garden. Interesting to record that from that time on two of the Lippok family were employed at the castle. What was also known was the early teaching in the family regarding the art of saving from their wages. Granddad also apparently discovered a love for singing which is interesting because he joined the church choir in his early twenties.

Count Renard passed away in 1874 after a relatively long life and was much missed not only at the castle but also in town and around his estate. Count Andreas Maria Renard was regarded as a generous benefactor to the town and estate. He had seen the world take the great leap from horse to steam engines. He had a reputation for being fair to his employees and labourers, often concerned when there was illness in the home, etc. Count Renard saw a need in town as it expanded, and by 1870 he planned and financed the building of a 'Gymnasium' {grammar school}. All pupils attended 'Volkschule' {public school} at age six, until fourth year. Those who passed the qualifying exams could attend the Gymnasium. All others stayed on until class eight. The Gymnasium was fee-paying, unless you qualified for a bursary or other assistance. Latin was obligatory, either French or English could be chosen. Count Renard's reputation as a benefactor is recorded in the annals of the town. He survived the opening of his Gymnasium by one year. In appreciation the Gymnasium was called 'Die Johanneum'.

With Count Andreas Renard's passing and the premature death of his son, the castle again required the appropriate Commission to establish the next rightful owner. It was Count Tschirschky who took over the estate. Through some distant relative he was entitled to extend his name Tschirschky-Renard. He had every intention to continue in line with Count Andreas Renard's plans for the Estate.

During his apprenticeship Granddad Johann made it well known that he was particularly interested in the garden horses. The head gardener obviously was aware of it. It was said in family circles, Granddad believed in God's wisdom that the coach driver for the garden horses was due to retire. Unknown to him the head gardener must have mentioned it to the estate Director. When the time came Granddad Johann was indeed given the offer to take over the garden horses, which he accepted with thanks. Marriage was not yet on his mind.

Everyone's life is shaped not only in the confines of our home, but by people and all matters around us. Life did go on outside the confines of the castle. There was the marriage of our Granddad-to-be. Johann had taken his time to choose the lady whom he thought to be the right one. At age 33 he married Thekla Pyka, age 24, on 13 February 1886. With both of them members of the church choir he must have had an eye on her as she too was about Granddad's height, six feet. Their marriage was blessed at the old Parish Church in town. Theirs would be a happy marriage and in the meantime their attention was to find a place where to prepare a home.

At the same time life outside the home was not all a march of glory. In politics it was certainly not a case of calm waters. In the land of commerce there was something of great interest to report. It was the completion of the railway line from Breslau to the town of Beuthen. It meant it was then possible to travel by train from Berlin all the way south, passing through the capital Breslau, on to the town of Oppeln, 30 kilometres on to our town Gross-Strehlitz and finish at Beuthen, at the border of Poland and the centre of the industrial area. Other connecting lines to the left and right followed. There were great celebrations say the records. Now one could travel by train from Berlin to Gross Strehlitz.

As regards the affairs of state, it was Chancellor Bismark who tried his best to negotiate agreements with neighbouring parties. He proved to be a shrewd negotiator and did achieve success with Russia and others. He wanted to achieve greater unity with some of the smaller German dukedoms. King Wilhelm I of Prussia occasionally had differences with the Chancellor, but did trust the man who often proved himself to be right. The unification of other German provinces allowed Wilhelm I to become Kaiser of the new German Reich. To mention just one anecdote regarding the Kaiser, commenting to friends he said: "It is not easy to be a Kaiser under Chancellor Bismark". Bismark was successful in persuading the Austrian Kingdom to join in an alliance with Germany and Russia. Russia and Austria turning eyes to the Balkans, caused fear of a possible war, but Bismark used his negotiating skill to good effect. Peace in Europe was worth more to him than the Balkans. The Franco-German war 1870/71 was a distraction from Bismark's idea of bringing small German dukedoms into a united Germany. When eventually the

Kaiser was offered the crown of the new 'German Reich', he hesitated at first, but did accept after giving it further thought. Bismark became generally known as the honest broker, which he was. It did not hinder Russia further directing its sights on the Balkans. Thus the Mediterranean now became a focal point for Austria and Britain.

Bismark began to see the danger of a war and turned his attention to a possible agreement between Russia and Austria to which Germany would add its peaceful intention; an alliance to calm waters. It was also an opportune time to make good use of new-found materials and energies, to develop the possibilities to make life less harsh for those whose life was hardest. Kaiser Wilhelm I died 9 March 1888 in his 91st year. Records tell of great sadness throughout the land for a much loved and much respected Kaiser.

A wave of hope in the successor Friedrich III was short lived, due to his sudden death only 99 days after his father. Confidence in the successor Kaiser Wilhelm II, a grandson of Queen Victoria, was at best mixed. There was hope that he would be the person to reconcile differences between the political factions. He enjoyed approval and cheering in political company. He loved riding in full regalia through the streets of Berlin, loved to be recognised and admired. Others were raising questions. His idea of enlarging colonies in Africa and his dream of his own 'High Sea Fleet' raised eyebrows in some government offices and in military quarters. Those who could not wait were the ever growing industrialists, like Krupp and Siemens who expanded rapidly looking even for military orders, which began to happen. For unknown reasons, the Kaiser with approval in influential Government departments, had decided not to renew the German-Russian non-aggression treaty, much against Bismark's advice, and eventually led to his dismissal by the Kaiser in March 1890. Among some of the competent diplomats it was viewed as a watershed between common-sense and madness. As expected by many it was viewed by the Tsar as an affront. The Tsar described the Kaiser as an uneducated young upstart. Russia lost no time and offered to join the 'Triple Alliance', Britain, France and Russia. Bismark viewed it with earnest foreboding. How right he was. Worse was to come when the Kaiser in October 1908, at an interview with his Chancellor regarding the encirclement of Germany, raised his voice saying: "You Englanders are crazy, crazy like March hares" {an undiplomatic remark that should not have got past the office, but it did, which led to its publication in the London Daily Telegraph, 28 October 1908}. Historians described it as the beginning of a downward trend in German politics. Comment regarding the Kaiser was heard among the people: "mehr Schein - als Sein" {more appearance - than being}.

This was the political scene as the Lippok family began to appear. Granddad's anxiety, or rather prayer, to find a home was granted when the elderly garden coachman retired and Granddad's hope was realised when told he could move into the vacated house in the garden. It was nothing grand, I suppose normal for the time. It had a large kitchen cum sitting-room and two bedrooms, paraffin lamps and there was a toilet, outside of course, plus a timber shed to house a pig, a goat for milk, chickens and a garden for himself. These were part of the perks and may well have been part of the wage. A fifteen minute walk took you to the town centre, church, school and castle.

Eight children were born in their new home, the oldest Valentin born 1888, Anna 1891, Franziska 1895, Franziskus {Franz} 1897 our Dad, Hedwig 1900, Vincent 1902, Paul 1905 and Elisabeth {Else} 1908. At least Granddad had a home, a bit crowded but that's how it was, and order ruled. I should mention it, like Granddad all were six feet tall, apart from Aunt Franziska. Rule no. 1 was stand and walk straight. It was adhered to by males and females. Both parents loved their children and did what was right which clearly showed as they grew up ready to apply for jobs. It was a home that had all the ingredients for happiness. The cottage, being on its own near the end of the castle garden, had ample space to have fun in a healthy environment, all around you only greenery, plants and all kinds of vegetables. The head gardener's house was half a mile away within the garden.

In the meantime Count Tschirschky-Renard declared his intention to continue to manage the estate in the late Count Renard's vision. It appeared that the staff around him were happy. An item of interest was the fact that Count Tschirschky-Renard had contact with the Kaiser's residence in Berlin. He also had long experiences of the valued potential hunting on the castle estate. After the first invitation, which the Kaiser accepted, followed another four visits between 1890 and 1905. Those were always grand occasions which the elder of my uncles and aunts could remember, even our Dad at age seven. Surely, you will not begrudge me moments of pride having had my family in close proximity to the highest person in the country?

On one of those hunting visits the Kaiser shot his 50,000[th] prey, a white male pheasant. A commemorative stone with an inscription is still at that place two miles from the castle. These were exciting occasions as two of our uncles were old enough to volunteer as beaters. Wonderful stories were told regarding my uncles earning their pocket money and food during the hunts of which there were many throughout the year, one of the advantages of being employed at the castle. The elder aunts also had opportunities by volunteering to help in the kitchen, rooms, or the laundry particularly during the shooting season. The large garden too needed help during ripening time, fruit and potato picking etc. Always welcome opportunities!

Driving the garden horses meant Granddad Johann would be required to bring all sorts of requisites to the castle. It was one of his jobs to move heavy wood containers with trees, palms, and other such decoration at the front of the castle in the springtime. During the days when the Kaiser came to hunt, there was more work for Granddad harnessing horses onto coaches to drive the visitors to the hunt area. An early rise was the order of the day, coaches had to be cleaned and prepared, horses groomed and hooves blackened. Uncle Valentin, the oldest, had the opportunity to see the Kaiser at close hand; so did the older daughters who helped as room cleaners. Our Dad was only seven when he too could remember watching at a short distance the party leaving the castle for the shoot. Invited counts and aristocrats would bring their own butler. If they travelled with their own coach, they had their own coach driver. The many bedrooms above the stables were well used.

Countrywide a professional huntsman had to serve a well organised apprenticeship. You were trained to know all about game and their management, breeding, feeding, etc., and also good knowledge of forestry, most intensively the knowledge of your hunting weapon. You also had to be able to play the hunting bugle, {not everyone managed to blow one}. On any of the large shoots there were many aristocrats, etc., taking part each with his own huntsman. A group of four or more huntsmen all in their traditional green uniform, would gather at one end of the castle and, with bugle playing traditional hunting tunes, march up to the castle at 6 a.m. to awaken the parties. By ten in the morning it was a beautiful sight to see gleaming coaches and horses.

Without any references to politics, My Story would be lacking substance, in so far as it affected not only our family, but everyone. While Kaiser Wilhelm was hunting at Gross Strehlitz Castle, the waves of his dismissal of Chancellor Bismark began to be felt in Europe generally. Bismark's ability to negotiate successfully in difficult situations no longer available, it was beginning to raise questions and unease about the Kaiser's ideas of Germany becoming a world power, 'A place in the sun', meaning colonies in Africa, and a Navy to match Britain was his ambition. Not simple foreign diplomacy, but it had to be world diplomacy. In spite of the Kaiser portraying himself as being worker-friendly, there was growing discontent regarding low wages and poor housing in comparison to the building of magnificent villas by industrial barons, whose hunger to produce guns and battleships kept on. As time went on the Kaiser seemed determined to prove his status. Whilst his grandfather had been an emperor of a plain and unassuming character, it became apparent that his successor was not. It is said that he muddled reality with pretence and revelled in self-esteem. Believing in military power and might, his attitude towards those who expressed caution, was dismissive, to the point of accusing them of abdicating their loyalty to the Fatherland. The result was the new German Federation and its policy 'to catch up on Britain', fostering expansion in manufacturing excellence; Siemens Electrical, Daimler Motors, etc. With the growing manufacture of steel, the Ruhr region competed with Upper Silesia in steel processing and manufacturing. The Kaiser and his dream of having his own 'High Sea Fleet', could become a reality. Thus, the encirclement of Germany was complete. More was to come, when later in the German parliament, most parties demanded the Kaiser dismiss his

Chancellor, von Bülow. Just as well, that no one could have foreseen the consequences the people and our homeland would witness in the next thirty years.

Where there is life there is death, and one follows the other irrespectively, the high and the low; and so it did around the Castle of Gross Strehlitz, when in 1908 Count Tschirschky-Renard passed away. The Estate once more was left with no rightful heir. A Commission had once more to determine the rightful heir: it was Count Karl von Brühl-Renard, a grandson of the deceased Count Andreas Maria Renard. The home of the von Brühl's is a well-known splendid residence in Saxony. The family had connections with Berlin and the Government elite. They also were benefactors in no small measure in the historic city of Dresden, Saxony. Extraordinary, miraculous, a few beautiful buildings were not badly damaged during the bombing of Dresden in 1945, others, expertly restored again. Granddad found Count Brühl friendly on his first meeting, when delivering at the castle. In due time having seen Granddad's deportment he asked him to be his second coach driver, which he did with style and pride.

Between the last few years of the old and new century there were some remarkable moments or events which I like to record for the benefit of our family and others interested. A milestone for our town in 1904 was the completion and consecration of the new Catholic Parish Church - a church, with a bell tower with four bells, and for the times, a much advanced organ. The town needed a new church with an impressive bell tower, complementing the Lutheran Church and the Town House. All three buildings survived the horrors of war in 1945. It also has a wonderful crib, with 'Josef' at four feet tall and the camel to match. It had been decided not to demolish the old church tower, as it seemed to be in a reasonably good state. It became the town's lookout tower for fire or whatever.

At the same time a far more impressive building was being constructed in our Silesian capital, the famous 'Breslau Century Hall'. The architect, Max Berg {1870-1947} had been commissioned to construct the first outstanding reinforced concrete round cupola building of such size in Europe, and the world. The cupola is 42 meters in height with 65 square meters diameter light admittance. The structure is supported on four half apses. The focal point of entry is the grandstand, with the then largest organ in the world. The Hall can seat 5,000 and standing 4,200, or 20,000 standing. It survived the Russian bombing and artillery pounding in 1945.

While the Kaiser's politics continued on a precarious road and certain sections of the public expressed discontent, others already talked of war, and in Berlin the high-life flourished. Trains were getting faster and the public were ever keener to travel by rail, even if only 20 kilometres, with the possibility to visit grandparents or friends. Train companies saw the chance and introduced three classes of travel. On went the building of branch lines like 'tentacles' over the country.

It seemed that the young Lippok family was growing up too by the beginning of the second decade. The boys and girls did well at school and some of them may even have qualified to attend grammar school {'Gymnasium'}, but for the lack of money to pay the fees. It was the time when Granddad's famous words were instilled in his children, backed up by his own tall stature: "Good manners, respect, honesty and carrying yourself well does not mean subservience, rather the first steps to promotion". It became the family motto and was certainly heeded, as well as being followed into the next generation, as we know, and it did us no harm.

One left school having completed eight years and having done well, which pleased the parents no doubt. It was now time to decide where to look for employment. The opportunities with Granddad Johann at the castle were more promising. There was always the garden for a start, which was not to be disdained or the stables for the boys, or the opportunities for the girls in the family in the castle itself, with staff leaving to get married or any other opportunities that become available.

Aunt Anna the eldest of the girls had taken up an offer from Count Brühl to go to his home castle at Seifersdorf in Saxony, to join the female staff there. It was to be a fruitful experience in a busy castle with constant important visitors. Uncle Valentin six feet tall at just 18 was keen to join the Horse Guards in Berlin. He preferred helping at the stables rather than the garden. Count Brühl was pleased to write his commendation and Uncle Valentin at nineteen left home for

Berlin. That meant two of the family had left home. Aunt Franziska had no ambition to seek employment far from home. The opportunity arose when the Head Forester offered Granddad the opportunity for Aunt Franziska to be housemaid at his home. She was happy to accept the offer. His spacious house stood in the large park. There was a large garden and a number of pens to keep poultry; also shelter for deer that needed nursing. The family always asked her to leave, seeing her having to work too hard, but she never did. There she had her own bedroom and sitting room. On her free days, Franziska could be home in 15 minutes. She never married.

Life went on in an orderly way at the castle and at home, disturbed occasionally by talk of war which apparently grew as time went by. Dad continued as a qualified gardener with Count Brühl. Other members of the family were still at school. Later they could find work in the castle's garden or as maids at the castle, when needed.

Then that fateful day, 18 June 1914, the assassination of the Austrian heir and his wife. Nobody could have guessed nor imagined how long or cruel the war would be. How far into the future would the consequences encroach? Twenty years later into my generation. With the declaration of war, the fate of millions was sealed. Old photographs of German conscripts travelling to the front in railway wagons with "See you in Paris, at the Boulevard", and "Home by Christmas", chalked on their sides. History books told us a different story and so did our uncles. Uncle Valentin, a regular and a corporal already in Berlin with the Kaiser's Horse Guards, was the first in the family to be sent to France and Belgium. There is a photograph of Uncle Valentin on leave after his 'passing out', cutting a fine figure in dress uniform. We also have a photograph of Uncle Valentin sitting casually in a reed-woven chair, in the lounge of a Belgian mansion, reading the "Belgian-Courier". He had been batman to his company commander {Granddad's teaching!}.

"Home by Christmas" did not materialise, for many never, on both sides. After some successes, winter had not produced the expected results, but it did not yet dampen enthusiasm. Life at home went on, not entirely in every home as the first casualties and death notifications arrived. Another year went by without the result that had been expected. One or two additional countries had joined the Allies. In the meantime, Dad had asked Count Brühl for a commendation to join the military horse-driving school, which he was happy to do, hoping the war would end before Dad was called up. Alas, it was not to be. Sooner than expected, the call-up notice arrived. It was for him to report at the Military Riding and Driving School, somewhere near Berlin. Dad was not entirely a novice regarding horses having gone out with Granddad often and taken the reins. The Lippok home was now in a position where space was no longer a premium. Worries had taken its place. On the subject of war, in a village only twelve miles away, a family said goodbye to three sons and brothers. After four years, only one returned to our future mother's home.

How many other families, on all sides, had to share such tragedy? Life at home had to go on, with Grandma and Granddad placing all their trust in prayer, that was for sure. In 1917 after training to handle a pair of heavier horses than those at the castle, Dad learnt how to drive larger military wagons fully laden, turning, twisting and reversing on narrow roads. He even had to learn driving two pairs in tandem. These were the interesting stories for us as children. After completion of his training, he was sent to the Serbian front. There he had to use all the skills he learned to drive wagons with munitions and other necessary materials soldiers needed, on narrow roads in hilly country. With deep ravines on one side and steep cliffs on the other, seeing a wagon in front of you making one mistake, or some animal causing a horse to shy and seeing it all slide down in a few seconds, with tragic results, was something you did not want to see again.

Late in 1917, just before his birthday, Dad contracted malaria and had to be sent back to Germany to a hospital that cared for malaria sufferers. Soon it was discovered that it was the milder infection. It was only in early January 1919 that he was discharged and sent home. At long last, the terrible war had finally ended. Uncle Valentin assured his parents he was well and had no scratch to show. He came home for a few weeks leave, as he had signed up for another year in the army.

Silesia had been fortunate in that the province had seen none of the horrors of war. Only the crosses placed at the cemetery for those who had not returned home - grandmothers missing their children and young mothers who lost their husbands and children their fathers. Yet, life had to go on. Dad continued his job in the castle's garden. Granddad Johann at nearly seventy years was still with his garden horses. Life in the country after losing a needless war began to get uncomfortable with prices rising and goods becoming scarce, also food and other items. While in the countryside, people had gardens, and as long as seeds were available it was not difficult. Not so in the cities. As for Upper Silesia politically, matters were becoming of serious concern. With the Treaty of Versailles and the founding of the League of Nations, Germany was allowed only a small army, to be at the disposal of the Government in cases of rebellion or revolt between different political factions. In larger cities, such rebellion was beginning to take place. In the meantime, we are in the year 1920/21. Far more concern for Upper Silesia was the demand of the Polish government, against the Treaty of Versailles, for the whole of Upper Silesia to be annexed to Poland. It was the British Premier, Lloyd George, who insisted on the resolution at Versailles to keep the peace. With the German government's strong objections and trust in British fairness, Lloyd George demanded and was granted a plebiscite to oversee a fair election, with representatives of both parties and the Commission.

To ensure there is no intimidation, a British and French military unit would be present. It was not long before a British company was stationed in Gross Strehlitz. The biggest surprise: it was a Scottish regiment in their traditional kilts and bonnets. The officers were billeted in the castle, occupying the free guestrooms, with the soldiers in the stable-boys' rooms and in a hotel in town. The Scots were most welcome visitors. Aunt Else had told us how the town square was packed, when on a Saturday evening the Scots played their pipes and drums and performed their dances, showing their colourful kilts. Seeing how much the people enjoyed it, they would again perform on Sunday afternoons to great applause. Dad and his two brothers, Vincent and Paul had great fun trying to converse. The reason for the British troops to be sent was the imminent threat of Polish insurgents trying forcefully to occupy Upper Silesia against the Versailles Treaty and cause bitter resentment leading into a shooting war. A French contingent was sent to the assigned

Polish area. There is one real episode on record of an occasion when Colonel Chrighton, the Scottish Commanding Officer, on his way to the Commission's Headquarters in the town of Kattowitz in the Polish territory, encountered a small group of Polish insurgents with rifles. Colonel Chrighton walked towards them, armed only with his baton, ordered them in military fashion to "drop their rifles", which they did. His bravery is recorded here and in Silesian history records. The result of the plebiscite was a victory for British fairness. Otherwise, who knows where I might be now or what language I might be speaking.

One other surprise in the family was when Aunt Hedwig, always vivacious, announced she would like to be a nun. For Granddad and Grandma, although active in church and choir, it still came as a surprise, up to a point. If that is what she really wants to try, why not? It seems they had taken it in their stride. "Try and see if you can stick at it, if not there will always be a home for you here". A cloistered nun was not what she had in mind; she wanted to be a nun in a convent that had a hospital where she could qualify to become a nurse. It was the year 1922 and by coincidence in town a new large, modern, half-moon shape, three storey red brick hospital had been built and put into operation. Might it have stirred Aunt Hedwig's interest in nursing? She went with the blessing from parents who were at one in letting their children go. Oh yes, and it had to be a Franciscan Order. To her they seemed to be a more relaxed sort of Order. {I got to meet her in person, thirty years later.} With an excellent recommendation from her parish priest and her acceptance she said "goodbye" and left for a nursing convent near Münster north-west Germany, where Uncle Valentin, her elder brother, trained at the Police Academy.

For those at home it was life as usual, apart from one day when Granddad Johann was not feeling well and it was agreed with Mr Ulrich, head gardener, that Dad should take Granddad's pair of garden horses to deliver whatever was needed to the castle and any other work. Naturally Dad was pleased as it meant he would be all day with the horses. That was his dream, to show the skills he learned at the military horse driving school. As luck would have it, Count Brühl on a walk outside the castle, watched Dad driving the horses placing flower tubs on their rightful places at the front of the castle. As he doffed his hat in salute, Count Brühl signalled to stop, telling Dad that Granddad should take another few days off, at the same time, telling Dad to drive the Count on his weekly estate visit the following day. One can imagine how that pleased Dad. That meant 9:30 a.m. at the castle with the open coach that had a fold-up rain cover, for the passenger of course! A round tour may mean fifteen miles, to visit four large farm units. {As a young boy, Dad had seen the tour before}. The Count's coachman is usually invited to the manager's house for a cup of coffee and home baking, while the Count is shown around by the manager, discussing progress, etc. The Count had taken notice of what Dad had learned at the driving school, and later in earnest in Serbia. He was impressed, suggesting that Granddad at seventy, should retire and Dad should take over. It must have made an interesting day for Dad, considering what the Count had to say to him.

At home, nothing stood still, with a growing family around. It was suggested to Count Brühl, by his butler, that Uncle Paul train as second butler. With another hunting date ahead, the Count agreed. Actually, Uncle Paul had felt a calling to study for the priesthood. Obviously, the family was not able to afford the fees. Their parish priest kindly offered to help. Unfortunately, the priest's sudden death put paid to that. He began his apprenticeship under the butler who apparently took a liking to Uncle Paul - not surprising, as I was to discover when I grew up, his polite and quiet, but firm voice and in his mind Granddad's family motto! An anecdote heard at family gatherings: on the occasion when the King of Saxony arrived on a visit, the butler thought fit for Uncle Paul, smartly dressed in his livery, to serve the welcome drink to the King. At the large entrance hall, he looked at Uncle Paul and simply said "Do you want me to become a drunkard?" Red-faced, Uncle Paul made a hasty retreat, not a good start for a young butler.

With the exiled Kaiser living comfortably in Holland, probably blaming everybody else for Germany's demise, the unemployment rate in Germany increased another notch. Inflation was rising ever more and discontent was all round. Politically it must have seemed an impossible problem to solve. With stagnation in manufacture, where is a government to find millions to pay the reparation fees? Who would want to be a politician? What about a nun? Aunt Hedwig seemed to enjoy her vocation so far and had passed some exams in nursing. That must have pleased her parents. What about Uncle Vincent, the third of the boys? It was said he was not lazy, but not yet for settling in anything particular. There were always odd jobs around the castle, but one thing was certain for him, gardening was only a way to make a living. What really fascinated him were those four-wheel motor cars, when they first appeared at the castle.

## 1923 The year of Franz Lippok and Anna Przibitny

It was in springtime when our future Dad and a friend were invited to a wedding celebration in the town of Tost, a small town some twelve miles south of Gross Strehlitz. After the Marriage Service in the church, the wedding celebration was held in the 'Gasthaus', {a large inn}, of the village where the bride came from. The 'Guesthouse' is where you would come for refreshments and drinks with your family including the children. The main room was large with tables and chairs along the wall where you sat as a family with friends. The centre was always left free for dancing. At one end was the bar where you ordered your drinks or one of the staff would come to your table for your order. Men might go in the billiard room to play and have a drink. Children would run and play outside, or inside if it was dark or it rained. Parents and children would always go home before eight o'clock. Apparently that was where on one such occasion our Dad had an eye for a certain young lady. In Scotland, not that many years ago, ladies and gentlemen sat on opposite sides on benches and you crossed the hall to ask the lady to dance. In Germany you made your way to the table where the lady sat with her friends and/or parents, you bowed and asked first her parents or her boyfriend if you may ask the lady to dance with you. Weddings in Silesia often lasted into the next morning, in those days even continuing after work next evening. Be that as it may, a courtship between our Dad and future Mum followed for some six months.

'Lippok Family Crest'

'My family in 1935
(from l to r Ursula, Mum, Engelbert, Dad, myself)'

Our future Mum was one of four sisters and six brothers whose father had a small farm. Two of her brothers had died in the war, only one could inherit the small farm, while two worked in mines, the other in the steel factory, commuting by train. One sister stayed at home to care for their parents, the others married. Dad made several visits by bicycle. They must have got on well and a marriage was proposed. Dad and Mum met as often as they could. In those days one would not travel fifteen miles every weekend, since Saturday mornings was still a working day.

At the garden and castle the normal routine continued. Dad had to get his plans prepared and start to save for the wedding. Compared with other young future bridegroom's Dad had luck on his side. Driving the Count around the estates, he got to know the farm managers well. To be driving the Count in those days you would be looked at in a 'higher' light. Once you have the trust of the managers, you might be asked questions about the estate or the Count's disposition on the day. Trust was most important when in such employment.

Dad was now age 26 and his parents must have felt pleased that he had found someone he could love and be happy with. Our future Mum's name was Anna, which pleased Dad greatly, so we have been told on occasions. In family circles it was because there is a mountain called 'Annaberg' {Mount St. Anna} which can be seen from all directions. It has been a place of pilgrimage, for two hundred years. Pilgrims from the beginning seem to have loved the place and settled, forming a village on three sides below the summit. Most of the homes offer bed and breakfast on days of pilgrimage.

It was time for Dad to turn his thoughts to the provisions he was to supply for his wedding. He must have done some arithmetic as to how long he would have to save to pay for his wedding. Let me remind you, this was 1923 with hyperinflation, where a hundredweight bag of wheat cost four million Marks. Dad seemed to have the talent to work matters out. He would need to save four million Marks for the wedding meal and drinks. Mum's wage was used for bed linen being her contribution to the dowry. It did not cost Dad any sleepless nights it seemed. Now that he had driven the coach several times with the

Count around the farm estates, he had got to know the managers quite well as I have mentioned earlier! Closer to the wedding, on one of those drives, he came home with several small bags of wheat. Together they amounted to a little more than he required and paid for the butcher, the baker and for the beer! The summer went on and Dad had already been given the dates of his leave. The wedding took place at our future Mum's parish church in the town of Tost. The reception was at the guesthouse in the same small village where Dad had met his bride, and which we got to know well as we grew up.

Sadly, the year, which was meant to be a year of joy, turned also into a year of sadness. Granddad Johann died at age 70, only three weeks after the wedding of Mum and Dad. He had come into the stable yard and collapsed as he dismounted from the wagon, {a fatal burst appendix, the pains of which he had neglected and not gone to the doctor.} At the funeral, all of his family was present except Hedwig the nun. As expected, it was one of the biggest funerals of the year, with the church choir, that Granddad led when there was no organist, singing the funeral Mass. As the congregation left the church, the parish priest noticed Count Brühl in a pew at the back of the church. His attendance was much appreciated.

Almost two months later, Count Brühl himself died unexpectedly at age 71, with no heir apparent. It seemed like a plague on the castle regarding rightful heirs. A younger stepbrother of Count Brühl, Count Schlieffen, also one of a widely-known family of aristocrats, with members in government and high ranking army officers was appointed to be the new occupier of Gross Strehlitz Castle. There he assured all the staff he did not want to make any changes, but would respect anyone who wished to move on. Thus, Uncle Paul was assured to complete his apprenticeship as a butler. It meant that Dad would still be second coachman. However, with Granddad no longer available someone else had to be appointed. Within a week, Count Schlieffen asked Dad to take the first coach and horses and drive him round the outlying estates. Dad being newly married and driving the new Count, must have made him sit up straighter and be in his element - showing off. Unbelievably, when they arrived home, Count Schlieffen, just out of the coach simply said to Dad "Lippok, tell Mister Ulrich {the head gardener}, from next Monday you will take the first pair and coach". With Uncle Paul as second butler and Dad driving the first coach, meant the Lippok family was established at the centre of the castle. What of the future?

In one way or another, 1923 had its share of joy and sadness about the castle. The hope among the employees was that Count Schlieffen would continue in the spirit of the late Count Brühl. As for the Lippok family, the year of 1924 began with Aunt Hedwig, a fully enrolled nun, now called 'Sister Gottharda', was preparing to leave Germany. She had been given leave to visit her mother and her brothers and sisters. Not to have seen her father again was the saddest part. She left with all their blessings. She and twenty other Sisters sailed to the US to their new convent and hospital in Wisconsin. Why go so far away? Is there something inherent in the Lippok family that makes them look further from home? As far as Aunt Hedwig was concerned, she had read about the Bishop of Wisconsin, born in Germany, asking nursing nuns to come to Wisconsin, to care for the many injured workers that were building the railroads in his diocese. There were not sufficient nurses there to care for the many injured workers.

Next, Uncle Valentin too had passed his examination as a fully qualified police officer and took the offer to stay on in Münster. It was there he found his 'Love' two or three years later. Now to the story of Uncle Vincent, who so far had not yet found his vocation, nor did he show any interest in looking for a wife. {By way of a reminder, I am quoting here family history, although it may not be unique, it has its own interest, which our children and grandchildren want to know about.} That changed with the younger Count Schlieffen. More visitors would arrive with their 'motor'. That was what fascinated Uncle Vincent. He spent his time helping wherever there was a penny to be made in the garden and at the castle, preferably. If you were looking for him, he would most likely be found with the driver of a visiting car. He would question them all about the technology, how things worked. He was hoping they would take him for a run in the park, out of sight of any castle windows of course, which eventually they did, seeing his interest. The family guessed it was only a matter of time before Uncle Vincent was on the move.

Aunt Anna, a housemaid with the Brühl Family in their elegant castle in Seifersdorf, Saxony, on one of her holidays spent at home, met a gentleman one Sunday after church. A friendship developed and with Aunt Anna returning to her place of work, letters began to be exchanged. The gentleman in question was Josef. Within a year Aunt Anna was to become his wife; Mrs Blüsch. Unbelievably, he too was a policeman. That made two police officers in the Lippok family. Uncle Josef was a policeman in the town of Beuthen, the 'capital' of the industrial area. You may recall I mentioned it before.

Count Schlieffen actually suggested to Dad by way of exercising the horses on his free Sunday afternoon, that he should take the second pair of horses and light coach to drive the twelve miles to Mum's village home, to visit her mother and her larger family. That was an occasion in the village. Nearly all the children came to Mum's home to admire the horses with their smart harness and coach. This must have made Dad feel very proud. In those days the appearance of a coach from the castle was a novelty, likewise a car, except one passing on the main road a mile from the village.

A good moment to report on Uncle Vincent. Count Schlieffen, aware of Uncle Vincent's interests, advised, with whom to get in contact in Berlin to find accommodation, and where he might then get further help in finding employment. Count Schlieffen gave Uncle Vincent a hand-written recommendation. Briefly, within a half year in Berlin he passed his driving test and became assistant driver to a well-known couturier in Berlin, attending and supplying the rich and famous. Uncle Vincent soon became personal chauffeur to the owner. Sometime around 1930 he spoke to a young lady he noticed occasionally visiting the shop. A conversation took place and a close friendship resulted. The lady's name was Meta and she was a seamstress. She invited Uncle Vincent to visit her at her place of work one evening, which he did. Uncle Vincent had not asked who Miss Meta worked for. It was a large house where she had a flat. With Meta working on a dress and Uncle Vincent reclining in a chair chatting away, the lady of the house knocked and entered the room. Uncle Vincent noticed that the lady took a good look at him. Before Uncle Vincent left he asked Miss Meta who the lady was: "Oh", Meta said, "that is Mrs Göbbels". Uncle Vincent apparently did not blink an eye, simply asking: "Mr Göbbels, Hitler's Propaganda Minister?" Later, Mrs Göbbels suggested to her husband that Uncle Vincent would make a far smarter chauffeur. Within the month he was Göbbels' new chauffeur. That was how Uncle Vincent was seen occasionally just a short distance behind Göbbels {there was one such colour photograph in our sitting-room}. Uncle Vincent seeing at close hand the direction the Nazi party was leading, had the opportunity and took it to be the Japanese Ambassador's personal chauffeur until his call-up in 1941. Sent to a unit at the Russian front, he survived the battle of Stalingrad in 1943 and was a prisoner of war in Russia until 1946/7. The Russian camp commander, able to read German, saw in Uncle Vincent's German ID card the notice that he had been the Japanese Ambassador's chauffeur and made him his valet in camp. Uncle Vincent insisted that's what kept him alive. He was sure his Russian camp commandant got him early repatriation back to Germany. He thanked God that he survived and that his wife Meta had survived the bombing and destruction of Berlin. They said it was a miracle to find a small flat. He had not seen his mother since that holiday in 1936. Eventually after Germany got on its feet again, Uncle Vincent noticed an advert, and called at a lady who had a high class ladies dress shop in Berlin and became her caretaker and chauffeur, with Aunt Meta as housemaid. A true family story, insignificant it may be, but recorded for those who have lived through such times after the war.

Time to return to family history 1925. As for Uncle Paul he had already talked to Count Schlieffen regarding broadening his experience and knowledge. Count Schlieffen fully understood and even suggested whom to approach with his commendation. Grateful for the Count's help, he was given the opportunity to be taken on as the livery butler with Prinz Löwenstein, at one of those romantic castles in Bavaria. The Lippok family is indeed spreading its name wider, but not before Uncle Paul had the opportunity, for the first time, to be a godfather to no less than Mum and Dad's first child - myself, born 8th June 1926. A notable year for me, especially as I was to discover twenty years later, that it was my honour to have given way and let our present Queen Elizabeth be born two months before me that same year. It had been my parents' wish that I be baptised 'Paul Aloysius' in honour of Uncle Paul. Indeed, I was pleased to discover that in any English speaking country the pronunciation of Paul would be the same. Within a week Uncle Paul left home, still unmarried. The Lippok boys seemed to take their time. Looking back, with five of the family having left home, one could have asked; is the Lippok family breaking up? One could also have asked, is it some foreboding of our beloved Silesia and its two thousand year history coming to a close? At least for the older generation, as the twenties came to an end, politically it did not look nor feel good with the strengthening of the Hitler and Stalin parties, raising their voices, vying for votes, when considering their radical approach.

Dad had been given accommodation in one of the estate's houses. The back faced the castle garden. At the front a two-yard wide pavement separated us from the main road. Our home now was an estate house where we lived on the ground floor which had two bedrooms and a kitchen. On the upper floor was one of the Estate Office employees and his family. Next to us was the second coachman's family. As usual we all had a garden and a shed to keep rabbits or hens. The house was linked to the castle garden. A good ten-minute walk took you to the centre of town.

The year 1928 was noteworthy. On the 20$^{th}$ of October my sister was born, the name given to her was Ursula, a healthy addition to our family. Not such a healthy year for the estate. Quoting from family memories, by 1929 it was becoming evident that Count Schlieffen was not the businessman to run his estate profitably. In fact, it transpired it was fast heading for bankruptcy. Those who had responsibility to try to save the situation took a decision. The result was the dismissal of Count Schlieffen. A temporary team was appointed to manage the Estate, including a competent man with a degree in Estate Management to take charge on the ground. With Count Schlieffen having returned to his home, Dad had been instructed to look after the stables and its small staff. There was a surprise when the decision became known that a Count Wolfgang Castell zu Castell was to become the new rightful owner of Gross Strehlitz Castle.

The name 'Castell' was not familiar here. Further afield it had no mean publicity. In fact the world over, for many years their name appeared on quality pencils, 'Faber-Castell' {due to a marriage of the two families} still famous for their quality today in the 21$^{st}$ century. The Castell family home is a small town in northern Bavaria. It is worth a description: by car, taking the main highway from Frankfurt eastwards passing Würzburg, twenty miles later turn right and then only five miles on you enter the small village called 'Castell'. It is one of the famous wine-growing areas. The village next to the castle are the original homes of the workers. The Castells are now well spread out in Germany, but the head of the Castells occupies the original family home.

On February 7$^{th}$ 1930 a brother was born for my sister Ursula and me. His baptised name was Engelbert. Strange, we never found out who had chosen his name, but it fitted him. Of course, with the change at the castle there must have been some anxiety among the staff. However, within a week or two the secretary and office manager spoke to the staff, informing them that there would be no changes for the time being and work was to continue as usual. That included Dad, who always told us how pleased he was since the Lippok family was now entwined with the castle for a century.

A new period had begun for us who were interwoven with Gross Strehlitz Castle. Mid-summer in June 1930, Dad was summoned to the Estate Office where the secretary informed him that Count Castell intended to come for an inspection and to get to know the estate's geography. With Count Castell arriving by train, it was Dad's duty to meet him at the station and drive him to the castle where rooms had been prepared for him. Dad's first impression was of a Count with good manners and an aura of aristocracy, at the same time one of a down-to-earth manager who immediately saw where drastic action was needed. Count Castell was six feet tall and wore a manicured beard. He hoped Dad would be happy to continue as his personal coachman. A pleasant rapport developed between them. Trust is of the essence in such a situation. It was a privilege for Dad to drive Count Castell around the large estate. He was full of praise of how the Count dealt and conversed with the individual farm managers, who in turn seemed confident that the estate would return to profitability. On arrival back at the castle he thanked Dad and hoped for a happy relationship. Count Wolfgang zu Castell-Castell had now officially become the rightful owner of the Gross Strehlitz Castle and estates.

Count Castell began to probe, ever so carefully on Dad's political stance; may I remind you it was 1930/31, politically it was seething in the country. Dad stated the fact that he was a Catholic and a member of the Centrum Party. The Count obviously wanted to know his closer employees' political stance to have a clear vision with the political scene in Germany so ominous. Within the year, he asked if Dad would mind if he called him by his first name, Franz. Dad took it as a compliment. After two or three months the Count had called in tradesmen, painters, etc., who were to prepare a few rooms for the Count to move in with his family. Early December 1931, before leaving to collect his family, Count Castell had even a bigger surprise when he asked Dad would he consider being his housemaster in the castle! That did surprise Dad, who could not answer for a moment, but was happy to say "yes" expressing his delight and thanked the Count, who immediately told Dad where he was to live at the castle with his family. He obviously must have asked someone who could convince him that Dad was a known handyman. It is understandable for Dad to be excited, wanting to get home to give Mum the news. It meant a larger apartment at the castle, a rise in wages, and for Mum, a shorter walk to the shops and church. Did Dad know that it meant more hours? Probably.

We have entered the third decade, and in 1930 who could have thought that it would end in the circumstances it did? As a five-year-old, in 1932, politics had no effect on my life. That was for the adults. We in Upper Silesia, as in many other parts of Germany, were spared the nastier political consequences. However, I do have vague memories of large groups marching and singing or shouting and waving red flags as they passed our house, with Mum quickly calling me in. Nevertheless, that should not prevent me from recalling the history of those few months when matters were heading for radical decisions to be taken. The bitter consequences of a badly thought-out treaty were threatening to tear a country and nation apart, with every party predicting catastrophe unless you voted for them. In the end, it seemed that the new National Socialist Labour Party (N.S.D.A.P. or Nazi) with Adolf Hitler as leader, and a strong Fatherland theme, had a chance. Its methods were not in favour with many. There was much apprehension not only among the churches. It must have been a trying time for the elderly President von Hindenburg; there was no other way and an election was called. Disappointingly, it did not provide a true result. Hitler's 'Brown-shirts' with their swastikas all over the place, playing incessantly the 'Fatherland' themes. The rising unemployment, the Wall Street crash and inflation getting out of hand had fed Hitler's ego to rouse the people. President von Hindenburg was forced to call a second election, which did not bring the hoped result and the sorry state continued. How long is this to go on for?

In January 1932, the Count had returned, and his family followed in a month's time. Dad had already received instructions to prepare the rooms for them to live in some comfort. With no central heating at the castle it was Dad's job to light the fires in those rooms that would be most lived in. He had also to ensure that the maids prepared the necessary rooms. The electrician had already been summoned to inspect and repair whatever needed to be done. This also applied to our new home to be ready for us to move in. There were a thousand and one things Dad had to find out and sort out. He had to work many hours in the evening, simply to find his way around the most important rooms for a start. It must have been extremely difficult to find his way where he had never been before. More often Mum had to put Dad's midday meal in the oven to re-heat it. It is just not possible for me to put on record all that he had to learn quickly, but the Count, and his family, were pleased and appreciative. Dad was grateful and a sound basis was established for working together. Even our new home was ready to move into. What a difference that made for Mum.

# Chapter 2

# My life began in earnest!

April 1932, school began after Easter, two weeks before we moved into our new apartment at the castle. I do remember carrying my two foot high traditional 'paper cone' with a few sweets, but I have never seen any of the better-off children having more than half the cone filled with sweets. It was a pleasant tradition anyway. Our school was the Catholic public school, administered by the state. Attendance was for eight years. Girls and boys had separate classes and entrance stairs. Four classes were allocated to accommodate the Lutheran pupils, and their own teachers. We always got on well and played together during break in the playground. School hours were from eight a.m. until one p.m., summer or winter, with a ten minute break every hour and no meals of course. Method of punishment, the cane! A short prayer was said first in the morning in each class. Thursday mornings 7:15 a.m., you were expected to attend the children's mass at church and be in time for school. It was not obligatory, but most of us went. As mentioned before, those who would attend Gymnasium left after Class IV.

**'Gross Strehlitz Hospital'**

**'Gross Strehlitz our Public School'**

Within two or three days, I noticed one boy in my class going home after school the same way as I did. Next morning I was walking that little bit faster to see if I could find out which house he would come out from. At playtime, I looked for the boy and was able to start a conversation. He seemed to be pleased since he too spotted me walking in the same direction. His name was Ernst and his father was a government employee at the Court in the Town House. Our friendship developed into a long lasting one to this day.

As there are no original pre-1945 photographs of the back entrance of the castle, permit me to digress for a moment. Referring to the picture of the former trade entrance of the castle, this was the sight that greeted me on my first visit to our former home after twenty three years, in

1965. I repeat my previous description of the back entrance, the central opening housed the large double cast-iron gates. On either side were pedestrian gates and the one on the right, had an electric bell which rang in our new home. Whoever was at home pressed the button/buzzer which opened the gate. The ruin next to the impressive gate frame was our home for only fifteen years, the Housemaster's apartment, to which I said goodbye in 1943, now a heap of rubble. Next to us was Uncle Paul's home. There seemed to have been no plan to defend the town, leaving the Russians just to walk in. Therefore it suffered no damage. The advancing Russian military recuperated for two weeks, occupying the castle. On leaving to advance towards the battle for Breslau, they totally torched Gross Strehlitz Castle and its contents, likewise every building around the town square, but not the Town House. Today the castle looks the same, gruesome and pitiful. However, all the buildings around the square have been rebuilt, by the now Polish population.

A recent published article by the London Times is appealing to save European heritage sites, the beautiful Silesian country houses. A surprising article which left me extremely proud to read this in a UK paper. Almost every town and in the countryside, Silesia had a grand country house, in Renaissance, Baroque, Neo-Classical or Victorian style. 'Rescue Silesia the Land of dying Country Houses' was the headline of the article.

Referring to my photo of the ruined castle destroyed in the heat of a war, one can understand, but letting historical and beautiful mansions simply fall into ruins is vandalism. One has to give credit to the present Polish government, now encouraging previous owners to invest and restore, or prevent further deterioration of those beautiful buildings. End of digression.

Towards the end of April 1932 we moved into our new home at the castle. That day was obviously not going to be like any other, excitement all round and I was only six. My new-found friend Ernst understood and on our way home we parted at the town square. From there I had only a hundred yards to get to the back entrance of the castle, where I pressed the bell button. After a few moments, the buzzer released the bolt and I pushed the door open. That was exciting for one experiencing it for the first time. I got home at twelve o' clock, had something to eat and, made myself as useful as I could, following a call from wherever it came from. Running upstairs and downstairs was a novelty. As a six year old, you were expected to be useful. Mum now had a large kitchen with a coal-fired stove. It had a two-gallon water container, which was heated by the coal-fire. That meant hot water for washing dishes and an oven for baking, a cold water tap in the kitchen, a scullery and a toilet. Upstairs we had two bedrooms and a spacious sitting room, which pleased all of us. The sitting room needed decorating. Mum wondered how often in the day the bell would ring, but she need not have worried. Interesting for us was the mirror fixed on the outside of the kitchen window, so that we could see who was entering after we pressed the buzzer. All this was fascinating for us kids at that time. I must admit, and I remember well, how proud I felt going to school next day through the castle gate, albeit the back 'gate'. Now it was only half the distance to school. It took some time to get into a daily routine. Sometimes Ernst and I would meet at the town square other times not. For Dad it was a real change from looking after horses and driving them around, whereas now he walked out of the house and was at his workplace. While he was used to lifting heavy bags, he now had to carry coal buckets to the various rooms around the castle, for keeping the fires going was part of his work. Before the winter, the Count had already talked to Dad about installing central heating sometime soon. Dad was pleased about that. The butler's apartment next to us on the second floor was still unoccupied. There was a storeroom on the ground floor. Here is the aforementioned hairpin, which was the passage to the rear of the castle. It led to the wood and coal shed, the large garden for the housemaster and butler and with ample room to rear chickens. Next to the gardens was the large castle drying green. Just a hundred steps on was the rear entrance to the Estate Office. All along on the left of the pathway to our garden and rear of the Estate Office was a fifteen foot high stone wall which was the rear of the shops and living quarters of the south side of the town square. The windows on their third floor allowed them to look down into our garden etc. It was a shortcut to the Estate Office, which the Count and Countess used, passing by our kitchen. In the passage, a door led into a well-equipped workshop for Dad to use. It was where he spent evenings repairing items and making toys for the Count's children. It was also where I first tried my hands at woodwork.

'Castle Gross Strehlitz'

'Count Wolfgang zu Castell Castell with
Counts Prosper and Ludwig'

'Countess Sybille zu Castell Castell'

'Counts Prosper and Ludwig (Lutz) with Schimpimpel'

Although the Countess, Princess Sybille, and her family had arrived in February, we had not yet met them. They had two sons, Count Prosper born 1922 and Count Ludwig {Lutz} born 1927. The Countess was the daughter of Prince Reuss with estates in Austria. Dad thought that we might meet them unexpectedly and advised we should just bow our head and say "Guten Tag" {Good Day}, and if we have a bonnet on, we should take it off.

Mum had already experienced how convenient it was to do the shopping when it took only minutes to get to the grocer, baker or any others. Equally surprising was the discovery how close it was to church; which played an important part in our family. {From the gate to the square, then diagonally and only a hundred yards across the square, a further hundred yards and you were at church.} Ernst and I would meet often at the square going to school and part when going home. A few weeks later I celebrated my seventh birthday with a cake Mum had baked in our new oven. I had invited Ernst and we had a good time. At the end of the castle, half way to the stables was a small area with a large sand box for children to play in. Ernst and I with brother Engelbert played there often after school.

Tradesmen moved in and out continuing to repair, renovate or renew as ordered by the Count. Dad was often inundated by questions from them, some of whom had never been in the castle before and got lost or accidently walked into the wrong room. In addition, Dad always told us how much he benefited learning from the tradesmen. Count Castell gave Dad a free hand to buy any tools he needed for his workshop. The countryside around us indicated that autumn had truly arrived and made thoughts turn towards Christmas. For millions there was very little to look forward to, with the national unemployment figures around three million. Those who lived on the land or were fortunate to have a garden might have been able to ward off the harshness felt by so many. We were fortunate, bearing in mind we as children were unaware then how others had it not so good. As Christmas was approaching Dad had news for us that we children would go on Christmas Eve to the castle to meet the Count and his family to wish them a happy Christmas.

Early December in Silesia snow fell before Christmas and there was frost. We had a small sledge which we made good use of. Frozen fingers and noses running was part of the fun. On December 6th, St Nikolaus was celebrated with sweets and ginger biscuits. A week before Christmas a wagon laden with Christmas trees appeared at the back gate. Two tall ones for the castle and one for us and one each for the staff and cook, the others were orders for the town. Miss Kati, the cook, was Austrian who the Countess had specially engaged because she favoured Austrian cooking. Miss Kati was a single woman and naturally jolly, as we were to discover in due time. This being our first Christmas at the castle we were to experience that there was a certain aura around. One of the perks working there was collecting a large fat carp for the Christmas Eve meal. Christmas in Germany is something special of that there is no doubt. On Christmas Eve at four o'clock, Dad led us to the castle to the 'Small Salon' to meet the Count and the Countess with Prosper and Ludwig, We bowed, shook hands and wished them "Frohe Weihnachten" {Happy Christmas}. It was quite an experience for us. Then the Countess handed us each a parcel wrapped in Christmas paper. We took our presents and said "thank you" and bowed, as Dad ordered. Mum was busy preparing the many different and special Christmas varieties of food. After we came home from the castle with all the presents from Lutz and his parents, Dad put them under the Christmas tree because we were not allowed in while 'Christkindel' was in the room, until after our meal. Soon after Dad came home we had our Christmas meal. Only after that we would all together enter the room and sing first "Still the Night, Holy night", then we looked for our presents. Once you were ten years old it was getting ready for church for the Midnight Service. Ankle boots was the order with snow lying at six inches, which was the norm in Silesia.

Christmas and New Year over, the attention in the family was directed to my godfather Uncle Paul who had progressed and was doing well in a widely known aristocratic family in Berlin. Count Castell on a visit to Berlin attending an important function on business met Uncle Paul acting head waiter at that function. At an opportune moment Count Castell asked Uncle Paul would he consider coming home to be his butler and personal valet? "I would love to come back home!" was Uncle Paul's answer. After a month's notice Uncle Paul, Aunt Magda his wife and their year old daughter Erika arrived early 1933. From that day on there were two Lippok brothers at the centre of the Gross Strehlitz Castle.

Spring 1933, Hindenburg had no other solution and was heard to say to those around him: "I suppose I have no other option, but to hand Germany to the Austrian corporal." Hitler on entering the Chancellery famously proclaimed: "Nobody is going to get me out of here alive". {What shallow bravery, when he, Hitler, only twelve years later, sat in a deep underground bunker in 1945, while his soldiers died fighting above, he simply took a fatal pill to wash his hands of it all.}

In early 1933 the unemployment figures rose to six million. By the end of 1934, almost two years later, it had been reduced to 2.7 million. How could that be possible? Hitler had time to think when writing his book 'Mein Kampf' {'My Fight'}. He did what he thought or others suggested when he took over to lead and rule Germany. He introduced a new currency and with one stroke Germany had no money to pay the Versailles reparations. A few capable economists, a massive building programme, modernising run-down factories, new technology, all that helped to achieve it. Hitler had one 'Schlagwort' {powerful slogan} for the people: 'Arbeit und Brot' {Work and Bread}. In truth, that was what the people wanted and needed.

One organisation that was soon established was the 'Arbeitsdienst' {Labour Service}. It was a compulsory six-month service for all males age 18, after you completed your apprenticeship, or you attended higher education. It was used for many projects: building bridges, sea-defences, helping to clear forests after storm damage, constructing motorways, almost a thousand miles by 1939. The Arbeitsdienst was run like a military unit. You wore a brown uniform with a ridiculous looking hat, boots and for exercising a new gleaming spade, the emblem of work you exercised with, just as if you had a rifle. The rules: behaviour, cleanliness and obedience. Accommodation was in well-built timber huts. New garrisons were being built and the resultant increase of the military lowered the unemployment figure. Hitler's 'National Socialist Workers Party {N.S.D.A.P.}' original appeal slowly began to show through that it had a nastier side as the years went by. It did raise eyebrows among certain sections of the population and began to fill others with consternation. Then there were those who shouted approval of Hitler's attack on Wall Street and anti-Semitic propaganda followed. He had been given a free hand.

Grandma, now a ten-year widow, was still capable of looking after herself in her old home in the castle garden. She was pleased to know that her son Paul was now the butler and the Count's valet. Grandma's fifth grandchild Ruth was born to Uncle Paul and Aunt Magda on my birthday, 8th June 1934. How wonderful I thought since it was also my eighth birthday. Now we had two cousins at the castle. The Lippok family at the castle was increasing!

By 1934, the 'brown shirts' S.A. {Sturm Abteilung}, 'storm units', called into being before even Hitler came to power, appeared in their uniforms at meetings to intimidate and disturb political meetings by other groups. On Hitler's appointment as German Chancellor, the S.A.P. became Hitler's 'mobile' swastika flag, increasing their presence by calling meetings every so often. Followed by the creation of the Hitler Youth, with light brown shirts and short trousers as the uniform. Far more offensive for many, was the introduction of saluting each other 'Heil Hitler' with the raised right arm, at any time of the day; in place of Good Morning etc. Can you imagine Mum going shopping in the morning greeting 'Heil Hitler'? Down here with us in Silesia it was not always obeyed. Even we as boys did not follow the 'rule'. Now in hindsight it sounds even more ridiculous. One by one Party offices had their office chief in uniform and if you had to go to see one of them for a reason you would certainly say 'Heil Hitler', because he sits there in a uniform.

Late 1934 was the first time the word 'KZ' short for 'Konzentration Camp' was heard. As eight-year-old youngsters we heard the word, but had no idea what it meant except you could be locked up. What else had the Party up their sleeve? There was the call for those whose family name did not sound German enough {for instance, like Polish migrants settled here long ago to find work} that they should go to the Registrar Office. There they would find the nearest translation into German; re-registration was free of charge. There were many who took up the offer, understandably, as some of the Polish names were very difficult to spell and to pronounce. This also applied to village names. It was the last straw. More disconcerting was the ever growing anti-Jewish propaganda by the Party, already well played before Hitler became German Chancellor. While on the subject, we had a number of Jewish shops in town and Silesia in general. In our town we had a dentist, outfitters, tobacco shops, and two grocers. Mum went to the Jewish grocer and I was often sent for additional goods. 'The last straw' was the beginning of intimidation of Religion, Catholics and Lutherans, when priests and ministers began to be intimidated if in their sermon questions were raised and issue taken with Party and State policies. In certain cases arrest and Concentration Camps was their end, as happened to one of our Priests, and the late Lutheran Pastor Niemöller.

One day Dad left a message with Mum to tell me to meet Count Lutz at the smaller inner courtyard any time after 2:30pm. You can well imagine my difficulty meeting a young Count. I need not have worried. His behaviour was absolutely 'normal' and he made me call him Lutz, short for Ludwig, his proper first name; and he would call me by my first name Paul. Lutz had already brought out two tin pedal-cars and without further ado he shouted "let's race!". The inner courtyard was ideal with its smooth flagstone floor. Having never been in one before, it took a few rounds before I got the hang of it. The last half hour or so he asked me to go with him inside to the playroom. It was the size of a large sitting room. Lutz showed me just a few of the toys we might play with. The children's nanny, Miss Agnes, always called when it was time to tidy up. Having done so I thanked Lutz and he in turn asked could I come the next day. Yes I would and left. It became a daily routine from two to four o'clock except Saturdays and Sundays. Understandably, Engelbert and Ursula could not wait for me to tell them how we got on. Occasionally Lutz would ask to bring Ursula and Engelbert with me when we played outside in the large sand box near the stables.

It was comforting for all of their staff that the Castells showed their stance towards religion by their regular Sunday Service attendance at the Lutheran church. The Lutheran minister was a regular visitor at the castle and the Lutheran community made up a third of the town's population. An amicable rapport existed between Lutherans and Catholics.

It is my pleasure to introduce important staff at the castle, apart from our Dad and Uncle Paul: Miss Pertal was the Countess' personal maid from Bavaria, who had been with the Countess for a number of years. Miss Kati, the Austrian cook, whose surname I cannot recollect was a jovial person, always smiling and handing out small tasty cookies. The children's nanny Miss Agnes. Then Herr Kanzok, an experienced coachman and chauffeur, also the stable manager. There were also two chambermaids and a kitchen maid. Those not from town resided in their rooms in the east wing. It is quite appropriate to mention the above subject at this time as I re-live the memories of my youth. What was much appreciated by the staff was the invitation to join the Countess on week days leading the half-hour morning prayer in the castle's private chapel {Mondays to Fridays} which Uncle Paul and Dad attended whenever possible. One could ascribe it as a personal statement in view of the then increasing totalitarian regime bringing disguised 'wedges' between state and religion. Anti-Jewish propaganda was now openly spread. At the same time Hitler did not dishonour his promise of work and bread, but the massive building programme had to be financed and three quarter of a billion Marks had to be borrowed. By the end of 1934 it was estimated it would rise to an alarming seventeen billion Marks. One does not have to be a mathematician to realise the cost of building miles of motorways, houses and new modern factories and accommodation for an increasing army and modern equipment. With all the countries that had suffered the horrors of war and loss of life, still trying to recoup their financial losses, there was the 'Führer' expecting the German army to be fighting fit within four years; "and his country bankrupt" was the comment heard at one's peril.

Hitler expected his army to do their bit with propaganda and coercion which they certainly did. It rang alarm bells at Bishops' conferences; both Lutheran and Catholic. The rhetoric against Marxism and the Jewish population grew louder. It was the beginning of emigration among the people, but too many did not expect the horrors that awaited them until it was too late. Our own Bishop of Silesia, Cardinal Bertram had a most able helper dealing with the Hitler regime, in Cardinal Count von Galen, Bishop of the Diocese of Münster. His family and his own war record could not be 'trampled' upon, as was his pride in his 'formerly' humanitarian country. On his mind was the talk of creating 'a pure Germanic race'. Over time his grew to be a fearless voice. The Lutherans were not behind for they too had their hero, Pastor Martin Niemöller. He was one of the first pastors and priests to be interned in those newly created Concentration Camps. What a black blot on a civilised country!

Advent time was just ahead and our preparations had begun. The traditional Advent wreath had to be made and help was needed when the Christmas ginger biscuits were made. How lovely. For me it would be a pleasant time; Lutz and I met already every second afternoon for playtime. It was wintertime with snow all around so Lutz and I played in the large playroom. Count Prosper suggested he would help to lay out the railway toys in the larger half of the playroom. I soon discovered why. It was not any sort of small railway you can build on a dinner table. From one of the large cupboards out came the rails, so many, I was sure there were miles. Then the coaches, twenty centimetres long I guessed. When the locomotives came, my mind boggled. It took us a few afternoon play days and I am sure Count Prosper had taken time to build more, while we played outside if it was dry. Eventually it was finished and what a display! The stations, the points, barriers, signals, etc. I knew my place and waited for Count Prosper to tell me what he wanted me to do. There was so much I was asked to do: setting the signals and points, eventually driving an engine and train. There was no end of pleasure. All the same every other day we had to be outside for an hour building snowmen or sledging, etc. When we could not go outside we had to come into the playroom. In place of toys we were sometimes asked to sit on chairs. Nanny brought materials out for us {black cloth, the size of our Mum's oven cloth} and she then explained what we had to do. We each got a needle and red thread. She then started with the needle to show us how to make small red crosses round the cloth, cross stitching. We were making 'Topflappen' {oven gloves}, a present for our Mum at Christmas and the Countess would on occasion join us as we worked.

Christmas 1934/35. On Christmas Eve we three children had to be dressed at four o'clock, ready to go over to the castle and led by Dad to the Yellow Salon. Dad knocked and opened the door and retreated while we were welcomed by the Countess, Count Wolfgang, Prosper and Ludwig {Lutz}. After a few questions, which we could answer, each of us was presented with presents requiring our two hands. We said our thanks as Dad had instructed us, bowed and quietly left the Salon. That repeated itself for ten years {only eight for me}. If only we had known the fate that awaited us, we would have cherished those moments so much more. Just as well none of us knew or could have even guessed. Still, even now after sixty years it is good to remember how fortunate to have been living in a place like that.

The staff were presented with their presents after us. Uncle Paul and Dad would then serve the Count and his family their Christmas meal, as usual, which was taken at 6:30 pm. I would have gone the day before to the estate fishery to collect our carp as part of the employee perks. Dad had already prepared the Christmas tree, hoping he would be home before eight for Mum would have our meal ready by then. All of the ingredients needed to be prepared in the early afternoon anyway. Christmas presents are always given by the 'Christkind' {Christ Child}. Santa Claus brings his few presents on his Feast Day December 6th. After our meal we tidied up and only when Dad called did we enter the sitting room to sing our Christmas hymn before we could look at our presents. Simple they were, but as much as our parents could afford.

Part of the Christmas Eve highlights was the Midnight Service at which the church was always packed out. Everybody wanted to sing the beautiful Christmas hymn, 'Stille Nacht, Heilige Nacht' {Silent Night}. Snow fell always before Christmas in Silesia. The stars bright in the wintry sky, a goodnight for us boys who had a torch or got a new one for Christmas. The competition was whose torch could best illuminate the top of the church steeple. Something one could not do half a century previously!

On Christmas day the Children's Service, was again filled with young people and grandmas, to visit the beautiful crib, with the babe, and of course the shepherds, the lambs, the big camel and the kings. How many more Christmases? As usual in the afternoon, wrapped up and with high boots, we would all go and visit Grandma and Aunt Else {Elisabeth, not married} in their old home in the castle garden.

Grandma would always have something special for us. Aunt Else's speciality was the 'Pfefferkuchen' {ginger biscuits}. In those days, small things were appreciated. Boxing Day was also a day of rest. Ernst and I would visit each other to admire our presents. School holidays were always two weeks, ample time to go with our sledges to the hill in the castle park. It was always packed with young and old. You had to be careful not to run into your neighbour. It was always well visited, because it was the only hill in town you could sledge on, which we did every day during the Christmas holidays. Of course the frozen lake in the park would be full of skaters, since Count Castell had ordered electric bulbs to floodlight the lake until 10 p.m. There were days when Lutz asked me to go sledging with him on a smaller hill within the castle grounds and he always insisted Ursula and Engelbert came with us.

January 1935. Ernst and I attended Catechism classes for one hour on Monday afternoons, the preparation for our First Holy Communion at Easter and Confirmation a month later. There were forty boys attending and as many girls. It was a sign we were growing up. There was something else that drew our attention, namely the appearance of soldiers, on leave we assumed, which had not happened before. Just ten years old, we did not realise it was the result of the increasing numbers of compulsory military two-year service.

1935, back to family. First, Uncle Valentin was now a police sergeant in Münster and probably will be moved to Düsseldorf. He too had found love and married a Westphalian lady, Therese. They had two children, our cousin Margaret and cousin Valentin {same name as his father}. Uncle Vincent was still in Berlin with Aunt Meta and chauffeur to the Japanese Ambassador. In summer 1935 his employer asked Uncle Vincent to drive him to Silesia to holiday in one of the famous and elegant spas in the foothills of the Sudeten Mountains. The Ambassador suggested while he is taking the waters Uncle Vincent take the car and visit his Mum, our Grandma for two weeks. I do remember the excitement visiting Grandma and admiring the car. Actually the car was one of the small models, well-polished and what a shine! We were allowed to look at it but never to touch it with our fingers. It was the first time we met Uncle Vincent. The Easter Feast had been celebrated in full splendour. Easter Monday was just like

Sunday, but for us boys there was the tradition to sprinkle the ladies and young girls with perfume. That is alright for those who work, but we had only pocket money which meant we had to water down our perfume. The girls knowing the game had no intention to stand and wait for us, it was a race to catch any of them. Easter Monday was also the day to look for the beautifully coloured eggs, everyone hiding his own gift of eggs for sister, brother or friend. Grown-ups and artistic children can produce some real gems. What innocent fun we had.

The Sunday after Easter 1935 was a landmark for those who had attended the Confirmation classes, because that was the Sunday our Silesian Cardinal Bertram would come to our church to confirm us. Our Lutheran friends had their Confirmation at a later age. For us it meant we would become a full member of the church and parish. It still is an indelibly memorable day for me. Not only the new sailor suit with short trousers, long black stockings and candle - how smart we looked on the day - it was also the Cardinal's presence and his personal words to each one of us with his blessing, asking each one of us, boys and girls, to be strong and guard our faith. These were not just words for the moment. As a ten year old you can distinguish when you hear a speech, is it calm and joyful, or is it ranting and threatening. Those must have been difficult, frustrating and worrying times for the Bishop and his flock. Young as we were, we began to feel the tension between Church and State.

Ernst and I met outside church and congratulated each other, although we had been sitting together in church. Naturally, both our parents met and approved of the Cardinal's sermon to the parents. Having wished each other a happy Sunday, we all went home for lunch including Aunt Else and Grandma. After a tasty homemade meal and short rest it was time to go to the photographer's studio for our family photographs to be taken. While we were away, Aunt Else prepared the afternoon coffee table with all homemade cakes and gateaux. Of course, we had invited my godfather Uncle Paul and his family to come down for coffee time. On behalf of his family Uncle Paul presented me with a 'golden' pocket watch, a pleasant surprise for me. I cherished it and wore it with my sailor suit. I purposely left it at home on my call-up and that was that. With the Easter holidays over, another year of school had begun.

'Gross Strehlitz my Post Office'

'Gross Strehlitz the Gymnasium 1870'

'The Town House'

'Ruin of our home & castle showing arched trade entrance, ruins of our home, and former guest rooms of the castle'

School life soon returned to normality as we settled into the new classroom. My friendship with Ernst continued, and the odd two hours' playtime with Lutz did not diminish our friendship. In regard to the political situation, there seemed nothing that could take us away from the daily school routine, other than the odd reference by those boys who had joined the 'Hitler Jugend'{Hitler Youth}. There was no enthusiasm among those of us who just celebrated our tenth birthday. Those in the Franciscan Youth Group continued to meet twice a month in the evening at the church hall. In fact there were other such groups in the parish for the over-fourteen year old girls and boys. All met regularly and enjoyed it, especially singing new hymns that were becoming very popular. There were a few young Christian composers bringing out new tunes and more appealing lyrics for the younger generation, to counter the flood of Hitler Youth being fed with the new, often rebellious, marching songs and rhythm, to oppose anything anti-state.

During the summer playtime with Lutz was as often as possible outside, racing in our pedal cars, or at the large sand box. Nanny would call for tidying up at four, the time for Lutz to go in for a 'Jause', that is Austrian for afternoon coffee, with his mother. Thereafter homework for him. Counts Prosper and Lutz were both educated at home by a qualified person, it was always a Lutheran candidate studying for ordination, but who had completed their degree course. They were addressed as Herr 'Candidate'. They had their own private room and took the main meal with the family. To allow them privacy, the other meals were served to them in their room. If we happened to meet them, normal courtesy prevailed.

During our summer school holidays I happened to meet our parish priest who asked me to become an altar server. My answer was a quick and short "yes". Could I come for the practice day next week? "Yes, thank you" and that was me ready to go. I learned quickly, having practised at home with Engelbert and Ursula. Within two weeks I served with an older server who had taught me. Soon I could serve on my own during the week at the early Mass, before making my way to school, and I loved it. "Showing off", was my sister's comment. A few years later I got my own back.

Late summer and something new and exciting for boys appeared with the arrival of the military at the castle. It was manoeuvre time. It was the first experienced at the castle, at least for us. Dad of course knew what it was all about. The castle was asked to provide accommodation for the horses and the soldiers. The officers were given the rooms used for hunting guests. All other military men and equipment were accommodated around the town. Occasionally a large column of soldiers and horse-drawn wagons would pass through, at other times military vehicles pulling guns. After a week they moved on. Manoeuvres would happen twice a year. The older generation kept asking, why the hurry? Of course it was interesting and fun for us boys to admire the cross-country vehicles and the military motor cycles, with their drivers showing off to us how they can handle them. The castle was always a useful place to house the field kitchen near the stables for overnight cover and water to cook and wash. As a near ten-year old, you just could not yet comprehend where all this was leading. One can only imagine what our parents and the older generations must have asked themselves: where is the money going to come from to pay for all the military equipment and at the same time hastily building new factories and more modern garrisons? And all started with a bankrupt country? Our parents knew more and more about credit finance and Government State Bills of Exchange. Although the earning power of the public increased, there was a lack of available goods in shops which left some extra cash in the household. This in turn gave the government the opportunity to siphon off some for the public purse by many appeals for contributions towards various social needs. Some of that was taken off to pay the country's debt, caused by Hitler's main aim, his 'War of Conquest'. My question is, could Hitler alone have thought out those tricks? Most of those of my age would remember that every winter on the first Sunday of each month, at lunchtime, a collector would call with his sealed tin, for our contribution to help the elderly, the poor and needy. That I suppose, was one way to save the state having to find money for the needy. {A glance into the future, I could not imagine that I would within four years actually open those tins}.

In the meantime, I could not persuade my friend Ernst to join me as an altar boy. He had a good reason. Within a few months he would leave our Public School to go to the Gymnasium {Academy}. As for myself, I really enjoyed being an altar boy, getting up occasionally at five thirty to be at church for six, run home and ready in time for school at eight am. I never considered it a problem. With Christmas 1935 approaching outside playtime with Lutz was becoming restricted, but it meant we would enjoy playing inside again. As the year before, we were shown something new to do for our parents by nanny. At our general playtime I must say how considerate Lutz could be when we planned a change of what to play. Dad had mentioned that a new tutor for Lutz would arrive after the Easter holidays. Prosper at the Gymnasium, would be leaving to attend an advanced Academy in preparation to take over his Dad's castle and estate one day. The first snowfall had covered the ground and the little hill had sufficient depth to allow us to sledge, in order that we might breathe fresh air into our lungs. Lutz invited me to ask Ernst to come and join us with his sledge. Ernst was delighted and we had good fun for two hours, and all went home to get our gloves and socks dried. We shall need them again. A Silesian Christmas Eve meal with its own special multi different dishes to go with the fish requires preparation the day before Christmas.

Christmas Eve has arrived. "Time to bath and get ready" came the order from the kitchen. 4 p.m., time to go over to the castle to be led by Dad to the Salon to meet Countess Sybille, Count Castell, with Prosper and Lutz, to hand us our presents. We said our thanks, wished them a blessed Christmas, bowed our heads, Ursula curtsied and we returned well pleased with all we got and showed them to Mum. While Mum got on with the final preparations, Dad placed them under our Christmas tree. Dad ensured that the larger tree in the Salon was securely fixed, ready for Prosper and Lutz and the Count himself to decorate the tree. Dad had decorated our tree and as always we were not to go into the sitting-room until the proper time after our Christmas Eve meal in the kitchen. Once the kitchen was cleared we went into the sitting-room, with the Christmas tree already lit we sang our 'Stille Nacht, Heilige Nacht', and then the presents. We were always grateful for what we got knowing that our parents could only give us what they could afford. Later the Staff went to meet Countess

Sybille, Count Wolfgang and their sons, and received their presents in the Salon, and once they said their thanks, they would all sing together 'Stille Nacht, Heilige Nacht'. Dad and Uncle Paul usually lead, both being in the choir, but that is not to take away from the capabilities of the ladies present.

Uncle Paul and Dad served the Christmas Eve meal to the Count and family. It allowed them to be home early for the family Christmas meal and then open the presents, all now well-practised. Soon it was time for us to go to Midnight Mass. As for me, I was looking forward to my first Christmas as an altar boy. Mass was celebrated in traditional splendour. Our large crib laid out as usual, with the central figure of the Holy Family, the camel and all the other animals already described before. The crib can be visited until one thirty a.m. then the doors closed. We young ones had our torchlight competition to reach for the church steeple. Then home for a short sleep in order to be at church by eight for the festive Morning Service. It was the tradition that on Christmas Day after dinner we would play with the toys we got, while Dad and Mum had a rest. We would go and see Grandma on Boxing Day. Because she was still able to walk to church we would have met her there. Also we would not go to the castle to play until after Boxing Day.

After Boxing Day we would take our sledges and go to the castle park to sledge down the hill. Frost? You never felt the frost. That was the way we grew up. Your red cheeks were from the effort to pull the sledges back up the hill again for the next run down. That's where Ernst and I would meet to have fun together. Next day we would meet again this time trying out our new skates, first of all trying to stand up and to balance on them and after a few falls, no need to be shy for we were first time learners. Then look for a space away from the 'professionals' to try to slide along a bit and eventually you would improve and slide along until you landed on your behind and quickly get up while looking around to see who might have seen you. By the time I was fourteen, I too skated until late 9 p.m.

It was the year when we, just ten years old, became aware of the remarks of a pure 'Germanic race', but what did that mean? Did we have to know? Of course we could not yet understand what pastors in church took issue with during their sermons, and why they suddenly were absent from the parish. Sometimes parents were not always taking care when discussing political issues, and not paying attention that we might innocently talk about it, when we should not. That is fine, but in real life a word spoken at supper time, eventually got out to people to whom it should never have got to. This was the beginning of the 'dark' days and we youngsters were sent outside to play when on one occasion a visitor arrived who we did not know. In fact he was a cousin of Dad's, who spent some weeks, months or a year in a 'Konzentration' KZ camp and had just been released. Obviously it was a conversation that could not be repeated to any other, under any circumstances. We were politely given instructions to play outside while Mum was making coffee for our visitor. It would have been interesting to know, but I did not remember to ask my Dad in later years when it would have been quite safe to talk about it.

1936 the year of the Olympic Games in Germany was a stroke of luck for Hitler, to show off his 'might'. There is a British newspaper photograph of Hitler, his bodyguards the S.S. 'State Security Unit', in their black uniforms and officials in their brown shirt S.A. uniforms, and others, as Hitler is descending the wide stone steps into the arena, with his familiar raised right arm in his particular style, only two other officials are in dark suits. I wondered if it was the photographer's purpose to show as if Hitler was entering one of his 'Nuremberg' annual military parades rather than an international sports competition?

We also have a newspaper article with a photograph of a young Jewish competitor in the Ladies High Jump. Her trainers were confident she would gain a gold medal for Germany. But just days before, a letter was sent to her regretting that her performance was not up to the standard of competing for the High Jump medal, and therefore could not take part. That lady is still alive in the USA.

Summer holidays! From this year on, my holidays will be spent at one of my aunts and her family in a relatively small village, only a mile from the town of Tost. The village name had a more Polish sounding name 'Pizarsowice' in earlier times, but in our time 'Schreibersort'.

It is where Mum was born and is most likely one of those villages founded by Polish-speaking migrants who found work in the coal mines and the iron works. They would have been given land to build their houses and some acres to cultivate for food. The family would have to decide who is to work the land, the father or son? The daughters would have to present themselves to find husbands. It is out of such a situation our Mum came, where one of her brothers agreed to take over the small farm after their father had died. The others had to decide what trade to be apprenticed to. The other side of the coin were the daughters. That is where the love of dances at weddings and the many feast day celebrations, which usually ended with dances that were always well attended. Since they were attended by German and Polish speaking males and females mixed marriages were normal. I could add there is the age old attraction, when two different nations meet. That is how it finished when Dad met Mum at a dance in a village he had never been before. As I have mentioned, one of Mum's brothers took over her family small farm, and others found work in the mines and steel works. Mum's oldest sister Marie married a railway employee who inherited a small farm from his father in the same village. They were able to keep two cows, a few pigs and poultry and a few acres of grass to graze the cows. They also had a few acres to grow corn and potatoes, a profitable additional income for Uncle Josef. They had four sons and one daughter and it was with those cousins I was allowed to spend three weeks of my six-week summer school holidays for five years. Cousin August was the second youngest and my age, his sister Agnes was the youngest. They had sufficient room to keep me and I was always welcome. The years I spent with them were some of my most pleasant times, as those with young Lutz.

Aunt Marie made sure I was enjoying my stay. At seven in the morning, cousin August and I would loosen the two cows and we had to lead them on a chain half a mile to graze for an hour and a half before taking them back home. What interested me was when I first saw in Aunt Marie's kitchen the 'Alfa Laval', or 'Alfa'. It is a hand operated gadget called a 'separator' {a centrifuge which separates the cream from the milk}. I enjoyed watching the cream from one spout flow into a bowl and the skimmed milk from the other. Alfa Laval was the manufacturing company. I loved to turn that gadget every evening during my stay. Next time I saw an Alfa Laval was eight years later and a few hundred miles away. I could not have guessed or imagined how useful my time spent with the separator and the animals at Aunt Marie's would be one day. There was no farm large enough in the village to have a tractor at that time. If occasionally a car appeared in the village, then children would leave everything to admire the car.

There was always something which both August and I could do. There was the barn, which needed preparing for the storage of winter fodder hay and grain. Where there is agriculture there are tools to be cleaned and oiled, for harvest is early in Silesia. Although a small village, it did have a bakery where you could bring your own prepared bread and cake to be baked. All the three weeks I spent with them, Aunt Marie always had slabs of cakes, which we stored under our beds. Well, yes, we were not always angels. Before I complete my resume of holidays with my cousins I would like to share what we could never do at home. Cousin August would collect a few eggs and we took them to the baker who would give us in return some fancy cakes, which we would enjoy while herding the cows in the afternoon. Surely, Aunt Marie knew, but ignored it? Soon it was time to go back home, a short half-hour train journey. Once every two months in the summer, we would take the train to Tost to visit Kleine Oma 'Small Grandma' {Mum's mother} who also lived in Schreibersort. We would be often a dozen cousins playing happily together, never dreaming it would all end in the most awful disaster at the end of the war.

Autumn 1936 and the Olympic Games fading into the background, life drifted on towards winter and Christmas time. We were still able to attend the Church Youth Group without any pressure from outside. Rumour had it, that the 'Boy-Scout' movement had to disband, which left us wondering who was going to be next. We had been slowly conditioned to fear; "Oh watch what you are saying", at home or outside. It is in hindsight that we can say that parents had an important role to play in those days. They had to decide where they stood in front of their children. Do we believe in a fair, respectful society regardless of faith, race or colour, or follow an ideology that will not tolerate any other? We as children were grateful our parents had chosen according to their conscience.

1936-37. With the first snow fall, Advent and Christmas followed its usual pattern. The two afternoon playtimes were taken up cross stitching as the year before. It left ample time for other afternoons to play in the playroom with one of the many different toys available. Count Prosper now fifteen was attending the higher grade Academy in Gleiwitz, the second largest city in the industrial region. Although Count Castell was succeeding in turning his estate into a formidable enterprise, it must be his wish to leave the estate to his heir, Count Prosper with a degree in management.

Mum's youngest brother Anton, unmarried, had been looking for work in town. An opportunity came when the town council finally decided to build an outdoor swimming pool, to be built close to the main road at the edge of town. Uncle Anton found a room to rent in town with a bedroom, small kitchen and toilet. During the Easter holidays I walked out to the swimming pool building and took Uncle Anton the lunch which Mum had cooked for him. It was an opportunity for me to have a look at the large display board. It will be a large complex with three pools, one for the swimmers with a 5 meter diving board, one for non-swimmers and one for the toddlers.

His having found work in town was a blessing for Mum and Dad because Uncle Anton was quite happy to help in our garden when the need arose. That does not mean that I got off scot-free. At ten and a half I began to show some muscles having done spade work before. The highlight of the year was the annual 'Deutsches Sängerfest' {the German annual song festival} to take place at the Breslau Football Stadium. Did I hear Dad mentioning it to Mum? But I never imagined he would go. When told the whole family would go - that was a surprise! What an opportunity, having never been to Breslau. Spring has passed, and summer half gone, when it was time to prepare for the weekend to get ready for the long journey, almost two hours. It was also Dad's holiday week. We kids did not have to worry about where to stay. We discovered that Dad had an aunt, {a sister of Grandma} living in Breslau with whom he corresponded at Christmas time. She offered Dad and all of us to stay with her for three days. The day arrived and off we went to the station and boarded the train. Once we arrived in Breslau, Dad found his aunt's apartment after a good walk. We were amazed just how large a city can be. Excitement all round. Next day, Saturday, when we got up, Mum was already slicing a loaf to make sandwiches. Breakfast, and soon it was time to go. Dad had instructions from our Great Aunt about the trams. That was a novelty. Not just that we saw one for the first time, but could actually sit in one and listen to the bell 'ding'. Would we ever travel again in one? Just as well I had no premonition of what awaited me in years to come. The tram came to a halt and everybody going to the Stadium got out here. We looked up from the outside to the height of the perimeter wall, where the top sitting place was. It took quite a while before Dad was directed to the top {that was the ticket we could afford}. We were happy, that's what mattered, although it took some time to get to the top. In the end it was the right place. After two or three hours of many choirs singing their best – with so many singers, - it really was a feast. There were many pieces we could sing with them: we Silesians sing wherever. Any small or large group out walking would sing. It was about one p.m. and we were hungry, so we had our sandwiches. Now in the distance coming closer and closer we could hear cheers, shouts of 'Heil, Heil'. We being at the top, had a free view for half a mile, as the first huge black open limousine came in sight. There were two side by side, and another two, then we could clearly see Hitler saluting on and on until out of sight into the entrance. We could hardly see now that he was too far away, but it did not matter, we had seen him. That was the biggest occasion we had ever seen as far as Hitler was concerned. Only eight years later he was no more. For Mum and Dad the highlight was the singing of such a variety of outstanding choirs. It was never forgotten. Before leaving for home we thanked our Great Aunt for a wonderful experience. Little did I realise the journey to Breslau, the farthest so far, had been like a test run for my future of which I knew nothing as yet. Once at home, everything quickly returned to its usual routine.

For my eleventh birthday in 1937 my Uncle Anton bought me a youth encyclopaedia which I found most absorbing and I thanked him for it. One of the most interesting items given was the news and pictures of the first television programme being shown in black and white in London of the Coronation of King George VI in 1936. I took the book to school to show it to anyone who wished to see and marvel at it {another personal historic event for my, as yet, unknown future}. At one of our playtimes Lutz mentioned to me his parents' suggestion that he should now begin to be taught how to drive the pony and light coach. The pony had a lovely fitting name - Schimpimpel - named because of its pure white coat. Lutz was to drive with the coachman at first to make sure he would learn properly under supervision. The pony had a very kindly face and was well behaved. Horses of course were no strangers to me, having been taken by Dad a few times on shorter drives while he was coachman. Within two weeks Lutz was competent enough to invite me to come out with him for a drive. Lutz was not allowed to drive on his own, nanny had to be with us. The coach with dual shafts was for a single horse and was of woven material, to make the coach weight lighter. It was a two-seater plus a single seat in the back. That is where I sat whenever I was invited. Well, this was my first trip and I thought Lutz had the confidence; the horse being in a dual shaft makes the steering easy. The route was always the same through the large park. To answer the unheard question, of course I was proud, with the odd walker stepping aside and doffing his hat. Returning back after an hour at the stable with an intact horse, coach and passengers, the coachman was pleased. We made our way up to the castle and I thanked Lutz and we hoped to do it again. Most days we still had an hour to spend in the playroom.

The Youth Group met once a month. Then one day in late autumn we entered the classroom in the morning and found the Cross removed and a portrait of Hitler in its place. At break in the playing field we heard that had been done in all classes. Returning to the classroom our teacher made us understand that the Rector's name was now 'Herr Bittner', with a warning not to make a mistake by calling him by his former name which had a Polish-sounding syllable. Mum still shopped at the Jewish grocer, as did other families. It was possible for someone actually to stop you in the street and question your integrity as a German, shopping at a Jewish shop. We still kept rabbits for the occasional rabbit roast and I had no problem going to the Jewish shop, just round the corner actually, who took all sorts of skins for cash which I could always keep for my pocket money. These were Jews who were, let's say less wealthy. Among the altar boys, we understood and could trust each other. In fact, we began to form ourselves into 'secret youth anti-Hitler party fighters', until some adult found out and quickly in no uncertain manner knocked our heads together. After a sense of bravado, we felt humiliated. People had to begin to be watchful, if you are not always agreeing with what was being said on radio and in speeches. We eleven year olds had to learn from our seniors; to keep quiet and attend Sunday Services and keep coming to the youth meetings in the Church Hall. That was also told to the youth girl groups.

Late October the piano tuner arrived at the castle for the annual tuning of the pianos at which time Dad always had a conversation with him while serving refreshments at break time. This time he had a special reason, the question being the cost of a piano for me, second-hand of course. The tuner was only too happy to accommodate Dad, because the tuner was actually from the piano factory. The deal was done and we were to get a newly overhauled piano. Where Dad got the money from we never knew, but our parents were savers, neither drinkers nor smokers. There was no doubt Dad would have got a bargain. Arrangements for the delivery were made. To shift a piano from the station to the castle could be expensive. Dad took a bit of a risk which Mum was apprehensive about. Only a stone's throw from our exit gate lived a slightly handicapped middle-aged Jew. We all knew him. Dad spoke to him and he was glad to help bringing his cart to the station. Dad and I first went to the station where he had already met the night railway porter {who knew Dad from church}. The cart arrived before midnight after the last train. With no one around, we four loaded the piano and off we went to the castle. I always thought it is by God's grace we never met anyone who might not approve of having hired a Jew. We arrived home and the piano was unloaded. Dad paid the Jew, end of story, and everybody was happy. This is how it was already in 1937. A few days later four kind helpers managed to transfer the piano upstairs into the sitting room. It was a beautiful instrument and for us an impressive piece of furniture. From that time I went to piano lessons. Dad knew well that if by any chance a policeman had met us, he would have gone out of his way not to see us, as there were police officers who still attended Lutheran and Catholic churches on Sundays.

Autumn arrived and no autumn manoeuvres took place around our county. Most weeks, Lutz and I, with nanny, had one or two drives with Schimpimpel. It was Advent time and nanny taught us again some interesting and useful stitches to make a Christmas present for our Mum. Lutz was actually very good at girls' handicrafts. We had to try to keep up with him. As for myself I loved my altar boy 'ministry'. As usual, our Franciscan Youth Group Christmas party was much enjoyed. Within a week, snow began to fall and as every year on Saturdays the sledges came out. With school in Germany finishing at 1 p.m. you could still find an hour sledging before darkness made you go in to your homework.

Christmas 1937 stood at the door and all the usual joys of looking forward to the feast began to reappear in our minds. It was the time for preparation as I have described before. As for me it was a busy time as an altar boy. There were many articles that we needed to clean and polish, especially brass. Dad passed on his experience to me. He gave me perfect instruction: how, what and what not to do! That year I was strong enough to help with bringing out the crib figures and putting them up.

Finally, Christmas came with its old tradition, and no one gave it a thought that it may not be so two years later. Remembering all this I am still the boy who tried to be the one whose torch was the best reaching the top of the church steeple, but once again it did not make it. That in no way reduced the fun with all of us friends. With boredom unknown, New Year was at the door with all its fun for the young, and for our elders and the thoughts of what the New Year would bring. For us youngsters there was still a week's holiday from school.

As the snow seemed to linger, Lutz suggested for next day a sledge ride with Schimpimpel, and would I ask Ernst to join after lunch time and to bring his sledge. Brilliant idea I thought and informed Ernst who looked forward to it. In the meantime, I searched in Dad's workshop for ropes to tie the sledges. We had three sledges, Lutz's, Engelbert's and Ernst had his. Next day we all got ready and made for the stables. We tied our sledges with the help of Herr Kanzog, the coachman. He then saddled Schimpimpel and tied him to Lutz's sledge. Off we went in great style. Let me remind you, we all knew how to steer a sledge with iron clad heels on leather shoes. Off we went with Lutz 'driving' of course. We crossed the main road into the large park where we had over two miles of roads to drive on. It was great fun, weaving with care. Schimpimpel had done well and we headed home. Before we crossed the road again we must have done something wrong and sledge after sledge turned over with everyone falling off. Schimpimpel galloped on with three empty sledges, until finally he stood at the stable door. When Mr Kanzog came out, he found none of the 'passengers' in sight, until four red-faced drooping heads came round the stable door. Lutz suggested meeting again next day, we all agreed. While those sleigh rides continued for a few days more, Ernst and I met after early supper at the large frozen lake to skate. Since Count Castell had strung light bulbs across the lake, the Gymnasium pupils with their expensive skates could show off their skill.

One afternoon in early March, with Lutz in the playroom, I was introduced to a lady whose name I could not understand: 'Miss Ida MacDonald'. She was to teach English to Lutz and Prosper. We were asked to call her Miss Ida, and told that her home was 'Schottland' {Scotland}. That meant for the second time in our town, Scotland was represented. Was it just a coincidence, or was it some other mysterious indicant? It was my first opportunity to shake hands with a Scottish lady. As regards her engagement, Miss Ida, was also engaged by the 'Prinz Castell-Castell' to teach English to his sons and daughters at their castle in Bavaria for six months. It proved a satisfactory arrangement.

After my twelfth birthday even Dad and Mum realised that I had better join Hitler's 'Jung Volk', the youngest group in the Hitler Youth, a boys' group for the over ten and under fourteens. This was to avoid discrimination by those whose parents were in favour of the regime. Learning discipline and comradeship would do no harm. The leaders were those over fourteen who had been trained before us how to stand still and rigid and march in step. We learnt new Nazi party songs, always in marching tempo, but also the old hiking songs, if the lyrics were suitable. There was a lot of physical fitness taught which did no harm; although we all grew up in an age where cars were a novelty and you were used to the outside physical life.

Far more disturbing was the imposition of the Party forcing the Jewish population to wear the six inch yellow Star of David, sewn on the outer garment - a most humiliating order for the Jewish population. In our parish we had two elderly Jewish sisters who converted to Christianity. In spite of this, they still had to wear the Star of David and it was embarrassing for all of us to see them enter church and to know that our people had forced this on them. It was good to see how the congregation reacted by greeting them as they walked in. Hitler's early declaration to his close political friends and military commanders was that he expected the army to be fit for war within four years. He also expected the German economy to be capable to sustain conflict. People can be blinded by rhetoric. One wonders was that what happened in Austria when Hitler felt confident to march into Austria in March to jubilant crowds. Hitler must have been rubbing his hands, a million or more new soldiers? Jubilant people, yes, on newsreels and in the press, etc., but what about those behind curtains and who stayed at home, not being so sure? Our older generation would have seen it differently.

During the Easter holiday, Sister Superior from the Convent school in town called at our home. They taught Domestic Science there, a two year course, to girls who had finished eight years at Public School. Sister had some news for my parents and me. The Convent had been given some money to pay for a boy, under fourteen, for a three week stay in a Catholic orphanage in Bavaria during the school holidays. Sister thought I was the right boy to go. That was a surprise! I had two months to prepare. That is some journey for a twelve year old boy, and I was ready to go.

At the castle, the Count had been ill and was sent to recuperate for a few weeks at Countess Sybille's Austrian home. In his absence, the Countess had a discussion with Uncle Paul and Dad about a wish she had had for some time, to have a public garden party in the small park. Both men encouraged her and the planning began. It had to be done during the Count's absence as he would not be too happy regarding the possible damage to the lawn. Encouraged, she summoned her Director and the preparations began. Bakers, butchers, ice-cream and soft drinks vendors were asked and supported the Countess. She wanted the stable boy to walk the Count's riding horse and take children for a ride round a marked area. The Countess also agreed for the chauffeur to drive the large car with children and parents for a mile or so round the small park. Count Prosper drove Schimpimpel with children on short tours. The local Red Cross was happy to attend, which was much appreciated. I was asked and able to help where I could. It was a huge success and blessed with sunshine. There were no injuries, only happy faces. There was never another opportunity to hold such an event. Next day two pairs of horses from the nearest estate farm and the right equipment turned the grass and the roads back into their original order. It was a one off event, for posterity.

No sooner was Countess Sybille's garden party over, but it was time for me to prepare for my trip to Bavaria. It was summer time, so shorts for the day and Sundays. Yes, I did get some pocket money for the journey and I had my homemade sandwiches. The train took us closer to the Sudeten mountains that gave me a grand view of their beauty, villages and churches to the right and left. Heading along in a north westerly direction, some passengers got off, others joined, and what was new? Their dialect, which I had not heard before, most I did not understand, yet we were still in Silesia.

After two hours or so we turned west towards Saxony, and the city of Dresden. My eyes barely moved from looking out of the window and made me forget to have one of my sandwiches. The train did not stop at every station. My interest in geography was being tested and I cannot describe my happiness when I read the stations and their towns. We stopped only once in Saxony, in the town of Bautzen. Within minutes I began to hear a different dialect. I was fascinated trying to understand what they were talking about. Soon it was time to prepare to get off the train and change.

Well here I am in Dresden. I often heard the name in geography and history lessons. I had one and a half hours till my next train. I felt confident, although often in my earlier youth I'd been shy. I ventured out of the station, always looking back, pin-pointing anything that I would recognise easily on my way back. As soon as you step out of the station you are confronted with a panorama of overwhelming architecture. There was not sufficient time to look, even at a small area - on my way home, perhaps?

We are off again, turning left in a westerly direction, with Czechoslovakia on the south side of the Sudeten Mountains. Within the hour we turn south towards Bavaria. Now I really have difficulty to understand the dialect. After an hour and a half we are at the Bavarian border, stopping at the town of Hof. Here I change into a slower train stopping at every station. My destination is Waldsassen, which will appear any time soon, so I get ready, reach up for my case and take my belongings off the rack. Journey's end, who will be there? Do they know when I was to arrive?

Not that many people get off and a young boy maybe 15 to 17 makes his way towards me. He asked me if I am Paul Lippok. I say "yes" and we shake hands. "Ah, now listen carefully and do not be afraid to ask if you do not understand". I wonder if I should ask for his name, but he has beaten me, telling me his name is Josef, "but in Bavaria I am Sepp". It took about a thirty-minute walk to reach the orphanage. Well, I am no stranger to religious Sisters, so I knew I would get a great welcome. A smiling Sister welcomed me and asked: "Paul, will you get homesick?" "No Sister". Sepp led me up to my room and made me feel comfortable. Supper is in less than an hour and a bell will ring. By the time I had unpacked my few possessions, had a good look around and out the window. The bell rang and I made my way downstairs and into the dining room. I carefully listened and watched the routine. All stood up and grace was said. Food is taken in relative silence and what we got was good and sufficient. You brought your dishes to the counter and I do not remember what we did after. Sepp, at seventeen years old, was to be our 'chaperone' rather than the 'head boy'. There were only four of us to enjoy the privilege of being the guests. Lingering in the playroom, we introduced ourselves and explained where we came from. It turned out I was the furthest away. The other three from Bavaria and from villages. Some of them were not that good at geography to know where Silesia was, I found that a bit strange.

After a sufficient supper {bowl of soup, bread, butter and a slice of sausage} it was time for a few table games, then night prayer and off to your room. Bedrooms were for four boys, I was with Sepp and two other boys. We each had our own wardrobe and within two or three days we gelled well together. I looked at it as some sort of preparation for Hitler Youth camps that I may have to attend some time. Morning prayer before breakfast, thereafter the older permanent boys like Sepp had certain jobs to see to. This being school holidays, some had gone home or away to start an apprenticeship {the reason for there being room for us to stay for a few weeks}. Sepp found me a useful companion, having discovered that I was well-trained not only in housework, but also at home in the garden and at my cousins on the land. We had ample time to go to the 'Sportfeld' to play football, which we played a lot. I aimed for a permanent place as goalkeeper during my stay. We also went for many walks in the hilly area. Waldsassen is mainly in undulating countryside. The Sisters had much trust in Sepp. That allowed us to go for longer walks. One day Sepp took us some three miles to the Czech border where we saw the barbed wire fences six feet high and other such obstacles {no-one could guess that all that would be run over within a year or two}. With Mother Superior's blessing and permission, Sepp took us to town. We had sandwiches and a bottle of water for our lunch. It was a most interesting day. Waldsassen has a very old and famous church, its architecture is well known far and wide. Sepp made an excellent tour guide.

The highlight of my stay here was a visit to a small village called Konnersreut, of which we heard a lot about at home. There was a middle-aged lady who had Christ's stigmata on her hands and feet which bled each Friday since early 1920s. The people who came on Fridays numbered three hundred. The Nazis had doctors examine her many times, but could not expose any facts to the contrary of a miracle. Sepp had Sister's permission to take me there on one of those Fridays. It was a two hour walk there and back. I make no apology. I am unable to deny the miraculous, nor have I any doubts. The name of the stigmatised lady was Therese Neumann. We visited the village on another day and Therese was working in her garden and was happy to pass the time of day. For me it was a memorable day. My whole stay there was an unforgettable holiday which widened my horizon. The effect of such a holiday and its experience is indelible in my mind. One other benefit was I came home a goalkeeper to be reckoned with. All too soon my time to go home had come. I found it difficult to say goodbye and to adequately thank them all, especially the Sisters. It taught me just how attached one can get to kind people. Sepp escorted me to the station, a wave and we parted, never to meet again.

The journey home was now even more interesting having seen, at least for me, such a large part of Germany. This time there was no opportunity to take a walk in Dresden: the connection to my train home was too short. The pleasure of travelling was raised by it being in daylight. I arrived home welcomed by my family. Telling them all about it took days. My first call next day was to say thanks to Sister Superior and I gave her a good report of what I had seen and enjoyed.

More political surprises in this year - the meeting of the Minister of War, General von Blomberg and the Chief of the Armed Forces, General Fritsch, with Herr Hitler raised eyebrows on hearing of the dismissal of the two generals, for expressing their doubt that the Armed Forces would be sufficiently ready for a massive combat. 'Lebensraum', 'space to live' became a new expression of Hitler's. This was now directed towards the east {Poland obviously and the oil fields beyond}. In the meantime, there began an agitation to stir up hatred towards Czechoslovakia for harassing the German Sudeten people - Hitler's propaganda machine in action. These were words over which many showed approval, but others who voiced doubts in whispers afraid to be heard. And there was us for whom school and playtime were more important. Although occasionally, now at twelve, you wondered why parents broke off a conversation as soon as we were in the room.

'My Story' continues. School holidays have come to an end and I am in my second last year. Count Prosper is continuing his academic year, after the family had a holiday at the Countess' family castle in Austria. Everyone at the castle is pleased and happy to see the Count in good health again. Lutz and I are enjoying our playtime inside should it rain; otherwise we play at the sand box with my sister Ursula and Engelbert joining us. Twice a week Lutz and I still go for a drive with Schimpimpel, with a new nanny, none other than Aunt Else, whom the Countess asked if she would like to be the nanny to Lutz. Now that Lutz is older there is not so much supervision required. Miss Ida calls in on us when playing inside. She stays for a while and talks with Lutz in English, as the playroom raises different subjects. Actually Miss Ida wanted me to join, for which I was rather pleased. I soon could say "Good morning, good evening, thank you" and a few words more. If only I had known what the future held for me. Other unexpected news was Uncle Paul had been called to do his two-month military training. We had one manoeuvre billeted for a week only. Apart from play I do have a serious time in my life. Church time first, and pocket money from helping at Baptism on Sundays at 2 p.m. I am getting to know church duties and the laying out of vestments and so much more. Moving the lever for the power to get the bells ringing I can do in my sleep. One other boy of my age and in my class has become an altar boy. He lives over a mile from church. We are on the way to becoming good friends.

Our Rector, who taught one hour on two days in the final year, class VII and VIII, entered our class one day and immediately enthusiastically proclaimed that "our Führer had at last intervened and moved into Czechoslovakia, to put an end to their threatening rough behaviour towards our Sudeten people. We should be proud to see our army marching into Prague". We just sat there not knowing what it meant and some teachers were notably less enthusiastic. All the newspapers had on their front page the soldiers being cheered by the people. The Czechs fist-shaking and spitting at our soldiers we never saw, of course, until long after when the real story began to emerge.

More interesting for the population was the meeting at Munich between the British Premier Mr Chamberlain and Hitler. Hitler proved a difficult 'partner' to negotiate with. Europe needed some stabilising politics. The Treaty of Versailles, which was always seen by Britain as a problematic nuisance, allowed Hitler to demand equal rights in matters of the military. Hitler must have made it extremely difficult for Chamberlain to come to a reasonable agreement and avoid another confrontation. What Chamberlain came home with, was a word that became infamous, 'appeasement'. Waving the piece of paper,

Mr Churchill, in a rage, immediately declared it a useless piece. How right that proved.

In the meantime Uncle Anton, Mum's brother, who worked at the new swimming pool the year before, had been sent to the town of Wolfsburg, to build accommodation for the new 'Volkswagen' factory workers. With Uncle Anton now working at the new car factory in northern Germany, it brought a new excitement into the family, at least for us children anyway. In 1938 there were only a few VWs seen so far south. In any case it was expected the factory would also produce vehicles for the military, staff cars for despatch riders and officers.

Hitler's meaningless declaration that the Czech people had nothing to fear was short lived, when Hitler ordered his troops into Prague, facing a spitting hostile population, deploring the fact that their country is to become a Protectorate under German authority. Next came the assassination of a German diplomat in France. An act of revenge against the 'Nuremberger Law' of September 1935, claiming only 'Aryans' have a right to live in Germany, all others are second class citizens {meaning the Jewish population}. Only those who could establish proof of Aryan ancestry could become public servants. The rage gave the excuse that the authorities had been waiting for, and led to Germany's darkest hour, the 'Kristallnacht', 9/10th November 1938. This is how it was seen and lived through in a Silesian town by me, a twelve and a half year old and my friend Ernst, on a normal late autumn afternoon.

It was around four in the afternoon when my friend Ernst called. He was not over exited but asked me to go with him to the town square as he thought something was going on. I put on my coat and told Mum I was meeting Ernst. When we arrived there were quite a few men in uniform talking and carrying large thick sticks, not walking sticks. As the minutes passed by, more and more uniformed {brownshirts} men arrived, the talking got louder and sort of aggressive as more people gathered. Within half an hour the 'Kreisleiter' appeared. He is the town and county Party official, who could override the mayor anytime in political matters. Shortly after, he mounted the steps of the Town House and burst into a raging speech, shouting and raving about things that were beyond us. But why those people with the thick sticks? He very quickly got to his theme; the Jews. Yes there was applause coming from Party members. He must have spoken for nearly three quarters of an hour for sure, when he ran out of speech material or whatever. Anyhow, Ernst and I could not make anything of it. Although we began to understand when Ernst thought; they are going to go for the shops. Surely not? That was when the Kreisleiter finished: "Now is the time to show enough is enough, arm yourself you know what to do!" With that the mob went for the Jewish shops around the square, beginning to smash the windows, broke the doors and ransacked the shops throwing everything into the street; and men who probably were not interested in the speech began to stuff their pockets and, how? Some had shopping bags to fill. There was the outfitters shop, the tobacconist, the grocer, the jeweller. Ernst shook my arm. Look up to the top floor where the dentist lives. Through the open windows came the expensive dental equipment.

We asked ourselves what on earth is the meaning of it all? Why? I suggested to Ernst that we go home and tell what is happening out here. Mum apparently had been out and heard bits of the commotion. When we arrived home and told her she went into a silent prayer. Mum thought we ought to stay inside. Ah well, young boys, curiosity took a hold on us, promising we will be back. The few yards from the castle saw us back watching the unbelievable commotion and chaos. Some elderly people passed by, barely taking notice yet shaking their heads. What they murmured we could not make out - disapproval? This disturbance must have gone on for nearly two hours, then the 'Kreisleiter' began to shout: "Auf zur Synagogue" {off to the Synagogue}. We waited till the mob had gone then we followed, forgetting that we promised to come home. A five-minute walk took us to the Synagogue, situated on one side of the square where the war memorial stood. There must have been an ordered detail of Party members long before us, because there was already a fire within the Synagogue. As we arrived a large fire was burning on the square with uniformed men bringing out more wooden benches and other contents from the Synagogue to be thrown onto the fire. The irony was that it took place on the War Memorial square, where the name of a few Jews were inscribed who fought and fell in the 1914-18 war. Suddenly, out from the burning Synagogue came the 'Kreisleiter' waving the Jewish Banner and shouting: "Oh Lord give us Moses back", over and over again until he threw it on the fire. Out of the blue, or by spiritual order, there behind us was Mum. We knew why she came and we followed her home. What she saw on her way to the Synagogue must have shocked her to the core. There was no mistaking tears were in her eyes. I said goodnight to Ernst, and was in bed within minutes. What an experience to have lived through. Next morning in school it was surprising how many boys in my class, who lived in the three satellite villages a mile from town, did not know what had happened the night before. They noticed the broken windows and saw the pile of ashes on the Memorial Square. They listened with astonishment at what had happened. The infamous 'Kristallnacht'. The silence from our class teachers next morning was surprising. Even today I wonder what went through the mind of some of the teachers. For myself, I was relieved that it was not one of the days the Rector had our class that morning. It surprises me still, how humiliated I felt. One has to remember the anti-religious attitude of those who wanted a different Germany began to create the rift, where old and young had to take sides and it became easier to define which side by listening to the Party. Now the state had the indisputable right to decide are you Aryan, or second class citizen. Those whose duty it was to warn against the state deciding who you are, took great risks. On the matter of who is to live and who is not, the Cardinal of Münster was not silent but outspoken. A much decorated soldier of the 1914-18 war, he was a thorn in the flesh of the Party, who dared not charge him for fear of his people. Just like his friend the Lutheran Dr Niemöller who with many priests also paid with their lives; not counting the number of those in 'Konzentration' camps. We as thirteen year olds began to know about these things.

The twice weekly half hour religious instruction in the morning had been abolished a year ago. In its place we had to write essays on Hitler's youth. History lessons were centred on the great Germanic achievements, like Frederick the Great and other such successes. While I liked history I favoured geography, although I had no special reason, at the time; but now I do. Within a few years I was grateful for such foresight.

Autumn and an eventful year were drawing to a close. There came one more surprise for all of us with the unexpected appearance of a possible sighting of a comet. What excitement, since we never had such an opportunity before. As you can imagine the reaction of the older people, their way of seeing where the politics of the present government is leading perceived the appearance of the comet as a bad omen. Two years later many could say "I told you so". Most of us looked at it as a privilege to be alive at that moment. Our teacher spent some time giving us a comprehensive lesson on the subject of comets. One of the suggestions from our teacher was to blacken a piece of glass by holding it over a candle. Today there are instruments to get a closer look. Friends, who have them, may invite you. With a clear night and no moon, we got a good viewing. Next morning at school, teacher and pupils shared our experiences.

Advent time and on 6th of December is 'St. Nikolaus' day. He is going to come again surely, since we felt that our parents would have something good to tell him about us, to be given some goodies out of his sack. On two afternoons during the week we were invited to join Lutz for nanny and Miss Ida to teach us with needle and thread to make something new for Mum. Quite often Miss Ida would speak with Lutz in English, at the same time teaching me a word or two. It was very kind of her and somehow I did enjoy it. It seemed unimaginable that it would ever be my second language.

Snow falling and frosty nights added to the spirit of preparation for Christmas. One other important and enjoyable time was the afternoons and evenings, helping Mum baking the traditional 'Pfefferkuchen' {gingerbread biscuits}, cutting out the different shapes we liked best. There was ample time to build snowmen, alternating with sledging with Lutz and Ernst. Our last debacle, with sledges and red faces, did not prevent us from enjoying ourselves, just taking more care. Too soon Christmas Eve was upon us and the well-known routine followed. Starting with we three youngsters getting 'spruced up' and making our way up to the Salon to meet the Countess and her family for our Christmas gifts. We gracefully bowed and said our thanks, and wished our benefactors a blessed Christmas. This was already our fifth Christmas reception at the castle, we were indeed growing up. At home it all followed the customary routine. A thought is always given to Grandma in the cottage in the garden, looked after by Aunt Else, who is still unmarried. We will visit them on Christmas Day afternoon, where Aunt Else will serve a delicious afternoon of 'Kaffee und Kuchen' {coffee and cakes}. The highlight will again be the Midnight Mass, for our Lutheran friends the 'Andacht' or midnight service. This will be my second Christmas as an altar server. So far on Christian feast days there has not been an attempt by the Party to disrupt the Christmas Festival as some feared. This may surprise many readers, just how much in our young teens, the conflict between the state and church had begun to form our opinions. For outsiders it might be difficult to understand the problems of those subjected to a political system, which was intent in displacing a traditional, civilised, accepted living pattern, and replacing it with an ideology where the individual has no right to question the hierarchy. It had been another happy Christmas and the rest of the holiday was spent as usual with Lutz and my friend Ernst sledging, often just down the little hill by the castle. More time however was spent inside the playroom and there was the duty to help Dad clearing the snow which might have fallen again. It was understood that I was expected to feed our rabbits and poultry, as well as fetching coal and firewood. Of course there was my altar server duty to fulfil at the daily morning services. At early Mass at five thirty there would be a number of people attending, the elderly in the main who were used to rising and others who would go straight after to work. Ah, yes, there existed a different attitude so many years ago.

Often I would just hang around and help our beadle during the school holidays, then home for breakfast. School holidays over, life took on normality. Although cars and trucks were no longer the novelty, four wheel sledges pulled by horses were very much in use on farms. The common four wheel wagons were quickly converted into sledges; steel studs were screwed on to the horses' shoes to prevent them from slipping. We may be living in a castle, but I grew up with horses in close contact.

Winter fading away and Easter is approaching and with it a busy time for altar boys to assist during the Liturgy etc. Just as important are the 1939 Easter holidays, and with it the end of another school year. There are those who will begin their first day at school, with the traditional cone filled with sweets and the occasional tear leaving mother. To remind you, Class VII and VIII are together, with the Rector being the class head and teaching one subject only, which I can no longer remember. Those of Class VIII will be leaving school, and starting their year on the farm before their apprenticeship. More important, just to show off, we will be senior boys starting our last year in school. Within two months I will be celebrating my 13th birthday. At the castle, Miss Ida will shortly leave for her six month stay with the Castell family in Bavaria. Here in the meantime the afternoon drive with Lutz and Schimpimpel continued. This being my last year at school it was expected that Dad and Mum would mention the fact and thoughts on what to do after school next year. What had I in mind? Nothing definite, I did have thoughts to try a career with the railways, not driving engines. There are other attractive opportunities as a railway employee. One was, free travel during your holidays. There is of course still the government rule, that if not a student you are obliged to do the 'Landjahr' a year working on the land with a farmer. You would have a year to decide. It was left at that, but never completely out of mind. Dad knew many farmers close to town, who have small farms. The thought of being closer to home in the evening was appealing. There was a maximum eight hour day stipulated.

The six-week summer school holidays had arrived. So far the weather was typically Silesian, with the temperatures between 22°C and 25°C, and the occasional one hour earlier home, if it went over 25°C. At the new excellent swimming pool there was ample time to spend an afternoon. The terrace with the tables and their sun brollies was worth passing a glance at ladies sipping coffee and ice cream. Holiday time arrived and there was some work to be done in our garden, with the help of Dad and his instructions. Dad's skill at joinery work pleased the Count getting small repairs done in an instant, anywhere in the castle.

As usual in the past few years I will go to 'Schreibersort' to stay with Aunt Marie and Cousin August. I was looking forward to operating the 'Alfa', separating the cream to make butter. Or, as I had mentioned before, herding the cows and taking a few eggs to the baker in return for lovely cakes. We will visit our little Grandma and offer our help to Uncle Thomas who works the small home farm. It will be harvest time and I will get to lead the horse, from which I get much pleasure. But all good things come to an end and so did my holidays. As I said goodbye to my cousin August, we were all aware of the fact that this was our last holiday because next year we will have left school and life will begin in earnest. As usual Dad and Mum took the train and came to visit mother's brothers and sisters, who came from their home for the family summer get-together. It had been a wonderful time on that last afternoon. Who could have known that was going to be the last of such a large family gathering? This time as we said 'Auf Wiedersehen' and God bless, none of us knew nor even imagined it would be the last time we would all be together.

Back at school and work, the days went by. At the castle there was the first shoot of the season. It was another of the many pleasant childhood memories. For the staff it was a busy time and late evenings. Uncle Paul had to stock up the alcoholic beverages. Dad had to get up early in the morning to see to a hundred and one things, so that everything got off to a good start. Can you imagine the numbers of boots and shoes there were to be cleaned after the hunt each day? We will miss the bugle wake up sound when after the week all have gone.

No sooner had the Hunt gone home, when an Army Officer arrived, requesting accommodation for officers and permission to park a number of vehicles about the stables. That meant there would be military manoeuvres taking place around us. Was that the time when Hitler's mention of 'Lebensraum' {room to live} meant room in the east, Poland? These were dangerous talks for the elders, and certainly not for our ears. But as a teenager, one began to question certain words that fell on your ears. But you did not spend your time digesting what you might have heard in passing.

This time at the castle it seemed to us that the officers' vehicles were larger, able to drive over rough ground. It is still in my memory the expressed surprise among adults why the manoeuvres were so close to the border with Poland, now? It was a reasonable question. The second Sunday in August was the day for the annual pilgrimage for men, old and young, of Upper Silesia, to the Franciscan Abbey on the Annaberg {Mount St. Anna}. Annaberg is a 1400 ft. high mountain in an area of undulating countryside in our county and less than ten miles from home. It has been a place of gatherings from ancient times, being visible from the four points of the compass. With the appearance of Christianity it had continued to be a place of meeting and eventually a place of pilgrimage. Franciscan monks settled there a few centuries ago. Eventually a church was built right on the top of the mount and dedicated to St. Anna. Through time people were drawn to the place. Roads lead up the mountain from three sides. Many of the houses have spare rooms to accommodate Pilgrims. Since the last hundred years a large variety of religious groups walked up to the Abbey, each group for its annual Pilgrimage. Visitors come to the mountain throughout the year to picnic or have meals in the few excellent local restaurants. Many visit the Abbey to pray and relax in the stillness of the place, with monks always available to talk. The view is outstanding. Only four miles away from Annaberg is the former German chemical factory that produced petrol from coal before and especially during the war. Built alongside the River Oder, the coal could be brought at low cost by boats, only thirty miles from coal mines. Let your thoughts wander. It is late autumn 1939 only a month before the war. It is the annual pilgrimage, for men of any age, the like of which Annaberg has never seen before or since, and that in the height and midst of Hitler's reign. Normally, between seventy and eighty thousand men, young and old pilgrims attend. They come by any means, including walking for miles to attend this pilgrimage. Miners in their full Sunday regalia with their brass band from thirty miles away, provided the energy for defiance. With the 'Kristallnacht' of last year, and the ever-increasing suppression of Christianity, an inner resentment of Nazism seemed alive. We, the Franciscan Youth Group of Gross Strehlitz had decided we would as before, walk the eight miles, leaving Saturday afternoon and hoping there would still be a place in the pilgrim hall to put down our blanket for a rest. Our Cardinal Bertram had pledged to attend the Pilgrimage.

Rumours that the Party might try and prevent the Cardinal from attending soon became true. While we the Pilgrims began to make our way to the grotto and the large gathering place, an announcement was heard from the loud speaker that the Cardinal might be arriving a little late. Rumour of the authorities putting diversion signs in some places, even digging up roads soon became true. Somehow news came through to the Abbey that the Cardinal had a two-hour delay in finding minor roads to negotiate. Over the loud speaker, a mighty "We'll wait" thundered across the plaza. That was the signal for the miners' bands to lead the mass of Pilgrims in hymn singing. Three hours later clapping hands indicated His Eminence had arrived. While our Cardinal was robed, a voice from the microphone announced that the number of pilgrims had reached 130,000. The roar and the clapping of hands were deafening. Cardinal Bertram, looking down to the assembled, seemed overwhelmed to see the defiance and took several minutes to compose himself before he began to pray. We all knew Hitler's S.S. dared not confront the miners. This indelible memory is still with me now.

With the defiant male pilgrimage fading into the background, comes the vociferous condemnation in newspapers and on the radio concerning the harassment of the German population in Poland. This could not be verified because of strict border controls. It was found to be untrue, by those who had contact with relatives across the border. Then came the bombshell, the signing of the non-aggression pact between Hitler and Stalin, late in August 1939, two nations thought by all to be deadly enemies. The day after the news was heard, our class was assembled outside the school to march off to the town's playing field for sport. Our gym teacher seemed lost in thought for a few moments, before he started to question if we had heard that particular news? Some had, most of us had not. He seemed so surprised, as probably many more people were, and in my memory I see him slowly shaking his head, from side to side in disbelief, as if we were not there.

Around the middle of August out of the blue military units begun to pass through our town, most at first with light weapons, etc. Within a day or two heavy trucks began to negotiate the town. We boys were stunned to see the heavy guns being drawn by large trucks. The front wheels were normal heavy pneumatic truck wheels, the rear were three wheeled tank tracks, in front sat the driver and two soldiers and behind the driver were two rows of four soldiers. We boys found it all exciting to see so many different motorised vehicles. At one point the whole procession came to a halt when one of the drivers misjudged the sharp corner and took quite some time to manoeuvre round it. A two-seat officer car had to wait beside us and they were listening to the car radio. Now that was the first time we saw and heard a car radio, how exciting. One wonders how many thought of the probability of a war. The Polish border was only a mere twenty miles away. More army transporters passed through next day. Changes had been promised when Hitler declared that within ten years Germany would be unrecognisable. Certainly there had been major changes, hardly any unemployment, a low crime rate, miles of new motorways and massive concrete defence works on Germany's western border. There was the arrival of the 'Volkswagen' VW cars for the people and all within eight years. Sadly, how much of that was not so good? Changes were becoming disturbing and unpalatable. 'Kristallnacht'? Why a Gestapo? Secret State Police? Concentration Camps? Even locking up his own people if you were judged not of sound mind!

Within a day or two another surprise, this time incredible and hard to believe possibly, news on the radio in the morning: "Polish insurgents in uniform have stormed the radio station in Gleiwitz with guns and shot some of the staff". By midday the whole of Germany had heard of the attack. From Berlin a hate campaign was launched immediately. Gleiwitz was the second largest city in the industrial region and close to the Polish border. Its radio station was the satellite station of the regional main station at Breslau. That was the opportunity for Hitler to march into Poland on 1st September 1939. In hindsight it was the beginning of the end of our Fatherland as we had known it.

What happened in reality? The truth for some reason could not be stifled of what really happened in our Upper Silesia, and soon got out, even down to us teenagers. Now of course it is well known that it was a set-up by special S.S. commandos dressed in Polish uniform entering the building shouting in sort of Polish, causing fright and confusion among the unsuspecting staff even firing real ammunition, with one of the staff having 'accidentally' been shot dead. Of course it did not come as a surprise, when a countrywide hate campaign was launched immediately. Jokes about it ceased abruptly next day when Hitler announced on the radio, "From today we shoot back".

With these words on that infamous day, Hitler tore up the faked promise at the Munich conference. He sealed Germany's downward fate. Far more painful, in the end he robbed us Silesians of two thousand years' labour of love to cultivate the land and build our homes. Just as well we did not know at the time, that within five years our Silesia would be lost to us forever.

Mum, who generally attended the weekday early morning Service, had just made breakfast for us and in a subdued voice told us that war had started. That is what the priest at Mass said and asked for prayers. There was silence in the kitchen, with us children not knowing what to say. Just finish your breakfast and off you go to school. With autumn sunshine and clear sky, as we approached the school we heard the advancing drone, and looking up watched the two-engine bombers pass over in a southerly direction. Ernst attending the Academy will call in the afternoon to 'discuss' the situation. Arriving at school, we found our teachers in a gloomy mood, with the exception of our Rector, who had something to say about patriotic encouragement for our army.

Coming home from school, we found Mum in subdued mood. The drive with Schimpimpel had been cancelled. My friend Ernst did call on us, which did not surprise me since I knew that their radio was superior to ours and he would hear more commentaries as the day went on.

Two days later, with our bedroom facing the back entrance on the second floor, I woke up hearing voices below the window. It was just beginning to get light and I decided to get out of bed to look out. Without opening the window I saw two people talking, one of whom I thought I recognised in a Post Office uniform talking to Dad. Not able to hear what the conversation was about I went back to bed. It made me think of a telegram, having seen a postman. Dad would have heard the bell and would have gone out to see and then pressed the buzzer. A short while later I went back to the window and recognised Uncle Paul with Dad and the postman, but could not hear their conversation. Coming down for breakfast Mum was in sombre mood and informed us that postmen had been out since the middle of the night delivering call-up papers. That was what the postman had been doing, bringing call-up papers for Uncle Paul. It was a bit of a shock for us, a new experience. Uncle Paul had few hours to gather his shaving and washing bag, pen, and knowing Uncle Paul a Prayer book would certainly be taken and photographs of his family. Before saying goodbye to his family he took time to say goodbye to Dad and Mum, but not to Grandma, nor the Count and his family, it being about five in the morning. That, he left to Dad to convey. Then it must have been time to say his last words to Aunt Magda. Mum and Dad obviously promised to be at hand for her.

For me, that was a bit of a shock suddenly faced with some of the reality of war. For instance, the little time he had to say goodbye to his wife, and his two young daughters. Uncle Paul had just celebrated his thirty fifth birthday. With hindsight one realises that happened to millions of families. {It happened to a family some 120 miles north of us. A young mother went through the same agony. When her husband was called up, she was left to manage on her own a small farm with two young girls, a child of three and a six year old who would become my wife sixteen years later.}

On our way to school we had to take care not to spend time watching the flight of bombers above us on their way to Poland, mostly the three-engine JU 52 with the 'corrugated' fuselage. The Stuka dive bombers we did not see. Within a day or two news spread that our troops had advanced far beyond the Polish border. The more serious news was, of course, the announcement of the British and French declaration of war.

Dad made an early start and had immediately taken on Uncle Paul's duty to serve breakfast. Count Castell accepted Uncle Paul's goodbye delivered by Dad, asking him to come to his private office room whenever he had finished his morning duties. Meeting Dad, Countess Sybille did express her gratitude and wanted Aunt Magda to know that she should stay in the apartment.

The German forces advancing into Poland, gave Stalin the opportunity he had waited for. He ordered his troops to advance into Poland and take back what had been taken from Russia in 1918. Although not openly mentioned, the possibility of Dad also being called up could not be far from Mum's mind. Dad called at the Count's office at the castle and seemed to have had an amicable, man-to-man talk, Dad telling us at supper that the Count thanked him for his willingness to take on some of Uncle Paul's duties. There would be changes in the running of the castle, and Dad was thankful for the installation of the central heating system. With the government's early appeal to save heating and light it will certainly help make Dad's work more manageable. Having been asked to practise 'black outs' before the war, now it was a regular routine every night. The other dark cloud over the castle is the age of Count Prosper, nearing call-up age. It all depended, of course, will Hitler be satisfied with Poland or is something else niggling him?

Sunday services were held as usual, with an increased attendance of women folk and a gap among the younger male population. There was something missing in the vestry and elsewhere. Rev. Langer our elderly parish priest took me aside and simply asked; "Can you take on the beadle's duties outside school hours?" "Yes of course" was my answer without hesitation or asking Mum. What happened? No guessing, the beadle had been called up. There really was nothing in the vestry or church I did not know about by then. At the first opportunity I called at Ernst to tell him my news. He and his family were active parishioners. Ernst's father would not be called-up as he was older than our Dad.

My next surprise, the leader of the 14 to 18 year 'Hitler Youth', met me in town one day and simply asked me would I join the Hitler Youth Fife & Drums band? "Yes, but I am not fourteen yet". "Oh that does not matter", because I would have to join them later anyway. I had occasionally tried the fife and was surprised how quickly I could play it and the tunes which I already knew by memory, being familiar tunes. Now I had to get a new uniform with band epaulettes. As for height, I was 5'10" and growing. My sister's remark, 'show-off'. Miles from Berlin in rural Silesia it is more important what you can do, rather than brandishing flags and running around in uniform. Of course you were more exposed as tambours major, because young kids run after a band. Oh there were laughs, "Look, the beadle with the Hitler Youth". While still on this subject, we played on occasions like Hitler's Birthday or political rallies outside on the town square, or in the new Public Hall at speeches etc. The fact was we no longer had a town brass band because the younger members were called up. We never played any new Hitler tunes; we preferred the old military and marching tunes.

With the Polish campaign completed and the Russian offensive regaining their objective, there was a silent 'peace'. The German authorities began the reordering of its Polish territory. The western area once under Prussian rule had again become part of Germany. The rest of Polish territory was governed by Polish officials, although under constant surveillance by German officials.

Even as a young person the kind of situation you found yourself in, with war and its accompanying new regulations, and forever exposed to political outbursts, you forgot you are still a teenager, at the same time beginning to think like an adult at times. With Christmas approaching nanny was determined that we should do something useful for our mothers. Again with Lutz, Ursula and Engelbert something useful and pleasing for our Mum was produced. Preparation for Christmas continued in homes where Christmas was celebrated because of what happened two thousand years ago. For the first time certain items were not available, others limited on ration cards. It was something the country had got used to. Our famous poppy-seed cakes will not be missing as Mum's parents, like so many others grew the cultivated poppy. The carp, we have been told, will be available as usual.

For me it was a time of change, as beadle I had to open the church in the morning. That was not difficult, but having to lock the church in the evening in the dark was. But then I had no choice, I had volunteered to be the beadle. This is how I did it. By all means have a laugh. I switched the main lights on, those that would not be so visible outside, and then I quickly went to lock the large front door and briskly made my way to the marble steps that led to the communion rail and altar. Facing the church I loudly call out, "Anybody in the church?" Waiting just a second or two for an answer I quickly made for the Sacristy, locked it and the outside door, and hurried home. Tough, if anyone had fallen asleep and did not hear me they would have had to stay till the morning. {It never happened to me, but apparently it did occur.} It could be eerie running home in a darkened town with dim lights now, but sprinting diagonally across the town square it took three minutes to get home. By 5:15 in the morning I opened the church again for the first Mass at 6 a.m. Getting up in the morning was never a problem for me, I was always in time for breakfast and off to school for eight.

# Chapter 3

# Our first Christmas in war time

Who could have known only a few months ago what lay before us? "What is awaiting us now?", these were the questions heard. A number of those over thirty years old who had been called up were demobilised and sent home. One other memory of mine was when our own town militia, no longer required in occupied Poland, returned to Gross Strehlitz. With the commanding officer leading, mounted on a horse, they marched through the town to be welcomed by the mayor at the war memorial to the applause of the townsfolk and we children had a day off school.

Count Castell thought it appropriate to the war effort to deliver his Mercedes car personally to the Military Commandant for Upper Silesia in Oppeln, twenty miles north from home. Expecting some appreciation as an elderly army officer, he expected to be driven home. Instead he received just a handshake and the door held open by an orderly. Unbelievably, Count Castell had to make his way home, as best he could. With no train for some time, the Count began to walk in the direction of home. Almost miraculously a car drew up beside him, it was the chauffeur of a fellow count who recognised Count Castell and drove him home. It was an episode that was talked about for a long time. Count Prosper has arrived home from the Academy for the Christmas Holiday. It will be his last year before going for special tuition on farming and forestry management.

Our school holidays had begun and I was able to be a full time beadle. That meant leaving home by 5 a.m. My routine was to open the church in the morning at 5:15, setting out the vestments, and preparing the altar for Mass at 5:30. There were quite a number of jobs a beadle was expected to do, apart from opening and closing the church. For example Baptism took place most Sundays at 2 p.m. There might be four or six baptisms all together. Each party would leave a tip for the beadle. A busy time lay ahead of me, until after New Year and I was actually getting some pocket money. Lutz and I still played together. When snow fell we spent time outside with sledges. There was a time after Christmas when I overheard Dad mentioning to Mum that Count Castell was not feeling well. Taking on Uncle Paul's position, he was closer to the Count, who had the absolute trust and confidence in Dad. Of course, it meant more work for Dad. On the political side it is worth mentioning that it should not have come as a surprise to Hitler, that Britain and France, honouring the Anglo-Polish treaty, declared war on Germany, three days after the invasion of Poland. The surprise of Russia's decision simultaneously to invade Poland resulted in the collapse of Polish resistance. Although not known to the public, rumour had it that just in time the Polish General Andres ordered his Divisions on a forced march toward the Balkans in an attempt to escape capture by Russian and German troops. His success did not become public for some time. Years later, he was known as the hero at the Battle of the Abbey of 'Monte Cassino' in Italy near the end of the war.

The Christmas holidays long gone and life enfolded into a workable routine. The occasional practice of the air siren going off without warning, and us having to go to the directed shelter added some variety to an otherwise normal day. It was the last Christmas of the turbulent thirties decade and entered the unknown 1940. For us young ones it was a novelty to write the new date. What our parents' thoughts were, we can only guess. One thing is certain; their concern would have been for our future. For me and our class there were still three months to go before Easter and for us the end of our childhood. Life will become serious. Yes, we were having our thoughts of what we may want to do. Thoughts about having to work on the land were in our mind, but also what after the year on the land? Most of us knew how hard it is to be a farmer.

At home serious concern about the Count began to worry Countess Sybille and Dad. He had been for a thorough medical examination and stayed in bed. It must have been something sudden and frightening because his doctor advised the Countess to write a letter to the military authorities for Uncle Paul to be granted compassionate leave to help in the care of the ailing Count. The Doctor would add his own report of the situation. It proved successful and within a few days, Uncle Paul arrived home. We were all happy especially for his family to have him home. Uncle Paul's presence was vital in the attention and nursing the Count required. His illness presented a crisis with the knowledge that Count Prosper was close to call-up age. Prayers were being said by all who knew and were close to the Count and were appreciated by the Countess. Playtimes with Lutz were curtailed now to a minimum.

Sadly, Count Wolfgang's health deteriorated rapidly and he died on 10th of February. Uncle Paul was permitted to stay for another two weeks which was much appreciated by the Countess and Uncle Paul's family as well as Dad.

After prayer at the castle by the Lutheran Minister, a dignified funeral procession followed to the mausoleum, a fifteen-minute walk from the castle. The coachman led the Count's own riding horse and Uncle Paul and Dad carried the Count's insignia on velvet cushions. I followed as the cross bearer {requested by the Countess}, followed by the Lutheran pastor and the Catholic parish priest. The coffin was draped with a large Swastika flag, accompanied on each side, by four uniformed S.A. Party members, {all against the Countess wishes, but unavoidable}, followed by the family and relations. Many estate employees and town members joined the procession. It was a cold frosty day with four inches snow on the ground. It really was a sad day for us all. With hindsight, it spared the Count from seeing his castle, including our home, totally scorched by the Russian soldiers advancing towards Berlin. Also the total loss of his estate at Germany's capitulation.

Life after had to go on, there was the castle and its estate, the life blood of the family. It was understandable that life was now subdued. The Count had died relatively young and had been only ten years at the helm, but what a turn round in the estate's fortunes. There were difficult times ahead for the Countess, especially with the prospect of

Count Prosper, now the heir, not being at home as often as necessary to provide the help his mother needed. The responsibility for the Countess must have been daunting, with Lutz only thirteen years old. She assured Dad that life would go on as before, for the sake of her children. Dad was happy to reassure her of his services, being the only adult male in the castle. The Countess in turn hoped we children would still be available to play with Lutz; but that would soon have to be my brother Engelbert since shortly my adult life will begin in earnest within a few weeks.

The Sunday after the Count's funeral I met Ernst after the Children's Mass to chat for a few minutes before I had to go and see to my duty as beadle for the next service, then home for dinner and back for baptisms. Count Prosper resumed his studies. Countess Sybille was now always dressed in black, a naturally graceful and elegant figure. For her it meant almost daily visits to the Estate Office. The Countess preferred the short route passing our kitchen window. If she saw Mum, she would always stop and talk to her. As time went on and spring began to warm the earth, snowdrops and other such flowers popped up. On the political front the winter calm seemed to lull us into thinking, is there an appetite for peace? But time did not stand still as it neared Easter and for us class VII, the end of school life. It will be time to grow up, or had we not learned already the serious side of life, because of what our political system was presenting for, and expecting from us? Dad kept on his mind my so-called problem where to find a farmer in need of help, to take me on to do my compulsory year on a farm. His prayer was answered when he met a farmer whom he knew, and whose chances were that he too may be called-up. The advantage Dad may have had in his mind was that the place was only a mile from home, in case he needed help, now on his own at the castle. Before the close of school I went to see the farmer to introduce myself, he recognised me already as the 'makeshift' beadle. I was introduced to his wife, but had not met any children. That was my first adult year organised.

Easter 1940 had come. School 'end of term' was always from the Wednesday before Easter for two weeks. Wednesday was also the day we received our leaving certificates. My memories serve me well, mine was above the seventy five percent. Easter is a very busy time for a beadle and it is good to have two weeks free to do my duty. There were rare times during the holidays to play with Lutz and go for a drive with Schimpimpel. Nanny was still our Aunt Else. Grandma still lived with her in the cottage, but was beginning to get frail and weak. It was my pleasure to take Mum's home-baked goodies to Grandma's garden cottage. On my new bicycle with dynamo lights and speedometer a run to Grandma through the small park across the main road and criss-cross through the castle garden was a treat {trying how fast I could be}. An unexpected official letter arrived at home addressed to Dad with a demand for a fitness examination by a military appointed doctor. This request came as an unpleasant shock. When Dad informed the Countess, her reaction was surprise and shock, thinking of the predicament it would cause her. The Countess decided she would ask advice from her doctor. Fortunately he was also our family doctor. The military had no record of our Dad having been discharged from military service in 1917 as unfit due to Malaria. The doctor's records were sufficient proof to satisfy the military for Dad to be classed as unfit for military service. The result added to the relief of the Countess not being bereft of a male in the house. True to her character, Countess Sybille indicated at once, that the life-style within the castle would be more austere and entertainment was thereafter kept to a minimum.

There were many times when I was needed to help Dad in the castle. I learned how to wash and polish glass and cutlery, and the cleaning of silver cutlery on a special pad before polishing. Later when the Countess might have family visits, Dad was glad to teach me the art of serving dinner {never thinking it would become useful a few years later}. It pleased Dad to see me actually enjoying myself; being a butler is a job of serving. I learned to enjoy pleasing people and it broke my shyness, for which I was very glad, not knowing how important it was for my future. Within a short time I had grown to almost six feet, and fitted into one of the liveries that hung in the butler's wardrobe. One never knows when something new had been learned it may come in useful one day.

# CHAPTER 4

# 1940 My adult life began

School firmly behind me, a pair of long trousers and a working jacket and a coat, just in case, in a small hold-all, and a good size sandwich {the mid-day meal was to be given by the farmer}. I mounted my bicycle and left home toward the stable and our sandbox, a couple of hundred yards through the park and on to the main road, from town to the village, just another hundred yards and I was at my place of work. It took just a short five minutes from home. I went in to the yard and was met by the farmer and was introduced to his wife who happened to come out of the house to feed the poultry. My face was familiar to both of them, having seen me as a server and now beadle at church.

I parked my bicycle in the cart shed and awaited orders. I do remember well the first job was to sort potatoes for planting shortly. The smell, or rather the air of farms was familiar. The village is one of those three satellite villages around the town, with small farmsteads to the right and left for a mile or more. Conversation at first was a bit slow in finding something suitable to ask that might result in a short conversation. At least I could remember my farmer's name; Herr Grushka, again not German enough for the Party. Knowing something about potatoes, I at last saw the obvious to ask, the name of the potato? I knew the names of three or four different varieties, and it worked. By continuing about my time spent with Mum's cousins in a farming environment, conversation led to the mention of Dad and his time with horses at the castle. From then on it was free sailing, so to speak. I added that I had reins in my hands with my Dad before I went to school, and on my holiday in the countryside, and occasionally drove Lutz's Schimpimpel, to which Mr Grushka admitted having seen us on many occasions driving from the large park back across the main road to the stables. So, what is farming work all about? It is getting hands dirty, being alert, not standing close behind an animal with your back to it and not letting a horse stand on your toes. Animals need cleaning, like our mothers had to do when we were babies, it also means lifting heavy bags with grain etc., and with the sun shining at its hottest on your back, do not cry if you got sunburn {look for Nivea cream}. Like a midwife you have to get up in the middle of the night and help to bring a young calf into the harsh world. That was what I did not have to do, unless it happened during the day, and it too came in useful six years later.

That's what Mr Hitler wanted me to learn, and for that only, I thanked him. Day by day I got to know Mr and Mrs Grushka. They had no children. There was also a good chance for Mr Grushka, in his middle thirties, to be called-up if Hitler continued playing with fire.

My beadle duties were curtailed to Saturdays and Sundays only. There was also a notice sent, from the Education Authority informing me that I will have to attend one evening a week a two-hour evening class, 7 to 9 p.m. at the local school in this village. These were compulsory lessons on subjects pertaining to agriculture, weights and measurements, etc., with a whiff of politics, thrown in. It applied to all trades in towns and cities.

On the political side, it seemed like a mysterious blackout; leaving the population guessing what next? Will there be an attack on France or England? We need not have bothered guessing for suddenly the 'Göbbels Propaganda Machine' occupied the newsreel with the information that Hitler ordered the occupation of Denmark, of all places, followed soon by the news, that Austrian and Bavarian mountain units were engaged with Norwegian forces. What was that for? Eventually we knew, to cut the supply of Swedish minerals, essential for the manufacture of steel to be brought to Britain. That was not so easily achieved as the planners had worked out. Apparently the Norwegian Brigade was not less efficient in mountain warfare as Hitler's Austrian or our Bavarians. Was it meant as a diversion from Hitler opening a western front? Suddenly everything exploded with the rapid occupation of Holland and Belgium, and a massive spurt to be in Paris by the 22nd of June. The superiority of Hitler's panzer units forced the rapid repatriation of British forces. We now know about the tremendous effort to get as many British forces as possible back to the UK successfully. Apart from the Dunkerque beachhead which led to the capture of a Scottish division, this turned out to be the end of the 'Blitzkrieg', a phrase coined by the head of the German Broadcasting Authority. Hitler's glory was getting the French to sign the capitulation in the same railway coach as in 1918. German propaganda at its best! Then the question was heard, "where next? Britain?"

The first few weeks on the farm have gone quite rapidly with the spring work completed, the rye sown and the potatoes planted. The fertiliser has been spread on the grass. All of course per horse, no tractors here, except one of the larger farmers who had two pairs of horses. One or two fields of grass will be left to grow, until it is ready to be cut to make hay for the winter. The other field is being used to graze the cows of which this small farm has only four in number. Worth mentioning is that in Silesia small farms do not have sufficient grazing ground. After milking the cows are taken out in the morning on a rope and grazed in the field for one hour, then brought back again, and the same procedure late afternoon in time for milking. One other important fact is that fields are not fenced. A strip of grass, three feet wide is the border line between each small farm. It is an amicable arrangement of long standing and never abused. That is the daily routine. Field work is done in-between those milking hours. I was seldom asked to do the milking though I had already learned at my cousins. Two months now in my new job, I am of course called by my first name, and I knew my way around. Not forgetting I had to attend the evening class and found it interesting. Occasionally the teacher would start a conversation on the main theme at that time. The air battles over Britain were much discussed. We did look at school maps to find the towns Coventry and Birmingham. It was difficult to figure out the teacher's political stance, not that it mattered because he did not refer overmuch to politics. He was a country school teacher and knew all the parents. Very occasionally he let something slip, which rightly or wrongly I assumed him as not being a fanatical

Hitler man. I do remember discussing the idea of Hitler giving Göring a sort of free hand to get on with the 'Luftwaffe' in the Battle of Britain. Unknown to the people of Germany, Hitler was concentrating on plans for his most ambitious project, code named 'Barbarossa', to invade and conquer mighty Russia. In hindsight I wonder what would have happened if the people had known about it? A dream too far in Hitler's insatiable pursuit of success where others have failed? Of greater concern was the rumour of the gradual removal of the Jewish population. We youngsters were not aware of what was going on, but it was a fact that the Jewish population in town had disappeared. Lucky were those who left Germany after 'Kristallnacht.' With a ruthless fanatical state security operation, we all had to be careful and live a life not knowing anything. More to the point at the time was the news reels showing the damage the German Luftwaffe caused on Britain. It should not be long before England surrenders, the Hitler propaganda machine was telling us.

Immediately the harvest had been completed, the dreaded letter arrived for Mr Grushka to report at the indicated command post within three days with his call-up paper. Wives and mothers lived at that time in constant fear that it would happen to them. We as youngsters could only feel a very small part of what it meant. Even on a smaller farm, like the one I was employed on, there is so much work that needs a man. It was my hope that Mrs Grushka would have felt assured that I would try and be of some use. I did not lack muscles and could place a yoke over the horse's head, even when it tried to be stubborn. Mr Grushka will be leaving in two days, and would give me some instructions regarding the simpler implements. Regarding the animals, there was nothing more to know.

It was advisable to bid Mr Grushka farewell the evening before, knowing that he had to leave early, before five in the morning. I suppose to make the parting from loved ones less painful, with young children still asleep. On my arrival at the farm Mrs Grushka had already done the morning milking. She seemed pleased that her younger sister might come to stay with her to help. The close contact with nature and animals in my school days seemed to have instilled a hidden love for the countryside and its versatility. Work on the land

and getting dirty I had experienced at my cousins. In any case, it is only for one year. Just how useful all this will be in the future, maybe revealed one day.

The war reporting has taken an unpleasant turn, now the almost daily news of the 'Luftwaffe' trying to bombard England into submission. Pictures in newspapers showing the damage done to the factories and other buildings, one would assume there are no more factories in operation in England. It is a topic which our teacher at those evening classes had to refer to, adding how efficient our 'Luftwaffe' is. There is a kind of 'camouflage' in regards to the losses of our 'Luftwaffe; but that is for private consumption. The occasional shooting down of one of the famous 'Luftwaffe' pilots cannot now be hidden, the answer was, to give him a hero's burial. An unguarded word could have unpleasant consequences. Occasionally you may hear such and such a person has suddenly disappeared. If they managed to get out of a nasty unfortunate situation they may return, but will not talk about it. They have learned their lesson. One might well ask what about the Hitler Youth, especially as far as I am concerned with my fife and drums. Still going on. We practise once a week to keep the officials happy that we are active. It is worth mentioning, that the Hitler Youth had an office and a full time official. To do what is a good question. Now, with so much austerity even his paper supply for keeping records and reports must be curtailed. Still there are always pamphlets and Party information, and warnings to take care: "Feind hört mit" {"The enemy listens!"} Setting politics aside since it does not bring in the food, life on the farm had moved on. Here now, I was able to take a man's place, well, more or less. I must not brag, my muscle size had increased and I was able to do almost every task that required a horse. I will admit that I could not yet drive the horse to plough a straight line. To do it requires a lot of practice. Mr Grushka's cousin did help out at the ploughing. There was for me one interesting break from my normal work. The brother of Mr Grushka had a horse-driven cart fitted out to transport pigs to market or to the slaughterhouse. Mrs Grushka asked me one day to help transport some pigs the following day. I agreed. It should be interesting. I had to be at the farm by six in the morning to drive the horse and cart. We covered a few miles collecting pigs here and there. To get the pigs into the cart might have looked hilarious with the first one, but I quickly cottoned on how to do it the easy way. Once the number of pigs had reached its lot, we drove to the slaughterhouse which I knew was close to the railway station. I also knew that it was a modern newly-built one. I looked forward to seeing it. My curiosity was unbounded. A pleasant surprise awaited me once we unloaded the pigs and secured the horse. We went inside. There was a huge tiled round basin with steaming water and a large number of mechanically humanely-killed pigs to get washed and at the same time soften the bristles. The walls were lined with ceramic tiles. To get the pigs out of the water and taken to an upper floor for the next stage was done mechanically. What was so amazing to see was the way everything was mechanised and quiet no squealing pigs. It was a most unexpected and interesting day with an unexpected bonus.

At home as the year progressed, our lives settled into an orderly pattern. We were fortunate in being able to rear a few rabbits, and chickens for eggs, and had the garden for fruit and vegetables. I did miss the holiday with my cousins and Grandma. At Aunt Marie's the oldest cousin had been called up. Any time there will be one or two other cousins called up as the war continues. At the castle there was only one maid as we approached the end of year. Others had been called to work in important places where the men had been called up. That resulted in the Countess talking to Aunt Else about the possibility of her working a few hours as a maid. Knowing that Grandma is getting old and beginning to fail, the Countess suggested that she might occupy the spare room next to ours, a former store room. When Dad asked Mum, she was happy to have Grandma closer and Aunt Else was happy to work in the castle where she would live in one of the staff rooms. Dad, Engelbert and I helped to clear the room and made it as pleasant as possible with paint and carpet. Grandma moved in shortly after Christmas when all was dry and pretty. It would not be me if I did not go and see Aunt Magda, to enquire if there was anything I could do since Uncle Paul could not be here for Christmas. Having had compassionate leave to care for the ailing Count, it was not expected that he would qualify for another holiday this year.

Returning home from the farm a week before Christmas, I was greeted with the news that a typist who knew Dad had asked if I might like to be the office boy in the Party's Social Office. There was no hesitation on my part, although I had preferred not to break the news to Mrs Grushka until after the New Year. I called at the appointed time to meet the manager who was a Party officer. I entered the office and was taken aback seeing six lady typists in a row. I was introduced as Paul Lippok, son of the castle Housemaster. At my interview the manager asked a few non-political questions and gave a brief resume of my duties and explained that everything was Confidential, - a new word, but I knew what it meant, since the same rule applies to the work of a beadle. He mentioned the wage for a junior office boy, but money really did not matter to me. I would have to use my own bicycle, and would start on 10th January 1941. It was my turn to raise the question about my uncompleted 'Landjahr'. I was to take a letter for Mrs Grushka, informing her that I would be officially released from duties. I remember feeling uncomfortable telling Mrs Grushka about my leaving in early January. She was clearly sorry and it did not do my emotions any good for I had not done anything like that before. I handed her the official letter, and she understood and hoped my new employer would quickly find someone to replace me at the farm.

Christmas time and I was able to do my Sunday beadle work and help a retired parishioner to get to know the drill. He will take over on weekdays, which fitted in nicely and I would still be free to take over on Sundays. Christmas 1940 was as happy as circumstances would allow. Ten months had passed since Count Wolfgang's funeral and the Countess appeared to have come to terms with her loss. She was in cheerful disposition when presenting us with her gifts. During the holiday week I found time to spend with Lutz admiring and trying the new toys. Do I hear an echo "at your age?" If you had lived at that time, you would soon have found out how short is the time from youth to shooting your fellow human.

There had been serious conversation with Dad and Mum regarding my future. I was interested in the Post Office and had thought about it seriously for some time. It transpired, providentially it seemed, that leaving Church one Sunday Dad had the opportunity to speak to the postmaster about my prospect of getting a Post Office apprenticeship. His response was positive. I completed an application form and was invited to attend for an interview. Sooner than expected, I called at the Post Office on the appointed day. I remember the interview well, albeit not in every detail. Was I nervous? Of course I was. The postmaster was of imposing stature and serious, but these were the impressions of someone who attended such an interview for the first time. The Post Office requires absolute honesty and integrity. With a prayer to the Holy Spirit, I must have given the right replies. By the end of January I had my answer: I was to start my apprenticeship at the Post office on 1st April 1941. It was to be a career for life with a state pension at age 60 and amounting to 70% of one's final salary.

It is 10th January and I had only a short walk to my new temporary job. I made my way up to the Party office on the third floor of the bank building, next to the castle's back gate. Knocking and opening the door I smartly took my cap off, and greeted the ladies at their desks. The typist who had spoken to Dad received me and introduced me to her colleagues. The function of the Party office was to provide help for needy people. The funds would come partly from the state, and from public collections for the war effort. Later in the morning I met the director. He was a distinguished looking gentleman; he welcomed me, hoping I would be happy in my job. This being the Monday morning after the monthly collections had been delivered to the office, the boxes were opened and the coins and notes were sorted and counted. On this my first day, I was asked to help sorting the coins and notes. How is it collected? On the first Sunday of each month a collector in his given area would call at your home, and shake his tin, into which you put your contribution. In our case, it was always the same familiar pensioner, and nearly always while we had our Sunday lunch. My first morning's work was completed by lunchtime, twelve to two p.m.. Those of us whose homes were close went home for lunch. All was different from farm work, it did make me think of those on the farms? Mum and Dad asked how I got on, to which my answer was "How easy to earn a wage". After lunch I was asked by which name I wished to be called. Taken aback for a moment, I said I would be happy to be called by my first name 'Paul'. I never worked anywhere surrounded by so many ladies and it took a bit of getting used to. Thanks to their friendliness, I felt I was losing my shyness within a few days. After lunch I was invited to call them by their first name, obviously with the title 'Fraulein'{Miss}.

Next there was a real job to be done, to take a pouch of letters to the County Council Office, only one and a half miles from the office. I got my bike and the office pouch and was on my way. There was a thin covering of snow and ice on the road. Half way from the office I landed on one side, my bike on the other. My first and only concern was whether anyone had seen me, but there was no one in sight. No damage done, I dusted myself down, completed my mission and returned to the office. Did I mention my mishap? No, my pride was the casualty. My prompt return surprised the typists. Confirming that I had indeed been to the County Office - the journey taking me only 15 minutes each way – I was told that the other boy took an hour. My pride was restored.

The first day passed quickly, closing time was 5p.m. and it certainly felt a good deal better than toiling on a farm. That was the moment when my conscience was pricked reminding me how busy they will be on the farm. Determined to try my best, I arrived punctually next morning, almost before the door opened. It was not long before I understood why the former office boy had lost his job. At my first task in the morning, I was shown how to sort and distribute the incoming mail. Returning after lunch I was asked if I would like to be shown how to work the hand operated adding machine. Oh dear, what is it and how does it work? My answer was yes, and instruction followed. Taking your time while you learned was important to avoid misprints or incorrect calculations. Concentrating, I found it gratifying to be able to use it. I was soon given small sums for adding and that was it. All I needed was to increase the speed, with the caution: walk before sprinting.

Realising how I enjoyed operating the adding machine the staff soon kept me busy whenever there was no delivering to be done. After I had received my official acceptance to the Post Office, I remember thinking how useful my work in this office would be to my new career. It is worth recording how we lived under a dictatorial regime, where even your religion was questioned and yet, although the Social Office was one of the many arms of the Party, I never felt I was being watched and was never asked to be politically active in any way. It was a case of keep quiet and just get on with your job. Gradually as time went on I was convinced that the manager was not a fanatic Party member; nor it seemed to me were the staff. It was good enough for them to know that I was a member of the Hitler Youth fife and drum band.

Winter had not been too bad, until there was a sudden fall of snow in early February and high winds. Large sections of roads were blocked by up to three feet of snow, a typical Silesian winter. Lack of manpower and snowploughs meant there was an emergency and offices were asked, more demanded, to send men and the over fourteens to the town square where they were issued with shovels and directed to follow the town's foremen to clear the high drifts. It was a break from routine and healthy, one may have thought. There was the odd remark heard, 'Why have the roads to be cleared, troop movements?' After three days we were no longer required. For us young folk there was still time for sledging and skating as usual. The problem was with the ban on lighting so you had to be careful not to run into each other, which was not difficult if there was a moon. It required care not to overshoot the roped off part where the ice had been cut for the brewery. The snow started to melt at the beginning of March, but I had to do a number of messages on foot because of the snow.

With only three weeks to go before I start my new job, or rather my career, there was an underlying feeling of sorrow leaving the Social Office after being called now 'Paulchen' by the ladies. I suppose if you are happy in your job and a good relationship has built up, it is inevitable to feel attached to people who respect you. I vividly remember the place and those good people after all these years. The reason may well be because of the non-political atmosphere in the office. All too soon the day of saying 'goodbye' arrived. My first call was to the manager of the Social Department whom I thanked for the opportunity to have worked here. He in turn understood perfectly and wished me happiness and success in my new job. Some of the staff who commuted by train will not see me again, unless I will be the postman delivering their love letters. The local ladies I will see on Sundays in church when I help out as beadle with my friend George.

# Chapter 5

# My Career at the Post Office

The Post Office, like the National Railway, was state owned and its workforce were all employees. You are an apprentice until you pass your final exam. Only then do you become a civil servant. On Tuesday 1st April 1941 I left home with my parents' blessing, and within ten minutes, I entered the Post Office staff entrance at the gable end. A few steps led to the entrance hall. The door on the left was the entrance to the general office, which occupied the whole ground floor. Ahead the stair led to the first floor, and the office of the Postmaster, and the telephone exchange.

On the ground floor the first door on the left was the main staff entrance. I knocked at the door, but there was no call to enter, until I knocked a bit harder and heard 'come-in'. I entered and saw members of staff dressed in post office blue placing letters in 'pigeon-holes'. Near the large window was the inspector's desk, who rose to greet me and shook hands with me, a pleasant welcome I thought. He asked me to wait, adding, that the Postmaster will come down shortly. There was a short conversation how my Dad was and how sad the Count has passed on.

The Postmaster entered and I greeted him almost standing to attention as is expected in public with 'Heil Hitler'. After a short few words of welcome he introduced me to the present staff getting their rounds organised. He took me to various rooms, with a short introduction, pointing out briefly what happened in each place. Then we went up to his office. Bidding me to take a seat he began to explain in detail the forms I would have to sign, and the rule of confidentiality and honesty. He hoped I would do well as a Post Office Apprentice.

He took me to see the Telephone Exchange; it surprised me just how many ladies were there. I thanked the Postmaster and made my way down to the secretary's desk. In my ear I still hear the final words of the Postmaster, "Honesty, good behaviour and respect towards the customers on and off duty is the prime rule, and dismissal is instant for any breach of the code".

The inspector was ready to take me round my future place of work. I had seen the sorting room for the daily deliveries. Next, was the larger room with the many pigeon-holes for outgoing mail, and the high table where the letters were being franked. Next to it was an area for sorting papers and magazines for next-day local delivery. Two doors from this large room led to the four Post Office customer counters, manned by second grade staff, {recognised by the pips on their uniform}. Back in the large room, a door led to the parcel room. It seemed a cold room, and had two counters, one receiving parcels from customers to send on, and the other to hand out parcels that had arrived and were usually collected by firms who had an arrangement. Another door led to the room where parcels are stored for delivery by horse and cart, and others to be taken to the Railway Station for transporting to wherever. It is also where the incoming mail and parcels were unloaded from the station. Letters from the town post boxes were collected three times a day. It was an interesting morning and I thanked the inspector who seemed to have enjoyed taking me on my introductory tour. The size of the Post Office surprised me. There will be a lot to learn. That was my first day in my new job. It was time to go home for lunch. It seemed to be a comfortable time-table for counter staff, eight a.m. to twelve noon, and three to five-thirty p.m. Books were balanced after counters closed. Letter delivery staff started at 7.30 a.m. until completion of their round {1.30 to 2.30 p.m.}. It was interesting to discover that all those who passed the second grade were permanent staff able to undertake any task within the office. In addition one could apply eventually to travel on long distance Railway Post coaches fitted out like a post office, sorting mail en route. I felt I would like that, but those carriages have no windows for security reasons.

It was midday break, from twelve noon to 3 p.m. I thanked the inspector again for taking me around and introducing me to the staff. My mother was surprised to see me home so early. Lunch was ready anyway because it was Dad's lunch time. He was delighted, I remember well, because he thought it would be an ideal occupation for me. I felt confident I would like my new job. After lunch I could not wait any longer at home and returned nearly half an hour early. There I was, my first day as an apprentice 'postie' feeling a bit proud. Yes, I was determined to succeed. Opportunities for apprenticeship in the Post Office are rare. The work does not require extraordinary muscle strength and the air in the departments is, to put it simply, fresh on account of the high ceiling. Postmen are known for spending free time in their gardens!

Let me tell you about the parcel delivery cart. It was a two wheeled closed-in cart with a door at the back, and twin shafts for one horse, a beautiful chestnut. The driver sat in the front under a tar pitched felt roof. The cart was that of a bubble cart, painted yellow and easily spotted. Entrance into the enclosed cabin was from the back. It had a lockable door, and shelves for storing parcels, and a seat for the postman when the cart may travel more yards without having to stop. In my time it was the same parcel postie I remember from my childhood. I actually had the opportunity to do the parcel delivery within a year in my apprenticeship.

I was taught to frank the stamps of the collected letter mail. A sheet of paper was laid on the high table, and the first thing was how to grip the hammer, identical to an ordinary hammer of which I was well acquainted. The ink pad on the right was embedded so it would not move about, and on the left there was a dish with water and a sponge. I was then shown how to hit the hammer on the ink pad then hit the pencil mark where the stamp would be. After watching my teacher carefully a few times, I was given the hammer and tried my hand. First I tried a few times without hitting the stamp, and then I tried to hit the template, not bad at all for a start. Having worked with an ordinary hammer before and not hitting your finger helps. I kept going for the next fifteen minutes and was surprised how many times I managed to hit the 'bull's eye'. To be six feet tall is an advantage. Soon it was time to move to the parcel counter. We introduced each other and my apprenticeship began in earnest! Learn to know where the parcels are placed once they come off the scales. This is the important instrument because that will tell how much a parcel is going to cost the sender to transport it to its destination. It tests how good your arithmetic is because at the end of the day you may be out of pocket money if the books do not tally. From the large sheet you read off the scale-weight, the distance line and the cost. Then parcels are brought to the despatch room. It is a quiet time until an hour before closing time. The mail van or bus, whichever is available, will take the parcels and letters to the station to meet the train for loading, then unload the mail for our office. The gentleman at the parcel counter could not have been more friendly and helpful. I found it incredible how much I could learn from him in those few hours. He asked about my parents and how I spent my spare time. His quiet friendly manner immediately made me feel comfortable working with him. In fact, his countenance is imbedded in my memory. Coming home Ursula and Engelbert were anxious to know how the day went and it pleased me to tell them how much I had enjoyed my day.

So, up at the crack of dawn, breakfast and I was on my way back to the parcel counter. But before that, I have not yet described the main entrance for important customers. Looking at a picture of the Post Office, on the right is the vehicle entrance and in the centre of the gable is the staff entrance. Looking along the front of the Post Office to the left is the customer entrance, five stone steps lead to the P.O. customer hall. As you enter: on the left are two parcel counters, straight ahead on the left the 80 locked customer P.O. boxes and to the right of it four serving counters. I was informed that two are always manned, the third at peak times only.

Two weeks had passed, and I began to feel totally at home at 'my' Post Office. I had been several times to the station and now know the system of taking letters and parcels to the trains and bringing the arrivals to the Post Office to be sorted and eventually delivered to the recipient. The first job was sorting the parcels that had been brought from the train station, putting them in order for the town's 'bubble' cart, or those that will be taken by the postmen on bicycles, to the villages, no more than four miles from the Post Office. A motor van will deliver parcels and mail to sub post offices.

Then there are those parcels which will be collected personally. The rest of the morning was spent at the parcel counter where I was given ample opportunities to serve customers. Every move was guided by my teacher. It is going to take a while before I may have a short stint on my own. Ah the words; attention, practice, confidence. There is a time for taking midmorning tea with everyone having a thermos flask and sandwich. The rest of the morning was spent sorting parcels ready for dispatch in the dispatch and receiving room. All too soon it was time for lunch. Close the counters and draw the curtain across the glass door. In the beginning I was back at the office at 2.30 pm to practise stamping letters. I had to make sure that my colleague at the sorting place did not mind. He was pleased for me to learn, the determination of youth, to be as good as the seniors, in due time.

Time to go back to the job I was meant to do. I had a most helpful person to teach me, Herr {Mr} Hubert. His surname was Hubert, and I will refer to him as Herr Hubert. The afternoon could not have started better when among the first customers was one of the ladies from the Social Office who was collecting their mail from their post box. She spotted me and wanted to say 'Hello' and told me, 'I looked well and happy'. That was encouraging. She will report back to her colleagues.

With uncles living far away in Germany and an aunt in America, from whom we had not heard since summer 1939, it is not surprising that geography interested me. With no customers in sight I thought to try sorting some of the parcels for transportation just to see how I progressed in memorising towns and cities. Germany's different counties are well known in my mind and I was reminded of my holiday trip to Bavaria. It gave me the opportunity to add cities and towns to my knowledge. The afternoon passed with normal customer numbers, it being the middle of the week. I was given a street map of the town and the town's three satellite villages. The idea is for me to study the street names of the town and at which end is property number 1. This knowledge will be valuable when it comes to my turn to learn mail delivery and the proper sorting of my specific round. Attention to one's job soon results in gaining the confidence to do the work without supervision. Of course it is going to take some time.

Gross Strehlitz is not that small. The parcel counter is obviously the less demanding in comparison. Within two weeks I was asked to manage the parcel counter on my own for a half day with help being just round the corner, so to speak. Two weeks later, I was asked to man the counter on my own for a whole week, my teacher never far away when needed. A few weeks passed and it was time to learn the basics of being a Briefträger, {letter carrier}. The difficult bit is knowledge of the geography of your route. That is why you walk with a deliverer for a few days when he will let you drop in letters after you make sure that the address and or house number is correct. If there is any difficulty for whatever reason, you knock and ask. When it is your first time on your own, you do not take chances. You just return to the Post Office an hour after the professionals. You dare not cut corners, but just keep going and every day you clip five minutes off. The Post Office supplied tunic, trousers, cap, quality boots, and a cape for rainy days. Mum thought I looked smart, and so did Dad, who himself knew how to wear his livery. Two days later I got my post bag and my tutor walked with me. As a raw recruit you feel a bit of a nit, because you have to look up at the house number, and sometimes they are not where you expect them to be, or they are missing, and then you look for the name on the letter box, if you're lucky. Some prefer a more exclusive site. Occasionally, they are just opening the door to go out to shop, it is your job to be the cavalier and greet the day. I was warned by my tutor to try to avoid getting into conversations, young or old, or your supper will be cold. Never cry, however you feel. Smile, you are a representative of the German Post Office. Posties have a reputation for being cheerful, helpful and never impatient or least they never show it. Do not be surprised, you will never be asked "are your feet sore?"

While we, especially in southern Silesia, were enjoying relative peace so far, our people in the west now had to fear what our Luftwaffe started last winter to do to England, {the bombing of factories and houses}. We need not have been surprised, when England started to retaliate. That is war, with planes you can bring it right to the door. Now even innocent people were suffering on both sides. There were many discussions in the office, yet one had to be ever aware to be careful what one was saying, for who may be listening.

I was young and could not take part, for the simple reason I was not long enough in the place to have any idea of current political viewpoints. I could guess reasonably accurately the stance of some of the staff, when I saw them at church on Sundays but that did not allow me to take part in discussing the rights or wrongs among my seniors. I can only add that the general attitude among most employees in this office was one of non-agitated political argument. Most employees were over forty years of age and many were veterans of the Great War. They would have their own views of what was going on. Younger employees had been called up for military service.

Two months on and I was feeling at home at the Post Office. The 8$^{th}$ June 1941 was my fifteenth birthday. Before leaving home that morning my family all wished me a happy birthday. Mum had baked my favoured Madeira cake and I looked forward tasting it at my lunchtime. After another pleasant morning at my work, I made my way home for lunch and a slice of that cake. Actually to be a baker was at one time a choice when leaving school. In hindsight I pulled the better straw.

Just when we were discussing the landing of German paratroopers on the island of Crete, there followed the most unbelievable radio announcement, of Hitler declaring war on Stalin, by sending his troops into mighty Russia, on 22$^{nd}$ June 1941. There was disbelief among those who would only voice an opinion to those whom they knew they could trust. Occasionally general comments were heard, never certain in either approval or dissent, sometimes recalling Napoleon's ill-fated attempt to defeat Russia.

When I arrived at the office two of the inside staff were sorting a number of identical letters which were 'call-up' papers. Now I knew what they looked like. It was not required that they had to be delivered immediately but with today's mail. As I walked through the office, there had been head shaking in private I noticed. What a time to be growing up! But life went on and my town delivery practice continued as I got to know the route, and I was reasonably pleased with myself. When asked how I got on? 'Great', I clipped ten minutes off my time. Soon I got to know every street and shop.

There was other news which a colleague in the paper sorting section told us, as he had read in one of the newspapers that a Prisoner of War camp for British war prisoners would be established near the lime stone quarry. There is a new modern cement factory close-by. So is the railway station for easy loading of cement and lime stones. We thought most likely those captured at Dunkirk. Apparently, there will be other POW camps within Upper Silesia. A sequence regarding British prisoners will appear later in 'My Story'.

More than six months had now passed since I began my P.O. apprenticeship. Then I was called to the Postmaster's office. Not aware of any misdeeds I entered with mixed feeling. I need not have worried. The Postmaster wanted me to know, that my apprenticeship was fully satisfactory, and mentioned my eagerness to learn. Also the inspector's report had confirmed the opinions of his staff. Of course I was pleased, and so were my parents. One successful achievement was delivering mail for one week in each town round on my own. My face had become more familiar. I had already done my training on country delivery, accompanied by a regular postman and sometime soon after, I had to do it on my own. Your bike is fully laden with a parcel carrier behind. You have to walk pushing the bicycle until some of the parcels have been delivered. That is one of the more difficult jobs for a postie. Not pleasant in rainy weather, as I had experienced it. The P.O. supplied you with a cape. It covered you, the front baggage carrier and the back wheel carrier and could be a nuisance in windy weather. There was a pleasant side to it when you were greeted by people who liked to see you, whether you brought pleasant news, or just passing by. Later I had to deliver sad news from the Russian front. That took a bit getting used to. It is the postman's duty to bring news good or bad. Among the staff it was predicted that sad news will increase with the growing resistance of the Russian army and the Russian winter. You will also be given letters for posting, which is part of your duty in the country side. You were allowed to accept tips, especially at Christmas time.

By then, the Post Office was fast becoming a familiar and enjoyable place to me. I had mastered letter franking at speed, and during Herr Hubert's holiday I managed the parcel counter on my own, to which I could be called to any time. There were many days when I spent time with my 'tutor' at the large pigeon-hole sorter, learning to memorise the whole board of nearly eighty compartments. It contained Germany's major cities and almost all of Silesia's main post offices. There is a correct stance to avoid moving too much and is less tiring. Standing with your legs slightly apart so that you can reach from memory the correct pigeon-hole to the right or left. That too I could soon manage on my own. To know Germany's geography of counties, cities and towns was what I was interested in. So far there had been no need for a reprimand, rather an enjoyable comradeship. In late autumn there was a vacancy in the delivery service. This time a lady was engaged as delivery postie. Apparently it was becoming necessary because of the shortage of men. While she was not a full Post Office employee, she had to take the oath of course.

At home, my friendship with Lutz continued at weekends, in a fashion. On Saturdays, Schimpimpel drives were still taking place but gradually lessened. Lutz no longer required his nanny. The occasional constructing of his magnificent railway was still a major attraction too. In late September or early October, the Countess planned a small celebration to mark Count Prosper's successful completion of his studies, with excellent results and his graduation. According to Dad it was a very enjoyable family feast with a few of their close relations. Needless to say it had been a busy time for Dad, and I was happy to help him with serving and clearing up. It had been a worrying time for the Countess. At the age of 19 Count Prosper could be called up at anytime. His call-up has already been postponed because the production of food on his estate had some priority.

Late November early December we had the first taste of frost and it did not take many days before news bulletins brought alarming pictures of soldiers struggling through mud in Russia. One picture I do remember well was that of a despatch rider trying to extricate his motorcycle and sidecar from a quagmire, helped by his comrades as the rain lashed down. Its publication was surprising! There followed a national appeal for the knitting of gloves and socks as the Russian frost began to show its teeth. Whispers were heard questioning who had planned the 'conquest' of Russia. Not having considered a Russian winter, the response from the people was instant. Within days, my friends from the Party's Social Office arrived with the first parcels for which there was no charge, but soon the Post Office could not cope with it all and parcels were collected at the Town House. It was not the shelling that wounded and killed but 'Jack Frost'. There was a lot of hidden anger when the request came for winter underwear. People who trusted their postman spoke about what their folks, sons and fathers wrote. By Christmas, the first letters arrived from those who had to be admitted to field hospitals with frostbite, and worse many soldiers had to be sent home to have frostbite amputations.

Christmas 1941/42 was the first in my working life with the Post Office. Staff had two days off at Christmas. Two staff members would be on duty during the day, replaced by one member on night duty. As a young recruit I was exempt from duty over Christmas and therefore could make myself useful at church. At home and at the castle it was as normal, but understandably the atmosphere was somewhat subdued. I still had time to spend with Lutz, at weekends. With Grandma now with us, it certainly made life easier for Mum and Dad, but it seemed Grandma was failing.

New Year passed. The snow lay deeper and the frost intensified. By mid-January many roads were blocked and with only one motorised snowplough in town there was a call for some commandeering from town and office staff who were supplied with shovels. It did not apply to P.O. staff. It was nothing extraordinary, for us lots of snow was normal, it was the lack of resources clearing roads of drifting snow.

Just before spring time the secretary had a talk with me regarding my training at the most prestigious counters where money is the most important item you work with. Stamps are sold, registered letters are dealt with, Post Office Giro, etc., and paying out pensions. My 'teacher' was one of the senior officers and of a friendly disposition. Of course there are always in any employment where there are the one or two with whom you do not try to tell a joke for fear it may be misunderstood. Having spent most time where money was involved kept my arithmetic ticking over. The time I had spent on the Parcel counter certainly will be tested. It was not only the handling of money but also the number of different forms and their purpose one had to remember. It would be a test for me to ascertain if I could be trained for the higher grade and that of course was the incentive for me to do well. It will take time.

Now at fifteen years of age, I understood that work and war and politics could not be separated or ignored when you are among men who had been in the Great War and took life seriously. Those who had sons in the military were undoubtedly anxious. In spite of the weather problems the renewed spring offensive seemed to drive the front deeper into Russia. As expected the Nazi media gave maximum coverage, {together with the accusing rhetoric} concerning Allied bombing on German soil. Of course there was no mention of Göring's plan to bomb Britain into the ground. The unexpected attack by Japan on Pearl Harbour brought the United States into the conflict and must have caused considerable anxiety among the German High Command. In the office our seniors were giving interesting opinions when discussing the new situation. I could not take part, only listen.

In spite of all the secrecy in the land and unknown to the general public, the sermon of Bishop Count von Galen at Münster, brought the horrifying medical experimentation on humans to an end, for now at least one successful intervention by a cleric. His sermon simply could not be completely suppressed. All Christian believers prayed for the Cardinal's safety. He was in the eyes of power a 'hot potato'. Worse was to come. There was a secret meeting of Nazi perverts, Himmler's cohorts at which plans to resolve the Jewish question were finally set in motion. To retain the strictest secrecy of their plans, names like 'resettlement' were used, and special S.S. units were created, their members seemed to have had no morals whatsoever. Rumours raged regarding a Concentration camp near Auschwitz, a Polish town some fifty miles south from us, thought to be one of the Jewish disposal camps.

In hindsight, it seems remarkable how in spite of ruthless state security, news trickled in whispers into the open, but kept to yourself. It must have been a parental nightmare to dare conversation where children were around, for fear you said too much. Having said that, we three friends did have our jokes about the political leaders, nor were we the only ones. Hitler did not know just how many there were who plotted to bring his evil regime to an end. We, the general public did not know. Yet there was the 'Kreisau Circle' who met in secret at a castle in Lower Silesia, which of course was not known, except to the few. Nor was it known of the arrest and execution of the Scholl siblings. All that was not known to the general public until the sad saga was revealed, and every German had to accept and come to terms with its enormity after the war.

The conversation at work was about the first US troop landings in northern Africa. Eyebrows were raised in the office; at the same time British troops had been able to contain our forces under Field Marshal Rommel. US units landing in Africa undoubtedly gave Hitler a headache, the campaign in Russia began to falter, much due to Russian resistance and the appearance of greater quantities of American military equipment, including American armour. That was the 'news' brought back by soldiers on leave from the Russian front. It was also rumoured that it might be getting more difficult to capture the city of Stalingrad with the danger of General Paulus' army being encircled by Russian forces, which did happen. A letter from Aunt Meta in Berlin confirmed that Uncle Vincent was to have been in that Army, that worried us of course.

My 16th birthday was on June 8th 1942. The following morning on my way home for lunch there was something about the home which I could not figure out until a few yards from the door. Dad came out and informed me that Grandma Thekla had passed away during the night. It was still a shock in spite of warnings by our parents. I had my lunch and made my way back to the Post Office. Colleagues' condolences were received for the family. Her funeral took place within three days, and I had been given leave to attend. Our Grandma Lippok has left us with wonderful memories.

A few weeks after my birthday the Postmaster summoned me to his office. I had completed my training at the front counter and my training officer had given me good marks. Just selling stamps was a cakewalk. I was not a whiz-kid, nor was I afraid of handling a few thousand Marks and took great care to ensure the books tallied at the end of the day. For my being called to the Postmaster's office was an unexpected surprise. As a result of my training record and the Postmaster's reports to regional office, it had been decided that I should take a two week intensive course for second grade standards in early July. The Postal College for Upper Silesia was in a town called Rybnik, some forty miles from home.

One other surprise was the arrival of a batch of Red Cross parcels. The Postmaster had a note with the details that these were 'Red Cross' parcels for the British POW camp at the stone quarry. These would be collected by the Camp after being informed by the Postmaster or Secretary. Within two days a troop of two English POWs and a German guard appeared with a German four wheeled handcart. I had the honour to 'oversee' the delivery. Just imagine the excitement, a sixteen year old boy facing a German guard and two British Soldiers in their own khaki uniform. It was my job to hand them parcel after parcel, at a guess, thirty in number. I indicated to them that I would stand at the top of the loading bay and swing the parcels for them to catch and place them into their cart. It did not take long before a smile was exchanged. What I can reveal now is that they were Scottish soldiers, but I did not know it then. I was too shy to say 'Good-day' or 'goodbye' which Miss Ida had taught me. I did regret it, but there were more opportunities to come and I intend to make up for it. Those deliveries took place twice in the year.

The time for me to prepare for the college arrived. I received a sum for return train tickets and pocket money. I did not have to take my ration book for the two week course. It was an intense and interesting course, and I tried hard to achieve good marks. It was a challenge but I was there to learn. For some reason, probably because of the short period, we did not form any close friendship, and perhaps because we all came from different towns. Also none of us had any desire to walk into town.

Two weeks intensive learning came to an end, with more confidence acquired. The journey home was pleasant to add to my unexpected travel list in my young life. Am I being prepared for something? My life got back into its normal routine, including the monthly evening Hitler Youth band practice which I actually enjoyed. Worth mentioning is the fact that there were fewer official gatherings now in the Party hall. Perhaps more serious matters regarding the war took priority. Hitler's birthday and two or three other official dates at which the band was required to appear and play, but I was still the Drum Major. Thank goodness there are no marching orders on Sundays. That would be the limit.

At the office someone asked 'did I not meet some young lady on my course'? My answer was simple; there was neither the time nor any inclination to go out. But what about here at home? Ah-well, my friends and I might have cast an occasional eye but there was enough to keep our eyes on other important matters. There was some frolicking by the three of us, at the war memorial close to a shop, where there was a young 'lady' of our age, but it quickly came to an end, without having exchanged a single word. Somehow none of us had any intention to follow it up; actually we wondered whether the lady in question was interested in any of us, just frolicking in front of her dad's shop? Those with higher education had no more time than us, who had an apprenticeship to follow. Also the idea of being called up played a part in our life. I still attended our Franciscan Youth Group. At one of those monthly meetings the ladies youth group had joined. I had a small round paper box which could be held in the hand without anyone noticing it. It was one of those evenings when we had my former piano teacher practising some Christian youth songs. At our short break, I turned the box in my hand upside down and for all to hear out of the box came the sound of 'Maaa--maa', hilarious laughter ensued, even the piano tutor could not restrain her laughter, and I was forgiven. It should not happen again. Only a miracle could make it possible to meet someone who had been there that evening. Oh where have they gone? Who had survived that awful time? To be a Franciscan Youth member does not automatically make you a saint. I had buried my shyness some time ago and always ready to join if there was a chance of harmless mischief. While on the subject of harmless mischief, I had this idea, while still 'Drum Major' of the Hitler Youth band, to ask my three friends to form a small dance band playing foxtrots, slow waltzes and quicksteps. I had my accordion, one other also a small accordion; the other was good at the mouth organ and the other our drummer. We practised in one of our friend's garden shed. Having had several practices within three weeks I had to appear at the Hitler Youth office. The Party appointed eighteen year old office manager left me in no doubt what will happen if I do not stop that vulgar music. I was old enough to know the consequences, that was the end of our 'dance band'. Oh yes, I said my prayer of thanks that my parents did not get to hear of it.

Only two months later one Sunday after High Mass, my friend George and I were at the church main door as usual about to close them after the morning service, when I spotted the two boys from the Hitler Youth office whom we knew well, clicking their cameras as the people walked out of church. George and I facing them, George said, "smile, you know fine there is no film in their camera, where could they buy one these days?" That's what the Party was good at, 'intimidation'. It was the sort of life we had to live.

Yet how fortunate to be living in Silesia when you hear about the insecurity of those exposed to air-raids like our people in Düsseldorf. It was brought home to us when Uncle Valentin wrote to Dad asking the Countess if it might be possible for his wife and their two children, cousins Margaret and Valentin Jr., to rent rooms in the Estate Secretary's villa? Dad had a talk with the Countess who was happy to oblige, as the upper story flat was unoccupied anyway. Dad sent the Countess' agreement to Uncle Valentin and within two weeks the family arrived and made their home just across from us, now we had two cousins, Margaret and Valentin to play with Engelbert and Ursula.

A month or so before Christmas, the Postmaster asked for me to call at his office. He thought it was time that I should be paymaster at the monthly pension pay-out. My most important assignment, normally performed by senior staff. The pay-out lasts from nine in the morning until twelve noon with each pay-out worth between ten and thirty Marks. On the day I prayed, and felt confident. The total pay-out amounted to fourteen thousand Marks and not one penny over or under paid. Yes, I felt great and have never forgotten that first achievement. The Postmaster then decided it was time for me to be on night duty. I had wondered when I would be asked. The night shift is from ten in the evening to six in the morning. A revolver is locked in a cupboard within the large main sorting place. My senior at the sorting place, some time ago had let me into the secret and how to use it.

Happily no one could remember when it had last been used. I would not be alone anyway because the telegraph upstairs was manned by three telephonists overnight. An interesting place the Post Office! With almost two years now at work here, I could be on my own at almost any place and loving it, and at that moment the future looked promising.

Aunt Meta in Berlin wrote that she had official notice that Uncle Vincent was presumed missing. He had left Aunt Meta a secret personal code, from which she could get a reasonable idea where in Russia his unit was. She knew therefore that he was in the Stalingrad area. Since the fall of Stalingrad, she could only hope. The defeat in North Africa was blamed on the recall to Germany of Marshal Rommel. Because with a merciless regime that will keep any bad news from the public, you have to use your own brain to work out a clearer picture. Strategic retreat could always be classed as either a clever or a desperate move. But veterans in the office could see a different picture. I had been asked how did we see the situation as teenagers with the possibility to be called up for front-line duty. As far as I am concerned, you just got on with growing up and looked after your apprenticeship. You really become used to the situation. I at least had never given a thought that I might see war and die.

Countess Sybille was getting very anxious about Count Prosper, already past his initial training. There had been no letter from him. She did confide in Dad when anxious. It was assumed that Count Prosper would be at the Russia front. Dad seemed to know that he was with the artillery, and had been promoted to sergeant. While on the military subject, when last we visited little Grandma, on our way from the station we noticed British POWs were billeted in the asylum in 'Tost'. They were sitting by the window and waved to us as we walked past, of course we waved back. There is a sequence to it.

The last Hitler Youth band meeting before Christmas passed without anything that might have caused anxiety, I was relieved. There was a light snow fall, otherwise Christmas preparations followed the normal pattern which included the carp for the Christmas Eve meal. Some of the exotic ingredients were not available. So far we had no experience of air raids. The week before Christmas the Postmaster asked to see me again in his office. It was twelve noon and the counters were closing. I knocked and entered and was asked to take a seat. I learned that I was to attend another course. This time it was in a place I had never heard of, nor had the Postmaster but he expected more details after the Festive Season. When the details arrived we were perplexed. It required a train journey to the city of Dresden, where I was to change and join a train south a few miles into the Sudeten, {now part of Germany again}. It required winter garments, long underwear, our strong winter shoes, gloves and winter bonnet. I was to leave the last week in January. This was quite a surprise, and a bit of a puzzle. Why be sent in the middle of winter such a distance, for an advanced Post Office course?

Christmas was celebrated in the usual spirit, with me helping out at church with George. Apart from spending time with Lutz, I visited Ernst and his family. Ernst had hoped to finish his education before call-up, he is nine months older than me, and would be called up before me. Christmas over and more snow fell without strong winds, so there were no blocked roads. I worked as usual, feeling really at home in the office. With Dad's help I felt I had chosen the right profession. Time went on and I packed my warm clothes. Frost down to minus 15-20°C is common for two months or more. On the day of my departure I received my return ticket, also my I.D. card. It was time to say goodbye to the staff, then home to pick up my case, ensuring that Mum's special Madeira cake is included then goodbye and off to the station I went. The journey took me on the same line as my journey as a twelve year old to Bavaria, that is until I reached Dresden. The difference was that this time all was white, the Sudeten majestically covered in snow. To see the expanse of the white Sudeten was quite something for a camera, which I didn't have! Which I have not got. Arriving at Dresden, I got off and looked for my train south to where I get off. At Dresden the station was relatively quiet, I first tried to find my bearings. My first call was the information kiosk, to find out my next train and what platform. Dresden is a large city. A helpful lady with a different dialect informed me, that my next train will be in three hours. So why not see a bit of the city, when I am here anyway? Stepping out of the station within a hundred yards one looks at the most beautiful massive buildings. School history taught us about the wealth of the Kingdom of Saxony. I could only afford a short glance at the 'Royal Church' from the former Catholic King. Saxony is predominantly Lutheran. I followed the map to the famous 'Zwinger', which you would need hours to see it properly. I could not even try to describe it. There was no time to see the famous Semper Opera, and sufficient other places to view within the station, and where three hours do not suffice. There was no point to linger on since I had to find my way back and the platform for my train. At least I know I will be travelling south which is leading in the direction of Prague.

What I found remarkable was the absence of commuters, neither men nor ladies. There had been a few when we left Dresden, but had they got off at stations not that far from the border of Czechoslovakia? I began to wonder had it something to do that we just crossed into Sudetenland, where it might be less populated. Anyway, with early sunshine the countryside covered in snow and the sight of the tree clad mountains all was beautiful. Checking again the name of the next station at which I was to disembark, I kept my eyes trained on the name of the next station, and this is it. Am I the only one to get off? Not so, there were a few young men like myself, and I soon discovered we were all heading for the same place. A gentleman on his bicycle was asked for directions, "Up the hill until you see a large Baude". Ah yes, Baude. Large timber houses for skiing, holidays and all winter sports, and for walkers in summer and where you get bed and food.

The higher we got the deeper the snow. Having asked where the others had come from, I learned they lived south of Berlin, but all from different towns. We all asked the same question: why a course in the middle of mountains? A twenty minute walk led us to our 'Baude' where an elderly gentleman greeted and welcomed us. He soon showed us our rooms. Those rooms are for four people, but all fifteen of us had been given a room each. A look through the window first, a romantic holiday scenery! The gentleman wanted us to call him by which he is known to all who come here: 'Bauden Father'. We were asked to come down in an hour to the dining-room for breakfast. I do remember we were all hungry and the meal was good, but we could have done with more. {Remember there was a war on, and ration books}. We waited in the dining room for the course master.

We were welcomed by a gentleman in his late forties and were told the daily routine: breakfast at eight, then a two-hour lecture, a coffee break, then outside for skiing instruction. Mid-day lunch was followed by another lecture and a further hour of skiing instruction. After that, drying clothes, supper and homework for one hour completed each day's routine, followed by free time and lights out by 10p.m. After supper there was no more food or drink to be had. Breakfast and dinner left us with a slight hunger, all of us agreeing that food rationing was part of the training here. My mother's Madeira cake I have cut into twelve slices, one per day for the time we're here, and I was determined to stick to it and proudly did. It is still a family joke.

In Silesian winters you always have strong leather shoes which allow you to clip on skis. Skis were supplied from the Baude. Bedcovers were feather beds, thank goodness because the heating was only just sufficient. Lectures on the Post Office were concentrated mainly on every day rules and regulations, in the office and with the public. That made our get-together in the evening more interesting, although someone had the idea this was to train us for delivering mail in snowy Russia, otherwise, why skis? Good guess! Personally I enjoyed myself, and being taught how to ski properly was part of that enjoyment. It was an opportunity I may never have had. As we progressed, our tutor took us on longer stretches on the down slope.

It became obvious that a few among us were not country wise, feeling always cold and grumpy about the food. Goodness, the country was at war and other people were worse off. Of course we could have eaten more, but that was a small price to pay for a winter holiday. It was simply the way I looked at it. I felt privileged to have been given this opportunity. To a few of us the question came up to ask our warden if there was a village we could walk to? Yes, was his answer and there is a pub where you could have a simple meal. We decided to go there the next day. Supper over we dressed up warm, it being quite frosty and got directions from our warden how to get there. It turned out to be nearly two miles, across fields on occasion, but never mind we found the place. With black-out you needed good eyesight to find the place, and after meeting one local person we did. A small village it was, but probably much patronised in peacetime. Entering and saluting, it was assumed we had come from the Baude and were hungry. What was an offer was homemade potato salad, a real German supper dish, with beer. The beer we declined, but were glad to have a slice of bread with homemade liver pate. There was nothing else to do; everybody seemed to be indoors so we made our way home. The joke was not to walk too fast or our energy would not last to get up to the Baude. If nothing else, it was interesting to have had the opportunity to talk to the locals and understand their dialect. Did we get into politics? No, nor did we venture out again to the village.

The course was coming to an end, with the general agreement that it was interesting for most of us. Personally I found it a fantastic experience, where I learned quite a bit for my future and how to get on with other people. I could go skiing at home, once I had earned sufficient to buy a pair. It was time once more to pack my case and to head for home after wishing each other good health, safe journey and war at an end before call-up? I can say I had been in Sudetenland. Because of a mad man's idea it will not go well with those people in only three years time. I can only say that now in hindsight. Returning to Dresden there was time for sightseeing and then boarded my train for Breslau. It was late afternoon when I arrived home happy to greet my family and looking forward to seeing the Postmaster and colleagues next morning.

Of course I did have a long and most interesting story to tell with everyone listening intently. It was my Mum who could not understand why all that money was spent to send us so far away, {she might have had a point there}. Anyhow, I slept like the proverbial log, but Dad the early riser made sure I got up in time. There was of course snow in Silesia as in the Sudeten. On my way I greeted the few ladies who were busy clearing snow from the pavement in front of their home.

Entering the office I was greeted cordially by all the staff and gave a brief summary of the lectures and learning how to ski. The reaction? Questioning and laughter! At the appropriate time I made my way up to see the Postmaster, who received me cordially and listened with interest to my report. The skiing lessons surprised him. The

Postmaster also informed me that another young lady has been taken on for mail delivery. Her home was only two miles east from town which takes her past the cement works and the Russian POW camp. Why do I mention it? Among the public there was an underlying apprehension regarding Russian soldiers who had been given a most dreadful reputation for cruelty by the Nazi regime. That led to local scares and fear should someone escape as they passed the camp. {The camp was a few hundred yards from the road and well fenced in. As a passing thought, I would have thought they would be glad to have work, some food and a place to sleep, rather than a battle field?}

Home life continued fairly normally for the time being. Not so for those who had to bear the burden of losing loved ones in the war and in air raids in the north and western counties. It was no longer possible to conceal the numbers of notices of the fallen which was rising as more and more confirmations are appearing in the obituary notices. With the Afrika Korps now on European soil in Italy, it meant the circle round German troops was shrinking. Well, what did we sixteen year olds know about 'grand' strategy?

Aunt Therese from Düsseldorf, who was living now in a flat at the castle, had a long letter from her husband, Uncle Valentin. He wrote that a few nights ago their house has been badly damaged in an air-raid. Their living apartment practically gone. However the cellar was not damaged, therefore all their important cherished stuff is undamaged. That was a bit of frightening news. Uncle Valentin apparently has a safe room in his Police District Office reinforced cellar. The situation on the eastern front was too disquieting, as it was discussed among the elder Postmen here. The occasional news of arrested Priests, whose sermons were deemed to be treasonable, reminded us that we are living in a totalitarian regime. Make a comment on such matters, and if overheard by the wrong person, you too would be for it. It brings me back to the day when the Propaganda Minister Göbbels spoke in Berlin in that great hall, filled with nothing other than brown shirts and S.S. black shirts with a sprinkling of wounded service men. When he, the then named Schreihals 'loudmouth', ended his speech with the question, "Do you want butter or guns?" "Guns!" they replied. "Do you want the total war?" "Yes!"

We heard it on the radio, and yes, many times quoted in newspapers too.

Spring was giving way to summer and Silesia continued to avoid the ravages of air-raids. As for me, I was now in my third and final year of apprenticeship. It felt I was fulfilling a senior position in the office. I was able to go wherever there was a need, including delivering a mail round, if someone fell ill. That includes the occasional paying out the Pension. The one topic I have not mentioned here yet, was the prospect of being called up to the pre-military service with the 'Arbeitsdienst'. I will be seventeen in two months time. That's a thought. One very pleasant newsletter came from Aunt Meta, that she had official news from the Red Cross, that Uncle Vincent was alive in a Russian POW camp. Aunt Meta will leave Berlin to come down and stay with the Head Forester, where Aunt Franziska is housekeeper. Their house is in the large park, a half mile from the lake and our home. Aunt Meta and the Headkeeper's family had been friends for a number of years. She will escape the air-raids, but for how long?

We had a beautiful Silesian spring again with cherry trees in full blossom. It is once more Easter time, the fourth of this war. Catholics and Lutherans celebrated Easter with special prayers for peace. The absence of male parishioners was noticeable. Prayers were said for those who gave their lives and those wounded, and others far from home. Easter had become a special time for us who are still safe. Everybody rejoices to greet a soldier on leave. Even us sixteen year olds are often thinking, when is it going to end, and how?

If anyone asked about winning the war, we were taught that it was safest to say 'I hope so'. It is almost impossible to describe how difficult it was for us youngsters, who already felt you are between two camps, especially if you believed in God. At seventeen and with a war on, you just do not know what a victorious nationalistic regime may go to? Surely, you could not expect us at seventeen, committed and active in the Church, to take a Christian flagpole and wave it through the town? Help; think of the consequences, with parents and sisters and brothers at home. Therefore, you just take life as it is in front of you, and hopefully a successful career. You are allowed to have a private view in state and faith and for the present continue to enjoy your work.

There is the possibility that a military call-up will come within the year, if the war should still go on. In the meantime there was a birthday to celebrate on 8th June, my seventeenth. It turned out to be something of a non-event, but my fondness for home baking was not forgotten. My skiing holiday did begin to fade, although the memories are there. Time I mentioned that I had more than one compliment that I looked smart in my Postman uniform, thank you. As you progress and reach a certain stage you get a golden pip on your tunic collar, both sides, for me in three years time perhaps? Stop dreaming Paul, there is a real world around you.

End of June and a shout came from the incoming mail sorter, 'Paul!' and I knew why he shouted, because like all of us he knew the type of envelopes. It was the call-up for the pre-military 'Arbeitsdienst', a unit established shortly after Hitler came to power to reduce the unemployment numbers. I mentioned it earlier you may recall, the brown uniform, the silly hat and the spade! Well, that was it then. I opened the letter and I had to report in ten days at the barracks near a small town, only a half hour train journey from home, or a two hour cycle run each way. My first duty was to go up to report at the Postmaster. Passing the inspector's desk I thought it proper to let him know. There was nothing anyone could do about it. The Postmaster on seeing the paper was disappointed that it interfered with my apprenticeship. But even he could do nothing about it. He encouraged me not to give up because I will pass my apprenticeship and will join the State Post Office. Whenever times will be normal again, we'll welcome you back. These were words of encouragement, what better. At dinnertime, I showed Mum and Dad my letter. As expected they were prepared, but not so soon. In the evening I called at George's, he did not get a call-up for the Arbeitsdienst nor did Ernst. Within a week Ernst received his military call-up and called to say goodbye, friends are parting with an uncertain future of seeing each other again.

In the Arbeitsdienst you learn how to be useful with a spade, pick-axe or brush. In place of a rifle you are given a brand new spade for drill. It was important that you keep the blade in new condition, in fact more dazzling than when new. How did I know? Because there was an Arbeitsdienst camp just out of town, and sometimes we watched them.

I took my leave from my colleagues and the Postmaster. I would see them when I come back. 'Arbeitsdienst' term is six months. That will see me back in November. One good point is that my pay would still be paid into my Post Office account. After work and supper I went to say my goodbyes to George. I had seen Lutz before that. It was a good opportunity to linger while at his home. That could mean we may not see each other until my return. My day for departing had arrived. In the morning I attended the 5.30 Mass and said my goodbyes to my parish priest. Back home for my breakfast and to say goodbye to Mum, Dad, Ursula and Engelbert. Ursula had just been accepted to attend a two year course at the Convent Domestic Science School in town. She was pleased about that. Dad called home just before I left to say 'goodbye' and mentioned that on a good Sunday they might all take their bicycles and come and visit me at camp. That actually is allowed on Sundays, the camp being only some fifteen miles from home.

There I was again, a short train journey to the nearest station from the barracks, then it was a fifteen minute walk to the gate of the barracks. Here you greet the Officer with the raised hand, signed the papers and were shown to your barrack. They were single beds and each had his 'Spind' a locker, 18 inches wide by six feet high. Before lunch the whistle ordered you outside to the parade ground. I do not remember the individual ranks but they were very similar to the military. The order was in three squads of twenty five each; name and squad number was given to line up correctly from tallest down. That done, it was a march to the Mess Hall. It was a case of getting used to military cooking. The afternoon was spent receiving our uniform of brown trousers and tunic, white and one grey underwear, two pairs of quality socks, a pair of shoes and a pair of calf-height boots, a work hat and that ridiculous parade hat. During and after lunch there was an opportunity to get to know each other. There was no one from my town, but all were from Upper Silesia. The surprise was 'ersatz' coffee, {substitute coffee} was available in the dining hall. A squad leader would call off and on with information.

My neighbour seemed to be somewhat confused, for want of a better word to sum him up. I tried to open a conversation, but did not get much of a response. I began to think he came from a village near the Polish border and I wondered if he had ever been far away from home. I did not want to give up because I began to feel he just was a bit shy. I guessed others might just not be too friendly. It pays to be six feet tall I discovered. There was a chance to introduce myself to my neighbour on my other side. Soon more of us got into conversation. Apart from the castle, my apprenticeship brought me into conversing with many people from different backgrounds. I asked my shy neighbour where he came from and was he in an apprenticeship? His answer was no, but that he worked on his father's small farm. That, I was sure was the reason. Eventually the order came to assemble on the parade ground. The camp commandant addressed us with some welcoming words, and told us we should look at our position as a preliminary training for military call-up. Each barrack squad marched to the dining hall. We had supper, not too much, then the call for the night roll-call and lights out. Rise and shine was at 7a.m. Wash, shave if you have to, dress and be ready to line up for breakfast. After breakfast, we were given the timetable by the so called 'sergeant'. Next, make your bed and stand in front of it for inspection. Then line up for roll-call and another short address by the commandant. After that, pure military drill, how to stand at ease, how to line up in a straight line, how to march in step. Well that we learned in Hitler Youth. My neighbour had a bit of a problem but he soon caught on. After dinner, we had a half hour rest, then out again and instruction on tools in small groups. That was a bit of a laugh with those who had not handled a spade or pick before. It is amazing what there is to know about a spade, and the variety of different spades. From that, you go on to the different forks, etc., all in order to know how to handle them properly and to learn how to make work easier by using the right tools and using the tools properly. You would be surprised what there was to learn. And also important how not to chop your leg off, and so it went on, not forgetting the morning fitness sport. Within the camp there was a large piece of land which was there to practise on with our tools. If you had a garden at home but got off 'scot-free' from helping, you were in trouble. In fact, it provided some real howls of laughter! Thank goodness my parents made sure we knew a thing or two in the garden, etc. I did my 'Landjahr' on the farm, and had spent time with horses at my cousins. Not wanting to show off, I had a lot to be thankful for in my early years of youth before joining this 'labour service'. There had been a number of occasions where I was called to demonstrate how quickly I could follow the instructor's orders. There are some at home who would not recognise the once shy boy of twelve. I should mention that I began to be grateful for opportunities and certain people who encouraged me to be active where singing and marching songs were called for. Walking in the countryside few or many, we would always sing, Germans do that, 'Valerie, Valera, ha ha ha' and so on.

Providence was keeping an eye on me when I was chosen among some thirty of us to pack overnight clothes and sent by bus to help fight a forest fire. It was some thirty or more miles away. Here is the interesting thing to recall. Our destination unknown I paid little attention to the direction where we were going, until I recognised that we were on the road towards my home. I suddenly realised and told my corporal we were getting close to Gross Strehlitz. In next to no time I pointed straight ahead to the entrance to the castle and home. The corporal asked the bus driver to pull in to park and I was allowed to run up the fifty yards and burst into our kitchen. My mother was perplexed, and just asked should she make me a sandwich? I said, yes please, while I explained the situation. Within fifteen minutes I ran back to my bus and thanked the corporal. I still think it was strange. Eventually, after another hour or more we reached our destination. Once we had eaten we took our tools and were shown what was required of us. We stuck our chest out pretending we were the boys and knew what to do. On the serious side we were shown what to do and told always to keep a watch in case a tree is burned through at its roots under the ground and could fall on us without warning or sound. That was an interesting lesson to know for life. We worked three days only, after which we were sent back to camp. The fire was out. It had been good fun and a break in our short time in the Arbeitsdienst. Arriving at camp, we had a story to tell. The fact that my shy neighbour was with us, gave both of us a chance to help him to open up.

Two months into my RAD {Reichsarbeitsdienst,} and my name had been called out again with another twenty at morning roll-call to assemble on the parade ground after breakfast. That we did and with curiosity listened to our commander. We were to pack our kitbag, including two sets of underwear, toilet-case and work clothes, in full uniform including that hat. We had to be ready to leave next day after breakfast. Now what was that all about? Are we about to go to another fire? Not likely, with two sets of underwear, and dress uniform. I did remember my writing pad and small prayer book.

Next morning breakfast taken, we were ready to go. I should mention the German kitbag is more like a large school satchel carried on your back, its proper name is Tornister, {a knapsack}. Assembled on the parade ground, we were inspected first to ensure we were properly kitted out. A few kind words from the commandant and the order to march was given. After a half hour march we arrived at the station. In time the train arrived and we were shown to our coach. Within a few minutes, we were on our way going north for a start. We did not expect to be told our destination but tried with humour to tease it out of the corporal. The direction was towards Breslau and I could name every station, almost, {my postal training}. The camp kitchen supplied each of us with a fairly large food pack. Did it mean a longer journey was the question we asked ourselves? We passed all the towns I knew as we slowed down; I recognised the station, Breslau. That was 80 miles from home. We have not yet been ordered to get off; so on we went still travelling in a northerly direction until darkness prevented us from guessing where we were. I knew the names of all the stations where we halted and point them out on a map. We were travelling on a normal passenger train. At some larger station we could get out for a walk on the platform to stretch our legs, while engines were changed. Remember it was still steam engines. We were now nearer Berlin that was certain. With darkness and ten hours or more travelling we fell asleep at last. All that way from the south. The train was faster now, and because we seemed to stop only at larger stations. Let me remind you it was in black-out times, so it was often difficult to read the station name. Anyhow, I must have been in a deep sleep. When I woke there was silence, it seemed everybody was asleep, and the train had stopped, probably a long time ago. Looking out of the window, there were a lot of rails. I thought we must be at a large station but beyond the platform. Dawn was beginning and in the distance I could just make out that there were houses. I ate a sandwich, and within a few minutes, as it got brighter, I could see what I had never seen before, the outline of houses that had been bombed, chimney stacks sticking out like sore fingers. The houses were without roofs like boxes without lids. I was sure no Silesian had ever seen what it looks like after an air raid. My thoughts were about those who had died so suddenly and children frightened or worse. Most of us on board had not seen such a picture and there was silence. It was probably our first encounter with the reality of war.

Soon we felt the hitching of a new engine and we were on our way again. After half an hour or so it was clear we were travelling west. After another hour an officer entered our compartment with news of our destination where we are going. Some surprise that was, we were going west towards the town of Emden, not far from the Dutch border. There was more, we would then be transferred to the Friesian Island of Norderney. I knew now where we are and where we are going, though obviously not our final destination.

We were getting close to the town of Emden and become aware by the braking. Just as the train slowed down to enter Emden station, and before we came to a halt we heard the air raid siren. The train stopped, doors were opened and people rushed towards a large building, the bomb shelter. Our officer, told us to leave everything in the train and follow the people into the shelter, children and women first. Just yards in front of the shelter entrance I heard the sound of a plane and at the same time a plane very low, skimmed across the station. No detonation which I had expected was heard and I was pushed and shouted at to get into the shelter. Inside we heard a dull explosion, or so I thought, and at the same moment I felt the vibration of the explosion in the shelter. It was a very strange feeling and I remember it well. After some fifteen minutes or so the all-clear sounded and the doors opened. Having experienced it for the first time, we found it difficult for a few minutes to adjust to normality. Our train stood there, apparently undamaged. It did surprise us how the locals behaved as if nothing untoward had happened, until someone told us this had happened several times before with single planes trying to bomb the single line railway to the coast and the ferry to the island of Norderney. I was surprised, once we got our thoughts together that the plane flew so low without being chased. Just think, I saw for the first time a British plane flying low over our heads. We lined up on the platform for a check if all present and correct. The officer was asked to go to the station office and returned with the news that railway engineers are on their way to repair some damaged rails caused by the plane. So that was the explosion we heard. We had permission to sit in the train and had our lunch pack. Still excited, I thought this was our 'Feuer Taufe' our {'battle baptism'}. True, that was indeed the first time an 'enemy' had attacked us!

After some two or three hours the signal was given to get back into the train, because we were going to move on. How far to Norddeich, the town where land comes to an end was my question to the ticket checker. "Twenty miles." I was happy with that. Looking out of the window, there were no hills to be seen, just green grass and Friesian cows. Get ready to disembark, we are at the end of land, was the command from the front. We assembled on the platform, and we waited for the next command. Our sergeant is chatting to one of the ferry boat crew, giving instructions most likely. I certainly was excited and remembered when I once had a wish to be a sailor. We were actually to be shipped across to the Island of Norderney. This should be interesting I thought. As we march on to the ferry boat, I looked ahead and saw calm blue water. It is summertime. To me it all seemed like a holiday dream. So it was! We boarded the ferry and found a seat. There are few civilians with us, and they were very quiet I remember, wanting to get home from work. In next to no time we were off with a blast from the ship's hooter. There was time to wonder if I might get seasick as the ocean seemed very flat and blue, but only the slightest motion, just to remind us we are at sea. Already the boat crew is indicating the island ahead of us. Time to leave the ferry, line up and follow the welcoming party, one sailor with no identifications as to his rank if any, no smile only a handshake with our officer, and off we marched.

We marched almost half an hour before we arrived at a place where there were a number of concrete huts, not in a closed unit, but each barrack a hundred yards from the next. With our leader and the sailor, we were led to our accommodation. Ten to each hut. Our accommodation was surprisingly pleasant. No complaints about the beds. The shower and WC were in one unit, a quick sprint from each barrack and there was a dining hall for our group. I remember that we felt it a bit cool, though it was the middle of summer. There was no heating and we were now a good bit north from home, and were surrounded by the North Sea.

Having rested for a while a call summoned us outside and a naval officer directed us to the Mess Hall for our supper. I still remember just how hungry we were. Nearly two days without a hot meal. The other thing I remember was that we all agreed that we could have eaten more, and that I recall, was the consensus for the duration of our stay. We comforted ourselves by blaming the fresh and clean air, enjoying a good sleep every night made up for it.

On parade after breakfast, it became clear that our officer was really not sure what we were on the island for. It was the topic most talked about among us on the journey to the island of Norderney. We seemed to live a life of questioning and making our own answers, building bunkers in the sand, or trenches in case of an English invasion? Having received no particular instructions, our officer thought it wise to issue us with spades, and lead us to a sandy area, gravitating near the shore, to dig a trench. It meant we could not be seen by the Navy personnel. Chatting away for over an hour our leader took a walk up the green slope to see if there was anything going on. He returned without having seen any one. That we found strange that none of the Naval Officers ever came near us, either to welcome or as someone suggested to ask us what business have we to be here, disturbing the tranquillity for them? Someone suddenly queried why are we not invited for lunch? So we dug around in the sand beginning to build castles. As the sun rose higher the temperature warmed up with it. We continued chatting away waiting for the lunch bell. We stuck the spades in the sand and discussed the thought. We kept looking to see a sailor. We were nearly half a day out here and never saw a sailor yet. Ah, the smart question on the possibility that the commandant and cook forgot that we are here? They are playing cards or having a nap, was another suggestion. At last a whistle blew and a shout came to go in for lunch. That was a welcome break. After a long lunch hour, we made our way back to the 'job', assuring our officer we are doing fine. Passing time during the occasional dig, one of us listened to one of the local passengers on their way home, who asked "what are you doing on the island? Coming from so far and not sailors? Building bunkers or what?" "Top secret", was our only answer. Locals were clearly bemused.

A week gone and it was Sunday. It was the day of rest and that's what it was, every day. My fellow traveller on the train was happy to join me on a walk in the afternoon on the island. We passed the scattered Navy barracks at a little distance, not to disturb their Sunday. Gerhard, my companion, saw a sailor coming out of a small building carrying a pole on his shoulder full of smoked fish. He crossed our path some ten yards from us without saying a word of greeting, far less offering a few of his fish. We just looked at each other in disbelief. Telling the story when we came back to our quarter it was taken as a joke.

What I found strange was that there were never ships of any kind to be seen out in the distance, until someone suggested there was the danger of being sunk by a U-boat. A sensible answer indeed. We passed time by playing cards. Those who were 'experts' enjoyed the chance of having ample time to enjoy the game. I could only join the simple games. At last we were given some newspapers which were welcome even though a few days old. I had managed a conversation with Gerhard a pleasant fellow member of our 'crew' while reading a paper and found him entertaining. It takes many conversations before you get a reasonable idea what you can talk about. We both felt a trust and friendship had developed between us. Both of us felt a need and found satisfaction to be able to discuss more serious subjects. The opportunity arose for me to dare ask him, if he was a Lutheran and at the same time letting him know I am a Catholic. "That's alright, I'm a Lutheran", was his answer. He lived not that far from my home. A relatively close friendship developed as both of us carefully opened up during conversation. Well into the second week here it became obvious that our situation on the island could not continue, unless some extremely secret operation awaited us. But who are we, to be told of some highly sensitive project? Our duty is, as we know well, to follow orders and leave the conducting to the conductor, {as in an orchestra}. Why worry, as far as I was concerned I could spend my time here to finish my half year Arbeitsdienst. But, hand on heart, I would have preferred to be at home in my Post Office. Therefore, if we cannot do anything about it let's be thankful for small mercies. I wondered why we never heard British bombers flying overhead on their missions. Gerhard and I did enjoy our walks on the soft fine grass and we had some interesting adult conversations.

Early in the third week at our morning roll-call we heard the sudden decision, we were to pack up, and we were going home. There were no air raids as we left the north. All was plain sailing and we got home next day. Back at camp it was fun to tell our tale to envious comrades. The normal routine resumed, as if we had not been away. Our training had become more interesting as we were often on really useful projects in our area, finding out how much we had learned. I often wondered what our friends may have achieved at their homes, digging or building. Just three weeks back at camp, our commanding officer left a message for me to report at his office after supper. First reaction was, not my name again, what have I messed up, or worse, some mishap at home. Or had I unwittingly said something somewhere? Yes, there were some butterflies.

I knocked at his office. When called, I entered and stood to attention as required and relaxed when told to. Next was a surprise when he suggested we go out and take a walk, it being a pleasant evening. Can you imagine the picture? There was I strolling on an early evening walk with my commander at my side. He asked about our 'trip' and I gave a short but honest report. He made no comments, but said, "Lippok, I had a letter from the Arbeitsdienst authorities that you should be released from your normal time of duty". This was a strange sort of situation and it felt as if I was walking beside my Dad.

His voice was measured and made me feel relaxed. I was then given the reason,"…..that you should be allowed to complete your Post Office apprenticeship, before a possible call-up". We kept on walking, with him asking questions, for instance, where do I come from, my Dad's occupation, do I like my choice of a career in the Post Office, and other such questions. I shall not forget him, after all those years I can recollect our walk. We parted with a handshake and almost a tear in my eyes.

Back in barracks, I had to tell my new-found friend that I would be leaving next day. The reaction was congratulations, and he agreed we had a wonderful friendship and wished it to continue. Alas, whatever happened we will never know. There was a war on and anything was possible, all of us would have had to face the 'enemy', some would return home, for others a young life given for nothing, but heartaches for parents. Hand on heart, I did enjoy the comradeship, albeit for only three months, but the prospect of being able to return to the Post Office was of greater importance. The possibility of being called up to military service within a year made the completion of my apprenticeship so much more attractive. The following morning I handed in my spade, uniform and that 'hat'. A half hour walk to the station and a less than half hour train ride, I arrived home to the surprise of Mum and Dad in time for lunch. You can imagine how pleased my parents were. Brother Engelbert arrived later from school and was equally surprised. I would see my sister Ursula when she returned later. I changed into my uniform and made my way to the Post Office to report to the Postmaster. He had apparently been informed, because that was the impression I got when I greeted him in his office, and we both were delighted. There was surprise among the staff and I wasted no time and I got a hold of the ink hammer and enjoyed franking letters which had accumulated on the table from the collections. The inspector would soon inform me where I would be needed the following day. The Postmaster had apparently organised the programme I was to follow.

My memory reminds me of a rather long and beautiful autumn with glorious colours in our garden and the castle park. Going on drives with Lutz and Schimpimpel was no longer possible, Engelbert took my place, and he too got on very well with Lutz. It pleased the

Countess to see Lutz having a male to talk to, now that Count Prosper has been in the Army for almost a year already. Miss Ida the Scottish lady was back with the 'Castells' in Bavaria. The weeks seemed to pass quicker as the autumn began to move closer. I called at the parents of my friend Ernst since I knew that he had been called up while I was with the 'Arbeitsdienst'. His parents were pleased I called, telling me Ernst is somewhere in training. They began to worry where Ernst might be sent to. At the moment only Italy or the Russian front. I got his military code to send letters and went home. Since coming home again there came another opportunity to meet the British POWs collecting their Red Cross parcels, if only I could say a few more words or even a phrase or two apart from 'good morning' and 'how do you do?' and 'thank you'. I had this inner feeling of pleasantness and the wish to exchange a smile. {The extraordinary sequence to this will be revealed at a later stage.}

Since my return I had been given another opportunity to manage the pension pay-out with a correct summary at the end. Towards the middle of November the Postmaster called me to his office after lunchtime. At lunchtime I mentioned to Mum and Dad that the Postmaster wished to see me after lunch. Returning to the Office I made my way up to the Postmaster's office, knocked and heard the 'come in'. No, I did not say 'Heil Hitler', I saw him at church on Sunday, that meant something in these times. He would not chastise me, he trusted me and I would greet him with 'Good Morning' whenever I met him on a Sunday at church.

I was asked to take a seat and he read to me the letter he had received from the Head Post Office for the Silesian Province. "It confirmed the completion of my apprenticeship on 30th November 1943. From 1st December I would be a civil servant of the German State, and my monthly salary of 105 Marks, would be paid into my Post Office Savings Account." The Postmaster continued to point out that in the event of my being called-up, my salary would continue to be paid. That was an unexpected and most wonderful Christmas present. The Postmaster stretched out his hand to congratulate me. The official parchment was wonderful. A satisfying job, a good salary and pension, and a good life to look forward to. Ah, you hope, like many others. But, while others are still shouting 'Heil Hitler,' not so few were saying something different, not in words but by their silence.

In the end, he who shouted loudest, took his life in a deep bunker, did not stand up and face the fate of millions, and took with him our future and our homes.

Coming home in the evening with my parchment in my hand had been a wonderful feeling to present it to my family. Engelbert and Ursula were home from school, with Dad following from the castle full of smiles and pride. Well, that was me ready to begin a new phase in my life; my future was laid before me. Will it come true? There is no sign of peace, but will it be really good for us? That was in the minds of many people. After supper I took my bike and cycled to share the news with George. Strangely, I do not remember what trade George went in for. Next morning after breakfast I did look in the mirror and thought, that blue uniform suits me, and off to work I went! The news had spread, congratulations followed and I was back at work. It was only natural to wonder what went through my parents' mind, after the initial excitement. Truly, I did wonder, was I showing off? Boys will be boys. Do girls not do that too? It will wear off, it always does.

Family-wise there was interesting news which was a surprise to be told that Aunt Else met a widowed soldier, through a friend of hers. His wife died after a short illness, leaving a family of two girls and one boy, aged between two and six. In short, they married and Aunt Else became their instant new mother. Was it that easy? I did not know, except Aunt Else's husband became our new Uncle Theo. His rank was Company Sergeant Major and his home only a bare ten miles from Gross Strehlitz. For Aunt Else, thirty five years old, it could not have been easy with Uncle Theo having had only two weeks leave. Uncle Theo had a degree in agriculture and had been manager of a large farm. I never knew where his unit had been. His marriage to Aunt Else proved providential, and reference to it will appear at the appropriate time in this story.

The Postmaster wanted me to be given a permanent place in one of the Post Office departments, sorting parcels or at one of the money counters. I was happy to start shift work in the out-going mail sorting room. I was just seventeen and a half and all of us at that time in history, young or not so young, had to learn that we were not masters of our fate, nor was God above, it seemed. That is what happened to me, when on the morning December 12$^{th}$, I was sorting the morning incoming mail for the delivery team. Unbelievably, standing in front of the sorting pigeon-holes, my name and address looked at me from one of the letters. My heart gave a jump. Recognizing instantly, I turned to my colleague, without saying a word. I held the notice in my hand, "Oh dear" was all he could say. I quickly collected myself but inside I was shaking. I unstrapped the next bundle and continued to sort and within seconds, there was another notice addressed to my friend Paul Apostel, this was his real name, the class mate from the orphanage, immediately in my hand the same envelope for my friend George. It seemed so unreal; I had been only two weeks in my first year as a qualified Post Office employee. Having finished placing the mail into their proper place, I opened my envelope and could not believe what I read; I was to report at the Paratroop Garrison at Gardelegen, north Germany. I could hardly wait to tell my friends in the evening. I was bothered by the thought why all three of us received identical call-up papers? Makes you think?

So, I had three full days to sort myself out. We can stop the clock but not the time. For the first time the morning seemed not to move forward at all. I felt composed although a bit shaken at first. I went to see our secretary who could not believe it at first, and suggested I go to see the Postmaster. I knocked at the door and entered, handing him my letter which he recognised, he just looked at me and shook his head, I thought. He was certainly surprised at what age recruitment is expected as the war wears on. Twelve noon and it is lunchtime, I got my bike and sped home. Mum and I waited for Dad to appear for lunch. Grace was said and we enjoyed what Mum had cooked. That was the moment when it dawned on me that soon I would not taste a home-made lunch. Time came before Dad was to leave to show him the official letter, a moment's silence and I said nothing just lifted the letter and Dad opened it for a few seconds and just looked at Mum, both were shaken, my lunchtime was over and I left to work. I am not one for volunteering for that sort of thing. Furthermore it was always understood that only volunteers could join the Paratroops. I never had any intention of jumping from flying airplanes! There was of course no mention that you will be required to jump off planes, question was do we even have any planes left? Ursula and Engelbert certainly will be surprised when they come home, and so they were.

At the office the secretary informed me that I should continue to work until the day before departure. The Postmaster had taken the details of my call-up paper in order to inform the Silesian Postal Office in Breslau. After supper I cycled at speed to see my friend George. Knocking at their door, George guessed why I had come and how mysterious that our friend Paul Apostel got the same letter and that I should have been the first to see their notice. I could only confirm that I did not see any other such notice, so why just the three of us together from the town. If you think about it, three friends, active in the church should have the pleasure to travel in our lives together. How long? One other mystery, will we ever know?

With Grandma Lippok already passed away it remained for me to see our little Grandma to say goodbye which I managed to do. I called at my Aunt Marie and her husband. Only their young daughter, my cousin Agnes, was at home. Her brothers, older than me, were already called-up. We do not know, but prayed it will not have been the last time.

The three days passed so quickly, taking leave of my colleagues and the young delivery lady from the small village, {Rosa was her name I believe}. Finally, to say goodbye to the Postmaster whose encouragement I treasured. Looking forward to see them all again, would be a blessing, and a miracle! Coming home Dad said that I was expected to say goodbye to the Countess and Lutz after supper. This I did, not expecting it to be emotional. She exchanged a few words with me, thanking me for the time spent with Lutz, then she handed me a tiny metal crucifix in a pouch. It was her own, bought on a visit to Rome before the war. She had it blessed by a monk-priest in Rome and wanted me to have it. What could one say to that? It is with me seventy years now. It was not in vain! That too has a sequel to it. I shook hands with Countess Sybille and Lutz. Sadly we were not to meet in this room again. Just as well none of us knew.

George, Paul and I had been to see our parish priest and his assistant. Having received their blessing we parted. What happened to the assistant? I do not know. What happened to our parish priest? You will find out. That was my last, very last evening in our home. If only we had known what lay ahead, we might have looked around and kissed the ground, to imbue it all the deeper in our memory. No one would have imagined that we would never again see the castle and our home, except in ruins, and without many faces we had known.

# Chapter 6

# My Military Service, at age 17

16th December 1943 - our day of departure has arrived. The train was due at 10.00 am. and I am about ready. My sister Ursula has to be at college by 8.30 am and Engelbert {in his last half year at public school} at eight. He is thinking about a printing career, we have in town a small printing firm which also prints the local newspaper. Engelbert had made some positive enquiries. While we siblings said our goodbyes, Mum had my breakfast ready. When will we see each other and where? It is not what you say, but what you think deep down; people do die in a war. Surely by the time Engelbert reaches his call-up age it will all be over.

At home, we three friends had to meet at the station. I had said goodbye to Aunt Therese and my two cousins from Düsseldorf. Now no tears, just kneel before Mum and Dad and receive their parental blessing. How a mother feels, I just do not know. Taking my small case, which will arrive back home with my civilian clothes once we're kitted out.

With that I walked off to the station which I had got to know so well loading and unloading mail and parcels from and to the station. I hoped, God willing, that I might return to my home station on leave. Till then letters will arrive here hopefully. At the station there were George and Paul. We shook hands and waited for the ticket clerk to appear. Soon with a quick wave to the station staff, we climbed on board. Third class carriages in Germany still had comfortable wooden seats. Our destination is our provincial city Breslau where we are to look for the garrison we are to report to. There had not yet been a fall of snow, just a light frost. We have our woollies, and 'long johns'.

Within an hour and a half we had arrived in Breslau. We left the station and followed direction where to go. Within fifteen minutes we arrived at the garrison. O yes, it smelled like a garrison. Led into a room and told to take a seat, we looked around. I thought there were not many recruits like us visible. I, the only one who had been called up for 'Arbeitsdienst' knew the order how to present yourself. Registration over, we were directed to the Mess Hall, for a meal. At the same time glad we were three who knew each other, it made such a difference. After all, we are only a few hours from our mothers' side.

So far we had not seen anyone from our town. Called to fall-in there were not that many of us. Has it got to do with us being an extraordinary unit? Now-now, do not show off. Later we were ordered to assemble in the Mess Hall to go to the counter and to receive our packed lunch. Soon the order was to fall-in, ready with our luggage to march off to the station. This time in military order three abreast, I guessed there were no more than thirty of us. By that time it had gotten dark and in black-out too dark to see anything of the town. At the station it was, 'stay in line and follow orders.' As the train pulled in, we were directed to our carriage, all for ourselves. There were many seats empty. I had been in Breslau before, but with the night drawn in, and the black-out you might just as well go to sleep. Yes there was a sergeant with us and kept an interest in us asking, 'are we alright, and do we know where we are going?' I said "Yes, is it not Gardelegen the town where the first Paratroops were trained?" 'Yes you are right'. At the Postal job you learn a bit about distances, it would mean we will travel through the night. I did not have a chance to tell Paul about my trip to Norderney with the 'Arbeitsdienst', which gave us now the opportunity. Our threesome friendship was unique and we found it pleasant to be together. The mood in the carriage was subdued, quite unlike a boisterous school outing. There was an obvious lack of enthusiasm for a life as a paratrooper. I have to come clean; there was a moment of some sort of enthusiasm to be a paratrooper. You could do nothing about it, so why not feel a bit 'superior' to be brave enough to be a paratrooper? Or just showing-off? Perhaps the fact that I was in the 'Arbeitsdienst' and found the comradeship not at all disagreeable, might have had something to do with it.

We also discovered that none of us had volunteered to join the Paratroops. Sheer lack of sleep got the better of us, although, while settling, attempts were made to lighten the conversation, rightly so, we could not pretend that we are some sort of outsiders, who do not want to mix. Paul II as we baptised him here, found the breakthrough to murmur, "What if there is an air-raid?" I knew well that to get to Gardelegen you would be close to Berlin to change trains. In any case if there is a warning the signals will go on red to stop the train outside a station. "Yes in a safe place, not to be run over by another train", laughter here and there. We are not the only ones who began to feel sleepy. We all knew Berlin is now on the RAF target list. Somewhere we came to a long halt. There had been a container brought through the carriage with coffee. Slowly we all woke up with the aroma wafting through the carriage. A couple of recruits were asked to distribute sandwiches. We got a beaker and filled it with 'ersatz' coffee. It was a most welcome break and the sandwiches were much appreciated.

It was still dark outside and impossible to see where we had stopped and where about we were. Not that it mattered. Sleep got the better of us and blessed the heating that was working. When the call came through to wake up, we guessed we must be close to our destination. It was five in the morning and still dark. As the train came to a halt, the order was given to disembark. It felt really cold as we got out, I remember. We lined up, make sure you've got your case and there was the command: 'March!' You could just make out where we were. After some fifteen minutes or more we seem to enter a garrison.

All was quiet, but a corporal came to welcome us. We were directed to a temporary quarter for now, get inside and make yourself comfortable. There were beds in it. The room, I remember, was warm and we just threw ourselves on the bed to stretch our backs. Most of us must have fallen asleep, because I remember being wakened by a military voice, and reasonably polite. The order was to get washed and shaved, if you need to, make the beds and prepare for roll-call. A corporal arrived and got us into line and counting found all present and correct, no one missing, and then we were led to the dining room. From it a pleasant appetising aroma wafted towards us. I remember I was hungry. The reason might have been that I kept some of Mum's sandwiches to have them later. I also remember the helpings were generous for the military. Well, you always could do with more, but we had to train ourselves. Get it into your head it is not going to be home from home. Thank goodness for the 'Arbeitsdienst' training. Thereafter, we were called and marched to our living quarters. The garrison had been built in the early thirties when Paratroops were first recruited. All was now new and modern in many ways. Before leaving the Mess Hall the order was to assemble outside to be given the daily routine:

- 07:00   Rise, ablutions and bed-making
- 07:30   Roll–call and breakfast
- 12:00   Lunch and free time till 13:30
- 18:00   Evening meal and free time till Tattoo at 22:00

I thought it was a fair time table, very similar to the 'Arbeitsdienst'.

We took our case and followed the 'leader' who took us to our proper quarters. It was a three storey building, if my memory serves me right. "This is your block, remember its number, just do not get lost". Then came the crunch, will the three of us stay together? That was one hope too far, pity, but you are away from mum's apron, so do not cry. Well what comfort, only four in one room, chairs and a table where four can sit and write to their loved-ones, lockers at each bed, wash-hand basin, hot and cold water. Each corridor had a shower room, with a small wash facility and the important toilets. As we began to unpack and agreed who would sleep where, we introduced ourselves and not one could I remember at first, except one, an Austrian Franz, who was happy to be called Franzi. After the first night, it was after breakfast on the way back to our room that I was able to get a few words out of Franz. In the first war Austrian and Silesian regiments were often placed next to each other. Not exactly useful information, but together they seem to have won more battles. We all agreed the central heating was the most appreciated 'equipment' in the rooms.

After lunch we had to assemble for the fun of being kitted out. I had already been kitted out in the 'Arbeitsdienst' so I knew the procedure. Only one other of my three comrades had been in the 'Arbeitsdienst'. That probably accounted for their initial reserve. There was the introduction to military discipline: the excess strength in the voice of the instructors, from the small Lance-Corporal to the Company Sergeant Major, 'assemble and line up for kitting out'. "Have you been through it before somewhere?" I asked my comrades. "No" was the answer of two. My advice is simple, at the counter the Quartermaster and his helpers will ask you your height, then he will get the kit from the back room and hand it to you, most likely adding 'Passt' {it fits} that is all, and you do not query it, the same with your boots. Next day there will be an announcement stating if it does not fit what you have been given, you get a chance to go to the Quartermaster and they will change it for you without a murmur.

Dinner and nap time over, this is it, remember what I suggested? The whistle blows, we make our way to the parade square and march to the Quartermaster store to line up and wait for your name to be called. March up to the large counter and give your height and size. It is December and winter in Germany, so it is woollen vest and long-johns. Next, two pairs of socks and shoe size, a pair of ankle boots with steel tacks. Finally you are given two Air Force shirts, an Air Force blue tunic and a pair of grey trousers. The grey trousers are to distinguish that Paratroopers fly and jump, and are fighters on the ground. Sign your name and march out to your room with a handful of clothes. Then the fun starts trying it all on. All I had to change were my shoes. The rest was alright. Our comrades were reasonably pleased apart from some minor changes, which we are going to change tomorrow. Undress and dress, try out what fits and what not. It was the opportunity to open up the reserve among us. I had a hunch that they may be students, while I had to do 'Arbeitsdienst' and at the Post Office you were forever in contact with people.

Day two, as predicted the chance to change what does not fit. Before supper time the order was to assemble on the parade ground in proper fitting uniform for the Commanding Officer to speak to us. I clearly remember the Major as a striking officer, a decorated veteran with the Iron Cross First and Second Class and the two inch broad white band on his left sleeve, on which the name KRETA in gold braid is stitched on, which every Paratrooper wears who had taken part in the Crete Island campaign. We already noticed how many of the instructors are wearing them. There had never been a parachute drop since. That begs the question why had we been chosen to join this 'unique club'?

The CO welcomed us and hoped we would be happy to be part of an elite branch of the 'Wehrmacht'. He was aware that few had volunteered and said he understood. However, he emphasised that to be a paratrooper required something special and, therefore, there was no question of forcing anyone to become an active paratrooper. Nor was there any shame in stepping aside, if one felt the role was not for him. Clearly a military tactician. Can one imagine who among three hundred recruits standing before him would be prepared to step out? That is, unless you were sure you would not be the only one?

This part of his speech remained in my memory for the simple reason that it was a strange way to look for paratroopers among seventeen year olds. Suppertime and after up in our room, we did get in a conversation at which, surprisingly among the three of us, thoughts were brought to the open which I did not expect so soon. All of us three hundred recruits had come from all over Germany. Franzi the Austrian kept quiet by himself. Personally I thought he might just be homesick, although his stature was that of a burly farm worker from the Alps. We will have to wait. This is the same situation again, do you try a political conversation or like me wait and see if others might just open a chink, from where you might know how careful or not you may have to tread? The Army was not immune from Party infiltration. More immediate that first evening was the question, who is going to volunteer to be the man to report in full uniform, "All present and correct" when the Duty Corporal comes round and everybody is in bed? Any volunteers? With empty looks all round it is just as easy for me to stay up and report since I know the order from the 'Arbeitsdienst.'

Day three, I think the corporal was happy last night when checking out our quarters. I suppose he did not expect a first class service, but he got one. Now our basic training would begin. Line up in the morning, grading was determined by height, myself at six feet in number one squad, thirty men, one squad, and three squads made up a Company. Start was usual, how to walk, how to march, keep in line, etc. Left turn, right turn, stand still, eyes right, eyes left. On command, march! All start with the right foot. Some rifle drill and so much more. Handling rifles, for some they were heavy, more muscle exercises were the answer. Not much shouting from the instructors on the first day. A routine had established itself within a few days. Standing to attention and at ease was quickly learned, so had the addressing of the ranks. Not forgetting, everyday there was half-an-hour sport fitness, very important. How quickly the days passed, and it was Christmas. We had sent our Christmas mail a week before, but no sender address was allowed, letters were stamped with an official number. For most of us this was the first Christmas we had spent away from home. We noticed that some instructors had been given leave.

There would be of course no opportunity to attend a church service, that changed when the Nazis took over. However, there were a number of mouth-organs among us, typical German, and no one objected to us singing our well known carols which we sung with unashamed emotion. We often managed to get several rooms to come together, or even in the Mess Hall, with some instructors joining us.

On Christmas Day the kitchen surprised us with their menu. Even traditional ginger biscuits were available. Our main meal was to a standard we could not criticise, we were grateful and congratulated the kitchen staff. Unfortunately we could not let our folks at home know our address in time. There was a war on and for Christmas letters to arrive late was to be expected. The second Christmas day was actually free, apart from roll-call.

The following days were different, all work and no play. Sometimes we spent a number of hours in the large training hangar. There was a really long table, long enough to lay out a parachute in its full length, parachute and lines 10 meters {thirty feet}. We were five or six in a group. The instructor showed us the most important job about parachutes, namely the folding of it. Each paratrooper, once he had been properly trained and passed the inspector's test, will always fold his own parachute, the one he is to jump with. It was not that simple for us 'kids' to learn how to fold the 'brolly', as it was nicknamed. It took several times just to get to know the feel of the light material, to fold it the way that once you left the plane the rip cord, attached to a rail in the plane will pull your parachute open, when you feel a slight jerk. It will slow you down so that you can land on your feet with your left hand holding the short submachine gun across your chest and your head tucked in to roll over forwards, or backwards which may happen. Take cover if you can, a one foot boulder being sufficient, until you hear your corporal give the command. Personally, I found it very interesting and looked forward to have another go at folding the chute. That did not mean I wanted to be a Paratrooper.

Time to get ready for lunch and then a half hour rest. Thereafter another afternoon exercising or inside the instruction room where there were blackboards and maps. Paratroopers had been given quite comprehensive lectures on strategy on a battlefield, mainly if landing behind lines.

Almost two weeks in Gardelegen brought us to New Year, which was a low-key affair as we were under 18 so no alcohol. In our room it did not bother any of us. My mind did wander home and to my Post Office and colleagues. So far we have not yet had a return to our letters with our secret address on. New Year in Germany is celebrated only on 1$^{st}$ January, so normal routine recommences 2$^{nd}$ January. We had a good look at an old Junkers 52 plane. The three-engined plane used for the Parachute troops until the newer planes became available. {The JU52 had been Germany's 'Lufthansa' passenger planes at first, I believe}.

One day we had compulsory 'First Aid' instructions which we thought was useful. In the afternoon the Instructor took us to a rusty JU52 that must have been standing outside since the Crete landings. The seats had been taken out. Paratroopers sat on a bench along the fuselage of the plane, leaving the centre free to be able to move to the door of the plane. As soon as you got up, you must remember to hook your line on the bar which was fixed to the roof of the plane. {It will pull your chute open once you are clear of the plane tail rudder.}

There was an interesting, or funny at your choice, incident at the evening report before lights out. It was Franzi the Austrian's turn. I lay in my bed and dosed away when I saw Franzi in his long-johns and woolly vest putting on his shoes. He then put on his uniform belt over his long-johns, then his helmet instead of his cap. I wondered what was he trying to do, is he not going to change, when I heard the Duty Corporal was about to enter our room. What is going to happen now? I feared the worst. Franzi stood to some sort of attention, saluted, but did not say "all present and correct" as you do. A few more seconds nothing happened. The corporal stood still for a short moment, looked at Franzi, and leaving just said "Go to bed boy" and left the room. None of us said anything. As you can imagine, we all wondered what was going to happen in the morning. Will Franzi be sent to the Medics or what? Nothing happened, everything continued as normal, including Franzi's behaviour.

3rd January and after roll-call, surnames were called out. Letters had arrived, including one for me from home. After breakfast I opened my mail and it was a Christmas card and a longish letter from Dad. He had bad news to report and I wondered how he felt. The Countess had an official note from Count Prosper's company captain informing the Countess that Count Prosper had been wounded in Russia a month ago. It required the amputation of his leg above the knee. He is out of danger, and further information will be sent from the hospital. The Countess indeed had news from the hospital with a short note from her son Count Prosper. A shock at first but relief with the latest news. It really could have been worse. Dad suggested the Countess see her Doctor to advise her on the possibility to travel to the hospital to visit Count Prosper. On receiving the Doctor's reply, she made the visit. That must have been a shock to everyone, according to Dad. The Countess now has at least an address to send letters to her son. As Dad says, for Count Prosper the war is over. He will now be looked after and the wound will heal. Dad is still the only man at the castle and will be trying his best to help the Countess in any way possible. Here at Gardelegen there was a lack of information. The radio in the Mess Hall is not always on. That left us with only small morsels of news. Had the Russian spring offensive started? The threat of a Russian offensive pushing our armies nearer towards the Polish eastern border could become reality.

We do wonder how long our training will be. The afternoon went well with more interesting instruction and more interesting stories from our corporal and his experiences on Crete and other expeditions in Russia. Our friendly Lance Corporal is going to show us how to land properly after you jumped from the plane. Always try to land on your feet, with knees slightly bent to act like shock absorbers, and roll forward onto your elbow. It is the machine-gun that is the tool you have to hold correctly and tightly, otherwise you will not be able to defend yourself when you land, not forgetting to release the clip to get rid of the parachute. This was what we had first practised, jumping from a platform near the roof of the hangar on to a thick bed of straw. We spent a good bit of time asking questions, since it was obvious that the Lance Corporal was quite happy to chat and tell from his experiences. A look at the clock and the afternoon had gone. Time to go to our room and get ready to fall-in at the parade ground to hear what the Commandant has to say. He simply addressed us and announced that we will leave the next day for new training grounds. He reminded us who we were and hoped we would do well, then wished us all good luck and disappeared. The Sergeant Major will give us instructions after supper. That was some surprise, and somewhat subdued, where to next? After all, all the actions are in the east, albeit now also in the south of Italy.

Next morning after breakfast the Sergeant Major gave us instructions that we should pack all our belongings into our knapsack, putting the food containers and cutlery into the pouch and attach it to your belt. Do not forget your helmet, ah yes, the helmet, now that was a surprise because we wondered what helmet? Out came the Paratrooper Helmet, it is lighter than the normal military and more comfortable because it sits on your head with straps to prevent it from flapping about when running with it. We were to leave after the evening meal. That is the Army, never tell you where to. Dismissed, we collected our belongings and stowed them in our knapsack. I went to see George and Paul in their rooms. We are of course in the same company, but we still could not figure it out how and why only us three from our home. All committed Catholics ready to defend the Fatherland. Then, George recalled the Hitler Youth with their camera at the church that Sunday Morning? Yes, it could have something to do with it. Oh, let's forget it. We have to go where we are being told to. However, we still have our faith and leave the worrying to 'Him' up there. Ready and correct we made our way to the Mess Hall to have our supper. When finished, we are to collect food for the journey, a surprising reasonably sized food pack. Up to our room to collect our belongings and down to line up for the command to march. What a blessing we did not have to take our rifle. Goodbye Gardelegen and within the half hour we arrived at the station. My first thought had been, watch where the train comes from, it may just be a hidden clue! It came from the East and I watched for the first half hour and it was still going west. Having passed Hannover meant we were still heading west. So far so good. Meaning we travel west, Hannover Station would be a good pointer, only if we stop to read the station. Someone in our carriage suggested that it would not matter as we would have to spend time in a garrison to be first fully trained. We never fired a shot yet on a rifle range. That was one way of looking at it.

Before boarding the train I had planned to see if I could take my seat next to Franzi. I was anxious to get to know him better. I first needed his confidence to talk to me. We travelled over two hours and still going west, a good sign. Our tummies called for our food packs to be opened, the field flask filled with coffee, although no longer hot would be welcome. Just a slice of bread would suffice. I learned from my former train journeys how tempting it is to keep eating up your ration early on the journey. Therefore, I am tough with myself and keep some for another time, who knows when and where we would get something more to eat. The time we stood at this station would mean there was an engine change. The good news so far is we were in west Germany. It is a middle size station and my postal teaching was paying dividends. We were in the Rhine-land, but soon it will be decision time, south to Italy or west to France? Suddenly a remark, maybe just another garrison in west Germany. We are in possible air-raid territories, unless the British RAF has a day off. Those who came from Berlin would have some experiences to tell. So far we have not heard a Berlin dialect. Certainly some from far northeast Germany. It was midnight and we stopped in one of Aachen's sub-stations, where we could actually walk on the platform, always in view of two corporals. Guessing our destination was the favourite occupation on the platform. An up-to-date newspaper would be most welcome. The order, time to board the train, again where to? My own hunch is Italy or France for training. Don't care as long as it is south. Before falling asleep I perceived the peculiar sound of wheels on steel crossing a bridge at slow speed, cupping by eyes against the window, there was no mistaking we crossed a wide river. It could only be the Rhine, which means only one thing; we crossed the river from east to west. Sleep really began to take its toll. We must have slept like logs when the train came to a slow stop. Early dawn and somewhere a voice was heard "we are in France." One could almost feel the relief. The platform was still empty except for two men in a strange uniform, French railway porters? Eventually the train moved on, we tried to read the name of the station but in vain.

With our compartment more than half empty and our half for ourselves, it offered me a chance to open a conversation with Franzi. I was curious and started small talk and tried to discover where in Austria he came from, seeing as I loved geography and could trace where his home was. I asked a question for which I apologized, but need not have done so, "Did you cheer and clap hands when Hitler marched into Austria?" A definite 'No' was his answer. Franzi came from a rural background. Then I asked "Are you Catholic?" "Yes" he replied. "So am I", was my reply. Such statements of us young ones in those times meant solidarity and trust. We knew where we stood with each other. Well, at least I hoped not to fall into a trap. I told him about our Countess coming from an Austrian aristocrat family. After a few more minutes Franzi whispered, "I hate this whole thing". With Franzi's remark we both knew where we stood. I seriously wondered if he had been trying to fake unfit for the military. "We are in France!", shouted one of our academic room-mates. The question then was, whereabouts are we? It does not really matter. Everybody got out to stretch their legs. We all tried to get it out of the corporals, "Where next?" in good humour, but they would not budge. Even if we knew who would know where in France it would be. Wait and enjoy the scenery. That meant we were not at our proper destination yet. It certainly was milder than in Germany. Back into the train. Our food and drinks are getting low, but we are 'soldiers' and have to suffer it. This is good training.

So we rolled on and admired the different scenery, and for me, the styles in agriculture, which interested me naturally. Goodness, how far south are we? The two wheeled carts with dual shafts and one horse was something new and interesting. We did not pass through any large wine growing area until later. In time it happened, the first vineyards appeared. The outline of a larger city is appearing as the train began to slow down as we entered the station. The corporals had already asked us to prepare for disembarking. Make sure nothing is left behind. We lined up on the platform and roll-call, all present and correct.

It was 5th January 1944 and a New Year had begun. We were in Angoulême, a mid-sized city in southern France. We barely attracted attention as we marched out of the station. We need not wonder, we are the occupying army. There was no singing as we marched along. Probably we did not wish to antagonise the inhabitants. There was an opportunity for me to enjoy our new environment. There were differences in the style of buildings and many granite villas as we entered an impressive wide avenue with grass and flowerbeds between the sidewalk and the road. We avoided marching through the centre of town, and soon the avenue narrowed to the out-of-town highway. Just ahead on the right we saw a large arched entrance, unmistakably the garrison. To the right and left of the arched entrance a ten foot high granite wall to encircle the garrison. We entered, passing through the archway into a large square, the parade ground. To the right and left the two-storey high dormitories. Straight ahead, between the two dormitories, was the impressive central building, for the commandant and officers, the administration offices, the Mess Hall and kitchen, and a ball room. The dreaded detention room and accommodation for equipment were on the right side of the main entrance and the watch and guard building on the left. The dormitory on the right was already occupied by a unit that had arrived a few weeks before us. Our company would occupy the dormitory on the left and we halted in front of it awaiting the arrival of the CO. We stood to attention as he emerged. He was a stern-looking decorated Major who would have been at the Crete island drop and, like all instructors here, would certainly have been at the Russian front. I felt sure he was a before-the-war veteran. His welcoming address was short. As a veteran in his forties, he must have thought he had been sent a pack of children, but a soldier with a heart, who deserved our respect. Having found our assigned space, we had time to unpack kitbags and place our belongings neatly in our locker. Testing the bed is always important {no 'Slumberland' quality but it will pass.} After such a long train journey the chance to stretch out is irresistible. The first day holds pleasant memories and I recall that dinner was good.

Angoulême is approximately 140 miles south of Tours, some sixty miles from Bordeaux, and a thousand miles from home, {which we were not allowed to tell our folks}. It is an ancient and historic town and it is said the garrison was built for Napoleon's troops. It felt and looked that way. Will there be an opportunity for us to see the town, although we are not on holiday here?

Daily orders followed the usual pattern:

| | |
|---|---|
| 07:00 | Rise, ablutions, beds, fitness drill |
| 08:00 | Roll-call and breakfast |
| 09:00 | Parade and rifle drill, etc. |
| 12:00 | Lunch and rest till 13:30 |
| 18:00 | Supper |
| 22:00 | Tattoo |

Thereafter we received instructions on a number of procedures. Sundays were free days, used chiefly for writing, reading, mending, resting weary bones, etc. No leaving the garrison.

Now a word about the living quarters. From the central corridor to the left and right were dormitories. Each dormitory contained six beds, small lockers and a table with chairs. Two single glazed windows, three feet wide, six feet high in each room needed replacing, but being so far south it did not matter. The doors were meant to last forever. Happily its facilities had all been modernised. The walls were very thick and one could sense the ghosts of hundreds of French recruits who through the decades since Napoleon had filled the place with friendship, laughter and tears. Now it was our turn. We understood we were here to learn how to defend our country from its enemies and how to protect ourselves, knowing that our opponent had the same responsibilities. We had to try to conquer our innermost fears as far as possible and to suppress totally our personal ideology and beliefs. That was where some of us were at variance with officialdom. The onus was on us, we had to learn how to survive! Military recruits who had not been in the 'Arbeitsdienst' found the initial training stressful. The commands of a squad's Lance Corporal were imperative and his toleration of mistakes was scarce. Many of us were not yet eighteen years old, and the weight of weaponry one had to carry required some fitness. It was a particular handicap for those whose life so far had not required physical exertion. Seven-mile marches would include instruction in orienteering, compass reading and distance assessment. The 45km {30mile} long marches proved arduous for many. Apart from your rifle or light machine gun, you also carried an ammunition case. Yes, there was a break for your sandwich and drink from your flask. From the last mile you sing your heart out and enter the garrison in style. I have to confess that I found a happy side to those route-marches; we were out among pleasant countryside, not spectacular, but with its own charm. Undulating green meadows and vineyards to the east of Angoulême levelled out westward, along the River Charente towards the coast. Those long marches were never without the occasional stamina test when the order came to put on your gasmask for several miles. That was not funny. By the way, the town of 'Cognac' was only some 20 miles away.

On one occasion I and one other recruit were ordered to accompany a truck to 'Cognac' with two instructors. We had to bed down on rags in the back of the open truck and had an excellent view of the countryside. To travel through the town was most interesting; at least I found it so. However often I tried I can only guess what we had to pick up. Strange that we were not asked to come down from the truck, just take the boxes and cartons that were handed to us and put them down and put a cover over them. I was happy with that because there was a certain 'streak' in me, a love to travel. Arriving home, all we had to do was to hand down the packages, it was obvious to us they contained bottles. We refrained from asking not wanting to be told 'none of your business'! It was a welcome break in a demanding routine, and I could say I was in 'Cognac'.

Not being permitted to break monotony with a walk into town was frustrating and the subject of much debate among us. One possible reason may have been to avoid antagonising an otherwise placated population. Although the Nazi propaganda machine did its best to keep at bay any knowledge of a French resistance movement, rumours did circulate. That was probably the reason why there were always double guards during the darkness.

After two months, permission was given to go into town. The advice was to go in pairs or more. The Commandant himself gave us the news one Saturday morning, making it clear that access to premises selling alcohol was strictly forbidden and so too was access by invitation to any disreputable house. We three, Paul, George and I invited Franzi to come with us. We knew full well that our instructors would be keeping an eye on us. We walked smartly down the street, not knowing a word of French, and the difficulties were immediately apparent when we stopped outside a small restaurant to survey the enticing display in the window. What do you say as you walk in? How do you ask for what you fancied? Easy, you point! More difficult though is the question of cost. Money was something we had not considered before we set out, so we decided it was better to walk on, rather than to make fools of ourselves. If only we could at least say 'Hello'. A couple of other recruits we met en route suggested 'Bonjour'. That was a start. Much to my disappointment it was decided not to go for a 'café au-lait' and 'gateau', but I spotted something I would enjoy for supper at a large cheese shop. "I am going in, anyone coming with me?" They followed me, not knowing a word of French. As I walked in I had to chance it and said as well as I could 'Bonjour', and pointed to one of the hard cheeses, and indicated the appropriate size. She understood my question and kindly inviting me to say "le fromage", I did and paid for an appetising piece of 'fromage'. Would I ever forget? It had been a memorable experience and everyone was clearly in favour of learning French without delay. During a happy evening we shared all the interesting and funny encounters of the day. Those of us who took the opportunity to explore the permissible part of town, enjoyed that bit of freedom being able to be part of civilian life, although you could not disguise that you wore the uniform of an occupying force.

Within the garrison we had no access to radios and news. Our instructors were not so handicapped and would sometimes discuss what was interesting to know. We gathered that the picture had changed somewhat. Africa was out of the equation, Italy had capitulated, and British and American forces were on the Italian mainland. The expectation of an invasion of France was no longer concealed and, as yet, there was no serious concern, or so it seemed, regarding the expected Russian spring offensive, which had begun, we were told.

There were moments when my mind turned to Countess Sybille and young Count Prosper who has been wounded and is alive, and hopefully will one day walk again even with an artificial limb. How many have this day already given their life or limb? Spring had begun a month ago, and it was so beautiful and peaceful here. Actually I almost forgot to mention that one day in January before breakfast we heard it had snowed during the night. So, most of us took the opportunity to battle it out in long-johns before racing upstairs to get washed and dressed for breakfast. By eleven o'clock it had melted in the sun.

At the end of March we were informed that our Vereidigung {'passing out' ceremony} would take place next Saturday. Goodness already. I did not think we were ready for it. Every recruit looks forward to this occasion with its promise of a day off and a special dinner. The important day dawned and there was extra effort required to do the spit and polish for the parade and ceremony. Rise and shine in the morning, breakfast, dress up and fall into a smart outfit. The flag was carried by a senior NCO, sadly for me, there was no band. The Commandant's speech was interesting and encouraging. He warned that much would be expected of us, and told us to remember the Fatherland. From today we were soldiers. For a few weeks the daily routine continued until we were summoned to an unexpected roll-call for news.

Within days we would leave Angoulême, for an unknown destination. All too soon we were to face the serious side of war.

Speculation and rumours did not help, but it created a home-made guessing game and passed the time. We have no choice other than follow other peoples' orders. As I write these lines I recall that time, and feel again the shock of confrontation with the truth and the seriousness of reality. What could you write home, except to tell your family that you will be moving again and to ask them to remember you in their prayers, knowing that is what they will do.

One thing I was certain of was that my mother would attend six o'clock morning Mass every possible day. This gave me courage and faith to leave my worries in safer hands, {as surely happened, or this story could not have been written}. I am reminded of an occasion when Dad told me in one of his letters that he had shown one of my letters to the Countess Sybille who read it and asked if she might read others. I appreciated her interest in me for she had many personal problems of her own. At a time of apprehension I was comforted. With hindsight I could have asked was this the journey of My Story or the story of My Journey? Either way, it had the potential of ending at any time.

It was the last days of March 1944, when the order was given for us to gather our possessions, and start packing. This time we had the additional weight of a paratrooper rifle to carry. Next day after breakfast we were in formation to move out of this interesting and peaceful garrison, and 'Adieu' Angoulême. One pleasant discovery for me was that our squad sergeant was travelling with us on this train.

Without delay we boarded the train, found our place and stowed our gear. Seeing the last dwellings of Angoulême fade into the distance one realised just how short our visit had been. We travelled in daylight giving an opportunity to enjoy the French countryside. After a brief stop at Tours we continued northwards then turned into a north-easterly direction. How I wished we had a tourist map! Lunch consisted mainly of sandwiches and lukewarm coffee and to pass the time as we travel may I introduce you to our unique German army Kommissbrot, the army bread viewed with disdain by many French and British POWs. It is made with one part rye and three parts wheat flour. With less yeast it is of a dense consistency requiring a longer chew, allowing a slice to satisfy for a longer period than a pure white loaf. We learned it was wise to chew each bite for longer to satisfy longer. It also will keep for longer days.

Franzi and I sat together, while friends Paul and George travelled in the next compartment. It was the first week in April 1944 and we were acutely aware of what lay ahead, the Italian campaign or the dreaded Russian front. It would be a decisive year for many of us. The train came to a stop late afternoon at Bar-le-Duc, a French city not far from the 1914-18 famous Verdun. The rumour was that we might stay here for a day or two, according to the corporal. We marched through the town to the garrison. Whilst our smart appearance might have been appreciated in any town at home, here it was totally lost on a disinterested and resentful population. On arrival at the garrison, we settled quickly into our dormitories, though ordered not to unpack. We were ready for our evening meal. Thoughts of home and our four-month absence from loved ones resurfaced. We spent a restful night, albeit interrupted occasionally by thoughts of the unknown 'where-to'. Morning call and line up for count and breakfast. After breakfast there was time to mingle and say our goodbye to our sergeant who seemed to purposely make for me to shake my hand. As he did so, I was sure as we looked in each other's eyes there was moisture in his eyes, and I recalled a conversation with him during a break on exercises in which he did not give anything away in words but in thought certainly, which never left me to this day. {As a Bavarian he might well have been a Christian.} Just as my two friends from home, George and Paul, did he survive the war? I will never know, sadly.

All practical matters were handled for us. We had just to follow the orders. Now we had time to dwell on our future, without the comfort of parental guidance. Our mood was subdued because we young recruits knew or felt that the possibility of the Russian campaign was not pleasant to look forward to. The order was heard to board the train. We left Bar-le-Duc in the late afternoon accompanied by new 'chaperones'. These new squad leaders could not divulge our destination and we had to assess things for ourselves, it passed the time. The train carried us eastwards for the first hour towards the border and the welcome sight of a German town. Nightfall and the blackout made it impossible to chart our progress. Time passed in the way it does on long journeys and one by one we fell asleep. At the last moment before sleep, I became the winner, I thought we were still travelling east. We all seem to have slept like the proverbial log.

The familiar sound of squeaking brakes woke us up one by one, and as subdued station lights appeared we were still unable to read a name until we came to a halt. One by one voices said, "Brenner Pass". I jumped up to the door to ensure we had heard right, and it was. I immediately convinced myself, surely we're on our way to Italy. There was no command to keep us from getting out. Guards were patrolling around the station building. Our new guards enquired how we were and promised that anytime we would line up for a hot meal, welcome news. We have reached the border between Germany and Austria, where not so long before, Hitler had met the Italian dictator, Mussolini here on this very station. The quietness changed to audible relief that it must mean we were bound for Italy. "Franzi" I said, "you are not far from home!". Then I found George and Paul to share the good news. Although I did not know it then, the Brenner Pass was particularly significant for me because it was here I turned my back on Germany for five years. By God's grace I lived to visit it when peace had been restored.

We lined up to follow the soldier in front and the aroma of the soup. It began to feel cold but we realised we have come from the south of France to the Alps! What was noticeable here, far away from battle fields the station lights were not darkened. Within a few minutes we entered the distribution centre to drink hot, thick pea-and-ham soup amid a much more relaxed 'gathering'. Having stretched our legs, we mingled and talked awhile. We enjoyed the two-hour break on the platform before we were commanded to return to the train. Issued with a new food-pack we settled down as we sped through the night, with an Italian engine I suppose. At this point, the distance between Austria and Italy is relatively narrow and one is soon on Italian soil. After a good sleep I woke to a rising sun and lots of green undulating countryside. I knew we must soon be in the Po Valley. I noticed, or so it seemed we are no longer moving at speed, an opportunity to see the countryside so much better. Travelling through the Po Valley one thought about a future holiday, while enjoying the privilege of travelling now in comfort, experiencing all of this gratis. Darker thoughts would then intrude; the plight of others, their discomfort, hunger, intimidation, and loss of life or limb, all the result of someone's crazy war that causes boys to grow up too soon.

We no longer travelled along a major rail-line when we finally stopped at a small station. There were few dwellings but we saw a small number of open trucks lined up, their khaki-clad drivers lounging alongside. It was late afternoon and very warm as we alighted. It was getting warmer, and we were in winter clothes. We lined up for roll-call ensuring everybody is still with us. The news was that these trucks were meant to take us down to southern Italy. Climbing aboard, we stowed away our kitbags and made sure our rifle and helmet was with us. The sergeant checked that no-one was left behind and we moved off. It was obvious at once that trucks were not particularly comfortable, but this was not a trip to a holiday resort. Kitbags and other essential gear necessitated our sitting close together.

The convoy rumbled along through the night. Progress was governed by the poor visibility from covered headlights which made speed impossible and there was only one brief comfort stop. Sleep was fitful and the journey seemed unending. We stopped at last just before daylight in a lay-by. As the sun rose over large hills we noticed that there was high ground rising from the road-side on our right, and a steep drop down to a valley on our left. There were trees on our left side and we were well camouflaged by nature. The reason for 'camping' here was the possibility of US reconnaissance planes on the lookout for troop movement. We would be travelling by night and staying under cover in daylight.

There was nothing to do all day, and I did not smoke and had no desire to try. I was surprised how few of us smoked. It was the veterans who smoked the pipe. To get off the truck and stretch your legs was bliss. I was interested in the country-side. It seemed like a holiday trip. We were allowed to walk up and down our column. After 'lunch' I looked across the relative narrow valley where there was a small house, where a man tended his flowers or something like a small vineyard. With our veteran standing close by I suddenly asked him, could I go across and ask if he would sell me wine to fill my flask? I went back and rested for a while. Having drunk my coffee from my flask and eaten a slice of bread, I told our corporal about my idea to go across the valley. To my surprise he said go, but no nonsense, "I shall be watching you". He gave me his flask and with my friend we made our way down the valley and up to the little house. What do we say? None of us spoke Italian. I managed some sort of greeting and held out our flask, asking "vino?" Saying nothing he took our flask and returned with the flasks filled. Not knowing what to say, I held out my hand with some liras, giving it a brief look, he took them all, at the same time retreating inside and closed the door. On our return we handed the filled flask to our corporal, and offered a drink to my companion. I could not believe that I was capable of such a thing. I was surprising myself. I shall say very little more about this episode. A most unpleasant journey it became as we drove through the night, longing for the convoy to stop for a break. The very thought of soup for lunch could not be considered, and I managed only a slice of our military bread. It was difficult to find a place where I could be without being seen! With daylight the convoy again sheltered under trees, which was a blessing. I found lying on the grass verge helped a little. That was the first and last time I drank Italian wine. It was sheer folly to have expected to get a decent wine.

We mounted our trucks before sunset. By day the temperature was noticeably warmer but as night wore on we appreciated our winter uniform. Our journey ended shortly before dawn. It got brighter with every minute. A call, this is it, end of journey. We left the vehicles taking all our belongings with us. We were in a grassy area and were led to a large brick building at one end which looked to have a number of empty rooms with an upper floor, it also seemed empty. We were led into this building where we found mattresses on the floor, a 'dining room' and a kitchen. Here, at last, we were kitted out with khaki shirts, tunic and light trousers and summer underwear, all the right size. Winter uniform was folded and stowed away in our kitbag. Now matters became serious, into the kitbag went all my personal items apart from shaving kit, writing pad, the Countess' cross and a photograph. All else, folded neatly into one's own kitbag. This is a serious matter. Our kitbag will be sealed, our name clearly printed inside and outside. It would then be taken by a truck to some collecting place, miles from here, so that it might be moved whenever the front line changes in order that should you be wounded or killed your belongings will be sent to your family. Quite a thought!

Before supper a Sergeant Major made a short speech. He informed us that we are now members of the 11$^{th}$ Regiment of the Fourth Paratroop Division under the leadership of the much-decorated General Gericke. Now we knew where we belonged! Eventually we learned that we would be assigned to the Anzio beachhead. The front line was only a few miles away. It also meant we were just south of Rome. Final 'exercises' took place half a mile from our quarters on a piece of flat wasteland and a small hill. I shall mention just two examples which keep occurring in my memory and have enthralled our grandchildren. The exercise was to attack the hill, on which an imaginary enemy was dug-in. The hand grenades we used were captured British egg-shaped hand grenades, and you had to creep forward and toss the grenade as far as you could with all your strength. The British hand grenades were lighter in weight than the German ones which meant you should be able to toss them further. Those who lacked sufficient muscle did not throw them far enough and the grenade would roll back towards the thrower, with disastrous consequences when primed. They were not primed for training. Some of us here could have done with some weight lifting at home. Thank goodness for my year on the farm.

The following exercise was how to survive a tank attack. A massive Tiger VI appeared, my goodness it looked fearsome. Supposed to have been the latest in the German Armoury. None of us had ever seen such a monster. To acquaint us with the roar of a tank's engine and its manoeuvrability we watched as it roared away a hundred yards on half throttle, then it turned on full throttle and stopped at a right angle almost instantly. We learned that to stay alive in a tank attack you had to make yourself as small as possible and to lie flat and still on your tummy in front of the tank caterpillar tracks if he is heading towards you. The driver will not have seen you, for he is scanning the terrain a good bit ahead. When the tank is about three or four yards from you, you roll away left or right from its tracks. It is safer by far to roll under the tank, which will not crush you because there are some eighteen inches between the ground and the smooth underbelly of the tank. The exercise for us was to go and lie flat in line with the caterpillar tracks, and when the tank is just four yards in front of you, you roll away from the tracks – the safest being to roll right under the tank – and when it has passed over, you can then roll over and fire a grenade at it from behind. 'Any volunteers?' I had watched the tank before and noticed the underbelly never bounced, that's why I wanted a shot. I looked around, no hand was raised, and I lifted up my hand. "O.K. you're sure?" the corporal asked. "Yes sir." I lay down some thirty yards from the huge beast of a tank in line with the 18 inch caterpillar tracks and looked at the tank twenty yards away when his roar went up, I kept my eyes focused on his tracks. He came straight at me and when he was four yards away I rolled twice before this beast went over me. Getting up I felt no spectacular feeling about it. "Want another try?" Yes, one other fellow recruit joined me. I think we both felt pleased. Would I do it again? Not at my present age. Exercises near a front-line, are not for the sport of photographers.

Within a week the day arrived when everything became earnest. We gathered our gear, which included a short handled lightweight spade, to dig-in when necessary. Two trucks arrived to take us wherever we were meant to go and our journey lasted about half an hour. We obeyed the order to alight and the driver kept the engine running till the last man was off, before he raced back into the distance. Obviously he was a veteran who knew that an enemy plane could appear at any moment over the horizon. This was our first lesson at the front, never linger in the open.

Now it was serious. We had to follow a veteran who went ahead of us telling us how to follow him exactly as he made for the trenches. Then we were divided, two of us with a couple of veterans. The trenches were dug out to almost six feet deep in a light ground. We were at the 'Anzio beachhead'. The instruction from the experienced veteran was clear, "you move in these ditches bent and never upright". The red house half a mile away is in British hands with a sharp shooter in one of the top floor rooms. If any of us is slow, or not crouching when moving in the trench you will not survive. The idea was to dig further trenches at right angles. It did not require us to work continuously, rather with lots of time in-between. Nothing serious happened here all the days we were in our trench. Going for food was the most dangerous, but we learned quickly, because Tommy was not sleeping. Our time here in this trench came to a sudden end after only a week. We were ordered to retreat during the early morning to some other place. A truck took us a few miles further south. It was hilly country, and as usual we had to jump out rifle and all, to let the driver get away. Here we were, a handful of recruits. Shortly a paratrooper arrived and made us welcome, and led us up a rising pathway. The path measured approximately nine feet wide; on the right was a two hundred feet drop to the valley, at a guess, three hundred yards wide, after which the ground rose again. More important was our position, where the height from the path was a straight ten to twelve feet high earth wall. The path went on for half a mile and more. Into this wall were dug out seven feet high caves. Ten feet deep and ten feet wide. A Lance Corporal greeted us, he then pointed to me and one other of us recruits to the first cave, two fresh recruits and two veterans of the Crete Para drop. Every cave had four very simple camp beds, two against each wall and a crude table, made from wooden boxes, and stood in the middle of the cave. We spent the first hour getting to know the other two veterans. Coffee was heated on a paraffin stove and we unpacked our rations. This helped to ease the tension and broke the ice. It was not easy for either, the veterans and us 'kids,' but surprisingly we soon gelled together. To our question "are the Engländer going to break out one day?", the reply was "maybe". "Where do you come from?" is a question that helps, unless your accent has given you away already. Being told we were in the second line and a mile or so from the battle front brought some comfort. One of us had to be on guard during the night for four hours with one of the veterans, then the other two. I drew the long straw and would be on guard tomorrow. I slept like the proverbial log.

 Next day we enquired about ablutions, "take your towel and toothbrush to the sparkling burn in the valley, and do not linger". I learned how to operate the stove. It had been drummed into us that every man depended on the others and we knew the importance of finding common ground and comradeship. Gradually we felt confident enough to ask who is facing us, British or Americans. "Never sure, they change", was the answer. There is always that gap between hardened and experienced veterans and young raw recruits. We could be a hindrance in difficult skirmishes with the enemy. It takes time to wear off; we have been warned by our instructors. I am glad to say within a week it did become very pleasant and friendly. Our veterans had been paratroopers since the beginning of the war. Occasionally the exchange of gun fire in reconnaissance skirmishes could be heard, and prisoners were taken by both sides. We did see a small group of British prisoners being led to the company field post. They smiled while shouting, "War finished, go home!" For now it seemed there would be little to do other than fetch water and go down to the valley to collect the daily rations. That was good to know for a start, and we waited to be told what to do. Without direction from our elders I found courage to ask which way to the toilet? Nature does not know there is a war on. "At the bottom of the valley, you'll soon see it, it has neither roof nor door." "Thanks."

Knowing we were at the east side of the Anzio beachhead, and in the second line, was comforting for now. We played cards, and it was difficult occasionally to pass the time since I was no card player. In the military that is a handicap but I took the opportunity to integrate and learn. The daily break at lunchtime meant that one of us had to go down to the valley with an insulated food container strapped on our back. A truck arrived and your container was exchanged for a full one. You collected miscellaneous items like bread, coffee and tea. Occasionally there were papers and other items of information and the occasional letter. Since we left France I had received no letter so far. It will take time to find us. It gave us an opportunity to quiz the driver on the situation and latest news including the truth of rumours. These encounters were hurried, because the drivers were always aware of the possibility of being spotted by enemy reconnaissance; yet they were a welcome interlude in an otherwise humdrum existence. We learned that since the battle of 'Monte Cassino' had been lost, it seemed the Americans and British were taking a rest to replenish manpower and supplies. But they would soon be keeping us on the hop. They are not that far away, if you care to look at a map. Our humdrum existence could not last. Politics were seldom mentioned and we listened enthralled to the veterans' account of their experiences and many adventures. They had spent time on the Russian front from the beginning of the war, but had a period of respite in Germany and France. To pass the time there was nothing to hinder us from visiting our friends in the other caves.

There was a story told as true about an extraordinary case regarding a new Paratroop unit next to us a few months earlier. The opponents were a British unit and, during the long spell of inaction, a way was found of communicating with each other to offer exchanges, German watches for British cigarettes. One simple 'Simon', apparently not very bright, but fearless in his way, was to be the go-between. A password and time had been agreed for 'Simon' to cross with the exchange. Apparently the origin began in the First World War.

One early afternoon, suddenly we heard the sound of a plane. We rushed out of our cave and there it was flying at very low altitude, just above height of the valley. The marking US made it obvious it was an American plane with twin fuselage. Obviously a reconnoitre plane. It was interesting since I had never heard or seen such a plane. Only later we wondered if we had given our position away by waving to it. Nothing happened during the next two weeks, and we relaxed. However, only two days later in mid-morning there was a loud explosion a couple of caves from us and seconds later I hear a cry. I ran out and looked up the path two caves from us, a young comrade was clutching his severed arm at the elbow and bleeding profusely crying out "My arm, my arm!" A small part of skin was holding his arm, a mortar shell exploded right in front of their cave. I held his arm and took him down to our cave where they had already opened a bandage pack. The shout for the Paramedic echoed in the valley. We bandaged his upper arm to stem the flow of blood, and I just managed to say "For you the war is over". I was surprised how quickly the medic appeared as I walked my fellow young recruit down the valley where the transport appeared. This was my first encounter with the wounds of war, and I was surprised to realise that I felt neither squeamish nor shocked. I was just propelled into action and did not think of the possibility of a further imminent mortar attack, which did not happen.

It must have been a single rogue which someone from the other side thought of sending a typical example of war. Aware of our dependence on each other, one reacted to the immediate need. The exploding shell reminded us just how vulnerable we all were, even in the second line.

Nothing happened until ten days later. The changing tide in my life, the quietness was broken. In the morning the order was for us to take our automatic rifle and our belongings in the small rucksack. A truck arrived and took us away from the hilly area to an open and flat area of fields where pioneers must have hurriedly dug trenches. These were too shallow, so with our short-handle spades we dug furiously to provide safer cover. It was mid-May and the Allied forces were heading for Rome. The advance had started in earnest. Eventually the order came for us to move and the last few hundred yards had to be completed in almost total darkness to avoid being sitting targets. As dawn broke we discovered we were behind a raised grassy bank only 18 inches high, which gave some welcome protection. Our platoon corporal knew there was a line of our infantry in front of us, and the plan was that if they were pushed back, we the 'Elite', would hopefully hold the line. That would mean to defend ourselves would require you to shoot your enemy! What a thought; and with no action to be heard, we began to relax. With the sun at our back, the corporal with me trained his binoculars on a distant object for some time. Before offering them to me he directed my viewing towards the large brightly coloured building far away; "Are you Catholic?" he asked, I nodded, "Well, you are looking at the Pope's summer residence, Castel Gandolfo". With his glasses I had the most beautiful and least expected present here to see, including Lake Albano. Was my guardian angel with me? I wondered? I felt privileged and was emboldened to tell him that our bread ration was very low.

The corporal agreed and seemed sure some would arrive with the warm soup. Food arrived late that evening and had to be collected some distance behind us in open and exposed country. You learn ingenuity during war, and we followed the corporal's advice by waiting till the setting sun was behind us, blinding the opposing side we hoped, before we went to collect the rations. It was quiet, almost too quiet next day. The corporal was of the opinion that the foe was regrouping or planning a new strategy. The veterans were puzzled that there were no reconnaissance planes around and no air attacks. We did see the vapour trail of bombers flying at high altitude from Italian bases towards southern Germany. They may well be on their way to bomb the last German fuel production refinery in Upper Silesia, only 15 miles from our home. Time to count our blessings, that we were for the time being, in a quiet and relatively peaceful place in brilliant sunshine. It will be my birthday at the end of the week. We had received no mail in the last six weeks. I felt sure there must be a few letters from home lying around somewhere.

Next day, 1st June 1944. The Allied forces were less than three miles away. We walked some two miles in a relatively flat area. Making ourselves as inconspicuous as possible we followed the dirt road across the terrain. There was a shallow ditch and a low embankment. Our first task was to dig ourselves a fox-hole for cover. Digging away into the hard bank, I must have been suddenly knocked unconscious. When I came to, I felt a searing pain in my back, turning to my companion I shouted, "do you see blood on my back, it feels very hot"? Thinking of blood running down my back, I was surprised that I felt no moisture. He confirmed that I was not bleeding. "Look behind you" he called, and there, several yards away was a mortar shell crater and on the road behind me lay a fist-sized lump of rock. This must have knocked me out for a short time, 'Lord' that was close, and no deadly shrapnel. You can be sure I did indeed say a short prayer. The pain had almost gone next day. We spent the night in our fox-holes keeping an eye open for any movement. Nervous tension prevented one from relaxing. We recruits had not yet met the enemy face to face. During the day the corporal kept surveying the area with his binoculars and we tried to relax. There were no troop movements and we could only assume that most of the German forces had withdrawn beyond the city of Rome, leaving us as remnants to slow our opponents advance. We were ordered to withdraw before sunrise next day.

3rd June 1944. We hoped our withdrawal was executed in such a way that the enemy could not see that we had disappeared. It took some time before we were out of range and sight and we sheltered under cover of small shrubs and trees. Within the hour two trucks appeared and swung round, engines running, a shout to mount quickly and we raced off at speed. We must have travelled almost for an hour, at least so it seemed. We came to a stop in an area of grass and gravel, surrounded by trees and shrubs. The driver kept the engine revving while shouting to jump out, which we did, and trying to reach for my rifle with one foot on the wheel he drove off with my rifle still on the disappearing truck. Within seconds the sound of an airplane, a US Mustang appeared over the open space firing a burst while disappearing. Surprised that he had not returned, we found ourselves among a large number of varying units of German soldiers. My memory tells me we all seemed to be in disarray with no officer to lead or command. There was I with no weapon to defend myself, or my Fatherland. Instantly one thought almost made me feel faint, because 'To be found in combat without your rifle carries the most serious consequences'. It seemed providential that there was no officer around. Also memory tells me there had been no casualties from the air attack.

Looking around, I spotted two paratroopers, easily recognized as 'veterans' who started to walk away in a northerly direction and I asked if I and one other junior who had followed me, could join them. They did not mind, but showed little enthusiasm. The suggestion was to walk and hopefully find a road leading in a northerly direction. It was obvious now that we somehow, miraculously or otherwise, had lost contact with our unit. If it had not been so serious for me to be totally unarmed, we had the appearance of a party of four on a summer outing. It seemed an unreal situation, especially since the seniors were not in a talkative mood. The two of us youngsters were asked to go ahead to see what is ahead. We spotted in the distance the countryside opening towards a suburban road. It was obvious we were on the outskirts of Rome. I could not believe it. Here I was half a year in the army and now walking into Rome without a weapon. It was Saturday late afternoon and not a person in sight, and a deathly silence. Are they all hiding in their home, and what were they frightened of?

Within a hundred yards or so I began to notice an aroma that reminded me instantly of Mum's vanilla pudding. Why such a strong aroma? I hurried my steps and came to a large arched opening between two houses. I told my new friend to stay outside, I could see he was somewhat scared. There at the side of the wide domed entrance stood an abandoned German field-kitchen; I opened the heavy lid and it was full of hot vanilla pudding, over ten gallons. And not a soul to be seen? Why did they not take it with them? It might have hindered them. I called my senior fellow soldiers, to come and see. They too, could not believe why they had not taken it with them? Well what a present. I filled my two litre dish, and so did the others. There were was not a soul in the street, and we wondered if they were simply hiding in their cellars. There was no sound of an attack or war. No one had ventured out to help themselves to a ready-made dessert? What experiences for me, still wondering why there was nobody on the street, or looking out from their windows. Very strange, no other soldiers followed us. Our 'seniors' suggested sitting a while on a bench to enjoy some of the custard.

The situation was unreal, without a thought in my mind. Suddenly, it came to me, I'm in the 'Holy City' and tomorrow will be Sunday, that was it. The sun began to set; our Lance Corporal suggested we call at one of the houses. I remember wondering what his intention was as he ascended the few steps and rang the bell at a door. A gentleman spoke to him and presently waved us to follow our comrade up the steps. Oh what a funny war! We were led into the kitchen and asked to sit down, extra chairs were brought in. The lady of the house offered to make coffee for us. We youngsters spoke no Italian but tried to follow it. The older veterans had been in Italy for a year or more and did speak some Italian and were able to have a conversation with our 'host.' Whatever our seniors said to them, we stayed overnight in the kitchen. We were tired and slept on the floor. At some stage the thought came over me that this was the first time we were civilians again after six months. What happens if the Americans come into town overnight? Anyhow before going to sleep I felt a need to ask if I might use the toilet, oh the custard. I say no more. But I did sleep well from about four o'clock. I gave spiritual thanks for the goodness of the people.

4th June 1944. Sunday morning dawned, in fact the sun was well up. The lady of the house had coffee ready for us. We wanted to make sure she understood that we appreciated what she had done for us, and with that we made our way out. We stood around for some time to find words to our situation. Question, are we the only German soldiers around the city of Rome? Where are the American forces? Why in the 'Holy City' are there no church bells ringing? Why is there no one on the street going to church, it is Sunday? A truly un-real situation. Above all, not a sound of war-noise.

What now, which way – where to? According to the seniors the enemy had not yet entered the city, and our units are north of the city, regrouping perhaps? Our seniors motioned us to lead on down the street. After a hundred yards there was an avenue to our left, I looked back and was given a sign to turn left. Admiring the villas and their gardens, a hundred yards or so on I turned round wanting to point out a villa to our seniors, but there was no sight of them. I asked my other junior to go back and see where they are? His two arms clearly indicated there was no sight of them. I run back, but they had clearly intended to get away from us, being just a hindrance to them. My predicament of having no weapon really bothered me. Added to that was the sudden appearance of two juniors out of the bushes from the villa across. In a state of fright they begged to go with us, no doubt having seen us being paratroopers. I had no option other than to lead and face the situation Friend or Enemy. You're supposed to be a man of faith and courage, well show it. Here I was in the 'Holy City', and I thought about the small cross which the Countess had given me. We stood uncertain as if waiting for a mysterious voice to tell us which way we ought to go. A northerly direction seemed preferable and the only answer, since that is the direction of our retreat to reform a defence line. That quickly went out of my mind. Strange, seeing the young in some confusion and fright gave me a feeling of superiority, where did that come from? Getting rid of those few seconds I went ahead where I thought I heard children's voices. I walked on past one villa on the right and found it was from the next villa. The drive to the villa was a hundred yards down-hill, where I could see the back of the villa with a large family gathering and the children dancing and shouting. I heard distinctly the words "Americano – Americano". As I walked a few more yards towards the villa, some of the children spotted me, and by some command they all bolted into the house. They obviously saw a uniform not knowing to where I belonged, they just looked for safety in the house.

I came up the drive and took a few more steps forward on the road; there in front of me lay a German light machine gun on the top of the three feet high wall of the villa on my left. No ammunition and no bolt, what a relief. I just took it in case we came across an officer. Some thirty yards ahead I noticed a road leading across our road from south to north towards the inner city. All the villas we passed the curtains were closed and not a soul in sight. It must have been around ten o'clock, with the sun shining, it is Sunday the fourth of June and no church bells in Rome, I still cannot believe it, why? I walked on, still not a soul in sight, my other 'juniors' following meekly behind. Some twenty yards from the T-junction I suggested that my three nervous young soldiers crouch down and wait for my sign, while I would go on to see what lay ahead and then decide which way. To the left is north into the city, to the right south where the British or Americans are coming from. It would be prudent to go left. I told my companions to stay back, and watch my signal. I placed my new-found useless weapon on the wall and, as if guided by my guardian angel, walked bent towards the junction. It was a four lane main road from south to north. There was silence, no cars, no footsteps.

Crouching on one knee I looked to the left for any sign, only deathly silence, and suddenly within a few seconds from the right behind me a voice called "Hands up!". It was in English. That I understood, I turned my head, and there was an American soldier, that I too realised. With their rubber soles he could not be heard, nor was there any other soldier. He saw that I had no weapon. I raised my hands, he pointed his rifle indicating to come to him. Still pointing his rifle, he asked in Polish "do you speak Polish?" Although I clearly understood his question, having learned a little at home, I stood still saying nothing. He was obviously a member of the Polish contingent attached to the Allied armies in Italy, {where the Polish army fought and won at the Abbey of Monte Cassino}.

Unknown to me at the time, that was the moment that changed my life. I always thought being in Rome a friend must have prayed for me. Think about it, two months in Italy and I have not had to aim at any enemy, or rather my fellow human being on this beautiful world!

# Chapter 7

# 'Captured', my life as a POW

Believing me to be alone, the soldier indicated I should walk in front of him. Within a few hundred yards, we were on open ground. Some fifty yards to the left was a 30ft high railway embankment. I was sure he pointed with his gun for me to walk towards a narrow opening in the viaduct where he would shoot me, in revenge for what we had done in Poland. I felt no fear whatsoever, nor did I think of pleading. I accepted he had a good reason. It was my fate and made my peace with my mother and my Maker. I had just taken a few steps towards that opening when the guard indicated to the right. I obviously had mistaken his signal. Ahead of us was a major road, and we had to wait. My eyes could not believe it, an almost constant stream of traffic, US military truck after truck of American soldiers. Followed by a row of tanks on transporters. When the traffic finally eased, we crossed the road, and there I joined a large group of guarded German prisoners. Having delivered me, my captor departed.

With hindsight I wished I had conveyed my gratitude for his treatment of me, which could have been so different. I assumed the Americans must have arrived at this point in the evening, and bivouacked before entering the city. Not forgetting an international agreement not to enter the inner city of Rome had been respected by both 'Parties'. Soon it was my turn to enter the building. An American sergeant sat at a table. I was ordered to empty my pockets and out came my handkerchief, my tiny rosary beads, that precious little cross from the Countess, a few German coins and my army identity disc, my total belongings! I gave my name and home address, which he entered on his list, suddenly he remarked in perfect German, "Ah, ein

Schlesier", {a Silesian.} It just about floored me; I was convinced he was a Jew who had left Germany at the right time. He could well have been living and had a business in Silesia. I was told that my name and address would be sent to the international Red Cross in Switzerland. With that I was dismissed and joined the fifty or more 'colleagues', now POWs. Sometime later two trucks arrived, and the order came to climb into the trucks. A guard sat on top of the cab facing us and we set off southward. "It's a mystery tour," some smart guy remarked.

Confronted with so many American military personnel and an incredible amount of massive armament, and the number of different vehicles travelling north, we voiced the comment "how can we win the war?" I understood that a new phase in my life was just beginning. A two-hour ride took us to the gates of a POW compound, enclosed by a ten foot high wire fence, and no barracks. It contained a large number of soldiers from various German units. We were directed to a wired section, given a blanket and told to hold on to it. The sun had set and we slept on the grass. It was summer and while the night was a bit fresh, I saw no reason for being miserable. After roll-call next morning we were issued with an American Army beaker, a combined spoon and fork. We lined up for our breakfast ration. This consisted of coffee, a tin of 'hash' and white sliced bread. The coffee was excellent after our own 'ersatz' coffee, the hash in a tin tasted good, but the bread was something we had never seen before. For us it was too 'white' and two slices were not filling. After the German Army's dense rye bread, one could eat a whole white loaf. Beggars cannot be choosers. An observer of human nature could see how some had been brought up at home. Here we were in a warm climate, the war at an end for us, and we were alive! Some people are never satisfied, I felt ashamed hearing the complaints.

Waking and lining up for breakfast on our second day 6th June 1944, the guards and a large number of US soldiers gathered round our compound were shouting in jubilation, "The invasion of France has begun. Germany kaputt. Soon we go home." That was some news, and the discussions in camp were something to have experienced, even for a young eighteen year old. It must have been duplicated in other camps. The discussions between those hardened Hitler believers of a German victory, and those who saw the beginning of a defeated

Germany were among some groups down-right dangerous. It gave me and others the chance to look for those with whom you would want to build a companionship in camp.

Two days on, Thursday 8th June 1944 was my eighteenth birthday I knew they would be thinking of me at home, surely wondering where I was. If only they knew. Perhaps within a month or two, the family will receive an official letter reporting me as 'missing,' but not where or if I am alive. We expected that we would be moved from here. Next day already, we had been instructed to make ready, and to take with us our blanket, beaker and the US Army spoon-fork on one metal holder. We were becoming accustomed to the American guards with their gum-chewing and obligatory spitting. I was taken by their confident expressions. Within these three days we have seen almost a hundred trucks, etc. After 'lunch' we assembled at the roadside in military order. A US corporal with a list counted the numbers as we climbed the trucks. All on board, the three truck convoy moved off. Two hours we have travelled and seen a bit of Italy to my enjoyment. The sun began to lower itself a bit; we are travelling south and a few more miles south of Germany. Someone's voice was heard, "there is the Mediterranean Sea". It was beautiful, after having seen the North Sea it is the second large sea I am seeing. Hey boys, the truck is entering the large harbour area. What does that mean? No one get off the truck until told. It is a large harbour, it must be Naples.

Without delay we were marched along the quay and boarded a large ship and went straight down into the hold. There was sufficient room to spread out our blankets on the steel floor. Most of us soon fell asleep. There was no food, but this was not a holiday. I could not sleep for thinking about our situation. I thought we would have been in an open camp at best with a tent. Now we are being sent somewhere by a ship? Sleep did get the better of us, and on wakening in the morning I missed an extra blanket. Some thought we were sailing or at least heard an engine. Of course you could not get up on deck as the hatches were covered. When the hatch by the steps was removed we found there were two toilets in the hold.

The Americans had appointed the most senior German NCO among us to take charge of prisoner discipline and order, and as interpreter for both sides. He had a good knowledge of English. In the morning we were permitted to go on deck for our rations and stayed in a well cordoned-off area breathing fresh sea air. Everyone had his own thoughts. For me, it was heaven and I felt grateful and in an odd way, free. Of course there was the uncertainty of what lay ahead. There was an island close by while we were at anchor and veterans from the Africa corps recognised it as Sicily. No one was allowed on deck from sunset until morning to ensure that there would be no attempts to jump ship and swim ashore. I had my first nautical lesson next day when, having remarked that we had sailed because the island was not the same, someone kindly explained that a ship at anchor moves almost 90 degrees with the tide, so you see a different part of the coast from the other side of the deck. That extended my nautical knowledge by a degree! Next day we did sail, but were not allowed on deck. The ship carried us through the Tyrrhenian Sea and far beyond. Late in the evening we guessed we were no longer sailing and some thought it sounded like hitting a pier. After two hour's wait we were ordered to prepare for disembarking, then the order to go up the ladder. Once on deck you did not know where to look first. It must have been midnight. We were in a large harbour that was very brightly lit. Word reached us from the front that this was Oran. We were in Algeria. As we marched along the quay a huge ship was docked beside us. From the front came the word to look up the side of the ship. Many hands pointed up, I looked up and read the name, "Queen Mary". She was awesome and everyone wanted to touch her but a rope strung three feet from the ship kept you from falling into the water. I was so close to this gigantic lady of Blue Ribbon fame. We seemed to walk a mile alongside her before we left the harbour to climb onto waiting trucks. As soon as we left the brightly-lit quayside, the night was pitch black and we travelled for an hour or more till we arrived at an American Army tent camp {something new}. Counted in, we were allocated to our quarters. Ten men to a tent, with proper camp beds, mattresses and a second blanket. Tropical nights can be extremely cold. No doubt, we all slept soundly.

Our NCO had been issued with a whistle to which we must respond and, obeying the morning whistle we were directed to the ablution facilities, {open air, of course, but with running water}. After roll-call we queued for breakfast and the familiar rations. We sat on benches at tables in the mess tent. The news that the camp provided laundry facilities was very welcome and drying clothes was not a problem under the Algerian sun. One felt that if every day was to pass like the first there could be no complaints. The only worry was that this 'luxurious' life might end if it was decided to hand us over to the French in the Sahara. It had happened, the rumour apparently was true. There must have been some 400 of us confined here, and a mood of resignation, or contentment prevailed. The camp had a double ten foot high fence. At each corner of the compound was a ten feet high by eight feet square timber guard box with a roof over it. No-one expected books or footballs to be handed out and the days would pass in the simple routine of morning roll-call, lining up for rations, and strolling round the camp. Lunch was soup and bread in your army plate or container. We watched the guard changing in the timber watch-towers protected from the scorching sun by a felt covered canopy. Of course, the perfect time for walks was during the evening when there was a welcome light breeze and searchlights illuminated our surroundings.

The night sky so far south was extremely interesting. We stayed confined here for more than a week. Towards the end of the second week, at roll-call after breakfast the order was to collect our few possessions including your blanket and assemble for leaving. A final roll-call and we marched out of the camp carrying our utensils and precious blanket. Trucks were ready for us to mount. Our destination was a railway siding a few miles away. A new puzzle, why boarding railway wagons in a goods train, some 25 prisoners to each wagon? Once twenty five were in, the doors slid shut. Being transported per goods train was a novelty. The next stage of our travels began. The wagons were 1900 models!

There were open slots near the top of each wagon and knot holes in timber walls and floorboards that had seen better days. These afforded practically no view. At least there was no animal smell, a blessing. Quietness had descended and nobody ventured to ask where we might be going, not one could have answered anyway. Perhaps we did not want to know? The unspoken words were 'are we to be sent south into the Sahara?' The train's speed was unimpressive and many hours passed without a halt. A different fear grew. Growing urgency caused us to find a way of enlarging some of the knot holes, and complaints about conditions increased. Someone began to use his fork to enlarge the knot hole and out it popped, to alleviate the situation. Late afternoon, just before dusk, the train seemed to slow down, and did come to a halt. The pop hole revealed open country. There were some orders being heard. Some time had elapsed and nothing was happening. 'The signal is on red', that was one possibility. All of a sudden we could hear the door sliding open in the next 'carriage'. After some time had passed our door was opened and we were told to get out and immediately realised this was at last the comfort break. The end of a break, and doors were closed again. Our next comfort stop was not made until early next morning. By mid-morning not a dwelling in sight as far as the eye could see but dried out grassy land. Just as well we did not have much to eat. Who said that? After sunrise another comfort break at last. Still desert but cooler temperatures.

Through the open slots some believed they could see less sand and more vegetation, and not long afterwards the first signs of civilisation appeared. The train slowed down as it travelled through a town. You can imagine the struggle inside the wagons to get a look through any small opening. Dwellings in the North African style could be seen and there were more people in the street. We assumed it to be a larger city because the time taken to steam through it. At last the train came to a halt and as expected a waiting time began. After an hour or more, we heard doors being opened and orders were given to take our possessions, we were ready to jump down from the train. It was clearly a sizeable harbour there had been a moment to observe the complexion of the multi-population around the harbour area as we marched some distance, before the front of our contingent came to a halt alongside a ship, not that large, I thought. Question was, what is it all about? The discussions now began in earnest, are we going to board one of those ships? Just then someone pointed to a sign on one of the harbour buildings: 'Casablanca', is that where we are? Yes, Morocco. We certainly did not excite the curiosity of the busy crowd as we marched in a haze of uncertainty towards a US freighter moored at the end of the quay. Navy personnel barely took notice of us as we were directed to the steps to board the ship. Once on board, we were guided immediately below deck. It was a large cargo hold with mattresses laid out. There were over fifty of us in our hold and it was a relief to discover toilet facilities in one corner. Later we discovered there were two cargo holds in the ship. By now it was late afternoon. Normal rations were sent down to us, the coffee in insulated containers. A hint of civilisation had returned. Our sergeant checked among us to see if any were sick. Sadly he had no other information to give us. Beset by questions and after long discussion of probabilities, sleep got the better of us, I gave thanks despite everything. Late at night someone thought the ship was moving. Tomorrow morning would be interesting.

Confirmation of that came next day when we were given permission to go on deck. We had sailed a distance we presumed, because all signs of a coastline had disappeared. Bright sunshine and a warm sea breeze greeted us, and the sight that presented itself was indescribable. We were surrounded by ships. We counted thirty with more in the distance. So this was how a convoy looked and now we knew how it felt to be in the middle of it. There were ships of every size and shape, each one sailing some two miles or more apart from its neighbour. It was yet another sight that none of us could ever have dreamed of seeing. One bright spark voiced the hope that a U-boat would not train its periscope on us; he reasoned that it would not waste an expensive torpedo on an 'empty' ship.

We had figured that the reason for our stay in Oran had been to facilitate the organisation of this convoy, gathering ships from various ports. I found everything fascinating and there seemed to be so much of interest. It was pleasant to be able to sleep easily at night in anticipation of the morrow. My new-found friend Hans and I had shared interests and spent as much time as we could on deck. We watched the crew performing their daily tasks and spotted a black crew member working on the superstructure. We tried without success to see what he was doing and eventually he came down with practised agility singing out to us "You going to America". What did Hans and I make of that? What a thought, we knew our course was westerly, he must be right.

On board this pre-fabricated US-built Liberty ship {informally referred to as a 'bath tub', because of the two holds in its steel hull} we continued to sail slowly westward. Our ship's engines were not powerful and the convoy sailed at the speed of the slowest vessel. We were at sea for almost three weeks, and in that time a fair amount of familiarity developed between us and the crew most of whom were black, something new for us. As the days went on, the black crews became friendlier by the day. There was the opportunity to learn rope-splicing by the black crew. Eventually more excitement to observe at close quarters the flying fish and other oceanic wonders. On one occasion, Hans and I joined other volunteers to help on deck, unaware of what our task would be. Hammers were distributed and we discovered we would be removing rust from the deck. Being young, we never considered what it might do to our hearing, because it caused some din! The work lasted for almost one week, between the hours of 10 a.m. and noon and after lunch from 2 to 4 p.m. For those below deck the hammering must have echoed and re-echoed around the holds.

One regular pastime introduced and encouraged by the crew was boxing. It was never my favourite pastime, but it was popular among smokers desperate for cigarettes. The crew provided tarpaulins spread on the hold decks, and boxing gloves for the contestants at these evening bouts. The crews climbed the superstructure, affording grandstand views and watched and cheered as the matches progressed. The number of loose cigarettes or packets thrown into the 'ring' depended on the quality and entertainment of the bout. That 'entertainment' continued all through the three-week journey.

The weather continued fair, and at intervals there would be alarm practices, when we had to descend quickly into the hold if a siren or hooter sounded. As each day passed we travelled further and further away from that part of the world where destruction of life and materials was still a grim reality. Europe was becoming a world apart and memories faded as the distance increased. Drifting on the ocean mile after mile further away from our loved ones began to occupy our thought of what they might have to go through?

We saw the convoy getting smaller as ships that had been close were no longer clearly visible or had disappeared altogether. It could have been that we were closer to the coast after three weeks sailing and those ships were heading to their allotted ports. It came as no surprise one morning to realise that our ship's engines had stopped. We were allowed on deck when the covers were removed. It was an amazing scene from the ship's rail, blue ocean for a mile or more, then a thin line of sandy coast and green woodland as far as the eye could see. Red-roofed dwellings completed a picture of immense beauty and I could have stayed all day looking at the scene and giving thanks for the privilege. We were below deck while the ship approached the quay. There, on the roof of a huge harbour-side store, I read the name: Norfolk Virginia. It was a most intensive feeling for an excited 18 year old, to step off the ship that carried us across the Atlantic Ocean, and for the first time put my foot on US soil, and it was not a dream. We marched along the quay with a slightly rolling gait of sailors newly ashore. There was so much to see, but we could not linger. We marched to a railway platform under escort by an increased number of guards ensuring no-one could contemplate escape. The US Railroad was still the major long distance transportation system; perhaps this railhead was used for the convenience of liner passengers? Now we were here and marvelling at the size of the railway carriages reversing towards us, towering above the platform, and we have not seen the engine yet. Everything now would be bigger. I could hardly conceal my excitement, looking at this monster of an engine when it appeared.

A burly US sergeant took roll-call and guards directed us to passenger carriages! We just could not believe it, POWs travelling what would be in Germany at least 'first class'? If you have travelled on the American Railway in the 1940s you may be forgiven for boredom, as I describe my first journey in the USA. It was not a boy's dream, this was reality. We were in normal railroad carriages with a corridor wide enough for adults to pass comfortably. Our seats were luxuriously upholstered. No more can be said, and the cattle-truck journey through Algeria is forgotten history. It was of no concern to us how long we waited for the train to move, but I do remember we each received a packed lunch and its quality and size and contents surprised us. Do they not know we are, POWs sitting in pure luxury and enjoying lunch? It was difficult to find some sort of reality in our situation.

At last, the train left the station to the unique sound of the US train engine's whistle and no one seemed to ask himself the question, 'Where to now'? We are half a world away from war. What a blessing. All eyes were fixed on the views from the large carriage windows as we left the outskirts of Norfolk in unbelievable luxury. Feeling and seeing it all around me caused my mind to think of envy, as everything around me is unbelievable luxury. Compare all this around us with our folks at home, and those who are left thousand miles away to defend our homes? Quite a thought.

We gathered speed as the city faded and we were in open country with a few more hours of daylight, still in brilliant sunshine. My memories of the countryside are deeply implanted, yet difficult to describe. The beauty was of a different kind yet very attractive. In the main, dwellings were of timber construction surrounded by lush lawns and gardens, and trees providing welcome shade. With darkness descending and after such a long exciting day we soon fell asleep. The night was comfortable and when we woke next morning the sun was already up. Two important luxuries had been discovered, the on-board toilet facilities, and a dispenser with iced drinking-water at each end of the carriage. We received a morning food-pack just before the train halted. We could not discover where we were, there was no name to be seen from our carriage. A black railway attendant entered and filled the water dispensers at each end of the carriage, including the ice container. An insignificant incident you might say, but this is 1944 and half the world is at war and here are we, prisoners of war in a comfortable train, treated as people on a holiday excursion. Although we were prisoners of war, the US Railway authorities regarded us as white passengers and treated us accordingly. What really got my back up was the discontented behaviour of a small minority among us who probably never had it that good at home.

How I wished we had some sort of map to identify the States through which we passed. We travelled still in a westerly direction through miles of open country with a lone farmstead here and there. Occasionally the railroad ran for miles beside the highway and cars would sometimes travel alongside at the same speed. Once, an open car full of young girls in colourful dresses did just that. They waved and waved, regardless of who it was on the train. It was my first experience of civilisation in many months and made a lasting impression. The second night passed, a new morning dawned and still we travelled. The temperature in the carriage was rising and I thought we must be heading into the central part of the United States. The lush greenery of Virginia was long gone. However, there was increased activity as our guards moved through the carriages telling us to get ready to disembark. The train slowed down and stopped in a railroad siding. As we left the train after such a long journey a brief look showed we were on a plateau. There was neither station nor town, but we marched into the hot air towards a huge fenced compound of huts and tents. US guards led us into our new quarters, single story timber barracks. To our surprise there was another compound next to us with an eight foot high wire fence separating us. It contained a number of German POWs of Marshal Rommel's 'Afrika Korps', who must have arrived nearly a year ago.

As we sat down and tried to comprehend our new situation and its uncertainties, we were ordered to line up. With our own NCO we marched to the Mess Hall for a meal. Outside, the heat intensified and we rested for an hour or two; or strolled around trying to acquaint ourselves with our surrounding. We learned that we were in a large base-camp some fifty miles from Oklahoma City. We fell into the routine with ease, roll-call, breakfast, lunch and supper on the first day. The food made one think of all our comrades still caught up in the fields of conflict.

We made our quarters ready for inspection by a US NCO accompanied by our own sergeant. We were not required to do any work, but those next to us left in several trucks each day. Boredom has never figured in my vocabulary, I was in a new land and totally different surroundings. Clearly we were not tourists, but I was disappointed that our destination was never divulged. Obviously one might try and jump the train or knowing we are now in Oklahoma State, meant we have crossed the mighty Mississippi, during the hours of darkness. What a pity! Things did become interesting when I heard that there were American newspapers in the Mess Hall, I felt like cheering! Lack of English did not deter us from flicking through the pages and examining the front cover with its sketch of the Allies advance in the invasion of France. Another interesting feature was the weather map which sufficed to establish at last where we were in this huge country. I decided I had to learn English. I was reminded of Miss Ida, the Scottish lady, who taught our Counts Prosper and Lutz. Where are they and how is Count Prosper? I cannot forget you so far away, and you do not know where we are or what happened to me. It was at that moment that I remembered my aunt is living in this country somewhere. Wisconsin was often in my head, I remember now. That means there are two of the Lippok family in the States. Not that far apart? What comfort. Within two days we had to attend at the Mess Hall for a photo take, while still in our uniform, me in my khaki paratrooper outfit.

**'Myself still in Paratrooper khaki in USA POW camp Oklahoma, June 1944'**

Notice how well fed we were after three weeks in this camp? After almost three weeks here and not required to do any work, it was not surprising when the order was to prepare our wash kit and towel for another move from here the morning after next. Next morning we were issued with a genuine US Army kitbag. So far we had little to fill it apart from a wash kit and a towel, but were asked to take care of it. I had a bunch of newspapers from the dining room to put into 'my' kitbag. Of course, no information was given, neither did we expect to be told. It is the Army way. One more night and wake up, roll-call, and breakfast. Thereafter line up with kitbag. The railway siding is reached within a fifteen minutes march. The carriages were there for the two hundred German POWs.

For myself, I was prepared for the luxury of another train journey. Yes, again, but this time where to? Settled in our carriage, I waited for that US railway hooter. There it was and we were on our way, with the sun well up to act as makeshift compass. We still travelled in a westerly direction; I noticed that a few companions had also taken American newspapers. I felt less guilty then, for I had taken one with the best weather map which included a southern US state map. I did hang onto it, and it proved a gem of a companion.

The State of Texas was next to Oklahoma, but our accompanying GIs gave us no information and darkness engulfed us before we fell asleep. Before that, the flat countryside of Oklahoma began to rise to more rocky ground. Later on after I had fallen asleep, there was a stop to replenish the water dispensers, and most of us fell asleep well before midnight. Waking early next morning we discovered we had halted, seemingly in the middle of nowhere to let another train pass. We were on a single-track line in prairie country. The sun rose and we received our morning sandwich-pack. Then word spread that we were in the state of New Mexico and now travelling in a southerly direction. I studied my little map in the paper and the state of Texas is also in a southerly direction. What does it all mean, where are we going? Far away on our right there were mountains and close by on our left was a high mountain ridge. I ask a guard and discovered that the high peak I could see was the 12,000ft Sierra Blanca. The scenery was so different from home; it looked and felt like real 'cowboy country'. What sights I am seeing! What a journey this is, and where will it end?

Our second night and we seemed to have stopped some hours ago someone said. As time went on we thought we are in a military compound or camp? We guessed that this may be where we leave the train. Not long after, the order to step off the train, carrying our kitbag with our few belongings, we entered what looked now like a large military base. It is 'FORT BLISS' El Paso, the word came from somewhere. We were two hundred POWs and our lengthy march ended when we arrived at a fenced compound encircled by wire mesh 10ft high. Our sergeant had a lengthy conversation with American officers before we were split into two groups of 100 men to a barrack. Each building had two floors, and fifty men were allocated to each floor. These barracks were standard American garrison accommodation. I was to occupy space in the second barrack, top floor. Inside, bunk beds stood on either side, with ample window space. A camp mattress on a spring base, and an Army issue khaki quilt made up the bed. There was sufficient space between each bunk. Right along in the middle of the barrack were tables and chairs on each side for every person, to write home or play cards. Washroom and shower and toilet facilities were on the ground floor. All that seemed 'luxurious' and so it was. My companion was a civil servant twenty years older than me, so there was no question that I would be occupying the upper bunk. Hermann was his name and he came from near Cologne. He was well-mannered and a committed Christian. How lucky could I get? I considered myself very fortunate to discover that others near me were also of the quiet 'type', and all around us, strangely, were non-smokers. Also, none of them showed expressions of pro-Nazism ideology. In addition my neighbour in the next bunk, and one year older than me, had secondary education including two years studying English. What more could I have wished for, in our new surroundings!

The daily order: 7 a.m. wake-up, ablution, 7.45 roll-call by our Company Sergeant Major, breakfast from 8.00 - 8.30am. There was no rushing, everything to be done in a civilised manner. There are four kitchens to cater each for one barrack of one hundred men. After roll-call our first breakfast. Eight to a table, on the table was a packet of 'Kellogg's cornflakes', our first contact with Mr Kellogg, a milk jug, sugar and salt. One of us collected a plate of bread from the counter, two slices per person, margarine and marmalade and the coffee jug. This was some luxury I thought, each table had to organise who cleared and cleaned the table, with your chair correctly in its place, and bringing everything back to the kitchen. The kitchen was staffed by our own personnel, a butcher, a baker and, if available, a cook. A US sergeant was in charge of two kitchens. Military cleanliness and tidiness was the rule. We looked in amazement at the modern kitchen and its equipment. There was lots of stainless steel equipment and utensils. Lunch was always a hot meal, meat often steak, potatoes and vegetables, finishing with fruit or occasionally a pudding. Supper was usually warm and included meat several days a week. Everything was clean; we had cutlery, cups and saucers. Brought up in a home where such luxuries were not available every day, the food we were given was much appreciated and thoughts of our folks who might well be in need of just a loaf stayed uppermost in our mind. As if drinking water was not enough, at each end of the kitchen 20-gallon containers of iced tea were available outside the kitchen every evening. Unbelievable, you might say, but true.

What interested me was the construction of US garrisons, every building was of timber construction. What was generally known in the US as 'clapboard' construction, which in Europe is known as 'shiplap'. There is so much wood in the US. The camp included a parade ground, administrative offices, the guards' and Commandant's quarters, two canteens and a chapel with accommodation for a chaplain. One felt aware of an invisible barrier between the veterans and newcomers, except when it came to sport. Two football pitches behind the barracks were fully used in the evening. There were four teams within the camp, I played a lot of football and soon got into the fourth team, gradually to the third team and, having been talent spotted, was given a chance to play in goal for the second team. No mean feat among four hundred men. Alas, pre-medal vision during the game, and my nerves could not cope. Letting four balls slip through my fingers, my shame and acute embarrassment put me off football altogether.

I reverted to simple card games and reading US newspapers of which there was a large collection of different views among the collection. During my time at Fort Bliss there was a flourishing theatre group led by a professional. They gave several performances and the Christmas show was attended by US officers and their wives. It was much enjoyed and they were intrigued and so were we by the costumes that appeared on stage. Where did the material come from, we asked ourselves, did the Commandant and his Officers rob their wives' wardrobe? One other popular pastime was the two-hour film show held in the evening, unbelievable luxury. A large screen fixed to the outside gable of the kitchen made it possible to see a different film almost twice weekly. We sat outside on our chairs and saw some wonderful films and got to know all the famous actors and actresses of the day. It certainly helped me in my early learning of English. My life within Fort Bliss was a happy time to the point when in the quietness of the evening you asked yourself, whether it was fair while so many in Europe were losing limb or life. How could you answer? Most of my comrades knew we were among the lucky ones. One would have been out of one's mind to contemplate escape by swimming across the Rio Grande into Mexico, especially when it was known that Mexicans would assist you, but then promptly hand you back and collect the 'bounty'. Fort Bliss was in our time 1944 to 1946 one of America's largest troop garrisons. It stands in Texas close to the city of El Paso. It is the triangle where Mexico and the two US states of Texas and New Mexico meet. We are in one of the US largest military reservations. A double ten feet high wire mesh fence was separating us from the US Army infantry training division. In the evening they would come over to us. They were recruits training to be sent to the Pacific front. It was not uncommon for a few recruits to come to the fence, questioning us about being in war, and what it feels like firing at your enemy, etc? Some did speak German either from school, most of German ancestors. A truly amazing situation.

Thinking about why we had been transported more than two thousand miles to Fort Bliss began to make sense, when one looked around this huge compound. In addition only fifty miles away is the US Air Force base. More about that later. A large area housed all the many storage buildings for food alone. Think of the uniforms, underwear, boots, etc., followed by sheds to store used clothes. Can you picture the large amount of residue that had to be got rid of? It was here where we were introduced to recycling on a large scale. Clearly it made sense to bring a number of POWs to earn their living in this complex. It would serve no purpose to list the many tasks to which we were assigned to. Suffice to put on record my contribution to the 'world's' first recycling programme.

A few days after our arrival we lined up after breakfast and were called individually to join a particular group. I was in a group of five and we passed through the gate, where a guard took a count. Greeted by a smiling civilian, who led us to our workplace, a small fenced compound. On one side a heap of glass, jars, bottles, etc., any size or shape. A mound of broken glass lay at one end. The 'Boss' introduced himself and gave each of us a low stool, a hammer tool and protective goggles, modern safety rule, for breaking glass into small bits. We made quite a din. This was where all discarded glass was collected and our task was plain. Here at El Paso (lat. 32º) the temperature was high and in open ground hot on your head. Next day our boss brought us sun hats. He made us down tools promptly to get to camp for lunch at noon. We were back at work from 2 p.m. to 4.30 p.m. and enjoyed a refreshing shower afterwards. In the evening when all the different jobs were discussed it was certain that we five had pulled the wrong straw. Next day we asked our boss, "how about a tarpaulin?", he would try to find something. It was not hard work but less pleasant was the steady din of glass breaking. You always longed for the midday break. Personally, I found the complaining an unwanted irritant. To my surprise after six weeks I was called to join another three to be taken to the large shed where all the cardboard was recycled. With us three we were eight to work in the shed processing used cardboard. I accepted it as a promotion since conditions away from the blazing sun into a large airy shed was welcome.

By now we were all well acquainted with the prevailing culture of recycling almost everything, rubbish was never left lying around. Our job here was to flatten all cardboard, put it into a hand-operated press worked by two men, one on each side. Secured when filled with two strands of wire and stored aside till ready for removal. On a certain day, one of those huge railway wagons appeared alongside the shed. Three of us to one barrow. Ten meters away from the sloping ramp, two of us on each side of the barrow, one steering and pushing. With the command 'push', three of us pushed the barrow up the ramp into the huge wagon. Our civilian foreman was pleasant and spoke good

German. At break we questioned him; he did not mind telling us that he had emigrated from northern Germany as a young man before the First World War, as he had no intention of being called up. A good rapport developed between us.

After three months or so, there was a pleasant surprise for those of us who cherished our Christian spirituality. The CO announced that there was now a Lutheran chaplain residing in the chapel house, a fellow prisoner who had been seconded from another camp. Anyone of any denomination could call on him in his room in the chapel. A service was announced for the following Sunday. Some fifteen of us, mostly Catholic met at the appointed time for a pleasant get-together. After the service the suggestion was for the Lutherans to meet the Lutheran chaplain in his house, while we Catholics met in the chapel, not all stayed on. It soon established that one of us in the group had been attending a Priests' Seminary in Würzburg Bavaria for two years before call-up. His name was Karl Boyer who agreed to be our 'chairman' and we two became instant friends. We decided we might organise something with the Lutheran chaplain's help and would prepare and hold Sunday worship led by Karl. I suggested Karl to ask the Commandant about the possibility of a visit from a priest in El Paso. It took a while but one Sunday a priest did arrive. His parents were German migrants and he spoke fluent German, at a guess he was near seventy of age. Another of those amazing coincidences in this American camp. During conversation with Karl and the pastor, we arrived at a point where we realised we could worship and converse freely without looking round to see if some 'Party' member was watching and listening. This new-found freedom was wonderful. Would this be something we could look forward to once we got home when a new peace is established?

The weeks and months rolled on into autumn and there was little change in the temperature and perpetual sunshine. Once again my name was called at morning roll and I was to join a group of five to join a detail of twenty that needed 'reinforcement'. A truck took us twenty minutes to a huge army depot. There were a number of large hangars. Outside, were hundreds of trucks parked in neat rows. These had been returned from the Pacific battlefields and our job was to remove all the wheels to be stored in the hangars. Those who worked here regularly went to their daily routine. We were taken care of by a burly civilian foreman who handed us to one of his crew to show us what we are here for. At the same time within a step or two the foreman put his hand on my shoulder and simply asked if I could drive a jeep. Hearing I could not, he said it was easy, and took me by the hand and walked towards a few jeeps. He must have been a man of faith to trust me. At the castle at home Lutz and I played in the car garage and moved levers and clutches. The foreman did not know that. "Get in, foot on the clutch and move the gear lever up and down. Now turn the key". Within fifteen minutes I got the hang of it, after going round in reverse for a turn or two until I found the forward gear again and that was me passed the test. My job was to transport tools from one location to another and bring wheels and tyres to the hangars. That job lasted about three months. I wondered would I ever have an opportunity to drive some vehicle at home again. What a schooling there was in that place. If you were really honest you had to ask yourself, what had you done to deserve such an interesting time. At the time I did not know the expression in English, "this is unreal"!

Reading the newspapers became a priority in camp after supper. I tried to assess the slow but growing push forward as our army had to give up territory. Far more worrying for us from eastern Germany were the reports of the steady advance of the Russian offensive towards Silesia our home. How fortunate by being well supplied with US newspapers, able to read in detail the state of the western and eastern front line. Hitler's rhetoric promising victory seems to fall on deaf ears. Yet, there are some among us who believe in this 'wonder weapon'. My friend Herman, on my lower bunk, and I have many interesting talks regarding the years of Nazism versus Christianity. We came to the conclusion, after having witnessed the overwhelming superiority of war material in the US that Mr Hitler's time is coming to an end.

Christmas 1944 arrived, my second Christmas away from home. Our kitchen boys decorated the Mess Hall beautifully. We could not believe what they managed to produce for our first festive meal in the USA. There was a kind of joy mixed inevitably with thoughts of Christmases long past. As a result of our talk regarding singing at Christmas Mass, and having told our El Paso priest that I could play the piano, he brought a US Army folding Harmonium for our Christmas Service and he'd keep it for us. My seminarian friend Karl Boyer and I prepared a Christmas Service with our well known German carols. It was a surprise to see the large number that joined us in the chapel to hear the Chaplain's moving words and to sing the Christmas carols we had prepared. A tear or two were inevitable even among hardened comrades. Many of us Catholics joined the Lutheran Christmas Service. It seemed like making a statement. For us Silesians it was especially poignant because of the questions about the welfare of our people which remained unanswered. Were they able to celebrate or were they far from home and seeking shelter in a stable somewhere, since the Russian autumn offensive aim would be to get as close as possible to the German border before the winter snows?

Yet here in the most peaceful surroundings life had to go on. For us and the US recruits, war was far away. Our detail was still removing wheels from trucks while everybody in the camp was occupied in a daily routine now well established.

In the second week of January 1945 the papers reported that the Allied forces had the German border in their sights on many places. An assault might begin any time, but heavy snow falls and the River Rhine could delay an attempt. For our folks in Silesia in the south, and those people in North and East Prussia, a far more serious concern was the Russian offensive continuing to progress towards the German border and our homes. According to the newspapers, which I read with intense interest, the Russian Army had not crossed the eastern borders between Germany and Poland. That would have meant our folks had been given reprieve to celebrate Christmas once more in peace. The Russian Army was encountering only weak resistance in most places. This could indicate a regrouping of our troops to prevent them from entering the industrial heartland, which would, at a stroke, deprive the German army from its last supply of fuel.

By early February the latest newspaper reports confirmed that the Russian Army had entered southern Silesia. Never could I have imagined that I thousands of miles from home, would read that my home town, Gross Strehlitz, had fallen into Russian hands. It was a peculiar feeling that came over me trying to imagine what that meant. A feeling of resignation tinged with the hope that my people might have had a chance to flee the Russian front. One wondered where could they really go. All that you could do was pray and hope. Here far away in Texas we read that our capital Breslau had capitulated and the whole of Silesia was in Russian hands. I dread to think what our people have to suffer while we live in pure luxury, and helpless. With the Russian offensive now on German soil our papers inform us that the Allied forces in the west were making gains towards Germany's western front. Germany's capitulation might quickly follow we hoped. For most of us reading about the Göbbels propaganda machine talking of a wonder weapon was not worth a laugh.

My affinity with Anglo-Americanism surfaced with the news and with it the concern about loved ones at home. I am reminded of Miss Ida MacDonald the Scottish lady teaching English. I felt sure she would have been safe at the Castell home in Bavaria. At the same time there was my Aunt Hedwig the nun in Wisconsin and I recalled my encounter with the British POWs at the Post Office, only a year ago. When our friendly priest from El Paso came to say Mass for us and I mentioned my aunt in Wisconsin, he asked for me to try and remember details of her.

I did and was able to tell him on his next visit that her name was Sister Hedwig Lippok, a member of the Franciscan Order, and she had qualified as a hospital sister and volunteered for service in Milwaukee in 1924. This information was sufficient, and within three weeks, I had my aunt's latest address. As soon as I was permitted to compose my next monthly letter, I wrote to her. She replied promptly, clearly pleased that I had done so. I was equally overjoyed, now there would be two of us sharing concern for our family's safety. I believe I was the only one who had a letter from a close relative in the US in this camp and I thanked our priest on his next visit, obviously he too was pleased to have achieved something.

The removing of truck wheels ceased. Our detail had been chosen for a new assignment. We collected our generous lunch-packs and boarded two military buses with a guard. The drive took us in a northerly direction into the US State of New Mexico, through a desert-like area known as the White Sands. The journey took almost two hours. On arrival, we were handed pick-axes and shovels and other such tools. Viewing the material stacked nearby, we guessed that our latest assignment was railroad building. We were divided into two groups and were guided and instructed by amiable and knowledgeable foremen. The area was quickly recognised as a huge Military reserve and building a railroad in the desert area of this huge military reservation was something of a puzzle. In due course the truth would be revealed. We did not realise at the time that this was where new weapons and rockets or missiles would be tested. Missiles meant nothing to us in the early summer of 1945. To think, that we actually worked on a very important modern project! It was here, at the north end of the White Sands base, that the first atom bomb was tested. Soon it might be spaceships? Such an interesting story for one's grandchildren, and I helped to build it. With increasing interest we followed the reports in the daily papers regarding the progress of Russian and Allied advances towards the German capital. Capitulation was certain and we just looked forward to the ending of destruction and misery in Europe. A mood of resignation and relief prevailed. The end was nigh for the regime that had fuelled fear and cruelly suppressed personal freedoms and religious belief.

At roll-call on 7th May the CO himself announced that Germany had finally capitulated and peace was returning to Europe. His announcement produced a momentary silence then applause except from a few hard-core nationalists. We were ordered to stay in camp for the day. It meant some of the delivered ration supplies had been removed and returned to the store houses. Film shows were suspended and the outside water containers taken back to the kitchen. There were a few guards around outside of our compound should hard-liners threaten rioting. The possibility would not have surprised some of us. No working detail was to go out. The guard towers around the camp area had doubled.

Normal work resumed within four days, and normal food rations returned after two weeks. Within a month the discovery of unbelievable horrors within the freed concentration camps were shown. The shame of it was felt by most of us, and for a few days newsreels of those horror discoveries were shown in place of the usual film shows. After a month or so, Hollywood films returned to the screen, the usual rations resumed, and our life returned to normality. Our detail went back to the White Sands to build that railroad with no adverse feeling. One day at roll-call I was unexpectedly summoned to the camp office. I had no idea what that meant and felt no guilt for anything. On entering I stood to attention and the sergeant handed me a parcel from my Aunt Hedwig in Wisconsin. Protocol demanded that I open it in the presence of the sergeant and I was acutely embarrassed, expecting it to contain food of which we had in plenty. It contained a shoe-box full of hymn sheets and German prayer books, just what we needed for our chapel services. The sergeant was interested to hear about my aunt and wished us happy singing. Only two months later, Aunt Hedwig sent me a letter, which of course I had to open with the CO in attendance in which she seriously proposed that I ask the CO to release me from the prison camp so that I could join the monks in the Franciscan monastery close to my aunt's convent. I did not feel I was ready for that. She was so kind, but oh the innocence of a nun. It did raise a laugh in the office.

One day while watching football outside, we heard the sound of a plane and immediately it swept over our heads at low altitude and unbelievable speed, obviously a fighter plane. We all saw that it had no propeller. Next day the local newspaper reported that the neighbouring airbase had taken delivery of jet fighters. Jets, what are they? My English teacher friend had a good explanation, "It has arrived before you hear it". In mid-July, our detail was informed that we would not be required at the missile/rocket range. Of course, no reason was given for the sudden decision and we speculated that there might be top-secret tests. However, I like to think that I had left an infinitesimal small mark in the field of early space research.

Within two weeks at roll-call, some fifty names were called out including mine to assemble at the sergeant's barrack. Lined up we were told to pack our kitbags, collect all our belongings and supplement our toiletries at the camp's canteen. This stocked a large selection of cigarettes Camel, Lucky Strike and Chesterfield, etc., perfumes, razor blades, aftershave, deodorant, etc., and snacks such as crisps and peanuts, all at low cost. If you worked you earned a dollar a day, one could shop for a dollar and got change. Because I did not smoke I had managed to save with ease. We had a whole day to get organised. The question arose, are we not expected to return to Fort Bliss?

The day of departure arrived and after breakfast and roll-call we were ready to board the two waiting buses. I always regretted that neither of my two friends were with me on those small 'excursions.' Because we had to take all our 'possessions,' we expected to be moved to a different camp. I had said goodbye to all my friends including my English 'teacher', and especially Karl Boyer, with whom I left most of Aunt Hedwig's song books, and hoped to visit him in Würzburg when we get back 'home'! I realised too late that I did not have his home address, but by then it was too late for my journeying had commenced and we were travelling comfortably in two buses with our guards, one in each bus and a relief driver, maximum speed in those days fifty miles per hour, often less for buses.

Leaving Fort Bliss behind after only one hour we crossed the mighty Rio Grande and a hundred miles on we were in Arizona. Thank goodness I remembered my maps. We settled down very quickly and in comfort. We passed through lots of cowboy country with the odd pasture areas interspersed by cattle ranches. Familiar countryside for us now. We had two breaks and bypassed Tucson and before nightfall we entered what we assumed was a small military camp, and so it was. The order was to take our kitbag and were directed to a couple of timber huts, and told we are going to stay the night. Stretching our legs we lay on the beds, shortly one of the guards came in and told us to make our way to the dining hall. I remember clearly we had been given a substantial supper. It may well have been that the cooks in such a small camp never met German POWs and served a normal meal. Good for them. We slept well, at least I did, when a bell rung indicating breakfast in half an hour. Entering the small dining-room, guards and us greeted each other and enjoyed breakfast. We were then told we will not leave today and will go and do some work. Our civilian foreman was ready to take us up. Only one guard came with us, there seemed to be a mutual understanding that none of us had any intention to forego a good life. We were given a packed-lunch and off we went. Whatever the reason we left the top an hour earlier. With the guard and our foreman in conversation on the downward way we were led aside from the normal way towards a long timber building. You won't believe it, the foreman thought he was doing us and the guard a favour by showing us what was in that long timber shed. The foreman opened the door, and the guard and we followed. The high pitched laughter and screeching from some fifty young Mexican girls, all in clean white dresses sorting and ironing clothes, greeting us was an unexpected interesting interlude!

Before lights-out the guards informed us we will be leaving after an earlier breakfast. We will be wakened early. Next morning our kitbag was ready for leaving, and that's what happened after breakfast. Where to sergeant? Wait and see. Yes, we got our lunch-pack. It had been a welcome break and again something interesting. I watched during the journey for more than an hour and we are heading west, see what happens after Phoenix. Some two hours later we had skirted round Phoenix and seemed still to be on the same highway, according to my map highway 10. We are definitely heading west now. It took me an hour to work out that it is some 150 miles to the border of California. California? Surely not! Travelling by bus one had more opportunity to enjoy the countryside although much prairie land. Late in the day we had just crossed the State border and there we were, in California! What a sight to have seen as we crossed the mighty Colorado River. It was almost nine o'clock before we arrived at another Army camp, this time a larger one, same treatment. But of course we do not know is this our journey's end. I can hardly believe that this is really happening to me. What am I seeing here as a prisoner of war? An early rise was the order, ablution, an excellent breakfast, all as in Fort Bliss, cornflakes, milk, butter, jam and bread, and two lunch bags; a longer drive this time? Time to join the bus, roll-call all present and correct. We are off again in good spirits, and sunshine. Are we going west towards the ocean? Or northwards? What does it matter, Los Angeles cannot be that far away according to my map, which has been passed round a bit as long as it was treated well.

Our two drivers seem to change more often; it may mean a longer drive and the reason for the two lunch bags. What is interesting is that after two hours I think the sun is more to the left of us; that should indicate we are travelling in a northerly direction, with the Pacific Ocean to our left. Information for anyone who might be interested. I am really getting my money's worth in regards to my favourite subject 'Geography'. Some sort of air conditioning must be installed since I feel that our buses are not uncomfortable to journey in. Yes, it feels warm and most of us fell asleep periodically. We were glad to see the drivers changing at their ordered intervals. We too had our comfort breaks. Noticeable was the increase of traffic and the ever increasing habitation. We must be getting nearer to the San Francisco area. After a beautiful sunset and having travelled in darkness, increasing interchanges with lots of illumination around made us wonder, was this really San Francisco? Next, our buses turned off the highway and within an hour we drove into a darkened area with lights showing a timber building, we have come to a stop. Another pre-arranged overnight stay? "No", said our drivers, "this is your home, folks" - end of the journey.

While the guards got out to greet a fellow soldier, we are to stay put in our buses. After a short time we were asked to leave our buses, with a warning not to forget our kitbag. A roll-call, followed with a short greeting by the sergeant; we asked and were permitted to thank our drivers for the interesting three days and safe journey. We did remark how civilised it all was. Our names were called out by a corporal, and shown to our tent, six to a tent. Our 'furnishings,' camp beds, small bedside cabinet, army issue folding canvas wardrobe, table in the centre and chairs. The need arose to check out the wash facilities, a stone building with the necessary and hot showers, perfect. Arrival in the dark meant we really did not know where we were. There were trees around and green grass, a change from Fort Bliss.

Everybody seemed to be tired and silence followed very quickly. In the morning it was a whistle that called us to rise and shine. The guard quarter and the dining hall were prefabricated buildings which could be dismantled. We were not aware that in one of our buses was a cook who will now be responsible for our fitness to do what we have been brought here for. Making our way to and from the Mess Hall, we looked around this camp and discovered beyond the shrubs and bushes we were "guarded" by a few magnificent Californian redwoods.

At the end of a bus journey of 1,200 miles we were ready to fall asleep on camp beds, and were too tired to get to know each other, most of us had not been in the same barrack at Fort Bliss. After breakfast we discovered we had a free day, an opportunity to get to know each other. All five of my 'comrades' had been in the other building in Fort Bliss, but felt we would get on together. Called to the Mess Hall the sergeant would be 'sorting' us out and giving us information about the place we arrived at. We were in the Napa Valley, which is some 29 miles from south to north and 9 miles wide. It is sheltered by mountain ridges on the east and the west. Beyond the mountain ridge west, is the Pacific Ocean, just 30 miles away. It was pleasant to hear again the singing of birds, a sound we never heard at Fort Bliss.

The fertile Napa Valley is cultivated by farms growing tomatoes and plum orchards. At the north end were some vineyards. Another day and night and it's off to work we went. Board the truck and soon the truck stopped. Myself and ten others were dropped off at a farm and greeted by the farmer. He and his foreman mustered us, and we were taken to a large field full of tomato bushes. There they are grown on low bushes in neat rows four feet apart. The foreman showed us what to do. You bend down and stretch your hands around the bush, lifting it sort of bottom side up, so that you can see lots of tomatoes on the underside. You pick only the ripe ones and place them gently in the box. Before you move on to the next bush, you must lift the bush back so that the tomatoes are covered again. One was expected to fill a quota of boxes per day, but we needed a few days' practice avoiding damaging the ripe fruit. A pleasant rapport was quickly established with the foreman and the farmer. We were allowed to eat some of the harvest. Later the truck would arrive and we helped to load the boxes. Having lunch out in the open with tomatoes, which we were allowed to take was great. Our foreman did drop a hint, that the farmer is expecting an improvement of filling boxes soon. Most of us returning home thought that it would take a few days for our backs to get used to the necessary bending, which we are not used to.

Arriving home at supper our guard excitedly told us that an Atomic Bomb had been dropped on Hiroshima with horrific deaths and destruction. It was expected Japan would now capitulate too. At last there too would be peace. In the meantime camp life and tomato harvesting continued, and lasting almost two months. At the end the farmer thanked us for our help. It was a gesture that made one feel valued. A small detail of our boys had the pleasure of harvesting grapes at the vineyards. They were allowed to bring back to the camp a few clusters of grapes to share with us, which we appreciated.

Our next assignment took us to a smiling farmer in his plum orchard. Plum-picking is something many of us have done at home; you climb a ladder with a pail and pick the fruit branch by branch. It is different in California where each orchard housed a hundred trees. Instructions were that two of you took a round tarpaulin about 5 yards in diameter with a half-way central split. Each of you took hold of a corner of the split and wrapped it around the tree. Then you shook the tree like mad. Plums would fall in cascades, sometimes on your head or down the back of your shirt. It is important to say that the trees were replaced before they were too old. You gathered the plums into wooden boxes and repeated the procedure, shaking the tree once more before moving on to the next. These were small plums to be dried and were not so sweet and were left to ripen longer before harvesting. Again there were quotas and if not fulfilled you worked an extra hour to encourage you to gain speed and fill more boxes. We replaced seasonal workers from Mexico who were experts; we were far less expensive labour. Our detail seemed to be the slowest and gained the title 'Moonshine Commando' because we arrived back at camp just in time for supper or later. It was our guard who got tired of staying on later with us. By the second week we had it fixed. Plum-picking went on until Christmas. Remember this is California. The farmer invited us to see the drying process. There were a number of six foot wide bins filled five feet high with millions of dried plums. You will surely have seen 'Del Monte' Californian prunes in the shops? You see them everywhere; I do hope that those we picked have all been eaten by now! One other farmer, after us having completed work in his orchard early afternoon, invited us to his villa. We sat on benches on the manicured lawn, including our guard, to be served cakes and ice cream, handed out by his wife. He and his wife chatted with us in perfect German, telling us their ancestors came from Germany and had farmed here since the end of the previous century. It was certainly the perfect location with San Francisco being only thirty or so miles away. Our guard too, enjoyed hearing us talk in our mother tongue. We thanked them and a hand shake and home we went. {I have re-visited the Napa valley after forty years, only to discover there were no more prunes or tomato farming, vineyards having completely taken over the valley.} Next time you buy a vintage 'Napa Valley' remember me!

Another Christmas and New Year 1945/46 has arrived, the second in the USA. Six months since the capitulation of my country and still no news, or any contact with our families. It came with thoughts of home and worries about the situation, particularly regarding Silesia our home. Press reports of forced mass migration from the German eastern provinces into West Germany, and the possible annexation of our beloved homeland Silesia to Poland worried us greatly. Someone with a legitimate reason may well ask for revenge for what Hitler's Germany had done. My faith dictates to pray and do not lose hope. To help to take my mind off the news, I have written one of my allowed monthly letters to Aunt Hedwig in Wisconsin, telling her not to write to me as we seem to be moving again. That is what did happen when in early January 1946 the order came for us to move camp. Kitbags on our shoulders we boarded two buses and left our beautiful Napa Valley. Napa Valley seemed to have had a strange effect on me of having loved to be there. Board the bus and off we went southbound again, to where we had come from, surely not? Our guard shouted and pointed to the right. In the distance was the Golden Gate Bridge and beyond San Francisco Bay and the San Francisco skyline in the far distance. What a sight, what a chance! After two hours or so it was clear we are travelling south through central California. The Californian sun is shining and we have not seen snow for almost two years. In spite of my road map I was not able to find which road south we are on, unless some sign of a major town would give us a clue. The temperature rose a number of degrees warmer than Napa Valley and the countryside was far less green. Fields on either side looked sadly in need of water. The cool drinks in our water containers seemed a luxury.

After our lunch and comfort stop towards late afternoon fields full of strange plants came into view. White flowers hung from the plants and we wondered what they were. Our guard obliged, "cotton, boys" he shouted, and we remembered the guard pointing them out on our journey north. None of us had seen cotton growing before. At last some brilliant guy had the answer. We had come as cotton pickers with no clue and no experience. Within an hour or so our two buses turned off the highway onto a tarmac road taking us to a farm. Soon, that's what it was, a large space of ground, with high-sided wagons and other equipment. We stopped beside a timber building, the office probably. A tall and broad gentleman appeared. With one voice we all said it, 'the boss'. A timber building with windows may well be our accommodation. A short distance away was our camp, encircled by the now familiar 8 foot high wire fence. Our guards led us to it and we soon settled in. Our guard confirmed that we were expected to pick cotton. Has any reader ever tried cotton picking? For the uninitiated I shall briefly describe the plant. A black pea size seed grows up to a four feet or so stalk and bush. Small branches grow outward bearing several capsules, the size of tennis balls, containing the soft wool-like material, and several pea-like black seeds. As the plant ripens the several segments on each capsule dry out, and eventually spring open and curl out, the points of each segments are needle sharp and make your finger-tips bleed until you have learned how to avoid them, and you do learn fast. The white soft cotton is there to be picked, and put into the six feet long cotton bag hung over one of your shoulders. You will also have to learn to pick with two hands, otherwise you will be a hundred yards and more from your pals. Never in my life had I imagined I would one day seriously learn how to pick cotton in California. You were expected to fill two bags a day, at first we managed to fill only half a bag or less. You can imagine just how much 'grumbling' there was among those who always found a reason to be dissatisfied. I never saw one of our boys fill two full bags. It was January and we had been given light summer hats. We were interested to see that black and Mexican seasonal pickers with their wives and children including toddlers, worked at the other end of the two-hundred acre field, more than half a mile away. When asked, why the separation? The foreman simply said "you're white", end of conversation.

Our living conditions were good and the ability to have a shower after a day's work in the hot cotton valley was a luxury. There was sunshine every day, peaceful surroundings and we were well fed. There were no playing fields, nor film shows. No time and too tired. There was cool water available at any time, but no iced tea. The fields where we worked on, were so large that we were transported by small trucks each day, returning to camp at 5 p.m. Evenings were spent quietly. Some played card games and others like me resting or reading the many papers and magazines provided by the guards. Letter-writing was restricted still to one a month, which facility I made use of in spite of not knowing if mail will ever be delivered. What I gained from my personal experiences was that contentment directed your thoughts to see and appreciate your surroundings whether amazing or mundane. I was alive and had seen and experienced so many things that others will never see in their lifetime. Here in this Californian cotton valley the year 1946 began in a mood of contentment that you are alive, you can do nothing regarding your situation. You can try to escape, but how far will you get?

Six weeks later in mid-February, our cotton-picking came to an abrupt end, when the sergeant announced this was to be our last day there. He could give no further information. After supper we enjoyed a shower and began gathering our small utensils to be packed tomorrow after breakfast into our kitbag. We made sure we had all our personal belongings ready to leave. Another move. Where to this time? We have seen and experienced already so much. The regret as so often, no camera to take photos. I always did say a night prayer, although short, of thanks for the unbelievable experiences and care-free life and the fair treatment at all times. It was quite interesting at times among ourselves how long it took to make contact with someone of your own disposition politically. It would be naive to assume that all political 'swastikas' had already been burned. However, I struck it lucky and there had not been one, who waved that flag openly. It was known that in certain camps it was not always so peaceful.

Breakfast US style, cornflakes and milk, bread, butter and coffee. On our way out, as usual we thanked the local kitchen staff after handing us our travel ration. On and on my life's journey meanders.

So let it be, I am prepared for whatever lies ahead, we gave thanks that the war is ended. We boarded our buses once more and, with a last look at the cotton fields, we headed north again. We stopped for lunch then travelled west toward what looked like a large blue lake. Our guards happily informed us that it is San Francisco Bay. This really was exciting. We had turned off the highway and after a few more miles had reached an Army base. We never had the chance to wave farewell or thank our guards and drivers for they left us immediately after we left the bus. We became aware that we were among a large number of POWs from different camps, probably from Oregon or other western states. After roll-call we had been led to our quarters. Now the guessing game had started with all sort of rumours, everyone had a suggestion or able to foretell. Supper and we let sleep get the better of us. After breakfast next morning we were addressed by a decorated Captain who told us clearly in simple military fashion that we were to be repatriated to Europe!

A shout of "Hurrah!" erupted. Everyone understood that we were going to Germany and almost as one the entire company of several hundred men raised their arms and cheered. We were called in sections alphabetically and made our way as directed to the quartermaster's stores, where our sizes were taken. Two pairs of socks and two sets of underwear. At two tables we were issued with a US Army shirt, trousers, tunic and greatcoat, all dyed black, and POW stamped on the back of the coat and tunic in a lighter colour. We suddenly looked like a different unit. Next, go to our rooms to change and drop our old clothes into a large collecting bin. Later on we had been directed to the Paymaster Office where ladies in US uniform sat at their desk to hand out our accumulated dollars, with a written confirmation of the sum given. After almost two years I received nearly two hundred dollars, accumulated because I did not smoke and was not excessive in spending on aftershave lotion, as quite a number did. We could now go to the canteen shop to purchase whatever we wished, razor blades, cigarettes, sweets and chocolate, aftershave, etc. I was by no means the only one who spent very little here. We assumed that matters in Germany would be especially difficult now and in the future more so.

Dollars would then be of high value. Before supper a so-called 'dress rehearsal' was called.

One of our sergeants took over the command to line up in the old order, then a count followed, and his dismissal was according to the old unforgotten dismissal. I was sure I saw an approving smile on the US Captain's face that we had not completely forgotten our military training. Two days later after supper the order was to be ready after breakfast, to leave next morning for transportation. We folded our greatcoats and other few things into our kitbag. Time to say farewell to America after almost two years. We were leaving and it is already springtime here. We were not told we are going home, only we were going to Europe. It will be the first step home.

Although burdened by thoughts of not being able to see my Silesia again, then I could look back on my time in the United States with very fond memories. I will remember it as a God-given pleasant experience for a young man, never ever to be forgotten. Thanks for the countryside I had the pleasure to see, but just that little bit more for the real friendship of the people at work, and not least for the guards, their friendliness and humanity, and most unforgettably the Polish US soldier who could so easily have fired that fatal shot at me, but instead it gave me a chance to thank him here now.

After breakfast and one final roll-call we boarded large buses and were transported down a highway. Might we get a view of the Golden Gate Bridge? Following the traffic we noticed that our convoy was following the shore road. After a few slow miles due to heavy traffic we stopped. We were not to leave our bus but could see that at the front our comrades were leaving their bus with their full kit. Whatever does that mean? We soon found out when it came to our turn to leave the bus, line up at the quay, and stand at ease. There was a large ship at the quayside; within a minute the news was we are going to board it. No time to wonder. Within the hour we were guided on board a former liner, turned into a troop ship. It had brought home veterans and wounded from the war in the Pacific. On this voyage hammocks would present us with no difficulty. We were experienced sailors! Ha Ha. "Wait and see", a voice was heard. Now the time for guessing, where to? Only one way to go, the Panama Canal, surely not? Where then? All the way to Cape Horn? That did not even receive a laugh.

We were allowed on deck, excitement was heard from those in front, there to see is the Golden Gate Bridge, and what a sight it was. There were the skyscrapers of San Francisco on our left and we passed under the Golden Gate Bridge towards the open ocean. What a sight, what a dream! {Many years later, my wife and I drove over and under it.} I recalled what I had read in my encyclopaedia, and I was sure the Panama Canal would be our route to Europe. It was getting dark and the skyline was ablaze with coloured lights for many miles and we would sail over three thousand miles to reach the Canal. The journey took us a week and a day. We were lucky for the sea was calm and there was so much to see. The variety of fish and their fun, {the entertainment I called it}. During the late evenings watching the lights of distant large dwellings and cities was a game of guessing because we had no maps. On this voyage there had not been boxing bouts. As a troop-carrying ship most of the tables and such other furnishings were removed to allow maximum capacity to transport troops from one continent to another across the Pacific. There were sufficient opportunities to sit and play cards, always a favourite with no other entertainment. I was never a card player, therefore I passed my time on the main outside, watching the Ocean, and trying to remember the different countries as we sailed past. I did not remember them all. By the end of the week we watched land coming closer as we neared the large bay towards the narrow entry to the Panama Canal. This was going to be my most interesting event to see it and how it works. The question was would we be allowed on deck at all? I need not have worried since there was a marked out area from where we could watch the whole operation. There were the locks of which there were three. The ship was guided into the locks and closed in. Everything here is done in a slow but precise manner, I had noticed. On each side of the locks were the locomotives, here called 'Mules,' who pulled the ship up into the next lock. Repeating this process twice more before we were free to move on under our own steam. It was fantastic to see. We were now two hundred feet or more above sea level cruising at the permitted slow speed not to allow the wash to disturb the shores of the lush green country side. There are such lakes at this elevation connected naturally or by human hands, creating the 50 mile canal. It took several hours to weave through the pretty scenery before we arrived at the other locks to lower us down to the Caribbean Sea and on to the Gulf of Mexico.

Sailing through the Gulf at first was a calm journey. Before sunset within minutes, the sky darkened and a gale force wind blew as I tried to negotiate some ten yards from visiting my friend in the other compartment to get into mine. The guard at the door was furiously shouting for me to hurry more, to get into my apartment so that he could close the door. I succeeded in offering an apology. One by one we all tried to keep our hammocks steady to get into them. Of course we helped each other. Long before the morning the path to the toilets became very busy. We experienced a force 8/9 gale according to the odd crew members we met. "Stay in the hammocks to keep the ship clean." It blew itself out within two days. Now it meant sailing for another few thousand miles back to Europe. Sailing up the Atlantic, it was natural that those personal worries we had suppressed would resurface.

One began to wonder where we would land and where we Silesians would go. I had left home as a 17-year old boy and was returning as a young man of nearly 20. I had to find my loved ones, and I wondered where they might be now? The Red Cross could help; those were questions which were increasingly occupying our minds as we sailed homewards. Especially those of us who come from eastern Germany like myself from Silesia and those from the north, like East Prussia. According to the news we read these last few months regarding annexation do not make pleasant reading. How would we find ourselves again? We have read somewhere that the Red Cross is much involved in bringing families together again. At least our names had been registered with the Red Cross.

After so long in warmer regions, we began to feel the difference in temperature. Are we anxious about our tanned complexion? Be honest guys, we had been spoiled, hand on heart, it is coming to an end. At least many of us commented that we need not worry regarding U-boats, they must surely know by now that the war is over. Into the third week someone with knowledge of star navigation suggested we must be getting close to the English Channel. Yet later, we were actually still sailing on a northerly course, it did not mean much as we fell asleep. Awaking to daylight morning, and with the ship's engines now silent, a scramble ensued to get off the hammocks and on deck. There on the roof of a dock-side shed we saw in bold painted letters: LIVERPOOL. No-one could be in any doubt where we were. We had docked in Britain. There was great confusion among us. The order to prepare to disembark was given. We disembarked after our last American breakfast, and were marched along the quay towards a railway platform. We were divided into two groups of 200 men each, before British soldiers directed us to two waiting trains.

We took our seats for the first time in an English train and again, were given no information. It was then that we all felt hurt not to have been given the opportunity to thank our Captain and his men who have accompanied us home. Rumour suggested that our ship was here to collect American veterans for return to the States, and we were going to the east coast harbour for repatriation to Germany. It was a pleasant day, sunny and not too cold. Let us remind ourselves, we sailed almost one month and it is here end of February and it's cold for us. Genial guards distributed packed lunches and our rail journey began without much delay. Though the guards could not or would not divulge our destination, I continued to travel hopefully. Always aware that with the sun always on our left we were heading north and not east. Drinks and supper-packs were handed round as the countryside became less populated and the number of sheep in fields increased. By now we should have been at an eastern port. Dusk became dark night and still we were travelling. We slept intermittently on the twelve hour journey then the train screeched to a halt in total darkness. Nothing happened for many minutes. At last the guards came into the carriage and we were ordered to take up our kitbags and leave the carriage. Stepping on to the platform there was a tiny light and a small sign bearing the name 'Comrie'. Where on earth were we?

We marched through the pitch-blackness towards distant lights and reached a small town, which we perceived to be Comrie. Once through the town and marching for another mile we passed through two sets of gates. Lights illuminated barracks of a strange design. We had arrived at a large camp. Shown to our quarters, we felt we could have done with food or a drink but it was well after midnight and we could not expect it. In any case, fatigue made us grateful to find a bed.

The duty corporal's voice woke us next morning for roll-call and breakfast. There was time to make our beds and examine the barrack, with its concrete floor and its curved corrugated-iron roof. There were two solid-fuel stoves, and tables and chairs. It was March but it felt cooler than we had been used to, in fact considerably so. That was not what occupied our minds. Our prime concern was why we had not been repatriated, as the US Captain had said?

We received an explanation later that morning. It had been decided that to alleviate the dire situation in Germany, lack of accommodation, etc., we would stay here for a while. To avoid boredom some of us might be sent to other working camps. The officer hoped we understood and wished us well. Personally, I felt he had spoken sincerely, almost gently. We had no idea of the conditions in Germany, since Hitler's demise. For the rest of the day we familiarised ourselves with our new surroundings. We discovered we were in Cultybraggan Camp, somewhere in Scotland. We learned that it was a famous military training camp, well known to many Scottish soldiers, and was the home of the famous Scottish 'Black Watch' Regiment.

In less than a week 150 of us gathered our belongings again and prepared for another journey. A fellow prisoner of war who was not travelling with us handed me a German-English dictionary that he had purchased in Fort Bliss. He thought I might like it and indeed it became a useful tool for me. I still have it. With four guards we headed for the station and boarded a normal passenger train with carriages reserved especially for us. It was another mystery tour but on this sunny day we felt like ordinary passengers and settled to enjoy the countryside and the unusual number of sheep. At home there had been few sheep on the castle estate. Our guards were friendly and even now I recall the sheer pleasure of the journey. The scenery was different with fewer farms and houses seen earlier. We had our packed lunch while we climbed to a height where snow lay over the mountains and around us. Once we started to descend the snow disappeared. It was all very beautiful. Strangely, I had not seen snow for two years. Suddenly there was the open vista of a large blue bay fringed by mountains. Sooner than expected we descended to sea level. A beautiful panorama unfolded before our eyes, and a large town appeared. It was obviously a bay of the North Sea. We stopped near a sign which read 'Inverness'. Other passengers left the train first, then it was our turn, and without delay we boarded another train. This journey was not over yet.

We had come a long way from Comrie but had further still to go. Life had already taught me the important lesson that if you cannot choose what happens to you, you can choose how to react, and I settled down to enjoy the very pleasant ride along a firth then across a winding river. But how I wished I had a local map! The train had stopped within forty minutes at a station and we seemed to have done a half circle facing east when we slowed down to stop at another station in the middle of a town with a name we could read without difficulty, 'Dingwall'. The name struck a chord, and I recalled school studies of the Celts and other northern people and their important meeting place being called 'Tingwall'. It was interesting for me, if not for others. The order was we were to collect our 'luggage' and to step off the train here. We mustered on the platform and marched away in orderly fashion, kitbags on shoulders. Some passers-by cast a quick shy look at us as we strode through the town. They had never seen a squad in black uniforms. Within half a mile we were in the countryside on the main road, so we thought. We walked for three or four miles in the spring sunshine and passed gentle fields with sheep and uninterrupted views on either side. Passing a village on our left we saw a number of huts just off the main road, another camp with many timber huts.

We were all tired after the long march. In the US we always had transport. We were assigned to our accommodation and instructed to line-up for food within half an hour. The huts were more comfortable than those at distant Cultybraggan and should be warmer, we thought. The countryside was pleasant and the flocks of sheep and herds of cattle in the surrounding fields would be welcome companions, reminding us of home. The meal over, we lined up for checking our names and home addresses. The rest of the day was ours and we learned we were in the German POW Camp 109 at Brahan Castle. This was a main camp serving several smaller ones. Some of us were selected for work at the camp almost at once; my name was not called out for several days. When it was, I found myself in a small group of fifty that would be moving on again. One of our number was a baker and had worked in the US camp kitchens, we had a cook! Shouldering our kitbags we were taken by truck to Dingwall station and boarded a local train. We travelled in reserved coaches alongside the two mile wide firth. Only a mile away we marvelled that the firth was covered with British Seaplanes. Retired from war? I recall us stopping at several small stations en route and was interested to see the firth making its way towards the open sea through a narrow gap between the headlands. Then the train stopped again at a very small station, where there was no village as such, just individual dwellings scattered here and there. 'Kildary' was the name of the station. Our corporal counting that every one of us came off the train, made us form a reasonable military group, following the corporal along a country lane with an odd house here and there, bushes and small trees on either side. We marched along for a mile or so then spotted some light coloured buildings to which we were led. There was among us one who could speak and understood English even I could say something, if not the usual hand signs. The friendly corporal confirmed that this was our new "home". Two barracks provided our living accommodation. They were prefabricated concrete buildings, which should be warmer. There was one toilet in each barrack. The main washroom was next to the kitchen and the guardhouse. Our cook inspected his new domain, indicating that both kitchen and mess room were satisfactory. Two solid-fuel stoves for each barrack provided heating. We discovered that Italian POWs had been billeted here before us, and had left a concrete Mussolini emblem on the gable of the kitchen. They also had constructed a nice timber roundel with a heather-clad round roof. This seating would be popular if we are still here in summer. Our sergeant seemed to have been at various war locations and he wore a couple of military medals. The sergeant and the two guards, whom we had met and shook hands, had their accommodation next to the mess room and kitchen building. Within a week one of the guards had left the camp. Our sergeant had given us a call in the afternoon where he gave us the routine and time table. From

Monday there would be two trucks here at the camp at eight o'clock. The driver will be given our name, and the address of the farm and farmer where to drop us off. The truck will start calling in the evening from the last farm drop in the morning, which the driver will explain to the farmer in the morning. The next day we remembered it was Sunday and there was a relaxed atmosphere and time to assess our new surroundings. Surely, we thought, this will be our last move. I spent precious moments in quiet contemplation, thankful for the blessings we had received and hopeful that soon I would hear reassuring news of the dear folks at home. Eighty per cent of us had not received any correspondence since becoming POWs.

A fairly informal roll-call was held after breakfast and there was a promised feeling among all of us of a pleasant comradeship with our guards in Kildary camp. The corporal explained that we were to be sent out to work on farms in the area and would be kitted out in British military uniform while working on the farms, saving our US black outfit for Sundays. Tongue in cheek, he suggested that our black Yankee outfits might be just the thing when we went out on the town! We helped the guards to lay out our new outfit: UK khaki shirt, trousers, two pairs of socks, a pair of boots and a tunic which had a bold POW printed on it. Changing into our new clothes straight away, we were amazed to discover that everything fitted. Gratefully we received official writing paper and envelopes, for which we had longed and made good use of it during the rest of the day. Perhaps this letter would evoke a response from our loved ones, and hear where they are? If there was no address on the envelope it would be directed to the German Red Cross. That was something positive.

We knew we must be ready for pick-up at eight the next morning and felt ready to tackle anything, rather than sit idly in the barracks. A second blissful night passed, the quietness interrupted only occasionally by the mooing of cows and the bleating of sheep and their small lambs, in the field next to our camp which was a novelty for us. Packed lunch in hand, we waited after breakfast for transport into the unknown. Two covered trucks arrived and the drivers received the list of our names and the places where we were to be dropped off. All on board and off we went discovering our view was restricted, apart from the open back.

What we saw from the rear of the truck was sufficiently interesting for our first day. For instance, those of us who are yet to be dropped off, as we turned a corner we saw a red and white painted high lighthouse and, what we assumed was the North Sea. We all had mixed feelings in anticipation and apprehension, especially those to whom agriculture will be strange and new. For those who had picked cotton it will not be much help. We all wondered how we would be received.

Soon we stopped again to drop somebody whose name presented the driver with some difficulty. A problem which will affect us more than the driver, who only has to call out a name. It will brighten the day. There was a lot of laughter. Sometimes three names were called out, and we rightly guessed that we had stopped at a larger farm. Gradually, we gained an idea of the countryside we were in. After an hour there were only three of us still aboard. Once they were ordered to jump off, I found myself on my own and began to wonder. The driver assured me that I need not panic. Houses came into view and I guessed we were on the edge of a town or village. We turned a few corners and the last of the houses receded from sight. The truck travelled uphill for about a mile. I got a grand view looking down onto the town and the sea beyond. We stopped, and the driver came round to tell me this is my farm. I jumped from the truck and felt confident to say, 'Good Morning' which raised a smile. The farmer offered his hand and I took it in the spirit it was given. The driver had given the farmer the paper with my name and camp number, and exchanged a few words with him, indicating that he would collect me at 4 p.m. I was eager to tell him that my name was Paul, pronounced much the same in English. The truck reversed and went off downhill again, {four years later, the driver and I were members of a local entertainment group}. The farmer, Mr Munro, led me the short hundred yards to the farm. He limped slightly, and I walked at his speed with him, {not knowing then that I was taking my first steps on soil that was eventually to become my second home}.

I was introduced to the farm labourer, Alexander Robertson, who wished to be called just Ackie and lived with his family in the cottage, where the truck had stopped. A quick look round the yard, ahead was the long implement shed, without doors, but it had a corrugated roof, for tractors and horse carts, etc. Next, the gate into the garden, with the two storey farmhouse with its back entrance. Taking a quarter turn to the right the drying green followed by the chicken and wood shed, turning further right are the sheep enclosures which brings us full circle with the 'steading' behind us. The cow shed, the stable for the horses, hay and straw shed. The upper floor being the granary.

Now for my first job. The three of us climbed steps to the granary where we powdered oat seeds with some insecticide and bagged them until noon. Mr Munro indicated that it was lunchtime, a one-hour break. I took my lunch-pack and was looking for a place to sit, the cart shed would suffice. Mr Munro beckoned me to follow him. I was led through the back door of the house into the lobby. Mr Munro, an easy name to pronounce and to remember, pointed to a table and chair to the right, for me to have my lunch there. I was happy with that, we are in a new environment that needs adapting to. A lady appeared bringing me a pot of tea, and milk and sugar, I did not understand what she said to me, a new voice I suppose, but I did have the presence of mind to say "thank you", which she acknowledged with a smile. I assumed she was Mr Munro's wife.

As soon as I had finished my lunch-pack, I went outside to take a closer look at the farm buildings. While there was time I wanted to look at the tractor and the two-wheeled carts. Interesting because in Germany we have four-wheeled wagons. The older tractor must be pre-war, because no rubber tyres. The last bay was fitted out as a smithy, I thought. Ackie, who just appeared explained that Mr Munro's father had been a blacksmith, at least that is what I understood. After lunch I was sent with Ackie to lift turnips from the field. I watched with interest as Ackie harnessed the horse 'Prince' and backed him between the shafts of the cart. Climbing on to the two-wheeled cart required some acrobatics, when compared with our larger carts. The turnips lay in rows, having already been clipped of their leaves. Once the cart had been loaded Ackie drove them up to the farm. I was to continue stripping the leaves of the turnips. The 'knife' that was used, I was warned is sharp, so take time to get used to it, was Ackie's warning. Ackie proved right and I took my time to learn. At three o'clock it was time for afternoon tea, but I did not feel hungry. I spent the fifteen-minute break practising with the 'clipper', the knife, and gradually gained speed after a few days. Both Ackie and Mr Munro spoke very clear English, which helped me in understanding what they said without too much difficulty. Actually much clearer to understand than the American voice. I remembered to tell Ackie that I was to be collected at 4 p.m., and making my way to the farm to pick up my bag, I managed to say "tomorrow" to Mr Munro and "goodnight", wondering was that the right word? I will ask Ackie tomorrow. Then I made my way to the end of the road to join the truck which arrived on time for my journey back to camp. On the way home I was the first to be picked up. I realised Mr Munro is getting short hours from me. Last off in the morning and first when picked up.

There was time for a wash before supper and afterwards we spent much of the evening exchanging details of our first day's experiences. Most were happy to have something to do, but those who were clearly town boys lacked enthusiasm for farm work. Rumour had it that we were to be paid £2 per week, which was good. One member of our group struck gold for he was working for two sisters, {retired school teachers} who had a large garden and required a handyman. He would make rapid progress soon receiving not only morning and afternoon tea but dinner as well. He became the spiv among us, polishing his shoes and carefully brushing his tunic after supper. There were no complaints about our treatment, and I can look back on my first day with contentment at the warmth of the three people I had met. Of course, I hoped that I would return to Viewfield Farm.

The journey next morning was quicker and when I arrived, Ackie was already carting turnips as I made my way to the farm. Mr Munro and I exchanged greetings and I slowly gathered that today I was to help him with his sheep. There was practically no sheep farming in Silesia, and I had only seen a small flock on the Count's estate and that only from a distance. This was going to be an interesting day. I felt honoured when Mr Munro asked me to call him by his Christian name, 'David'. Anybody could pronounce that name. He was already gathering last year's lambs with the help of 'Flossie', his black and white dog. The job I finally understood was to separate twenty five of the best from the flock. I helped where I could and the chosen yearlings were penned, while Flossie guided the others back to their field. It was most interesting to see a dog working with sheep, amazing! At tea-break I asked Ackie why he spoke so much louder to David than to me, and learned that David had a hearing problem. It explained why he sometimes did not answer when I asked for instructions while sorting the animals. At four o'clock my truck arrived and I climbed aboard and made the journey close to the lighthouse and back to camp for a wash and supper. There followed the exchange of what everyone had not experienced before. Some comments were worth a good laugh, but others complained over nothing. That too is understandable if you had never handled a horse or any farm animal previously.

It was Thursday in my first week at Viewfield Farm, and David asked me to help him drive his little flock of sheep to the market in town. During our mid-morning break, a short description of the town as told by Ackie: The town itself had its own Provost and court. It lies at the south of the Dornoch Firth, {the town of Dornoch is only a few miles across the firth on the north side of the firth. It is found on any atlas, where not only Scotland, but Great Britain is at its narrowest between the North Sea and the Atlantic}. Tain is a market town in the Easter Ross area of Ross-shire.

I looked forward to my first excursion. We set off after the tea break and I was instructed to go ahead of the flock and close any gate of a field that might be open, and the flock run out of control. It is down-hill for a mile before we had reached the first houses. Now I had to ensure that no garden gate was left open. If so, I had to close it, to keep our sheep from entering the gardens, and helping themselves! Then walk through the town, after a hundred yards we turn left fifty yards on, turn right, always down-hill a hundred yards we cross a road, this was where the dog had to prove how good a sheep dog is. The large building we pass on our left is the 'Academy' {secondary school}. Two hundred yards on we have reached the Mart. There were many pens and sheep, and farmers, a noisy place of farmers talking and sheep bleating. I had not yet learned to recognise lambs from grown sheep. Now came the surprise with David asking me to make my way home to Viewfield! I might have stood there with my mouth open, but I realised David meant it and thought nothing of it why I could not just walk home on my own! So I marched off, sorry in a way not seeing the fun at the mart.

Having made mental notes on the journey through Tain, I found my way back to Viewfield without difficulty, enjoying every moment and pausing to admire the vista, the expanse of the coastline, the shining firth and the distant lighthouse at Tarbat Ness, the place Ackie informed me. At the same time I realised here was I a German POW, walking freely through the town on my way home. An extraordinary feeling. As I walked home I met Ackie with 'Prince' the beautiful big black horse with a cartload of turnips and walked with Ackie to Viewfield. Ackie informed me that turnips were called 'neeps' in Scotland. I also asked Ackie if the lady of the house was David's wife. To my surprise I was told she was David's sister, Miss Ella, who kept house for him. Neither David nor Miss Munro had married. It was lunchtime and I helped Ackie feed the horses, yes there were two horses here on the farm, Prince the black young horse and the older light coloured horse. Having been told by David to have my lunch in the lobby where there was a table and chair, within minutes Miss Munro brought me a pot of tea with milk and sugar. I had no difficulty to say, "thank you very much", remembering Miss Ida MacDonald from the castle. As I walked out after my lunch, a car arrived from which David emerged. It was simple to understand that David had been given a lift from a farmer friend. Before he went indoors for his lunch, he showed me the turnip shed where the turnip slicer was, and how to slice the turnips to fill the wire baskets. These would be fed to the cows in the evening. One more job learned. So far I had not yet done any work with the cows. There were six in the shed and two of them milking for the house and Ackie. Milking was done before I arrived and after I left.

After dinner David and I went to erect some lambing shelters in a field close by. April is lambing time and there were a number of sheep. David explained that the first lambs were expected within days and the shelters were protection for the new born from cold spring winds or even snow. We were working with corrugated sheets, wooden posts and large mallet. I managed to make myself understood asking how many mother sheep there were? 'Hundred and twenty' David said. Now, I must have spoken loud enough for David to have understood my question. I was pleased. Sooner than expected I spotted the camp truck coming up the hill from town, to pick me up again. I said my 'goodnight' and made my way to the road. How quickly the day had passed. David still had the cows and his pigs to feed while I was driven back to camp for supper. Again, the evening passed pleasantly, after an enjoyable supper. I should mention there was coffee and tea available for us to make. One other good point was that there was no high fence around the small camp, only the normal three feet high field fence to keep the sheep out from messing up our place. Now we had even more questions, and answers to none of them. One thing we learned was to have patience and matters will be resolved. At least we were alive and living well under the circumstances. Those of us from the eastern German provinces were eager to hear about Silesia's annexation to Poland and the resultant deportation of its people to West Germany. Now we had even more questions, and yet answers to none of them.

Returning to Viewfield for my second week I looked forward to lambing time and I found helping David with his 'midwifery' a pleasurable new experience. There was the occasional difficult lambing, but all had survived so far. But we are not half-way through. David, in spite of his difficulty in hearing is happy to talk with me, maybe even appreciating my asking questions? Spending several hours in the day with David at lambing I am very much aware how difficult it must be for him to catch a sheep. Therefore I took the opportunity to outrun David when trying to catch a ewe that may need examining for one reason or another. In an instant, I realised that this is where I could be most useful, in situations where it was more difficult for David. At the same time giving me a chance to show gratitude for the food given at break and lunchtime. I am glad I thought about it. I learned that a mother sheep may die during lambing or she may reject a lamb. If rejected, then the lamb had to be bottle-fed. One other extraordinary surprise was when David skinned a new-born dead lamb and put the skin on an orphan lamb. I watched with interest, as he took it to the mother of the dead lamb, who smelled the woolly skin of her dead lamb and immediately let the orphan suckle, taking it on as her own, pure magic and one of nature's tricks. My goodness, what a lot I am learning here in Scotland. Before long we had another orphan to bottle feed. It gave me the opportunity to speak to Miss Munro asking her in my funny English if I could give the bottle to the lamb? She was happy to oblige and watched me try and said "very good", with a bit of a laugh. Feeding had to be done three times a day and I asked to let me do it again at lunchtime.

I spent most of the week helping David with the lambing and helped Ackie when needed as he finished carting neeps for the mother sheep, {ewes in Scotland}. We sowed oats using the tractor and seed drill. That was a job I had already experienced during my 'Landjahr' after leaving school. It was a busy time on the farm and had another enjoyable week. I spent the weekend quietly doing some washing and going out for a walk. Walks were permitted, but there was a restriction to two miles only, which we observed. Men passing on bicycles even raised their hand in greeting which was appreciated; my new found friend and I walked two miles on one of the two roads from camp. It seemed that most of us would keep our places of work where a good relationship had been established. David and Ackie soon realised that I was no stranger to farm work and had the necessary strength. By the same token I considered all that I had learned in the last eighteen months. With lambing completed, bar one or two 'stragglers', grain sown and potatoes planted, what was next?

There was always a local spring holiday on the second Monday of May. On that day, so Ackie informed me, a few ladies from town would be coming to help planting potatoes, to earn extra housekeeping money. We had a few days to prepare the seed potatoes for them and I was told that Viewfield planted a ten-acre field. Most of the crop would be sold to England and some kept for next year's seed. On the day of planting, Ackie went down to town to bring the ladies up in the cart. This was the first time since my call-up two years ago that I worked with ladies again. It took two days to plant the field and it was pleasant to be called by my first name.

All the cows were now out in the fields until autumn. Summer had arrived and compared with Texas it was more pleasant here. For some of our boys, it was not warm enough. You cannot please everybody. My leaving an hour before stopping time did occasionally interfere with the task in hand. It was pleasant being involved with the lambs, watching them grow from week to week, observing the little groups as they gambolled and raced alongside the fences. I found that particularly fascinating to watch, never having seen such frolics before. The two milk cows had their own pastures next to the farm, making it easy to bring them in for milking, which David did in the morning and Miss Munro in the evening.

Now next in line was the task of sheep shearing and I looked forward to this. Even though I knew nothing about it, I felt it would be interesting. I arrived with anticipation and greeted David and Ackie confidently now in English, "Good Morning", as they handed me tools to be taken up to the place where shearing would take place next to the chicken shed and the sheep pen. The tools are the shears and every shearer brings his own. According to Ackie they are farmer friends of Viewfield. Then there is the heavy wool-bag measuring some 8ft in depth and 4ft wide. The strong bag was hung on a beam. One other tool was a pail with black paint. That is to mark the sheep after it had been shorn and before you let the sheep go. The mark for Viewfield is a six inch V, which I thought was for Victory, until Ackie, among hilarious laughter put me right that it is for Viewfield.

The two shearers arrived and shook hands with me, which I took as a most friendly gesture. It was agreed that either I would catch the sheep in the enclosure and bring them in turn to the shearer, or climb into the bag and pack the wool. Since I was taller than Ackie I would go into the bag. Everybody was happy and the 'fun' began. I discovered that sheep are not that keen to let anyone grab them and bring them to the shearer! Held by the shearer the sheep is shorn from the neck downwards till the fleece is off in one piece. One of the helpers rolls up the fleeces as tightly as possible and hands it to the person in the bag. The wool is trodden down inside the bag until it is full. Shearing must be the hardest job, because sheep are not always placid and may try to take off at any moment. After two hours, shearing is not kind to your back, because you are mostly bent doing this work. I was happy doing what I was asked to do and felt that I was part of the team. I kept watching the shearers. Tea time was ten thirty and Miss Munro called me to fetch the tray for all of us. I was asked a few questions which I could answer but I have to learn a lot more English. In the late afternoon a visiting shearer, a friend of David's, noticed my interest and invited me to have a try at shearing. It was important to get the feel of the shears, because the spring reaction is strong and the points of the blades extremely sharp. He held the animal for me and showed me how to let one's hand rest on the sheep's skin when shearing, to avoid nicking. Damage is sometimes unavoidable if a sheep gets restless and attempts to get away.

Whenever there was time, I was allowed to try again. By the third season, if I am still here, I would be an official shearer, thus letting David have an easier job. I hoped to be home before that? Viewfield had some 150 sheep to be shorn within three days, and everybody hoping it will stay dry. The ability to shear a sheep at a respectable speed would boost anyone's morale. At lunchtime while the shearers had lunch in the kitchen, Miss Munro kindly handed me a plate of home-made soup, and tea for my sandwich at my usual place in the lobby. I found it very moving to be treated like an invited guest, and how I wished I could let my people know that their prayers for me were being heard. Incredibly I was at the end of my third month at Viewfield and feeling part of the staff.

Resting on Sunday at the camp, I decided to go for a walk in the sunshine and quietness of the countryside. I strolled along the narrow lane and found a patch of grass to sit on. I had my small prayer book and read for a while. Two and a half years had passed since my last letter from home while training somewhere in France. It was a time for quiet contemplation, and loved ones were uppermost in my thoughts. They had been spared all the air-raids endured by the western provinces but in the end faced the equally frightening threats from a hardened army from the east which had fought for four years in appalling conditions, while their people were subjected to the atrocities of Hitler's S.S. Our people must have feared revenge, unless they could flee and seek refuge into western Germany. Had they suffered? Were they alive? It is the overwhelming helplessness that got to me.

Here I am in the Highlands of Scotland now with peace at last, being fed and a roof over my head and I can sleep in peace. I would be repatriated one day I hoped. Here in peace I am filling in the time mastering all sorts of skills as a farm-hand while still a prisoner of war. I mulled over all these thoughts. I was the only foreign worker among people who had to earn their living from the land. They did not know my background. They had their own wisdom and judgement and expressed it in their daily life by kindness and a willingness to accept me as an equal. I in turn followed my natural instincts and the example of my parents and appreciated all the kindness I received. Was this the beginning of a growing affinity towards the people and the country around me? At that moment a career in the Post Office was very much in the background. At least for the time being.

Returning to the work in hand, it was time to thin out the turnip seedlings. It was much more comfortable here than in Silesia, where because of the smaller farming units that sort of job required bending so as not to leave large gaps between each plant. Here it was done with a long-handled hoe. The tool required practice to gain speed and not leave too wide a gap between the plants by uprooting too many. This job gave me the opportunity to talk for hours with Ackie as we worked. David was at a disadvantage as he could not hear and join in, until we raised our voices. One can imagine how difficult it was to have a reasonable conversation with us. However it was surprising just how much I understood because Ackie spoke very clearly without any accent or dialect. Ackie confirmed that in these parts of the Highlands, the dialect was not difficult for a stranger to understand. So I was in the right place to learn English. Before harvest it was hay making in good dry weather. Ackie took out the grass cutter to oil the moving parts, while David and I continued singling the turnips. Ackie soon moved out of the yard, and drove to the field to start cutting the lush meadows. Once the grass has dried it would be taken to the end of the field and stored in a round stack coming to a cone shape at the top. After the hay was safely stored, it was holiday time for Ackie. It seemed that neither David nor Miss Munro took holidays, and I would just carry on, since there had been no mention of such luxury for me, at least so far not.

This is an opportune moment in my employ at Viewfield, to let my readers have a brief bird's eye view of the approximate extent of land and family involvement. David's father, John Munro Sr, bought Viewfield Farm, the farmhouse, outbuildings and land in 1895/96. The grounds extended to 55 acres arable and 30 acres heathland up towards Tain Hill. In the mid 1920's Mr Munro Sr. bought the 40 acres of Abbotshill farm, adjacent and northwest from Viewfield. A further 45 acres was rented in 1930 from St. Vincent Farm, also adjacent and to the east of Viewfield. Thus Viewfield provides a stunning view of the Dornoch Firth. There were four brothers and three sisters. David and Miss Ella, took over working the farm, the others did well in Education, Medicine and Commerce.

Mrs Munro Sr. died in 1939; her husband Mr John Munro Sr. died 30 March 1946. I arrived at Viewfield one week later, thus my arrival was timely. It became an embedded talking point.

For a week now Miss Munro had surprised and delighted me by providing me with a full lunch. I too was relieved, for the possibility of not returning to Viewfield could have arisen if the Munros had no need of me during the holiday period, and I would have been moved to another farm. Just a minute, so what? Might I have been disappointed? Or could it be that I began to feel an attachment to the place, Viewfield? As it turned out, David had a number of jobs for me during Ackie's holidays. I was able to clean farm machinery where my youth and height was useful. Fenced-in fields were not common in Silesia, but I soon got the hang of mending fences. There was also more work among the sheep. First after the holidays we dipped sheep in a wooden bath, 6ft long and 3ft deep. I had no idea what it meant, until Ackie explained it simply, the sheep are going to get a bath, a cold one. It was necessary and I was told compulsory, to prevent nasty sores and remove various bugs. One person would grab a sheep and bring it backwards to the bath. David, in a waterproof coat, plunges the animal into the bath, where the sheep would turn itself round and climb out on the timber ramp.

While Ackie was away David and I often worked together, which helped me in improving my English. So much so, that we were able to speak about our lives well enough to get the essence at least. I had found my 'volume' for David to understand me. For instance, I learned that David had served in the 'Lovat Scouts', a Highland Regiment, for a time during the Great War.

When Ackie returned we began the final preparations for harvest time. We sharpened the scythes, which I already knew something about and earned an approving smile. The scythe was used to cut a two yard wide swathe round the edge of the cornfields, to provide the start-line for the binder. Otherwise the tractor would drive over the corn on the first round and three hundred square yards of corn wasted. That was the first job that Ackie and I were to do. When it came to cut the corn, Ackie took his seat on the binder while David drove the tractor. During our coffee break I managed to let David know I learned that on my compulsory land year after school, "you know all about that" he beamed. Both of them looked in awe, seeing me gathering the cut and bound sheaves and put them in the proper position to dry out before being taken in. Yes, there was a bit of showing off when I saw them smile. No sooner than we had our afternoon tea break, when half an hour or so later, my truck appeared and it was my time to go home. Back at camp two days later after lunch the corporal asked me to his office, and I wondered what the reason was. Imagine my surprise when he suggested that I take one of the two bicycles belonging to the camp to get to Viewfield earlier in the day. He thought the farmer would like me to come a bit earlier. I was amazed, but quickly accepted and was 'instructed' to take the best one. David was delighted when I told him next day that I would be arriving by bicycle on the morrow. After lunch he took me to the front of the house to point out a short cut from the road I should come. It would be a shorter road than the truck uses in the first place. Within a week we made a start cutting the oats as the weather was perfect. Oats were the only cereal grown in Viewfield, for neither wheat nor barley were great croppers here. Just as well, since barley is not pleasant to handle.

The tea break half way through the afternoon was very welcome and Miss Munro had put a flask of tea and a scone in David's bag for me. Time flew and it seemed that we had hardly started harvesting. I had my bicycle so did not have to go until an hour later. Shouting a quick "cheerio", I left the field, another day had passed.

Next morning I breakfasted, collected packed lunch, set off and pedalled for a mile and a half till the road climbed steeply for some two hundred yards. I had to dismount and walk. For two further miles the road climbed gently uphill and thereafter it was downhill all the way to Tain. It was an extraordinary sensation as I free-wheeled through the countryside on my own, feeling free as a bird, the roadside gliding past. Soon I arrived at the water reservoir, a mile before Tain, and turned off the road where David had suggested and arrived at Viewfield forty-five minutes early. I parked the bicycle in the shed and went merrily off to work.

The sheaves were damp from a shower during the night, so Ackie and I continued lifting the cut sheaves from the ground and 'stooked' them to dry. Back home sheaves were all stored in a barn, but here I discovered stacks were built at the side of a field where the threshing will take place. I looked forward to seeing how the round stacks were built and I learned that sheaves are laid round and round till the stack is twelve feet high, then keep stacking creating a cone-shape top. If I am here next season I hope to build one. Harvesting took us almost to the end of September, a month later than in Silesia. Next, it was time to prepare for the potato harvest.

It was at this time that among the mail I was handed a letter when I arrived back to camp for supper. The envelope bore my name and letters of identification and an official number. Turning it over, I almost fainted for it bore my brother's name as the sender. It had been posted in Wildeshausen Germany, a place unknown to me, though one fellow 'prisoner' thought it sounded like a town in northern Germany. I vividly remember opening the envelope with trepidation and wondering what it might contain. It promised to confirm the survival of at least one member of my beloved family.

A translation follows:-

> *My dear Bruder {Brother} Paul, I hope you will receive this letter and will be able to read this letter in person and good health. The important part first; Mother and Father are alive and well. They still live in the old 'Heimat', but it is no longer our home; it now belongs to Poland. Our Sister Ursula has been evacuated with the nuns and other pupils before the Russians came. I have made contact and she is in their Mother-House in Munich. I am here in*

*the town of Wildeshausen in the county of Oldenburg, some 35 km south of the city of Bremen, maybe you have a map? With me is our Aunt Else with her three children. Her husband Theo, our new uncle, is apparently also a prisoner of war, but we are not sure of where. We will keep in touch with the Red Cross. That is where we got confirmation that you were a prisoner of war in England. I have already sent a note with that news to Mum and Dad, but will they get it in this mess of confusion and hate? I have to thank Aunt Else that she kept insisting to the Polish Officials, who dealt with our transportation to the West, and claimed otherwise, that my name was on the list and she needed me to help with the children. Finally, late at night when the officials were tired they stamped our papers. We were still anxious until we got on to the train for West Germany. We are here with hundreds of people from Silesia. Someday I will tell you what a catastrophe Hitler's war caused for us Silesians, maybe you heard? We were allocated to this house which belongs to a bachelor. We have one large room with a stove for cooking and a small room next to the cowshed, {but there are no cows} for the five of us. Our mother was keen that I should try and go with Aunt Else because there is no future in Silesia. However difficult and not much food, but we are free here at last. The English soldiers and officials are very helpful and kind. There is not much work here yet. The town was not much damaged. Our home and the whole castle was burned down, also every house around the Town House Square when the Russians left. Mum and Dad have one room at a Great Aunt in Rosnitau. You know the little village just 3 km from home. A Great Aunt of Dad's, who thinks you remember her, has given them one of her two small rooms. Dad is helping a local farmer who knows him and Mum helps on the field, so that they can get some food. If you get this letter, please write back that we know where you are. The post is very poor, but by the grace of God, and we had much experience of that, your letter may arrive however long it will take. We long to hear from wherever you are. Love from us all. With God's blessing, thanksgiving and great joy, your brother Engelbert and Else's family.*

What a surprise and what an evening to read the letter, there is only one thing one can do, to thank God for such wonderful news, the family alive and well, although scattered. How glad I am that they now know that I am alive and will soon hear where I am. So our home and piano is gone. I slept peacefully, and was full of joy and thanksgiving as I cycled to the farm next morning. I was able to make David, Miss Munro and Ackie understand that at last I had good news in the letter from my brother. I was so happy and content to return to the daily chores at Viewfield and to tell my good news. I was now involved in various new tasks, such as brushing the coats of last year's calves to prepare them for the local Mart later in the autumn to sell at a good price. David and I were to sort out thirty or forty of the best new lambs to be taken to a special Mart some twenty miles north. I am told that it's supposed to be the largest in the Highland area where some 30,000-40,000 lambs change hands and that there will be a number of them coming from all around the northern Highlands.

October approached and it was time for the potato harvest. Viewfield's ten-acre harvesting would be quite unlike the potato harvest in our garden at home and on the small farm in my 'Landjahr'. Ackie told me that David tried to gather his potatoes during the aptly named "Tattie Holidays" when the school pupils provide the labour force. I looked forward to it and the day arrived when Ackie picked up the boys and any ladies from town who wanted to earn some money. Each was given a 'stage', measured and marked out by David. Ackie drove the tractor with the potato harvester, and I with Prince pulling the cart, picked up the full baskets, emptied them into the cart and brought the load to the end of the field where a pit would be made. The children quickly got used to me, a German POW and able to speak a bit of English, soon a rapport was established.

They quickly lost their reserve and gained the confidence to call me by my name whenever a basket needed to be emptied. I was not shy to point out if their stage was not properly cleared. They, in turn, began to complain that their stage had been wrongly measured. I took this growing familiarity as a compliment. I offered to prove that, by spread-eagling, I could grab the spokes of the cart wheel with my hands and feet and let the horse move forward as I turned three rounds, their eyes popped and I was accepted as just another big boy among them showing off. They clearly hoped for an encore every day, but once was enough, we had a job to do. My brother's news certainly brought in me a new spirit of joy and absolute contentment. Many a household in Tain had heard about me by now. I was beginning to make my presence felt as 'Paul the Jerry from Viewfield'. The job ended when the last potato was lifted and the pit frost-proofed covered with straw and earth.

Within the week, I had difficulty understanding a letter that David showed me one day at the end of October. His explanation was understood, but hard to believe. Apparently, if a farmer had a cottage or bothy available to accommodate a POW, the prisoner might be allowed to stay there, calling at camp only on Saturdays to show he was still in the district. The day after, David and his sister made it clear that they would be happy to have me and I could stay in the house with them, if I would like that and be happy. I was overwhelmed and thanked them, "yes I would". Then I worked for the rest of the day and cycled back to camp in a dream. Others at camp had also had offers of accommodation in small empty cottages, but it seemed I was the only one privileged to reside within the farmhouse.

The next day had special significance for me as possibly it may be one of the last days when I had to cycle from camp. Autumn was approaching as I travelled along Scotsburn Road and paused again at the highest point, where Tain and its surroundings came into view. There was nothing to conceal the vista as I pedalled along and viewed my situation. I am now already six months at Viewfield, and there is an established familiarity between us since a while. It could not have been easy at first getting used to the presence of a foreigner and former enemy, now living in the same house, the family home. Nor was it for me, the first week anyway. Therefore I was particularly pleased when Miss Munro showed she was not afraid to venture out when I was around. She 'bravely' attended to her hens and any other chores at the farm, eventually saying "Hello, Paul". Thank goodness for my parents' foresight giving me a world-wide familiar first name. Now I was accepted, not only as a stranger, but as the junior farmhand at Viewfield and to live in as a member of a family unit. Short spasms of thoughts did occupy my mind, from a profitable career at the Postal Service, to the two-year gap of wartime and as prisoner of war, and now farming occupation, which in the present circumstances I also seem to enjoy. But with no sign or word of an end as POW living as usual, was fine by me.

I knew how useful my past experiences had proved to be since I first set foot on the farm. I could perform many daily tasks without supervision while David did his regular inspection of the sheep and cattle. Ackie was preparing to start the ploughing for next year's corn, the potato pits were covered and the corn stacks had been thatched with straw to protect them from the elements. The daily round became a preparation for the coming winter.

I parked my bicycle and David returned from his long walk among herds and flocks at lunchtime. Then it was arranged that I should bring my belongings with me on the following Monday and move into Viewfield. I wondered how I would feel living in real family surroundings again.

My last Saturday in camp! Is it really my last Saturday in a POW camp? My mind was fully occupied throughout that weekend, apart from my answering my brother's letter, drawing a home-made map where he could find Tain. Then I took a final Sunday walk to quietly reflect on the two and a half years since my travels first began. Even after sixty years, memories return whenever I pass the derelict remains of my Kildary Camp.

## Chapter 8

# My home at Viewfield

Monday morning dawned. I no longer recall the exact date, but I remember the last breakfast and handshakes before I climbed aboard the covered truck with my modest kitbag and the bicycle, which the corporal insisted I should keep, when I am sent home. Well that was a good present since it was as new. As we travelled around the Fearn peninsula my comrades were dropped off, and finally there was just me aboard as we drove through Tain up the hill to Viewfield Farm. The driver off-loaded my bike and kitbag and I thanked him before he drove away. {Unknown to us we would meet again in due course.} I took my possessions and parked my bike in the shed as usual. Putting my kitbag in the lobby, at the same time I announced myself with a "good morning" to Miss Ella, who returned my greetings. I quickly resumed my daily routine, now so familiar. Ackie was already ploughing a meadow for next year's corn as I tackled a number of jobs about the farmstead. David set off on his daily inspection of the animals. Ackie's reappearance on the tractor indicated it was lunchtime. He assured me that all would be well and just then David called me indoors for lunch, which I was to have with him and his sister in the kitchen from now on. I was shown to my seat at table and was immediately aware that grace would be said. I was not sure how to convey my approval, but a nod did the trick, and I managed to explain that it was something I had always done at home, and quietly to myself daily. It was not difficult for me to express my thanks and enjoyment of the meal as I left the kitchen to return to work.

    Miss Munro handed me a thermos flask of tea and some cake. During the afternoon I mended a fence which some sheep had broken through in their belief that the grass was greener in the adjoining field. I had no idea that sheep would do that. Do we humans not do that too? David dismissed it as a common occurrence due to old fences needing renewing. Before the afternoon ended I went back to the steading to feed the pigs and prepare the feed for the dairy cows. I saw Miss Munro with two milk pails and offered to carry them, but she declined and I did not insist this time, but I was already sure I will take over milking. Supper time was approaching and I spread fresh bedding for the cows then accompanied David into the house. As we passed the dairy I noticed that the Alpha separator had been used and it gave me the first opportunity to suggest that I might use it next day.

At supper I tasted Miss Munro's girdle scones which, with homemade butter and marmalade, found a ready customer in me. A real opportunity presented itself when it was time to wash the dishes. This time I stuck to my demand, explaining that it was a task I had done at home. I remembered that the separator had also to be washed and I recalled its various bits and pieces at my favourite aunt's farm. Miss Munro showed me how to dismantle it, and I watched carefully so that I could remember the sequence for re-assembly. It was a practical way for me to show my appreciation. I was amazed to discover that Viewfield had neither water mains nor electricity. This was something I had never experienced before. Paraffin lamps had to be prepared every day by Miss Munro, and a pump in the house brought water from the nearby well. Ackie had to carry water from the pump to his cottage, a distance of some 100 yards. This really did surprise me.

Supper was over and the dishes washed and put away. David and his sister sat on either side of the warm stove; I sat on the other side of the table facing the stove. Behind me was the large dresser on which stood the wireless with its accumulator; that was another piece of unfamiliar apparatus that had to be recharged regularly at a local garage. David sat reading the Aberdeen Press & Journal while Miss Munro suggested that she show me my room and the rest of the house. A bathroom with bath and closet adjoined the kitchen. Along the lobby towards the front door, on the left the living room on the right the dining room, and the staircase to the upper floor. There were three large bedrooms and one small single bedroom which was to be mine.

It had a single bed, a wardrobe and a small table, and good size bedside cupboard. Until my demobilisation I felt I could happily settle here. I did not know then, that destiny had decided that Viewfield would be my home, for how many years to come? Miss Munro decided it was time for an end to formality and I was to call her by her Christian name, but I felt for the time being it would be correct to address her as Miss Ella and everybody was happy with it.

David was still reading his paper when we returned to the kitchen. Miss Ella attended to other chores, while handing me the previous day's newspaper. David interrupted from time to time trying to tell me interesting stories as best he could. It soon proved to be a successful way to learn and to improve my English. Sometimes I understood a fair amount and at other times not that much. The fact that I would now have to speak English only should help.

As the weeks went by I began to be more confident to read and asked for confirmation of a word as I thought it to be correct English, only to find Miss Ella erupt in hysterical laughter. This was to change in due time as my English improved by having to speak it continually now. To be with Ackie was also an additional learning opportunity by hearing the spoken word from a different voice. As evening drew on I began to realise that David's deafness was such that Miss Ella had to raise her voice a few decibels for her brother to hear her. I understood I must do so too and soon got used to raising my voice and facing David when talking with him. I gradually began to realise that Miss Ella would spend quite a bit of time in silence, in the evenings especially, while David was engrossed in the paper. I had thought about it and wondered was my coming into this house providential in enlivening their quiet evenings; especially the time now after the loss of their Dad? It did make me think especially of course of my coming here just a week after their Dad's passing. Officially, we had no permission to go out after work, indeed I had no intention or desire.

That was not adhered to by a number of my fellow POWs. Later in the evening Miss Ella would make a pot of tea with biscuits or other home baked cake for us, which I was told is a long standing tradition, and I soon found a liking for it. It became for me the hour when to retire to my room. David suggested that while he milked the cows next morning I should have breakfast then put the milk through the separator. Miss Ella showed me that breakfast consisted of porridge oats, home-baked scones with butter and Lyle's golden syrup, tea or coffee (Camp coffee). The menu met with my total approval and I bade them goodnight. I set the alarm clock on the bedside table and slept soundly at the end of another memorable and exciting day. Everything worked according to plan next morning.

By the end of November the cattle had been brought in, though weather conditions here were mild compared with our Silesian winter, when snow could fall from the beginning of December. There was certainly no doubt that I had fallen naturally into the Viewfield routine and all because of my background knowledge of farming from my summer holidays with my cousins in the country with our Mum's relations and hands on during my 'Landjahr'. Week by week I was increasingly aware of my total inclusion in my new-found home. Of course, I waited for further news from Engelbert, who will be surprised to find where I am. He will certainly be surprised and remember Miss Ida MacDonald the English teacher at the castle; and more surprised of my long journey to Scotland. It is only natural to think of my family as we come closer to Christmas,

Mentioning Christmas to David, I was surprised to learn that in Scotland it was not celebrated as a feast, nor will there be a holiday. Here in Scotland we celebrate New Year with two days' holiday. That was a real surprise until I had mentioned it to Ackie who explained that in England Christmas is one of the major feasts with two days' holidays. The second day being Boxing Day. It is one of several differences between England and Scotland that I would discover as time went by. The passage of time was measured by the arrival of Sundays when we three took breakfast together later than usual. I well remember the first one and the pleasing moment when Miss Ella asked if I minded that David read a passage from the Bible. I found it profoundly moving to be included in this family custom. Christmas passed and as usual made my private meditation in my own lovely room with its enviable view. I also decided that my cows would have a double ration of turnips and hay as a Christmas present. I have been described as a romantic and make no apologies. I loved my animals and the idea of a present appealed to me. When I told Miss Ella she was almost in tears and I wished her a Happy Christmas. It did momentarily cause me to think about Christmas at home where our parents would celebrate it.

New Year passed quietly at Viewfield although listening to the wireless introduced me to Hogmanay, and of course to Scottish dance music, which became a must on Saturday evenings.

There had been family visits, like that of their younger sister from the Black Isle and her four boys (including Peter, the youngest, to whom I would become much attached). A regular Saturday visitor was Miss Ella's older sister, whose husband farmed Ardjachie, just outside Tain. Social callers were an elder of the parish church, Mr Gibson manager of the Linen Bank who brought the Communion notice. The Minister of the Church of Scotland, the Rev. Mr Begg, called at regular intervals and always shook my hand and spoke several minutes with me. One other caller was Mr Fraser, the manager of the North of Scotland Bank, of which the Munros were clients. At most of these social occasions I was encouraged to be present at the traditional tea. And after tea, now that it was accepted that my job was to do the dishes, I no longer had to insist on doing them. I mention this in particular, to help you to understand that I was treated by David and Miss Ella as part of the family, later, almost as the 'son' neither ever had.

The New Year (1947) began and the weather was relatively mild till January 30th David woke to find snow piled high against the back door. I had been aware of a gale blowing during the night but the view from my bedroom window was obscured. When I looked outside at breakfast time I thought for a moment that I was back in Silesia, I had not seen snow like this for three years. The blizzard continued, but David did manage to milk the cows and I put the milk through the separator before we went out to feed the animals. When Ackie arrived we tried to clear some sort of track along the steading, to the chicken coop and up to the house. After our mid-morning break we devised a plan to get to the sheep. I did not understand that sheep could survive this sort of weather, but told not to worry, only wait and see. It was obvious that Ackie and I could shovel a path to the cowshed and the stable, then to the cart shed. We needed to get the tractor started. It took a number of turns before it came to life. Tractors in those days had no hoods. Next to the door at the cowshed was the shed where turnips were stored for the cows. Ackie and I started loading the trailer with turnips. We put on coats and bonnets and went out to the fields, here the snow was at least a foot or more on the ground. I was on the trailer throwing off the turnips while Ackie drove the tractor while the snow blew incessantly around us. We watched as the sheep battled with difficulty through the drifts to get to the turnips. I was fascinated how those sheep nibbled at the turnips. Their determination won the day and I wondered if their efforts and the nibbling of solid frozen turnips helped them to keep warm. The blizzard lasted all day and well into the second night. Amazingly, it was absolutely calm the morning after. The third day there was total calmness and a brilliant blue sky. A transformation that lasted till the snow began to thaw in early March. There was nothing else one could do on the fields and it was a case of the tested daily routine bringing hay and turnips to the sheep and feeding the cows inside their places. I busied myself by clearing a path to the poultry sheds. The mile from Viewfield to town was blocked for vehicles, that is to say for cars. After a few days we got into a well organised daily routine. I managed to provide a reasonably smooth path for Miss Ella to get to the poultry sheds. I made sure I locked the poultry sheds in the evening, not for fear of stealing which I was told does not occur, but the possibility of a fox having a try with the snow cover.

One morning the local county road employee called, having walked up the road from Tain. Somehow he knew about the used railway sleeper we had and suggested we make a snow plough with it for the tractor to drive it down to clear the road. Ackie and I suggested to David that we could do it. David agreed and we went to work immediately. I had no problem with a hammer and saw; by lunchtime we had the wood cut and would 'knock' it together after lunch. This we did and Ackie got the tractor to hitch it on and off we went. It worked and we cheered ourselves. Next day we drove into the sheep field and ploughed a track for them so that turnips could be dropped on a very thin layer of snow. Hey presto!

Just as we were about to turn for home we heard the sound of an airplane, a Dakota, coming from the direction of the large Air Force station some eighty miles south-east of us. As it came closer at a low altitude we could see an Air Force man standing at the open side door waving to us. They were flying hay bales north where they had snow drifts and sheep were not able to find fodder. This lasted for a few days. I noticed how much of the feed was trampled underfoot in the deep snow. At that time Tain had only one snowplough used for the main road first of course. Consequently all the town's side roads, including the road to Viewfield, remained completely impassable. After three weeks a squad of men started clearing by hand the deep drifts that blocked the route.

Shopping was done on foot, and on one occasion I was asked to go down to the Butcher and the Co-op bakery to collect provisions that Miss Ella had ordered by telephone. I called at the bakery on my way home and the manager recognised me. He handed me the provisions and wrapped up a small Madeira cake to eat on my way home. Such a kind gesture made a lasting impression.

Towards the end of March I received a second letter from my brother. It included my parents' address. Engelbert warned me that any answer from them might take some time, providing that my letter was actually delivered in the first place. Strictly, I was not allowed to write, but with my sender's address as Viewfield, I hoped at the local Post Office it would be treated as a normal letter. It is wonderful to have, at long last, contact with the family. We hope that a steady regular mail contact between my brother Engelbert and myself will develop as time will allow. Thanks to Engelbert having made contact with our sister Ursula, we now know she is in a Convent in Bavaria. This was indeed good news for the three of us knowing we are well and good to know where we are and able to correspond. As our brother Engelbert said, our parents will be very happy we three are in contact with each other. It seems that our sister Ursula has made the decision to become a nun. This to me is totally out of character as she was a vivacious fourteen year old aiming to be an actress!

Providence clearly had other ideas, but I was confident that she would make an excellent teacher. The following is an abridged record written by Engelbert, recalling the traumatic weeks in 1945.

> *January/February –June 1945 at home in Gross Strehlitz; Silesia*
>
> *Our sister Ursula arrived unexpectedly from Breslau, where she was studying at the Convent's domestic science college. A great joy for us to be together at Christmas time. Only my brother Paul was missing. Declared officially missing, but where? Aunt Else with her three children were also living at the castle in one of the staff rooms. So far, Silesia had been spared the trauma of air-raid destruction and loss of life. Now in everyone's mind was the Russian winter offensive which step by step was gaining ground towards Silesia. Midnight Mass was not to be missed. It was exceptionally well attended with a number of soldiers on leave.*
>
> *Our parish priest delivered a poignant, occasionally dangerous sermon. Walking home after Mass we met our Lutheran friends after their service. In most people there was the silent thought of unanswerable questions. Yet no one knew that we would be celebrating our last Christmas as Silesians and that it is going to be the end of a thousand years of history of our ancestors. Immediately after New Year, I and other boys of 14 to 16 years were ordered to dig trenches for our retreating army only ten kilometres from home. It was to provide readymade trenches for our soldiers. It only lasted two weeks after which I was allowed to continue my only four month printing apprenticeship at the local Printer. Returning home one day towards the end of January, a totally unexpected surprise was to greet Uncle Theo, husband of Aunt Else, on leave. As a Sergeant Major with five years military experience, he saw the situation differently. He wasted no time to visit the local military command office after the meal. Greeting his comrades and asking regarding the situation, their quick advice was: 'Kamerad, go home, get your family out and across the River Oder. We have already sent our families away a day ago. Trains are no longer moving. We expect the Russians will be in town within twenty four hours or less'. Returning home Uncle Theo lost no time to speak with Dad and I about what should be done. First the mothers were to collect some*

*warm clothing and pack as much food as possible. Dad said that the Countess, before she left the castle two weeks ago, had told Dad that he must take the pair of horses from the stable and take the most useful coach to take his family to safety - wherever. Dad actually thought of getting everything ready then letting Uncle Theo and myself take the cart with the people. Dad was then going to put on his livery, receive the Russian officer and show him the castle. Uncle Theo in military fashion told Dad not to be a fool; the Russians will regard you as an officer and shoot you before you open your mouth.*

*Dad made his way to the stables and gave the horses a double ration then handmade a few bales of hay and bag of oats and greased the coach's wheels. All jobs that Dad could do blindfolded. Early in the morning Dad, without sleep, went to the stable to harness the horses. I went down to help Dad to load the horses' feed, and then we were ready to go to our home and began to load the coach. Into the coach went Aunt Else, Uncle Theo's wife, their three children, our Mum and the cases with extra underwear, real important papers and Dad remembered the photo album. The coach was the one that always brought the food to the shoots, therefore, it had a rainproof canvas roof. Dad in front had no cover, but he had a waterproof feet cover and coat. Uncle Theo had Dad's bicycle and I my brother Paul's great bicycle with a speedometer. Dad knew the road to the River Oder well, so did Uncle Theo. We even had room for two featherbeds which you can squeeze into a small cushion when travelling. I cycled quickly to my employers to explain my situation and said my goodbye. Up in the dark wintry morning with -8°c, Dad had already fed the horses and arrived to start loading. Before locking the house, Dad had a last look at our large picture of the Last Supper hanging in the living room. Then it was time to lock the house and Dad took the key for the castle. We were on the road within two hours while Uncle Theo and I cycled ahead to see if the road was fit for travelling. Able to cycle we were happy with the conditions of the road, after the heavy snow fall last few days.*

*The road having been used by fleeing travellers before us helped. We aimed for the nearest crossing westward which we reached after three hours - a distance of 20km. The soldiers helped us to cross with* more wagons arriving. They already had the order to blow up the bridge, but thought it could wait a while. We stopped at the nearest large building to use the shelter and have some of our refreshments. Dad fetched water for the horses and at the same time ate his sandwiches. No time lost we were on our way. We just passed Uncle Theo's home country, but he thought it prudent to keep going. He and I cycled ahead to a large estate at which he was well known. It meant for our family another three hour drive. Uncle Theo and I arrived to a warm handshake from the Manager who was surprised to see Uncle Theo. Matters between the two men were discussed and quickly organised. We would stay here overnight. Uncle Theo, in uniform, managed to stop one of the military scout cars when they recognised Uncle Theo's military rank. They were of the opinion that the Russians were not going to advance for a few days, but suggested to try and make towards the Sudeten Mountains. With Uncle Theo not having been on leave very often since marriage to Aunt Else, I did not get to know him well. This changed since he came home so suddenly on leave a few days ago and having been together the last two days he treated me as an adult as he got to know me at close hand. In the meantime the Manager of the estate asked one of his employees to take me with him and prepare a place for our horses and wagon, while the Manager and Uncle Theo organised a place for the rest of us. There was a large room above the stable for Aunt Else, the children, our Mum and for us men. We were given fodder for our horses and would take as much as we could tomorrow.

The time preparing passed quickly and it was not that long until our wagon arrived. Once we told them that this was where we would stop the first day from home, smiles and silent prayer of thanks were said. We men got the ladies and children up to the loft where straw and blankets soon made an attractive change from our featherbeds. Try and think as an adult how your life can change within twenty four hours? From 'luxury' to beggars looking for a place to lay your head on. We had already agreed that I would get up in time to feed the horses before breakfast, to allow Dad to have a longer sleep, but care and worry made him rise and he felt better to do something useful. We had been given a stove for our ladies to prepare breakfast.

*While the ladies cleaned up Dad and I took care of the horses and soon had them harnessed. The Estate Manager made sure we had taken fodder for the horses. Important also to have a tin of grease for the wagon wheels and it was time to move on. Dad suggested we go slightly north to his older sister Anna and her husband Josef who was the Police Inspector in a town almost a day journey away. After our midday break it was decided by Uncle Theo that it was too close to the city of Breslau which Hitler had declared as a fortress meaning that from that particular day no one could leave or enter Breslau. Uncle Theo's prediction, that the Russians will destroy it and a lot of unnecessary lives will be lost, came true.*

*We turned left towards the mountains which were still two days journey or more away. At least the roads were passable and not too much snow. We were heading now towards the Sudeten Mountains, still in the far distance. We had also of course Uncle Paul's wife Aunt Magda and their two daughters. We seemed to make good headway. Uncle Theo again took me with him to scout ahead and with the road tarmac in good condition we went a good bit ahead. The two of us had a field flask and a sandwich just after mid-day. Within the hour the country became more undulating. We had to quickly find a kind farmer who would offer us shelter for the night. They were now still almost two hours behind us. With Paul's bicycle and being twenty years younger than Uncle Theo, I had gone a mile ahead when I saw a large farm. As I came alongside I got off my bike and pointed to the right as Uncle Theo arrived. It was a two storey farmhouse which, counting the windows, must have a number of rooms. Uncle wasted no time to make his way to the front door and introduced himself as being on leave, but would have to depart within a couple of days. The gentleman he spoke to was the farmer who introduced himself as Mr Peters. While listening and having been introduced I was impressed at Mr Peters' attitude and he offered us a little cottage next to the farm.*

*While Uncle Theo and Mr Peters made their way to the cottage, I went to the roadside to await our wagon. It took another half hour before in the distance I recognised our wagon and horses. As they drew nearer I pointed with joyful gestures to turn into the spacious yard.*

Dad brought the horses to a stand and jumped down to hear the good news to have found a 'St. Joseph's' stable.

We introduced each other thanking Mrs Peters and their two teenage daughters. The Peters seemed surprised how far we had come. Dad was proud to show the horses to Mr Peters and his daughters, the Count's riding horse, feeling sorry for it having to pull a wagon. Mr Peters showed us the stable for our horses and where the straw and hay lay. In the meantime, Mrs Peters showed Mum, Aunt Else and Aunt Magda the cottage which they could call their own for the time being, whatever that may mean. Later in the evening I was allowed to listen to the men discussing Mr Peters' offer for us to stay put for the time being. Uncle Theo concurred on the grounds that should the Russians overtake us, which in his opinion would happen sooner or later, then it would be perhaps less stressful. The Peters were happy for us to stay. Uncle Theo reminded us that he would have to leave in two days. That was an awakening reminder and the day arrived sooner than we hoped. It was not a pleasant parting for Aunt Else or Uncle Theo. Too imponderable what is to become of us? Parting after his short marriage with Aunt Else and his three children could not have been easy. We would try and help that was certain.

If that was not enough only two days later a German Unit arrived and the Officer commanded that we must leave within twenty four hours as the area would be mined to slow the Russian advance which is certain to move within days. Dad and Mr Peters had little time to ponder where best to go for a safer place, if there is one. Mr Peters decided a route which was not too steep for the horses and less visible from the more busy road, which the Russians might miss and could be reached within one day. The best of plans could be wiped out by a sudden Russian advance from anywhere. We had to take the chance. The women had to be ready that night for leaving at dawn the next morning. Everything worked well and we were off, sharing the thoughts we had when leaving: 'how will we find it, if and when we return?

After two or three hours the road began to climb, not yet bothering the horses. That did not last long, when we came upon a small river crossing which our soldiers were about to blow up. They urged us to hurry or we would also be blown up. We crossed it.

*A little over half a mile later they blew it up, shying the horses for a moment and on we went into the distance.*

*An hour and a half later we came to a small village with homes more spaced out. We managed to find a pleasant elderly couple who had an empty clean barn with lots of straw where we could sleep. The children slept in a small room at the cottage. There was also a space for our wagons and horses. The elderly couple had given up farming a few years ago. The Peters were also given shelter less than half a mile from us. We soon were organised, the horses fed and watered and I am sure they must have been tired.*

*No news of the situation around us was available. The Peters came over and also had not heard. Two days ago we could hear some artillery, but impossible to tell from whom. Out of the blue a small group of German soldiers appeared from nowhere as our little group called at the small inn in the village. We hoped to hear some sort of news, but none. The soldiers warned us to clear all the alcohol from everywhere. For our safety no Russians should find any. They would be the last German soldiers we would see, the Russians may miss us, but we should not bank on that. We helped the innkeeper right away to pour all the alcohol in the latrine.*

*Unbelievable, within two hours suddenly a Russian officer entered the inn looked around and demanded 'Schnapps'- German alcohol. The innkeeper showed him the shelves and cupboard, and a few bottles of very light beer. You could feel the tension in all of us as he looked around and looked at me; I was scared and almost wet myself when he gripped me by the arm. It was clear he was going to take me out and shoot me taking me for a soldier who had changed into a civilian. My Mum risking everything went to the officer pleading in her broken Polish that I was still a schoolboy and her only son. He took a side look and saw the young woman who had tried to hide behind one of the older men. He let my arm go and went towards the young woman in her early twenties, grabbed her by the arm and took her outside. We all stood in silence and prayed for that lady. It was time we all went away to our beds.*

*I had a very disturbed sleep and awoke early, but did not go out. It was wintertime and still dark. Seeing daylight I washed in cold water and dressed. I went outside carefully, first looking if any*

*Russians were around, seeing no one I went to the water pump. Just then I heard steps and quickly turned round, it was the young lady that the Russian took outside. I, only just eighteen, had heard enough and knew what the lady had gone through. Our soldiers whom we met as we fled always shouted hide the women. I had the presence of mind to shake her hand, she could say nothing. As one after the other of us appeared to wash, it was believed that the Russian front had moved on, meaning we were no longer 'protected' by our soldiers, we were from now on at the mercy of foreign people. With Uncle Theo gone we had to make our own decisions and decided to stay for another night before biting the bullet and trying to make our way home to whatever condition we may find it. We spent the day checking our wagons, greased the wheels, collected some straw for the home journey and packed our few belongings. Uncle Paul's wife, Aunt Magda and our two cousins were somewhere in this part of the world, we hoped they were safe and well among their relations.*

*After four months in no-man's land, Peace at last! What does it mean? We will find out. Together with our friends, the Peters family, we left after breakfast saying goodbye and thanking the elderly couple for giving us shelter and their kindness. Our worry was where to find bridges to re-cross the river? It would be a longer journey. In the next town we were stopped by Russian guards and our papers were checked in case we were Nazi officials. We were given an official Russian permit to travel home. Relatively trouble-free we arrived back at the Peters' farm. It was late evening and we accepted their invitation to stay overnight. We had passed through some parts quite untouched by war and others completely devastated. The Peters were glad to find their home intact.*

*Parting from them next morning was a heart-breaking good-bye, us trying to thank them for their kindness and hoping to see each other sometime again. With a thought and a prayer of thanks for being alive and hoping that this awful disaster was behind us, everybody wanted to get home, no matter how we would find it. Along the road and in the fields lay the remnants of war. Most of the material would eventually become worth looking for, to sell as scrap to buy bread. We were now on the road we had travelled three* months ago. Late May the days are longer and we reached our river again, the Oder.

This time it was a major crossing and important Russian check point. Our Russian documents were being checked and approved and as we were about to leave a Russian officer noticed our Count's good-looking mount, 'Pusic'. He made us stop, looked into the horse's mouth and ordered Dad to loosen the animal. He gave Dad a much heavier horse. Throwing his saddle onto Pusic's back and fixing the harness and bit, he swung himself in one go into the saddle, pulled sharply on the reins and we watched with tears in our eyes as Pusic galloped away happy to be again a riding horse. We were happy to be on home ground. Alas, not for long. Stopping at another control post we discovered it was manned by Polish militia. They checked our documents and our vehicle for useful things which they took. We men were separated for deportation to Russia, leaving the women to drive on. By chance a young Polish officer noticed that the women could not handle the horses and called us back to take the reins. Our two horses were taken away and we were given one lighter horse. We could only give thanks for guardian angels. We learned the value of prayer as we drove once more on familiar roads. Tears flowed as within the hour the steeple of our sacred Annaberg came into view. Then again just three kilometres from home, our church steeple in view, but not for long as we met a lady and asked about the state of the town. She advised us not to proceed, telling us that the town centre was almost totally destroyed. So too was the castle. The Russians had torched the town centre. The church, thank goodness, was undamaged. Later we learned that our parish priest had been shot while trying to persuade a Russian soldier to spare four teenage girls he was trying to molest or worse. It gave the girls a few seconds to run into the crypt to hide. How sad, our parish priest. Having heard such bad news, Dad immediately thought of his Great Aunt who lived in this little village we were just entering. We stopped at her cottage and it was an emotional reunion. Confirming what the lady on the road told us, the Aunt offered us accommodation in her small flat. Our prime thought was how to live now. Dad was well known in this village and went straight to the larger farmer to ask if there was a possibility to have room in his stable for Dad's horses.

> *There was a great welcome of seeing each other and the answer was yes. While Mum went up to Aunt's flat, Dad and I parked our castle wagon and got the horses into the stable. Right away it felt like we were among our people and a weight fell from our shoulders. Dad and I went up to Dad's Aunt and he remembered being there many times. Let's call her our Aunt, I must have met her somewhere, you must have met her because she said so. The coffee was ready and there was some food, but what was uppermost on our mind was the relief of having a place to shelter and to sleep. Two hours ago we stopped at Aunt Else's husband's home, where she found a place to stay with her children. It should be easy to get in contact with her when needed. Dad with his horses and I were willing helpers to the farmer.*
>
> *So my dear brother this is our brief 'story' of what happened here in our 'Heimat', which it seems it is no longer, Hitler and his cohorts have robbed us of it. My dear brother Paul I hope this will help you to think and feel with us about our homeland that was, but will never be forgotten. Most of the farmers had stayed and still had their little farms. We were grateful to share the little that our Aunt had and we learned from her that most of the townsfolk had gone away. We were advised to learn to speak Polish, however poorly. With all we have been through, it no longer matters. Here we are not Germans now and this is no longer our beloved homeland.*
>
> *With God's blessing, your brother Engelbert.*

Although I was so glad to hear from my brother how the family had survived their ordeal, his account of the flight from the advancing Red Army made very disturbing reading. I was intensely aware of my own good fortune and could certainly count my blessings. While my future was unresolved, my warm acceptance by David and Miss Ella, as member of their own family, meant that I enjoyed the comfort of a safe home and a fulfilled life, at least for the moment. Miss Ella one evening must have felt confident to tell me that she had many years ago voluntarily given up a promising friendship and marriage in order to look after and care for her parents. Knowing how difficult it might be since David would not get married, Ella now looked at it as a happening through divine intervention, my coming to Tain. These were certainly comforting and extraordinary words to hear.

Now I was confident enough to perform many tasks around the farm without supervision, and my English was improving. I read more and more, and I liked to listen to the wireless in the evening, enjoying even the Saturday weekly "McFlannels" a soap opera. Listened to Scottish dance music on Saturday nights and got to know the different bands by name. I have now been at Viewfield for almost a full year. The snow has melted and spring had arrived, and soon we would be lambing again. Ackie was ploughing for the first spring sowing and I, with 'Prince' between the shafts, was carting turnips from the field. After lunch I changed horses, giving my beloved 'Prince' a well-earned rest and harnessing our older horse to continue my task. David came down to the field to help me load the cart. We had lifted only a few turnips, when by chance David saw smoke coming from the stable. The smoke got thicker and, leaving David in the field, I ran towards the steading a distance of some 300 yards. The fire was well alight, and clearly I was too late, my faithful friend 'Prince' was already dead in the burning stable, where the fire had started from. Not able to untie him was a devastating blow, he was already dead.

Alerted by Ackie's wife, Miss Ella was frantically trying to untether the cows, but I made her go outside and managed to free the last cow and get the pigs out safely into the yard. Now it was time to get myself out, for the flames were spreading unchecked and dry worm-eaten rafters were beginning to collapse. Miss Ella was clearly exhausted and frightened. She leant against the cart shed and I went to her, but before I could say anything she hugged me and thanked me for arriving so quickly. It was a moment of unexpected affection and meant so much to me in my situation. I walked her to the house just as David came round the corner with the horse and cart.

The fire brigade arrived to tackle the blaze, and onlookers came up from the town. There had not been a large fire like it for some time. David quickly assured the police inspector that I was clear of suspicion. How the fire had started would remain a mystery. We had no electricity, and I had left the farm before David and Ackie. Hasty arrangements had to be made for the two cows to be fed and milked, and it was decided they could safely graze overnight in the paddock. At supper I had already prepared what I felt I ought to say regarding my position, thinking that David would have no need of me and that I should go back to Kildary camp. There was an emphatic "not on any account" and David insisted I would now be needed more than ever. I was satisfied to know where I stood. I had often helped my Dad, who was skilled at carpentry, the saw and hammer were tools I knew well. It is far more important to record fate's timely intervention.

The neighbouring Mansfield farm had been rented to a farmer in town. The tenant's lease would end on the May term date. Its owners decided to sell the property and agreed it would be advantageous to separate the farm from their big house in the sale. The private building was a large two and a half storey house, it was a mansion passing as a castle with its flag tower. Built from the beautiful sandstone quarry on Tain Hill, it stood on eight acres of ground, with the farm buildings right at the edge of town, with the police station across the street. Next to the police station is a pleasant two storey stone built house, belonging to the farm, occupied either by the farm tenant or the manager. The first thing David had to do was to telephone his solicitor. He would call after office time, which he did. The solicitor informed David that Mansfield House and the farm will be sold, and that the house and farm will be sold as separate items. Sale will be by auction. Miss Ella told me that their solicitor is hoping David will place an offer. Apparently the out-going tenant had left the grounds somewhat neglected.

In the mean time we had to fix up some sort of cover to take the milking cows in for milking. Here something extraordinary happened; I discovered an interest in working with wood to build a temporary wood shed from some of the timber which had not been badly burned. I looked around until I had a number of timbers to make a start. I could do with a sharper saw, which I mentioned to David and he soon brought me a new one from town. Anytime I was not needed, but especially in the evening, I began to be really good at this joinery lark and the shed began to look like one. We soon needed to look for a place where we could have one solid place to fix the shed to it. That we found, and after a week we had a new cowshed to avoid getting wet when milking.

David was keenly interested and made an offer for the Mansfield farm. The acceptance day for offers was a nail-biting one. But it was also another personal red-letter day for me, because Miss Ella kept me fully informed of their hopes. On that important day in the morning we all kept fingers crossed. When David came home to lunch there was no decision. The offers were still being negotiated. Later in the afternoon when David came home again we were told that things looked promising. The reason for optimism was that Mr Cormack Snr, the solicitor, would be calling at Viewfield in the evening. While I got on with the daily afternoon chores and milking, Ackie had arrived home at the end of the day, asking me if there is any news. I only knew that matters have not yet concluded. Miss Ella had provided an earlier supper for us. While I got on with washing the dishes and separator, Miss Ella prepared the lounge for the important meeting. I knew my place and had ample work to pass the time outside. David had already bought a good hand saw and a hammer since he had seen what I had done in getting some repairs to essential small shelters, etc.

A car had arrived and I took it to be Mr Cormack since David had led him to the house, while I continued with what I had been working on. With daylight hours so much longer than at home, it allowed me to keep going happily. Eventually Miss Ella came out looking and calling for me. I was about to go inside when David and Miss Ella escorted Mr Cormack Snr. to his car. Miss Ella immediately introduced me to Mr Cormack who was happy to shake my hand, remarking that he had heard about me. While David escorted Mr Cormack to his car, Miss Ella wasted no time to let me know that David had got Mansfield Farm. In all humility our parents instilling manners and respect certainly left its mark in us, and I had often reason to thank them for it. It was a momentous moment, even for me, since I have been treated as one of the family. Now we have a place to put the animals under cover in winter, when it comes and if I am still here. David will have a meeting sometime with the present tenant to discuss the changeover. There is the matter of leaving the house next to the police station. With summer time there is no need for the cattle to be inside. What David would need to do is to find additional farm-workers. Mansfield farm lands are of course next to Viewfield grounds. We are curious who will buy the big house?

After Mr Cormack's departure, at supper discussions took place and I was able to suggest that I could do the morning milking and separating before my breakfast. This I thought, would allow David to have his breakfast, and time for preparatory work for Mansfield? After a moment of silence, David and Miss Ella surprised me by saying it would be a good idea. For David it meant to engage three additional workers. One additional tractor driver, a cattle man, {herdsman} and a general farm worker. I would be the hands at Viewfield. David had already brought his idea before us at supper time, that he will eventually get in contact with a builder to erect a new farmstead.

So, I will be the man at Viewfield and available to work with the others at Mansfield whenever necessary. It would mean that I would leave whatever job I was doing around 4p.m. and head for home for the evening milking, etc. Ackie of course had been informed in the morning. David is going to get a mechanic from Munro's Garage in Tain to get the old Ford tractor fully operational. The iron wheels on both tractors have to be replaced by pneumatic tyres for use on the road. To get from Viewfield to Mansfield steading you must have rubber tyres. Meanwhile, attention had to focus on current tasks, lambing was in full swing. This year I learned how to skin a stillborn lamb and place its skin on an orphan lamb or one of triplets, trusting that it would be accepted by the ewe as her own by the scent of their coat. Farm animals and their behaviour never ceased to interest and educate me. Feeling more welcome within the household, I felt free to spend time after supper mending, fixing and making things that are necessary after the fire.

Regarding additional labour Miss Ella mentioned that David had engaged a middle-aged farm worker, Jim Patience, who delivers milk in town from another farm, to be foreman, and tractor driver. Ackie would continue as tractor driver. According to Miss Ella, David will need a cattleman for the additional animals that will be housed at the Mansfield farm in town. When Ackie did not get to be the foreman he gave notice to quit. Ackie left within two weeks. The little roadside cottage became vacant for a shepherd. I was asked to remain in the house if I was happy. Jim Patience was appointed foreman and soon moved into the beautiful two-storey stone farmhouse. Peter MacLean, the new cattleman accepted good living accommodation in the farm building that faced Scotsburn Road, and the police station. John Corbett, the new tractor man, moved into the cottage next to the Masonic Hall.

David's other priority was to buy another car, for his 4-year old Hillman had suffered the same fate as "Prince", perishing in the fire. It was but two years since the end of the war and new cars were few and far between to be had. David tracked down this old green 1936 Morris and bought it from Corbett (the builder) where it had been under cover during the war years. It was a beautiful 10hp car in near-mint condition. David was aware of the improvements his new property required, but essential work had to be done on Mansfield grounds. Some acreage had been sown by the departing tenant, but David required land to be prepared for an additional turnip crop and he wanted to plant an extra ten acres of potatoes. Some of the newly acquired fields bore evidence of neglect. Weeds had been creeping into Viewfield ground, fencing also needed urgent repair or replacement. Behind the Mansfield farm steading one field separated it from houses built pre-war on Craighill Terrace. Integration of the extra acreage was natural since there was one wire fence between the border fields.

After term day and the tenant had left, David took me for a first look at Mansfield farm, and I was anxious for him to show me the buildings including the foreman's house. When I met our new fellow workers I was surprised that they had already heard of and seen me, that was except Peter the cattleman. I hoped they would accept me as a fellow worker, and in no time at all we were at one. Singling turnips provided the best opportunity to develop a good working relationship as we toiled side by side along the rows. I took a particular interest in Peter in an instant, perhaps because of his hearing difficulties, and I used the skills I had developed when talking to David and did so when talking to Peter. As we worked there was no lack of general gossip and fascinating topics. I quickly learned about all manner of interesting local matters. We worked as a team, and I was pleasantly surprised.

David bought more sheep and cattle for the extra acres of grazing. We were preparing for the additional mowing and haymaking. My learning of each new skill improved and likewise my confidence. Now my bicycle came to its own when leaving the field at four to get up to Viewfield for the milking. Going uphill was a bit of a drag. With good weather it was hay making time and here I learned how to build haystacks from our foreman Jim who was happy to teach me. We fixed that by building our stacks side by side.

At lunch one day in August Miss Ella handed me a letter that bore my parents' new address. At long last I had something tangible now from Mum and Dad after three long years! I found it emotional to read of their thanksgiving and joy to know that I was safe and well. Father had written the letter and he told of the indescribable sadness that so much was changed and lost forever. They lived in a state of uncertainty, but they thanked God for knowing we children are well and looking to the future.

*"I have a job now in the stone quarry to which I cycle every morning. You Paul know where it is. It is quiet here in the village and we know the people. They all accepted Polish citizenship and are left in peace in their own home. They are working their farms with my help, which pays for our food. We have enough to eat. Your mother cries every night, missing you all and praying you will not lose faith. 'Keep trusting God'. At least we still have our lovely church, but now we have to sing in Polish. We had to learn proper Polish! We look forward now and hope for your letters. It will make us so happy to know you are well and have a job and are not hungry. With all our blessing and prayers; yours Mum and Dad."*

I had a glad feeling and my steps were lighter as I went back to work. We were in touch again. I was full of joy, and the sheep shearing was done without my injuring myself. We picked the lambs for the special Lairg lamb sale. I then learned that if you ask a farmer about prices and he says "not bad" he really means "pretty good". All our men are having their holidays. I thought they settled down well, at least we hoped so. The staff took their annual holiday before the harvest, and David bought a second hand Land Rover, like the US Jeep, from Corbett, the builder. This is the ideal vehicle for farm work and David made sure I learned to drive, in the field at first of course. I have no licence yet. This was not difficult, for I had driven American jeeps at Fort Bliss, remember? Mr Corbett the local Building Contractor came to view the gutted building at Viewfield. In time his drawing of the new steading arrived for David to have a look at it, making sure I too had a look at it. I studied it at great length because this was the first time I have seen a professional drawing. With David's approval an estimate is expected soon.

Miss Ella must have given some thought to my Dad's letter and asked me one evening if I thought they would accept some of her parents' warm woollen underwear that had never been worn? I wrote to Mum and Dad asking if they were permitted to receive parcels and, after the usual lengthy delay Dad wrote that parcels were allowed and there was every chance they would receive them. Miss Ella's kind offer was accepted and she and I got together items that would make the permitted weight. I wrapped the parcel carefully and posted it with my blessing and hope that it would arrive safe and sound. In those days you took chances, but life without hope is not worth much. Weeks later we received a moving letter of thanks to Miss Ella. Dad's letter of thanks to Miss Ella was one of his special ones. In time other parcels made their way from the Scottish Highlands to distant 'Polish Silesia'. It was clear that Miss Ella got great satisfaction out of Dad's grateful letters. Young, energetic and the weight of uncertainty about my family now lifted, I was ready to play my part, firm in the knowledge that all the terrible things done by Nazi Germany were not held against me personally, I looked forward to the start of harvest with our new 'crew'.

Fate decided to intervene with a letter for David and one for me informing us that my repatriation was to take effect from November 1947, in three months' time. An addendum indicated that if both parties agreed, I as a prisoner of war may be given permission to stay and will become a civilian on the given date. In the meantime, I had to provide the authorities with a written address of where in Germany I was to be sent. A joy for most undoubtedly, but a dilemma for me? Should it be? Or do I know the answer, or am I sitting between two stools?

# Chapter 9

# Demobilised and content to be in Tain, Scotland

To be absolutely frank to myself and to my readers, my initial feelings were to stay on. As I began to think, I asked myself, why the hesitation? It occurred to me could it be that the fact that by now I was living in a family environment, created by two kind people, David and Miss Ella. It would undoubtedly have been different, were I to lodge in a farm cottage fending for oneself. My so called 'adopted parents' were happy for me to be going home, but said I would be welcome to stay, if that was what I wanted. I asked to be given time for me to write to Engelbert to let me have a non-emotional answer in regards to my being able to get a position at a post office. Also, could I find suitable lodgings in his town or district? I knew they themselves were short of much. I indicated that if his answers were negative, then I had already been offered work and a home at Viewfield.

Engelbert's answer arrived within two weeks. He said that he wrote unemotionally, that priority for employment with the Post Office was for the time being for former employees with families or for invalided veterans. Qualifying numbers had been increased by the influx of many thousands of refugees from Silesia. Accommodation was difficult to find unless one took a job in the countryside. While the family would love to see me, I would have to work at whatever I could find and try to find a place to stay. Obviously Engelbert would help in that matter. The situation was in fact a lot worse than Engelbert described. With this knowledge, I decided to ask if I might stay with David and Miss Ella and was left in no doubt that they would indeed be happy for me to do so. That was to prove some time later to have been for me, what I like to call, a 'monumental' decision!

David and I wrote our letters recording our decision that I would like to stay in Scotland UK and would accept Mr David Munro's offer to be taken on as his employee. David wrote that I would become a registered employee. As such I would receive the going rate for a farm worker and be covered by National Insurance. I would also be given accommodation within the employer's private residence. Both of us waited now for the official reply, this would come from the offices for Agriculture in the County town of Dingwall. The demobilisation was a matter for the Government and Military Offices. When reporting at the camp my sergeant knew already of the situation and was curious if I had made a decision yet? My answer was yes and that made him shake my hand. This was part of my dilemma. You may remember my soft feeling when the English soldiers, pardon, I now know they were Scottish soldiers who collected their Red Cross parcels.

Workers' hours did no longer mean anything to me at Viewfield. If you feel being treated as an adopted son you act like one. I consider that from now on, my Military and POW life had come to an end. I have been treated with fairness and human respect, which alas some of my people had totally ignored, to my shame.

I had a home and work I enjoy and was once more a normal human, free to go wherever I wished. That was a wonderful realisation. All would become fact once the official formalities were completed and the official letter would arrive. Meanwhile, more important there was harvest to be gathered. This should be interesting with five of us now on the field. The old tractor has been serviced and cleaned ready for driving away. David had bought a good used trailer which will now be necessary. Jim our 'grieve' {foreman}, will build one stack while Peter our cattleman and the oldest in our team will build the other stack. Now we were a team of five in the fields. David will drive the other tractor. It was time to bring the sheaves of grain to the place where the stacks were to be built. It requires one on the trailer with his fork throwing one sheaf at a time to the stacks. To toss a sheaf correctly requires practice, it should land right beside the kneeling builder, or there will be a complaint, or bad language. I volunteered to toss sheaves to Peter the cattleman, and we worked well together. I had watched Peter all day, while at the same time concentrating that I could place each sheaf as neatly beside Peter as possible. We reversed roles the next day. Peter was in his late forties or early fifties, and building stacks was the more difficult job. Your first stack may resemble the leaning Tower of Pisa, Peter was quick in calling if I should get out of plumb. If you have some idea of a plumb-line you quickly learn, which I was desperate to do. Of course I did have a head start at Viewfield the previous year. With that harvest completed, the potato harvest got into full swing. The former tenant had an auctioneer engaged to value the potato crop while still in the ground. David and the former tenant have agreed on the auctioneer's valuation and left the potatoes for us to harvest and the later sale. It will prolong harvesting the additional potatoes, but it will also provide greater earnings for the children and adult pickers from town. This was the first autumn harvest on the enlarged farm.

Our working routine was well established. When I had completed morning milking, I made my way to the dairy room. I sieved the milk and filled the milk pails for Jim the grieve and Peter, also the other tractor driver Dave had his breakfast and then left by car with the milk pails for Mansfield farm. David will discuss the order of the day with Jim and the others. I was free to do any other job requiring attention at Viewfield or to join the rest of the team in the fields till it was time to return for evening milking. I used my bicycle when convenient.

A letter arrived for David in early November. He was to take me to the Department of Agriculture office in Dingwall for my official registration as his employee. Formalities completed, I received a government form to take to the local police station. We returned to Mansfield farm and I went across the street to the police station to see Inspector Fraser in the office. By now I was well known to him, and for the right reasons! I knocked at the door and greeted the inspector, and handed him the form. He studied the form, signed it and smiled while shaking my hand, he wished me well. I walked across the street and found David talking to Peter our cattleman and we drove home in time for dinner. Miss Ella was clearly happy to look at the form which said I was a civilian again. An official form from the authorities will follow. It was another major landmark in my life, and all three of us enjoyed dinner. I was no longer a prisoner of war! Frankly, I had not felt like one for a year.

My wages did enable me to purchase tea and coffee and other useful items to send to my brother and Aunt Else in Wildeshausen, and my parents. I knew they could, if they wished, use them as barter for other essentials. This may interest some of you, in 1947 a loaf of bread here in Scotland cost eleven pennies {twelve pennies in a shilling}, and petrol was four shillings a gallon. My wage then was four pounds and fifty shillings per week. I had no deduction for income tax, nor did David deduct anything for food and board. I was able to save all my pay. And yes, I refused every cigarette I was offered.

Before Christmas-time, now that I could 'roam' about free in the country, I asked Miss Ella to try and enquire if there are any Catholics in town, which she was happy to do while in town to do her shopping. Miss Ella had on occasion a reason to go to the Chocolate Shop, of which the owner was Mr Pieraccini, an Italian. Miss Ella simply made for the shop and Mr Pieraccini was happy to oblige and told Miss Ella that apart from himself there was the dental technician, Mr Louis Bain, whose house is the cottage next to the Royal Hotel. Miss Ella was delighted to bring me the news. I wasted no time after supper and cycled down and found the cottage. I knocked at the door and introduced myself, I was invited to come in and meet Mrs Bain. In brief, Mr Bain was happy that with me there are now three Catholics in town, and the times for service are on the first Sunday of each month ten o'clock at the chapel in Invergordon. Christmas Eve Midnight Mass was at St. Lawrence in Dingwall, the county town. I thanked them both and promised I would call again.

In regards to our repatriation to Germany and the number of my fellow POWs, I have no idea how many there are around the Tain area who wished to stay. Some will look for employment with the contractors who are building the new Hydro Electric Power stations, earning higher wages with lots of overtime shifts. That does not appeal to me. Two weeks before Christmas the official signed forms from the Government have arrived, which also included the notice and time table for our official repatriation to Germany in early January.

It means that every German POW will be repatriated to Germany. Those who have signed the contract form to come back will be issued with the return ticket form at the official office at the German border.

**'Myself in UK de-mob suit Tain 1947'**

**'My POW camp Kildary, Ross-shire 1946-1947'**

We all had received our 'demob' suits last week at our camp. Very smart double breasted herring bone pattern, grey, and quality cloth. I did not waste time and made an appointment with the local photographer, Mr MacLeod at the Grove, High Street, to be photographed that I may send photographs to my parents and other family members, as they might not recognise me!

The integration of Viewfield and Mansfield had been accomplished smoothly and the whole team had bonded easily. I do not remember the exact circumstances, but one day Miss Ella asked me to end formality, insisting I was to call her simply 'Ella' and it felt so natural now, to my surprise.

Now free to travel, I cycled to Invergordon for 10 o'clock Mass on every first Sunday of the month. Having milked the cows and fed the animals, I washed and was ready to leave home by 9a.m. It was a twelve mile journey each way on a level road, apart from a one mile uphill on my way home. On coming home by 12 noon, Ella's homemade girdle scones, and our own butter, 'Lyle's' golden syrup and Camp coffee never tasted better!

As I had already found out that Christmas is not celebrated in Scotland, I took my bicycle to the station to enquire about train times. There was the evening train to Dingwall, the Ross-shire county town, but I would have to wait after Midnight Mass for the first train in the morning at 6.30. I had ample time before Midnight Mass. As far as Catholics are concerned, we are in a Diaspora. We had a wonderful service, and the church was almost full. In my thoughts I was many times at home. Only one hour separated us. I felt great. After the Christmas Mass, the parish priest, Rev. Father Stuart welcomed me, asked where I came from and wished me a happy Christmas in fluent German and looked forward to see me on the first Sundays of the Month at Invergordon. We bade each other goodnight and parted. I was aware that the last train north left Dingwall Station at 10.30 p.m. I just walked the streets of Dingwall which were relatively quiet. I returned to the church and fell asleep on the steps. I was still a shy boy but happy. The night was unusually warm, and I found the time passed relatively in comfort. I made my way to the station and arrived in Tain a happy man in time for the milking. I managed not to tell anyone how I passed the time. That Christmas stayed as a permanent memory in my mind. Actually I had my Christmas Day as a holiday, by not doing any other work apart from feeding my animals double rations. I got a 'kick' out of knowing my animals too enjoyed

Christmas. Instead, here in Scotland New Year is a two-day holiday event. Should a Sunday fall between the two days, then you still get your two days off work!

Let me tell you a true in every sense Christmas story here in North Scotland. The Presbyterian Minister of the church that was only two miles from our POW camp spoke fluent German and took to visiting the camp and spoke to the boys, and asked would they like to come to his church on Christmas Day and sing a few German carols during the service? The reaction was positive and that's what happened to the enjoyment of the congregation who had a fine table with food prepared afterwards.

Ella's elder sister is married to a local farmer, Mr Fraser whose farmstead is only three miles west of Tain. It is a long standing arrangement that Mr Fraser would bring his wife on Saturday evenings to Viewfield. He himself would go back to his home and return a couple or so hours later, in time to join for the tea that Ella provided. I am of course expected to take part, and not simply because I insist on doing the dishes afterwards. The benefit as far as I am concerned is my ear was exposed to more variety of voices. Of course I am being asked to join in the conversation when appropriate. I would spend a certain time in my room writing or reading before returning to the kitchen in time to help set up the table for tea, Mr Fraser would have arrived, while the conversation continued. Naturally, I would clear up after and do the washing up.

It's January 1948, just after New Year a letter has arrived from the Authority regarding our repatriation to Germany. We are to be at Dingwall railway station on the 20th of January. David had received a copy of my letter. There was some excitement in Viewfield. In the meantime it was work as usual. The weather in January had been much milder than last year. My life was settled and there was much joy in the house when my parents' letter arrived, full of thankful words prayers and good wishes to Ella and David. Dad would love to come over and help on the farm. They gave thanks in church for such needed goods, having lost everything. Later in the evening our conversation concentrated on my return to Germany. For a start David insisted on driving me to Dingwall. Those of us who will return will be issued with a return ticket at Harwich where we will leave and return.

My only concern was to assure David and Ella that I was grateful for their kindness and they were happy to welcome me back to Viewfield. It was a clear understanding between us and no further words were needed. All our attention concerning Ella and I was what could they gave me to take with me, and what is there that I should buy and fill my case with. I had of course my US Army kit bag, but to take a small suitcase might also be useful. Ella still thought about her parent's clothing. Could I take some with me and send them from Germany to Poland? It did make sense and I took a small parcel with me to Germany. In the meantime at Viewfield, the conversation turned often to the anticipated possible sale of Mansfield House. David and Ella would be told by the solicitor as soon as a buyer had been found.

My time for repatriation to Germany arrived. It was my intention to take the minimum of clothes for me in order to have more room for all the useful items for my brother Engelbert, and especially for my Aunt Else and her family, not forgetting sweets and chocolate for the little ones. The day has arrived to say goodbye to Ella with my promise to return as promised. The employer was asked to accompany the former POW who opted to return to Britain, to Dingwall. We met at the station where a number of us had arrived. The Official from the Department of Agriculture was ready to check us out who intended to return and exchange a paper with our employer. One other Government official checked us out to confirm all were present and correct. It was time to say goodbye to David who left to go back home. Time for us ex POWs to board our reserved compartment on the normal train to Inverness where we joined a larger group of ex POWs. Checked out again we boarded our two carriages attached to the normal passenger train to Aberdeen on the east coast. Entering Aberdeen we realised that it was a large city. This time we had some military guides to check and put us in order. It was clear that the numbers of us now swelled to require a special train of five carriages, to which we were guided to board and take our seat. I sat with the others of our Dingwall and Tain group.

Within some fifteen minutes, we were on our way to Harwich in southern England. It should not be a surprise that I was more interested in our travel than playing cards in which I have little interest and would frustrate my partner. I had long studied Britain's Geography and could follow our journey. It had to be passing through Edinburgh, which happened through the night. More of a pity was having missed the fantastic Forth Rail Bridge. Why was I so fascinated? Because we had an eight by six inch picture at home of it and I used to look at it often. I never dreamed that I might ever see it, but now the possibility is there on my return journey. On a long journey like this it is almost impossible not to succumb to sleep. The longer nights in the middle of winter add to it. Although most of us had brought a sandwich, the appearance of coffee or tea with rolls in the morning was welcome. Being a special train it should mean fewer stoppages at stations, meaning we will arrive in time to board the mid-day ferry to Holland, that being my guess. That is what happened as the train came to a halt at the seaside terminal. On disembarkation we lined up in military order and answered when our name was called. A boarding ticket was handed and officials led us to the boat, not having been on one since we arrived from the US at Liverpool two years previously.

Without any delay we sailed out once more for a six hour trip to arrive at The Hook of Holland. Disembarking and count all present and correct we were led to the carriages that will take us to the German town of Bentheim just over the border. This is for many of us a first look at Holland something new to enter in our travel book. Not many had wasted time to have a snooze on board ship and like me had enjoyed the sea and walk round the ferryboat. The six hour crossing passed quickly and by midnight we reached the German town of Bentheim and we are back on German soil. At one stage I had expected a possible shout of 'Hurrah' being back on German soil again, but that was not in any of our thoughts apparently. Why? I suppose everyone had thoughts of meeting our loved ones once again. End of journey, and a march to the garrison for the final line up at the desk where everything will be sorted out. Here now we met for the first time the new post-war German officials, together with the British representative. Once the count proved correct we were led to the comfort and rest rooms and refreshments until eight in the morning when a wakeup call will be heard.

It has been a long journey and we enjoyed our German breakfast again. I hasten to add this not to belittle British or rather the Scots porridge breakfast. Now the serious side with a few official Recorders taking our names, former home and present addresses, name and address of parents or relatives to which we hope to go. Those of us who will be going back to Britain were guided to the appropriate desk, where everything was sorted and our return tickets to this place. It is possible that some may change their minds and will not return. The Recorder then sends you to the appropriate desk where you will get your travel ticket to the nearest station of the address you wish to go to. We then were given our official travel ticket to the nearest station. I made my way to the station and awaited the train I was advised to take. My journey took me to the north German town of Wildeshausen at which I was told I should arrive by lunch time, a mere two and a half hours travel. The country side is fairly flat and in the main agriculture. Having asked the guard if I am on the right train, he assured me I am, and in twenty minutes it will be Wildeshausen. And he was right as the train slowed down I read the station sign and prepared to leave the train. I had to ask the station guard the direction to Deeken Strasse. I thanked him and I was on my way. One more question for direction and I stood before Aunt Else's door and knocked. When it opened, one look at me and Aunt Else flew at me to welcome me with a long hug and tears rolled from both of us. Aunt Else had already prepared lunch for her three children returning from school. Although they expected me they had never seen me. Lunch was stretched to include me but seeing the situation, I suddenly did not feel hungry. Later I opened my case and gave Aunt Else the goodies it contained for the children. In a small way I was discovering what life was like for refugees from Silesia. Having lived through traumatic times, it's not easy to look unmoved at things one has not seen before. The children were most appreciative. Fredrick the oldest, now almost ten years old, is followed by his two younger sisters Hildegard and Rosemarie. As a reminder these were Aunt Else's adopted children whose mother died while they were very young. Uncle Theo their father, met Aunt Else through a family friend of his. Uncle Theo was twenty years older than me, and had also been called up at the beginning of the war and was desperate to find a mother for his three children.

Returning from work Uncle Theo was delighted to see me, and since we had never met before welcomed me with open arms. Uncle Theo was always appreciative of Engelbert, who was allowed by the Polish authorities to accompany Aunt Else because of her three adopted very young children, when forcefully deported from Silesia to Germany here in Wildeshausen, while Uncle Theo was still a POW. The house they live in is owned by an unmarried middle aged farmer. He himself lives on the upper floor of this house. Aunt Else and family were allocated to live down stairs with a good sized kitchen, a smaller bedroom and Engelbert in a small former storeroom. Engelbert has cleaned and repainted it. There is room for Engelbert and myself to sleep in. The kitchen is indeed a busy place while I am here. Uncle Theo with a family and elder age was given a job as a Postal mail deliverer. My brother Engelbert had been fortunate to have met at church the owner of the local printing firm. A chance conversation with Engelbert when he mentioned his few months at the printing firm at the old home, led to the offer of an apprenticeship in Herr Klein's printing firm.

After an apprenticeship, Engelbert managed to qualify to study at a college to gain a degree which in the end secured him a management job in one of West Germany's best daily subscription newspapers, the WAZ. Having looked around the town during the next day or two I mentioned to Engelbert my concern regarding the old cooker Aunt Else has to cook on for a large family. Now including me, albeit for only three weeks. It was one evening I asked Engelbert to go with me to town and have a look at a shop-window where there was a stove on display. He agreed and we made our way, while I was not sure on which street I happened to see it. Engelbert knew immediately and while we looked at it I asked Engelbert would that be the sort of cooker that would make a difference? Without any hesitation he could confirm that it would, and I in return mentioned that it would give me great pleasure to buy it for Aunt Else. I still had my 95 US dollars and my English pound notes both of which had a great value over the then German mark. There was an opportunity to speak to Uncle Theo in regards to the cooker, without giving anything away to Aunt Else. Uncle Theo's deliveries finished in the early afternoon and that is when we will go and call at the shop. Which we did and I asked

Uncle Theo to tell me if that particular stove would be the right one? The shop owner did his best to assure us what the cooker will do and that there was a guarantee. The price was mentioned and I had figured that if I showed my Dollars there might well be a good deal in it. I took my 95 dollars out and held it before him. I said go ahead count them. He gave me five dollars back, and we shook hands. It would be delivered tomorrow. It was one of those enamelled white and black cookers with an oven. According to the master it is the latest of the new improved models just before the war. We had to get permission from the landlord who was very helpful and wished us good luck. Aunt Else could not believe it at first, when the delivery came next day to fit the stove in. It was pleasant for me to see Aunt Else's look of thanks.

I had no difficulty in passing the time in Wildeshausen, for during the day I tended to explore the town, which had suffered very little damage as any resistance was hopeless as the war was about to finish. The surrounding countryside is practically flat. In our old home we had a more beautiful undulating countryside. Although it was the end of January the temperature was mild, and free of snow and ice. The absence of snow made it pleasant to explore on foot. Engelbert had arranged for Uncle Anton, mother's youngest brother to come and visit us when our sister Ursula is here. He had asked to let him know when I would be here, and we should expect him in a day or two. Uncle Anton, you might recall, had worked at the Volkswagen Factory and had been called up just at the end of the war and released at a small town near the Dutch border. His friend had a small farm. On their demob the farmer, knowing Anton could not go back to Silesia asked him if he would like to come and work on his friend's farm. Anton had no other place to go to and accepted the offer, and found a kind home and work. He did not marry either.

We still have something pleasant to look forward to when our sister Ursula is expected to come to Wildeshausen for our much looked forward reunion. Engelbert had found a place for Ursula to stay. Ursula is now in her preparatory semester as a primary school teacher down in Munich. In the meantime Engelbert and Aunt Else's friends across the street, who are also farmers, invited them and me to join them on Friday evening at their favourite 'Gasthaus' pub in town. Aunt Else was pleased about that and hoped we would have a pleasant time. Friday evening Engelbert and I made our way to the Gasthaus where the friends had reserved our seat and table. Engelbert warned me that I would be offered more than I could consume without beginning to feel unsteady.

I thought it to be wise not to put on my demob suit, since spillage is possible. We arrived at the place and Engelbert soon found their table. We greeted and I was introduced to many. The mood was already in full happy swing. With Engelbert being here more than a year, the numbers that greeted him followed that I would shake hands with many whose names I would not remember. The waitresses were busy and the music being played includes many old tunes that are still familiar with a mixture of the latest in jazz. I did not have to get up to invite a lady to dance as there were males and females who wanted to know where my home was. Where do I live now, and if so how did I get there to Scotland? Followed by the sure fire question what do the Scots wear under the kilt!

I wondered how long before I would have to get up and invite a lady to dance, I have tried to spot the lady that did not sweep round the dance floor eyes closed as in a dream. I could not prolong it to get up as everybody on our table is on the floor, pointing to certain ladies as they twirl around on the floor. Courage brother, you have to try, which I did and got away with what I could do, explaining that I play music for dancing, the cause of my poor dancing. At least in style I could bring the lady to her seat and not forgetting to thank her boyfriend for the permission given to dance with his lady.

I had hardly sat down when the announcement was 'Ladies Choice'. I saw it coming when one of the ladies seemed to walk towards me, surely she could not have seen me on the floor at the last dance, there was no escape route left but to get up and offer the lady my arm and on the music went. Another Strauss waltz, actually it went better than expected, but oh dear, to look at those who dance every week. At the end I returned the lady to her table and her companion, said the formalities and returned to our table. Some of our company thought I did well. It was an act of bravery. Actually rhythm and timing has never been my problem, it is the coordination of my feet that require practice when I return to Scotland.

As the evening wore on I had very few more dances as people kept filling my glasses. Finally I was in need to make my way to the gent's rest room, oh dear. I hear Engelbert's voice; watch how much, but too late. Now there was only one thing I could do just walk out and try to get home, how to find my home here was the question, how I found Aunt Else's home after a mile walk, was the great miracle. Thank goodness I found the right bed. I never heard anyone come home. I still ponder over it, after all those years ago. I slept the sleep of fairies. How did I find my way home was the question next day, "led by my guardian angel" I replied. I did sleep past breakfast time and enjoyed my coffee and had no longer after-effects. Tomorrow it is Sunday and it will be a larger family with me being here, as we decided to go together to the same Mass.

This is the first time in church in Wildeshausen, and I was amazed at how many people of our former home town Gross Strehlitz have been at church. Now settled here, all that must have been a colossal undertaking for the authorities to accommodate several million refugees from eastern Germany. Engelbert said many locals were not pleased to have us come here, but that is past now.

Even before we came close to the church there were the odd family or single person who recognised Engelbert and were from our home area and much handshaking followed when I was introduced and some actually remember me as the young altar-boy and others from the Post Office. It was wonderful to meet and recognise each other. It extended even longer after the service. It was a mixed feeling with Scotland far away from here. At long last it was time to go home and enjoy breakfast together. After breakfast I asked if I can help but there was no room for all of us. Aunt Else was warning us that it is going to take another week to get to know the new cooker. That was the least we worried about. It was a good time for me to go for a walk with my new little cousins who were enjoying taking me for a walk.

It also gave me an opportunity to speak more German; at the same time we had fun to teach them some easy words in English which they found interesting since they are now in their second class or above. Neither were they shy to ask me questions regarding the difference between Scotland and England. We arrived home for lunch at the right time with a mixed wafting aroma of soup and gravy. Aunt Else certainly had earned our applause. She in turn thanked me for the cooker. The gentleman owner had given half of the house garden to Uncle Theo and Aunt Else to cultivate for vegetables and fruit. That was a great help to supplement their food ration which was still in operation in Germany for certain items at that time. After coffee time Engelbert and I went for a walk, the weather being kind whilst in Silesia our old home may have lots of snow now. There had not been a letter for Engelbert from our parents, although they know that I and Engelbert are together at last after five years. More important than anything is the fact we and our parents are blessed to be alive after all that trauma and anxiety for each other. We both spend the evening writing a note to our parents, which they will be pleased to receive.

While Engelbert will be at work I will try and make myself useful in whatever way I can. In the meantime I will go into town and purchase a few cards to send one especially to David and Ella. They might well wonder how I was received and also whether in time may change my mind and not go back to Scotland? A legitimate question surely, but that I cannot see for the time being. Therefore a few postcards will confirm that I will be back. In the meantime we are all looking forward towards our sister Ursula coming for our so called reunion, none more so than myself. It was my privilege to meet Ursula at the station. I gave myself sufficient time to walk along the platform. Wildeshausen is not on a mainline therefore single track line. Time is up and German time keeping is working again. And there she is our sister Ursula, I see little change but of course she might have grown in every way from fourteen years old to nearly twenty now. Well, here at last we are embracing without words from both of us. "Grüss Dich Gott", "God greet you", and at last here we are looking at each other and no other words will come out. Before we cover a hundred steps we are exchanging words that closed the ring of a five year separation. Sadly not at our home which we left in hope, alas it was not to be. As the good Lord says, we are only 'guests here on earth'. Ursula has become a lady of twenty years, and seemed joyful. We walked and talked about everything but not in detail, it seems that is common if you have not seen each other for a number of years, everything wants to come out at once. We passed through the town and are on the last half mile to Aunt Else's home. The welcome for all those who passed through a traumatic time is and has to be emotional for both parties to get out of your system what has been fixed in you and waiting for the opportunity to be released. Aunt Else and the children were at home to welcome Ursula, who had seen them on what was for all of them the last Christmas. That wonderful moment which is still being replayed as those who are still held in Russian camps are released at a very slow pace.

**'Germany, January 1948 –family reunion with Ursula and Engelbert, our first since I left home in 1943'**

It is Uncle Theo who arrives home first with Engelbert following by 5.30pm. I was absolutely happy to be just sitting and listening what everybody had to say, simply because I have not been at home when matters of war became the nightmare that had been prophesied by many in secret and under the threat of instant death. Our sister Ursula had been evacuated to a convent school in Bavaria before the Russian front entered our Silesia. During the week that Ursula stayed here, I had many conversations with her while Engelbert was at work. I had to tell her my story and my present plan to stay with my adopted Scottish family. Ursula is hopeful to become a teaching nun for classes one to four. She is being trained at a convent in Munich by nuns according to the national official training certificate. Final examination is by a Government inspector. Now I know exactly what I have to pray for. During the conversation with Ursula I was able to detect that she has it clear in her mind what is before her and what her aim is. Our Mum in her letters to Ursula has given her strict instruction not to become a nun simply to please Mum, which is the last thing Mum would want. I too was extremely satisfied to have had that talk with Ursula while we had the chance. However, I could not bring our conversation to an end without enquiring what happened to our sister's dream of becoming a film star when she was fourteen? She who was always leading her friends to play acting, and ordering them about. But then that dream too collapsed.

While Ursula was still with us, Engelbert had invited our Uncle Anton, Mum's youngest brother who lived at a farm near the Dutch border to join us. One can understand that for him it was an honour to be invited to come over to Wildeshausen and 'kill two birds' meeting both Ursula and myself. Uncle Anton often spent some time with us when we were at the castle. We exchanged a lot of stories and experiences. Uncle Anton wanted to know all about Scotland and what I was doing, with Ursula enjoying listening and asking question after question. Anton too found my story quite interesting. Our Mum too will be happy to know that her brother spent time with all of us. The weekend passed so quickly and we said goodbye to Uncle Anton and thanked him for taking the time to visit us, and hoping to see each other sometime soon. Within a few days it was time to bid farewell to our sister Ursula also. I was hoping to see all of them sometime again now that we have met at last. I will be leaving my folks as a free man again, with hope that we will see each other. Now it was my turn to say 'Auf Wiedersehen', goodbye. There was every reason to hope that we will see each other again.

We had a real good last evening including toasting each other and Aunt Else thanking me for the multi-plate and coal fired cooker which also heats the kitchen, with coal being relatively cheap in Germany. While I was there a few items were taken off the food coupons, slowly the country will get back onto its feet again. Together we thanked the Almighty, for we really have been blessed. And we remembered those in our wider family who had to give their life for nothing. I encouraged Engelbert to prepare to come to Scotland to visit me, and wished him all the success in his apprenticeship. After a good sleep it was my time to get up, dress, have the breakfast Aunt Else cooked and then the farewells. Engelbert and I said our goodbye and God be with you on your journey. Our sister Ursula accompanied me to the station. We had purposely gone early to the station to have more time to talk. If Ursula's plan comes to fruition then I will come to her great day in three years time. The train approached the station, stopped and I boarded to open the window and kept waving until we both faded into the distance.

Arriving at our German border town Bentheim it was back to the office where we have received our train ticket to 'The Hook' for embarkation to Harwich. With the formalities over we were asked to sit in the canteen and refreshments were free for us. I seemed to have been one of the earliest who will return to the UK. Less than a third appeared to return to the UK. Time to board the train for the Hook of Holland and the night ferry to England. Crossing the channel was good and on arrival at Harwich it was back to the hall where the formalities took place 3 weeks earlier. It transpired that there were actually over twenty of us who will travel to Inverness with a number to eastern Scotland.

Having arrived in London we boarded the night train to Inverness. Those travelling east will change at Edinburgh. An uneventful and restful journey and typical February weather awaited us in Inverness. There was no snow and a watery sun was rising as we changed and made our way to the north train, arriving an hour later in Tain, now my home. What I had to do was to bring my case and bag up to our

Mansfield farm where David or I will pick it up later. A brisk walk a mile and a bit took me to Viewfield where I arrived just before lunch and knocked at the door purposely to surprise Ella who wide-eyed received me with a hug and happy to see me as I had promised.

We talked intermittently while Ella continued cooking their lunch. At the same time, against my pleading she added what-ever now to have sufficient for the three of us. While I sat and kept Ella entertained with all of my news from one to another, David walked in with my case. He had called at Mansfield after me and was told by Peter that it was my case and I have arrived home. I liked that, 'arrived home'! Thus life at Viewfield fell into its normal routine. Here we were again all three of us at lunch and all three of us trying to tell our news and asking questions. After lunch I was the first off the table determined to wash the dishes which I did before taking my case up and changing into working attire. I came down with my few gifts from Germany. For Ella among some other small items a silk scarf with a German pattern, and for David a carved black horse, and there had been a few small items given by Aunt Else's children. Although small, it was appreciated.

It was only natural that I would change into my working clothes to do the evening milking and the usual routine. After supper there were a number of questions and we ensured that David could join in. I had important messages of thanks from my people for all the goodies Ella had given for my people.

Ella and David wanted to tell me that the uncertainty regarding the sale of Mansfield House had finally been resolved when David received a call from his solicitor that it had been sold. That was interesting news indeed. David received confirmation that a Mr and Mrs McDougall the new owners were hoteliers from the Scottish Borders and would move in within the next few months. This is my short description of Mansfield House. The main entrance to the grounds is a short mile from the town centre. Two wrought iron gates six feet by ten feet high were fixed to two sandstone pillars, and each pillar had an eagle on top. The oval shaped drive-way leads to the main entrance. It is a two storey house with two rooms above the second floor creating a tower impression on which is raised a flagpole.

It was a private residence to one of Tain's worthy members. Mansfield House stands on eight acres of ground. It's worth mentioning that Tain Hill is blessed with a quarry for fine yellow with the occasional reddish sandstone. Almost all pre-war buildings in Tain are of Tain sandstone. Quarrying ceased before the war.

During the war Mansfield House was occupied by a detachment of the Norwegian Brigade, and visited by the then King. After the war a large detachment of Polish Brigade were housed in corrugated barracks on Mansfield ground next to the mansion house, while the officers were accommodated in the mansion itself. The Polish detachment left before the sale.

Important to point out that Mansfield House and its grounds are now surrounded by our Mansfield farmlands. David noticed one day passing that a removal van was unloading at the mansion, assuming that the McDougalls are moving in. Telling us at lunchtime we took it as interesting news. Life at Viewfield is in great spirits all working together. Lambing, sowing grain and the fun planting potatoes with me getting to know the plant names and my English improving by the week. What I find on reflection in the fields amongst the animals is my sheer contentment. My visit to Germany and the establishment of a real family circle after those horrible years. Yes it does include our parents, although still separated by political borders but connected by the written word. A few days later David was passing the back of Mansfield, saw a gentleman walking about and stopped, assuming it to be Mr McDougall. David spoke and wished him a good day and the introduction followed. The gentleman was indeed Mr McDougall. Both men were interested in each other. During their conversation, Mrs McDougall also came out and both were delighted to have met their neighbours. On parting, Mrs McDougall offered an invitation for David and his sister to come down one evening, soon.

Within the week Mrs McDougall had phoned Viewfield to ask if Ella would come down with David for a chat. An evening had been arranged and while David declined to go, because of his difficulty in hearing asked Ella to take me with her. That is how it all began! I drove the car and we arrived at the front door thinking it is more appropriate. Mrs McDougall came to the door and Ella introduced herself and me as the German who is living in Viewfield. Mrs McDougall seemed quite happy and thought I would be good company for her husband. Having met them and introduced each other, we chatted together around all the preliminaries, as I called it. Mr McDougall suggested the two of us men to go in the small sitting room which turned out to be a small bar. The two of us got rather quickly into a conversation because for a start he had been a regular in the army for ten years before the war. There was topic number one, while Mr McDougall went to fetch the whisky for us. We got on in great style, I tried to sip my whisky very slowly, and a very amiable time we spent, never running out of topics. That was when Mrs McDougall called us for tea. On leaving, the invitation to come again soon was genuine.

Ella taking the passenger seat right away left me to drive the mile long quiet road to Viewfield. Ella informed me right away that the McDougall's intention is to turn the house into a hotel, of which the town had a need. Before leaving we were shown briefly round the house and I was very impressed by the immaculate and beautiful woodwork. The building reminded me greatly of our castle in Gross Strehlitz. On our way out I talked about our castle. Mr and Mrs McDougall listened with interest, especially when I spoke about my family's service with the nobility.

We did visit the McDougalls almost every three weeks. Naturally, visits to Mansfield House were less frequent as the summer season approached and the farm began to demand more time. Important to mention is that the building of our new farm building is progressing, not at the speed I expected. Apparently it is a kind of local sickness occasionally leaving to go and start somewhere else. Lambing always presented difficult moments which sometimes required the vet's help. I recall the occasion when David was absent, overseeing progress at Mansfield, and I needed help with a troubled ewe. Mr Sutherland the vet arrived and his examination established that the lamb intended to exit the wrong way round. He knew of my keen interest in animal husbandry and had previously shown me how to deal with lesser problems. This day was no different until he unexpectedly ordered me "Paul, roll up your sleeve, scrub your arm and do exactly as I tell you".

I did as instructed and gently entered the sheep's womb until I felt the lamb, and guided by the vet I turned the little one back to front and he or she soon saw daylight, it was a female. Soon it was cleaned by its mother and suckling. This was yet another occasion when people went out of their way to teach me skills I never thought I would learn. I did feel a bit proud of myself, and thanked Mr Sutherland. Animals on the farm are alive, and other health problems do occur. If you can solve it then it leaves you with a wonderful feeling. It is not just nailing a loose board back again.

Lambing season finished. Potatoes planted, and sheep shorn. I felt confident that my farming apprenticeship was just about complete. David had hardly any need to tell me what needed to be done, and I shared in domestic tasks too. One summer day I remember I came upon Ella about to tread blankets in a galvanised tub at the front door where nobody ever comes. It seemed too strenuous a job for a lady and before you could say "Amen" my shoes and socks were off and I felt brave enough to lift Ella out of the tub and put her on the mat and I was enjoying stamping away in the suds. Afterwards she and I put the blankets through the hand-operated wringer, still no electricity at Viewfield yet. Who else remembers that annual chore? It was my job until electricity became available.

Corresponding with our parents in Poland is still a two week journey one way, but at least letters are arriving. Now that Silesia had been claimed entirely by Poland and democratic government had been replaced by a Communist regime, one wonders how the population is going to react to it. However, there was some good news from our parents. When the new Polish priest in our old parish church heard that Dad, a regular attendant at church, had been employed as housemaster and butler, he offered him the job of full-time sexton. Dad's smart appearance and experience would certainly be an 'asset' to the parish. He was happy to accept the offer, because the job included a comfortable flat, within a house beside the church. This would make a marked improvement in my parents' standard of living, although, and Dad would have known that, it requires him to be available at odd hours.

At Viewfield, with all harvesting completed and my corn stacks built solidly and vertically plumb, my own interests were expanding.

There was always a need at the farm that required joinery which caused me to acquire a good book well-designed in drawings and instructions. My interest was further stimulated watching the craftsmen rebuilding our farmstead. It was inevitable that I should look for an equally good masonry book, before I ventured to build our new sheep dipper. In the eyes of David and Ella it was my first masterpiece. The construction of a new and larger concrete sheep-dipper, or you may call it a sheep bath, was desperately required. It is a chemical wash mixed with a lot of water to kill or make harmless any pests which attach themselves to sheep. It is a strict annual Government requirement. My taking over the sheep dipping task from David was much appreciated. I drew up my own design having put sheep through the wash for two years now. It proved a success and I did not get wet anymore.

Listening with growing interest to Scottish Dance music I began to test myself playing on the piano in the house. There were several sheets of Scottish Dance tunes which I tried to learn. Not easy, but through time I got more interested and it resulted in my buying a second hand accordion I saw advertised in our local Ross-shire Journal. How fortunate that there should be a piano here at my adopted parents' home. It was pleasant of Ella telling me how wonderful to hear their piano being played again; it would do well for it. Both David and Ella were pleased to hear me learning Scottish music. For some reason I found playing Scottish tunes on the accordion easy, and I made good progress and kept practising. In the meantime David had arranged for me to pass my Driving Test. On the day Ella came down with me as required. My Test Official took me round the town. Half an hour or more I arrived back and was handed my pass certificate. Ella saw me hold my pass paper and a smile she could not hide. Another achievement in Scotland. I thanked David and he himself was pleased that I had made it. Of course having driven on fields made a difference. It should be an advantage with Mansfield farm almost in the middle of the town.

Another evening visit to Mansfield House, or rather now Hotel had been arranged between Mrs McDougall and Ella. "Well Paul, now that you passed your test, drive me down". This I did in the 1935 green

Morris. After a short introduction Mr McDougall and I retired to the small bar. Declining the offer of a more potent whisky I preferred a beer. We soon found ample material to fill our time. From farming to horses, the army, and a tour of Mansfield House to see the inside. Considering that it had had a number of different military personnel, it was in perfect condition, despite having been used by the military, the Free Norwegian army, and officers from the Cameron Highlanders.

We joined the ladies for tea before leaving for home, but not before Mrs McDougall told us that she had an enquiry regarding a possible forthcoming wedding in the hotel. Having heard about my Dad and his family working in a functioning castle, Mrs McDougall assumed I would be well versed with manners and etiquette and would I not be able to wait at table! Such a suggestion took me by surprise but strangely not perturbed. Surprisingly my presence of mind made me say that I could ask my Dad for some very useful instructions. Mrs McDougall in an instant suggested that I should do that. With that, Ella and I left for home. Of course not before I held the door open for Ella to enter the car, now that I have a British Driving Licence. Ella of course thought it a good idea to ask our Dad. With that we arrived home and I was fast asleep in no time.

An official British driving licence, my personal 'monument' the sheep bath at Viewfield and now the possible promotion to be a waiter in Tain's new hotel, in addition to my frequent appearance in town in connection with our farm, makes me feel I am now a permanent fixture in town. In the mean time I expect a letter from my parents with Dad's instructions regarding my acting as a waiter. Since Mrs McDougall had telephoned the wedding is booked, I made my way down to see the Gents Outfitters, MacKenzie, {a true Scottish name}. As expected, after I introduced myself, the questions were asked, where I live now, and where in Germany? Half way through my explanation Mr MacKenzie stopped me and began to tell where he had been held as a British POW in Germany. It made my hair stand up. Mr MacKenzie was one of the British prisoners who were billeted in rooms of a hospital we had to pass when visiting our Grandma on Sunday afternoons! There they were on the second floor, sitting at the windows, smiling and waving to us as we walked by. I could not believe that Mr MacKenzie was one of those who waved to us. We could not decide who was more surprised while shaking hands. Mr MacKenzie mentioned certain features of the hospital exterior, which removed all doubt that it was the right place. He then enlightened me that their's was the Scottish Highland Battalion that was captured at Dunkirk in 1940. A most unlikely coincidence and I should not be surprised to meet a number of them in town. Perhaps even the one who collected the Red Cross parcel at my Post Office, I had mentioned already. Mr MacKenzie took my measurements, and I should have my outfit in time. Within the month I had my Dad's detailed lesson and advice, and I have two people at home in Viewfield to practise on.

According to David it has been a good harvest with regards to grain and potatoes. So were the returns on lambs and cattle. Before Christmas we will have dressed a few tons of potatoes to send to England, with our 'Golden Wonders' to be best suitable for chips.

Talk about surprises, I had not mentioned it so far regarding Ella and her shopping habit on Tuesday and Friday afternoon driving herself by car. It was on such a day when she met a gentleman whom Ella knew, wishing to speak to her regarding the German that worked at Viewfield, yes, me. Somehow he heard that I have an accordion and am learning to play Scots tunes. Could Ella ask if I would come and visit them with my accordion? Yes, she would ask. Their name was Ross also a typical Scots name. It resulted in my going to call on the family, and introduced myself. A pleasant family with four boys, no daughters, Mrs Ross right away suggested a cup of tea. Well here I was trying the impossible. Mr Ross played the fiddle, and their oldest son Ian, the drums. Shortly after, one other gentleman arrived, who was introduced as Ackie Ross who played the button key accordion. We thought not to waste time and it was first names only. Ackie was far ahead of me regarding Scottish tunes. I played off sheet music of course, Ackie by memory, and played well enough to play at dances. If I could learn from Ackie to play some Scottish tunes and some German Waltzes we could play at a dance in one of the small halls in nearby villages. We had a few weeks' practice and thought we were good enough for the small hall. Actually there was a piano in the hall on which I could play to accompany Ackie. We got applause and managed a good last waltz. On our way home was the next surprise when Ackie asked where my home was. Lo and behold came the next surprise. Ackie too was one of the Scots captured at Dunkirk, one of the Scottish Highland Division, but his camp was a good thirty miles from my home!

Ella called at the outfitters to collect all the articles for me to try on at home and make a note of all that may need adjustment. Well the two of us had some fun, the outfit was similar to what I wore at home when helping Dad at the castle. We laid it all out on the large table in the dining room and began to put it on. In the excitement I almost forgot to say, "Turn round please" while I put my trousers on, hilarious laughter from Ella. White shirt next and black bow tie, ah yes, of course braces with the trousers is a must in the profession. Dad had told me that already at home, but made a note in his letter of instructions. I was grateful for Dad's instructions. I could well imagine the church at home never having had a smarter beadle than Dad. Now the tuxedo with shining lapels, it all fitted perfectly, that's when I heard Ella murmuring "if only I were thirty years younger"! Thank you, what a compliment. I never had all these opportunities to feel happy and content since I left home. There you are, I am ready for the wedding to please the hotel and the bridal party.

In the meantime farming work has to be the priority since that is where I earn my wages and pay for lodgings and food, all be it in kind. The annual cycle on the farm and that of nature might be repetitive but like life could still be unpredictable, rain when it should be sunshine. As long as one accepts it as something we cannot change, then there should be no reason for not being content. That is what happened this year at odd times and yet every crop sown brought results. Hay was made, corn cut and harvested and stacks built, and potatoes lifted, some pitted away from frost. Most sent or will be in the spring-time to England. The rebuilding of our farmstead is now watertight and we will be able to bring the usual animals back up to Viewfield. There is a need for some wood work to be done which I will do during the winter months, if the contractor does not appear.

Regarding my first officiating as a waiter at a wedding at the Mansfield Hotel I am most happy. Ella thought it should be 'proud' in place of happy, that all went well with me. No spillage of any kind or anything sliding from the large platter. What about my English? Well, that surprised me, everything that was important to announce I managed as well as I could. There is only one explanation, and that is the fact of my having to talk to Ella and David all day instead of in German if I was still in camp. They in turn are exceptionally clear in their expression of the words without any accent. Could it be that their grammar is of a higher grade? Considering that two sisters and one brother were teachers, and two brothers were managers in India, then perhaps so. Normal life on the farm continued in Viewfield and down at Mansfield. In view of the extra work within the larger acreage David engaged a shepherd, with the cottage here at Viewfield being free since Ackie left. A good middle aged couple with no children.

It was the middle of November when unexpectedly Mrs McDougall telephoned Ella. The Town Provost and Town Clerk had called at the hotel, with a most interesting proposition. Could we, Ella and I call at the hotel in the evening? That was the news when I came for lunch. Yes we could go down after supper, sounds interesting. That was alright with David, who too was curious. I took the car out and down to Mansfield the two of us went. Evidently pleased to see us so soon, went somewhat excitedly into the business why she had called us. We learned that there was to be an important civic dinner at Mansfield House Hotel on New Year's Eve 1948, provided Mr & Mrs McDougall could take it on. This is what it is all about. The Tain council planned and had agreed to honour two former provosts of the burgh in the town. Mr W. J. Munro and Mr W. Fraser had between them, served 60 years on the town council. The function would also be attended by the Right Hon. Peter Fraser, the Prime Minister of New Zealand from 1940 to 1949. It was hoped that the new Mansfield would be able to provide the facilities and the dinner. That was some surprise!

Prime Minister Peter Fraser attended Tain Royal Academy and was a native of Hill of Fearn, a village not five miles from Tain. Mrs McDougall asked would I be the waiter in charge with two capable ladies assisting? Feeling confident I said yes and was looking forward to it. I was excited and honoured. The McDougalls were delighted and offered, nay insisted to have a cup of tea before leaving for home. On our way home, Ella remarked how good I had carried out my instructions at the wedding. I wrote to Dad at once for any more important instructions and other fine details of finesse suitable for more honourable guests. David and Ella were very happy for me, and Ella even offered to help in the hotel kitchen if required which pleased Mrs McDougall and hoped Ella would come down with me. While waiting for Dad's reply, Ella kindly provided her best china to practise with on the dining room table at Viewfield. Ella clearly revelled in the preparations, declaring there had not been such excitement in the house for some time. It would not have been easy for Ella after her Dad died to be alone with David who could not sustain a whole evening just talking. A question arises, was it fate? I prefer and believe providential matters intervened. Why only a week after the funeral of Mr Munro senior, should I arrive almost out of the blue at Viewfield Farm? Where within a short time the place became a temporal home for me in the real sense of the word? There is food for thought. It is not only an invisible imaginary feeling of a family union but a tangible existence, where thoughts and matters are openly exchanged. Here are two people who by their behaviour and words made me feel I am part of that unit. No harm in losing oneself in a little philosophising?

Within four weeks I had a letter from my parents. They are always happy to have letters from their children to brighten their day. Just as I am glad to hear from my sister and brother. They are well and the parish is appreciative in regards to Dad being the smart and efficient sexton. They have sufficient food, their small garden is productive, and with many baptisms and weddings the historic habit of an 'appreciation' is still honoured. So far good news, to make us glad. Dad was glad and proud to hear about the exciting event to be, and sent a special list and small sketch to make sure I will not let the 'profession' down, Dad's little joke, but he meant it! All I have to do is practise here at home. I showed it to David and Ella who seem to be happy for me that I am given the opportunity to enjoy myself outside the farm. The dining room table is there for you to practise, were Ella's last words.

Winter had begun and all our cattle were safely inside. Most of the potatoes were dressed, bagged and despatched by rail to England.

David would reserve a wagon at the station and we took the 'King Edwards' to the train, loaded them aboard and carefully lined the wagon with straw, a rule to guard against frost. Farmers had the responsibility to ensure their potatoes arrived in England frost-free. Lambs were also transported by rail, in their thousands after the Lairg sales in August /September. Tain rail station was a very busy place. 'Beel the Hen' was a favourite station guard who kept us in order. Does anyone else remember him? And what about Mr Bett, who delivered goods and parcels around the town, with his horse and four-wheeled flat cart? He too was a memorable character. And what about the little group of folk of local fame who on street corners debated strongly and often effectively, with the odd contradiction amongst themselves, which was entertaining if you happened to pass, before moving on.

My second year Christmas at Viewfield, Ella did not mind at all me putting little Christmas reminders like pictures and my Christmas cards on the dresser and found it rather pleasant. I expect there should be more Christmas cards and letters for me, as all our letter writing begins to let people know where we all are. I will again go to Midnight Mass in Dingwall and will find transport back home. Most certainly my animals at Viewfield will know it is Christmas-time, and there will be extra rations of food. On Christmas Day I will not be expected to do any other work apart from milking and feeding. Christmas Eve in the afternoon when I clean the kitchen coal fired stove, I shall listen on the radio to the German Station, to all the Christmas carols in song and music, it becomes very moving, yes, even soldiers can shed a tear or two. I had heard it often said by British soldiers that no one celebrates Christmas like the Germans. There will certainly be a Christmas spirit at Viewfield with Ella producing something special like it was last year. It does not look like it will be a white Christmas this year.

My fellow workers at Mansfield farm will be working as normal in the meantime. I have to get serious and do a bit of juggling of dishes, cups, etc., only a few short days left, until December 31$^{st}$ or as in Scotland Hogmanay. What excitement, what a surprise serving a Prime Minister. How fortunate that I should experience such an honour. Mrs McDougall invited me come to the hotel to get used to the surroundings and to rehearse various procedures and etiquette that my father emphasised were so important. We wasted no time, there was much to discuss and in my opinion the geography is paramount. Where are coats, etc., to be hung, pre-dinner reception room, etc. The dining room general layout, relatively not difficult, as the number of guests are of no concern. According to the total number of guests submitted by the council, a long table will allow every guest to be in view of the Prime Minister. Having been MC and head waiter at weddings gave me an advantage of a pre-visionary set-up. Just as important is the knowledge of the drinks requirement, especially any personal requests. We spend some time to familiarise myself with the dinner service to be used.

Friday December 31$^{st}$ 1948 finally arrived! Ella drove me down to Mansfield in the car and would return later to help in the kitchen. My assistant waitress, whom I had met at our rehearsal, was naturally nervous but my English was good enough to assure her she would be alright, after the first fifteen minutes. I was ready to receive the guests, I bowed and indicated the ladies to the waitress and myself attending to the gentlemen, with the Prime Minister actually extending his hand to shake mine before I received his coat and led them to the reception room. At the appropriate time I asked for attention and bid them to the dining-room where my lady helper attended to the ladies, I to the Prime Minister Peter Fraser and the other honourable gentlemen. Having assured myself I asked for attention and with a slight bow announced, "Honourable Sir, Ladies and Gentlemen, the Grace!" From then on, all went like clockwork, bar the minor unnoticed hiccup. I stayed at my post while speeches were being delivered and pictures and presentations signed. Now let the Queen be toasted, I am ready. At the end we all had our tea and looking back, there were no serious trip-ups, success!

Mansfield is the most prestigious hotel in town. Mrs McDougall showed her confidence in me by saying she hoped I would help out again in similar circumstances. She felt certain that business would improve, and she was right. Having been asked regarding my remuneration I had no idea and was asked to call within the week with Ella. That we did and I could only say 'thank you' to Mrs McDougall and yes, I would be happy to help out when ever needed. That was the time when I spoke to Ella about my opening a bank savings account with the then North of Scotland Bank in town. Ella suggested when next in town she will call and make an appointment with the Manager Mr Fraser whom I have already met on his visits to Viewfield. Soon my savings were earning interest. My waiter's outfit was back on the hanger in my wardrobe. In the morning back in working clothes and happily engaged in my daily tasks. Still thinking occasionally how Dad would have been proud to have seen me following his instructions. There were a number of photographs taken where I would have been on it, but so far none have come my way.

The rebuilding of our farmstead seems to be complete according to the contractor, not that it is, but we have not seen the contractor or any of his tools which would have been some indication that they might actually turn up again. In the meantime I had discussed with David in regards to my finishing some of the outstanding wood work which is needed. David understood and suggested I go to the Ironmonger and buy what I would really need, it will go on Munro's account. That I did and have now some good carpenter's basic tools. It meant I could now do a number of jobs within the steading, fitting pens, etc. Apart from a few light snow showers and odd days of rain, winter passed quietly and spring arrived, at least so it feels for the time. After all it is only middle of February.

This is an opportune moment to mention one other of Ella's occupations that I have added to my interests by taking on the churning of butter. Having practised with the wooden "scotch hands", I soon was expertly shaping the general oblong half pound blocks of pure farm butter. On her regular Friday shopping day, Ella took four to six half pound blocks down to Mr Leitch the grocer, together with surplus new laid eggs. While on the subject of butter I ought to confess that there was a day when I blotted my copy book a year or more later. One cold day I churned in the kitchen. The churn holding ten litres, sits on a timber frame, with its two steel axles sitting on a round steel bed. The handle is fixed to the centre of the barrel. In the winter time the butter may take longer to separate from the milk. A cup of hot water added to the cream in the churn does the trick, most of the time. You have to let it stand for fifteen minutes or more, leaving the lid a half inch open with the locking lever on half click to let the gas escape. I did all that and let it stand for ten minutes or more. This time the churn stood in the kitchen because it was warmer which helps. I read the paper for a while and went back and took the handle and turned the barrel round and a streak of buttermilk ran along the floor and up and round the ceiling before I stopped to close the lid! Probably a cup was lost. But I had to hurry before Ella returned from whatever she was doing outside. Too late to shout do not come in, she entered while I just cleaned the last few inches. One look and Ella burst into uncontrollable laughter and had to sit down on the chair.

It was one of a number of incidents we laughed about in the last two years. Snow no more than four inches and no storms made movements on farms and country roads possible. Wintertime is taken up with feeding those animals kept inside and sheep outside with turnips and hay. Inside, cows in calf will drop their newborns. An early warm spring might be used to hire a threshing machine for two days when we are all busy and may thresh six corn stacks. The grain stored in the granary, and straw baled and stored under cover to bed the animals inside during winter. Now a well-run routine.

Ella and I had paid Mansfield Hotel a visit after Ella having had a call from Mrs McDougall again. As usual I sat with Mr McDougall in the comfortable small bar room, discussing the visit and reception of Mr Fraser the local boy becoming Prime Minister and other topics past and present. Called to join for tea with Ella and Mrs McDougall we recalled the reception in honour of Mr Fraser and it was good to hear that Mr and Mrs McDougall thought it went very well. The town clerk, on behalf of the council sent a thank you letter to Mr and Mrs McDougall and staff, which was appreciated. Addressing me Mrs McDougall had two enquiries regarding weddings to be confirmed soon, looking at Ella at the same time, it was Ella who answered it should be no problem for me to be available. It was understood that David and Ella were happy for me to sort out my helping at Mansfield Hotel and my farm duties at Viewfield.

Their attitude towards me willing and enjoying helping out at the Mansfield Hotel stems from a talk we three had in a close family atmosphere. To both of them I had only one answer, yes I am content and happy to be in their company. We had our nightcap and content to carry on with all of us knowing life will continue as it is. David and Ella are happy to see me enjoying the occasional time out at the hotel, knowing that my work on the farm is taken care of. David and Ella are well informed with regards to my attitude towards alcohol and pub life, both are struck off my list, as are ladies for the moment. The point is, I am still living my youth that Hitler has ruined, although that is past. More concern is the question of my parents, which my brother Engelbert and I will work on to bring them over to West Germany. While Engelbert does the ground work I can help by sending what they need. With regards to food, it is not so much the bread, flour, and potatoes, but the spices, coffee or tea, also quality British underwear for Mum and Dad. My help is in paying for and buying what they need. Let's remember they, like so many, have lost everything except what they had worn when they fled from the battle front. From the Polish authorities there is no hope of an early movement regarding repatriation of our parents. Brother Engelbert too, is still in need of help.

Back to the present, my interest in some form of motorised transport for myself was growing. My accumulated savings allowed me to turn it over in my mind. Sunday attendance at church, and the 22 mile round trip doing it in some comfort like a car, is somewhat appealing. Having mentioned it at table, David and Ella preferred to let me make the decision. Having scanned the local Ross-shire Journal for adverts, I pinpointed the following advert, motor bike for sale: 1936 Cotton 250cc, this is now 1949 remember. A phone call to the advertiser informed me of the cost which I thought was what I could afford to spend. I took the evening train to Golspie some 30 miles north of Tain to pick up the bike from the garage which was right across from the station. The train south was due in half an hour. The guard helped me to put it into the luggage van. The time was 10.30 pm. when I arrived in Tain. The local station guard recognised me and obliged by helping me across the off side rail and up to the platform. It took me a few kicks before the engine started. I first began to doubt if I could make it start. With nobody around I managed to drive all the way up to Viewfield without meeting anybody. The engine had a high pitch when driven and already had foot gear-change. Cotton was a famous family for building racing motor bikes. Within six months however the clutch had let me down. That was the end of motorbikes for me. I had no option but to get the clutch repaired and advertised it in the local paper, and an interested party collected it. I determined I would be more careful how I spent my money. I learned a lesson and my dream for motorbike transportation was gone. I was mature enough to guess what my 'adopted' parents thought. It will be a car the next time.

Farming is where my food and lodgings comes from. No more disasters with the butter churn. Spring calving complete without need for any veterinary help. It must be really serious when I will not interfere with nature and call for the expert. There were the usual difficult births, but if you put your heart into the job and are willing to learn from those who studied how to put nature's quirks right, and they trust you that you will go only so far, then a trusting relationship is established. Sowing of oats was completed, and potatoes planted. Threshing of last year's grain stacks has been completed. The last sowing of turnips was completed last week. In two months we will be all in the field singling the turnips. A job which can be boring, but it does not have to be. With five of us, one behind the other with your six inch hoe blade, you knock out six inches of the two to four inch high seedlings, leaving one seedling every six inches. No one ever can make it so accurate. With two or five behind one another there is never silence. Everything is put right, from politics to sport and scandal. In between there was the important sheep shearing at which I replaced David who appreciates my taking over from him as it goes for his back! Yes, that's where it gets you, alright while you're young. One of our staff, usually the youngest and fittest catches the sheep in the pen and brings it to the shearer. You start at the top, the sheep's neck but quickly you are in a bent over position. The shears' springs are pretty strong to squeeze. Not all sheep are docile before the shearer, and will wriggle to get away from you. One person rolls up the shorn fleece and hands it to the chap who is inside the six foot wool bag to pack the fleeces down. There is tea time at ten, lunch by 12.30 and a 'cuppa' in the afternoon. By five thirty your back will say enough is enough. Hopefully the next day will still be dry to finish the job.

'Building corn stacks with Jim (foreman) on left, myself on the ladder, and Peter'

'Feeding time, one of seven 'orphans' at Viewfield Farm, 1946-1964' and 'Miss Ella, home from shopping'

This is the year 1949, and at the end of June I received one of our Mum and Dad's letters, now at regular six week intervals. Among the general news was the most extraordinary information. Dad, still the sexton, found himself in a conversation one Sunday after church with the Bandmaster of our former Town Brass Band, Mr Hlubeck. We all knew Mr Hlubeck as we ran alongside the band when it marched through the town. The band had over forty members; almost all of them were church members. The band used to meet pilgrims a mile or more out of town on their way home, leading them in rousing hymns back to town. Straight into church for the last rousing hymn accompanied by the band. But they were also the official band playing at marches on any occasion of 'Party' gatherings, during Hitler's time. Also in the band were some members who played and marched in the band because they loved to play, and were secretly not Hitler supporters. Mr Hlubeck was a civil servant in the German Railway office at our railway station. He owned a beautiful house and a large garden. The following is Dad's information in his letter: "Mr Hlubeck was asked by the Polish speaking members to stay and adopt Polish citizenship, and was promised that he would be employed by the new Polish State Railway in the administration office, and to be the band leader. Also that he would keep his house." His love of music had won them over.

According to Dad's letter the two of them often meet after church for old times' chat. This time however their conversation regarding sons became the subject of more details when it transpired Mr Hlubeck son is also a POW in England. When Dad mentioned that I was in Scotland, that was when Mr Hlubeck remarked that in his son's letters he does mention 'Schottland'.

What a coincidence, I knew Herr Hlubeck's son Georg {George} very well. For a start we were in the same class until class four after which Georg went to the Gymnasium, {Grammar school}, like my friend Ernst. Georg was also in the Catholic Youth Group. We did not become close friends in the same class, like I was with Ernst. I wasted no time to write to Dad to let me have Georg's address. Georg studied music more seriously, encouraged by his dad no doubt. I remember Georg playing our large organ occasionally in Sunday youth services.

When Dad's letter arrived with Georg's address I discovered that Georg worked on a farm near Crieff, 17 miles from Perth and only some six miles from Comrie, the POW camp we arrived at after we came from the US. I wrote to Georg and had an immediate reply. Georg was surprised to receive a letter from Scotland and someone with whom he went to school at our former home. He invited me to his wedding in four weeks time. Naturally, I accepted his invitation, and thanked him for it. David and Ella too thought how extraordinary things can happen. I asked David and Ella if I could have that weekend off to attend the wedding and it was understood that I should go. In the meantime there were my daily chores.

While the other 'squad' on the farm see to it that the hay stacks are netted to prevent high winds blowing the top off, David and myself were busy separating the best lambs from the flocks and putting them on fields with better grass, to bring them up to a standard that will fetch a better price at the season's first sale. The grazing here on the hills in the Highlands is the reason for seeing sheep wherever you travel. Some 25 miles north from Tain in the middle of the hills is where the auction mart holds their sales. Some thirty thousand young lambs change hands. Most going south, some as far as England to graze and put on weight. The breed favoured here are Cheviots.

My going to Georg's wedding will occur while the staff will be starting their two week holiday. David insisted on taking me down to the station. The train arrived on time and I took my seat. One travels in comfort even in third class with upholstered seats, whereas in Germany it was still shaped wooden seats in third class. That has of course changed once the country got on its feet again. We arrived in Inverness, yes the city of the world famous, Loch Ness Monster. This is where you join the train south to Perth and Edinburgh and beyond. If there is a need to ask advice or other I would have no difficulty in asking or making myself understood. Therefore getting off at Perth and asking for the platform to Crieff was simple. If you use a map we are travelling south west, if you continue you will arrive at Glasgow. The twenty minute journey to Crieff gave little time to view the scenery. I reached for my overnight case and leaving the train I had to ask which way to the farm I had to find. The station guard as usual in true Scots fashion most obligingly suggested a taxi as it is nearly two miles. No thank you I've got time and used to walking at some speed. A few clouds in the sky, I spotted a farm in the distance and there I was. Getting close I asked a farm worker if I am on the right place? Yes, and he knew Georg Hlubeck and pointed to the cottage nearby. I knocked and out came Georg whom I would have recognised instantly.

We greeted each other and could hardly believe that it is real to have met in a totally strange new land so many miles from home. I met his bride-to-be and should call her Lena, I assumed short for Helena. Yes, I was ready for a cup of coffee, even if it were Camp Coffee. It was obvious that the couple had much to do for their wedding tomorrow. Georg explained that it would be at the local Registrar's office. His future wife was from north-west Germany, and obviously Lutheran. That was alright by me, and no wish to go into that. I became aware that the couple needed time to be on their own. It was not difficult for me to entertain myself, telling Georg not to be anxious about me as I understood quite well how busy they must be and I would love to have a look outside in which I am interested. Georg explained that they will stay overnight at his friend, also a German POW, and is also married to a German lady. I was given to understand that in the city of Perth there are a number of German ladies employed at some woollen mill. I was given to understand that German ladies meet at a Dance Hall and have refreshments. There were and still are ex German POWs who got to know the place and join the ladies. Understandable, that is where closer friendships began, and some do end in marriage.

Some went back to Germany if they had parents there or a place of work. Georg and his friend stayed on. Lena showed me where the coffee, bread and other food was. I assured them I would be alright, and will have a walk round before darkness. I wished them well and look forward to see them tomorrow. That would be after their marriage and meal, etc. I was interested to see around this farm, the owner I was told lived a mile or so away from this place. My immediate impression was of a poor example compared with farms where I am up north. There is a need for some tidying up of rubbish and order in general. Before going to sleep I had a closer look and wondered why the division of the three rooms in this cottage was of a four inch timber frame and lined with timber boarding, and why is the dividing timber wall only seven feet high, leaving a space of one foot at the top? One could hear every whisper. Poor Georg, what would your dad have to say if he saw where you live, compared with your former home?

I slept well and made my breakfast and my bed. In due course I dressed in my Sunday suit and waited to be taken to the reception. I did not have to wait long when a taxi called for me to be taken to the reception. Congratulating Lena and Georg, I was introduced to Georg's friend and his wife, both of whom I found pleasant to talk with. It was good to hear everybody speaking German. Eventually it was time to say goodbye to Georg's friend and his wife. A taxi brought us home.

Lena prepared a supper which we enjoyed and drunk a toast. It was embarrassing to sleep in a room with an open space at the top of a timber wall next to a newly married couple. I had decided to leave in the early afternoon to allow me to get back to Tain in the evening. Lena, now Georg's wife, prepared breakfast for us and I began to question Georg regarding his present employment and accommodation, giving small hints at what it is like up north where farm cottages had been modernised before the war and is still ongoing. Surprisingly, Georg listened with intense interest. Eventually I did mention if he ever felt to come up north I would be happy to enquire at some of the larger farms locally. It was only then, that I mentioned the possibility to re-awaken our band. At that point Georg raised his eyes and smiled. Lena who had been listening just said, anything would be better than this. Georg obviously did not have any thoughts on returning to Germany for the moment. Lena prepared a simple lunch for which I thanked her, and we all hoped to see each other again. Mentioning the fact that when we write to our parents they will surely be elated. Time to say goodbye and we will hear from each other. Having arrived at my home station, a brisk walk soon took me back home to everyone's delight. Within an hour I had recalled my surprising trip. Yes, I recognised Georg who had not changed since we saw each other last. Their supper over, all I asked could I make myself a homemade wheat scone with butter and golden syrup and a cup of tea? "Why, have you already forgotten where everything is?" Laughter!

Ella and David were quite happy for me to enquire around the local farming community for any possible opportunities. For that I shall have a look at our county weekly newspaper adverts. Pure tiredness made me excuse myself and made for bed, barely remembering that I undressed, but had managed to set the alarm clock.

I had a refreshing sleep and I was ready for my usual routine, the milking, and all that is involved, including the milk pails for David to take down for Jim and Peter. Then I made my breakfast. I have not yet described to you my Scottish breakfast. There is the common porridge made with oat-flakes, and milk, or the other recipe I do is Brose, pure Scottish, finely ground oats in a ceramic bowl and boiling water poured over and eaten while hot with salt, sugar, milk and a spoon of cream as I do. During my breakfast I had a quick look at the paper in question and there, lo and behold was an advert for a farm worker to work with the cattleman. Almost too good to be true, I showed it to Ella who on reading it suggested it be worth a visit. It was one of the larger farms in the area of Easter Ross. I better own up now, six months ago I bought my first car, a 1936 BSA 10hp estate car. A beautiful maroon two door model, and already with a pre-select hand operated gear lever. A totally unexpected remark my buying a car might cause the Munros thinking they are paying us too much. That I found very disturbing at first, until I was able to collect my thoughts and replied that I neither smoked nor drank nor spent on any other unnecessary items.

All my work now at Viewfield after three years, is now a matter of routine. Viewfield, by the grace of God and the parent-like atmosphere created by David and Ella, has become a true home. After supper, the Alfa and dishes washed I started the car and was off with a prayer to see Mr Scott the farmer. The farm is only six miles from Tain. With hope I rang the bell. I introduced myself to Mr Scott and mentioned that I worked for Mr Munro at Viewfield. Mr Scott knew of Viewfield and Mr Munro. It was for me to give a summary why I was calling on behalf of Georg and the circumstances. Mr Scott seemed pleased with my petition and said, "Yes, but I would prefer if you came." To be told that would floor anybody surely! In two sentences I was able to convince him why I could not accept such a surprise offer. With that we shook hands and I would let him know as soon as I heard from Georg. Before it was bedtime I had written the letter detailing the weekly wages and the cottage, and the job as assistant to the head stockman. The cottage is one in a row of three, within a small village with a grocer and baker. Also within the village are a small hotel and pub, and a doctor's surgery. The train station is three miles from the village. In brief, Georg had replied by return and was happy with the information and could I inform Mr Scott of Georg's acceptance with his enclosed letter. That I did and was pleased to hear Mr Scott's agreement. An unexpected surprise in Georg's letter was the question if I could possibly try to find a similar job for his friend and family, whom I met at Georg's wedding? Miracles do happen when I had another look at the job offer page. Much to my surprise I was able to accomplish a similar situation for Georg's friend at a farm only three miles from Georg. Suffice to say within the month, both families had taken possession of their job and accommodation. Georg's senior cattleman could not be more helpful for Georg to settle in. Georg thanked me and was pleased to have made the move. Thereafter I visited Georg every two weeks if possible. Georg and his wife Lena found the daily bus service to Tain convenient for shopping, etc.

Having that interlude behind me, unknown that there will be consequences, life at Viewfield my 'home' moved on in its normal way, apart from any extraordinary things, such as helping Ella beating the mixture for a cake, which was a wedding cake for Mary, the lady who was good at reading our tea cups. The reason why I mention it is to prove that even with my help, or because of it, matters can go wrong. This happened this time. On examination in the morning the cake had fallen in. Panic stations? 'No, do not worry Ella,' there are two days before the wedding, I will finish my chores, and will be back in less than an hour. You look out the butter, sugar, eggs and flour. I will be back and whip it up again; there is no room for panic. The kitchen was warm enough which will help. Next the white of the eggs and beating them up, was also my job. This time let's make sure the oven is really up to the right temperature, if slightly higher the better. There was nothing more I could do and continued my outside work. I happened to work up and about Viewfield so when Ella came out to look for me I went in for my mug of tea, my first look was where the cake stood, there it was perfect and I could put a wager on that this time it is not going to sink. Mary is to marry an ex Polish soldier who decided to stay on in Scotland. Next day was Sunday and the first of the month, church at Invergordon, only twelve miles from home and I have my car now, what bliss. Because of having a car I am able to give the Fraser family a lift to church and back again. Their home is half way from Tain and a lovely family, often inviting me to have a cup of tea on our way home. There are three sons still communicating, and we see James and his wife once a year.

December 1949 and another year is drawing to an end. I had recently met my friend Ackie Ross, the accordion player in our recently formed band. He talked about music and was quite excited when I told him about Georg and his musical talent. Ackie was all for it for me to ask if Georg might be interested in forming a Scottish Dance Band? Georg was delighted to join and to be our band leader. He could also have my 120 base accordion, and I would play the piano. I made a point to visit Ackie and gave him the news and he was absolutely delighted, and would speak to David Dundas, whom I have met before and plays Scottish fiddle music and the saxophone. Ackie also thought that Ian Ross the drummer we had, would also love to play, and having spoken to him was happy to join.

Here is the surprise. When I mentioned to Ella I had spoken to Ackie and the news about the new band, she was equally excited for us and asked me, "where are you going to practise?" I had no answer yet. What followed was no surprise to me, "just bring them up here, there is the piano, will that do?" Yes, thank you, and next day I went to see Ackie and he too was over the moon. I drove over to Georg and he was delighted. Georg can come in by bus and I will bring him home after. We had our first practice within the week. With no-one else having a car it was me who provided the transport. Georg and David came in to Tain by bus, Ackie lived in town and I picked them up in town while Ian could walk up to Viewfield unless it rained. To summarise, our practices worked to everyone's satisfaction. Ella had already mentioned that we could provide a cup of tea and a home-baked buttered scone or cake. That was what we did at half time, and everyone was delighted. David often sat in and enjoyed listening to the music. At that time Tain did not have a Scottish Dance Band. We would not have a practice during the Christmas-New Year holiday.

Ella and I paid a visit to the McDougall's shortly before Christmas who had phoned for us to call on them. As expected they had a number of enquiries regarding Christmas Dinners, etc. Would I be available was the question, to which I could reply with a yes. Some for lunches, and others for the evening. Ella's side look towards me meant, 'of course,' and I could do with the money. All that was followed by Mrs McDougall bringing out more news. A farmer called one evening booking a dinner or something, also mentioned that at a local farmers' meeting the possibility was mentioned of having a farmers' light dinner and dance, or a dance mainly from the Tain and surrounding area. We had mentioned the possible formation of a Scottish Dance Band and could now confirm it was happening. Mr McDougall who had joined us for tea out of the blue surprised us saying, "why not call it 'The Mansfield Accordion Band'?" And without hesitation I said "yes". Should the farmers' idea be of holding an evening dance here, we can also supply the ready-made band? Why not? There was food for thought. On our way home Ella and I talked about that idea as a possibility. Before parking the car in the garage we looked at each other, remarking what a great name for a band!

December on the farm, anything that should be under cover and secure had been done, that should include as much as there is room for storing food for the cattle. The male sheep have been with their ladies for three weeks and if nature keeps its promise there will be lovely cuddly lambs in April.

There should be no need for me to be unduly repetitive reciting my monthly or yearly farming sequences anymore. My home life at Viewfield is ever expanding because of my now having a car. For instance I was able to attend a County Choral concert a good few miles away, bidding Ella to come with me which I knew she would enjoy, and indeed we did enjoy it. One Sunday afternoon I was able to drive the ten miles or so to see the Tarbat Ness Lighthouse. That was interesting to find that it stands at the edge of a small peninsula. Its height is impressive; I have never been so close to one. I will certainly observe 'my' lighthouse when the lights are on which we see so clearly from Viewfield. One sure place to take my brother to, if my plan comes to fruition. Christmas and New Year has come and gone. Attending church by car is such a joy, in addition giving others a lift is a bonus. I did of course visit Georg and his wife who is expecting a baby in summer, and took some goodies with me. During our conversation Georg did mention that he actually enjoys playing music again in a band. He is happy with the musical talent we are and looks forward to our first performance. Georg thought by the end of January or beginning of February we should have a programme for one evening. We were all surprised at Georg's musical talent. By the way I should mention that I am often invited to drive Ella on her visits to her sister and her husband with whom we discuss farming and politics, etc. It helps to improve my English.

New Year passed and we had our first practice in the year 1950 an interesting new date when writing a letter. Everybody seemed ready to go. Georg obviously had practised from my Scottish Dance Book. Georg is also ready to accept any help from Ackie or David Dundas regarding Scottish tunes and their rhythm. Georg admitted he is now listening to the Scottish Dance Music programmes on BBC Radio Scotland. Georg is also keen that we should play more Viennese waltzes.

When Ella and I last called at Mansfield Hotel, an interesting discussion resulted with the McDougalls, Ella and I agreeing to name the band 'The Mansfield Accordion Band', and Mr McDougall brought a small glass to drink to the band's name. When informed at our next practice all agreed. It was decided to place an advert in the local Ross-shire Journal. At our next practice I told the boys that Ella had offered the Viewfield telephone number on adverts and letters, and especially bookings. The familiar atmosphere made David Dundas call for a vote of thanks for Ella's offer to allow 'Viewfield, Tel. No. Tain 116' to be on our adverts and paper heading, also any bookings. We also discussed and agreed on a fee to cover our cost including the transport which I will provide at a rate less than hire, even when I bought the larger 1936 Morris 6cyl 18hp car to help transport all the band's kit. On mentioning Tain Telephone Office, I wonder how many people in Tain will remember the little telephone exchange in the late Mr Tree's living room as I do. Only one person at a time was needed to operate connections.

'The Mansfield Accordion Band, l to r myself, Ackie Ross, David Dundas, Georg Hlubeck, Duncan Mackenzie'

'My 1936 Morris Estate 6cyl 18hp'

At the end of January on wakening I became aware that there was a high wind blowing. With my bedroom window facing east I was not aware that it had blown a hurricane until I was ready to go out to milk and I felt the strength of the storm and the damage it had caused. I made my way to the cow shed and sheltered from the still strong wind, and turning towards the cart shed I could not believe my eyes and saw the corrugated roof in one piece of the thirty yard long cart shed lifted and fold over the eight foot high wall into the garden. Almost unbelievable for me too was to find around the farm house six thirty foot tall trees on the ground. David said such gales are not a rarity, but never had there been so much damage. I wondered that none of the chicken houses fell over. It will take months to fix the cart shed roof. David thought he will have to get a contractor in to fix the roof. After a further walk round our new farmstead there seemed to be no other drastic damage. I made my way to do the milking in order that David could go down to town to see if there was any damage to Mansfield farm buildings. I was able to reassure Ella that there was no damage to any of the chicken houses. Repairs could only be done in between farm work. Some important repairs might be requiring tradesmen. Any small important items could be stored in the new farm steading upper floor. David had arrived back for his midmorning cup of tea and reported that there was no damage to any of the farm buildings. He did however see the odd chimney pot on the ground in town, and damage to the odd hedgerows. All the sheep are in order. David thought we both might go to make sure the gates are all closed, otherwise they might loosen on their hinges, and sheep wandering anywhere. That's what we did. The tractor drivers bring the hay and turnips to the sheep in the field, which is part of their job in wintertime. The storm has gradually calmed down, by dinnertime you might still lose your hat. Next day life at Viewfield returned to normality.

It was the middle of February that we had our first band engagement at the Mansfield Hotel. The first of the Farmers Dance engagements, and everybody, the farmers, the hotel and we in the band could look back on a successful first night. Georg with his specific Viennese waltzes had his reward. We thought it was a success as a number of partakers came to thank us for an enjoyable evening.

While on the subject of a successful evening, it was almost two years later that it had been suggested we should apply for an audition at the BBC Scotland studio in Aberdeen. We did apply and were given a date for an audition. The well-known Herbert Wiseman was adjudicator, and after our session we were asked to go for a cup of tea at the BBC tea-room and have a practice in one of the studios to relax, and come back when called. Alas, we had to admit we were beaten by the Wick Scottish Band, who were soon heard on radio. We did not try another audition. We talked about it at great length at Viewfield before we commenced with our practice session. I do remember some interesting comments were discussed. With that we enjoyed Ella's tea and scones. We had already played at a number of local dance-halls. We had achieved spreading our wings, when in early summer we had a date some thirty miles from home. It was at a village hall where one of the hall committee members heard us play nearer home, and found our telephone number. It had been a most enjoyable place to have played in. David thought it partly due to our style and again it was Georg's Viennese waltzes that made the difference, emphasising that David with his violin and Ackie's button-key accordion added to the over-all harmony. Worth recording at the above engagement at that time, we had to hire a car from our local garage and their driver. At the end of the dance there was tea and sandwiches for the band. It was beginning to get bright up north here when we left for home. The gale force wind blew stronger and stronger, and by the time we were a few miles from David's home the wind had blown the entire hedge along the length of a field on to the road and blocked it. There was nothing else for it if we wanted to get home, everybody out, all of us in evening dress, had to clear the road before we could proceed. On one other occasion in summer, I was on my way home from a dance and could not believe my eyes. When half a mile from home, I spotted one of my milking cows grazing in the middle of a field of ours, with the gate wide open. There was nothing else for it, I had to stop, dressed bow tie and black suit and got her out of the field back on to the road home, with me following behind in the car. Arriving home she just walked into her stall. How did she open the gate of the field to take a long walk? All is possible with animals. We must have been a hilarious sight!

Do I hear a whispered question dear reader? When do girls come into your life, Paul? A legitimate question, for me not difficult to answer. There was hardly time in my busy life to look in that direction is one reason. It did not have to be, it was my choice. Let me remind you, I was seventeen and a half years old when called up, then front line service, followed by two and a half years as a POW. Those were three years of my life without meeting or speaking to a lady. These were important years in a young man's life. Wasted? No, I learned much in those years. Once a 'free' man again, I did not know where my family was, alive or not, my homeland taken away. It took a while to find my family again. I found a new place in a new country, and been given a home and work, by two people of my parents' age. All I wanted in my new found freedom was to learn how to live a normal life again, and with my wages help my family to build their life anew. I hoped I will know when it is time for me to find a companion to share life with. I was gaining confidence making full use of my growing English vocabulary. I always remember my Dad and my Godfather Uncle Paul's advice, never equate serving with servility. You provide a service for which the recipient may at a convenient time thank you. A smile and a word are appreciated most of the time. That has proved itself during my attending at functions at the Mansfield Hotel. Elegantly dressed ladies have a number of times flattered me even at table by asking, "are you Welsh?" or "are you from the Isles?" Even "what a lovely accent". Well, there is no finer compliment. I hope to see my parents first. Would someone want to marry a German at that time? Occasionally it did happen.

And so back to the farm. The builders had returned to re-assemble the cart-shed roof. I was able to do a fair bit of joinery inside the new steading. There is now much more room. We now have even a garage for two cars, one of which I am allowed to use for my car. We are in the early nineteen fifties and at last David took delivery of a new black Hillman Minx. At last the new post war car models are being produced; the delivery problem will no doubt still take a long wait. Better news is that at Viewfield we have a new coal fired kitchen stove that heats a several gallons copper water tank. Let me remind you that there is still no electricity available to Viewfield, although it is only a mile and a half from town. Nor is there mains water supply as yet. The well holds very good water and never goes dry, even in hot summers. One consolation is that in the kitchen we have a hand pump to fill the cold-water tank in David's room, and do not need to fetch water from the well. Not so good for the shepherd in the cottage, who has to come the hundred yards to the pump for every pail he uses.

There are official plans drawn up and County approval for a main water supply and a line of Hydro Electric Power. David enquires periodically every half year, promises are made, but not kept. It is an eternal waiting game. The stove in the kitchen is a big improvement since it has facilities to heat water. It does not require much muscle power to pump the water up to the tank. Having mastered lambing, sheep shearing and stack building with Jim our foreman, I do occasionally have to take on the tractor work during the men's holiday. Often I do the evening round of the fields to see that the animals are safe, to allow David to rest in the evening. Occasionally I may use the Land Rover when I am lazy, or if a field is further from 'home'. Occasionally David took me to the Mart at Dingwall, the county town. It is interesting to try and follow the bidding to buy or sell animals; auctioneers have a language of their own. Even without the band, boredom is not in my vocabulary.

Summertime, but no heatwave as yet. School holidays do not affect us, apart from potato harvesting. Ella had a phone call, from her and David's younger sister Terry, whose husband has a motor car repair shop, and also owns a farm. Their home is on a peninsula called the Black Isle across from us some forty miles away. Ella did mention that her sister Terry, the youngest member in the Munro family, is not that well and she wondered if their youngest boy Peter could come over for a time during the school holidays? Although Ella had asked me, she knew that I would love to have Peter here. I have met them several times on their twice annual visits to Viewfield. Actually I had on two occasions been asked to spend two week-ends with the family. There was no question other than Peter would come over to stay with us at Viewfield. These are the names of the four boys, starting from the youngest, Peter, Keith, Charlie and John, no girls, plus parents arrived on the Sunday. We greeted each other, Peter just eight years old eyed me up, and when I suggested to come with me to help feed the chickens, he did not hesitate and came with me, so the others and we had a good time playing games. The ice, which never was, had been broken. Leaving his parents and brothers, Peter did not shed a tear and was happy to follow me as my younger 'brother'. Language was no longer a problem either. I need not ask, Peter just followed and helped at milking time. There was something about Peter.

Peter slept in the spare bedroom. While we sat in the kitchen having our nightcap, and David reading the daily paper, Ella admitted to worrying slightly about her sister Terry's health. She still enjoyed taking the bookings for our band, although there is a bit less of it in summer, but she had two or three bookings for the wintertime already. That is apart from any bookings for the Mansfield Hotel, which may allow me to earn extra money towards the cost of running my car.

Peter and I in the meantime, were enjoying getting to know each other, creating a basis for a good friendship. Ella and David enjoying watching us two becoming almost like brothers. Even I was surprised how smooth we glided into a companionship. It did me good and made me think, what is my life here all about? There has been one such moment in the field, when the view down towards the shore of the calm blue firth, reflecting on the mountains along the shore as far as the eye could see. Leaning on the gate of the field, lambs two months old gathering in groups of ten, more or less, deciding suddenly to run along the fence as far until one leader gives a command and all turn round for the race back. Getting back their breath, all decided to run and find their mums to have a drink. Well, seeing this you cannot but think, is there someone preparing a special life other than what you are happy with? Was I dreaming? Certainly not, but I did spend time in thought, should I just be grateful for all the goodness I had been given and follow the way I am being guided? I may eventually find out.

School is about to begin and Peter had been collected by a visit of his parents and brothers. I was thanked and invited to take my car and come over to visit them over to the Black Isle. That I did on several occasions. It became a lifelong friendship. Unexpectedly I had a letter from our parents from the old home. It was pleasant to have a sign from them. Dad seems to have a poetic gift when writing his letters to us. They are thinking about us, hoping we are all well. Dad is thanking providence for having got the chance to be sexton and enjoying it. He is seeing it as some miracle that he should have been given the opportunity as someone who had seen the church being built as a six year old. Dad often finds our mother crying while she prays, missing her children and unable to help us. In our letters we try to assure her not to be so worried about us. We are all well off compared with them. The onus is on us to keep sending our letters to assure them of our love. Ursula our sister and I are well aware that Engelbert is keeping in contact with the authorities finding a way to get the Polish Government to issue the necessary authority for them to leave. As our Engelbert says, we are not the only ones who still have relatives in our old homes who want to get out to where they speak the mother language. At least the three of us agree to continue in prayer and hope. This is the opportunity where I can publicise that it was my intention to visit my brother. I spoke to David regarding a suitable time, after we got the hay in? Yes, that suits him fine, and I will get a ferry booking for one. I will find out next week. Mr Fraser, Viewfield's Bank Manager and family friend called one evening to discuss private matters and tea afterwards. As usual I was asked to join for tea. We have met before at Viewfield, somehow accidentally my planning to visit Germany came into the conversation. Mr Fraser immediately gave me the name and address of the Travel Agency in Inverness, and that I should ask to speak to the Manager. How lucky can you get? That I did, and was indeed introduced to the Manager who advised to take the ferry boat from Hull to Hamburg. When the time came I received my booking including the train journey, Tain to Hull and return. At Hamburg I would buy my rail ticket from Hamburg to Wildeshausen and return via Hamburg. The day arrived and I was off, with my adopted parents wishing me well, hoping all will go well and look forward to see me return.

It had been a wonderful reunion with my brother Engelbert and Aunt Else with Uncle Theo, and their three children whom we adopted as our cousins, remember? There was a lot to talk about as you might guess, our parents for example. Engelbert is very active in contact with the Polish government, regarding the permit to bring our parents to West Germany. According to Engelbert it is a matter for the Polish Government and the West Germans to find a way. Silesia at that time was still not absolutely a Polish Territory. Britain and the USA had not yet agreed to full annexation of Silesia to Poland, and the reason for each Government holding on to any possible leverage. Patience is asked for. Engelbert is enjoying his apprenticeship at the printers. The owner, an active catholic in the local church, is very pleased with Engelbert and his ability and interest in printing. He also feels for Engelbert's longing to get our parents over to the west. There was a surprise for me which they were all quiet about in case it might not come off, namely the arrival of our sister Ursula from Munich on a two week holiday. Could there be anything more wonderful? How pleased our parents would be for us. The day of her arrival was a family reunion in every way. Ursula looked happy and over-joyed that the three of us have had our second reunion. What a joy that would be for our parents, once we send them a letter and a photograph. I had bought a German camera, so I would have some good pictures. There were many topics that the three of us talked about. There was me, already almost four years at Viewfield in Scotland, living in a family atmosphere, able to send useful items to our parents and here to Aunt Else. With myself perfectly happy because of my extraordinary situation. A situation I had already indicated. Ella, the sister, who had forfeited love and marriage to care for her brother who managed the family farm. Because of a war, which nobody wanted, a young man was ordered to work on that farm. By an extraordinary fate a developing situation merged somehow into a quasi-family unit. After six years from home, a disastrous war, and the loss of my homeland, these caused any vestige of a Post Office career to fade. It was the cause of an intensive exchange of our innermost thoughts. While Ursula and Engelbert had reached a point where their future is relatively clearly visible, mine is not. Its advantage for the moment is my fortunate position in being able to provide physical help to our parents and brother in sending parcels and small sums in their need.

Ursula is being cared for by her Order which also takes care of her educational requirements. Ursula led us in to a short prayer of thanks for a meaningful exchange of thoughts and especially the physical coming together. All three of us will send our own personal letter, which we know would be a joyful present for Mum and Dad, their longing to see us is their pain. The meeting of us three was a time of very inspirational and encouraging hope within us, that one day our prayers will come to fruition. It was good to see that our sister has not lost her particular humour, her love for singing and her ability to find instant joy and a leading relationship with children. We need not worry, she had not changed, I am sure she will make a much-liked children's teacher. It was time for me to say goodbye to friends of my family here that I have been introduced to. My train for Hamburg will leave early in the morning. I had said goodbye to them all, while Ursula saw me to the station, and me leaving out of sight. Ursula has at the last moment confided that God willing she will do her Profession to be a nun in two years time. Where will I be? Good question.

Another calm sailing back to Hull and a train to Tain in Bonnie Scotland, and back at my 'family' to a joyful welcome which made me feel good. I made my way to my bedroom and hung up my Sunday clothes and back into my working garments ready for that cup of tea Ella had prepared. There was time to start telling all about my travels and my reunion with my sister and brother, sufficient to tell for many hours. It was getting towards evening milking time and I used it to have a walk round to see if all is still in order. Soon I called the cows from the paddock and got on with milking I was sure the animals have recognised me, probably never even missed me. That's how quickly one can get into the well-known routine. After our supper I literally had to fight with Ella for my dish washing job. Having completed my chores, and David having had a read of the daily paper, I was happy to tell him about my visit to my family in Germany. David found it all quite interesting and it gave me the pleasure to answer any questions he asked. I was ready for an early bedtime and excused myself to my room. In no time I was away in a dream.

Saturday early evening at supper, everybody listens to the half hour Scottish dance music on the radio. There is now a large variety of Scottish tunes that are now familiar to me. It was important that I visited Georg to report that I am back and that Ella had a couple of bookings for dances at places out of town, which was good news. A normal Saturday night with the appearance of Mrs Fraser, Ella and David's sister, and Mary who will be reading our tea cups and telling us our fortunes. This was always good fun and entertainment for David. The longer time is spent on the local news and general 'gossip' in town. Mrs Fraser's husband Donald will call later in time for tea and taking them home again. Mr and Mrs Fraser have one daughter, Christobel a beautiful young lady she is going to be.

With my new camera I took several photographs of our town and from Viewfield the fantastic view of a panorama from left to right, the visible town and the blue firth and northern hills. Worth taking a few of the most important interesting places in town. In the centre of our small town is the Town House. It houses the council chambers, and their offices. It also has the required places for the court which sits in town weekly. It is a Royal Burgh due to the local historic Saint Duthac, and the shrine to where the King of Scotland had come on several occasions prior to the reformation. The Town House is apparently a replica building from a German town house, but I was never able to find out where. One other historic item is a piece of tapestry attributed to St. Duthac, some ten feet high and six feet wide, hanging among other such items in Cologne Cathedral, I have yet to see it there.

A lovely letter from my parents awaited me when I came home for lunch this day. They were pleased to receive the photos I had sent them of Viewfield and the Highlands. Now they could visualise my new life. They and others to whom they showed the photographs were intrigued to discover just how many facilities were available in our small town of which I took the photographs. It had seven hotels: Mansfield House, the Royal, the Balnagown, the Railway, the Temperance, the St. Duthus and the Star Inn; six banks: the Royal, the North of Scotland, the British Linen, the Commercial, the National and the Bank of Scotland; five churches: the historic Collegiate Church of St. Duthac, the Parish Church, the Free Church, the Free Presbyterian and the Scottish Episcopal Church. No Catholic Church at that time. A former church had become the Town Hall and all these facilities and its historical importance make it an impressive town worthy of pride and a visit.

The year 1951 has gone and 1952 had started with a number of engagements for our dance band. Winter brought nothing extraordinary, and spring too had seen the new lambs having a great time in the fields, having real races which are amazing to watch. All the seasonal work went on in orderly fashion. Any free time I busied myself with joinery work of all sorts of repair or new work, of which there was a lot. Ella had longed for things to be done in the garden and inside the newly refitted cart shed roof. The highlight during the summer of 1952 was the arrival of my brother Engelbert on a two-week visit to Viewfield, which we had talked about during my visit to him last summer. Engelbert was quite surprised at the beauty of the part of Scotland we lived in. The fact that we lived some four hundred feet above sea level added to the attraction looking down to the shore, and then the view of the firth and the hills to the left. Yes to have a high lighthouse you can visit was another bonus. I took Engelbert to a number of interesting places, including the west coast. Engelbert and I also visited Georg Hlubeck our band leader, and his wife Lena. Georg was very much interested to hear from Engelbert about the flight when the Russians entered our home town. Did Engelbert have a chance to see how much damage was done if any to Georg's home when the Russians came in? Engelbert knew of course where Georg lived and so it was someone who knew and experienced what had happened at that time. There was a booking for us to play at a dance in a village called Inver, only five miles from home which I had almost forgotten until Engelbert asked about our band. We managed to fit everyone and everything into the car. On arrival while we unpacked and set up our equipment, I spotted 'Ginger' a redhead ex German POW who too was well known, because he played for the local football team. He also followed our engagements enjoying Georg's waltzes. I made for Ginger to introduce Engelbert to him. Ginger delightedly shook hands with Engelbert and would look after him.

Engelbert in turn was no shy boy and looked forward to see the local 'talent'! Right away he found it strange that the men all sat on one side of the hall and the ladies on the other. Next there were no tables where you could sit together and have a glass of beer or whisky. That was his first opener of the custom. Clearly determined to enjoy himself, he boldly went across the hall, bowed to a lady {they do not do that here}, and asked her if she would dance, took her arm and led her onto the floor. At the end of the dance he offered her his arm to escort her back to her seat, bowed and thanked her. His style ensured that he enjoyed many dances that evening! Many eyes were raised, but Engelbert continued. I wondered what will happen when we announce a Scottish country dance. We need not have worried, Ginger in good form, took Engelbert with him and two ladies obliged to dance with them. Ginger of course knew a bit and helped Engelbert to enjoy the fun. Of course you change many partners during the dance which adds to the fun. We all agreed it had been a very successful evening and congratulated Engelbert and his success with the ladies. I noticed that he gallantly attempted to engage his various partners in conversation despite his limited English. We entertained Ella with a full report, Engelbert himself trying occasionally to fill in details of amusements with his added comments. She found it hilarious and clearly imagined the conversation among the girls at their work next morning. Engelbert was determined to walk to town, and took the opportunity while purchasing souvenirs to practise his English in the shops. It was sad that his holiday was over so soon and he had to leave for home, but not before he had washed and polished my car. Ella made up a packed lunch for him, including some of her famous scones, for which Engelbert had quickly acquired a taste. I drove him to Inverness station where we parted. We vowed we would see each other the following year at Ursula's special day. To get to the station we had to cross the River Ness in the middle of town. A bare hundred yards before the bridge we had to stop to allow a massive lorry with a covered large boat to cross the bridge and then do a tight turn towards the river. Before we parted at the station everybody knew it was the speed boat of Mr Cobb, to break the world water speed record on Loch Ness. A historic moment for us. Unfortunately Mr.Cobb died when the speed boat exploded and crashed.

Settling after my brother's visit, I was acting now as a full family member, able to take over the more tiring tasks from David. Lambing was well behind us, so too the harvest and the potato picking. As another Festive Season approached the band's bookings increased, and functions at the Mansfield already heralded a very busy time. Since I did not smoke or drink, I was able to afford to run my car and also add to my savings in the bank. Running a large car may not be the wisest thing.

The year was to end on a solemn note with the tragic and untimely death of King George VI, and Princess Elizabeth's immediate accession to the throne. Here on the farm, frost and light snowfalls made it a comparatively uneventful winter.

What lay ahead in 1953? The familiar farming year had begun. Spring cultivation was complete and the animals were outside again in the meadows, enjoying fresh grass and warming sunshine. How pleasant I found it to be surrounded by God's nature and to be a part of it. Returning for dinner one day, Ella gave me the exciting news of a booking for our band to play at the Town Hall in early June for the Ross-shire Scottish Country Dance Society's 'Coronation Dance'. What a feather in our cap! We started preparations for our important engagement. I had to practise on the piano and I had made our music-stands which were approved by all. Soon the day of the Coronation Dance arrived. We set up the stage and our audio equipment and the adrenaline began to flow. We took our seats and struck up the prescribed march. The doors opened and the dancers entered, the men in their colourful Scottish kilts and the ladies in their likewise colourful dresses. Eight abreast taking their places for the customary reel. Dressed in their various tartans, they were a sight to behold! From beginning to end it was a truly remarkable and memorable evening for us, and to play for star dancers had been especially enjoyable, but alas it would never be repeated.

Only a few months later, fate struck our band leader Georg a crushing blow. With his wife and young daughter, Georg was visiting his friend and his family on their farm barely half an hour's walk away. For some reason, never established, a fierce fire destroyed Georg's cottage and all their possessions, including my accordion. More by God's grace, the adjoining two cottages were saved by a quick response by the fire brigade. In short, his wife did not want to stay and Georg had to seek new employment which he found in Cambridgeshire. Georg and I have never met again. The band completed any bookings that Ella had taken. It was a sad parting but we understood Georg had to do what he thought was right. To stay on here would not have been a pleasure. The band was no more, and David and Ella were equally saddened, for they would miss the musical evenings we had all enjoyed together. In due course the Tain Scottish Dance Band was formed, with Ali McGregor at the helm. They eventually had achieved what we could not. They have been heard on the radio many times and for many years.

Then it was time for me to prepare for my trip to Germany to attend our sister Ursula's great day. I changed my large car for a 1938 Morris 8, having decided to be brave to travel by car. Mr Forbes had the garage next to the Mansfield farm, and I entrusted my little car to his expertise ensuring I could travel safely to Germany and back. I joined the Automobile Association and decided to leave my adventure in their hands, yet I could not blame Ella for being apprehensive about my bold plan. Considering a journey from the very north, to the port of Harwich, more than six hundred miles! She provided all the food I needed, including my thermos flask. It was understood that I would buy any of the goods that would be of real value to our parents to be sent from Germany. I also remembered to bring something for Engelbert and Aunt Else and her children.

Sadly, two months before my departure Ella had a phone call to visit her younger sister Terry, the mother of Peter and his brothers. The anxiety was caused by a hospital examination. A conversation at table regarding Ella's visit to stay a few days at their sister, had our assurance that David and I would manage to look after ourselves. Would David be happy with my cooking? That was solved by David having his lunch at his sister's near town. Cooking a lunch for myself I had already learned at home, neither was there a problem for me to provide supper for the two of us. House work is a 'cake-walk' for me.

Ella left two days later and life at Viewfield kept running smoothly according to the arrangements made. After four days Ella arrived back home with a worrying look, but hopeful with the hospital treatment bringing the hoped-for results. Life at Viewfield continued in a relatively hopeful atmosphere, with my trip to Germany to go ahead as booked. Within two weeks it was my time to load my car and say goodbye, with Ella and David wishing me 'good luck'.

With my tickets, money and my German passport, I said my goodbye and off after early breakfast on the road to Harwich. In 1953 traffic was light, the number of trucks minimal and restricted to a speed of 30 mph! There were, of course, no motorways. I had to travel through the night and slept in the car when needed. I arrived at

Harwich at 9 o'clock next morning. I found a garage and got my petrol tank filled. I went to the office to pay and handed my pound notes over the counter, and was taken aback when I was informed by the attendant that he did not take Scottish banknotes. Stunned, I asked for advice and was directed to the Post Office. The garage attendant drew a sketch map on a piece of paper and advised me to take the car to save time. I was puzzled but had no option. At the Post Office the cashier just shook his head and changed all my Scottish banknotes, and I went back to the garage to pay my dues. In case you have not realised, the pump attendant actually let me drive to the Post Office without having paid! I could have just driven on to Harwich, it never entered my head to abuse such trust, but that's how it was in those days.

**'My first international venture by car in 1953. Harwich to Hoek van Holland with my 1938 Morris 8 (as yet no roll-on/roll-off!)'**

Arriving at the ferry pier my little car was lifted by crane into the hold (no roll-on roll-off in those days). Six hours later, equipped with my map I headed for northern Germany and Wildeshausen. As I drove through Holland I found that the road signs were for the most part the same as the German signs. Their roads were very good. I stayed for two nights with my brother and Aunt Else before we headed south together for Munich. Engelbert was an excellent co-driver. This was my first attempt to drive a car in Germany and with the steering wheel on the other side, wrong side. This was 1953 not 2000. With Engelbert following the instructive map we arrived at Munich, and found the Convent College with its modern church. There were several cars parked and as we locked the car Engelbert noticed Mr Klein, his employer, park his car. Mr Klein, also a member of the parish in Wildeshausen, had been given an invitation by Ursula on account of him having taken on Engelbert as an apprentice. This was the first time us being at such a service, seeing our Ursula taking such a courageous step. We were humbled by the participation of our Countess Sybille, who was not only delighted at Ursula's invitation, but also as a token for the years of service of our family, while the Countess and her family were at the castle. What a delight to have met the Countess after the trauma seven years ago.

The service, in which Ursula professed her vows to become a nun, was a time of joy for us, because we knew it was what she wanted. There were moments of sadness when we thought of our parents, pain and disappointment because they could not be present and share the happy day. For our Mum and Dad it was a day of agony between elated joys. The fact that our Countess Sybille followed our sister Ursula's invitation and came to the service, was taken by all of us a sign of honour. We greeted her, also on behalf of our parents with the respect she deserved. After all, all of us saw the castle for the last time in its splendour before leaving it to the wanton flames of war. The Countess' new home was near the city of Frankfurt. We sat together at lunch at the convent which was an excellent opportunity to meet one more time and remember more pleasant times. Countess Sybille was accompanied by her former Lady-in-waiting, Miss Klara Pertl, whom we knew so well. It was this family reunion that added much value to the occasion. It is difficult for a stranger to understand the joy to meet once more in peacetime when many had to forego such joys. This one-off unexpected occasion to meet, we will remember forever. After an invigorating coffee and tea, we had to face the so often moment to say goodbye to each other. Our parting from Ursula was not so difficult, since the three of us are happy in our present lives, and are thankful for the opportunities to meet again. We had every reason to be thankful for such a happy day.

Engelbert and I stayed over-night in an inn and had an opportunity to be with our Ursula for two hours in the morning. That was a bonus for us. Eventually it was time to say our goodbye and waving us off as we turned to join our road for home. We arrived back home at the now new hometown of Wildeshausen. I had another week to stay with Engelbert. The drive home provided an excellent opportunity to talk over each other's more immediate future. Engelbert had no intention other than to extend his printing profession by a possible two year course in the Printing College. Engelbert is in his last year of his apprenticeship and may well look for a new and larger firm to expand his knowledge. He certainly would want to climb the ladder. Of course we talked about my situation and did not find a definite way forward. It was time for me to thank Engelbert for all his help and kindness, as well as for the understanding between us. As for marriage I could not give Engelbert any further information, since I live a life with the Munros in a family atmosphere, with a definite feeling of being treated like an adopted son. It was time for me to thank Engelbert and everyone for all they did for me, and say goodbye and God bless. The handshake and hug, then get into my little 'Morris' and I was soon out of sight until the next time. The sea crossing was calm, if only the Cambridgeshire country roads were straighter, it reduces the speed considerably. No dual carriageways all the way north. But one day perhaps? I arrived home safe and sound, to a meaningful welcome. I felt in good spirit having been at Ursula's great day, and that talk with Engelbert on our way home, made my drive home so pleasant.

Ella had remarked one day how easy I made their life. To hear that, really got to my heart. That is why I felt good to have arrived home again to a warm welcome. Ella quickly made a new pot of tea for all of us, thus, I quickly came down to earth again. David's welcome was warm and meaningful, which felt good. He does depend on my taking on many of the heavier jobs; he is showing the occasional weakness without letting it be known. Family life continued as if I had never been away. Late, but not yet bedtime, yet I had to admit that I felt it was time for me. That was understood and I added that tomorrow morning it will be as usual, me doing the milking, etc. With that I bid them goodnight and off upstairs I went. I set my alarm clock, and within minutes I was away with the fairies.

In the morning, fit after a good sleep, I started where I left off. I doubt if the animals missed me. They love anyone that feeds them. I felt happy and everything was ready for David in the morning. I had my breakfast by the time Ella came down to wish me good morning and asked how I felt? My answer, good. I had already extended the greetings from my people, not forgetting Engelbert's special greeting

I am also in demand more and more at the Mansfield Hotel where they are sought after for functions or weddings and any kind of large or small celebrations with invited guests. It is certainly widening its reputation. Functions were being booked for the winter season at the Mansfield Hotel which would keep me busy.

The latest! I discovered a liking for painting, decorating rather than the artistic. Ella having seen my painting the new doors at the new steading soon found sufficient opportunities for me to start work inside the house, mainly where mistakes would not be so noticeable. Later, when it came to tackling the front door, Mr MacLeod from the paint shop in town was happy to give me useful advice and instructions. The firm was busy and I was willing, so he showed me how, then left the tools and let me get on with it. Sand papering first, not too hard or there would be marks. Finally I managed to grain the door and a clear varnish finish to the satisfaction of the master.

Occasionally, I did find myself questioning where my life might lead and whether I was satisfied for it to continue in the way it had evolved so smoothly during six years at Viewfield. My happy life here on the farm was clearly far removed from the career I had envisaged with the Post Office. It was just a thought; meantime I was kept busy with the customary tasks and the farming routine of autumn and winter. Functions at Mansfield Hotel provided me with additional pocket money and provided also wider contact with folk outside the town. I still wondered vaguely about the future, and it seemed I was not alone in thinking about my future where it might lead.

One cosy winter evening in the New Year of 1954, David, Ella and I were relaxing after supper. While David was reading his newspaper, Ella and I were chatting away. She suddenly asked me, if she may, "*had I ever thought about my future and marriage?*" Surprised I certainly was, equally I thought how gracious of her. It was what Ella said next that struck a chord. She told me that she and David were facing the fact of growing older. David was supposed to take life easier and this he was able to do with my presence. It was likely the farm may have to be sold some time, because no family member seemed to be interested in taking it over. I appreciated her concern and realising just how much she and David cared about me, was comforting. It was understood that our conversation demanded my absolute confidentiality, just as I was trained for. The fact I had been leading such a comfortable life contributed to my feeling that time was on my side. I had years ahead of me. Hitherto I had never made decisions, events and other people had determined what happened to me. Now I would discover that thoughts of a future for me should stimulate my thoughts. Back to Germany? For me, the principles of a Christian marriage after courtship were special and I felt confident that I would be led providentially along the right road. It had always been so for me, on my so far relative short life's journey, but now perhaps I was required to be put to the test! Where to?

The probability that Viewfield would one day be sold did raise the question of whether I would then be prepared to work for some other employer? It raised doubts which needed serious consideration. As Ella added, "there was no reason to think that changes were imminent", and I had no idea what my first step should be, so I put the idea to the back of my mind, literally leaving my life in my Maker's hands.

Religious authorities in Germany had been asked to appoint an English speaking Lutheran pastor based in Edinburgh, and a Catholic priest, Fr. Dumont based in Bradford, with responsibility for Northern England and Scotland. They provided spiritual care and help where needed for the large number of young German women employed in the jute mills, for au pair girls, and for former German POWs like myself, who had stayed on in Britain. I met Fr. Dumont when he first came to visit the north two years previously. He met the few of us at our Parish house in Dingwall. We had twice yearly meetings, one of them near Christmas time. After the service we would have coffee or tea with our home-baked Christmas baking by the few German ladies up here in the north. He always brought a copy of one of the Catholic monthly newspapers, "Mann in der Zeit", 'Man of the Times,' printed in Germany mainly for us younger generation like me. It contained religious news and articles, political comments if applicable to church matters, excellent new material after the dark times for Christians under Hitler. It had a half page designated for young men and ladies, seeking to correspond with likeminded persons, for friendship and possible marriage. That section I ignored apart from the occasional passing look. There is a reason why I brought the above to your notice now!

This being early April 1954 and two months after we had that talk regarding the concern about David, the farm and its future and mine. For some reason Fr. Dumont had decided to visit us at Easter time. Our parish priest Fr. Davies was happy to allow us to have our meeting in his spare sitting-room and as usual Father Dumont in good spirits gave us a good talk and lots of interesting information about the re-awakening of the Christian Youth movements in Germany, etc. We also have a chance to meet with our other German Catholics, who live and work in the county. As usual we all brought our baking and coffee while we chatted away with Father Dumont joining in. He also always held a Sunday Service for us in German. The time does pass more quickly than you think and we began to collect our belongings and assured Father of our appreciation, bidding him a safe journey and hope to see him soon again. Father Dumont and I chatted a while longer and made sure I had my newspaper, 'Mann in der Zeit,' before we shook hands and his blessing for my journey home. I thanked him and we parted. Our parish priest Father Davies happened to come out and we chatted a while, including my active part in teaching hymns in our 'satellite' church at Invergordon, and other small items before it was time to go home.

Here is the miracle. If Fr. Dumont had not come that month I would not have received that particular monthly paper! Wait and see. I arrived home just past supper time, which I did not need, but was grateful for the cup of tea. I did go out to take a look at the animals to make sure all is well before bedtime. I also gave Ella a brief resume of our meeting and thought of going to bed, when David wanted me to have a read on some interesting government article regarding farming in Scotland. In due time I was ready for bed and did so. After a refreshing sleep it was back to work, resulting in a normal day. After supper clean up and wash-up, normally I would have read the paper I brought home, 'Mann in der Zeit' in the kitchen. This time, I took it up to my room and read it there. For the very first time, I did not ignore the half-page section of personal advertisements. I began glancing at each line, without any thought or particular interest, except one small notice that made my finger return to it, the size of it was 2 cm x 5 cm – barely 1in x 2in., not particularly eye-catching, except that it had been placed by two lady-friends, which had no real influence on my sudden decision to read that notice. Gradually though, my eyes kept returning to that advert until I lost any resistance and cut it out and wrote my reply to it. Unbelievable? Yes, I posted the reply to that advert next day. The reason for posting it pronto was that the paper was six weeks old by the time it reached Scotland.

# Chapter 10

## The Authentic Advert

> **The authentic Advert April 1954**
> **2 lebensfrohe Mädel**
> Freundinnen, kath., 21/1.68, wünschen, da es ihnen in der Diaspora an kath. Herrenbekanntsch. fehlt, wirklich echt kath. Jungmänner kennenzulernen, die Wert auf christl. Ehe- u. Familienleben legen. Bildzuschr. unt. 399 an MiZ.

Two friends, full of the joy of life, catholic, 21 years, 5`9"

Would like to correspond with young cath. men, who truly

value Christian Marriage and Family

Reply with photograph to: MIZ nr 399

'Newspaper Advert'

'Ehrentraut Krause – introductory photograph'

I had no desire to look for any special advertisement, and yet, there was this one whose simplicity struck me, leaving me, the reader, in no doubt as to the ideals they lived by and desired from anyone wishing to reply. I hesitated momentarily since the paper was several weeks old, was it worth replying? Then I seemed to hear a voice: "Is it not what you are waiting for? Are you not a committed Christian, who had secretly hoped to find someone one day? Well, lucky you, not one, but two are looking for you. The notice clearly said what is expected of you. Reach for the pen and ink". This I did!

This is a translation of my reply:

> *Tain, Scotland 14.06.1954; Grüss Gott.*
>
> *Dear Friends, {at this stage names were not published} you will be surprised to receive a reply to your advertisement from so far away in Scotland, where men wear the kilt. A German priest visits us twice a year and brings the 'Mann in der Zeit' for us to read. The Priest is Fr. Dumont from the Rheinland and is appointed by the German Bishops to look after the German Catholic ladies and men who work in Britain, that includes 'Schottland', from where this letter comes. When he comes and visits us, we meet in our parish house; have Mass and Kaffee und Kuchen afterwards. It will not surprise you when I say that he always brings the 'Mann in der Zeit'. Fr. Dumont has been in the UK since 1951. It means we know him well. You probably would like to know more who it is that sends you a reply? My sender detail gives you already my name. It is best to start from the beginning, if I may? I was born on 8$^{th}$ June 1926 in Gross Strehlitz, Upper Silesia, which you know is no longer part of Germany.*
>
> *My father was Housemaster in the castle at Gr. Strehlitz, under Graf Castell zu Castell until forced to flee from the Russian front. I completed my apprenticeship with the Post Office and looked forward to a good career, but because of Hitler, I was called up when 17 1/2 years old. I was only five months in the army when I was captured by the Americans in the outskirts of Rome. I spent almost two years in camps in America, {El Paso, New Mexico, and latterly in California}.*

> *After the war I was brought back to Europe in March 1946 and sent to the North of Scotland in a small POW camp. Two barracks for fifty men and two Scottish guards and a sergeant. The nearest town is called Tain, (from the old Viking 'Tink', I think). Tain is some six miles from the camp and right at a bay on the North Sea, with some 2,000 inhabitants. I work on the farm belonging to Mr Munro and his sister Miss Ella. They are my parents' age and neither are married. Mr Munro does not hear very well. After a few months we were allowed to live in the farmer's house, if they had a room. Mr Munro and his sister were happy to have me live with them and treat me like a son. My parents are still in Gross Strehlitz, where my father is Sexton in our old Parish Church. Ursula, my sister, is a nun and domestic science teacher in Bavaria. My brother Engelbert is a printer with a newspaper in Düsseldorf. I have a car and go to Mass on Sundays some 18km away from Tain. The catholic Diaspora causes problems in Scotland too, as you wrote in your advert, there are no catholic girls in our church to meet. I play the piano and the organ, not professionally, and I like singing. I do not know if I want to stay here, but I trust my faith and hope that I shall meet someone like your advert speaks of. Maybe I have written too much and I know I may be too late with my letter, but if you would like to hear more about Scotland please let me know. I always had placed my trust in the One who cared for me and never disappointed me. My greetings to you.*
>
> *With God's blessing, Paul Lippok, Viewfield Farm, TAIN, Ross-shire, Schottland.*

With a prayer and hope, I completed the letter and went down to the kitchen, where Ella had just made a pot of tea. I was happy to share details of my introduction to the ladies venture and remember Ella was clearly pleased for me. We both knew that our relationship would change sometime. A year or so earlier we had an in-depth discussion concerning my personal attitude about marrying a Scots lassie. Choice there was aplenty, of that I was well aware. Ella had understood my attitude and belief. For me a mixed marriage between Protestant and Catholic was not the ideal. Could I be sure that a

Scottish wife would adapt to a German environment? Especially if not able to converse in German. Having posted my letter and hoping for a reply regardless what, there was work to be done and a wage to be earned. Lambs were growing up, sheep shearing, turnip singling and watching as young lambs grew more and more cuddly, all helped to fill the days of waiting. I also developed my new idea of trying to cultivate button mushrooms in one of the disused Mansfield sheds. Straw is what you need and of that we have aplenty. Three weeks had elapsed and no return for my effort so far. Life goes on.

Early in July I returned home for dinner as usual. Ella was busy at the stove, not saying a word but pointed to a letter which lay on the dresser. It was addressed to me and I did not recognise the handwriting. It was then that I remembered my answering the advert and according to Ella, I blushed. My curiosity was aroused and I saw that the sender was an Ehrentraut Krause of Deister Strasse 62, Hameln, of 'Pied Piper' fame.

My heart skipped a beat and I was grateful when Ella suggested I should read my letter in my room after dinner, which had just been laid out as David entered. It required some control not to rush through the meal, but I also did everything I normally did after dinner before I went upstairs clutching the envelope, opened it and started to read.

> *Hameln, 29.06.1954. 'Grüss Gott' {God greet you} Dear Mister Lippok,*
>
> *Thank you very much for your letter which came as a surprise from so far away. We did not know that the 'Mann in der Zeit' would be read in Scotland. My friend left it for me to answer your letter. I thought it was interesting, so here I am. You asked if you are too late? I hope not, at least not your letter. My friend and I had a number of replies sent to us by the Newspaper, 46 in total. Yours was one of the last three. My mother took the bundle and handed them out, one for my friend and one for me. That was fun. Of course, not everyone attracted us. Who will be the right one will emerge. We can only hope and wait. Would you like to enter into an exchange of thought with me? It should be possible to a certain extent,*

> *but not continually by letter only. Perhaps there might be a possibility of your visiting your family in Germany during the year? Let us see how we get on. You have already introduced yourself and I shall do likewise. For a start this is my surprise for you, I and my friend are Silesian girls. I was born actually in the Trebnitz hospital, the place of our Silesian patron saint, Hedwig which you no doubt will know about. We, my father, mother, my younger sister Annemarie and I lived in the village of Kapsdorf, which is halfway between our capital Breslau and Trebnitz. We had a small farm, where we lived happily until that dreadful January 1945 when, in that cold winter, we had to flee from the Russian front. I shall say no more at this stage. After our expulsion we were sent to live in this beautiful town of Hameln. I am sure your people will know the story of the "Rat Catcher"? I am a qualified shop assistant in gents' outfitters. I am also active in our church and a youth group leader. I love singing, but do not play an instrument. I took dancing lessons and my favourite dance is the waltz. At the moment I am attending English evening classes but I am only a beginner. You of course, will be very good now, since you speak it all the time. That should suffice for today? Enclosed is my photograph.*
>
> *Greetings, Ehrentraut Krause, Hameln, Deister Str. 62, Germany*

Of course, I read the letter several times. There was something in the words of Miss Krause that appealed to me. It did not seem to be a negative reply, rather an invitation to tell the young lady more about Scotland and my life among its people. I thought also that her question about the possibility of my visiting family in Germany was something positive. I read it as an invitation to meet if I cared, even though I had to assume I was facing competition, considering the number of replies the two friends had received. Miss Krause's letter gave the impression of an outgoing person with the will to make the best of life; it would be prudent not to let my heart beat faster. Miss Krause seemed to be an active and busy person within her church community. Also enjoyed dancing and I felt that her Christian faith and ideals were woven like a thread throughout her letter. I knew that my second letter would be on its way to Miss Krause without delay.

*Viewfield, 4 July 1954 Dear Miss Krause,*

*Ehrentraut, what a wonderful name your good parents gave you! I believe your name can be explained in two sections, 'Ehren' meaning honour, and 'Traut' meaning trust, am I right? To have received an answer from you to my letter was welcomed. Of course I would love to tell you more about myself and my life here in Scotland. Before I go on, I must tell you how much pleasure it gave me to read that you too, are also Silesian. Why? Because, as I explained to Miss Ella my adopted 'mother', my reason for not having thought about a relationship here with a local lady was, that I left Silesia when it was still peaceful and beautiful and not ravaged by war. All my experiences so far give me the strong belief that my life has been guided by providence. It was a surprise indeed to read that you are a born Silesian. Like an unexpected voice calling from our old 'Heimat', Homeland. It does sound like a call from heaven. Could it be? You purposefully did not disclose it in your advertisement, yet something made me reply to yours and none other. Perhaps the idea might provoke a thought in both of us? If so, please tell me. What are we doing on the farm at present? Have you ever seen over a hundred sheep being shorn of their wool? You start by gathering them into pens at the farm, then someone will bring a sheep to the shearer and he will shear it within ten minutes, that is if he is very good. Actually that is what I am doing these days. I have learned to shear sheep very quickly to help David who was finding it more difficult. I read with interest that you had a small farm in Kapsdorf; it means you know what it is all about. No lazy Saturdays or Sundays. It must have been very hard on your mother when your father was called up. Having to work the farm and take care of two children. I can imagine that you as a twelve year old would have been already a help to your mother.*

*I spent my school holidays on my Grandma's small farm, where I learned all about farm work. Not wanting to show off, however, I do everything on the farm here. Something different now, we have Mass every Sunday at 10 o'clock in the morning in a town 18 km from Tain. I used to cycle there every Sunday, now of course I have a car and I am giving a family a lift. The mother actually comes from the Sudeten and married a Scottish soldier who was a British POW*

> *in Germany. I think her mother is now in West Germany, I think in Stadthagen? I hope I have not bored you, but I do enjoy writing to my family so I get carried away. It will be my pleasure if you wish to know more from me. May God bless you and keep you, greetings to your parents and friend until the next time? Yours sincerely, Paul Lippok.*

At Viewfield, Ella had asked me would I please send my parents by way of a letter her's and David's gratitude for what I did all those years, especially for the following. Not that many months ago, sadly Ella and David's youngest sister Terry had died as feared, at the early age of forty five, leaving a grieving husband and four young sons. The youngest boy Peter was only ten years old and he was of particular concern to Ella. She wondered if she should take him into Viewfield for a year or two. I knew what I had to do, and supported the idea, assuring her I could be an older brother to him. That made Ella very happy and appreciative. I knew Peter since he was three.

Peter had been with us now for two years, with me playing the older brother. After homework, Peter would waste no time but looked for me to help me. He loved to come with me in the Land Rover. We both enjoyed our games of football around the farm, and he liked to help me feed the cattle or accompany me in the Land Rover when I checked the animals in the fields each evening. We played football with two trees being the goal posts, that and much more. He is due to start in the Academy at his home and will leave us to go with many memories. {After fifty years we still write Christmas Cards}.

# Chapter 11

# Correspondence Courtship - Abridged

So far, three letters had exchanged between Miss Krause and me. I did not know if I was the sole recipient of her lovely long letters, but was happy not to ask. In any case it's early days. I actually enjoy the mystery. It was a joy for me to discover that we clearly shared the same principles and precepts. In the pages that now follow you may read our personal correspondence and see how our friendship blossomed.

> *Hameln, 13.07.1954 Dear Mr Lippok,*
>
> *Thank you for your letter in which you told me so much about Scotland. I am slowly building a picture of your life from the details you have given. I shared much of your letter with my parents and we all found it so interesting. I hope you will not be impatient with me if I keep asking you questions when something is not clear to me. You asked us to be honest in our search to know each other and that makes it easy for me to tell you that I do not believe I am willing to be a farmer's wife. I am not afraid of work but have been medically advised not to lift heavy items. Please do not misunderstand me; I am not sick but would not want to compromise joys of childbearing and motherhood.*
>
> *I am happy to tell you about our new church in Hameln. The town and its surrounding area are predominantly Lutheran, but the Catholic population increased from 600 to 8,000 when we, the displaced Silesians, arrived. County and government helped financially to cover part of the cost to build a new modern church, which we love. It was consecrated less than a year ago and so far there has only been one wedding. It was interesting to tell my parents*

> that you play the piano and the organ. I understand, you did say not professional. While I do not play an instrument, I love singing. We sing a lot in church at the youth services and any other services as you can imagine. We Silesians are born singers, are we not? Let me know if I am right? May God take care of you,
>
> Yours sincerely, Ehrentraut Krause

---

> Viewfield, 18.07.1954 Dear Miss Krause,
>
> May I wish you a happy and pleasant Sunday with your parents, sister and your friend Gretel. We also enjoyed a warm sunny Sunday and naturally I was at Mass with Mrs Sellar and her two children. I am teaching Peter, the older one, to be a server. I admit I let my thoughts reach out to you in Hameln, when you too would have been at Mass. May I thank you for your open and honest letter, which left me in no doubt of your integrity towards courtship before marriage. It strengthened my resolve to continue to share with you my thoughts and expectations. Thank you for sending me the photograph of you. It reminds me to mention that, from my letters so far, you will have gathered I could not offer you a bed of roses. To achieve that would take some time yet and would require the help of a companion. Miss Ella and David wonder how we are progressing and the continual arrival of your letters seems to reassure them that I am still in the race, am I? You ask about the farm, the lambs are growing and the hay will soon be ready and stacked for the winter. I find it wonderful that you will have no difficulty understanding what I am talking about. I almost forgot your questions regarding my room. I have finished papering it, although it is a small room it is comfortable, and I see your smile every time I walk in. From my bedroom I look out on to the blue water of the firth and when it is dark the lighthouse blinking light shines into my room. By the way, I have not told you that I earn extra pocket money by being the butler at functions in the Mansfield Hotel that is also on our land at the edge of town. This will suffice for today, may God be with you and your loved ones. God bless you and your family, Paul Lippok.

*Hameln, 22.07.1954 Dear Mr Lippok,*

*Thank you for your welcome letter. I find it interesting to learn about life so far north. Thank you also for the map of Scotland and the dot that told me where to look in an atlas. It made me happy to receive your answer to my letter. I wanted to be absolutely honest with you in my conception of Christian values and human values in general. It helped me a good deal to appreciate where you stand. Having read your letter twice over, I did appreciate your honesty. In my work I have to bear so much untruthful and unwelcome language which is against all my principles. I just have to close my ears because I have to keep my job to save for my future.*

*Our Dad was called up in 1939 when I was 6 years old and my sister Annemarie three. We saw him only once a year for a short time during his leave. Even then he was busy on the farm helping when on leave, giving Mum her instructions how to do things on the farm. It could not have been easy for our Mum, working the farm and looking after us. I had to help wherever I could after school. It was seven years later in July 1946 when we were all together again and our prayers were heard that Dad had survived the war. Thanks be to God. You would like me to tell you about our flight from the Russian front? I feel this is not the right moment, do you mind? I would prefer to hear more about your life, work and attitudes; the other can wait for a more appropriate moment. Before I forget, may I congratulate you on your names-day St Paul? Next time I will let you know my date. I could write more about what I am doing every day. Tomorrow I will be working late because I have to work during the night to help the decorators changing the two large shop windows. It is tiring work. We are also expecting visitors for the day who is Dad's cousin. This will have to do for today.*

*Yours sincerely, Ehrentraut Krause, do you like my first name?*

> *Viewfield, 28.7.1954 Dear Miss Ehrentraut,*
>
> *Thank you for your welcome letter. Now that I have your smiling photograph, I know who I am talking to. Thank you also for all the news of your varied daily life in Hameln. I worry that you are such a busy lady with all the youth work, and your full-time job, yet you still find time to write to me. I hope you had a rest after your night attending the decorators? To answer some of your questions, my father was Housemaster in the castle owned by Count Castell-Castell. The Russians burned down the centre of our town and the castle, which included our flat. My parents opted to stay and had to accept Polish citizenship. My father was very fond of our mum's family.*
>
> *They all had small farms and spoke a bit Polish. Father was then asked to become the Sexton in our church, where I was altar boy, and that made him happier. My brother Engelbert is sure he will get them out of Poland one day, hopefully. That will be a wonderful day for all of us. I have not told you my parents name, my father's name is Franz and my mother's name is Anna. I have not seen them for nearly eleven years. Engelbert was born in 1930 and is in the printing trade in Düsseldorf. He is not married taking his time to choose; actually I have not heard of any girlfriend. Our sister Ursula has made her final vows as a nun in Munich. Engelbert accompanied me when we went to the very moving ceremony at the convent. Actually our Countess Castell, now living near Frankfurt, came to Munich to the Ceremony, where we both wept because our parents could not be with us. Ursula will teach Domestic Science and English to the junior class. Who knows? You might meet her some day? That will do for today. May you and your family have a pleasant weekend.*
>
> *Yours, sincerely Paul Lippok*

At Viewfield we were enjoying a pleasant, dry and warm August in Tain, which raised hope for an early harvest. The team returned from their annual holidays and began the usual preparations, the checking of binders, the sharpening of all-important blades, etc. There being no combine harvester yet, scythes were still used to cut round the edges of the cornfields. The annual lamb sales began at Lairg and David hoped for a good financial return. Having worked with lambs for six years, I judged ours to be above average. At long last the reconstruction of the steading had been completed. I had acquired a really good handbook on joinery and will enjoy doing more joinery on several projects still requiring attention. The correspondence between Miss Krause and me seems to be leading into a fascinating but still only possible courtship, despite my assumption that even now I might still have a rival, or two? Any suggestions?

> *Hameln, 07.08.1954 Dear Mr Lippok,*
>
> *Thank you for your kind letter. I hear that you are well, and I too am well although we have been busy at home. Were you hoping to have a letter from me? I should have mentioned in my last letter that we would have a very important birthday celebration last week. It was Dad's 50th birthday. He looked forward to a party and we wanted to make the best for him. We had many family guests, some coming from afar. Annemarie and I helped Mum with the baking, but I must admit it was chiefly my sister, who did a two-year course in housekeeping. My friend Gretel's birthday was on the same day so she joined us as usual. After we washed up I took time to read your welcome letter. On Wednesdays at 6 a.m. we have our monthly Youth Mass. It is always well attended and as a group leader I try to be there. You must know that many people in Germany start work at 7 a.m. I am tired, but would like to finish this letter to you because I had no time to do so yesterday as I promised. I would have liked to be at Fr. Leppich's talk. You heard of him I am sure. He is so good at speaking to the youth after Hitler's disaster. The youth follow Fr. Leppich in thousands. He is a very down to earth speaker to the youth, us! I am sure he comes near from your former home?*
>
> *I have just attended the wedding of my friend from the dancing class. She married a nice young man who has a good career in a bank. Her parents have a furniture business so she will move into a completely furnished home with a modern kitchen. Please understand, I am not envious. Thank you for your few English lines, I could read most of it.*
>
> *God's blessing and greetings, sincerely, Ehrentraut Krause,*

*Viewfield, 15.08.1954* Dear Ehrentraut Krause,

"Whatever worth we are in the eyes of God, that's how much we are and not more. He who created me in my entirety will also demand me back in my entirety". Ehrentraut, it is my seventh letter and like yours it seems we are still in a mood to find out about ourselves as time goes on. It gets only more interesting to find out about your life and your mind, which I find fascinating, do you feel the same? Since you keep replying to my letters could I ask would you mind if we drop the use of the German 'Sie' and use the German third expression 'Du'? Please be so kind and let me know.

I do enjoy getting and reading your letters and hunger for more if you keep on feeding me with yours. After all in the eyes of God we are brother and sister. Somehow I have the feeling you will not rebuke me. Ehrentraut we are at the start of harvest here, yes a good three weeks behind in Germany, so if my letters are a bit shorter you will pardon me. The forecast is for good harvest weather, but one never knows. It will be pretty hot with you in Hameln, it is important that you have a good holiday. I can well imagine you are looking forward to get away from thinking about your shop and seeing something different, other people and scenery, and change of air. Actually that brings me to tell you I am seriously thinking about my coming to visit you and Hameln and say 'Hallo'? Please let me know what your thoughts are? Let me stop here, and wish you happy holiday, and I wait for your return, one never knows whom you might meet? Many greetings to you and your family, and your friend Gretel, Yours, Paul, and may the good Lord take care of you.

Oh how lovely; your letter arrived before posting mine. What a lovely surprise to get those lovely blossoms, all the way from Germany across the sea. I can only think what a lovely romantic thought, but I dare not think beyond that, for the time being. It did not pass unnoticed that you should have thought to send me so soon the blossoms and the photo of Rüdesheim, thank you so much. I shall close my letter for Miss Ella to post it when she goes shopping. May the dear Lord protect you and bring you safely home after a restful and refreshing holiday.

Yours, Paul.

*Hameln 19. 08.1954. My dear Paul,*

*You certainly caught me by surprise; but to be honest, I have seen it coming. I feel I have no option but to follow suit and avail myself of our German "Du". I do agree with you Paul, we have reached a stage when it has become appropriate to informally address or talk to each other as close friends. Thank you so much. That is my holiday outside Hameln gone, and we will see what time off I might be able to get when you come in October. Are you looking forward to it? My second week after my tour I am spending at home doing housework for Mum. Mum does clean the hall way in this four storey house to help with the rent. Our parents have gone; or rather we have helped them to go, to the Harz Mountains where they have never been before. They had sent a card and are having a good time. My sister Annemarie has taken her holidays to spend at Krefeld near the Dutch border, where she attended the domestic college. I now have to try and cook for myself. That is not so difficult, enjoying eating it alone is. Could you not come and try my creations? You would like me to tell you more about my holiday tour? Just a few appetisers then I retire to bed as I am ready to fall asleep, Goodnight my dear Paul, there! I said it. Good Morning Paul, after breakfast I want to finish this letter so that I may get it posted on my way to work, you do not want to wait too long for a letter from me, do you? By the way, my friend Gretel and I will go to see the 4-hour film "Gone with the Wind", have you seen it yet? Let it suffice for today. The post box is just around the corner on my way to work. My holiday report will follow. With my best wishes,*

*Yours Ehrentraut, if I can be it?*

---

*Viewfield. 25.8.1954 Grüss Gott, My dear Ehrentraut,*

*I think yours is a lovely name, I have never heard any other lady being called that at home. Thank you for your newsy letter which makes me happy. Here at Viewfield, as in the rest of Britain,*

> the harvest is in full swing; the sun shines; everybody in summer shirts and feeling good. As each field is cut closer and closer the rabbits keep hiding towards the centre, until soon there is nowhere left to hide. They run out and we try to catch them. Other news, I keep up my correspondence with my parents, sister and brother. Engelbert talks already about accompanying me. He could take Gretel out? What do you think? Sorry, I must go out, some clever or a known trouble maker of a sheep has broken out through a loose fence, and the others follow, as the proverbial story says.
>
> My dear Ehrentraut, sorry I had to stop yesterday when those sheep broke out of the field and then it was late evening. Now bless you on this beautiful Sunday afternoon. Thank you for your kind and very thoughtful letter which has arrived within three days. I had every reason to think about you more intensely at this morning's Mass. You really pinned me to the wall didn't you with your probing thoughts and uncompromising questions. It confirms my suspicion that you are serious in making me aware of your conviction on Christian marriage. May I suggest when I am in Hameln with you, we take time and the two of us talk earnestly just you and me alone, Yes?
>
> Yes it is true that in the back of my mind occasionally I had that thought of marrying a Silesian lady, who had lived through the trauma at the end of the war, wondering how it could happen, Ehrentraut. Miraculously now it could happen? Patience is not a problem for me. I wait dear Ehrentraut until we meet in October, only two month away. Then we will be able to hold hands and, while looking into each other's eyes, heart and mind will say yes or no. Until then, we keep our thoughts and words crossing sea and sky, yes? Best wishes to your parents, Annemarie and Gretel.
>
> Let's hope the weather stays, then the harvest can finish and I can think about booking my journey. In the mean time I hope you will keep looking for my letters, as I do?
>
> Sincerely yours Paul.

At Viewfield things looked favourable for completion of harvesting by the end of September. Allowing for an early start on lifting potatoes, in October. Having talked about my going to Germany in the second half of October, David and Ella assured me that I was not to worry and I felt free to start making my travel plans. I do admit getting excited at meeting Ehrentraut. She was clearly someone special, a strong character full of profound thoughts, who is not swayed by dubious ideas, giving them a hearing, while standing by her own. Yet, she lives in the world as it is, enjoying selected films, attending all the church's youth festivities including dancing. Happy attending dancing classes, waltzes being her favourite. Oh dear, I require some urgent practice!

> *Hameln, 28.08.1954 'Grüss Gott', dear Paul,*
>
> *It is Sunday afternoon and I am sitting in our living room drinking coffee on my own, wishing you could join me for a cup, and I have some cake from the baker in our house. Did I mention that half of the first floor is let to a very good baker who has a great variety of cakes? He is open on Sundays from midday till 4 o'clock. You must try it when you come.*
>
> *Paul, I am very grateful you have answered my questions so honestly and convincingly. You have strengthened my thinking and I really look forward as you suggest to facing each other and discussing our thoughts and beliefs when you are here, it will be interesting. I shall follow you and be patient until you come, only a few weeks now. I feel sorry for your little lambs being taken from their mother, and am glad you have told me about them; because the thought came to me that is how it is with our own mothers, who are so close to us while we are inside them. Once born we are no longer one. It is the first parting which must be felt at first, but soon forgotten when we can hold them close. That is how I imagine it, you with your lambs will understand.*
>
> *That brings me to the film "Gone with the Wind". A powerful film, and it made me think a lot. Sometimes I felt not good, because it brought out war as it really is. You know a good deal about me to understand that some parts of the story did not agree with me, but I realised that's how life is sometimes in our world today. The colours and scenery were stunning. You will have seen much of it in real life. Maybe we shall have time to talk about it when you are here. Were you surprised to get a card from Stadthagen? Gretel and*

*I went by bike to see Mrs. Milas, the mother of Mrs Sellar from Tain. A lovely grandmother. She told us more about where you are and about you. Oh, oh! She was surprised and pleased when I said I brought greetings from Scotland and asked if I was your bride? Can you imagine, Paul, how I felt? I'll tell you when you are here. She insisted on making coffee for us, for which we were glad. It takes two hours one way by bike. She told us a lot about Scotland and especially about Tain. Oh dear, all that came out about you. I will still welcome you in Hameln. She sends greetings and you must visit her when you come here. We could do that one evening. We arrived home safely and were tired but enjoyed the trip. Now I hope to get to bed early, because Gretel and I have agreed to attend the open buffet and dance celebrating the feast of St. Augustin, our church's patron saint, I will pray for you. Please pray for me and keep well.*

*With all my best wishes, Yours, Ehrentraut.*

---

*Viewfield, 10.9.1954 My dear Ehrentraut,*

*Thank you for your very interesting letter in which you told me so much about your work in the parish youth group. It made me quite envious, for it brought back so many memories of my time in our church youth group. In our day one had to be so careful, because of the constant listening and probing of Hitler Youth members, some of whom barely knew what fanaticism really meant. They posed a constant threat and, when I look back, I believe we must have been close to being reported by them for disobedience against Party rules.*

*There are too few of us here to have a youth group; but how wonderful it must be to feel free now and to organise all sorts of helpful meetings and conferences on Christian faith and morals. It does me good to read your commentaries and reports; they allow me to share in your work. I am quite sorry I cannot join you and help in the young male groups. It tells me a lot about your nature and unshakeable faith. I feel compelled to tell you that you are the sort of person I would love to share my life with. I hope you do not mind my saying this, but it is the truth. Just to change the subject, are you beginning to count the weeks until I start my journey to meet you? Now the weeks can be counted in single numbers. You did mention that I should give you some idea of my expected accommodation for the time. It depends on how long you would like me to stay, a week? One thing is sure since my brother would like to accompany me, a double room, nothing expensive so long as it has a bed and heating just in case the weather turns cold. Engelbert feels he could keep Gretel company while you and I try to find time for ourselves. That is, unless you take one look at me and your mind and heart tell you that I am not the one, then we would only send Christmas cards to each other. It was great to hear you actually did go and visit Mrs Milas at her home. You did well cycling the two hours to her home. So you found out all about my terrible things I never told you about? Is it worth my coming to see you? Well, I am coming anyway, I want to meet you. There you are. You know I look forward to hearing from you soon; but do not give up precious sleeping time to write to me. You really should not give up sleep, for it is the body's best medicine. All my greetings to your family and to Gretel (as yet unknown).*

*Yours sincerely, Paul.*

---

*Hameln 13.09.54   Grüss Gott, as we say in Silesia, My dear Paul, What is the matter?*

*I am waiting for a sign of life from you. I do hope you are well and it's just that you are so busy at the harvest. Or worse, have I somehow offended you? That is the last thing I would do. Please let me know soon; a short note will satisfy me. I can certainly understand how busy farmers are during harvest. I remember well at home, when the two of us had to look after ourselves, because mother had to help in the field. I also had to look after my little sister, especially during the war years, when our Dad was away. At least we had a young Polish boy to help with the horses and the heavy work outside, sowing and harvest time, and feeding the cows and horses. Something I have never told you: My job after school was* to look after the goslings herding them for an hour on the grass patch. My other weekly job was to sweep and clean the footpath outside our property on Saturdays. Every time I had finished raking it neatly someone would walk along ruining my pattern. I shall never be able to forget how hard Mum had to work while Dad was away for five long years. Yet she still had time for us to take us in her arms and tell us a story. Looking after my sister perhaps, made me grow up sooner. Then in the last half of 1944 I went 7km by train to secondary school in Breslau. On the way home the air raid siren would go off and we had to run to the air raid shelter. Enough of that, or we might talk again in years to come; perhaps?? We will soon know, yes? Yours sincerely Ehrentraut, greetings from Mum, Dad and Annemarie, yes and Gretel.

---

*'Viewfield'* 17.09.54  "Grüss Gott" dear Ehrentraut, as they greet in Bavaria and often in Silesia too.

One day I will tell you of my school holidays in Bavaria, yes? Maybe? First of all thank you for your worrying letter which could have told me something, that you can tell me when we meet. Yes, I thought how loving, should I say it? That you worried about me not having had a letter from me. I could read something into it, but should I risk it? Please, never think you might have offended me; I do not think you could. Yes, work and repairs on machinery kept me up late in the evening. The weather has let us down. A blessing we got the grain harvest just in, but the potato lifting might be a problem. This would not be the first time that potato lifting was late. Rain is the problem, not the cold or heat. Determined patience is what a farmer needs. I am sure I will see half of the potato crop lifted before I come to meet you Ehrentraut.

I am sorry that you should have worried when there was no letter. In one way it made me feel warm inside, but I cannot think how you possibly could offend me? So if it happens again just go to a *dance or read one of your interesting books. Better still go one day early to bed to be well when I come to stand before you and be approved, by your family and friends, oh and your parish Priest?*

*I have spoken to Mr Taylor, who owns the Ford garage, regarding hiring a car from him. I know him well because I play the piano for his wife who is a very good singer in Mr Taylor's small concert party. There is also a gentleman singer, and a comedian, who was the driver of the truck that brought us to the farms from camp, and me to Viewfield, it is a small world. I will let you know Ehrentraut if I come by car or by train. My heart is trying to tell me I could be falling in love with you. Caution prevents me from believing it. Your principles on true love, trust and faithfulness in marriage, plus your spiritual values you uphold interest me so much which keep drawing me to you. Could I be the only contender? I must not chance my luck. Dear Ehrentraut, for today to you and your family all my good wishes.*

*Yours, Paul.*

---

*Viewfield 19.9.54    Grüss Dich Gott, My dear Ehrentraut,*

*Thank you for your long letter with so much news, almost like a daily newspaper. I just love to read your letters and all they contain. There is something special about hand-written letters: they are so much more personal. I would go so far as to say they could speak to the reader of Love. You might care to comment on that next time. Will there be a next time? I sincerely hope so. How do you cope with all the work you do in your spare time, and still write wonderful letters? I have wondered a few times whether you are trying to make the time pass quickly before you give up your daily job for some other occupation? Please do not misunderstand my comments.*

*Thank you for copying the articles on the main issues you hear at your youth evenings. You ask would I be interested. Without question, since it brings back memories of my youth meetings, when we had to be especially careful under Hitler's regime. But remember, I was at an age where 'pigtails and aprons' were not discussed at youth-groups under fourteen. It was interesting to read about the Sunday afternoon cycle ride with your group. What professional planning for the visit to some beautiful towns and villages around Hameln! That sort of activity does not happen here. I recall how we used to cycle to various shrines or beautiful churches in my youth. Dear Ehrentraut, you manage to bring back so many lovely memories for me. My dear, I have read your letter twice over in the quietness of our surroundings here. Before I say my prayer of thanks for another wonderful day, I could not glide over your account of a comment made by your branch manager at a recent staff party, when he remarked, "Ehrentraut has changed somehow, is she in love?" With whom? I venture to ask. But you go on teasing me, "is it noticeable?" In all honesty, I cannot answer that because I have experienced nothing like it before. However, I'll be reckless and enjoy it as being directed at me? Should I have done that? In a few weeks' time I shall know? I am glad that you enjoyed your weekday excursion to Fulda and the annual Catholic Gathering with your group. I shall follow the commentary in our Scottish Catholic Observer and answer some of your questions so far as I am able. God bless you, dear Ehrentraut, please remember me to your parents and Annmarie and Gretel.*

*With all my love, yours Paul, am I?*

---

*Hameln, 24.9.1954. My dear Paul,*

*Thank you very much for your long-awaited letter, I began to worry about you, in case you were not well? If I do not hear from you in good time, I get anxious what might have happened. You work with strong animals and machinery. I enjoy reading your letters; I have already built up a strong trust in what you tell me, your outlook and for me important your understanding of my views, apart from my religious convictions!*

*In your writings you express what I have prayed and hoped for when I began to think about my future as a possible mother. The fact that you are patient with me I count as a bonus. I am glad you are able to proceed with your corn harvest, so that I can look forward to meet you. You must have already good experience in building your corn stacks. As you know here in Germany it all goes into barns. You asked if Gretel has found someone to correspond with, yes she has, so far they are still corresponding. We two are close friends in our outlook and convictions, but do differ occasionally. My parents are a bit unhappy with my youth work and now the letter writing. They worry that I may not get enough rest and sleep. But that cannot be helped as long as the 'bird' has not left the roost. Yes, I do have to write often late at night and at times at breakfast to make sure the letter goes off. My Dad says that I am married to my youth work. The other day he again told me that I am married to my youth work, saying that my future husband would have to book an evening a week ahead to talk to me.*

*By the way you have not yet made any comment regarding my brown eyes? I know it is only a black and white photo, do you think they suit me? I am happy with them and thank God I can see. Well if we keep on writing the way we do I may have to give up some of my outside work; and should I get married then there would be no time for youth work. Oh yes you have not told me the colour of your eyes, please do. I will guess, but will not tell you now. At least I am glad you have time and still interested to write to me, it helps me to think and imagine about you when the decorators come in a few days; and I have to help and clean up after them. I will not get home before one in the morning, totally 'kaputt' – tired. Still, these days, as Dad says, better to stay with them if you can because it is not so easy to get another job in Germany once you are a qualified shop 'Assistant'. Dear Paul, are you counting the days until your 'Urlaub' holiday like me? My Dad said something about my spending money on holiday travel, thinking I become a travelling aunt {Reise Tante}? Perhaps that's what he thinks when I keep writing to you. We shall see sometime soon? I will be going to our Youth Centre in Woldenberg in two weeks time, but you will still get your letters, if you will still be looking for them. I pray that our good Lord cares for you while you build corn 'steeples'.*

*Your Ehrentraut.*

At Viewfield, slowly but surely we brought the harvest in. I would be leaving for Hameln on 27th October, and it now seemed likely that the potatoes too would be lifted and safely stored before my departure. I confided in Ella that I believed I may have fallen in love, while Ella had been wondering when I would tell her. Ehrentraut, while keeping her cards close to her chest, there is the occasional slip of a word causing me to wonder what am I to make of it? I am in no hurry to ask, for I had discovered just how indescribably wonderful and beautiful it had been to get to know her by letter. I would not have wanted to miss this experience and saw no reason to force the issue. We have been corresponding for four months now and, God willing, we shall meet within the month. In the meantime let correspondence continue.

> *3.10.1954 'Viewfield' Dear Ehrentraut,*
>
> *Many blessings I wish to bring you my dear Ehrentraut on this sunny Sunday. Of course, I had every reason to think about you and include you in my Sunday prayers at church. I had Mrs Sellar and her children with me. May I say it? How I wish that one day you would sit beside me as we make our way to Mass. It would certainly be a good day for taking in the harvest but here that is not done on a Sunday. I am glad about that, not because of having a day off, for after all, cows have to be milked and animals fed. Thank you for your letter filled with so many interesting thoughts which resonate in my mind and heart. You seem so eager to absorb as much as possible from your attendance at weekend seminars, presentations and talks at your much loved Woldenberg Youth Centre. Perhaps we will have time to visit it together during my stay. I fully realise it may not be 'Me' that you choose. I shall keep knocking at heaven's door, or should I give up? No, no not so fast. Thank you for reminding me of the great tradition in our Silesia, the Rosary Devotions during October. My parents will surely be praying for us, and missing us. They know we two are corresponding and will be happy for us to find our way. Thank you also for the beautiful autumn flower. I shall certainly keep it well preserved within your letters. Who knows, might it not be possible for us to look at it together in years to come? I am not dreaming, simply wishing. Am I permitted to wish?*

*You have a pretty full programme ahead with the Parish Parents' Evening and all the other youth evenings. Must I remind you again to go to bed early?*

*It was good to hear that you are happy now that you know so much more about me, particularly what wind blew me to Scotland. Yes, it has been a long journey, but you too have travelled far. I have looked on my travels as my journey of life, and now it feels as if I may reach my destination in a month's time? Please do think about what I have just written, or? Could it be a happy ending in Hameln? I leave it in the hands of our Creator with whom 'we' seem to have a special relationship. That brings me to your question I have not yet answered: the colour of our eyes. For a start looking at your photograph morning and evening in good daylight yours are 'deer eyes', not the dark colours, more like the friendly deer we had in the castle's park. I am convinced when I shall look at you real for the first time, your eyes will sparkle in matching your hair which is dark, not jet black? My sort of blue eyes will fade with the blue grey sky. You too take care and keep well for me,*

*Yours, Paul.*

---

*Hameln, 6.10.1954 Dear Paul,*

*Your welcome letter gave me much pleasure, thank you. Your letters certainly encourage me to answer them as soon as I can. You seem concerned about my work with the young people and the occasional unpleasant times at the shop. Please do not be worried about my missing sleep. I am just one of those who need more sleep than most people. You are right, I am sure, that sleep might be the best medicine for me. Our Parents' Evening was another great success, and we had fun. I thought how lovely it would have been if you and I could have danced a waltz together. Let us hope it may happen. I am pleased you liked the card I sent from our Youth Centre. We have new shop assistants, replacing others that have left. We shall see how we get on. I hate the constant lying to customers. It is totally against my principles, but if you have the opportunity to* learn a trade you have to take it, there may not be another chance. I should never have been a shop assistant. Enough of that!

My other friend, Dorle, went on an exchange trip to Stoke in Staffordshire without a word of English and enjoyed it very much. She suggested I start to take lessons. Whatever does she mean? Do you realise this is the 6th of October and there are still four week to go? Does it test your patience too? You do not mind if I ask and wonder whether you might be disappointed? Some men in the shop claim I am a "prickly character". Perhaps it is my forthright attitude. I am confident that we are at one in our understanding and resolve to enter marriage if that should be mutually agreeable after our long-awaited meeting? Do not be over anxious about the approval of my parents. I have shown them your photograph and trust my modest ability to perceive that they will approve if I am happy. I was so pleased to read that your mother had been on a pilgrimage to Trebnitz and the shrine of our Silesian patron saint, Hedwig. That meant she passed by our old home. It is a pity I did not know, for I could have sent her some information about Kapsdorf.

Just a few lines more to let you know what has kept me busy these last two days; one evening I spent with my colleague's wife who has some worries regarding their ten year old son who may have to go to a clinic. We do a bit of needle work on something that will be useful one day? Now I'd better listen to you and get off to bed. Next Sunday I will go again to our Woldenberg Youth Centre to attend a lecture for young people, including those preparing for marriage, it should be interesting. These days there are so many disturbing distractions on radio and on television, though many of us do not have it yet, {television that is}. Please take care and keep well. I hope you will soon complete the harvest, dear Paul, because I want to meet you soon.

God bless you and me, yours Ehrentraut.

*Viewfield, 12.10.1954. Grüss Gott, my dear Ehrentraut.*

*I can no longer suppress my excitement when I look at the date and am reminded that it really is only two weeks until the day I shall say goodbye to Ella and David and take the road to meet my love! I really cannot say just what I wish, not yet, but I am quite happy to live with the joy of anticipation. It is not that difficult to be patient and joyful. Your last letter, for which I thank you so much, contained hints that you too are anxious to meet. I love your suggestion that we go for a run to see your Diocesan Youth Centre. Nothing would give me more pleasure. The corn harvest is completed and we start lifting the potatoes in a day or two. It no longer matters to me if the weather suddenly stops the lifting. I have my tickets and, God willing, I shall be on my way. How does the song go? We both know it, "Mein Schätzlein kommt von ferne, Oh-ho Oh-ho – {My treasure comes from afar}". Ella thinks I may have fallen in love, what do you say to that? What if I have to fall out again? You asked if we have a radio in Viewfield. Yes we do. I always listen to the German programme at Christmastime, which inevitably draws tears when I hear our carols played and sung. I shall bring your Dad something Scottish.*

*We do not produce wine in Scotland. Whisky is a pure Scottish product. Would Dad like that? I shall bring some to taste. What is no longer a surprise is your schedule for next week. It means you will be late again every night! No wonder your Dad is afraid you are becoming a travelling aunt. I know you like to get the most out of your admirable youth work and I might as well say it, since the thought has entered my mind, it seems to me you would be the ideal person to continue your work here in our small parish in Scotland! You might comment on that when we meet, yes? There are many questions for us to think and talk over I am sure, will we have time? Should I have asked for more time? There is still that unanswered question, dear Ehrentraut, or am I so blind or frightened not to read or feel the answer in all the words you speak in your letters? Could this be the reason why I long so much to receive your letters? Please do not comment on what I have just written. I would rather wait to hear them whatever they are from your own lips and feel the breath whatever you may say to me; that way I will remember and feel your voice for ever. We have this wonderful word in German: Vorfreude, anticipation. That will have to suffice for today. May the good Lord take care of you for me, yes? My best wishes to your parents, sister and friend. Thank you for inviting Engelbert.*

*Yours, Paul.*

---

*'Viewfield', 17.10. 1954 My dear Ehrentraut,*

*Do not panic by getting a second letter from me within a few days. I am well and happy, but I did not want you to be anxious if you should hear about us in Schottland suffering heavy rain falls. Foremost important is that my plan will not be affected. In fact it was David who first assured me that my timetable should stay as I have booked my travel date and that potato harvesting will go on without me. That was the news I wanted you to hear and read from me. Regarding our Aunt Else, now that we know that Engelbert would like to come with me - and he thanks you for the invitation - it is a good thought of you to suggest Engelbert and I could visit her while you are at work. We would be back by the time you come home from work. Engelbert and I do wonder if Gretel has found someone to correspond with. Sorry, we are just curious.*

*I hope our good Lord has blessed you with good health, so important for our special day when by the grace of God we shall meet. It is good that we are kept busy, to help us pass the time. Thank you for your lovely news-filled letter. You are the busier person by far. You write so natural, as if you are telling me all you have done while I stand close by. You enjoy to the full the work you do with the young people. Ella and David are well and send their greetings and good wishes. My parents' letters take less time to reach Britain which is good, because I get a feeling of nearness. They are well but missing us and they are glad we are all well. They keep asking how we are progressing. I can only answer that we are looking forward to meeting each other for the first time later this month.*

*Regarding the tractor-man whose cottage in the town had been flooded in that awful rain, he has given in his notice, but will not be leaving till I return to the farm. David enquiring at the town council was told a vacant town flat was available to move into. That solved a significant problem for David. I am making progress in my mushroom business and getting results, I think I need help? Ella will pick them and will bring them to the grocer. I hope to break even. Mansfield House Hotel is still providing me with additional income from weddings and other formal functions. Can you imagine what goes through my mind at weddings, seeing a young couple celebrate their most important day? It is bedtime for me and you, and that is what you should do, yes it is an 'order', sorry but I thought it would do you good. Strange and wonderful, we have never met and yet we talk as if we have known each other for some time; in a way we do. Blessing and a 'Gute Nacht' Ehrentraut keep well; with all my love yours, oops, am I allowed to say that?*

*Yours, Paul.*

---

*Hameln, 15.10.1954   Grüss Dich Gott, 'God greet you'? Is that right? My dear Paul,*

*How exciting! In ten days we will look for the first time into each other's eyes full of admiration and joy, that is how I imagine it, and you? I am always glad to hear that you keep well, just in case the bad weather should cause you to feel ill. That would make me sad now that we have gotten to know each other and discovered some of our feelings for each other. Heartache or yearning I may tolerate. You must know by now how keenly I await your letters and love to read your news and your opinions which echo so much within me and make me feel and speak of love. Am I right? So far I have not had the opportunity to ask my 'boss' how many days off he will give me. A longer weekend would be nice but we will have two Sundays anyway. Mum accompanied Gretel and me to the town's newly-opened Youth Culture Hall; funded by the town of Hameln to encourage the interest of our young people in the old fairy-tales, which our grandmothers used to tell. A sad dying culture. Classical music and poetry were performed, good books and pictures and the revival of ballads. A lovely evening and I was happy that Mum could come with us. I am sure you would have enjoyed it, especially if you could have been at my side? Thank you for the photo of yourself and Engelbert. You look so serious, does Engelbert always laugh? Gretel has asked me if Engelbert will accompany you? I will attend a very interesting talk at our Youth Centre next Sunday. I do not want to miss it, but you will have your letter because I have an hour's wait for a connection at the station and will have time to write. I enclose a very informative article on sexual matters, which was part of one of the lectures for young people looking towards marriage. It is written by a well-known doctor and I would value your comment on it. May our dear Lord take care of both of us, now that we at last might meet, with my best wishes, your Ehrentraut.*

---

*Viewfield, 22.10.1954 My dear Ehrentraut,*

*This is probably my last letter to you before I leave on the most important journey in my life so far, and for the first time I find myself unable to find the words I want to say to you. There is so much within me to say or rather shout out for you to hear. I should not be presumptuous. Ella has been trying to tell me to slow down, because I keep finding jobs in the house that I wanted to do before I leave. Now to respond to the copy of the Youth Breviary, which I promised I would do. I admire your trust in confronting me before we meet to state exactly where I stand on the subject and principles on Purity before Marriage. To leave you in no doubt, I wish to reassure you by repeating my agreement with you in these words: "If it is God's will, that a child shall grow up in the womb of a committed family, it needs both father and mother, who as legitimate married members, husband and wife, have the right to use the determinant organs to effect new life". You and I are not immune from irreverent talk, pictures, newsprint, etc. No one is spared the struggle to resist those temptations to preserve purity of the body. I can do no better than follow your wise words as you signed yourself off in your letter: "That is how we want to keep it, by helping each other, victory is assured". What am I to read from those last words? This is a powerful statement Ehrentraut, which should leave no one in doubt what is expected. Anyone still in the running with me better look out and read the fine print. That is my advice, because I am still in the running, am I Ehrentraut?*

*Thinking about the subjects, we have written and thought about, I am looking down into our garden from my bedroom window; there is a rose outside, its bud still tightly closed and patiently waiting until it's time to unfold and reveal its beauty. Could I impatiently break it before it is ready to unfold itself? No indeed. While you, dear Ehrentraut follow your daily routine as you must, I have to think seriously about getting my belongings together for the journey. Time may fly, and I am still hoping to travel by car. I will send a short letter within a few days. With my best wishes to you and your Mum and Dad and Annemarie, always thinking about you, yours Paul.*

---

*Hameln, 23.10.1954 My dear Paul,*

*Your letter arrived this morning after I left for work, and my lovely mother had placed it in the favourite place where I would look first when I return for lunch. Thank you for your kind greetings and concerns. I am well and so far it has not been too stressful in the shop this morning. When the shop is not busy the men try to tease or impress with double-meaning jokes and comments. These I ignore as their inability to find a more interesting topic. Is there something about me that makes me hold off these days? Could the manager's remarks made about my being in love have something to do with it? Soon we will know if you and I have reached our goal and find out who has won? I do agree with you, it is time and we are at the stage when we are ready to know. I have never in my life read so many interesting and thoughtful letters and have enjoyed it. I have kept all your letters, every one of them. They were thoughtful and thought provoking. Our destiny is not being decided here and now. For that moment we still need more patience. At the*

*Youth Centre it has been interesting and inspiring as usual. Dear Paul, how I had wished for you to have been there with me. So often it seemed as if I was hearing your letters whenever we agreed on delicate topics. I would have liked a few more girls of my age group to have come with me here. How often I could have told them that there are true men who believe and live a life we heard about that day. I am so glad I went because there was so much to listen and hear that constantly made me feel you're beside me listening with me.*

*Gretel and I were at the dancing class yesterday, learning old and not so old German folk dancing, which I really enjoy. Sadly the boys are not interested, and we girls got on with it on our own. Pity you cannot stay a few weeks then we could go as a couple. Would you like to dance with me? Leaving the hall with my best friend I was glad I had my mock-leather raincoat and my bike. It rains nearly every other day in Hameln, if that is any comfort to you. Now my eyelids are drooping. It is almost midnight and I must rise early tomorrow. I can hardly believe that in a few days I will look into your eyes, and you into mine. What will we be able to say to each other? Have you thought about what you might say to me? I do wonder sometimes how many happy people have met like us. I hope it will be a lovely surprise for both of us. I appreciate your comments on the subject of purity before marriage. We are adults and I feel we wish to follow the same guidelines, yes? I am not tired of writing to you, but I am happy that at last I will hear your voice. May God protect you on your journey to me.*

*Yours, Ehrentraut.*

---

*Viewfield, 25.10.1954 My dear Ehrentraut,*

*This then is my last letter before I am able to reach out my hand to you. The clock is ticking far too slowly and to calm me down there is only one thing left to help, find something useful to do. All the words you have written to me carry the seal of a true friend, who reveals honesty, clear vision of what she or he truly believes and knows exactly right from wrong. You show respect for all fellow-humans and have all the qualities of a true comrade, a companion at whose side I would love to be for the rest of my life. Even a friendship can last forever if that is to be. There, I have said what I wanted to say.*

*Now I will give you the address of my brother's friend: Fam. Metzner, Düsseldorf, Ackerstrasse 49. I will pick up Engelbert from there, so if you need to give me any message you can send a note to that address. May God bless you and your family, and thank you for your prayers for my safe journey.*

*Yours Paul.*

# Chapter 12

# First visit to Hameln and my Love

It was October 27th 1954, our mother's birthday and I am about to begin the journey that may change my life as I live it now, and earnestly prayed for. A life that started in distant Silesia, God's beautiful never forgotten land. Through bitter pain and tears half way round the globe to the Highlands of Scotland. Now at last it is leading me to the unknown German city of Hameln. I was about to meet Ehrentraut a living, throbbing Silesian heart, that had been forcefully taken from home and resettled in a strange land. Will we find ourselves compatible? I feel I know her although we have not met and we have not yet heard each other's voice. Latterly we had exchanged written words that could have been construed as love, but I was convinced that Ehrentraut's fundamental attitude is such, that the word Love is not to be used lightly. For myself, I believe to experience love at its deepest meaning can be possible only by mutual understanding and common consent.

I had collected the car and hoped it would not let me down. My case was packed. Ella was baking some of her tasty girdle scones and other goodies for my journey. By having a car one has the opportunity to take many useful items like coffee beans, Scottish bake-ware, cigarettes, packets of tea and more, which are all still scarce.

I spent most of this last day doing whatever I could indoors and on the farm and retired early, hoping for a good night's sleep. Morning came and I had completed the milking and other chores by 10 a.m. Saying my goodbyes, I assured Ella and David that I would return. Young Peter waved me off and soon the steading was out of sight and I was on the road to distant Harwich. Recalling last year's trip, I hoped to travel an average of 40 mph. Ehrentraut's prayer is with me for a good journey which started well and it was a bright autumn day. If only the motorist's dream for a road-crossing of the two firths could come true! Leaving Inverness the capital of the north behind, I faced the long, quiet, yet beautiful drive through the Highlands and the Perthshire hills. Having to queue for the next ferry across the Firth of Forth was a welcome pause. This being my second visit, I was able to negotiate Edinburgh with ease, and headed for Newcastle. I took a longer break before midnight and slept till 2 am. Ahead lay the notorious "Doncaster Bottleneck" and the country road between Cambridge and Harwich. I wasted no time and continued the long journey. There were a few anxious moments en route, but I arrived at Harwich quay with more than an hour to spare, which is not that much, ferries do not wait for you. Cars were hoisted by crane into the ship's hold and, after a six-hour sail, we arrived at the Hook of Holland and passport control. Soon I was on my way to Düsseldorf to meet my brother Engelbert. The Metzner family (relatives of Aunt Else's husband Theo), with whom Engelbert lodged, welcomed me and offered me the sofa overnight. Mrs Metzner had a breakfast prepared and we expressed our thanks. Leaving a token from my Scottish collection then the hand-shakes and we were off. It was wonderful to have Engelbert at my side to keep us from falling asleep. I found it difficult to suppress my excitement at the prospect of meeting Ehrentraut when we finally departed. Quickly I realised we are on a motorway and Engelbert ordered attention on my part. He will keep pointing out the country side and any news he may remember. We had two stops for a break at motorway service stations. How glad I was to have Engelbert's company!

It was a fair day of sunshine and occasional showers. Negotiating the traffic raised a fear that we would not arrive in daylight. The traffic did increase on the motorway and we were not correct in timing our arrival. Darkness had descended and we had to slow down on account not knowing the road. The last twenty miles were on a minor road, and darkness had arrived as we neared Hameln. Since we were to arrive by train there was no need to have known any road instruction. Therefore we had to keep asking directions in town. I was not too perturbed not having let Ehrentraut know, yet she may have gone to the station for nothing with all sorts of possibilities going through her mind. That's when I got worried of Ehrentraut thinking I got cold feet. I could feel my heart was beginning to pound. We had arrived at last!

The names of the residents were displayed beside the entrance; the Krause family occupied the fourth floor. Engelbert pressed the bell button for Krause. Only a few moments and the buzzer responded. Having locked the car, I followed with the cases while Engelbert held the door open for me into the hallway. The light was a bit dull I thought, to save electricity I am sure. Having straightened ourselves, I took my case and was just at the second step when behind us the front door opened. Both of us turned round a bit perplexed and as the door closed we realised it was a lady, and from her photograph I instantly recognised that it was Ehrentraut. I put my case down and made a step towards Ehrentraut, stretching out my hand to greet her "Ehrentraut"? "Yes" she answered, not so sure of myself I asked, "may I kiss you", Ehrentraut's answer was quick and decisive, "No, you have not met my parents yet, this is the second time I have been at the station, follow me!" A sailor will know the feeling when the wind drops and your boat is going, nowhere! It dawned on me; I had not sent Ehrentraut a letter informing her that I will not be coming by train but by car. It made my tummy turn, how could I? Such a disaster.

We reached the fourth floor and Ehrentraut introduced us to her parents. Herr Karl and Frau Gertrud Krause welcomed us and we were led into the sitting room and invited to sit down. Conversation soon got under way with questions about our journey. Common ground was quickly found, because we were all Silesians and refugees with the shared loss of home and identity. While Ehrentraut helped her mother to prepare supper for us and set the table, she found opportunities to join in the conversation. I hung on her every word for one special reason. As she spoke, phrases in her letters to me came into my mind, her voice matching exactly as I had always imagined. I took the first opportunity to quietly ask for pardon having forgotten to send that note. I was forgiven, I thanked the Lord.

Presently we were asked to take our seats at table and Ehrentraut led us in saying the grace. We two sat opposite each other, which was more comfortable. Introduced as the mysterious suitor, there I was having my first meal with Ehrentraut and her family. I was glad that

Engelbert was with us, for my thoughts were all over the place. He engaged easily in conversation with her parents leaving Ehrentraut and I free to look at each other across the table and to wonder what was in the other's mind. I relaxed a little in the warm and pleasant atmosphere and ceased to dwell on my lapse at the front door. I began to feel better, we had at last met. I wondered if I could read something from her eyes or expression that conveyed a shared happiness. It was a joy for me to experience such emotions for the first time in my life. What really tugged on my heart and mind was Ehrentraut's voice, it moved me to the core. Having expressed my thanks for the meal, it was natural for me to offer help afterwards, but Ehrentraut's reply came quickly and raised a laugh, "No thank you, you can do that in Scotland". We all agreed with Herr Krause's suggestion that a 'schnapps' would be appropriate before retiring and we toasted "to the future" at Ehrentraut's suggestion, that was the moment for me as a sign I might be forgiven! Sleeping arrangements had been taken care of by Ehrentraut; Engelbert would sleep at a neighbour's house, while I had been allocated the foldaway bed in the living room. There was the traditional handshake with everyone, then Ehrentraut indicated she would see us next day at lunchtime, and bid us 'Gute Nacht'.

The understanding expressed in our letters, that we wished to take our time and enjoy each other's company without complications, produced an almost tangible aura of calm joy between us; and I was content to wait for the moment that would surely come. It made me happy to allow Ehrentraut the freedom she needed to get to know me as the person I am, rather than the picture she had built from our correspondence. During conversations while I watched her and listened, I would begin to understand how Ehrentraut saw and was resolute in preserving her principles on marriage. She needed time to be sure of her love if there was. Before falling asleep that first night, I thought about the events of the evening and I remembered what I wrote in one of my last letters comparing Ehrentraut with that beautiful rose not yet ready to be cut. I shall be patient, for then there is a whole life before us to enjoy.

A refreshing sleep after two tiring days on the road was most welcome. It was Saturday morning, and Engelbert and I had breakfast with Frau Krause. Conversing with her was easy, for we had many common subjects that threatened to occupy us far longer than time allowed. She spoke of our patient corresponding and how often she had to remind Ehrentraut to stop writing so late at night. I resisted asking if Ehrentraut might be in love with me, because I wanted Ehrentraut to tell me herself. My brother and I went for a walk in the town, leaving Frau Krause to get on with her chores. I dismissed the idea of seeing the shop where Ehrentraut worked, considering it unwise without having asked her. There was so much to see in historic Hameln, it is an immensely beautiful town.

We were surprised how quickly the morning had flown. Returning 'home' we found Ehrentraut had already arrived. I wished her a belated Good Morning and enquired if she had had a good day. "So-so" she replied while donning an apron to help her mother. Herr Krause returned from the allotment and we had much to talk about. Happily Engelbert was not word-shy and I had time to watch Ehrentraut as she went about her chores. I enjoyed watching her and thought it the most natural way to strengthen a loving friendship between suitor and his desired lady. Ehrentraut informed us that we would meet her friend Gretel {Margarete} that evening.

**'Ehrentraut on holiday in Frankfurt'**

'Ehrentraut on first day of school Easter 1939. "There are only a dozen sweets in my cone and 8 years at school; I'm determined to fill it with all I can learn in that time"; and 15 years later we were married.'

'Ehrentraut in fancy dress as a Geisha Girl'

A late lunch was served (the menu was one of Herr Krause's favourites). This time I was allowed to help Ehrentraut after the meal, which gave us our first opportunity to converse undisturbed. We began by exchanging our thoughts on the long period we had spent trying to form a picture of each other from the contents of our letters. We continued towards the more-serious aspects that Ehrentraut had raised and which she wished us to talk about person-to-person. It was good of the others to have purposely given us the space we needed to draw us closer in mind and heart.

Later the doorbell rang and we're introduced to Gretel. Ehrentraut first met Gretel in the Silesian refugee camp in Hameln, where both families had their allotted living and sleeping area close by. Gretel, the same age as Ehrentraut, and her mother had traumatic experiences during the Russian invasion of Silesia. Being of a more vivacious nature, Ehrentraut befriended the shy and quieter Gretel, and their friendship exists to this day.

Gretel was the second person in that momentous advert inserted by the two friends. As yet, Gretel had not found someone for serious correspondence; but Ehrentraut assured me that she had no ulterior motive when inviting Engelbert to come to Hameln if he wished. However, Ehrentraut would be delighted if he would be company for Gretel while Ehrentraut and I could have the opportunity to spend time with each other. With all of us now together, a most enjoyable evening it turned out to be. Serious exchanges of views were occasionally outweighed by humorous contributions. It was truly a happy family affair, and Ehrentraut and I held hands for the first time for all to notice. Once more we raised our glasses "to the future". Again, it was Ehrentraut who took charge, reminding us that tomorrow was Sunday, when we would all meet at church. I was to take Gretel home, with Engelbert beside her on the back seat and Gretel giving me directions.

Sunday 31$^{st}$ October 1954 was the day I had longed for. My happiness was complete as I walked to church beside Ehrentraut. We clasped hands most of the way. It was the day that both of us had spoken about and hoped for during recent weeks. There we were Ehrentraut with a young man sitting next to her in the pew. Who could understand how important and deeply moving it was for both of us? After the final blessing, "go in Peace", and the organ playing us out we left our seat and I do remember a moment of hope inside me and a distinct feeling that, by God's grace, Ehrentraut and I would return some day to this church. It was to be expected that Ehrentraut's young friends would want to meet and shake hands after church. I was introduced to a number of them and for many it was a surprise. They had never seen us together before and Ehrentraut had not yet made our friendship public. You could not blame me for feeling pleased with the attention. Gretel was invited for afternoon coffee. Arriving home, Ehrentraut and her mother began to prepare lunch. I offered to help in setting the table. The aroma from the kitchen promised something delicious for lunch and it was. We men congratulated the ladies for an enjoyable meal. While her parents had their customary afternoon nap, Ehrentraut and I attended to the clearing up and prepared for the afternoon coffee. I suggested Ehrentraut should have an afternoon nap which pleased me when she said "yes" and did so. It was another opportunity for both Engelbert and me to enjoy talking about our family and our sister Ursula. To forestall Engelbert's question, I was pleased to tell him that we will confirm our love and hope of marriage. Engelbert and I also discussed some sort of plan for the two of us. Ehrentraut had already told me that she had to work on Monday but would get Tuesday, Wednesday and Thursday off. We decided we would go north on Monday to see Aunt Else. I would return to Hameln in the early evening, and Engelbert would stay there and leave next day to return to work in Düsseldorf.

Engelbert indicated that he found Gretel of a friendly nature and might come again to visit her. Ehrentraut's father after his afternoon rest, came into the sitting room and suggested for the three of us a 'schnapps' to aid digestion, it would be appropriate. Soon we were wishing each other "good health" and the young pair Ehrentraut and Paul, 'prost'. Earlier than expected, the ladies returned and had no difficulty realising what we had been up to, and demanded to be treated likewise. It allowed us to have a second toast, this time I held Ehrentraut close to me, and looking deep into her brown eyes, I whispered, "to us".

The doorbell rang, and it was suggested that Engelbert should go and invite the visitor in. As expected, it was Gretel. Was someone enjoying a bit of secretive scheming? With all of us now at ease, including now Annemarie and her friend Heinz, a congenial atmosphere soon became an intimate family afternoon. Hearing the latest family gossip, and Engelbert recalling his first visit to Scotland and the odd hilarious experiences he had. Sunday afternoon passed very pleasantly. Ehrentraut and I, with the help of Annemarie, prepared the afternoon 'Kaffee und Kuchen' {coffee and cake time}. In the kitchen there were looks, smiles, the occasional accidental touch, but above all the sense that this day would not end like any other. The many letters between Scotland and Hameln must have done the preparation. It was proving to be the pleasantest day in every way. From the fourth floor, it was possible to see the sun still above the steeples. Gretel thought it time to go home and Engelbert offered to escort her. Gretel was pleased to accept as someone remarked "you will be quite safe".

There was a chance for me to ask Ehrentraut for both of us to go for a short drive, to get some fresh air. Hoping it would give us a chance to say something to each other. Ehrentraut put a light coat on while I took mine. After Gretel and Engelbert had left and said goodbye we followed, before closing the door Ehrentraut shouted "we'll be back for supper", with that we closed the door and made our way down the stairs and into the surprisingly mild air. Closing the house door, we crossed the street towards the car.

I opened the passenger door and bid Ehrentraut to take a seat; I closed her door and went to the driver's door, laid my coat on the back seat and got into the driver's seat. I put the ignition key in its place, for a few seconds I could not turn the key, I looked at Ehrentraut at the same time asking, "where to?" Extraordinary, suddenly our eyes seemed to freeze for a few moments, I placed my left arm around Ehrentraut's shoulder, at the same time I held her right arm in mine, and I simply said, "I love you Ehrentraut, do you believe me?" Ehrentraut did not answer, just put her arms round me and we both felt that in that first 'kiss', it was our pledge for life. Ehrentraut's first words were "I was beginning to wonder, when you would tell me that you love me?" Typical practical Ehrentraut!

We spent the next hour in the car holding hands in a feeling of warmth never experienced before. Not surprising since it was for both of us the first falling in 'love'. Simultaneously we began to recall when first we had begun to look more eagerly for the next letter after the first three months. With Ehrentraut expressing amazement that I still feared competition! Having spent nearly an hour talking, we concluded that our coming together was the ever-closer compatibility in our personal conviction of faith and morals followed by love. These were the fundamental building blocks for my marriage; Ehrentraut said it, adding that she believed I was not leading her on. I recalled the letter in which Ehrentraut wrote of the time when her shop manager made remarks to the staff, "Ehrentraut has changed lately. Could she be in love, yes?" I had wondered if it could be me. Ehrentraut confessed her surprise that I did not comment on it. "You should have known by then" she said, "It is not in my nature to play games when loving someone." Remembering other such artful and subtle references caused much laughter and delight until I remembered Ehrentraut's promise that we would be back for supper. I locked the car and we turned to each other and embraced, we kissed, it was our first embrace in the open world. It was dark and there was no one around to witness our sheer happiness.

Before we climbed the stairs we simultaneously recalled my arrival and Ehrentraut's refusal to kiss. Now she placed her arms around me saying: "Jetzt sollst Du mich küssen - now you may kiss me". As we entered she took the initiative, kissed me and announced, "Yes, we love each other". Her parents seemed especially happy for us, wishing us well. Supper was already on the table and Engelbert had returned. Herr Krause agreed with Ehrentraut that we should all drink to happiness and our future. So far, it was one of the happiest days of my life. That memorable evening was spent in an atmosphere of sheer delight, for our happiness was infectious. My eyes never leaving Ehrentraut, I was briefly carried away with thoughts of our future. My prayers had been answered and I have found someone from my homeland. Someone to love and cherish and with whom we can remember and sing of our home of old. Of course, I returned quickly to the present when remarks were made about the lateness of the hour and the fact that there were those among us facing work in the morning. Ehrentraut and I embraced and kissed each other goodnight for the first time.

After breakfast next day Monday 1st November, All Saints Day, we all attended the morning service at the Parish Church. Engelbert rode Ehrentraut's bicycle while Ehrentraut and I walked arm in arm to church, I walked as if on air! Coming out of church there was the opportunity for Ehrentraut to introduce me as her friend, which having been a first for me, made me feel quite proud. Engelbert and I wished Ehrentraut a good day and I will look forward to see her at home in the evening. I remember it clearly, Ehrentraut was just about to mount her bicycle when one of her shoes came off. It was Engelbert who lightning-like took two steps and picked up Ehrentraut's shoe and put it on her foot. It's still haunts me that it was not I who came to Ehrentraut's aid. It could have been my first act of gallantry to rescue my bride-to-be in public. Engelbert had said his goodbye to Ehrentraut, his hopeful future 'sister-in-law'. Both Ehrentraut and I loved that remark. Since he had planned to leave for his home from Aunt Else, she made me promise to drive safely. Engelbert and I walked to the Krause's to say that we were on our way to visit our Aunt in north Germany, and that I would see them all in the evening.

Our car journey took some 90 minutes and it was good to meet Aunt Else and our cousins again. Naturally she was eager to hear the news from Hameln and shared my joy. We had dinner and coffee, and all too soon it was time for my departure. I wanted to return to Hameln in daylight. Engelbert was to stay overnight and return to Düsseldorf next day. Farewells were said and Aunt Else was keen to know when she might meet Ehrentraut and asked about a wedding? We will let you know, with that I left on my way back to meet with Ehrentraut. I had arranged to meet up with Engelbert at Düsseldorf on my way back to Scotland. I returned safely to Hameln and Ehrentraut's welcoming embrace and lingering kiss. She was clearly looking forward to her three-day holiday, and so did I. A week is a very short time, especially for Ehrentraut and me. I began to regret it that I did not take a week longer to stay here with Ehrentraut. But then, I was not sure, although hoped that we would 'melt' into the true friendship of love, which has happened. A longer time alone would allow us to exchange many questions and thoughts to test our compatibility. With Ehrentraut's help we should find a way to decide how best to spend the precious three days that remained. She asked if there was anywhere I particularly wished to visit. My knowledge of the district was none, but I indicated I would love to see the Diocesan Youth Centre, which she had mentioned so often in her informative and fond letters. Ehrentraut's kiss confirmed that was where we would go and it was clear she wanted to take me to the place so that I may know in Scotland where Ehrentraut might be when she tells me.

The sun was shining next morning and it seemed that the heavens were trying their best to ensure our enjoyment of the day together. Traffic on the road was light and Ehrentraut had no difficulty keeping us talking. Indeed, there was so much we wished to say to each other now that we were alone. We were constantly aware during our conversation how honest and sincere our twice-weekly correspondence had been. I drove us through picturesque villages and undulating countryside in its full autumn glory. The time passed quickly and within an hour and a half we reached Woldenberg. A secluded stone built large house within the grounds of a medieval castle. I parked the car and followed Ehrentraut into reception, where we were welcomed by a cheerful lady. She of course recognised Ehrentraut and they chatted amicably until I was belatedly introduced by a smiling Ehrentraut as her close friend. That gave me that pleasant feeling of belonging to someone.

Ehrentraut showed me round the Youth Centre and I had the opportunity to recall the times she had written in detail about the many hours she spent there. I was just about to ask where the chapel was when Ehrentraut pointed to it. She stepped ahead to open the door and led me in. Would she offer a prayer that she may have found her true companion in her life in me? Those were really precious words to hear from Ehrentraut. Which of course I was not to know. We paused awhile in mutual prayer of thanks giving. Suddenly I felt within me that this was the place and the moment to take her hand and asked, "Ehrentraut, I wish to marry you, Willst Du meine Braut sein? – will you be my bride?" There was the briefest pause before she whispered, "Yes Paul, very much so". Tears of joy followed, as with one mind we sat down in the pew all by ourselves, except the One that brought us together now happily watching over us, for 60 years.

On our way out we thanked the receptionist and sat outside on a bench in the warm sunshine, reliving the important moments we had just spent. A place and time full of romance and simplicity. I must add that we always remembered it as the place where the open 'ring' from the small advert to this place here finally closed. The few passers-by had no doubt we were a couple in love. There was time to have something to eat before we headed for home. Ehrentraut suggested we drive through the city of Hildesheim passing by its beautiful Cathedral. I was surprised to see how much the city bore the scars of war air-raids. Ehrentraut snuggled as close as it was wise and safe to do and we held hands whenever we could, seeking words that adequately described what we felt about this day and ourselves. We reached Hameln again as the sun was setting. A very warm welcome home received us from now Mum and Dad.

Ehrentraut helped her mother with final preparations for supper and her father abandoned his newspaper and fetched beer glasses. After supper he returned to his chair to listen to the radio, while Ehrentraut suggested her mother should join him for a well-earned rest. We two felt it was our turn to wash the dishes and tidy up. Ehrentraut was eager to tell her parents more about our day and the pledge we had exchanged in the chapel at Woldenberg. They shared our happiness offering their congratulations and good wishes, both parents indicating they were not surprised.

Of course, it would be my duty to follow the custom and formally ask Mum and Dad in person here, for their daughter's hand in marriage. That called for the traditional toast, and Ehrentraut thought a stronger drink was called for. Her father directed her to fetch the best spirit {not schnapps} and the best glasses. Annemarie and her friend Heinz were present. We could not have hoped for a happier ending to a day we will remember for the rest of our lives. When her parents had retired for the night we sat together reflecting on the day's event. Clearly we had moved a stage further in our relationship and would have to consider the way forward and the practicalities of what was to be our life together. Tiredness overcame Ehrentraut and our shared embrace and goodnight kiss allowed us to retire happily.

I woke from a restful sleep next morning and heard Ehrentraut preparing breakfast. Her parents had already left. She suggested we spent time within the town, later visiting her place of work and meeting her colleagues. It was another dry day and we set off at a reasonable hour to make the most of it. I was entirely dependent on Ehrentraut as my guide. We strolled along one attractive street after another discovering and enjoying their ever-changing beauty. I am familiar with Bavarian architecture but in Hameln there is a distinct difference. I quickly realised it would take many days just to explore every street without even entering the many interesting buildings on either side. I saw the River Weser but time did not permit a river cruise, the shortest requiring at least one hour.

Ehrentraut wished me to meet her Oma, her maternal grandmother and this we did next. She was a small lady with a cheerful disposition, reminding me of Ehrentraut and invited us to join her for coffee. When we left we promised she would see more of us in the future. Now we realised we must hurry if we were to pay the expected visit to Ehrentraut's colleagues at the shop before it closed for lunch. We reached the shop and entered. I had a strange feeling seeing the place where she worked and the people she wrote about, but now I would be able to visualise the scene next time Ehrentraut writes to me. I was introduced to the shop manager and Ehrentraut's fellow assistants. I answered their questions and took the opportunity to recommend Scotland for holidays. Praising its walks and scenery, and of course its famous whisky. It was approaching time for the shop to close, and time for Ehrentraut to see to the shopping we were to take home. Ehrentraut informed me later that she had been congratulated on her choice. Naturally I was pleased.

Mum had lunch ready for us and after an enjoyable meal with her we insisted she take a rest while we cleared up and washed the dishes. That done, we continued our tour of the town. After several stops to look in furniture-shop windows I began to wonder if Ehrentraut was showing the natural instinct of the bride-to-be. It pleased me to think so but I refrained from commenting. Having seen a number of other shops and interesting buildings, including the beautiful Lutheran cathedral, we decided it was time to return home. We both knew there would be other opportunities for further exploration in the future.

Ehrentraut's Dad came home from work and the four of us spent another pleasant evening together. There was a cosy family feeling. On completion of our chores in the kitchen, we joined her parents and the conversation turned to plans for Ehrentraut's last free day. We decided to make no real plans for Thursday. Ehrentraut would like the two of us to visit her favourite uncle Paul, her mother's brother who lived nearby. I was aware suddenly that our time together was running out and I would be leaving Hameln on Friday afternoon. The realisation produced butterflies. Yet, despite these feelings of dismay and sadness, the evening ended happily with the traditional nightcap, and another opportunity for the two of us to linger awhile after Ehrentraut's parents had discreetly gone to bed.

At breakfast on Thursday Ehrentraut asked if I had any thoughts or preferences concerning the day's activities. I invited her to choose. Her view was that because we had so little time, it might be wise to stay indoors and talk while her father was at work and her mother busy elsewhere. Now that we had agreed to marry there was a wedding and more besides to think about. I agreed, and was reminded of what I had perceived from Ehrentraut's letters a sense that she was someone whose circumstances had caused her to become a mature adolescent in her early youth. Though now she was someone in love, her feet were firmly on the ground. Aware of this I tentatively suggested that an early wedding might not be realistic. Ehrentraut replied quickly and emphatically, "I still have to work and save for my dowry". Relieved I answered "so do I." I told Ehrentraut that before I left to meet with her, David and Ella had mentioned that should we get married and wished to continue in their employment, the small cottage close to the farm would be available for us.

Obviously surprised, her eyes sparkling, Ehrentraut leaned over to kiss me and ask "does it mean we would really have a home?" When I indicated that I did not know if she could consider moving so far to live in Scotland? She replied: "Where you are I would love to be, as the song says". I did not mention that the farm and its cottage had neither running water nor electricity although both amenities had been agreed, signed and scheduled for installation, hopefully within the coming year. Of course, I would enlighten her before I departed as it would be crucial in coming to a decision. Our conversation had turned naturally to the subject of accommodation and my possible reemployment in the postal service in Germany? On this matter Ehrentraut confirmed Engelbert's warning of the continuing difficulty regarding housing in the new western Germany. Also that reinstatement in the postal service was offered only to married postal staff from the former German eastern provinces, Silesia, etc. "You will have to tell me more about Scotland," was Ehrentraut's closing comment before we made our plans to visit Uncle Paul that evening. We were welcomed and I soon felt they were a wonderful couple who seemed to be very fond of Ehrentraut. They had no family. We hoped to see them again.

One important question remained for me and I knew I had to ask it before I returned to Scotland. My memory of the moment is very clear. I held her close and asked, "Dear Ehrentraut, you must tell me about the time when you had to leave the old home until you arrived at Hameln?" "Must I?" she replied. "Yes please, Ehrentraut, it is important for me to know. Should we go for a walk or a drive?" "In that case, we might just as well stay here at home, we are alone, and the others are away". We sat down and I listened intently as she spoke.

"It was Sunday 14$^{th}$ January 1945 and my twelfth birthday. The snow lay well over my high-laced shoes, winter as usual in Silesia, as you will surely remember. On the sitting room table covered with one of Mum's beautiful tablecloths lay a book or two and a flowerpot containing a lovely blue Alpen Veilchen {cyclamen}. Alas no tokens from my Dad, who would have remembered my birthday, but 'field post' always took so long and, of course, we never knew where he was. These few gifts from Mum were untouched and, looking after the farm, she obviously had no time to bake a birthday cake. Anyway, snow or no snow, it was back to school next day by our little train to Breslau. We always hoped there would be no air-raid siren for none of us liked the sound of the sirens, when we would have to run for the nearest shelter, hoping the train would wait. Home was 9km. away.

On the Thursday morning we were told there would be no school for the next few days. We were not told why! Over 10cm of snow had fallen. At home Wenzel, our young Polish labourer, told Mum he had seen some people loading their wagons, at least that's how it looked. Later that day our village mayor {Mr Horn, the village Party official} came to tell Mum that we had to vacate the village next morning, and she should prepare and load our large wagon with essentials for the journey. He also told Mum she would not be permitted to travel with us, for there had to be room for relatives, two cousins {pregnant mothers} their children and an aunt. Wenzel would take us to our Grandma nearly thirty kilometres. We at least knew we had close relatives to go to, others did not. The rumours about the Russian advance soon got round. Wenzel had to ensure that oats and hay for the horses were loaded on the wagon, and our clever Mum got us to help by collecting our dearest toys. I looked at once for my favourite doll. Mum filled the large trunk that grandfather had made, also finding room for farm records among warm clothing and other essential items. The traditional feather bed would be squashed into a relatively small space in the open wagon; it would certainly keep us warm on the journey we had to face. Mum coped heroically with all that had to be done so quickly; and I helped where I could by looking after my young sister, Annemarie, and feeding the hens. Mum said very little, and must have worked until late. Next morning Mum rose early to milk the eight cows, and get the milk into the churns to be collected later. We never knew if the milk ever was lifted that day. I clearly remember Mum holding us both close before we had to climb onto the wagon. She kissed us and traced a cross on our foreheads as we said our goodbyes; somehow there was no time for tears. Recalling it now, it must have been the same for Mum every time Dad departed when his leave was over.

Our journey had begun aboard the wagon driven by Wenzel, there were three mothers, two expectant and nine children including Annemarie and myself. We found we could not cross the Oder in Breslau, because all the bridges were ready to be blown up. It took more than an hour down river before we found a ferry that was still operating. Like a miracle it was able to take the horses and wagon across the river. For the first time we all met the reality of war, we heard the older ones saying. Our aunt knew the way to Grandma's house, but first we had to look for a place to spend the night. Allowing at least one hour before darkness, we stopped in a village. One of Mum's cousins tried twice before a lady agreed to let us stay. She offered us a large empty room in the farmhouse and the stable for our horses. I am sure Wenzel must have been very tired, more than us, but he unharnessed the horses and made sure they were stabled and fed. He offered to sleep with the horses, on straw and a blanket, because he too was afraid someone might just steel them overnight. I still remember now, how lucky we were to have had him to drive the horses for us. We were also wondering how our Mum was doing. It may have been just as well we did not know, but still hoped she was well. Thank God the lady allowed us to use her cooking stove to make some sort of meal for us. Of course before that we had to bring straw into the room and laid our blankets on. Most of us slept well, Annemarie needed comforting for a while, but after we had eaten we curled up and fell asleep. In the morning we woke up when our elders had breakfast ready. Wenzel had already fed the horses and when asked how he slept? "Very well" he said. Of course the usual farm noises reminded us of home, and I wondered how Mum was doing?

Thank goodness there had not been another snowfall during the night. I kept telling Annemarie that we will soon be at Grandma's. We made good headway, thanks to my aunt who knew the lesser known roads, because the main road would be busy with military traffic, or Russian planes. After several short breaks we children gave a happy yell when told we will be at Grandma's in an hour or so. God be thanked when we entered the large farmyard making a noise over the cobblestones. Well after lunchtime Grandma was at the door looking somewhat perplexed. When she recognised that it was us she came straight towards us with arms outstretched to embrace Annemarie and me as we jumped from the wagon. The farm was worked by Uncle Robert and his wife Agnes. They could not believe the Russians were so close. You Paul, as a prisoner so far away may not have been aware of what information was withheld and what Hitler's propaganda told us? Here in Silesia we were far from air-raids or signs of war, until suddenly so close that it was frightening.

While Grandma took us children into the house, Wenzel was introduced to Uncle Robert who helped Wenzel to unhitch the horses and took them into the stable. The elders had to find places for the others that came with us. I was thrilled that the two of us would stay with Grandma. There were other relatives in the village who were able to give rooms for the other mums that came with us. Yes Wenzel too got a place to stay and be fed with one of our relations. We were too young to worry about how long we would be living here. Since I had been at Grandma's before I knew the places where we could play and where not. Electricity and water supplies were still working and the radio was listened to by the elders. What I understood was that schools were already closed and the elders were talking about who had left the village a week ago or more. The teachers, and all other well-off people were heading to safer places in the west. That's why there were a number of empty houses around, which refugees could use to stay a night or two. Two days later in the afternoon when playing outside we suddenly heard a voice which I thought I knew and there was Mum walking into Grandma's yard. Can you imagine how we dropped everything and raced into Mum's arms? Grandma quickly made some food for Mum. Then she and Wenzel with our two horses walked two miles to the main road where our second wagon was left by Mr Horn who had hitched his second pair of horses to our second wagon with the rest of our stuff. He apparently moved further on. Within two hours Mum and Wenzel arrived with our wagon and the rest of our belongings that Mum had taken. Two days later we began to notice our soldiers passing by; also one small military car drove fast past us driving north. Later in the day a small group of our soldiers stopped to ask for water to fill their field flasks. They warned us they were the last German soldiers in the vicinity, and were moving further north. They told the elders they could not help us anymore, and warned them to get rid of all alcoholic drinks, warning them to hide away all woman and young girls. Now everything was hurriedly organised. Wenzel fed the horses while the elders loaded the wagon with essentials. Grandma came with us and we made good headway before we had to stop at the next large farm and asked for room. The men were told there is a large empty house the owners had left many days ago, just go and settle in. That's what we did. The horses were stabled and we all rested in the large house. Beds and sofas, chairs and tables were there so we could sleep. We were tired and slept peaceful till morning. There was no shooting or any other noise during the night

Next morning the ladies made some breakfast and Grandma led us all in prayer. After breakfast the elders were discussing whether to go further towards the mountains or not. The decision was not ours any more, as someone said the war has passed us, we may not be in Germany any more. While Wenzel fed the horses he heard a car coming along on the street with a few Russian soldiers to whom Wenzel waved greetings. They in return, shouted "war finish soon, Germany kaputt". Wenzel waved back, and it was he who suggested the war was finished for us here and we should go back home. The elders decided yes to go back to Grandma's home but not to our own home on the other side of the River Oder. That's what we did and arrived at Grandma's farm before darkness and without any damage, everybody thought that there had been no shooting or fighting here. We were all thankful and began to clean everything although it was as clean as when we left it two weeks ago. Next day it was Wenzel on whose eyes all of us looked when he decided it was time for him to walk home. He thanked us and wished us well telling Mum to greet Dad when we see him again. With that he waved goodbye and disappeared forever. Mum thanked him especially in hope that he will find his people in good health. For us it was the beginning of a new life. We as children could not take it all in, but I as a twelve year old began to understand what the elders were thinking. The news had trickled through that the city of Breslau, our capital, is more than half in ruins including the beautiful cathedral.

Well my Paul, how about a cup of coffee and then the rest to satisfy you. I do understand that you want to know what we went through while you were safe in America. Well, is the coffee alright?

Life began to take some sort of order. The men worked the farm as usual; the country seemed rather quiet with fewer people around, no cars to be seen. In June somehow we were told the war is finished,

Germany no longer as it once was. On the following Sunday the little church was nearly full. The priest invited all to pray thanks for peace and a better future, that's what we all hoped for. Three months later, Mum decided to take a chance and tried to walk all the way back to our old home, which was a brave step. But my uncle insisted he go with her, it was far too dangerous. They made it. The extraordinary was almost unbelievable. The door of the house was as we left it, locked. Mum tried the key and it opened. When Mum entered she found everything the way we left it. My little cyclamen was all dried up on the table and my books, my birthday presents were still there, the way my Mum had placed them. Nobody had entered the house. The animals were gone and grass and weeds began to grow. Wasn't that strange? Mum collected small items as much as the two of them could carry and closed and locked the door with a blessing and returned safely home at Grandma's. We now lived in some sort of no-man's-land. There was no police, no school or teachers, no post office or post deliveries, no shop, if there was a shop it was totally empty now. Mum and my uncle took the small roads to be less recognised and not possibly molested or more. They arrived safely and told their story.

Where did our elders get food from? Everybody did have some food pickled or in glasses, of course we on the farm had animals to kill, hens and rabbits. We will never forget the winter of 1945- 46 when hard frost penetrated the potato pits and half the store was unusable. During the potato harvest in which we all helped, I suddenly collapsed and fell to the ground unconscious. My Mum was called and I was carried home to bed. I came to, but felt very ill. It was frightening for Mum because there was neither a doctor nor any other medical person around. Everyone searched for any kind of medicine they might have stored away and lucky someone suggested to cycle to the next village, where there were a few nuns in a small convent. The nun who came had some medical training and was certain I had contracted typhoid. She asked for hay seed, boiled it and put it in a hot bath. I was laid in the bath for some time, and the process was repeated for several days until the poison found its way out. According to Mum, the Sister had little hope for my recovery. {At this point Ehrentraut had to stop, tears and thoughts overwhelming me, is that why I had not looked for any other in those years until we looked and found each other in the end?}

Eventually my skin became tanned all over from the hay seed. One day when I was getting better I sat up in bed for a while, but soon had to lie down again. Within a second of my lying down a piece of shrapnel half the size of my hand came through the window and embedded itself in the brick wall right above my bed in line where my body and head had been seconds before. Our people did not know that our soldiers had laid mines in the field below the farm. When Mum came in and I told her she nearly fainted. Twice my life had been saved within a short time!

"A miracle indeed, does it explain why I was not interested in marriage so far, until you were ready Ehrentraut to look for him, whom the good Lord thought was the right one, and so too it was my time to look for you. Here we still are, sixty years on. After all that, we are happy to believe in miracles."

Within the year in 1946 a notice appeared in the village and all of us as Germans had to register and the follow-up was that the Land of Silesia was to be cut off from Germany and become part of the Polish nation. Unless you accept Polish citizenship you will be transported to Germany. You were allowed to take with you only what you could carry. You Paul were far away from Silesia so it was impossible to imagine what it felt and meant. On the given day we walked with what we could carry to the station and a train took us to West Germany. At the first large station in Germany we had to get out and a short walk to a large hall where we were deloused first, then registered and given the papers where our new home would be. That was to be Hameln, the Rat Catcher town and here we are, my Paul."

How did I feel? Speechless is the true answer, because what sort of words could one find to counter such experiences? All I could do was put my arms around Ehrentraut and we spent a few minutes in silence, after which Ehrentraut reminded me that we had promised to visit Uncle Paul and Aunt Lehnchen who welcomed us warmly. Having arrived home, I switched off the engine and took Ehrentraut's hand and I just wanted to say "thank you for giving me your time to tell me what I needed to know before we have to say "Auf Wiedersehen". Yes I was at peace. Mum called, supper was ready. You told me what I had to know and I am happy now, and at peace now. That is why I never felt a desire to look for a life companion, until that tiny 'ADVERT' in a newspaper!

We spent the remainder of the evening with Ehrentraut's parents, who had waited patiently for our return. Although Ehrentraut had to work next day, I hoped she would be permitted to come home for lunch and have the afternoon off. My incidental remark for Ehrentraut to visit Scotland was lost among other topics; I tried again and succeeded in expressing my wish for her to accompany me tomorrow as far as Düsseldorf. It was understood that I was to provide Ehrentraut with a return rail ticket to Hameln. My idea was not dismissed, it may well have been thought 'daft' by others. For me every hour spent in Ehrentraut's company was priceless. The hour was late and before we retired for the night I thanked Ehrentraut's parents for their hospitality and for welcoming me as their prospective son-in-law. It was my duty to promise that on my return to Scotland, by letter I would ask Ehrentraut's parents for their permission for Ehrentraut to be my 'Bride'. Ehrentraut too had an early rise, shops open at 8 a.m., but we lingered for a while before kissing each other goodnight. Ehrentraut, the stronger, perceived a tear in my eye and quickly wiped it away, she wagged her finger saying "no, no tears let's be strong Paul, I too have to be without you".

It was Friday, 5th November 1954 and the day of my departure. The purpose of my visit had been primarily to ascertain our compatibility; I had come with no assumptions. Though enjoying our exchange of correspondence and finding in it increasing interest and warmth, there could have been a number of good reasons why burgeoning hope might have died. Sheer honesty had in fact forged the bond between us, and so much greater therefore was my joy to discover we truly loved each other. Parting so soon would be difficult but bearable with looking forward to a future, better still a life together.

Dad was already leaving for work. We exchanged good wishes and he surprised me by saying quietly, "take care of our daughter". He departed and the three of us enjoyed breakfast together, aware of time passing too quickly. Mum tidied up and Ehrentraut got her coat before we descended the stairs together. I fetched her bicycle and with a last kiss she cycled briskly away hoping to get the afternoon off. My few possessions were easily packed and I included a few local goodies that I had bought for Ella and David. When Ehrentraut's Mum returned from her daily chores we sat together to enjoy a cup of coffee and the little plate of cakes she had brought up from the ground floor bakery. Our pleasant chat centred naturally on Ehrentraut and I was moved when she remarked, "Paul, let me tell you that I felt a while ago that Ehrentraut might be falling in love with you before she met you face to face. Latterly the first thing she looked for was the place I always put your latest letter on." I knew she was happy for she smiled. She further confided that Ehrentraut was her closest companion as she coped with being both mother and farmer, while her husband was away in the army. When she concluded "I am sure you will make each other happy," there was no need for me to add any comment.

While lunch was being prepared, I moved my few belongings downstairs to the car, checked and filled it with fuel. Climbing the stairs again I heard Mum say "Don't worry, Ehrentraut will get the afternoon off". Then the door flew open and Ehrentraut threw her arms around me saying with glee, "yes, my colleagues even wished me a safe journey, so long as I am back at work tomorrow". Aromas from the kitchen prompted us to sit at the table to enjoy an unmistakable Silesian lunch. We said grace, and remembered my parents who, so far away could not share this happy moment. Ehrentraut promised to write to them on Sunday. Lunch was delicious and Mum was warmly congratulated. Ehrentraut wondered what to wear for our journey; I suggested a coat for certain - something warm during the drive. The moment to say goodbye had come, and I thanked Mum for allowing me to love her daughter. We embraced while tracing the traditional cross on our foreheads for a safe journey. Mum was persuaded not to come downstairs to see us off. "Well, my treasure, with God's blessing here we go. I cannot believe that only a week ago I first met you in the hall. One week later we have confirmed what we hoped might be true, we love each other."

I might have regretted that I had not asked to come to Hameln for two weeks, but our spade-work had in the end proved that the seed of love had been sown. Here, with Ehrentraut at my side there was no room for regret. We are both young, fit and happy. The miles passed quickly, for we had much to talk about. As I had promised myself, I told Ehrentraut about the lack of tap water and electricity in the cottage which hopefully, would soon be remedied. Ehrentraut's attitude was frank, "Every beginning is hard, I know something about that" and the matter was closed. It was a good moment also to let her know that there was no question in my mind about her return to Hameln, I would drive her home. Her remonstrations gradually subsided when I pointed out that I could not rest knowing she might languish in a coach for hours alone. What did appeal were the extra six hours I could be with her. Her sparkling eyes said more than words. Ehrentraut certainly revealed herself as an amiable and entertaining conversationalist. It was not surprising that the hours passed pleasantly and the miles so quickly. She read Engelbert's instructions on how to reach our destination, and with traffic not too dense we arrived in daylight.

Mr & Mrs Metzner made us welcome and it was a joy for me to introduce my bride-to-be. A meal was shared when Engelbert arrived and a happy four hours until it was time for Ehrentraut and me to depart. Ehrentraut thanked the Metzners for their hospitality and me for their insistence to call on my way back for breakfast before leaving next day for the ferry. Arm in arm Ehrentraut and I made for the car and were soon on our way. It was a starry night for lovers to drive safely home.

It was relatively easy to follow directions to the motorway that led to Hameln. At this time of night it would allow a comfortable speed to complete the journey safely. I told Ehrentraut that if she felt tired she should not fight it, but she had no wish to waste the few precious hours remaining. I used the opportunity to talk about Scotland and her possible visit to see Viewfield and Tain. It was also essential for her to see my present home, meet my people there and form a clearer picture in her mind. She could then think about it at home without any pressure. Naturally, I saw it as my duty and pleasure to arrange her travel and tickets for the journey. Ehrentraut clutched my arm. "Oh, my dear Paul, to come and visit you? You would really like that? What more could I wish for? My head is in a whirl!" If only we could have stopped, I would have held her close but we were committed to a timetable and good sense prevailed. For Ehrentraut there would be the matter of obtaining holiday leave, but with Christmas and New Year approaching the coming weeks would provide happy thoughts and dreams for the future. Daylight was breaking as we left the motorway.

In Hameln early workers were already leaving their homes. I stopped the car and we were locked in an affectionate embrace on the pavement. Ehrentraut, again the stronger, whispered, "no tears, Paul. Thank you for your love and for making me so happy". We had to part, there was a lingering kiss before she waved and smiled while walking away. I watched her close the door, started the engine and drove away. It seemed that angels had kept an eye on us and I arrived in Düsseldorf at the Metzners in time for breakfast. I had stopped for coffee and a sandwich on the autobahn. Engelbert and I had hours to chat and I gathered that he intended to go to Hameln at New Year. Of course, it was time to leave them all too soon. They waved as I drove off for the ferry at the Hook of Holland.

Passport control at the Dutch border was relatively swift and even a German passport presented no problem when travelling to the UK. It was an uneventful drive on Holland's motorway to The Hague and the port. I had slightly less than an hour to spare so was grateful for a trouble-free journey. I had booked a cabin which allowed me the opportunity for a refreshing sleep, even if for only five hours. The weather continued fair, favourable for my 24 hour drive from Harwich. Safely on dry land with passport controls behind me, I drove north. Anyone who travelled north on the A1 and A9 in those days will remember what a drag it was! Because it was Sunday, traffic was light and there was a 30 mph speed limit for all lorries, I entered Viewfield just as David was about to start Monday morning milking.

It was pleasant to be so warmly welcomed by him and Ella who had got up early during my absence to make David's breakfast. I gratefully accepted their suggestion to rest and take it easy. The evening was spent giving a full account of my trip. They were obviously anxious to hear all about my first meeting with Ehrentraut. Deeming it unnecessary to divulge details, I let them know that we had fallen in love and were happily looking forward to marriage. Without pausing for breath I added that Ehrentraut hoped to see

Scotland and felt happy about the cottage. To have David and Ella's approval and their obvious sharing of my joy made me feel real good.

I planned to write to Ehrentraut at the first opportunity and wished I had put pen to paper on board the ferry. Here several days of welcome sunshine had dried out the rain-soaked fields I had left ten days ago. Of course, my fellow workers were keenly interested in the outcome of my trip and wished me luck.

I found that in the first few days back at Viewfield my thoughts centred on Ehrentraut with a new intensity. We had both built up a version of each other's identity and had only a week in which to seek and find each other. It had surprised and delighted us both to realise just how close to the truth our 'ground work' turned out to be. Now I was experiencing the wonder of a friendship that had blossomed into a love of such depth as to be almost supernatural. As I walked quietly through the fields ensuring the well-being of the grazing and resting animals, I would rest on my crook in the autumn sunshine and cast my eyes towards the deep blue waters of the Dornoch Firth and the softly shrouded hills of the northern counties in the distance, and I would picture Ehrentraut enjoying this scene someday. The stillness and undisturbed beauty contributed to my deeper contemplation of the familiar landscape, allowing a fleeting moment of hope that Ehrentraut will find joy and happiness here. I had written to Ehrentraut and waited impatiently for her letter. Our love and mutual pledge of faithfulness, would now allow us to communicate and converse with unencumbered ease. In spite of being so many miles apart, in Spirit we were truly together on the road to fulfilment of our love.

I had been home for a week when David and I returned for lunch as usual in the middle of the day and were greeted by Ella. I noticed the now familiar special smile as she looked first at me then glanced briefly towards the kitchen dresser. I knew at once that Ehrentraut's letter had arrived. I derived great pleasure from waiting and did not open it just yet. I would do so when the last of the day's chores had been completed and I could read it undisturbed in the quietness of my own room. The anticipation was understood by David and Ella. This letter was special, for it was the first since our pledge to love and marry, God willing, and I opened the envelope with anticipation.

*Hameln, Saturday 6.11.1954 My dearest, dearest Paul,*

*How happy I was to receive your letter and know that you returned safely to Düsseldorf and crossed to England. I went straight to bed wondering if I could sleep, but I must have been tired from all that happened in this last week. Mum had to waken me after only two hours. It was difficult to concentrate at work and I was glad it was Saturday, and only a half day. I kept hoping all would be well with you and that the car would bring you home to Viewfield without any breakdown? Were Ella and her brother happy to see you? I am sure you will tell me they were, how did they react when you told them that we will marry? How I miss you, my Love if only you knew!*

*It is late and I have to go to bed, Mum worries, I'll continue tomorrow Sunday. In my thoughts I hold you, many kisses and wishing you 'Goodnight', my dearest Paul,*

*Your Ehrentraut.*

---

*Sunday, 7.11.1954 My Love, and dearest Paul,*

*Surprise, I managed to go with Mum and Dad to the late Service, we had dinner and I went straight to lie down and slept for three hours until almost past coffee time. Now I am writing to you while I enjoy the moment but I think how lovely it would be if you just came in to join us for coffee before going for a walk together. Do not get sad. We have our pledge and must be brave and patient. I do so miss you; my heart was aching when going to Mass without you at my side. We did this only a week ago and I cannot help thinking just how more wonderful it would have been this morning, now that our love is confirmed. Dad went to Berlin to visit his cousins and we hope he will be back tonight. But now I have to say goodnight again, imagining how sweet your kisses would be if you were here. How comforting it is to be loved by you. Will there be a letter from you soon? I do hope so. Your ever loving Ehrentraut and all the family who know how I long for you.*

> *Viewfield, 11th November 54 My dear Ehrentraut, my Love,*
> 
> *Winter evenings do not have to be regarded as a cause for depression on the contrary, I find it stimulates thoughts of love to put on paper and that is what I am doing now to thank you and to answer your letters, two against one of mine. It worried me to hear that you have battled with a cold and I am glad to know you are feeling better. Please do not say 'I should not have told you', for that would defeat our pledge to share and keep each other informed of whatever burdens us. There is little news here that may be of interest to you. I was asked to be a waiter at a function of the local Farmers' Club, at the Mansfield Hotel where I usually earn my pocket money. Such funds are now for our future home. That reminds me to let you know the cottage can be ours if we so decide. Am I right to say we did already say that we would be happy to have it. I am asked to send you greetings from Ella and David whenever I write to you. My best wishes to your Mum and Dad from me, for you how many kisses? You choose. Keep well and praying for both of us, Forever yours, Paul.*

The daily routine continued at Viewfield, heavy rains did not affect us to any great extent due to natural drainage off the sloping fields. We listened with interest to reports on the radio of extensive floods in other parts of Scotland and south of the border. There were many opportunities for me to pursue my interest in woodwork and repairs that constantly require attention around a farm. Such skills would be important if the cottage will be our home. Thoughts about the future reminded me that I am no longer responsible for myself alone. Ehrentraut's next letter contained exciting news.

> *Hameln, 12.11.1954 My dear Paul, my Love,*
> 
> *I hoped to have had a letter from you yesterday. Please do not be angry with me for being such a 'Nimmersatt glutton'- waiting to devour every word you write. Your letters tell me always so much about you. I will try to be satisfied with whatever you send me, but be warned, I may not succeed if you keep sending me so much love*

*and consideration. Now I cannot wait any longer to bring before you my proposal in answer to your surprise invitation before we parted that I should come to visit you in Scotland. If only you knew how I felt to hear you say this to me the words and the thought that you longed for me to come to you. Once I had settled after you left, I thought about how many days I could gather without touching my summer holidays next year. The possible days amounted to two weeks if I can make up some overtime. I could not wait to tell Mum, and as I put my arms around her, she whispered how happy she was for me and that I should come to you if you wish it. Now I am so excited and cannot wait for your answer. Oops, there I go again! Can you forgive me? At coffee-time we listened to the radio and heard the Water Music followed by Strauss waltzes. I closed my eyes and imagined us dancing together. Mum smiled and knew where my thoughts were. Time to finish. Gretel is calling for a short walk before it gets dark, as usual greetings from Mum Dad and Annemarie.*

*With lots of love, your faithful Ehrentraut.*

---

*Viewfield, November 1954 My dear and precious Ehrentraut,*

*Thank you for sending me such great news about the possibility of your coming to visit me. What bliss to see myself mirrored in your eyes! Now we have yet another reason to pray that it may come true. You mention February as a possible time and that would suit all of us here. Your concern for Gretel is something I wish to share. She should certainly not be led on in a half-hearted relationship with no future commitment. Please do not hesitate to keep me informed and do not be anxious, for I will be circumspect when next I write to Engelbert. It would be natural for me to ask my brother how his friendship with Gretel is progressing. There is of course the fact that they really had not yet met that often. Remember it took us six months and forty letters to find out if all was true what we wrote to each other. Engelbert also has the opportunity to meet with his friends in the different church Associations for Men, etc. which I have not got, and that does take up time in evenings. When it comes to letter writing then I know I win hands down.*

*In the meantime, I have written to my parents and my sister Ursula, giving them a comprehensive account of our first meeting. Our discovery that by God's grace we were meant for each other; and how we pledged our love and agreed to marry. I wait for their reply. Please be patient if I stop here today, you know now that I love and enjoy writing to you. Although it may repeat itself over and over, but as you so beautifully said it in your letter they are the building blocks of our love. I can only add that Homes for love are also built with hundreds of bricks. It is a wonderful thought to think that our letters are our building blocks of love Ehrentraut. Make sure to give my greetings to Mum and Dad, not forgetting Annemarie. From me all my love Ehrentraut, your loving Paul.*

---

Hameln, 24/26. 11,1954 My dearest Paul,

How I wish I could say that personally, but my written word will have to do, thank you for your lengthy letter. I love to share the details of your daily life. I do not regard your letters as a substitute; rather for me they mean your real presence as I read your words and lift my eyes to look at your photograph. I wish to ask you a question, which you must answer honestly, do you have to pay surcharges for my bulky letters? Remember, truth only, I do not accept lies! So you are already working things out for our meeting next year. I am excited and my heart beats so quickly.

I felt that the photograph of you with Engelbert is not quite you, so I have replaced it with one of you on your own, which I prefer. Now, after me clearing the table, you and I are alone together. Earlier I made supper for Mum, Dad, Annemarie and her boyfriend Heinz, who have gone into town to see the musical play "The Flute of Hameln" presented by the youth of Hameln. I felt *it was a good opportunity for the four of them to go together. The musical is supposed to be very good.*

*Soon it will be Advent, a busy time for me. I shall not enjoy the three Advent Sundays before Christmas, when all shops are open from lunchtime till 7 p.m. We have to tidy up after closing time and do not get home till 8 p.m. Did I hear you say it will pass the time for me? There will be a number of preparatory events for the youth groups during Advent. The favourite with my group is to carry a statue of Mary from house to house in the evening and sing a few songs and an Advent poem or two. People who wish us to visit on a particular day put their names on a list at the church door. Come and join us, you will enjoy it especially with me at your side! My dearest, if you could feel how much I love to write to you. I know that to talk with you would be ever so much better; but, like you said, let us be grateful for the ability to put on paper what is deep in our thoughts. I expect my folk to be back any moment and it is getting late. I have to say goodnight, and looking at your picture, I feel your kisses. I pray always that you keep well for us.*

*Yours with a hundred kisses your loving Ehrentraut.*

---

*Viewfield, 28.11.1954 God greet you, my sweetheart Ehrentraut,*

*Many thanks for your loving and warm words again in the letter I received yesterday. I read it with great joy until I discovered that it finally dawned in some people's minds that you are taking a risk with me. I feel quite proud to read how you defended your corner and coped with Gretel's Mum's assertion, "How could you go all the way to Düsseldorf with him when you do not even know him? He could have just dropped you off and left you stranded there." Well, you did take a risk poor Ehrentraut! What will happen when Gretel tells her mother that you may actually travel to Scotland on your own? I look forward to that comment. Having said that, it made me think that there may well be other people even within our families with similar thoughts, I had better be prepared.*

*It had never occurred to me that you might ask what I am doing in the long winter evenings. Which is a perfectly legitimate question to ask an unattached, not anymore, young man. I better be prepared, and have my list prepared. Remember how I asked, almost begged you to tell me how you and your Mum and sister Annemarie managed to live without your Dad and with little food for a year and a half. Far from your own farm and house, fields and animals all left behind, and simply taken away from you, without any recompense of any kind; which generations had tilled by the sweat of their brow. Finally taken away from your mother earth, with only what you could carry driven to a new, strange place. It was that thought in my mind that I might meet someone like you and give away all my love to make up for all that pain. It took me almost seven years of prayers to find you! During that time I pursued several interests, my car, the dance band, the many opportunities to act as waiter at weddings and social functions. I consider all those years a busy waiting time until that miracle when finally you and I were extraordinarily brought together. My treasure, all these pursuits still occupy my time to prepare for the day when we become Husband and Wife. Now to the matter of your coming to Tain. It gives me great pleasure to tell you that Ella is really happy that you should visit Scotland. I have not mentioned accommodation yet and would prefer you to stay in the Mansfield Hotel where I assist as waiter at functions. Mrs MacDougall the owner would be delighted to let you have a room. Also, Mrs Sellar would want you to stay with them. There is time to settle the matter. It is time to put our arms around us and say with a kiss, goodnight, your loving Paul.*

---

*Hameln, 6.12.1954 my dearest, dearest Paul,*

*Do you remember the date? Yes, St. Nikolaus. Were you not frightened as a child? My thoughts as usual are with you, wondering if you will be putting a plate out, hoping he will leave some goodies for you. I am going to put a stool out and shall peep through the curtain to see if you are there? Or should I come over? Do you have St. Nikolaus in Scotland? Tomorrow is our first open Sunday, 1-7 p.m.*

*at the shop. I will be too tired to write to you after. My Dad would not be pleased - thinks I will ruin my health. Will I be forgiven? Also our youth work will require a number of late evenings. It all keeps me occupied, and I enjoy the company, the fun and the spiritual side of it. Importantly too, it helps me when my heart is so yearning for you. How happy you have made me telling me about my visit and where to stay. It makes me feel warm around my heart to know that you care for me. I love to tell my Mum about my love for you because she is so happy for me and loves to share my joy with her. For me she is a comfort because Mum knows when I miss you. You are not to worry!*

*We know that mail from Poland takes more time. We thought your parents, hoppla "my future in-laws", would have written by now? Dear Paul can I ask you for a favour? Is it possible for you to frank your letters with a few smaller values? Roland, the son of my friendly colleague, is collecting stamps and I give him yours when I visit his mother, Frau Meissner. We both like needlework, it is important for brides? Keep guessing? I would love to send you a Christmas parcel, not too large because the postage would gobble up more than it's worth. I would bake some of our traditional Pfefferkuchen, ginger biscuits, and when you taste them you will have a piece of me inside you. I will also send a parcel to your parents in Poland. Hopefully it will get there. Again, it is nearly midnight.*

*With my prayers, and all my love my dearest, yours Ehrentraut, + + more?*

---

Viewfield, December.

My dearest Ehrentraut, It will probably require more than just wagging my finger if you will not stop writing to me at midnight. No excuses just lay aside the pen and continue when next you have time. It does worry me because your sleepless hours may well damage your health. That is the last thing we want when you are going to be busy in the shop. Please think of our future, end of lecture. I am ever so glad to hear you are well again, but be careful. Yes, I would indeed love to have a small parcel of your ginger biscuits for Christmas, to share with my adopted parents. Next Christmas might I be able to help you to bake them? Beware, I do learn some baking here at Viewfield, Ella is a good teacher. As for my parents, I am sure they would be delighted to receive a Christmas gift from you; they would look at it as a 'Weihnachts Geschenk' Christmas present from their future daughter-in-law.

You asked how Christmas is celebrated here. You will be shocked. While England celebrates Christmas for two days as in Germany, in Scotland it is like any other working day. We Germans could not believe it. At the time of my first Christmas in Viewfield, I went back to camp to meet and greet my friends there, wishing them a blessed happy Christmas. They had to ask the Camp Sergeant for permission to take Christmas Day off and work instead on January 2$^{nd}$. The sergeant was happy to oblige.

You may be interested to learn that the nearest Church of Scotland {Presbyterian} was only a mile and a half away from the camp. The Minister at that time Rev. Ronald Walls spoke German well and went to meet the boys at the camp and held a short service in German. That was an unexpected event and the boys enjoyed it and thanked the Minister. Two days later Rev. Walls asked the boys if they would sing a couple of German carols in his church at his Christmas service. The camp sergeant agreed provided Rev. Walls brings all of them back. {Twenty years later I had the pleasure to meet him when he visited our Catholic Parish here in Tain, as a Catholic Priest. A friendship that lasted for many years.}

But let me tell you how I celebrate Christmas here. As a member of the family I do all the necessary jobs, feeding etc. On Christmas Eve I attend Midnight Mass in Dingwall. On Christmas Day I make sure all the animals get a double ration of feed from me, a ritual I began at my first Christmas here. We get two days off at New Year which I ignore. My dearest Ehrentraut, do not be too disappointed. I am not sure how you will react to this. All I can do is place myself completely in your hands and await your letter. What I have learned about you is your total honesty in all matters. There is a thought that came into my head; might it not be possible that you could actually become a new changing light in our parish here? In my thoughts I embrace you lovingly with numberless kisses. All my good wishes to Mum, Dad and Annemarie, your own Paul.

*Hameln, 19.12.1954 My dearest Paul,*

*You worry too much. How could I not understand? Promise me you will not do it again my dear. I had already written my letter in my mind whenever I had time to think about you, and it is well known that nowhere is Christmas celebrated as in our homeland. If only you could be here on Christmas Eve? Can you imagine all of us gathered together, you in our midst in our living room enjoying our traditional Christmas meal, the Christmas tree decorated and the beautiful candles burning, singing our favourite Christmas carol? Then it would be time to get dressed to attend the beautiful Midnight Mass. That is how I imagine it with you at my side. But promise no tears! If we are blessed we will have our own Christmas together next year, am I right?*

*Please do not worry that at present the shop manager will allow me only four days off. I will have a word with the shop's owner when he comes to visit in a few days' time. Also do not worry that I might find the countryside around you too quiet. If I look around there is a lot of artificial excitement and I do not enjoy today's hustle and bustle. Will you think about me when you light the first candle on your Advent wreath? Do you even have one I wonder? Perhaps that is something else for me to think about next year when we hope to be together. My dearest love you will have to be patient for the next few days. I will be rather busy not only in the shop but also in my youth work. I am also trying to crochet something for my sister Annemarie, which could be for her dowry.*

*Now goodnight, may my prayers, love and kisses be with you, Yours, Ehrentraut and my family.*

---

*Viewfield, 20.12.54 My dear Ehrentraut, and Mum, Dad and Annemarie,*

*The angels sang "Glory to God in the highest" and in that spirit of joy I send my happiest thoughts and blessings for a happy and blissful Christmas to you my Love, Mum, Dad and Annemarie. I hope you are all well to celebrate this most wonderful feast. Of course, in spirit and in deep thoughts I will be with all of you all who welcomed me into your family. At the same time I remember my parents, so long parted from us, Ursula and Engelbert. I believe my parents have sent you their best wishes. They were pleased to have your photo and thought you must be a happy person. You are right, Ehrentraut, our thoughts will cross the miles over and over to reach each other. It is a truly lovely thought. Thank you for your two letters, giving me details of all you are doing in your parish and the youth group with all the preparations for the celebration of the festive season. I am happy to know you love singing, I am sure you and I will be singing hymns in our church, that's my feeling and belief. You really should listen to your Dad and not write so late into the night, since you have to be in the shop by 8a.m. You must have felt shattered to learn that your manager is allowing you only four days to visit me. You have not given up and will ask the boss next time he visits the shop hopefully before Christmas. I join you in your prayer for success. Now it is my turn to pour out all my love to you and your folks. Enclosed are my notes of what happens on the farm, and how my animal family up here in Viewfield will know that it is Christmas. Of course those who are down at our Mansfield farm will not be so lucky because in Scotland it is not a holiday. In England it is celebrated as at home in Germany. You will of course get an extra Christmas letter. It is my turn to pour out all my love and kisses to you, and 'ALL' your loved ones, yours Paul.*

---

*Hameln 22.12.54 My dearest Paul,*

*Thank you for your lovely thoughts. You should know by now just how much I like to read of what you are doing. I tell you everything; that is what our love is all about. Now I have to warn you, this will be a shorter letter because of all the preparation in our youth club for the great feast. We organise the beautiful half-hour service at the crib before Midnight Mass, which is always appreciated by the congregation. Do you have something like this? Maybe, when we are together? Would you like that? These are tiring days in the shop and our practices are late. I have to stop dear Paul, it is nearly midnight, sorry I am falling asleep.*

*24. December, Christmas Eve. 1954 My dearest Love and Paul,*
*I never thought my future husband would be called Paul. Just a few very important lines at 4.15 p.m. Today we closed the shop at 2 o'clock and wished each other a Happy Christmas. Before I started my journey homeward, I enjoyed a brief moment to think that this will surely be my last Christmas at the shop. On my way home I called at the hospital to visit the mother of one of my friends. She has a broken hip and her daughter is working in New York. I am glad I did, for she was so happy to see me and, of course, I had to tell her about you, and us, and how the two of us are getting on. Can you imagine how happy and proud I was to tell her about us? I can hardly hold the pen because of my joy I am coming to visit you! My boss called at the shop yesterday and, though not over-enthusiastic, he said YES but the days will be taken from my summer holiday. That did not dismay me, since I may hand in my notice by that time. I could jump for joy, you too? We will see each other in less than two months. What a present! Our prayer to Mary has been answered. I'd a feeling she would help. I have to be patient to wait for your letter, but better still, your telephone call on Christmas Day. Oh, to hear your voice! I must get going now. There is still so much to do. I hope you have a full bus when you go to Midnight Mass. Happy Christmas, from your deepest love, Ehrentraut to my deepest love Paul, not forgetting your adopted parents Ella and David.*

---

*Viewfield, Christmas Day 1954 My Love, dearest Ehrentraut,*
*What can I tell you? What a Christmas to be joyful about, now that I have been given the most precious and loveliest Christmas present: my Love Ehrentraut, that name is tagging at my heart. I am in my room and the clock says 4 o'clock in the afternoon and I sit here and look at your photograph. I try to fathom what has changed. Eight years have passed without outside encouragement or any personal wish to change my way of life. The time passed in a life of work and many different interests, all of which provided fulfilment. Then came the moment when I answered the invitation in the newspaper. I see it now it was a call to change direction, face*

*a different way of life, a challenge to seek nature's most beautiful gift: 'LOVE', now personified in you, Ehrentraut. I found a love that I could never have imagined until I held your heart close to mine and our lips touched. At last, it was you who has given me the real purpose in life, to love and care for you. For that I will need your help.*

*I bless this afternoon and the stillness that surrounds me. My adopted parents are in the kitchen, reading the newspaper or whatever. As usual Ella provided an excellent Christmas dinner for us. Having our own dairy cream, I had a good helping with the pudding. I do not know if I ever told you that on Sundays before breakfast David always reads a passage from the Bible. I remember on my first Sunday here, I was asked if I minded and was pleased to answer that I was happy to be in a Christian family. I will close now and attend to the milking. I shall continue after our phone call. Do not worry for Ella is very happy to allow me to phone you. It does not cost a penny. Until later.*

*'Joy to the world' so the carol goes. How wonderful it was to have had the opportunity to speak and hear each other. I had no problem to recognise your voice. My heart almost lost a beat when I heard your voice. We will do it again on your birthday. Joy upon joy to hear that your boss gave permission for the two weeks. Now 'Mein Schatz' we can plan your visit. We will enjoy two Sundays together. I too could have cried out. Now we can really plan and I know what I have to do. I am so happy for you and so excited that I will finish my letter and hold my pillow tight, imagining it is you. With love and kisses yours Paul. Greetings to your parents and Annemarie.*

---

*Hameln, 29.12.54 My sweet dear Paul, my Bridegroom do you mind my calling you so?*

*I am writing this letter in fits and starts because of unavoidable interruptions. Although I was missing you, we did have a happy Christmas. During the meal everyone agreed how enriching your presence would have made it all; but that is the pain that those who love deeply must bear. I could not help myself when I looked at your picture on the shelf and thought that it could have been your first Christmas amongst a family for twelve years.*

*I am sure though that Ella would have made the occasion special for you and David at Viewfield. We had a generous Christkindl. My Dad got an electric shaver from us, which pleased him. Myself, I got the first Christkindl of goodies from my Love so far away. Thank you my Love, can you not feel my arms around you and our hearts beating? I received some very useful things for my dowry, which we both shall share in the end. My parents gave us two bedcovers with matching damask pillowcases, a silver candlestick and a bed jacket. Annemarie gave us a white damask tablecloth with six matching napkins. With my Christmas bonus I bought the twelve spoons, knives and forks we chose from the catalogue I sent you. Yes, we need a lot more I hear you say.*

*After Midnight Mass I did not get much sleep for a dozen of us went as in other years to sing Christmas carols to the prisoners in the jail. How much they enjoy that? I will not be there next Christmas. Last, but not least, did you hear my heart flutter when I heard your voice on the telephone saying "Hello, my dearest Ehrentraut"? It helped me so much to be able to answer you. We could have talked for ages, but let us be happy with the time we had. Please thank Ella for me.*

*My Love, my own, take care and do not forget how much I love you, Your Ehrentraut.*

---

*Viewfield, 29.12.1954 My dear, dear Ehrentraut, Mum, Dad, Annemarie and her friend Heinz, to all of you from me and Ella and David, we wish you a happy and good New Year. From me to you Ehrentraut I send a few special kisses which you may pass on to others, only family of course!*

*Although we have this year three days of holiday, it will be a rather busy time for me. In the business of farming there are always animals that need to be fed, think of mothers at home? The sheep are outside in fields. If it interests you or Dad, fodder has to be brought in to last over the holiday period, in case there should be a fall of snow. In addition I shall be busy in the house, helping Ella to bake and feed family visitors who always come for New Year lunch, afternoon tea and supper. Viewfield is of course, the home place, and I am glad to be able to help. Young Peter will be coming with his father and his three brothers. How are you getting on with the* choosing of your engagement ring? I am quite excited for you. Shortly after New Year, Ella will be away for a few days in London, visiting her younger brother. David makes his own breakfast and will get his lunch at his sister's farm, just two miles from Tain. I will take care of our supper, I am quite good at baking girdle scones. One day you will taste them. We look forward to your coming to see where I live now.

Dear Ehrentraut, I will visit the travel agent and arrange the booking for the Holland-Harwich ferry crossing, reserve your overnight cabin, a rail ticket to London and tickets for the London-Inverness return journey. Can I ask you to enquire about the return journey Holland Hameln or would you prefer me to try to arrange that from here? Please let me know. Regarding our official engagement, are we agreed for it to take place here? I think your idea makes sense. We can invite friends here for a small party, as hardly anyone will travel to Germany for the wedding. This then, my treasure, will be my last letter in this momentous year for us. May the good Lord keep you and with all my best wishes and kisses. Your own loving bridegroom Paul, also to Mum, Dad, Annemarie, Heinz, and Gretel, especially Oma and family.

'New Year 1954/55 at the Krause Family, from l to r Mum Gertrud, Ehrentraut, Gretel, Engelbert, Annemarie, Dad Karl, Heinz'

*Hameln, 29.12.54 My dear sweet love, greetings from all my people.*

*First of all, "Ein frohes gesegnetes Neue Jahr" a happy and blessed New Year to all your people. Everybody hopes you are well, just as we are in Hameln. First I would like to thank you for your Christmas card and the most wonderful poetic words addressed to me. It moved me so much and I had to read it out to all at coffee time. They thought it was fitting for me. It was the icing on the cake. Do you have a saying like that? You know tears do not come easily for me, but this time nearly. Is our life always going to be so romantic? Better not, we would not get much done.*

*We all visited our relations as usual. There are a number who came with the same transport from Silesia. We always visit Grandma Mum's mother and gave her your special greetings. She is rather small as you know, but a wonderful grandmother who looked after us so well during the hunger years. You can imagine how interested she was to hear how the two of us are getting on. I felt so warm inside telling her about us and that I am going to see where you live. I told her too about our plan to get engaged. I could not help myself and invited her to our wedding. She smiled and promised to pray for us. She decided you must be alright for me when she saw how I love you. Come to think of it, I never said anything about Engelbert and his visit to Gretel and us over New Year. It was quite funny in a way when suddenly about lunchtime on Friday he marched into the shop with a huge smile on his face. He threw his arms around me announcing "I've made it". I was glad for Gretel and I am sure you too would have been pleased, we were all glad that Engelbert made it for Gretel's sake to have company over New Year. We all will have a good laugh when we toast each other, you and I will do it with closed eyes imagining we look in each other's eyes. You told me that you have three days off, not here. You mentioned in your last letter you will soon look for my travel tickets. It was lovely to read that. That must do for today, your ever loving, Ehrentraut and you wished me to say, your Bride. God bless us all.*

*Viewfield, 8.01.1955 My dearest Ehrentraut,*

*Thank you for your long letter written with so much love. The way you write makes it seem as if you are sitting beside me talking. If I close my eyes it seems I have the good fortune to hear you on the telephone. Your kind words give me the opportunity to share the good time you had over the New Year. Engelbert's arrival must have pleased you so much for Gretel's sake. Your detailed description made me feel I too, was right among you, it was a pity we could not exchange our personal good wishes with a kiss. Time will remedy that. It did please me that Engelbert was made so welcome: a special thanks to your parents. Gretel's happiness matters to me too. In spirit I was with you all. There can be no doubt that Engelbert is thinking about our parents so far away. He has the idea that sooner or later it will be necessary for him to initiate a possible legal extradition for them from Poland to Germany. I freely admit that Engelbert would make a far better negotiator than I could ever be. He is a man of the world while I live quietly at Viewfield. I imagine that, being a light smoker, he might make full use of the opportunity to use western cigarettes, etc. to negotiate with Polish officials. Of course, all that is in the future. Now to the important point: As arranged I will again on the agreed time phone you to wish you a "happy very happy 22$^{nd}$ birthday", you will hear my kisses.*

*Well, my loving bride, you certainly know how to raise my excitement by wasting no time in introducing the practicalities of marriage, the need to begin amassing domestic items for 'our home'. It gave me great joy to hear that my parents' letter to you confirmed their happiness to welcome you as their first daughter-in-law. How wonderful that sounds. I am sure I will have my letter telling me of their joy arriving any day. Finally, as promised, I am happy to tell you that Pastor Günther will try to come up to bless our engagement. What do you think about that my Ehrentraut? You will get more details about your travel arrangements soon. I am sure there will be something about the engagement ring in your next letter? I close today with a lingering kiss until you struggle for air.*

*With all my love and kisses, your loving 'Brautigam' Paul.*

*Hameln, 15.01.1955 my dearest Paul,*

*Thank you for your long letter. It made me so happy to know that you enjoyed reading about our New Year celebrations without you; but I do not want to dwell on your absence lest it makes me sad. I missed you so much. It is more joyous by far to thank you for wishing me so much happiness and love on my birthday by letting me hear your voice on the phone. Dr and Mrs Siemens left us alone in their room and all our guests came down to hear you wish me happy birthday; and the doctor's wife has indicated she will be happy if I ask again to use their telephone. If only you could imagine just how difficult it was for me to concentrate at first. I have never spoken to anyone so many miles away, and you were not just anyone! For me it was the highlight of my birthday and you could have heard my heart beating. Now I long even more to come to you and be held in your arms.*

*The time for my journey across the sea to you is getting nearer. The lovely news is that Engelbert sent me a letter telling me not to worry because Mrs Metzner's relative Stan (Stanislaus) will be waiting for me when the boat train reaches London. Stan has indicated he is happy to help and you can imagine how that pleases my parents. They have forgotten that I have travelled on my own before my trip to Italy. You I trust will be waiting to pick me up when I reach Inverness. I do miss you my Paul*

*Now that the sales are behind us, there is not much pressure of work in the shop. One of my favourite colleagues had to be rushed to hospital, appendicitis I believe. I'll visit her within the next few days but just now there are a number of events with the youth group that will require my help in the evening. Please do not worry; it helps to pass the time. Now let's talk about my engagement ring. As you know I am not one for extravagant jewellery and prefer the one without the diamond mount, please. You know we need all the money we can save. I will let you have any important matters in my next letter which you shall have within the week. Imagine now it is only a matter of a few weeks and I can fall into your arms, will you hold me? Let me hold you in your arms while I close my eyes and feel your kiss goodnight. Your loving Ehrentraut.*

*Viewfield, 17.01.1955 My dearly beloved Ehrentraut,*

*Thank you for your loving and newsy letter. Every time you express your love for me I am amazed and humbled. The details of what you do at home, at work, or with your youth work within and outside the church, show me that you do not stand still, which to me means 'determination' to get out of youth-life as much as one can. Now I read that you are attending cookery classes. Please do not overdo it. You cannot afford to get ill again. I am sorry to learn that your father is unwell. Please convey my best wishes for his recovery. Somehow David and Ella missed the weather forecast on the radio, so it was a surprise to find myself stepping out into four inches of snow at milking time. Since there had not been a drifting wind, it will not cause major problems. It will require loading the tractors with turnips, hay and oats to feed the sheep in the field. You asked me some time ago to tell you how I pass the day, because your father is interested as a one-time farmer. You do not need to feel sorry for the sheep outside, they are happy as long as they are fed. More important for me to assure you not to be worried about your winter journey. I am sure the snow will melt away soon.*

*The good news is that that all your travel documents will be sent directly to you by the travel agent, and in good time. The joy of anticipation is growing day by day. More good news, I heard from Stan confirming he is free to meet you, and awaits details which I will pass on to him soon. Regarding presents for the Sellar family, please do not buy any other than the Hameln Pied Piper figures, because they really want to pay me back for taking them to church on Sundays. More news; I have received the itinerary. You have a second class cabin on the boat, and your seat is reserved, only promise you will always ask the guards on the platform, do not be shy, they will love to hear your voice. That is all for today, with my blessing and good wishes and a long embrace. Yours, Paul.*

*Hameln, 24 January 1955 My own dearest Paul,*

*If all goes well, I can throw my arms around you in only three weeks time. I must not think too much about such joys. I thank you again my dear for your informative letter and enjoyed reading all about the sheep, I read your account to my folks who enjoyed it too. I will be good and not worry about the snow. I have to confess to you that I had to stay in bed for nearly a week. Something called 'false flu' is going round northern Germany and it caught me too. Thanks to Dr Siemens and his care, I am allowed back to work next Monday, and providing my temperature stays normal there is no reason for not travelling. Gretel called today, unlike me, she does not get regular letters every week, but at least Engelbert does write to her. She called to ask if I would accompany her to the pre-Lent Carnival Ball. I have to ask you, my Love, on one knee at least for permission to attend? It will be my last as Fraulein Ehrentraut, one day to be Mrs Lippok? I look forward to the arrival of my travel documents. I am sorry I am jumping about a bit, but I have just remembered to ask you if you had thought that your birthday congratulations were the last on my own? God willing, in a year's time you can congratulate me when you wake me before setting off for work, a lovely thought and something nice to pray for. I am romancing. You could still wish me happy birthday when we meet soon. Would you like that? Back to reality. I intend to dress simple and sensible making sure I am warmly clad. As you rightly say, one can never be sure what to expect of the weather in February. I have made a few more purchases for us, plain good quality cutlery, they will last a while, yes?*

*My parents-in-law have sent me a lovely letter, your Dad wants to know my height and my age, you 'Lausbub' rascal, never told them that? At least they did not want to know my weight. What I appreciated is that we have their permission to get married and happy with their daughter-in-law. Please let me tell you about a small book with the title: "We are enclosed by a holy ring". It contains the letters of a young bride and her fiancé while courting, both committed Christians, while he was a pilot in the war, sadly killed before their marriage. It belongs to Gretel but if I can find one I will buy it for us. I wrote to you that we have to send a notice of our 'Engagement' to our relatives and close friends, or we'll never hear the end of it. It cost DM14.85 for forty copies. That can be done after I come home again. We can make up the list when I am in Scotland. Tell me how much money can I bring into the country? Or how much do I need? Let me know soon. Enough for today, with many good wishes from all my family, Kisses for you, and imagine my arms around you, Your true Ehrentraut.*

---

*Viewfield, 19-29.01.1955 my dearest Ehrentraut,*
    *I am glad and thankful that you are feeling better and ready to return to work soon. Thank you for your concern about me but, with the snow practically gone and the temperature around 5-7°c, our life here has returned to normal. Ella is back in her routine, telling me that young Peter is relatively happy among his three elder brothers, obviously missing his mother. There is every reason to be grateful, especially now that you have recovered. Mrs Sellar and her husband have been asking about you, and they insist that you must not think of bringing presents. They are only too happy that you bothered to visit Mrs Sellar's mother and hope you may do so again. Now for news that should make you feel better. Our parish priest, Rev. Fr. Davies, is looking forward to meeting you and will be happy to bless our engagement if Father Günther is unable to come. He has never had an engaged couple seeking a blessing during Sunday Mass and is hopeful people might learn from it. You are already putting your mark on our parish! Pardon a few notices just in case, in toilets 'Free' means frei, 'Engaged' means besetzt. I keep forgetting that you found your way round Venice and returned on your own without having to be sent home with a label tucked on your chest. Sorry, Verzeihung!*
    *In case I have not mentioned it already, I have made enquiries at the National Hotel in Dingwall where our parish church is, and have booked dinner for the two of us after Mass. Would I be right in thinking it would be nice for just the two of us being together, yes? You mentioned the Carnival please go to it, dress up as you usually do and take Gretel by the hand and have fun. Please, do not forget I am still your fiancé! I expect a photo of you in your outfit*

*afterwards. Might Engelbert be coming to the carnival? Doubtful I suppose but still you never know. Only two weeks or so and he will be celebrating his 25$^{th}$. I must remember to congratulate him. Oh yes, are you getting used to being twenty two? The weather is better and the sheep can nibble away at the short grass. Of course they are still getting their daily ration of turnips. Those who carry lambs have to build up their milk supply before their lambs appear in two months. Thank you for telling me how you keep your eyes open for any bargains towards your dowry Ehrentraut. Mrs McDougall asks if we would like to hold our engagement party in their hotel, she was delighted when I said yes. We will have to pay only for the food. I will pay for the drinks. I thought that is good of them, what do you think? You really must ask me when to send some money over, you cannot always use your hard earned money, please do let me know! I have also received your itinerary; Your ticket on the boat is for a second class cabin. On arrival in Harwich you will find that the train to London is not that far away, and a large number of passengers will be looking for it. Your seat is reserved, but do not be afraid to ask, they are always helpful. Stan will be waiting in London. I am so glad that you are really coming to see where I am living and work. Also it will give us a chance to talk in depth, regarding our wedding in Autumn? This will have to be all for today. May the good Lord keep you in his care, greetings to all as usual especially Mum, Dad and Annemarie, your loving Paul.*

*Hameln, 4-10.02.1955 God greet you My darling Paul,*

*I found it in my small English/Deutsch dictionary. Am I right, it means Liebling? do you like me to call you thus? All in the Krause family hope so. Here we are all pretty well on the mend. Everybody is back at work. Back at the shop I discovered that there had been three of us off work. Just as well our mid-season sale is not on till next week. I had a slight tummy pain, and was worried in case my boss might change his mind about my holiday; but all is well. I am looking out what I might be putting on and taking with me. I shall heed your advice and not pack too much.*

*Well, you did say your people are not so fashion-conscious as here in Germany now the economy is improving. Thank you for all the things you have already organised for us and our enjoyment. I really would like to give you a hug after reading where we are to have our church blessing and the following dinner. It is what I would like: just the two of us for the meal. To be together is worth more than anything to me. I do miss you so, but I am going to be brave. Do I understand correctly that we will have a party for our friends in your hotel? Does that mean we will meet one evening and have a meal and drinks there? We should send invitations, that is something you could organise. It makes sense and should be fun to get to know them all. That would be an occasion for which I should bring a dress? Our family, especially Mum, are so happy for me, which makes me feel good and is the strength of my love for you.*

*For me to be in church these days is the place where I can be on my own to ponder quietly on the wonder that I should become someone's wife and, with grace, a mother. Can you feel my love, my dear? Do you occasionally also have a funny feeling in your tummy whether all this is real or are we dreaming? Then I see your picture and your letters and know all is true. I could never have imagined that what I say in my letters could make you too feel warmed as if by a cuddly shawl. At your suggestion I will bring a pair of strong shoes. My loving 'Lausbub' rascal do you want me to bring my cocktail dress? Why not, it is not heavy. Time now to go to bed do you not think so? It is nearly midnight and I pray may God protect you for me. Hold me and I will kiss you goodnight. Your ever loving Ehrentraut, until we embrace in Inverness yes?*

---

*Viewfield, 7.02.1955 My Love, my dearest Ehrentraut,*

*This is my last letter to reach you before your departure and I hope it finds you in good health and feeling better by the day. Thank you, I too am fine. So are David and Ella. The weather is holding up fine and we just have to trust and leave all in the hands of providence. Here the last information concerning your journey. Almost all the cabin staff speak German, for the toilets: Ladies are*

> *Damen. I am sure you know it. Make sure you find the Dining-room (Ess Salon) and have something to eat. Any announcements over the 'Lautsprecher' loudspeaker in English will be repeated in Dutch and Deutsch.*
>
> *You may already have all your documents and tickets. When you arrive in London Euston there is no hurry to get out, for the train stops there. Stan wrote to me and you will recognise him when you get on the platform. He will be at the barrier wearing a yellowish camel-hair coat, no hat and will be looking for your dark hair and hazel eyes I am sure he will notice you. Keep your return ticket! Stan's full name is Stan Chapman (Chap - wie Tchacha der Tanz). He is going to take care of you all day and take you to the train for Inverness. When you wake next morning you will be travelling towards the blue bay and hopefully arrive within minutes in Inverness, I'll be waiting for you.*
>
> *I am confident you will have no travel problems; but a tip from Ella, put some Spalttabletten in your handbag in case of headache. As a precaution, I will pray to Saint Christopher to bring you safely to me. With that, I embrace you and gently kiss you, Your loving Bridegroom, Dein Schatz Paul.*

At Viewfield it is February 7th, my brother Engelbert's 25th birthday. The last letter of my instructions to Ehrentraut has been posted. David and Ella's new Hillman Minx was delivered this week and, as agreed, their four year old Hillman is to become my new car at a very reasonable price. It is in excellent condition because I have been looking after it. David has a Land Rover for all farm work. How fortunate that I should have now a post-war car after the number of pre-war models. It calls for a discussion with Ehrentraut while she will be here for our Engagement. The lurking suspicion is there, should I have spent my money on a car while trying to save for our marriage? We shall certainly talk about it.

I thought it wise to have a good store of animal feed so that I gain extra time in the evening to be with Ehrentraut as soon as possible. One has to plan ahead when in love. I am happy that my bride-to-be will stay with the Sellar family. Mrs Sellar speaks fluent German and, as I have mentioned before, her husband Bob was a POW Seaforth-Highlander captured at Dunkirk and in a camp near Mrs Sellar's home in eastern Germany. Now I could give Mrs Sellar and her children a lift to church on Sundays. On our return I was invited in for a cup of coffee and was shown the room reserved for Ehrentraut. Back home I could not help but think and hope that all had gone well with Ehrentraut on her journey and that she had been met by Stan, as agreed. At lunch, I sensed that Ella and David were aware of my excitement. She asked, "are you able to eat your lunch?" It saddens me that David could not hear or join in any conversation that Ella and I had. We have to raise our voices to include him. Ella and I always bring him into our conversation when it is appropriate to share articles we know or guess he would be interested in. It has to be said David himself demands our attention when he comes across an article he could share with us. After supper I completed my last inspection of the animals in their quarters across the yard.

In my bedroom I laid out my clothes for the morning for I intended to leave immediately after my morning chores. Ella called that the kettle had boiled and I hurried downstairs. As we shared our night-cap drinks there was an opportunity for me to ask David what his newspaper's weather forecast said, "Getting cooler and a low approaching" he said. It might get wintry. Electricity and television had not yet reached Viewfield. I could not settle so decided I might just as well go to bed and try to sleep. To my delight I had a very good sleep as I discovered in the morning.

# Chapter 13

# Ehrentraut's first visit to Tain and our Engagement

It was no surprise that I was wide awake before my alarm went off on the Monday morning. Before David had risen I was already out among my animals, busily feeding and milking, and not particularly aware of the darkness or a light intermittent drizzle. The chores completed I returned to the house to process the milk. David had his breakfast and was about to go out when we met in the lobby and wished each other a good day. David hoping I have a good run to Inverness to meet Ehrentraut. My turn to have breakfast, washed and dressed for my journey. Ella reminded me to ensure I took a blanket with me, good thinking, no heaters in many cars yet. Just after 7a.m. I said goodbye to Ella, like a mother, she reminded me to drive carefully. Within minutes I was on my way. The drizzle persisted and ahead of me was the 45-mile journey through four towns and villages. As I approached Inverness my heart was beating faster. I could not ignore the drizzle which was heavier and increasingly mixed with snowflakes.

As I entered the town small patches of snow already lay here and there. I was some 15 minutes late as I approached the station. There stood Ehrentraut already on the pavement in conversation with a lady. I stopped and called her name, stepped out and flung my arms round my Love. She introduced me at once to the lady who had been her companion in the sleeper compartment and had been so helpful. I shook the lady's hand and thanked her. She declined the offer of a lift, a relative was on his way to collect her. We said our goodbyes and I guided Ehrentraut to our new car. She was pleasantly surprised.

My precious cargo and her luggage safely on board, we were on our way within minutes. We seemed at first to keep excusing one another because we were both asking the same questions but, having left the town behind, we began to relax. Ehrentraut took the initiative and slid closer to me along the bench seat.

As we crossed the river I told her it was the Ness flowing into the North Sea. She heard about Loch Ness and its monster. A few miles on, I apologised for the wet weather and lack of sunshine. The car did not have a heater and I suggested Ehrentraut use the blanket because our journey home would take more than an hour. I asked her what she thought of the scenery once daylight arrived. "I thought I was in Switzerland. There was a lot of snow on the ground and the trees and bushes were thick with snow. It looked beautiful" she said. I was stunned and wondered if it might snow down to our level?

Ehrentraut was in her element telling me all about her journey leaving home, the train, the ferry, how useful the overnight cabin was without her becoming seasick, and how Stan spotted her at Euston Station. The sun was shining in London and telling me how Stan showed her a number of interesting places and took her for a meal in a good restaurant. They had afternoon coffee at his house before he escorted her to the sleeper train for Inverness. Stan spoke fluent German, which made the day so much more interesting for her. I resolved to send a letter of thanks to him at the first opportunity.

Ehrentraut led the conversation and asked many questions. The sight of sheep and cattle outside in winter intrigued her and I explained that their winter coat protected them. I drew her attention to the narrow gap where ships enter and leave the Cromarty Firth. She was keenly taking in the different scenery, the sea and hills. "Soon we will be home, Ehrentraut my Love". I said, she responded at once "How wonderful to see another country, the different style of building". "Is this Tain your new home, Paul? Thank you for bringing me here." How wonderful to hear Ehrentraut's voice.

"Yes this is our Tain Ehrentraut. I just bypassed the High Street and drove straight on until here we turn left into Viewfield Road. If you walk straight up a mile you are in Viewfield. We are stopping here because the house on the right is where the Sellars live, your home for two weeks. A kiss first before we go out to knock at the door. Look, Mrs Sellar must have seen us she is already opening the door, so let's go and greet her, but first a kiss". The door opened and Mrs Sellar embraced Ehrentraut warmly and guided her inside while I took Ehrentraut's case inside and closed the door. Mrs Sellar insisted that I stay for lunch, which was about to be served. She expected Bob to return from his milk round shortly. Mrs Sellar showed Ehrentraut the bathroom which was important after the drive.

We sat down to lunch when Bob came in and greetings and welcome were exchanged. With lunch enjoyed, it was time for me to leave. How fortunate that Ehrentraut had already met Mrs Sellar in Hameln. Of course Mrs Sellar spoke perfect German which would make matters so much more pleasant. I had to go and thanked Mrs Sellar for her tasty lunch. Ehrentraut saw me out to have our embrace until I call in the evening. I told her she should take Mrs Sellar's advice and rest in the afternoon. Back at Viewfield I garaged the car and met Ella in the kitchen. She was eager for news of Ehrentraut's safe arrival; and I apologised for missing lunch at home because of Mrs Sellar's pressing invitation.

I changed into my working clothes and wasted no time in getting back to work. After supper I completed my usual duties and had a quick look in the newspaper for tomorrow's weather forecast. Ella was looking forward to meeting Ehrentraut and I reached for my coat. At the Sellar's, I found Ehrentraut in good spirits and certainly better for her rest. I had not seen or talked to Bob for some time and sat with him for a while. He was an active politician and town councillor and I always enjoyed his commentaries and arguments regarding local interests. It was Mrs Sellar who intervened, fetching Ehrentraut's coat and suggesting that Ella might be waiting? We said goodnight to the children, Denise 7 and Peter 9 and I asked at what time Ehrentraut might be locked out? I indicated we would return no later than 10 p.m. and was told the door would be still unlocked.

It was dark as we made our way to the farm so nothing could really be seen. Naturally, Ehrentraut was apprehensive and I took her hand in mine. She need not have worried for David and Ella received her cordially. We sat together in the kitchen and our conversation went much better than I had expected. I relaxed because my translating was relatively easy and what could have been a difficult first visit turned into a light-hearted pleasant meeting. Ella and Ehrentraut exchanged questions on various subjects, many of which resulted in hearty laughter when the meaning had been misunderstood. David joined in occasionally. Ella soon suggested we had tea, keeping the atmosphere amicable, often due to Ehrentraut with her gift of finding a question or other. As expected Ella had produced a selection of her favourite baking. My offer to clear and wash up afterwards was appreciated but gratefully declined. All too soon it was time to take Ehrentraut back to the Sellar's and Ella made sure before we left that Ehrentraut knew she would always be welcome and expected.

There was a chill in the air and no moon as I escorted Ehrentraut to the car. I folded my arms around her and we kissed, Ehrentraut responding fondly. I knew that my bride-to-be had made a good impression on Ella and was able to dispel her own anxiety. Inability to converse in the same language does not make things easy at a first meeting, but Ehrentraut was not shy to use a word or two that she knew in English. We clung to each other a while longer, to catch up on the kisses we had missed since our first meeting three months ago. Ehrentraut became concerned that we should not be late returning to the Sellar's. I felt she needed to catch up on her sleep and I wrapped the blanket around her before we started on our way. As we left the farmyard I asked Ehrentraut to look ahead as we rounded the stable. The headlights illuminated the little white cottage just fifty yards away. "'What a nice little house" she remarked, "That is our cottage my Love". As we turned right and motored down Viewfield Road. Within minutes we arrived at the Sellar's and since it was at the respectable time of 10 p.m. we allowed ourselves a while to say goodnight. Between intermittent kisses I suggested that, all being well, we should drive to Dingwall on the following evening to see Father Davies at the Presbytery to discuss our engagement service on the Sunday. I had already contacted him and he would be at home. "All being well my dearest, I will call for a few minutes after lunch tomorrow. If I am unable to come down, I will call to collect you by 6 p.m."

Eventually we went indoors to greet the family. Of course, the children were in bed, but I thanked the Sellars and gave Ehrentraut a final hug before departing. Within minutes I was back at the farm and talked a while with Ella and David. Clearly Ehrentraut had made a favourable impression. They judged her to be down-to-earth and completely unpretentious and I was pleased to hear their opinion. Before saying goodnight I thanked them, especially Ella. Then I checked with David that nothing beyond our usual winter routine was planned for the morrow. I retired happily for a good night's sleep.

Tuesday morning dawned. There was no sunshine and, happily, no rain. I hoped Ehrentraut had slept well. After her bout of influenza shortly before her departure I wanted her to recover sufficiently to enjoy the two weeks in a different environment and hoped fresh sea air would do her good. While attending to my duties my mind kept turning to Ehrentraut and what she might be doing and I was able to visit the Sellar's briefly after lunch.

I rang the doorbell and there stood Ehrentraut with that smile of hers, quickly lost as our lips met. She had been allowed to sleep as long as she wished which she did and planned to walk up Viewfield Road with young Denise and Peter during the afternoon. It was time for me to go back to work after a final embrace and lingering kiss. The afternoon passed quickly, work being completed in good time and supper as usual. Washed and dressed I left Ella and David and drove to the Sellar's. Bob opened the door and, welcoming me he added that I was lucky to have found Ehrentraut. Denise and Peter assured me that Ehrentraut was ready just putting on her coat and there she was, with that smile. Bob suggested I take a front-door key since I had mentioned we might call briefly on friends on our way home. A wave to Bob at the door and we were soon in the car. Ehrentraut wrapped her blanket round her legs for after sunset the air had become more chilly. The novelty of having my Love so close to me and to hear her voice right beside me caused me to stretch out my hand to assure myself that Ehrentraut was there beside me. Who could blame me? "A pity it is so dark to see much, but we are on the same road we travelled from Inverness. You might see the firth glimmer as we get closer to Dingwall," I said.

We made good headway and arrived at St Lawrence's Presbytery in Castle Street just before seven o'clock. Father Davies welcomed us and ushered us into his sitting room. I introduced Ehrentraut and he clearly wanted to know more about her. I did as best I could, not forgetting to tell him of her close involvement in her Parish Youth activities. Ehrentraut was able to say, "Sorry, I do not speak English," clearly regretting she could not join in the conversation. Speaking on our behalf I let Father Davies know what it meant to us both to have our engagement blessed during the Sunday Mass, confirming the importance we attached to our commitment especially because of our unavoidable separation until our marriage. Father Davies expressed his joy and emphasised that engagement was a first commitment and pledge of our fidelity in the preparation for marriage. Engagements can be broken but hopefully it can be used to help and encourage those planning to marry. We joined him for a cup of tea and went on our way content.

We called next at the National Hotel to confirm the booking for our meal on Sunday. Ehrentraut met the receptionist and thanked me. "Even this small gesture makes me feel so attached to you as your future wife" Ehrentraut said and I found this very touching. Within twenty minutes we arrived at Ruth and Dominic's home in Alness and made welcome at this hour. Ehrentraut was taken to see their daughter Sabina, just going to sleep, then we spent a very happy evening with them. We discussed our engagement party and the Sunday Mass. Ruth asked Ehrentraut might she like to spend a couple of days with her. Ehrentraut was overjoyed to accept. Happy with our plans and progress, we left for home, and on arrival did not linger too long before we kissed goodnight and hoped to see each other tomorrow.

I was awoken on the Wednesday morning by the wind setting a branch a-tapping at my window. I became aware that the intermittent light from Portmahomack Lighthouse did not illuminate my room. Taking a closer look, I realised my window was covered with snow. My spirits sank, it was what I feared most, a blizzard and Ehrentraut here on holiday!

A blizzard it was, two feet of snow at the door, the fifty yards to the cowshed had a foot of snow. Until proper daylight it was impossible to know what conditions there were. As I crossed the yard the snowflakes were not falling but being blown horizontally. David and I surveyed the farm road after breakfast. Already there were high drifts and we knew that was how it would be on the Viewfield Road right down to town. The Land Rover might not make it. I suggested that David phone the Police Station in the hope that someone might walk across to the Mansfield steading to ask Jim our foreman to send a tractor up to Viewfield. Within the hour our young tractor driver appeared. Half way down the road there were high drifts. He had opened the gate into the field and re-entered the road again at the top gate of the field due to a large drift. Having made a track with the tractor, we felt the Land Rover would be able to make it for David to transport the milk and discuss with Jim how the day's work could be organised. The Mansfield crew would have to bring hay and turnips for the sheep.

The blizzard continued and I felt it was a pity that the Sellars had no telephone, but I consoled myself with the thought that Ehrentraut would not lose heart, it's what we had in Silesia every winter and for two months or more. At lunch I mentioned to Ella that I would walk down to town that evening. It was all I could do, no chance of using the car in these weather conditions. When Jim appeared with more animal feed he confirmed it was possible for me to walk into town since I was young and fit. "Will we meet your lady soon?" he asked. I completed my evening tasks and after supper Ella insisted that I waste no time but get on my way at once. She kindly handed me samples of her home-baked wheat girdle scones and pancakes with our home-made butter. I donned my woolly hat, coat and rubber boots, and collected a pair of slippers. Clutching these and the gifts for the Sellars and Ehrentraut, I stepped into the snowy world and I must have made an interesting ghostly figure as I scrambled over fields and fences.

My path was a straight line towards the street light nearest the Sellars' home. One moment I was running and the next I was tripping and falling over a frozen molehill. Nothing would stop me on my way to my Love. Shaking off the snow from my coat and boots I pressed the doorbell and within seconds Bob received me saying "I knew it could only be you. With no-one betting against your coming, we just waited for the bell."

I removed my outer garments and asked Bob how he had coped on his milk round? Ehrentraut quickly appeared and locked me in a tight embrace for a lingering kiss. We all relaxed in the sitting room until it was time for the children to go to bed. Bob and Mrs Sellar offered to leave us alone in the sitting room but we opted for the kitchen where we could sit and make notes at the table. We sat there alone and my apology for the weather was dismissed at once. "Paul, my dearest, I will be here for several days. Snow? Have you forgotten just how long the deep snow lasted at home in Silesia? I have my snow boots with me, and that is it!" Ehrentraut thought I looked happier than when I came. I proposed that we might walk over to the Mansfield Hotel tomorrow evening. I had telephoned Mrs McDougall and she was looking forward to seeing us both to talk about our party. Tuesday or Wednesday would be fine and Mrs McDougall had suggested a warm buffet, a sweet and tea or coffee afterwards, but we'll talk about it when Ehrentraut and I come over. "It sounds good to me, I am happy with it" Ehrentraut said, followed by "I can hardly believe this is happening to me. Do I need to tell you how much I love you? I know what you are thinking, pity our parents cannot be here, they will be at the next celebration".

The time passed far too quickly, but life is like that. We re-joined our hosts, Mrs Sellar made hot drinks before I had to take my leave and head for home. Thanking Mrs Sellar and Bob, Ehrentraut saw me to the door. We just hugged and kissed, wishing each other a goodnight. As I made my way up, I was sure the wind began to drop and stars begun to be seen. Slightly out of breath I trudged uphill through the snow, arriving at Viewfield in time to say goodnight. Before I fell asleep I earnestly prayed that the blizzard may die down, no more snow please, I closed my eyes and slept.

Next morning I was glad when I saw the stars and no wind except more fallen snow. I cleared my path to the milking cows, and after breakfast I cleared paths all over the place, the hen houses and in the yard to avoid getting shoes too wet. The sun with its increasing strength will help. A totally blue sky and vision unhindered, a white countryside with the blue mountains on the left, and straight in front the blue firth. A scene worth seeing! I am sure Ehrentraut will take a walk up the road, the Sellars' house is actually on the road to Viewfield which I had explained to Ehrentraut. Thank goodness she had brought her high boots. I was feeding sheep with hay in a field beside the road, when I spotted Ehrentraut with the two Sellar children, making their way up the road through the snow. Schools had to close after lunch. I stood on the road and waved them on. The children recognised me from a distance and said it is Paul. Ehrentraut had not seen me in my working clothes so could not guess that it was me. It was half way up where there was a bridge, crossing the burn. Of course I took Ehrentraut in my arms. It was mid-afternoon with sunshine and no wind, all white. Ehrentraut thought how wonderful to have met me at work. Now she will have a picture in her mind when she will think about me at home. "What a blessing" she said, I took her in my arms and said "I'll see you later when I walk down". My walk down would allow me to check things out, regarding my plan how to take the car down from Viewfield, if the snow plough does not appear soon.

The day's work was done and we shared a hearty supper that Ella had prepared for us. On completion of my evening chores I got ready to walk down taking my lighter shoes in my rucksack. I told Ella that Ehrentraut and I planned to see Mrs McDougall regarding our engagement party. I might be late, but home by midnight. On arrival at the Sellars' I was met by a smiling and excited Ehrentraut. She told me she had been in town and had enjoyed looking at the different shops. "Imagine," she said "I managed to read and understand some of what was displayed in the shop windows. I must have learned something on my short English course. I took a short walk up the road just past the houses. What a wonderful sight! Looking down to the sea, how beautiful and blue it was, then on the other side were the mountains all white. It was just as you described in your letters. My dearest Paul, thank you for having me here with you." I was delighted to hear it from her own lips but enquired "Did you make sure you were warmly dressed?" Ehrentraut replied, "Yes I did, my husband-to-be." We chatted for a while with Bob and Mrs Sellar then made our way to the hotel to see Mrs McDougall. We enjoyed our walk up to the hotel, walking arm in arm in the frosty air. We took advantage of the opportunity to steal a kiss or two. Welcomed by Mrs McDougall, I suggested we sat in the kitchen, which I knew would be warmest. After a brief exchange of opinions on generalities and the weather, we told Mrs McDougall that we were happy with the arrangements she had proposed. Our choice of Wednesday evening for the party met with her approval. She suggested that I show my fiancée round the hotel while she made tea. I was grateful for the opportunity for Ehrentraut to see the place where I served at so many functions. It pleased her, for now she would have a picture in her mind when I next write about a function at the hotel. Thanking Mrs McDougall for the tea we left and stepped out into the cold air. The full moon had risen in the east and we stopped to look up at the sky, thinking how beautiful it was. Ehrentraut declared she had never before seen so many stars. Time allowed us to walk deliberately slowly arriving at the Sellars at a respectable hour. We shared a warm embrace before ringing the bell. I offered my thanks and declined the offered nightcap and Ehrentraut guided me back to the front door where we bade each other goodnight.

Friday morning brought another lovely day, blue sky, keen frost, the sun about to appear and not even a gentle breeze. I hoped the fine weather would continue. The farming community in the Highlands have a well-established method of coping with winter. For the second day we heard the approaching sound of RAF planes carrying hay to isolated flocks of sheep in the far north. The crews standing at the open door waving to us as they flew by at low altitude. Here at Viewfield the established routine worked well, our sheep content in the fields. I did not linger with my lunch so that I could work out my plan in my mind, to see how I might get to town in the car. It would be fairly easy going on the packed snow all the way down to the bridge over the burn, then slowly negotiate my way through the gate into the field then keep to the track made by the tractors. The last thing I want, is to get stuck in the up-hill field on my way home. Once I got down I would leave the car at our Mansfield farm under shelter with anti-freeze added, and just walk home.

Dressed for the weather after supper I prepared to go forth, Ella gave me half a pound of our homemade butter for Mrs Sellar and with the blanket under my arm I was just about to open the car back door when Ella called me back. She held the 'piggy', the earthenware hot water bottle and suggested it might be useful in the car. What a brilliant idea! I went back to the kitchen to fill it with hot water and wrapped it in the blanket and took it into the car. Hmm, why did I not think of that? I closed the garage door and offered a prayer. Off I went confidently or more in hope, that I would arrive safely. I did. The plan worked. Congratulating myself I rang the bell, by now I had my own signature bell ring! There she stood, my Ehrentraut, with that lovely smile.

We closed the door to keep the cold out. As on previous evenings we stayed a while playing with Denise and Peter, but declined the offer of a cup of tea. Bob gave me a comprehensive brief on the conditions of the main road and important side roads. Apparently, our farm road should be cleared within the week. Making sure that Ehrentraut was dressed warmly, I led her to the car. She was delighted I had managed to arrive safely and we took our seats. Ehrentraut was somewhat puzzled by the lumpy blanket and unexpectedly her hand made contact with the hidden piggy. I quickly apologised "Sorry, I forgot. It is my piggy to keep you warm." Long laughter ensued and, still amused, she took a closer look at the piggy and approved its worth. It was quite dark and there was no-one to be seen on the main road.

I had planned a short drive but decided we must stop and talk. After all, time was short and we still had much to discuss. Apart from our engagement, the more important subject was our wedding. We needed to plan our future together face to face rather than by letter. Ehrentraut was happy to start married life here in the Highlands, and it seemed that mid-October would be a suitable time for our wedding. By then the grain harvest would be completed and the potatoes would have been brought in. David and Ella had offered the little cottage rent free, for our first home together, "Paul, my dearest treasure, you know I love you and I want to be where you are, and be with you when life may not be smooth. We have our faith and our promise. I remember you wrote to me early on, that you could not promise me a bed of roses; but I too had to work, at home on our farm when very young and later earning my living as a shop assistant. I did not grow up in a castle… oops, pardon me! You know how I meant it. Just hold me tight and tell me I am right, I am used to hard work."

Clearly Ehrentraut's thoughts mirrored my own. It was a moment of truth and time well spent. We sealed it with a warm embrace and headed home with a genuine prayer of thanks. Bless her, how lucky I am, a precious wife-to-be with her feet firmly on the ground. How much more meaningful our forthcoming engagement will be. Back in town I left our car at the Mansfield farm. There was room for it in the garage beside the tractors where it would be safe, and useful if there should be more snow overnight. I took our blanket and rolled the hot water bottle inside it to carry home under my arm. As a reminder our Mansfield farm buildings are directly opposite the town police office. The inspector's living apartment is on the upper floor. The offices and the two cells are on the ground floor. We had just come out of the farm to walk home when Inspector Thomson emerged from the police station, an opportunity to introduce Ehrentraut to him. He reached out his hand and greeted her in perfect German, "Guten Abend, Fraulein"! Ehrentraut was surprised and noticeably pleased. The inspector looked at my bulging parcel and I told him it was a harmless 'piggy'. "Goodness, at your age with a pretty lady at your side, what do you need that for?" I translated the inspector's words and it had Ehrentraut in stitches, we three parted amid laughter, eternally remembered. I escorted Ehrentraut to the front door, but did not linger too long. We agreed that our time spent had been useful, perhaps I might call briefly during lunchtime. We parted with a kiss in blissful happiness. Myself with the piggy under my arm began my walk up to Viewfield my home, in snow a good half hour.

Saturday morning dawned. The sky was blue and the frost revealed nature at its most beautiful. I completed my chores and made sure there was extra fodder {to save time on Sunday}. I spent the afternoon with Ehrentraut, and returned for evening milking and supper. In brilliant sunshine I walked down and soon rung the bell at the Sellars' house. Ehrentraut was waiting, her cheeks still rosy after a brisk walk in town with young Peter and Denise. She told me she had slept well, giving credit to the fresh clean Highland air. I suggested we visit Willie and Agnes Pirrie in Invergordon, fellow parishioners and close friends of Ruth and Dominic. Willie was employed as a gardener at the mansion of the owner of the local distillery. Willie also had been captured at St Valery in France and was a POW in a camp somewhere in Silesia. I helped Ehrentraut don her coat and had to decline Mrs Sellar's invitation to join them all for supper, explaining that I had to return to the farm to attend to the evening chores.

We walked to Mansfield farm for the car and set off to visit Agnes and Willie. I proudly introduced Ehrentraut to my friends who also knew about our friendship. An amusing and interesting conversation followed with Willie keen to use what he could remember of his German vocabulary. The tea Agnes provided was much appreciated; and I must give Ehrentraut credit for her courage in trying to ask questions in English. It gave her the opportunity to offer an invitation to attend our forthcoming engagement party, which Agnes and Willie gladly accepted. We told them we would be attending church on Sunday at Dingwall, where we hoped to confirm our engagement and receive the blessing. Ehrentraut made sure in her own way that she enjoyed meeting them and hoped to see them at the party, and said our goodbye. On our way home Ehrentraut assured me she would be happy to have friends like the Pirries, which pleased me very much, thinking of the future when Ehrentraut will have to find new friends. {Little things like that are so important when having to find new friends}.

While I left Ehrentraut at the Sellars for supper I made my way up to home for the evening milking, etc., and supper. David told me he had not expected me and was prepared to do my work. That led to a discussion of plans for the morrow, when I would be in Dingwall. David promptly undertook to take on my chores. That is how it is in farming as in family life, animals and children have to be fed.

Ella called that supper was ready. I declined the offer of the piggy and indicated I would not be late returning. I left my good shoes in the car and put on my rubber boots and walked down and was soon at the Sellar's door which opened before I was able to ring the bell, a smiling Ehrentraut had been watching at the window. I managed a fleeting hello to Bob and Mrs Sellar and we made for the car. I warned Ehrentraut, "My sweet Ehrentraut, no piggy today". "So I will just have to sit closer to you" was her reply. {With bench seats in the front in those days that was possible.} Welcomed by Dominic, we soon found sufficient topics and reasons for conversing entirely in German. That made me think that perhaps, in the early days, Ehrentraut might feel more comfortable if she could converse and confide in the vernacular with Ruth. It was a thought that should not be lightly dismissed. After all, Ehrentraut would be undertaking a major life-change. It amused me at first to watch her at play with little Sabina. Then it struck me that I was watching her 'motherly instinct', of course she had to look after her younger sister while her Mum had to work the farm while her Dad was at war, I pondered on this later at home.

Bedtime for Sabina made us realise that it was time too for us to leave. Dominic assured me he would bring Agnes and Willie to our party on Wednesday. Ruth clearly liked Ehrentraut and confirmed her earlier invitation that she should stay with her for a day or two. It was arranged that I would drop Ehrentraut off on the journey back from Dingwall tomorrow. Ehrentraut had a friend. We thanked them both for their hospitality, wished each other goodnight and home we went. Within half an hour we arrived home, and knowing that tomorrow was a most important day for us, we parted. "Oh, Ehrentraut, how I love you." "And I love you too" Ehrentraut replied. Goodnight.

Sunday 21st February - that most special day in my life so far. I was up at the crack of dawn and saw from my window that it was frosty promising to be a bright and sunny day. I wasted little time and completed my morning duties knowing that I need not worry, for David would attend to things for the rest of the day. With breakfast over I prepared to set off with David, who was going to Mansfield with the milk anyway, and would drop me off at the Sellars. Ella's good wishes were ringing in my ears as we departed. Bob had seen me, and opened the door, saying that Ehrentraut was almost ready and had slept well. I declined his offer of a door key, because Ehrentraut would be staying for two nights in Alness with Ruth, that's when my Love appeared and handed me her overnight case. It was time to say goodbye and we were soon on our way. Ehrentraut recognised various landmarks and as we drove through Alness I pointed out the road that led to Ruth's house. The town of Dingwall was quiet when we arrived and within minutes we were outside St Lawrence's Church, where the first parishioners were arriving. Some came over to shake hands, allowing me the opportunity to introduce Ehrentraut and to tell them why we were here. With Ehrentraut on my arm we made our way into church.

There was time to compose ourselves and quietly meditate. Shortly before the service began Father Davies came to greet us. It was impossible for us to resist the occasional moments when we could turn to smile at each other and hold hands. It was a normal Sunday Mass. At the appropriate moment we were invited to go forward to the altar rail where Father Davies said the prescribed prayers and we exchanged our simple vows. Ehrentraut's engagement ring was blessed, I placed it on her finger, and exchanged a deliberate look. Still holding hands, we returned to our pew, both feeling that something inexplicably wonderful had happened that had united us.

Having attended services at St Lawrence's during the years, I knew many regular parishioners there. Many waited outside to meet Ehrentraut and congratulate us both. Father Davies was there too among his flock and we thanked him for making it so beautiful. He expressed the hope that he might see us more often in the future. Eventually we took our leave and made our way to the hotel where we were welcomed at reception and shown to our table-for-two. We had fun with the menu since it took a while for me to translate and a patient waitress joined in our fun and laughter. We enjoyed what we had chosen and moved to comfortable seats afterwards to enjoy our coffee. The room was cosy and warm and we used our time to talk. Ehrentraut had many questions, for which I was glad. Ever since I first heard Ehrentraut's voice, I was fascinated by its particular resonance, which has that explicit effect on me, wanting to hear her talk. When it was time to depart I paid the bill and we returned to the car. Making sure my Love was wrapped in the blanket, we were soon on our way. Our journey was a leisurely one so that Ehrentraut could see the hills and view the narrow entrance to the Cromarty Firth. Before sunset we reached Alness, where the Stoltman's door opened to a friendly welcome, and an invitation for afternoon coffee, but not before their 'official' congratulations.

Ruth was keen to know how our engagement ceremony was received by the parishioners during Mass. Also to hear about the meal at the hotel. Since there was no language barrier Ehrentraut was able to tell all in great detail, which seemed to be her speciality. I spent time playing with Sabina and chatting to Dominic. He was working on contract on road maintenance. His work was at a standstill because of the winter weather, so like the rest of us, he too had hopes for an early thaw. Ruth insisted that I stay for supper; I accepted, anything to prolong the time spent in Ehrentraut's company! While I helped to set the table Sabina took Ehrentraut to see her little brother, three-month old Bernard in his cot. As usual Ruth provided a splendid supper and afterwards Dominic suggested I should have a nip of the local brew. I did see Ehrentraut wagging a finger at me but she relented when she saw the small glass. All too soon it was time for us to leave. Ehrentraut, who was to stay two days with Ruth showed me to the door where we parted. "My dearest love, I will miss you. But we should be happy for we both have our strong love. Remember this day when you say your prayers; Goodnight, and God bless, drive carefully!"

I motored home and parked the car at the Mansfield farm and made my way home. Passing the Sellars' house I did call just to let them know all went well and Ehrentraut will report when she comes back from Ruth. I in great spirits and under a clear sky and a bright moon was back at Viewfield within half an hour. I was not surprised to find David and Ella waiting for me. It was a pleasure to recall our important and wonderful day and they listened with interest. It was after all the first time they had heard about a church engagement ceremony. I declined a nightcap and felt suddenly ready for bed, but sleep evaded me as my thoughts began to recall the day. I could hardly believe that a week had passed since I held Ehrentraut in my arms at Inverness station. A happy week undoubtedly and a red-letter day for both of us as we pledged to walk together in spirit for the next few months on the way to our union as husband and wife. Eventually I slept well and felt the better for it.

David had mentioned that straw and grain stocks were beginning to run low and a thaw would be welcome to allow for a day's threshing. A quick look through my window next morning confirmed we had another frosty day with bright sunshine. The threshing would have to wait but there was always a variety of jobs within the farm buildings when the ground was frozen or covered in snow. I continued with my normal tasks, and thoughts of Ehrentraut were never far away as I worked. I suggested to Ella that I could do the churning and butter-making since I was not going out. She gave me a knowing wink and clearly had guessed that I was missing Ehrentraut. She and I frequently saw the funny side of things and shared jokes freely or laughed at each other's misfortunes. I think I helped to brighten her day, for David's deafness prevented him occasionally from sharing in jokes and laughter. The churning completed, I received a phone message from Ruth telling me not to collect Ehrentraut from Alness next day. Instead Ehrentraut would travel by bus and I should collect her at Tain bus station. Good thinking, well done, Ehrentraut!

Tuesday dawned and my first thoughts were of my Love. The morning passed and after dinner Ella asked if I would like an earlier supper that evening. I declined but said that I would like to meet Ehrentraut at 4 p.m. when the bus arrived in Tain. No dispensation was needed for the adopted son. I waited for the bus from Alness and saw my Love among the descending passengers. I stretched out my hand to help her and, of course, we kissed not caring who saw us. We agreed she should return to the Sellars to rest, and within minutes I led her up the steps just as young Denise opened the front door. We kissed and parted, and I drove home to complete my day's work, promising to return after supper.

There were many important practicalities that we needed to sort out before Ehrentraut's departure, and although both the Sellars and my adoptive parents would willingly have made a private room available to us for these discussions, we felt rather uncomfortable with such an arrangement. My solution was simple, without motoring any distance the Town Hall car park was the ideal place. Snug beneath the blanket warmed by piggy, Ehrentraut opened our conversation by telling me about her short stay in Alness. I was reassured that, despite missing me for two whole days, she and Ruth had got on very well together. Ruth and her family had fled from eastern Germany and lost everything. Her young husband Dominic a Pole, spoke fluent

German. Conversing in German had made it easy for Ehrentraut to ask and answer questions as she learned of Ruth's own experiences when she came to Scotland. Ruth's reassurances and friendship had clearly given Ehrentraut much-needed confidence to face her future in a different environment. "So, my dearest Paul, I will be happy with you at my side, the two of us together in love and faith. Now put your arms around me, you deserve a kiss or two."

We did not intend to stay out late and practical Ehrentraut admitted reluctantly that it was time to go home. Two hours had passed quickly as we talked about what lay ahead of us. In the next seven months we could converse only by letter. We agreed that the German word Vorfreude would be the key as we coped with the separation that faced us. It would nourish our love in depth and strength from the words we exchanged on paper. The invitation to join Bob and Mrs Sellar for a nightcap was welcomed. Our conversation touched on the realisation how quickly time passes, Ehrentraut's visit would end in a few days. But tomorrow's engagement party would be one other highlight, and a timely reminder to retire early this evening. Ehrentraut escorted me to the door and the keen frost discouraged lingering farewells. Back at Viewfield I found David and Ella waiting and anxious to catch up on news. It gave me an opportunity to convey Ehrentraut's thanks for their offer of the cottage. She thought it would be pleasant to be surrounded by the fields and farm animals, especially the young lambs next spring. I did add that she hoped there would be electric power installed by then. It pleased them to hear what I had said. We were all ready to retire then and I was grateful when David told me he would see to tomorrow's evening milking.

Wednesday morning dawned, frosty and promising. The sun was about to rise and the winking light of the lighthouse still beamed intermittently. The snow was not going to disappear yet, but continued high pressure enabled morning chores to be easily done. After breakfast I tended Ella's poultry flock and an amusing thought flashed through my mind: thank goodness white hens do not lay white eggs in snow. After dinner I visited Ehrentraut to make sure that there was nothing needing my assistance. She assured me that all was in hand for our party, and Mrs Sellar had offered help if need be. Reassured I returned home and the afternoon passed quickly. Then it was time to see to myself and, well-groomed and polished, I presented myself for inspection before Ella and David. They approved. I had invited them to our party but they declined and I understood. They wished us well and, after a final check that I had my wallet and my keys, I left the farm. Arriving at the Sellars' I was able to greet Ehrentraut properly, as expected, and we were soon heading for the hotel. Bob and his wife would follow us shortly.

We met Mrs McDougall in the hotel kitchen, where I offered my help, "You have a day off" she said. So I helped Ehrentraut to remove her coat and thought how pretty her dress was and how beautiful she looked. I felt so proud and happy. I looked over the table prepared for our guests and Ehrentraut brought me a complimentary apéritif as we awaited their arrival. I had the opportunity to show her the rooms on the ground floor used for weddings, receptions and dining. In a short while the bell rang to herald the first arrivals.

We assembled in one of the small rooms, greeting each other and relaxing as we sat sipping apéritifs served by Mr McDougall. Ehrentraut welcomed Ruth and Dominic Stoltman, Willie and Agnes Pirrie, Louis and Mary Bain, Bob and Gertrud Sellar. Ehrentraut was at ease having met them all before. Conversation was easy for Ehrentraut is a gifted communicator, and Ruth and I were there to help out when necessary. When invited to the dining room we took our seats at an oval table which allowed us to sit comfortably and in view of each other. It was the moment for Ehrentraut to present her engagement ring to the approval of all guests. With my fiancée at my right it was my privilege to say Grace and formally welcome our guests to our engagement party. We had a very good meal, and before long one of the guests proposed a toast. Others followed creating a most agreeable atmosphere that was well interspersed with hilarity. With general consent we dispensed with music and dance, enjoying the friendly atmosphere of our informal gathering. At the appropriate time Mrs McDougall served end-of-party refreshments, and all too soon it was time for those with young children at home to take their leave. We thanked our friends for joining us and promised to see each other in church on Sunday. Ehrentraut would be able to say 'Auf Wiedersehen' then, until her return in October as my dear wife, God willing.

When the last of our guests had departed we thanked Mr and Mrs McDougall for ensuring that our party had gone so well, all acclaiming the event as a great get-together. We promised to call again before Ehrentraut's departure on the following Monday. Before I drove us away from the hotel we held each other in close embrace. Ehrentraut wished to thank me, but I gently placed my finger on her lips. It was my turn to congratulate her on her beautiful dress. It complemented her sparkling brown eyes which enhanced her lovely smile "Ehrentraut, I could fall in love again - but I have not fallen out of love. All were impressed by your vivacity and how you brushed away the occasional language difficulties with your sense of humour. Oh how I will miss you!" Ehrentraut reaffirmed her love for me, "dearest Paul, by now you must know just how much I love you. It is the love from which we shall be nourished while we wait for that lovely special day in autumn. Now count the kisses with one breath and then we must go home. Goodnight, my treasure, mein Schatz. I had better go, or might find myself locked out. Then you would have to smuggle me into Viewfield, and Ella may not approve. God bless, dear Paul, I cannot wait till I will see you again tomorrow."

Our road now cleared I garaged the car at home again and found the house door still unlocked. I might have guessed, David and Ella were still up. Jokingly they expressed their surprise that I was sober. They were interested to hear how the party had gone and I was happy to entertain them with a detailed account of the evening with our friends. I told Ella and David that Ehrentraut would have liked them to join us, maybe next time? Thanking David for stepping in for me and my evening duties, I bade them goodnight. Sleep did not come easily at the end of such a lovely day.

Thursday morning came and the weather was still cold and dry. David asked me to take the tractor and trailer to fetch various items from Mansfield farm. En route I decided to stop at the Sellar's, expecting everyone else to be up and about since it was 10.30 a.m. However, Ehrentraut had taken the opportunity to sleep in. Mrs Sellar suggested I went upstairs to waken her. I climbed the stairs quietly and gently pushed the bedroom door open. A voice I recognised said "Stop creeping about, just walk in, I am awake". I entered boldly. "Good morning, Ehrentraut" I said. "May I kiss you in bed?" She replied, "come here, my mother did that before you", laughter ensued. I explained my unplanned visit when Mrs Sellar called to come down for coffee. At first I declined but relented since I did not work the fixed hours of the rest of our staff. By that time Ehrentraut had followed in her housecoat to join us. I departed after enjoying my cup of coffee and expressed the hope that I might see Ehrentraut at Viewfield when the children came home from school. "Yes you will". Having lingered for some thirty minutes, I then made my way quickly to the Mansfield steading to do what David had requested. I had a long chat with colleagues who had yet to meet Ehrentraut and hoped to see her before she left for Germany.

At the end of the working day, I went back after supper to see Ehrentraut. Young Peter answered the door and invited me in. I sat a while with Bob and it was pleasing to hear that he and his wife had enjoyed the party. Bob enquired about the cottage and asked about the installation of the long-awaited electricity, there and at the farm. I said that installation had been promised for mid-summer. Then we debated about the preference for electricity or tap water? The consensus was a unanimous "both" if possible. That was wishful thinking, but Ehrentraut's timely reaction at being happy so long as one was installed for a start, indicating her willingness to sacrifice comfort for love and being together, spoke for something. We excused ourselves and took a walk to watch the moon rise. We had an invitation to join Bob and Gertrud for a nightcap and promised we would not be late.

Ehrentraut suggested a walk through the town as we stepped out under a brilliant star-studded night sky. I was happy with that and off we went arm in arm, my beautiful fiancée close beside me. She assured me she was warmly dressed and we stopped occasionally to look in shop windows while Ehrentraut compared prices and clearly enjoyed being outside in the clear Highland air instead of being stuck all day inside a shop. My intention was to lead her around Tain's streets so that she might find her way about on her own. Ehrentraut discovered that the historic Town Hall and the Court House opposite the Royal

Hotel, could be a useful direction-finder on the homeward route to the Sellar house. On our return we enjoyed sharing the welcoming nightcap, and then it was again time for us to part. I headed for home after Ehrentraut's warm embrace.

Friday came. The air temperature had stalled at -7°C and farming routines continued in their unchanging and unhurried way. With the muffling effect of thick frozen snow it is possible to imagine the peaceful hibernation of nature. It recalled wintertime in Silesia for both of us. There was not a lot of time for imaginings and day-dreaming for that afternoon. Among sundry other jobs we were all occupied in moving hayricks into a more sheltered position in the field. Ehrentraut was spotted as she walked up the road with little Denise. She waved frantically and succeeded in catching my attention and that of my colleagues. Soon I was introducing my fellow workers to my fiancée.

She stayed until it was time for me to return to the farm for my evening chores. We planned to meet again after supper, Denise turned shyly away as Ehrentraut and I kissed goodbye. She accompanied Ehrentraut down the farm road, clutching her hand after a brief snowball fight. We were reunited in the evening and Ehrentraut was happy to stroll round the town again. She proudly informed me that she had been shopping that morning buying cards showing the beautiful local scenery and the unique Highland cattle to send home, with greetings from both of us, of course.

My fiancée truly amazed me with her practicality and common sense in our various exchanges concerning not only the preparations for our wedding but also our married life together. I was bothered about the cost of the wedding reception, because Ehrentraut's parents were slowly recovering from their losses and were still building their own new home after the war. Ehrentraut did not see that there was a problem. Ehrentraut declared that these days few people could afford a hotel venue so they cleared a couple of rooms for the day, problem solved. That's what we will do.

As we ambled back from town I mentioned that Ella had invited us to accompany her when she visited her older sister Mrs Fraser, on the following afternoon. The Frasers farmed just outside Tain. We were to visit their daughter and her two-month old baby. I had accepted the kind invitation on behalf of both of us and was pleased that Ehrentraut looked forward to meeting other members of the Viewfield family. Back with the Sellars, we shared a pleasant hour till it was time for my departure. Ehrentraut escorted me to the door in the established mode.

I awoke on Saturday morning with a glorious view of the winter wonderland outside my bedroom window. A clear blue sky greeted me, and a mile downhill beyond the town I saw the firth stretching far into the distance, a pencil-sharp line indicating where the sea and the snow-covered hills met. I was so happy that Ehrentraut had seen this beautiful view in its winter coat as lovely now as in spring or autumn. A thin veil of cloud dimmed the scene momentarily, reminding me that Ehrentraut would be leaving in two days. This was not the time for gloom, as Ehrentraut said "let us rejoice for the gift to have seen each other for two weeks every day, and we will share in spirit, our embraces and kisses to be counted for each week, during the seven months we have left to prepare for our most important day when we will become one heart and soul; so let us be grateful, my very own Paul for those memorable two weeks." These surely were words of wisdom and practicality. It was time to begin my day's work.

I collected Ehrentraut after lunch and while she fetched her coat Mrs Sellar and Bob and I agreed that it had been a good two weeks despite the snow. As we departed I remembered to mention that Ehrentraut would be having supper at Viewfield. Ella was waiting for us and we were welcomed by the Frasers on arrival at their farm. We were introduced to Christobel the young mother, and her baby boy. Things were not as difficult as I had imagined, for Christobel and Ehrentraut managed to communicate with little help from me. While tea was served I relaxed, it was clear that Ehrentraut enjoyed meeting other people because it gave her the opportunity to hear the same words spoken in English by different voices. It was a very enjoyable visit and we expressed our thanks.

Back again at Viewfield Ella started preparing supper. I changed my clothes and Ehrentraut accompanied me as I busied myself with my normal evening duties. Ehrentraut remarked that she had not been close to livestock since she had to flee with her family so suddenly in January 1945 leaving belongings and all their animals behind. It must have stirred many disturbing memories for her. She waited patiently until my chores were done then we went indoors together. Soon we were all sitting down to supper. Supper prompted Ehrentraut to comment on Ella's homemade scones and jam and our own butter. Ella was clearly pleased and amiable conversation led easily from one topic to another. David asked Ehrentraut a few questions, which I translated. He also broached the subject of electricity and water supplies and expressed the hope that installation would go as planned. He assured us the cottage would be available, because Mr Renwick the shepherd, was retiring within the month.

David hoped I would definitely be staying on at Viewfield and that we would find the cottage acceptable. Ehrentraut suddenly confided she felt to have become part of my adopted family already.

Because we planned to attend Mass in Invergordon at ten o'clock tomorrow, a Sunday, we had to decline Ella's pressing invitation to stay for the entire evening as Ehrentraut wished to have a bath and an earlier bedtime. I promised that Ella and David would certainly see her again on Sunday evening. We lingered in the car for just a few minutes recalling the day. We felt extremely happy that the evening had gone so well. Ella and David's warmth and goodwill were reassuring. I promised I would arrange dinner for us after Mass and reminded Ehrentraut that we were expected at Ruth's for coffee afterwards. I asked Ehrentraut to say goodnight to the Sellars for me. Before we parted she said "Thank you, my dear Paul, for the wonderful time we have had or, rather, that you have given me. With every day that passes I feel assured that the good Lord is looking after us. We will make it together!"

Sunday dawned and I was up early for morning milking. I had a light breakfast and let Ella know that I had not forgotten that we would join her and David for supper. The sun was not so brilliant this morning yet the temperature was rising at last. I drove down to town and soon Ehrentraut was welcoming me. Wishing the Sellars a happy Sunday and reminding them that we would not return till late, we were soon on our way to church. We were greeted there by the first arrivals. Soon Ruth and Dominic arrived and also the Pirries. Father

Davies welcomed Ehrentraut and announced our engagement to the assembly, we both loved it giving us a warm feeling that we were now both members of the parish community.

After Mass all members of our small congregation shook hands with Ehrentraut wishing her well and hoping to see her again before long. "God willing, my Love, we will be back here in November as husband and wife" said I. I particularly wanted Ehrentraut to meet a family who had already heard so much about her. Mr & Mrs Fraser and their three sons. Ian the oldest was my age. They were a very friendly family and I felt they would also be good friends to Ehrentraut. They live half way between Tain and Invergordon. One of their sons, James and his wife, still visit us to this day. It made me happy to hear Ehrentraut say "What a pleasant surprise, all the people so friendly and welcoming me. They make me feel already a part of them. I am beginning to believe I could be truly happy here, my dearest". It was time for lunch and we walked to a hotel further down the High Street. It was a pleasant place and served a good meal. Afterwards we had coffee in the lounge where one could rest and enjoy the comfortable seating. There was little time left to talk about our love and other serious subjects and we made our way back to the car, doing some window-shopping on the way. In the car with time to spare we continued discussion about furnishing our first home. We agreed that Ehrentraut would be in charge of domestic matters and would scout around various shops that had experienced staff to advise and assist. I knew that Ehrentraut would certainly not give up her featherbed. Being totally unqualified in that department, I caused some laughter, and Ehrentraut reminded me that featherbeds are single size only and I ought to mention that, if some relation should offer a choice of wedding present.

It was time then to make our way to Alness and we took the shore road from Invergordon. Ehrentraut found it very interesting although it reminded her that in not so many hours she would be crossing the sea. Sadness threatened to overcome us, then practical Ehrentraut insisted we look for the joys to come. How true! Shortly afterwards we arrived at Ruth and Dominic's door. We were greeted by the aroma of coffee wafting round the room. Lifting Sabina, Ehrentraut was rewarded with a beaming smile. Setting her gently down, she was handed Sabina's three-month old brother, Bernhard. She cuddled him too and I found the sight deeply moving. The ladies had much to talk about, and Ruth gave Ehrentraut further useful information. I enjoyed chatting with Dominic, and the time just flew by. We had a time table to say goodbye and Auf Wiedersehen.

Ella and David were waiting to welcome us, and soon we were sitting comfortably at the supper table. I told Ella how our day had gone, and David said I must take tomorrow afternoon off. Once I had explained what David said, Ehrentraut thanked him in perfect English which pleased David greatly. We talked at length over many things regarding our wedding in autumn and our getting the cottage for our home. It was a conversation that pleased Ehrentraut because we spoke in earnest about our home which will be there for us. A home which is the dream of every young bride. Aware now that time was running out with Ehrentraut having to prepare to leave tomorrow, it was time to thank and say 'thank you' for the food and good news regarding our 'home'. It was a case of saying "see you back in the autumn". Ella's good wishes for a safe journey and a welcome return were ringing in Ehrentraut's ears while I took Ehrentraut to the Sellars. On the way there was no mistaking that a slow thaw had set in. Bob and Mrs Sellar were expecting us and a low table in front of the settee had been set for the nightcap. Ehrentraut appreciated such hospitality and thanked 'Trudi' as Mrs Sellar had insisted on being called thus far. We recounted the details of our day to Mrs Sellar, and Bob. It was not my intention to stay any length of time and I stuck to my resolve. I thanked them both for their hospitality to Ehrentraut and myself. Then I took my leave of Ehrentraut with an embrace and a few words about our programme next day "Yes my treasure, I'll be ready to leave for Inverness after lunch. Thank you again for a lovely day. Now, no tears, let us be brave! Do not forget to give Ella and David my thanks, let me kiss you goodnight, and may God bless you and me." One final wave and I was on my way home. There was no doubt about a thaw having set in.

The dreaded day had arrived, Monday 28th February, and after two weeks of brilliant sunshine, it was a dull and cloudy morning.

It matched the sadness all around. After lunch I was acutely aware that now I had to collect my Love. There was time for me to accept Trudi's offer of coffee. Then Ehrentraut checked that she had packed everything and prepared to thank Trudi for her kindness and hospitality. Mrs Sellar waved aside her gratitude, saying she would appreciate Ehrentraut visiting her mother again when she could. Ehrentraut said it would be a pleasure, for it was only a two hour cycle ride from Hameln. Mrs Sellar was very pleased.

We had allowed ourselves an hour in the station cafe before the train left Inverness. We made good headway for the road was now completely clear of snow. Arriving at the time we hoped, we made for the cafe and found a table in a quiet corner where we could sit close together undisturbed. "Well, here we are, my Love, happy in this new and important stage in our life, let's call it our pre-nuptial life for it sounds better than waiting time". "Dearest Paul, we have pledged our love and faithfulness before God, that is good enough for me. I trust you and I want you to trust me. That is what makes me happy and it is what makes our waiting time as I have read somewhere, though I am not the poetic type, a road through paradise; do you like that? It is time for me to thank you for the lovely time I have had. Someday I will tell you how much I appreciated having been able to come and see where you live and work; and if there is nothing better, for now I am happy and look forward to being with you here. I know now how it must have felt for Mum to wait a year before Dad could come home on leave. Now, my Love, I may not have so much time to write to you often with all the work you have given me to prepare for our wedding, it will certainly help to pass the time."

Then it was time to check when Ehrentraut could board her sleeper compartment. The guard indicated that the compartment would soon be ready, a half hour before leaving time. There was a final check, to make sure that tickets, passport and ferry bookings were in order and safely concealed in Ehrentraut's handbag. We found the reserved compartment and, enfolded in each other's arms we held each other closely, we could not say anything more and there was no need for words. It was time to go and we shared a lingering kiss in one last embrace. She slowly wagged her finger as I tried hard to suppress tears and then we parted. The doors closed and with a final wave I watched until the last coach faded into the distance in the quickly falling twilight. I got back to the car and sat for a few moments in the solitude that enfolded me. I started the car, aware of the empty seat beside me, I arrived home and was greeted with understanding smiles of comfort. Ella had completed my usual evening jobs and thought we might just as well have our nightcap which had the soothing effect I needed, and wished my adopted parents goodnight.

It was the first Sunday of March and I had already sent a letter to Ehrentraut a week ago. I had this brilliant idea to send Ehrentraut a letter, which I hoped would have been delivered before Ehrentraut's arrival, hoping it will have the effect I wished when she arrives. The thaw had set in and the snow is disappearing. When I awoke, I saw at once that it was a dull morning. The lack of sunshine mirrored my own mood. New hope and anticipation scattered the gloom as I busied myself about the farm. I worked happily away, at the same time allowing my thoughts occasionally to centre on the wedding and our future home.

Mr Renwick, the elderly shepherd planned to make his retirement home in the north and intended to leave Viewfield at the end of April. It was firmly established that Ehrentraut and I wished to make his little cottage our home and plans could now be made. Much depended on the installation of water and electricity but other matters that concerned me could be resolved in the meantime. I intended to keep Ehrentraut fully informed in the letters that would pass between us in the coming months.

> *'Viewfield' End of February, dear Ehrentraut, now it should be my 'Bride',*
> 
> *We are truly engaged to marry: is it not wonderful? If all went well, you should now be home, safe and sound. I look forward to your telegram confirming this. Can you imagine how I felt when you left? I waited till your train vanished from sight, then I got into the car and sat for a few minutes looking at the empty seat beside*

me. Remembering your words before parting: "Courage, no tears". I started the car for my journey home and arrived safely. David and Ella understood how I felt and I was glad to join their nightcap. I reported to David that the roads were all clear again. David and Ella thought you would be a good companion for me. I did enjoy hearing it from them and it lifted my spirits. I took my leave and said that life here would continue as usual tomorrow.

There is something I must tell you. As I was doing my final check to ensure the animals were settled for the night, I looked up at the sky and there among the dark clouds was a large patch of clear sky in which the stars were glinting. This patch of twinkling stars appeared to me to be a sign from heaven. I thought again of your words and resolved to be happy and joyful and think of our future together, I shall remember this as a sign from you cheering me up. Your engagement ring is the visible sign too of our pledge and love for each other, now for all to see. I went to bed content and had a good night's rest. Your inability to write often to me is understandable. Your first task will be to write of our engagement to the many people we listed. Then there are your Youth Club evenings. Then there is the lovely 'engagement' tradition to provide coffee and cake for your colleagues at work and for friends and relations at home. Am I not getting off 'scotfree' here while you are doing so much for us? It does worry me that you should have to do it all without my help. I know your Mum and sister Annemarie will help. So please take my wish seriously when I say write to me twice a month only, now that I know how busy you will be. The vision of our future for the next few months is relatively clear. You have already proved just how busy you will be. You have not the help of your husband-to-be as you should, so please, to ease my conscience just send your love for me in prayer, and it will give me the joy I need my dearest Ehrentraut, your husband-to-be, Paul.

*Hameln, March 1955*

My dearest, how I long for you! It is the same longing when you left me after our first meeting in Hameln. I was so sad then, time was so short for us. I never told you but I had already realised then that I had fallen in love with you even before we met. Now I am so happy because our engagement has sealed our love that has come true. I like to think that I have found that jewel of love and trust. Promise me you will not be sad, you are mine and I am yours. Before I start the second round of our correspondence I want you to know my innermost thoughts now that I have safely arrived home. I have been with you for two weeks when we could meet every day and in the evening, what a blessing and joy that was for me. It made up for the short time we had together when you came to Hameln to meet and greet me for the first time. Now I want to thank you most of all for making my visit to you so carefree for me by your absolute fidelity to our obligation before marriage, so thank you again my husband-to-be for making my visit such a joyful relaxing 'get to know time' with you. Our waiting time without kisses and embraces will be so much easier to endure until autumn. Of course I look forward to read and hear from you now that I know your voice, what you have to tell me.

Now to the necessary 'mundane'. I do hope you received my telegram. I arrived home at 6 a.m. My sister opened the door when I rang the bell. She was surprised, and my parents were up as usual, getting ready for work. As soon as I had greeted them I could wait no longer to show them the ring. They are so happy for me, and I am sure my sister is a little jealous. See what happens in a year's time. Mum insisted I eat something first, and afterwards I needed no persuading to go to bed, where I slept soundly till four in the afternoon. Now about my journey, I knew I would miss you so, and I was glad you had booked a sleeper for me. Within minutes I was asleep. In London I was quite proud of myself. I managed to ask for the boat train to Harwich and people were so helpful. A gentleman sat opposite me in the carriage and soon we got talking. He was a Dutchman who had brought his son to London to study at university. I was glad of his company for other men joined us later and I would not have been too happy on my own. I intended to remain on deck on the ferry since it was a sunny day; but, after a while, I did not feel too good and went to the desk to ask if I *could have a cabin for myself which I got. I slept for three hours which made me feel much better. The train from Hook of Holland terminated at Lohne in Germany after 1 a.m. and my train to Hameln did not depart till 4 a.m. By 3.30 a station official suggested I could sit in a carriage. I was glad, as you can imagine. On arrival I took my case and walked home. The rest I will tell later. Sorry, my dearest, I could not finish my letter last night. We had visitors and Gretel was among them. She was over the moon to hear about us. It will take many hours yet to tell her everything. She was glad to tell me that Engelbert had written while you and I were together. Before going to work this morning, Mum made some funny looks towards the shelf where your picture stands. There I spotted an envelope with your handwriting. What a lovely surprise, you rascal! You must have written it on Monday while I was still with you. How caring and sweet of you. I had to read it at once and kissed it because your hand had written and sealed it.*

*Then I had to pedal hard. I could not be late. Can you imagine the staff taking it out on me? Ehrentraut late for work after her holiday! Mr Meissner is one of the senior sales staff. I visit his wife regularly and we do needlework together. He keeps the 'smart guys' in check; but they all gave me a welcome and when I showed them my ring they were really surprised. They all congratulated me and, when I returned after lunch, they asked what they could contribute towards our engagement. They stated a sum, and I had already something useful in mind, a coffee service for eight. Their contribution would suffice for half and I will buy the rest. Now they know we are serious about each other. Tonight I attend my cookery class, and there are several youth group meetings in the evenings ahead, some of which I have to organise. One most important task I have to concentrate on is the printing and dispatch of our engagement notices, and thereafter the replies and thank you cards for any presents there might be. So, my dear Paul, I shall be busy but happy for it is, for both of us. I certainly could do with your help but, alas, it is not possible. I miss and long for you. Time for me to send you all my love and thank you once more for two wonderful weeks during which I got to know you so much better. Your ever faithful, Ehrentraut, greetings from Mum Dad and Annemarie.*

*Viewfield, 15.03.1955 My own dearest Ehrentraut,*

I am happy to have received your telegram. I am sure your family is happy to see you safe home. Here the snow has gone completely and we are back in the old routine. Now I feel as if I have lost a large sum of money, talk about feeling empty? But your letters will soon sort that out. The fields are drying out and we shall be able to start cultivating the land again. Your Dad will know all about that. It is my intention to write soon to my parents in Silesia and my sister who, I am sure, would love to hear how you and I got on here in Tain, and especially to hear of our engagement. Just now David is calling me and I know that it means we expect the birth of a calf, I might as well say goodnight, my treasure, and join him as the midwife.

Dearest Ehrentraut, I am happy to report 'that mother and baby are fine' and doing well. This is a happy and blessed Sunday. I got your lengthy letter and you are so right. It does feel different now talking to each other this way. Do you also feel a closer bond is affecting our thinking and feeling when we write? Thank you so much for your travel report, and thanks be to God that everything went well for you, apart from the long wait at Lohne for the train to Hameln. Thank you for describing your homecoming and the showing of your ring. It made me quite proud to read about the surprises it caused. David has spoken with our retiring shepherd. He leaves us in April, and we can definitely have the little cottage. It really means we have a home, not every young married couple is so lucky. I wait now to hear what you think. In the meantime I will make a drawing of the cottage and its dimensions. I have made drawings like that before, and the measurements will be accurate. You will have something to show to Mum and Dad and whoever, and you to think about it. It is so important that we do not have to search for a place to live close to my work. Actually we will see each other when I am passing and, I will be home for lunch. I have thought about us a lot especially in regarding our home. I include a separate sheet with this letter, regarding our home, to share my thoughts with you. A basket of kisses or narcissus? Both come with my deepest love. With all best wishes to Mum, Dad, Annemarie and Gretel; especially you, my Love, your loving Paul.

*Hameln, 13/14.03 1955 My dearly beloved Paul,*

*I am sorry that you had to wait a day or two longer for my letter. It seemed as if a seven day week had shrunk, and I needed a few days more. Of course I know you love to read my letters, but there was much to catch up on after those wonderful days I was allowed to spend with you. By now you know all my hobby 'excursions,' youth and church work. In addition this week we had our last cookery course. It is always an enjoyable end of term day with us cooking and baking for the event. It really was good fun enjoying our own cooking. We received much praise which made us proud. If you had been here you could have joined in, would you have liked that? More importantly was 'our' engagement party on Saturday, which required some organising. Because we as a family had already talked briefly about our wedding, we wanted to try out the seating at home, we expected to have some twenty guests. So we cleared some of the light furniture out of the sitting room and joined two tables with a wide board. It worked with great approval, even our Dad was impressed and made him think, what?, yes, our wedding. You see my love, I thought about you writing early on how you enjoy joinery work, so I thought what would you do? I could be a match for you? OK, perhaps your work mate. It was left to me to buy the assorted slices of cold meat and 'Wiener' sausages to be heated. I made the potato-salad. My sister and I helped Mum to do some baking for the later coffee or tea. I had to prove my cookery lessons. In short, it was a happy party and we had several toasts to you 'in absentia'. There were moments when I thought tears were not far away. Our guests were mostly relatives who had been invited. Then my close friends and I, and very importantly, my dear Grandma. She was the first person I visited the day after my home-coming from you. She is my favourite and she thought if I love you so much, you must be the right one for me, was it not sweet of her? I loved her even more for that, and I told her so. Don't you think it was a useful exercise my dear husband-to-be? May I remind you when on one of those occasions we sat in the car and talked about our wedding month and date? Did we not agree how important the 15$^{th}$ of October would be and forever a joy to remember on* *our anniversaries? Also when we came to the conclusion of the practicalities for our guests: (a) Saturday a day off work anyway, (b) travel for those who will have to come on the Friday and could return on the Sunday. Of lesser importance perhaps, friends and parishioners who would like to come to the church service, or just come to see us coming out after the service, coming to see the man from Scotland! That will be our argument when next Dad and I will talk again soon. Mum is on my side anyway. Further my Love, Dad was surprised how our engagement party had sufficient room, after we had moved the furniture about a bit. Now our neighbour, Frau Bethke is also on my side suggesting some pieces of furniture could be moved into their home for two days, "with the approval of her husband". What do you think about my 'planning'? Yes, occasionally I do wish you were here, but do not think it makes me sad, no, because I love you dearly. An honest love is more important to me than wealth, which sometimes does not always bring happiness. Paul my dear, sleep is overpowering me. Remember me in your prayers as I do, do not doubt my love. I do however think about my parents-in-law who may have something to say something about our wedding on a Saturday? It might be advisable for you to write soon including, if you have not yet reported about our engagement party. I am sorry but now my eyelids are really falling down meaning to close the 'shop', my dearest Paul goodnight, may God bless our Love and us when we meet in our prayer.*

---

*Viewfield, 25.03.1955 My very dear Ehrentraut, my Love,*

*Thank you for your most interesting letter that contained a wealth of love and surprises. Before I continue, I first have to tell you of my concern regarding your health. You seem to be what is called here a 'workaholic', someone who does not stand still. What energy and even more dedication you put into the organising and preparations for our, yes our engagement party, and I am not there to help you, even to lay a teaspoon on the table. All that on top of your dedicated youth work, and then you tell me of the occasional unpleasant teasing and comments from your colleagues. How do I* feel? On my own here with ample spare time to help you? It does bother my conscience quite often, my dearest Ehrentraut. Please do take care for your health's sake. I am left speechless by what you, and your family have managed to do to entertain so many friends and family. Words fail me except to say thank you and your family. How can I ever repay it to your family? To you when we are in our own home? I wish I could in person congratulate you on planning such a successful engagement party in a small area. That is worth a medal, I better watch I could have opposition here with you. Truly, I had no idea what is involved in being engaged. I could not believe the number of well-wishers who gave us such useful presents. Now you have to send them all the 'Thank you' cards in both our names, yes but with me having contributed nothing. Please say a thank you from me to anyone of those kind people you may meet, but especially Mum, Dad and Annemarie.

It seems to me every time you cycle to town you keep looking at windows, walking into shops to ascertain the quality and worth of the goods that are on offer. I am amazed the list you have enclosed of the items you have already bought or received as presents. The one thing I have already discovered about you, Ehrentraut, is your knowledge of quality and purpose of cutlery, kitchen utensils, and the many different items needed in bedrooms, etc., my mind boggles. For the record, here is a very short number of items on your list you have sent, the first our framed 'Home Blessing', to be hung in the lobby to be seen by whoever enters our house, first things first with you; how right. Then it goes on: 6 damask covers, 9 pillowcases, bed sheets, 3 tablecloths, 6 hand towels, coffee service for four. These are only nine items of the 35 listed in your letter, now you are casting your eyes on cooking pots.

It amazed me by the generosity of your guests and friends to present us with so many useful items to start a home. Honestly, I am at a loss for words on how energetically you 'throw yourself' into the preparations for our wedding. Little wonder it makes me feel like a lone person on the side-lines just looking on. My only hope is to be able to make it up once we start our life together. Here is some news what is happening at the Farm. We had a number of calves, the mother sheep are getting extra food to make sure they will have milk for the young lambs. The tractor men are busy getting the ground ready for the sowing of oats, and we have a few of the corn stacks to thresh. Not forgetting our hens are increasing their egg production. Now my Love, here is something we can earn by keeping a few hens to lay eggs for us. Would you like me to talk about what we can do for us when we move into our home? Please tell me, just remember how much I love you, my own Ehrentraut, and convey my best wishes to Mum and Dad, as I am now to call them, and Annemarie, and why not her friend Heinz, also not forgetting Gretel. Yours truly, ever loving Paul.

---

Hameln, Passion Sunday, 1955 My dear Paul, no, my dear 'Lausbub' rascal, why?

You'll soon find out. Thank you for your letter, how I long for them because they tell me of your love for me. How is your 'young family' doing? Any more calves? When do you expect the first lambs to arrive? At last the cold and sleet have gone and spring is beginning to return. With all the snow and frost when I was with you in Scotland I did not feel so cold as here. Well what did you make of our 'engagement' party here at home? Everybody thought it was great, only pity you could not have been with us. Dad now has fewer reservations about having our wedding celebration and meals here at home. Frau Bethke's offer to store some of the furniture did help to convince Dad to come round to our way of thinking. As he rightly says, you are not a rich farmer nor do I inherit a rich dowry. After corresponding for eight months, you ought to know I am not one for insisting to be seen as a bride; folk can come to the church and will see us there.

Now to your peculiar second letter to get that out of the road or rather out of your head. Am I wagging my finger? Yes I am! I could not understand what made you write such a letter, if you were so sure of my love? Under no circumstances will you get my ring back, that is mine and will stay on my finger. My dear Paul, our engagement on that 'sacred' Sunday for the two of us was not some sort of comedy act or game for me. May I remind you in one of my early letters I wrote to you and I meant it, I would never play games *with true love. No my dearest Paul, I will not stay on at home after our wedding just because you may not have the cottage completely in order to carry me over the "Schwelle", the threshold. I know you would like to offer me as good a home as possible, but do not forget how our people including your Mum and Dad over there, had to start completely from nothing? Must I remind you again how I had to help our Mum on our small farm, looking after chicks and geese, sweeping the yard, and I was not twelve years old? Remember our first few letters after you answered our advertisement? What was it that neither of us wanted to discontinue the correspondence? Rather we were both interested to find out who we really are? It seemed I was beginning to fall in love before seeing you. You had better prepare, I am travelling with you to our new home, like 'pioneers' who emigrated to a new world. I know now, how beautiful nature is where you are and I will be happy as long as you are with me. With you I will not be lonely, I want to build with you our home, and glad to leave the shop, etc. behind me. Parents too, like their 'birds' to leave the nest sometime. Come to think of it, it might be quite romantic with an oil lamp! We just have to go to bed early! Now listen, did I make myself quite clear? It is getting late again and Mum is anxious that I go to bed. A look at your picture in front of me makes me long to hold you close to me and shower you with kisses. Take care and remember me to Ella and David, your ever loving bride, who does not ever want to lose you. Goodnight, may our guardian angel watch over us, I'll continue tomorrow.*

*Next day in the evening. Back to business, I looked in one of the shops and saw a lovely rust-coloured blanket and liked it very much, thinking it would be useful over the couch when you take a rest after lunch. I shall go in one of these days and enquire regarding the price. More good news, Dad has a workmate who will be coming with his wife for supper and a drink to toast our engagement. He offered to make a trunk for us. He is a joiner in the firm Dad works for. The owner has several grocery shops. He actually gave Dad a beautiful large bouquet for our engagement. I am so pleased about the trunk. He will have it ready within the month which means I could then put already some of the presents we have received into the trunk. At the moment our cupboards are getting short of room. Are you pleased with me my 'Schatz' treasure? Are you getting prepared for Easter?*

*We too are practising in our youth group. This will do for now, happy Easter to all of you, more in my next letter. Many greetings to everyone that know me now, Your ever loving, Ehrentraut.*

---

*Viewfield', April '1955 to my Bride-to-be, dearest Ehrentraut,*

*Glad to hear you are all well in Hameln, enjoying the first fruits of spring flowers battling for their places to be viewed and admired by people who were glad to say goodbye to winter and looking forward to the explosion of spring colours. Well, we are not so far behind, although I had not mentioned it, I did spend quite some time in the garden. Ella is very appreciative that I quite enjoy pottering in the garden. In fact my dearest Love, I have acquired quite a bit of knowledge and love for our garden here. There is a fair size garden attached to the cottage; if it interests you or Mum and Dad, the most common and loved spring flowers here are the snow drops and the daffodils. These of course we used to have in masses in the castle's park.*

*That will do for an introduction, now to the 'painful' bit. Your answer to my second page I raise my arms and bow before you; for the first time I ask for absolution. I do feel a bit like putting on sackcloth and hiding for a while. But then I learned something else in the last few months, your determination when you will not bow down if your conviction tells you so. Am I forgiven then? Actually it showed my total lack of knowledge in matters of 'love'. Do you remember when we met first in November during our conversations you wondered that I had not detected that you may have fallen in love with me several weeks before we met? Well, I suppose the hesitation was primarily that of not wanting to be disappointed. I will admit to having felt very much drawn closer to you which I told you when we sat in the car that particular 'Sunday' in our life, when first we kissed. So, are we the best of friends again my dearest 'treasure'?*

*What about our sister Ursula, have you had a note from her yet? Neither have I, from Engelbert I have not heard for a while now, hoping that he is sending even short letters to Gretel but at closer intervals. What about my parents? Nor have I received a note from them but I'm confident it will arrive soon. I bet they will ask you why we spent money on our engagement party? But it would be wonderful for us to remember it in years to come. By the way, before I close it struck me that Engelbert, now that we have a certain date for our wedding, is more than ever determined to try to move heaven and earth to find a way to bring our parents out of our old home of Silesia to be at our wedding; don't you think that's what he'd want to do? It is almost impossible to get a visa just for a visit; you know those authorities? They know we would never let them back again once they are over here, in the West.*

*There is other news I like to tell you about the cottage. Mrs Renwick met me going for water and we chatted a while when she told me that they will be leaving here and retire up north where they have a cottage. Mr Renwick should have retired a few years ago. David is happy knowing that I can do all the shepherd's job. This is where I say, I love you and wish you were here to hold you in my arms. So, that is some positive news my treasure; I will be able to start some work at the cottage in a few weeks. Freust Du Dich schon mein Schatz, are you joyful my Love? Oh, I almost forgot to tell you our first lambs have been born, is it not lovely to have Easter-lambs around us? Think of it, if all goes well you will see many in a year's time? Oh and how wonderful you can see me in or out of dreams where in the fields I will be among the lambs, to be 'Midwife' occasionally. Now I wish you my dearest Ehrentraut and all the family and friends a very happy Easter, your own Paul.*

---

*Hameln, Palm Sunday 1955 My very own Paul,*

*My best wishes from us all here at home on this, quite spring-like Palm Sunday. Sometimes, like today especially at church I missed you painfully. Oh what I would have given to have had you beside me to share the beautiful liturgy. I consoled myself thinking next year, will it be at the Invergordon Church? It does not really matter as long as we will be together. I'll comfort myself and sing* to you, "Wenn ich ein Vöglein wär flieg' ich zu Dir!" {If I were a little bird, I would fly to you}, would you like that? Oh, did you meet Ruth and Dominic at church this morning? Did you give the Sellars my good wishes, and did you give them a lift? Thank you for your lengthy letter it was comforting to have and read your letters, often I read them again before I fall asleep, and I sleep better.

So you would like me to forgive you for being a 'bad boy'? I can say that in English! Do you really expect me not to forgive you? When I knew you did not mean it? Yes you are forgiven you 'doubting Thomas'. Pity you cannot get a hold of me and hold me and give me that kiss of peace? Of course I told my Mum, she just looked at me, shook her head and simply said "Oh Men", and laughed. I learn from her about you men! I am pleased about the trunk being made, but we will probably have to send it by rail and boat. That will be something you will have to decide when you will see it. Here we are all well and glad the little snow is gone, and everything looks so much more like spring. Do not forget to tell me when the lambs are being born. For today we all send you our best wishes, I shall write soon. As usual, it has been a busy time for me and the young folk taking part in the Easter rituals at church. I was aware that it was my last Easter in action here and my thoughts wandered frequently and I wished you were at my side. This would be a good time to be with you, to enjoy the good weather and watch the new lambs playing in the fields. Just think, if all goes well I will share the enjoyment with you in six month time. And now, I, Mum, Dad and Annemarie, wish you my dear, and all at Viewfield and all who know me now a blessed Easter. Your very own love and bride-to-be, Ehrentraut.

*Viewfield, Easter 1955 'Gesegnete Ostern' Blessed Easter my dear Ehrentraut and bride-to-be, also to Mum and Dad, Annemarie and Gretel also Engelbert if he should appear.*

*No doubt, you would have all met at church. Today I have given a lift to Mrs Sellar, Peter and Denise. Friends and parishioners whom you have met send their Easter greetings to you; wishing you being well and full of the joy as when they met you here. It felt like a real welcome to you which made me happy. Thank you so much for your two letters. Sorry I did not answer yet because our first lambs had arrived. That will mean a busy time for David and me, working in a 'tandem' fashion. It is understandable that I as the 'youngster' will take care of the difficult births or trying to catch any sheep or lamb that might need some attention. Shepherding for me, although not brought up with sheep, has become a most gratifying occupation. Especially because of my ability to attend to certain difficult situations, owing to Mr Sutherland the vet's encouragement and teaching. God willing, next year you will be involved in bottle-feeding lambs when necessary, you'll love it. My dear Love, thank you for the parcel which contained such useful and tasty articles, by that I mean the edibles, especially the sausages, and also Ruth's knitted bonnet and the sweets for the children. I gave it to them all today after the service. All are thanking you from the heart. Mrs Sellar's gifts I gave when I picked them up this morning. While we are on the topic of the Sellars, there is news. Bob has got a new job driving a van with groceries to sell around the villages near Tain. They are very pleased, Bob no longer has to get up at five in the morning, and it is a better paid job.*

*There is also good news for us 'mein Schatz' my treasure, Mr Renwick has retired and will be leaving for his new home north this coming week. I went to see them last week and had an interesting chat with him and his wife. Mrs Renwick is glad that at last they can look forward to retirement. That means the cottage is our first home, and on your behalf I thanked David and Ella. We can now plan in earnest; once you tell me if that is where we should start our life together. That is the news for today. We wish all of you good health especially you my Ehrentraut all my love, Your loving husband-to-be Paul, a word you already know in English. For Dad, lambs are dropping out by the dozen and so are calves here and down at Mansfield. I just thought of it, if I mention Mansfield you can separate the farm in town and the hotel which makes it simple for me when trying to tell you anything interesting. By the way, I must tell you something that was pleasant for me, it was a thought out of the blue I imagined seeing you walk in the High Street shopping for us, it was a wonderful feeling. To all of you good health and a lingering kiss for you, your loving husband-to-be Paul.*

---

*Hameln. Easter 1955.*

*My dearest Paul, there are many other names to call you by, as my own Love, today I let you choose one and let me know when next you write to me. Let me thank you first for your 'Easter Greetings' and the interesting words you had for me. They made me feel so enveloped in you, and I realised just how gracious the Lord has been to allow us to meet in the manner we did. Like you, I am forever grateful. Being grateful is what my family and those you included in your Easter greetings wanted me to thank you for. Yes, as in other years it was a busy time for me, and my fellow young people, to take part in all the Easter rituals in the church. Thinking it will be my last Easter here in action! The many times when it was difficult for me with my thoughts inevitably wandering to you, wishing you were at my side. Again thank you for your letter which allowed me to take part in your visits to Ruth and Dominic. Thank also Agnes and Willie Pirrie for their good wishes.*

*So this would be a good time to be with you with the good weather and the many lambs playing in the fields. If all goes well I will share the enjoyment with you in less than six months time. How happy I am to tell you that the joiner has brought the trunk in the evening after his work. I was already home so I could thank him profusely for such an excellent piece of 'furniture'. It is as beautiful as it will be useful. Now I can stow away everything I have, and all we got as presents in boxes, and which I crammed in my wardrobe. Enough about the trunk for now, and instead* to let you know something about our visit to Wildeshausen. You 'Lausbub', you rascal, you secretly arranged that Engelbert should take me to Wildeshausen, approximately 80 miles north of Hameln where Engelbert and Aunt Else with her family were resettled after being forced out of Silesia. Mr Albrecht, Engelbert's friend in whose car they came, has friends in Hameln you might recall. He took Gretel, Dorle, Engelbert and me to meet your Aunt Else and family. Now at least I have met some one of your family. Else being your Dad's youngest sister. Engelbert introduced Gretel as "meet my Gretel". We really had a good time. Good food and before leaving, her husband Uncle Theo played the guitar and we all sang our well known folksongs. Painful for me as everybody wished you were there with us. You can imagine how I longed for you to be with me when Engelbert and Gretel sat beside me in the back seat and cuddled. I closed my eyes and thought of your kisses. Thinking about it is a good time to say I love you and my good wishes and prayers go with you. My Treasure this will have to do for today, many greetings as usual from my family, please think of me. Your very own, Ehrentraut. PS. It was good that we agreed to reduce our writing, it does save time to concentrate on all the work that is building up, which I am sure you too did not expect, preparing for marriage. Especially when moving so far away. I still keep an eye out for any useful and of good value articles we still need. I am always thankful when you tell me that you are well, now for me too. I love you dearly and happy when you send me your letters in which you tell me of your love. Many greetings to all I now already know, your loving bride Ehrentraut, and from all in my family. Greetings to all.

---

*Viewfield, May 1955 to my beloved bride-to-be, my dearest Ehrentraut,*
    Thank you again for your interesting and newsy letter as always. I am glad to hear you are well and had a good time visiting our Aunt Else. Oh how the tears were beginning to flow reading how much you enjoyed singing our beloved folksongs with Uncle Theo playing the guitar. As you know well, I would have loved to be with you all and enjoyed the pleasure beside you. I did not look for more

excitement here, due to the fact that we are only a 'family' of three with a certain age gap. Add to that the remoteness of any neighbours and you have the answer. In all my years prior to our meeting, I did not feel in any way deprived of a 'normal' life, simply because I chose neither to smoke, nor to go to the pub, nor ladies' friendship. But reading the enjoyment you had on your trip, triggered my mind to recall my so far quiet life discovering its reason, namely to await you my Love. I cannot think of a better explanation. Yes, we did have the occasional glass of sherry and much laughter. There was also our Mansfield Accordion Band; my extra work in the hotel and the car to see farther afield. In other words I had ample choice to pass my time, and in any case as I said once before somewhere, that I enjoyed the freedom from other distractions. In the end it all came together in a most extra-ordinary order, or manner. It all came before me in a most pre-arranged guideline. With hindsight it seems clear that those early years when others got married, I was, without my knowing, being 'groomed' {'vorbereitet'} for a life with you dear Ehrentraut. Whatever else anyone may say, I shall not be shaken from my conviction of what I said. As I now look back, waiting for you was one of the most pleasant times for me. Little wonder how I yearn for your letters now, allowing me fully to take part in your daily life. There is an addendum though, it's my real worry, are you risking your health writing these letters at all hours? Please Ehrentraut, now that you have to do so much work for us, you and me, would you PLEASE reduce the number of your letters! We have met and spoken eye to eye yes, and kissed, so please do not worry me and rest more, if that is possible in your busy life. Even without a letter I know you love me, now promise.

Was I not pleased to read that you went with Engelbert and his friend to Wildeshausen to meet our Aunt Else and her family. You were quick in 'seconding' her two little girls to be the flower girls at our wedding. Trust you to grasp the opportunities. Oh yes, to sit in the back seat with Gretel and Engelbert cuddling would have an effect on you, with me miles away. It's great news that you got your trunk, how wonderful. After hearing what you have already for your dowry in presents and your own bought material, your Mum will be pleased to have her space back in the wardrobe, etc. Before I close to let you know, we have over 200 lambs and one black one *with a white dot on his head. You'll see him, yes him, when you are here. That is what I wanted to say to you today. Tell Dad potatoes have been planted, and the oats sown too. Also the cows are out on the fields all day and night. That means less work for me. I have to think about new mushroom beds for us my treasure. Please take care, remember you are my Love, and thank you for your lovely goodies in the Easter parcel. Ella and David send their greetings. From me with all my love and kisses your Bridegroom, Paul.*

---

*May 1955 My dearest Love, Paul*

*My love and greetings I send you from a heart that misses you so much every day. Thank you for your lengthy letter which helps me so much because I just love you to tell me what you are doing there so far away from me. It is no longer so painful because now I can visualise whatever you try to tell me. I suppose it is the same for you, now that you have been here. Thank you for your concern about my overdoing things; only do not be too anxious as I do stop when my body tells me. Otherwise you will not get so many letters from me, have you thought about that? It is my only contact with you.*

*Last Thursday my friend Malve and I carried our Catholic Youth 'Banner' at the wedding of a former group leader. Standing there during the service I thought about you and me as you can imagine. The bride was a good friend and she had asked me some time ago. I thought how nice, as it would be my last time. The next time I hope to be the bride and I have already asked Malve and one other of my group to be banner bearers. Just think the time will pass between now and October. While on the subject of weddings, I am happy to let you know that at last your parents have answered me, apologising for their delay. Although not too happy at first with Saturday, they could understand after giving some thought and reading my explanation. Now my happiness is complete. Pity is that they did not mention anything about being allowed to come to the wedding. Probably too painful without some sort of hope. As you said, we had better leave it with Engelbert. Saturday evening we had invited the last few friends to celebrate our engagement.*

*Annemarie and I baked and helped Mum prepare the cold and warm buffet, before the cakes, gateau, coffee and drinks to toast you again. You just have to drink at our wedding to make up for the ones you've missed. That reminds me, Engelbert was not pleased that I had not asked him regarding the printing of the Engagement cards. You and I never thought, but we have now promised we will give him the job for our wedding invitations, etc.*

*Last Thursday Annemarie, Heinz and I went to a demonstration on cooking, with the latest 'Jena Glass' cooking utensils. Very interesting and much less messy for cleaning, and lighter than the steel pots. We thought it a great improvement and ordered two for us. Gretel and I accompanied our friend Gertrud home. Time for bed, it will be a busy day in the shop tomorrow. Choose how many kisses, may God take care of you, your Love Ehrentraut.*

---

*Viewfield, June 1955. hallo, my own 'Schatz' my Ehrentraut.*

*Happy Sunday to you especially, but no less to 'my family' which in their generosity have taken me into their midst. As time goes on, I find it more difficult to reciprocate your tireless reaching for the pen to assure me of your love. How could I ever doubt your love my sweetheart? You just seem to throw yourself into our life together, all be it in spirit for the moment. I do try not to be despondent realising that your life is revolving around many more people than mine. I have my animals and they too make a noise trying to tell me something, I respond in a way that does not make me a hermit.*

*As usual my Love, thank you for your letters, the number of which have overtaken mine. When, oh when will I be able to recompense you for all the work you do for our future life? At least, you still find time to spend on your youth work and especially visiting and going out to meet your friends. Now you know about our cottage which is to be our home. I am glad for you because it must be a worry for young brides not to have a home to call their own. Actually I have more news for you, namely that David* was asked to arrange for an Electrical Contractor to wire up the farmhouse, farmstead and the cottage. Ella and David were excited to tell me this and hoped I would let you know. The question remains when will it all be connected? As soon as I see a man dig a hole and put a pole in it, I will phone you. To answer your question regarding 'our' mushroom enterprise, the preparations are complete and beds with the spawn are laid out in one of the old Army huts. Can you remember the huts on the right side coming down from Viewfield just before the hotel? A test bed is already showing signs of mushrooms popping up, fingers crossed. That reminds me I always wanted to ask you have you noticed on your walk up the road the half round huts where I grow the mushrooms? How did we miss that? Here our last few lambs are being born, as usual there are always 'stragglers' two or three weeks later, nature's way. For two of the bottle fed lambs, I managed to find a 'stepmother' who had a dead lamb. Fields are sown for oats, and the potatoes are planted. We get our potatoes free and a litre milk, and the cottage free. For that I will still take a visit round the fields in the evening, at which you could accompany me; a nice walk before bedtime.

This is important that you too have at last had a letter from our parents. According to your assessment they may not have been so sure about our wedding on Saturday, but accepted your detailed explanation. Their reply to me was a slightly less enthusiastic one; but finished with their blessing. On the matter of being allowed out, they had not much hope Mum will storm the heavens to be sure. It is a good note to stop and say our goodnight, we no longer need to get up early. It was good of you to tell me you still keep active in your youth group, even if only occasionally. So what? Are we going to have some of the latest quality Jena Glass dishes? I am going to send some pound notes over to you Ehrentraut. It makes sense for you to have pound notes while the exchange rate is to our advantage. My greetings to Mum, Dad and Annemarie and all the others I know. To you my very own Schatz, Ehrentraut, greetings to all and your goodnight kiss, yours, Paul.

*Hameln, June 1955 Happy Birthday My Darling Paul,*

*How is that? Still, I prefer Mein Schatz, my treasure. Thank you for your kisses, greetings and most of all, your love for me. This letter in return, carries more love than you and I could carry together. I hope you have something to celebrate your birthday? If not I will bake a cake for you, I cannot wait for that. Let me ask you, did you remember what sort of time it is? Not the clock, but time to celebrate. Imagine, it is a year since Gretel and I placed the advert in the Mann in der Zeit magazine? After we had already been sent over 40 replies in the first batch, you 'lonely' and last, arrived three weeks later; and you, shyly hoped not to be too late. A number of letters later, we agreed it was all providential, and today we are surer than ever and happier for that. Let us congratulate each other and thank God for it.*

*My Love, since we cannot celebrate together for real, it gives me the opportunity to say a few words that come from the depth of my heart, and are important for you to know what I felt in my heart. My dearest Paul, I want to thank you for your honesty, that you expressed in the letters, and shown to me when you and I first met in person in Hameln. I said it before and say it again; only a few months ago, at your home in Tain, when you made our short two weeks together so easy for me to fully enjoy being held by you in warm embraces, without my ever having felt apprehensive. It was that freedom which made the short time we could spend together such a heavenly time for me, from which I 'feed' while waiting for our day when we can fully give and thank each other. We are both human beings and have proved we are capable of loving. We are not immune from human passions, and virtues which we wish to respect and have so promised ourselves.*

*Yes, I am happy now my dearest, and hope my greetings will arrive for you to know my thoughts are always with you and yours mine. We may think October is in the far distance, not so my dear Paul. I have spoken to my parish priest about our wedding day. As expected, he was surprised our wishing to get married on a Saturday, which is not yet so common. Having explained our reasons like the number of relatives having to travel he understood and was happy. So that is sorted out, because booking early dates is wise.*

*Now for more important matters which include you. For the church wedding I need my Baptism Certificate and yours. I have mine, but you would have to do something soon because yours will be in your old parish. Your Dad as church officer will be able to get it for you. We hear it so often how long and difficult it is to get documents out of Poland. For the German State Register Office you have to get a Statement that you live in Tain, Scotland, that you are single and not married!! You had better find out, if from the British Authorities I need a document that I am allowed to come in and live in Britain as your wife; make sure!, I do not wish to be sent back at Dover to find my way home! It is time that you find out what further documentation we need for Britain, even for yourself. We surely must be registered in England or Scotland? Documentation can be slow at times. I had to write this letter in stages. There were a few matters to be seen to. Now my dear Paul how many kisses? You choose, time for bed, Dad says high time. Goodnight. Your loving Ehrentraut.*

---

*Viewfield, June 1955 My Love, my Ehrentraut,*

*We both hope for each other that all is well with us, and so far we have been blessed. Thank you again for the time you spend telling me the story of your daily very busy life. I am beginning to fear that you are actually far busier than I am. You must be tired in the shop so many hours on your feet? I do begin to get worried for you, and then you still take time to send me all your love by staying up so late. Yes, it does worry me, because I am quite capable to figure out the time you spend in a day. Dear Love, one letter a week would make me happy, because you already spend a number of hours on our marriage 'business'. Now greetings and kisses to you my dear from sunny Scotland. Sorry to hear that you had rain for several days, good to hear it had changed for the better now. Being so many miles further south you will have it much warmer soon. Here we are all well and I am happy to report the lambs are growing and frolicking, and can get quite cheeky. Next year you'll enjoy them with me. Thank God you too are all well and busy, so you told me. Just in case I should forget, thank you for the interesting pocket travel book of Germany. It was lovely to tell me of the pleasure it gave you seeing a flock of lambs on your walk last Sunday. Made you 'homesick' you said - for the lambs or for me?*

*My goodness you were busy in the shop, placing a delivery of 680 shirts in their right place. Might you sell them all by the end of summer? At the end of your summer sales I am interested to buy one, see what you can do. By the way, when I show Ella your letters, it amuses her no end at the number of words you send. I am quite happy with that, knowing I am so happy to tell her it is full of news of what is happening around you; with a quarter page where you tell me how much you love me. The goodies you send me were meant to be something special for me, besides your love that is attached. What a pleasant surprise, since I never expect parcels. I know you are the 'rascal' who is spending your hard earned money on me. Thank you for surprising me again. Makes me think, time I come over and take you with me over to the cottage, now that it is empty and our home.*

*Regarding my parents' concern about us getting married on a Saturday, the tradition in former Silesia is that celebrations go on till next morning, and this is still the case with the Polish population now settled in our old Homeland. After the church service the bridal party and guests gather in the local restaurant, which always has a dancehall. In the evening, more guests and friendly villagers arrive. Dancing until the morning, and as often as not, commencing again next evening. If we were to have that sort of celebration, we would not be able to have a Saturday wedding, because of our catholic traditions on Sunday.*

*Of course it is for me to write to my parents and lay before them how it will be with us. For your perusal, in short this will be my reply: at 9:30 a.m. the compulsory marriage registration at the official local office, then home to dress the bride; full church service at 11a.m. Then home for celebrations lasting no longer than 1a.m. Sunday morning, but the Bridal party may leave earlier by 11p.m. Saturday evening. Our guests are in the main elderly close family. No dancing, only Bridal dance under veil, after the veil is removed from the bride by the bride's friends and held up for bride and groom to dance under, in the hallway or where there's room. Do you approve? I shall elaborate on that of course in more detail. The page is full, only enough room to let you know that I love you deeply Ehrentraut, thank you for your love, greetings to Mum and Dad, Annemarie and Gretel and others. Take care and rest, remember I am concerned that you try to do too much. Greetings from Ella, David and the Sellars, Your loving bridegroom, Paul.*

---

*Hameln, June 1955 my dearest Paul, my Love;*

*Oh how happy you made me telling me more of what you are doing, it makes me feel so much closer to you, distance becomes no object now, because I have a very clear picture after having been in Tain with you. Please keep telling me and I can then feel so close to you. Alright, the country was all white but it is not difficult to imagine it now being green. All of us here hope you are well and so are we all. Now from all of us we send our best wishes on your birthday health and happiness. This is your second birthday since we first met, all be it by letter. All my personal good wishes, and God's blessing from your own Ehrentraut. I will be thinking about you on this day, and you about me please, yes? So you now have three black sheep, are their mothers black too? Dad is quite interested to hear what happens on the farm, as an ex farmer he should be. Last Sunday we celebrated Mother's Day, so Annemarie and I cooked the dinner and yesterday baked a cake for coffee in the afternoon. We all slept after dinner. Pity you could not be here for afternoon coffee and gateau, just what you would have loved. We all went together for a walk after coffee to see what Dad had done already in the garden. My own Paul, I could not help thinking this was my last Mother's Day here for me. Item by item here in my life will come to an end. Moments of sadness will soon be replaced by a new deeper and greater love for each other, as we grow together to fulfil God's given purpose, the joy of new creation in a loving family. Oh the joy building our own home made me feel quite tingly inside. In the evening I started writing but Gretel came and that was that. my Love,* thank you for writing to your parents regarding their serious concern for us getting married on a Saturday. Of course I understand that it caused you concern at their stance. I pray that they will understand after your explanation. Although I thought of asking you, what about us changing the day rather than upsetting them? But after having thought about what you wrote, we will wait for their reply. Much to my surprise my Dad is now of the opinion that the Saturday is after all a most suitable day for our wedding. What you and I thought all the time, because guests who have to stay the night could go to the late Mass on Sunday, that is for those who wish to, and have a much more comfortable journey home on Sunday afternoon. As you said let's wait for their reply. You did say that Engelbert will write too? Now I realise why you wrote to Ursula, she too may have questioned the Saturday. I feel confident Ursula will understand once she reads your explanation.

On Sunday we had the Bishop of our Diocese (Hildesheim) confirming nearly 300 children here in our new church in Hameln. I suggested Gretel to represent the senior youth group to meet the Bishop. Yes my Love, I slowly make my 'retirement' felt. Oh, I nearly forgot to tell you that my other best friend Dorothea, we call her 'Dorle', insisted on making my bride's dress. So now it is getting serious! We are going to choose the material soon. Dorle is a dressmaker. So, 'mein Schatz' my treasure, no peeking?! Did you send the shoes your Mum asked for? Ask Engelbert if you cannot get something suitable, she is waiting for them. I will send a special Birthday card to you. This will have to do for today, bedtime Mum is calling. I give you all my love, yours Ehrentraut.

'Viewfield' July 1955 My dear Bride-to-be,

There are so many love-expressing words with which to greet you, but first thank you Ehrentraut for your kind wishes on my birthday, it was the first time a young 'Lady' sent me a birthday card including the warmest wishes and kisses; as if that is not enough, there was a beautifully decorated birthday parcel, and that was the first time I had a parcel sent to me by a wonderful lady. Thank you my Ehrentraut my Love. It is a wonderful feeling to be loved. Even in the necessary mundane work and practicalities our love is expressed. It is my hope that you are all enjoying good health and hope, my Love, that my letters arrive in spite of the rail strike we have here. So far your mail is arriving almost as normal and I thank you for the time you give me to let me know how much you love me. It is so easy for me; when it is lunch time I do not have to walk far, while you have to cycle home, morning, noon and evening. It is the reason why I am concerned about your well-being. It was kind of Annemarie's Heinz to spend some time helping Dad digging in the garden. To answer your question, I will prepare a piece of ground to plant some vegetables, like carrots, and lettuce. Potatoes we will get from the farm. Please do not give up your visiting your colleague's wife, Mrs Meissner, with whom you spend valuable and useful time at needlework, all for the good of us. More pleasing was your decision to 'let go' in stages your commitment to the youth. I can well imagine your parish priest's disappointment seeing your loss to him and the parish. How wonderful that you are so pleased with your trunk that your Dad's colleague made, you must be pleased that you have a place where to put your presents and all that you already bought yourself. It all seems our dream is coming true. As a reminder of my first letter, "Liebes Fraulein Krause", Dear Miss Krause, and now one year later, 'My beloved Bride Ehrentraut'. I could not help but recall it thus! So my true Love, thank you for your love and good wishes for both occasions, which we hope to remember in so many years we may be granted. A special thank-you to Mum and Dad for giving me you, yours with many kisses and a 'spiritual' embrace. Yours, Paul.

*Hameln, July 1955 Grüss Dich Gott (May God greet you) my Paul, my Love,*

*So far this week there was no letter for me, my dear mother tries to console me. She knows how I feel when she has no letter from you to put on the shelf under your picture. Your railway strikers do not seem to know how much heartache they cause to loved ones. Here they call it the 'English disease'. You do seem to have strikes more often, I should be getting a few letters when it is all over. In one of the Barracks here there are Scottish soldiers. Their Pipe Band often plays in the town centre on Sunday afternoon, to which a lot of people go to see and cheer, especially if they perform a Scottish dance. Amazing that I should be living soon in their homeland?*

*Yes 'Mein Schatz', my treasure, this is our first year since we met. Our miracle became true, as we used to say. Pity we cannot celebrate together with our folks. On Sunday at coffee time, we shall have a drink to celebrate with you being with us in spirit, and really close to me. I shall be brave and keep any threat of tears back as I look at your eyes in the picture, and think if only I could rest in your arms and feel your warm lips on mine. In less than four months now my dear. I feel so overwhelmed when I think how much we share already. It helps me so much in our time of waiting, until we can give each other completely in unencumbered joy.*

*It seemed to me this morning like a miracle, with the chance and the sudden urge to go to church for the evening service to offer our thanks for bringing us together. I felt so warm inside me and so joyful for such a wonderful gift, our love for each other. Do you feel like that sometimes? Then tell me please. Thank goodness, our waiting time does not stand still. Do you remember how we sat in the car with the 'piggy' keeping me warm, and we talked about many things. Among them the realisation that we could not ignore the fact of life that there might well be times when our love will be put to the test. Then we shall recall the resources we have built up during our waiting time to stand the test.*

> *Oh yes, I want to tell you how glad I am to be able to share our thoughts this way with you. It gives me the opportunity often to mull over them when cycling to and from work; yes I know what you think, I certainly do watch the traffic! How about my little birthday parcel? Did the postman deliver it? There is nothing in it that could go off, but I would be disappointed, it was meant to be my surprise birthday present. Dad is asking how the mushrooms are doing? Please let us know.*
>
> *So we do have a home now and you have drawn a plan. I am anxious now to see it. What did you plant in the garden? Does it mean we can plan for our new home? If so will it be possible to tell me what you feel regarding electric or gas? It will be important for choosing the kitchen utensils, like cooking pots. Germany has already some very good quality goods compared with what Trudi Sellar had or Ruth. Now my eyes are closing and you realise how I need sleep I send all my love & kisses, your faithful bride, Ehrentraut.*

---

> *Viewfield, July 1955 my most beloved Ehrentraut, just three more months, and then?*
>
> *You tell me, just come and fly into my arms. What a wonderful God who knew what his loving creatures needed. Especially those whom he brought together in a most extraordinary way like us. Senses that are able to communicate with each other in a most intimate fashion, Ehrentraut. Thank you for your three letters which got caught up in the strike. My special thanks for your goodies for my birthday, all arrived in perfect condition and it required some restraint on my part not to over indulge, rather retain some for a longer time! Thanks to you, Mum, Dad and Annemarie for their contributions.*
>
> *So what is the situation over your way? I wait curious to hear if you have by now received my missing mail? My dear Love, you wished to know how 'our' mushrooms are doing? With the sun*

now at its strongest, inside the hut it is very warm during the day, and makes the mushrooms pop up. I have to go down every day to water the beds and pick mushrooms twice a week. Ella takes them down to Ross the grocer when she does her shopping. He can sell all we can produce. Soon I will have earned back what I had paid out, indeed we should have our own mushrooms when we return from our wedding. Growing mushrooms turned out to be an interesting hobby. I am certain you will actually enjoy picking our own mushrooms. Amazing how British prolific strikes are making headlines in Europe, quite rightly so. It is an almost inborn ailment. My documents are in order. Yes we can plan for our home. You will soon have my drawing. It will be nice for you to play around with our furniture.

To your important question of whether gas or electric cooking. We have really only one choice, namely electric. It would make more sense to have only one source. An additional gas supply would have to be propane, not really beneficial, my dear Ehrentraut. In the meantime I will call at the electrical shop to have a look at what is available regarding electric cookers. For the moment it is more important that the actual power will be available before we come back after our wedding. My advice therefore is do look out for "electric" cookery utensils, because that is what we are going to have. David has already instructed the local electrical contractor to come up and make a plan of where all is going to be fitted.

Just in case I forget, our German Priest, Fr. Günther was up and we had a very pleasant afternoon with him. We were all there, Ruth and Dominic too, I gave a lift to George who enjoyed it after his illness. As you can imagine Father Günther was very much interested in how we are getting on, regarding our wedding, and sends you his best wishes. The pages get quickly filled; still you have always so much more interesting news to tell me. May the God who brought us together continue to take care of you for me. As always, many kisses and all my love that this letter is bringing to you, and greetings to all others, and my best wishes to you my Love, Paul.

*Hameln, July 1955* My dear Paul, better still, my Love and Bridegroom.

*After a year and so many words you must believe in my love for you. Just as I believe in your love for me, for which I give my thanks to our dear and gracious Lord every time I spend in his house and at night, when I give my last look at your picture before I close my eyes, and ask to take care of you for me. It is reassuring for me that you too keep looking at the calendar and mark the days as they disappear towards our day when you will appear again at Deister Str. 62 and ring the bell. Thinking about it I get all tingly inside me. We all are blessed with good health and glad to read so are you. My Love, your sister, I am allowed to call her Ursula, wrote me a letter in which she wanted to assure me that your parents will understand after you had written to them and explained the situation, and that Ursula's letter to them will have reassured them. That was real good news for me. However much she would like to be with us at our wedding, she does not want us to be disappointed if it is not to be. There will be chances again to get to know me.*

*Oh what a shame, you taking the wool off your sheep? I hope they will not catch a chill without their winter woollies? Now that the rail strike is over you may send some coffee and tea over which we could keep for the wedding. But as I said before, not over the limit for customs. Next question, how are you progressing regarding the important papers, without which, no wedding? You don't want me stranded at the pier? How about the black suit? It really is necessary, everybody says you're handsome and it is expected! Engelbert asked me to tell you to write to him as he may have no difficulty to procure one for the day. So, please do that. Annemarie told me that one of her work colleagues had offered to come and cook for us. That would be very helpful because Frau Bethke remember, our neighbour has also already offered. You may have to explain that in Tain if that is not known; that at smaller weddings in the house of the bride, friends offer to cook the meals in your house, it is a beautiful tradition. Of course as Germany is rebuilding and people will earn more, then that too may no longer be the norm.*

*The other matter I would like you to give a thought to, is who do you wish to invite to our wedding from your side? I am glad to bring those matters to your attention because it makes our waiting time feel less distant, bringing some urgency into it, only two months now! You keep telling me how you long for me, and it is the same for me. I am convinced now, that I was born for you, to love you. I just love to think Jesus knew who he wanted me to care for, because that is why he kept you hanging on, not to be caught by someone else. What else kept you cocooned among your cars, band and hotel duties? Am I forgiven? Please, do pay attention to my questions. Now that is a big order for you, please see to it. Just hold me close to you, and a long kiss, Your faithful, loving, Ehrentraut.*

---

*Viewfield, July 1955 Greetings to you my dear Ehrentraut in hope you are well.*

*I need not ask, you are busy and thinking all the time about us. I said it before and will do so again, busy on our behalf while I seem to do practically nothing for us. From a sunny Scotland my greetings fly with love to the beautiful town of the famous 'Rat Catcher', in the hope to find you well and in good spirit. Please accept my thanks for what you are doing for us. I really should be at your side, and I ask myself, will I ever be able to pay you back? I really pray that I will not fail. If it sounds like a confession, then I am pleased to know that you understood.*

*What have I been doing since my last letter? As I said the sheep shearing is over and the wool bags have been collected. With the weather being favourable we will be starting to make hay. This is a pleasant job, no noisy machinery which allows us to talk, no, not all the time! On a good sunny day I may wash the blankets, which are really the bed covers as you experienced when staying with Bob and Trudi Sellar. You did mention that they will be coming over to Germany to visit Mrs Sellar's Mum and Grandma to the children. I am sure you will invite them to come to Hameln that you may show them the beautiful town. They will appreciate that for having given you a holiday apartment so to speak. That is something we have to do yet, for you to show me the town proper, may I suggest perhaps next year?*

*Regarding the situation with my birth certificate I have written to Engelbert as he should be able to tell me how to go about it. It was unfortunate, and I could do nothing about it as my papers were in my kitbag which I never saw again. Goodness knows where in Italy they are now? Engelbert knows how to go about it in Germany. I expect to hear from him soon. Next week I will go and see our Police Inspector Mr Thompson, whom we met with our piggy. Regarding my black suit that is organised. The other important item you have mentioned is the list of my guests to be invited. I shall attend to that right away. Actually their numbers are small since they are all from the Lippok side. Any invitation that could be considered from here would decline on practicalities and cost. Regarding Aunt Else and Uncle Theo, I suggest inviting her own two girls only. It will be wise for me to send Engelbert my list to have a look and let me know should someone be added to our list. My dear bride I shall close my conversation with you for today because David is across the firth visiting his farming brother. I promised to take the last check on the animals in the fields. One last sentence, over a year ago I wrote a letter to a Miss Ehrentraut Krause, today it is 'My dear bride'. My heart is pounding, can you hear it? With God's blessing and all my love, let me hold you close, your husband-to-be, Paul.*

*PS. "Be careful on the bicycle".*

*Hameln, July 1955* My beloved Bridegroom, my own Paul,

Every time I read how you love me, my body tingles all over. I hope you feel the same when I send you all my love to you. Did you remember to change your calendar? Now only three months and with God's grace I can put my arms round your neck, close my eyes and feel your lips again, and I will not have to let you go again! Please keep telling me what you are doing and where. I love to follow you, now that I have a picture in my mind of where you live. I now know your home, the fields and the sheep, it really helps me when I miss you. Only I never saw your fields in green, have you thought about that? Only white fields, is it more beautiful when all is green?, I am sure it must be. Dad was pleased to hear that 'our' mushrooms were doing well now, and that the investment is paid and from now it is profit. It would be lovely to have some mushrooms when we come home, this time together. So that's how you celebrated our first anniversary of us having got to know each other. While the four of us had drunk a toast to our future, you enjoyed your home made 'Schlagsahne' (whipped cream) and peaches all on your own. How I longed to have been with you, I dare not tell you.

Have you celebrated, even on your own, our Saints' names days? Peter and Paul and mine St. Ehrentraut after yours. Last year we just exchanged two letters, twelve months later as my bridegroom and I your bride. I had to go to Mass on your Holy Day to give thanks for such grace. There can be no doubt that our marriage began in heaven. It is a wonderful thought and I know you agree with me. All that is part of the ever growing strength of our love. Back to earth now, oh I must tell you, yesterday one of my elderly lady colleagues, with whom I get on well, asked me if I would go for a walk with her after work, which I did. She was very much interested in more detail about us. She found it intriguing and at the same time wonderfully interesting. She actually admired my courage to follow you to Scotland, so I invited her to visit us. She thought we were brave and wished us well, which was nice of her.

Before I forget, let me tell you that I bought the black shoes for your Mum, soon my mother-in-law. My Mum came with me to make sure I got the right ones, also for quality. I have sent them off with some small items, useful for cooking and baking, like spices, *herbs, etc., to make up the weight allowed. Now pray that they will get it all intact. One hears some extraordinary stories. Engelbert advised me what to send as we do not have any relatives over in the old 'Heimat'. Oh, I must tell you, my colleague was interested how we manage or feel, having only seen each other a few weeks in our year of courting. So I told her that with both of us enjoying writing a lot, we probably discovered much more about ourselves than if we had been seeing each other every week or so. That both of us felt our love growing more intensely and deeper as well, it is also a real test for our fidelity and faithfulness. Was I right? So you tell me! That must be all for today, yes? My eyes are closing, I have to kiss you goodnight and look at your picture on the shelf. Your loving bride Ehrentraut.*

---

*Viewfield, August 1955 'God greet you' as the Bavarians would say, my own dear Ehrentraut,*

*Courtesy demands appreciation for gifts received, letters in our case, and I wish to do so now; thank you for your last two letters. Within these last few weeks, when we reflected on the anniversary of our miraculous finding and meeting, a desire came over me to reflect on our past year on a particular theme. It happened on a brilliant summer's day while doing some repair work up on the field above Viewfield. I sat on a rock, having my midmorning tea and sandwich at 500ft altitude, and a panorama of more than 180°. From left to right one can see and count seven counties, with the deep blue firth in the centre, which you saw in the winter when you were here when all was white.*

*There was no hurry and I had time to admire the stunning scene and let my thoughts wander, if only I could whisk you over here, like the lark that just settled on the fence not that far from me. Yes, I can hear you saying, "but I am not a lark". That was the moment when my thoughts turned instead to your letters which flutter across the sky to me twice weekly. Do you know that you have sent over 130 letters since the first, addressed to 'Mr Paul Lippok', until the last just two days ago addressed to 'My loving Bridegroom'? How do I know this? Because I have kept every one of them!*

*In every letter I see that bright smile I saw when first we met. In every letter you send, never is there a word of despondency, or sadness; never even a disguise of disgruntlement or boredom. In every letter there is your untiring information of what you are doing. In the evenings the time you spend with your youth work, only when your eyes refuse to go on, will you stop writing. Never once a complaint or unkind remark about anyone. Untiringly, many words of how much you love me. Also constantly the encouragement for both of us to strive together on the road to our predestined long-awaited bonding of our marriage.*

*All this has been on my conscience for some time, but I never felt the right time until now. My dearest Ehrentraut, I have emptied my heart to you and contentment is a satisfying feeling, of course it would have been wonderful to have had the opportunity to tell you all this in person. But then I wonder would not the temptations to steal an embrace and kiss intrude and disrupt the continuity of thoughts, so important don't you think? Are you telling me something? Before I close my eyes and hold you close to me for you to kiss me, let me tell you that I will see Inspector Thomson sometime next week regarding your permit to stay here after our marriage. He is asking for you each time we meet. This is a good moment to assure you that you need not worry in regards to our German nationality. Never in my nearly ten years here have I ever heard a derogatory word or comment. It is saying a lot about the people I live, work, sing and play with; and I can assure you, in next to no time, you will be asked to join in.*

*Here is a recording of mine when calling at our Police Inspector Thompson regarding counter-signing the validity of my official documents and my clean record. I thanked him and he said "bla bla bla what made you go for a German wife? Are there no good looking ladies around here?" Talk about pulling the rug from under my feet. Perplexed and thinking of an answer, I replied "yes, but if my wife decided at some stage to go back to Germany it would not be so difficult." After a few moments of silence, Inspector Thomson replied "well, you may be right, actually we could do with some new blood around here. Good luck, I'd like to meet her again when you come back with your good lady." Thank you, how pleasant can people be. Please tell Dad haymaking is going well and we have put all the sheep and lambs through the disinfection 'dipper bath'. The oats are ripening earlier this year. I wonder could this be an earlier harvest than usual? Fingers crossed, it looks like it. Yes, I am so happy I told you all, so now once more love and kisses, your loving Paul.*

---

*Hameln, August 1955 Sunday my beloved Bridegroom,*

*Only two more months, and I cannot believe it. I bring and send you graces I prayed for you at this morning's Mass. Oh my dear Paul, how I always miss you at my side in the pew, ever since the first time I experienced that overwhelming feeling of belonging together when you came to me for the first time, nor forgetting the first time in February in Scotland at your church. That was a long sentence but I could not stop until I got it out of me to send it to you. But we must not despair, every week is bringing us closer and closer.*

*Next week it will be busy in the shop, so I decided to write to you now. We all had our Sunday rest, what do you call it, 'forty winks'? With the reasonably good weather our Dad was busy in the garden after work, no wonder he looked forward to a rest. We had our Sunday Coffee together, Annemarie's Heinz was here too and now they have gone for a walk. Why not pick me up? I am ready to go. But I promised to give you a report of this year's "Silesian Folk meeting". It's held every three years, this year it was in Hannover. Since it is only a half hour train journey from Hameln with reduced price rail tickets the whole family went. There must have been two thousand people!*

*Each large town had its own tent and the smaller ones shared. We soon found our village, and very quickly people found each other. Some we have not seen since the forced removal in 1946, others have died. I have not met any of my friends from school, since we were only a small village anyway. But we met up with a number of our relations, some of whom had not been settled in Hameln. On the information list I found your tent, Gross Strehlitz was only two tents from ours! So I went over just on a chance, since I do not know anyone from your town and Engelbert had not got in touch with me that he might go. Lo and behold, as I looked around I spotted Engelbert at a table with Gretel sitting beside him having fun and laughter! So, I hid and crept up on them unnoticed till the last moment. Wagging my finger at Gretel for not telling me, we hugged and laughed heartily! Of course, I had not seen Gretel all week for her to tell me. You can imagine among the laughter there were many tears. People who lost family members, neighbours and friends in the tumult of the Russian invasion and the hunger year until we had to get out of Silesia. And then there is the joy of meeting someone you never imagined of ever seeing again. If you had been here we would surely have met with some of your class mates, or people who knew your parents or yourself from the Post Office. No point in losing a tear, my Love, I hold you very close to me because I know this would have brought memories back to you. I am happy I did what I promised you. It was good to see Engelbert, who told me that he has a black suit for you which he will have when you call for him on the way to me in October! I have to say goodnight and sweet dreams. Your ever loving, faithful Ehrentraut.*

---

*Hameln, August 1955 my dearest Paul my Bridegroom,*

*First of all, again thank you so much for your precious words of love that mean so much to me. Suddenly another month has gone, and it comforts me that you too are longing for our 'Day'; it is the feeling of togetherness that gives us the strength. The spiritual togetherness at Sunday Mass, and you not being at my side is the time when I miss you painfully, and love is tested in strength and intensity. These are the moments that confirm your love for me; you keep assuring me every time that your mind, heart and hands appear on paper consoling me. I had wanted to tell you these thoughts of mine many times. Great joy my darling Paul, a letter from your parents thanking me for the parcel I sent with the black shoes for your Mum, now also my Mum. They fitted with room for an inner sole which made them very comfortable to wear. The extras, herbs, etc., I filled in to make up the weight were not disturbed and most welcome. I am so happy that I could do something for them. Thanks be to God, because the letter for me from your Dad was most welcome which set me at ease now that they understood. Having had your letter and Ursula's as well was wonderful. Have you now sent the invitation to your side of the family? I have not got their addresses, nor do I know them, except Tante Else. Don't forget, time will move on now. I have sent my documents for approval to the British Consul in Hamburg and expect them back soon. As for my wedding dress, it has not been started yet, the reason being that Dorle is on holiday with friends from Norway. She does not want us to worry as she will have it ready in good time. I trust her, she knows. What saddened me is that she will not be at the wedding because she is going to work in Norway for a rich family, the contract starting before our wedding. My dear bridegroom you said you would send me the sizing pattern for my wedding ring, please do that soon, you know time passes now? I have not yet seen Gretel since she returned from her holiday in Düsseldorf with Engelbert. You can imagine that I am anxious how they got on. She did send a card saying she is enjoying it, so we all hope. In the end, it is they who must decide. I sincerely hope so, you know how anxious I am that Gretel should be told quickly one way or the other.*

*First I have to thank you for your awaited letter, but more so for the phone call, to hear your voice again was the highlight of the day. The tingling sensation within me did not leave me until I fell asleep. Mum and Dad are so glad for me. They know I shall leave them, but they are happy for me that I have found you. Dad is always happy when you tell something about the farm. You having two binders means to him that you must be on a larger farm than he thought. Going back to the cottage, I was so excited that I can tell everyone who may ask, that we have a home and garden of our own and a fantastic view of mountains and blue ocean. Sheep, lambs and cows around us. You also wrote we will have our own mushrooms when we arrive home. You seem to be more than just 'cow-boy', pardon me, if you are able to do so much for our cottage. First, do not worry if our home is not yet perfect. I like to be part of our two 'love-birds' team. I really could not wish for more. Like so many who left home for America to start with little.*

> *Back to the important thing and your invitation list. I have mine complete. Yours will not be that many. My friend Malve, who worked in Cambridge to learn English booked herself in to visit us next summer, what do you say to that? That must do for today, my Paul. I always pray for you, your bride, Ehrentraut.*

---

> *Viewfield, September 1955 my deeply loved, Ehrentraut;*
>
> *Thank you for your comforting two letters of love this week. Here are the sizing patterns for your ring, send them back with your next letter. Not surprising with the questions and instruction as our waiting time is shortening. At least you are well, with all the thinking and planning, which to my regret has been left to you alone since I am not there to help. Thank goodness the weather was perfect on the day when you had to entertain the Sellar family and their Grandma, showing them your beautiful town. Yes, I can well imagine that the boat trip would have gone down well with the children. I will soon be told when next I will see them. Oh, and thank you for telling me of your surprise at the 'Silesian Gathering' spotting Gretel and Engelbert there, which you had not been told about, but in the end it must have been fun to be at it. So far Engelbert had not told me, I would have asked him to look for anyone that might have known me, and then he could have introduced them to you. Now my true Love, time is suddenly beginning to intrude on our life in earnest. Enclosed is my list of guests who will certainly attend. We can assume that my friend Ernst and his wife will not be able to attend according to his letter. We do appreciate the kind offer by Heinz's parents of a room for Engelbert and myself for the two nights. No, no, rules must be obeyed, no bridegroom to sleep under the same 'roof' as the bride!*
>
> *Engelbert has resigned himself that permission from the Polish Authorities for our parents will not be given. It does not mean that Engelbert is giving up, on the contrary; regardless of how long it takes. You asked about 'our' garden, yes we will have some carrots,*

*leeks and lettuce. Strawberries in the farm garden are ripening, it takes longer here. Are you sure your Dad picked as many strawberries as you said? Yes, indeed I do spend time in the cottage, 'our home', cleaning, repairs and some painting. Do you know what is strange my Love and Bride? I find myself occasionally stopping and thinking, asking you 'what would you like here or there, a shelf there, another here, and what about the colour?' It felt strange and funny, much has to wait until you are here to tell me what and where. My other suggestion is we fill the trunk with as much soft and light material and pushed hard in; like our featherbed etc., to cut the weight, since the trunk will go by train and boat. The heavy items like china pots and pans can go in the car, so also our clothes. Regarding our sister Ursula I have written to Mother Superior, but I am not very hopeful. If she allows one it will establish a precedent that might create future problems. Do not despair, dearest, it might be a reason for a honeymoon trip? As regarding your dress, Dorle will brook no argument and will make your wedding dress before she goes to work abroad. You had a talk with your parish priest and all is organised for our most important place that day our commitment at church. Of course we have to go in the morning to the Registrar for the state registration. All that in only a few weeks now. Oh how strange? I just recalled when you wrote that one of your aunts received your engagement notice, she refused to accept that you should marry a farm worker! How degrading for a small-holder's daughter...I felt low when I first read it though, you dismissed it in your letter in an amusing manner. What did I do to deserve such love? Your two feet are firmly fixed on mother earth. God be praised for your pragmatic outlook on life. Oh, before I close, I understand the groom has to provide the bridal gown but is not allowed to see it before the day, that's fair, a surprise to look forward to. Time to say goodnight with all my good wishes to them all, to you Ehrentraut all my Love, take care for me your*

*Paul. xx.*

*Hameln, September 1955 my Love mein Schatz (Treasure) Paul*

*'Das ist der Tag des Herrn!' You still remember that first line? 'This is the day of the Lord', surely you have sung it too? Can you guess my reason why? Yes of course, the official handing in of my notice. This was a day when I really longed for you, to be here and to hold me. How I needed you today, I would have given anything to have had you here to support me in so many ways. My Love do not worry, be happy that it is fulfilled, I am on my last few weeks at the shop. If I need you I go for one of your letters to hold it to my heart and all is well soon. My Mum was very helpful, but it was your heart I needed to feel. Most of the staff had kind words apart from one of the men. But I stood firm and did not show my annoyance. The good wishes from Mum, Dad and Annemarie soon brought me the comfort I needed. Now all I look forward to is your promised telephone call tomorrow evening as on my birthday. With your love that you send to me in every letter across the waves, it will help me through the last few weeks until I say my final goodbye to the shop.*

*My treasure you are busy for us doing things in the cottage, I know you are trying to do your best but as you suggested I am happy to look forward to help you in matters where I might well have other ideas of where and what I would prefer. These are the things that make me feel I am part of you. I cannot forget how little we had when we left home and came to Hameln. Can you imagine how good a feeling it is when I can answer, yes you've got a job and we have a home. Many young couples are not so lucky.*

*A number of our guests have replied positively to our invitation and as is common asked for a list of items that would be useful for us. Some of them have indicated a sum they wish to give, and for us to decide for what we need most of, or towards whatever. Others have indicated the particular gift they intend to give. Your plan for the sitting room to do away with the open fire and replace it a free standing modern closed fire, which has a door that can be opened, sounds OK with me, since I know nothing about those things. You wrote that it is now settled that we will have an electric cooker. Should anyone of your family and guests ask what we still need or would like to have then I can get in touch with them, that is provided I can have their address. This week I am going to a cooking demonstration with my group, it will be one of the last meetings with* me. They tell me they will miss me and might not join another group; that would be a pity. But I am starting a totally new period in my life where I want to fulfil my birthright, if it is God's will, to be a wife and mother for you.

Going back to the cottage, my dearest Paul, you did say it is settled and we have a real home, our own home. You say every gadget requiring power must be electrical. Any pots designed for gas cooking can be changed without difficulty. Oh my dear Paul, it is a lovely feeling to be preparing for our home. Dorle is back from her holiday and is ready to get on with my dress. The two of us went shopping together to get the bits and pieces required but, here is a laugh —so far in the whole of Hameln I have been unable to buy a suitable pair of white shoes, can you believe that? Yes and my close friend Malve insists on being a banner bearer at our wedding. With all my love your bride Ehrentraut.

---

*Viewfield, September 1955 My Love, dearest Ehrentraut,*

Thank you for the mail I received with great joy and gladness for you. The day you so long had yearned for has finally arrived; and you have lived through it. The congratulations expressed by your colleagues were appreciated, and I see you marching on with your head held high. That was a day I should have been many miles nearer to you to hold you in my arms - soon, soon. Now we can count down in earnest the weeks, and soon the days when I will ring the bell and you will come rushing down to open the door and our arms clasping us together, just think.

But before that happens there is a mountain of preparation to be done, and as I said before, it will fall on you to see things are done. You at least are happy now that the material for your dress is bought, and Dorle is confident it will be ready in time. You wanted me to tell you how things are here in Viewfield? As I said before, this is the hottest summer with no rain. The result of that is, this will be the earliest grain harvest since I came here in 1946. We spent the last week with all the staff, getting the two binders ready to start next week.

*You will have got the sizing pattern for your ring, and whenever you have decided, send it back. The lady said they can make small alterations and we should not worry. I must not forget to bring them, is that what you are saying to me? Thanks for letting me know that your Passport is valid till next year. Now, important to tell and assure Mum and Dad that the new car is all paid for. Mr Taylor the Garage owner has given us a deal for a new Ford van which we will pick up in London, where we will change the car. I got the booking forms for the ferry. We will take the midday ferry with a cabin. Telling you this is giving me a strange feeling. It must be the fact of doing things for us together. You must tell me how you felt reading this?*

*Oh, I nearly forgot to tell how overjoyed I was about you telling me that our Dad has written a letter to you. A letter which made you very happy because it was assuring you that they loved you and are praying every day for you and me. That's easy for them when Dad is the fully paid Sexton in our big church. Apparently the priest who engaged him five or six years ago was of German parentage. But of course Dad had to learn Polish, by now he is fluent I would guess. Pity I could not be with you listening to the radio, those wonderful songs I know; the Strauss Waltzes which our band played here a lot by request once we started. Franz Lehár, and his lovely light opera tunes, and most popular the 'Merry Widow'. How wonderful that you are already collecting your records for packing. Time for milking, dear Ehrentraut, let's close eyes and kiss goodnight, your Paul.*

---

*Hameln, September 1955 My dear Bridegroom,*

*What do I have to thank you for first? Your letter, or the telephone call? For both of course, but to hear your voice was the highlight of that day and the day after.*

*Paul my love, I appreciated your wanting to talk a few minutes longer, it gave us the chance to sort out a few important matters right away. It is now less than six weeks, who could blame us for counting. Have you asked David yet about your holiday time? It would be good to know for me, then I could make a large cross on the calendar and strike the days off like on an Advent calendar. Keep telling me what you are doing on the farm. I enjoy knowing because I have been there and can picture it. My goodness! So we are having a number of mushroom beds, and according to you there should be a good crop for us when we get home. Will it be my job to pick them? I would love that, the very idea that I could help you appeals to me. In the meantime here I am not idle as you can imagine. The other day when I spoke with my parish priest I remembered to ask him if we could borrow 25 chairs for our wedding. Of course we could. So one more detail resolved. At the same time he asked me if Fr. Davies spoke German? I said no. Apparently our parish priest must inform Fr. Davies of our intention to get married here in Hameln. I suppose formalities have to be adhered to.*

*That will have to do for today. Now, we both know what we have to do, with all my Love, your bride.*

---

*Viewfield, September 1955 My dear Love Ehrentraut,*

*A strange feeling this is indeed, since I have never been exposed to such emotions. Can you imagine, soon we will be giving each other our 'Ja' word?! What does your mind and heart say? I would imagine it will be the same as mine, and that would be 'wonderful'. Yes it is true this is one of the last letters that will fly across the sea. No need to speak of love, time or longing any more. Our aim and destination is in sight as our hearts beat faster. To God be praise and thanks, wonderful thoughts they all are!*

*But now there is almost suddenly a feeling, I must not lose sight of reality. For a start I am sure something you did not think about? In our shed we have a ton of coal, and a farm trailer full of wood blocks to keep us from freezing. As I once said, we will remove the open fireplace in the living room, build up the opening and get an enamelled free standing fire which I have ordered. The danger is that I might have taken on too much before we arrive. If so, you would be a handy helper. David enquired regarding the electricity. They promised it will be done before Christmas. That is a bit of a disappointment. Ella wanted me to tell you that the chest of drawers in my bedroom is ours if we have use for it. I thanked her and said yes. For its age it is in very good condition and will be useful for us. What do you say? That brings me to tell you about a bedroom suite I saw in the furniture shop. In light walnut veneer, a large wardrobe, a smaller one for gents, and a chest of drawers with a large mirror, at a reasonable price. I called at the shop and said proudly, I would call with 'my wife to see it! Yes, 'mein Schatz' – 'my treasure' the cottage is empty. I have the key, and can get in and out as I want. You are right, we will have electricity, that is certain, in regards to your cooking utensils. I doubt if I will be able to install the new fireplace. When we are in the cottage my dear I will no longer be in Viewfield in the evening and dinner time but at "HOME" with you and free to fix our house after work, with you cooking something for me and helping to hold a hammer.*

*I nearly forgot, if you had been here you could have taken a basket of six pounds of mushrooms to Mr Ross, worth DM13, not bad! Another will be ready in four days. To your question on one of the important forms regarding my profession, just put down what I am, farm worker. Let them wonder if they then see us with a car. Let's see in ten years time? Another thing, my tailor-made suit is ready; fits like a glove. Well-made and very good material, and you the expert, will be the judge. Something else, it is now certain our Mum and Dad will not get permission to come, so I will make up a parcel to the maximum permitted weight with those things they cannot get. Ella will bake a raisin cake that will keep for weeks, so that they could have a celebration on the 15th October, in spirit with us. Dad had written that he will phone from the parish office. Their parish priest offered it to them. Aha, so your Dad expects Engelbert and me to dig his garden to help pay for the wedding? I am ready. Tell me, am I supposed to buy presents for the bridesmaid? We have covered a lot and thinking about you Ehrentraut, only two weeks and you can say goodbye to the shop. Until then you will be busy at home more than in the shop according* to your letters? It is a strange feeling to realise it is one of the last letters I shall send you my Love. There are always greetings from Ella and David. Come and lay your arms around me, your very own bridegroom, Paul.

---

*Hameln September* My 'Darling' yes? Paul, my Bridegroom and my Love,

Soon I'll be introducing you as 'mein Mann' my husband, how my heart tingles! We all hope you are well and that my prayers are answered. Thank you for your letter filled with love and the interesting news from, our new home, Viewfield. You have finished cutting the oats and are beginning to bring it in to build those 'round houses', as I used to describe them when I saw them outside in February.

Yes my dearest Paul we have come a long way, fifteen months and well over a hundred letters each. They contained a lot of love and trust in each other; where did our strength come from? The creator of you and me. Oh, if only I could be in your arms at this moment, but soon, in three weeks time. That reminds me, might it be possible for you to arrive on the Monday? It has been suggested that we young folks, you and I, with Gretel and Engelbert to go to the theatre to see the 'Barber of Seville'. It would be wonderful to have been once with you, Gretel and Engelbert! Yes, a busy time is in front of me as you can guess. I have to send my application for my new Passport, as I will be then 'Frau Lippok' after our wedding. Please remember to send me the other forms I asked you to fill in as soon as you can. Otherwise we may not be able to get married.

A surprise arrived two days ago a letter with DM100, from a Mr Mosler, do you know him? He is from your town in Silesia and had been on a visit there, and met your Dad whom he knew. So Dad gave him the money to send it to us for our wedding. They should not have done it, but I can imagine they would not want to miss such a chance. I shall thank them on our behalf and that we have received it. Now I have another surprise for you, can you *guess? In Germany the groom pays for the wedding dress, and you are still a German. No, you do not have to pay for her underwear! Tomorrow I go to Dorle to pin the hem of my dress, now that I have my white shoes. Even in Hannover it was difficult to get a pair of white shoes. The day after tomorrow I go to see Dorle to celebrate our going away, she to Norway and I to Tain. We discovered we will be on the same latitude. See how busy I am, tomorrow I have my last youth group evening and farewell party. Thank you for your brilliant idea of bringing a few dozen fresh eggs from your own hens. They will be larger than those we get here, a most welcome present. You better beware, you may have to teach me again to kiss and cuddle you. I spoke to Engelbert about your picking up my young cousin Christel on your way here from Krefeld which is on your route. Engelbert says yes. I will write to her and tell her, we have the address which I will send to Engelbert. Surely you will be in touch with him to know where to pick him up? He says he will meet up with you near the Dutch border? You can see how much we have to sort out. Please forgive me, but my eyes are starting to close, as you 'order' me, only one more letter! I love you dearly, may our good Lord care for us, your Ehrentraut.*

---

*Viewfield, September 1955 Meine geliebte Braut, my beloved Bride Ehrentraut,*

*This may surprise you, but I have actually organised my work in order that I may have time to concentrate my thoughts on this my last letter in our long journey of seeking and finding love. Recalling the day when looking through the paper, 'Mann in der Zeit', I glanced at the 'Friendship seeking' column, my eyes fell on this one and never moved from it. Only two thoughts crossed my mind, am I too late, or should I? It was the invisible hand that moved my finger to answer. After eight years bachelor life, interspersed with Military service, and prisoner of war in a far distant land. Working with animals, and other interesting experiences, other than lady friends, miraculously my hand reached for the scissors, the rest is history* now! These are words for posterity my dear Ehrentraut. Now after seventeen months, with only two short visits, we shall by God's grace stand before the altar to be declared Man and Wife. Those, my dear Ehrentraut, were my thoughts throughout the day.

Thank you for what should be your second last letter. When you receive this from me, you will have said goodbye to your colleagues and shop with relief. But you will not have any rest, very busy in fact when I read through all your letters. So far the weather has held good and all the grain is secure. If the weather stays as good, we will start lifting potatoes. David and I are agreed, that should the weather break then regardless I will leave here as planned. Therefore do not worry one moment. I will leave here on the Saturday and take the ferry on Sunday to be with you Monday evening. Engelbert and I will pick up Christel as planned.

In order to avoid custom duties I have sent a parcel to Engelbert, one to Gretel and one to Heinz, and one to you, while I bring my permitted quota, and whatever else I mentioned in my last letter. Our rings are safely put away among all the important items to get me through to you. Fr. Davies read out your names perfectly in the banns. We have many well-wishers in the parish, and many more who are looking forward to welcoming you here. Is it not wonderful? Others you will leave behind who will miss you very much. Finally, there is only one wish, to love you and that it may grow throughout our life. It has been an intense and interesting experience; and an extraordinary test, - but we have won through, providentially guided and helped; and our soul and minds are united. We have fulfilled our commitment, as you said when last we spoke.

The only downside, for me disappointing, is that our new home is not as complete as I really had hoped it would be. Not even the electricity will be connected. But there you are now, comforting and encouraging me to wait until we are together, and you to be there to help and pacify me. Can we really put pen and paper aside? Not quite, other people will expect to hear from us. Yours Paul.

Hameln, Tuesday 11.30 a.m., 27*th* September 1955 my dearly beloved Bridegroom, my Paul.,

Bowing to your wishes this will be 'our' last letter - my writing and your reading. It pains me that you will be without a letter of love from me, but I respect your wish. There is a double portion of love in this letter for you, happy? My dear Paul, can you imagine, how wonderful it feels to be writing to you at this hour during the week? At home in the middle of the morning. It is a taste of how it might be when I am in my, 'our' own home. A colleague, Miss Grüne, was here last night. The two of us were busy baking for our small leaving party, which we plan to give after the shop closes. We laughed a lot about ourselves, the shop, and some of the colleagues and glad that we are out. She too is getting married shortly. Tonight Mum and Dad were due to go to the Theatre to see a new play, but Dad already backed out of it and Mum will stay in. So Gretel, Malve, I and Annemarie will go. In two weeks I will go with you! How I look forward to it with you at my side. The few times we walked together I felt so proud at your side. Can you understand? Not many people have seen us together yet, it is a pity but do not worry! Thank you for your letter which told me so much of your great love for me. With you at my side I feel fulfilled. If we do not forget 'Him', he will not forget us. Some of my friends and relatives do wonder at my courage, others are rather sceptical. Our young priest had a bit of a problem when reading our banns, he was not sure how to pronounce Tain, yet so simple. Probably shyness made him to pronounce it wrong, most people would not have noticed.

We had a letter from the Metzner family from Düsseldorf. They are pleased to accept our invitation, asking if we need a mincer or bread slicer? I asked for the latter. Your cousins, Ruth and Erika are disappointed that they cannot come because Erika too is getting married around that time. They did say that theirs is a small family wedding, must be why you or Engelbert never got an invitation. Now, about the work in our cottage. I am wagging my finger; I am good at that, not to worry if all you intended to do will not be ready. I am willingly prepared to class ourselves as pioneers trying to build a new life somewhere. I am surprised that our mushrooms are doing so well. So there will be some left for me to cook and bring to the shop.

*That is how I will get to know the people. Remember when in Tain I went on my own to buy cards to send away?*

*Finally, please will you promise me that you will go to bed early. Do not worry about our new home, but more importantly drive safely, so that my arms may receive you well and joyful. May our guardian angel watch over you, and blessed Mary, protect you for me. In spirit I gently trace the sign of the cross on your forehead, and thank you for patiently waiting for me.*

*In love I wait for you, your ever-loving Ehrentraut, your bride.*

# Chapter 14

## Preparation for our Wedding, Viewfield, Scotland

**Friday, 7ᵗʰ October 1955**

Friday evening as usual for many years I have completed my evening tasks with my animals, and was ready for supper. The three of us, Ella, David and myself, enjoyed a pleasant conversation. We had much to say to each other; I to remind Ella that there will be a few pounds of mushrooms ready to pick and would she take them down to Mr H. Ross the Grocer, ensuring that she keep some for herself and David, otherwise they might spoil. David was adamant that I should not worry about my not being here for the potato harvest. David will take me to the station in the morning. Time for me to go up to my room and start packing; Ella gave me some useful goodies and her favourite sultana cake to take with me. It was Ella's usual good-will and well-wishing to the bride. In the process of packing my cases, my eyes were drawn to different aspects of my room; at one point to the window by the intermittent light from the Tarbat Ness lighthouse. Just then I stopped and realised, I was in fact clearing my room where I had lived for eight years, the place where I wrote and read many letters, to my parents, to friends and of course to Ehrentraut. It has been my real home for all that time. When I return with Ehrentraut, we will have our own new home. This is the beginning of another chapter in my life. I had better get going, any moment Ella will be calling that our nightcap is ready. It was a good opportunity to thank them both heartily, as they reciprocated which I really appreciated. Wanting to finish, I said my goodnight, and it was not long before I fell asleep.

## Saturday, 8th October 1955

David did the morning milking while I got ready for my journey, making sure nothing was missing while Ella was busy buttering her girdle scones for me to take on the road, there was none better for me. When it was time to take my cases out, David arrived for his mid-morning cup of tea which he took while I loaded my cases. There was no time to lose in saying our farewells, all three of us hoping for a safe return. My itinerary in short: change at Inverness for the London train, arriving at Euston late evening. Get a taxi to take me to the garage where I would pick up my hire car. It will be midnight by then probably. By way of a reminder, this was in fact my first visit to London. However, I had studied a London street map seriously, and had my directions to get on to the Harwich road in my mind, reminding you this was 1955. With this mental picture and carefully watching direction signs, not easy in the dark, I managed to keep on the route. Traffic being light in the middle of the night, there was no reason for me to hurry. Out in the country I found a convenient place with an open cafe to rest, and took the opportunity to have a hot drink. Returning to the car I had no difficulty in falling asleep for an hour or so, before continuing my drive to Harwich.

## Harwich - Sunday, 9th October 1955

Arriving at the port, with the formalities completed, I was guided to the queue for the car to be hoisted into the hold (still no roll-on, roll-off yet). Once on board I asked for a cabin, and for a few shillings was given one. Before having a rest I decided to go for a light breakfast. Returning to the cabin I soon fell asleep, not before setting my alarm clock, which did ring at the appointed time. I had allowed time to have a coffee and sandwich before disembarking. Docked in Holland it was time to go onto the quayside to pick up my car. A quick look round to check for any scratches or damage, and I was on my way.

With intermittent sunshine it was good driving weather. Having passed the city of Utrecht and Arnhem, it had got dark. It was not long before I crossed the border into Germany. After one and a half hours I arrived at Engelbert's in Düsseldorf. He prepared a supper during which we discussed leaving next morning after breakfast. First, we had to pick up Ehrentraut's cousin Christel, which could be reached within half an hour. Having had a good sleep, I felt fit for the drive to Hameln.

**Monday, 10th October 1955**

This was how things worked out on the day. Leaving as planned, we soon reached the place where we collected Christel. She must have kept an eye on the door because it opened rather quickly after Engelbert rang the bell. We introduced and greeted each other, and once everybody was seated we were on our way. It was not difficult for Engelbert to entertain us, and especially Christel while I did the driving. It was now motorway, of which Germany had vastly more miles than in Britain, all the way to Hameln. We soon got to know the close family connections between Christel and Ehrentraut's family.

Driving conditions were excellent and after two hours we had a comfort stop and light refreshments, before continuing our journey. Sometime later the first advanced warning exit sign for Hameln appeared. A few minutes later the exit to Hameln. Only 30 minutes later and we entered Hameln. In a minute or two we were in the centre and entered Deister Strasse and within seconds stopping at number 62. I claimed my privilege to press the bell button, twice, as secretly pre-arranged. The buzzer went and I pushed the door and made for the stair; and at the same time I could hear hurrying feet coming down, and at the second flight a pair of arms flung round my neck, lips pressed prevented me from saying anything. At last I could breathe and two brown eyes looked into mine, and then Ehrentraut said, "Now you are really mine and you will never leave me again". Words I have never forgotten. By now Christel and Engelbert had passed us by and climbed the stairs to see 'Mum' Krause, Dad was not home from work yet.

Ehrentraut and I in each other's arms lingered to savour this so long anticipated moment. These were not moments for words, which neither of us could find. Soon, we too climbed the stairs and faced 'Muttel' (Ehrentraut's mother Gertrud) welcoming me in an affectionate motherly embrace. A moment I cannot forget, it was an embrace of a motherly 'welcome home' to the family. Our final goal or dream, or whatever better word there is, has been reached at last! While a warm drink was being prepared, Engelbert and I went down to bring up the rest of the luggage and parked the car at its place as instructed by Ehrentraut. She and I used every opportunity, however short, to touch hands or a hug to relieve the tension after so many letters and waiting. Within the hour, Annemarie arrived from work and we greeted each other fondly, with my welcoming her as my lovely 'sister-in-law'. Soon Dad arrived home and we greeted each other warmly. While Dad and I sat down and chatted, the ladies prepared supper for the now larger family, with Christel eager to help, mother being Christel's aunt. Ehrentraut and I touched briefly on matters concerning our documents and Ehrentraut suggested we ought to see the relevant officials the following morning after breakfast. Her reason for this was that with our both being German nationals and both leaving Germany to live in the UK, certain important paperwork was needed.

Engelbert offered to help wherever there was a need. At some stage he would try and call on Gretel. We gave thanks for a sumptuous supper, with Ehrentraut impatient to show me 'our trunk'. It really was a professional piece of joinery. It was a happy moment for me to thank Dad for his effort to negotiate with his joiner friend. Sometime later Annemarie's boyfriend Heinz arrived. Dad thought it was appropriate to celebrate the happy 'reunion' and all of us agreed, followed by a united 'prost'. As had been arranged Engelbert and I were to stay for the pre-marriage days at Heinz's parents. With all of us feeling the need of sleep there was no lingering, we wished each other goodnight. Ehrentraut and I were allowed a few seconds more on our own for our goodnight kiss. Heinz, Engelbert and I soon arrived at Heinz's parents' home. We were warmly welcomed by Mr and Mrs Pothe, and guided to our room, followed by an invitation to join them for a welcome drink. Mr Pothe actually is employed by the British military at the local garrison, and offered to drive our car on our wedding day, driving right hand vehicles at the garrison had been useful. There was no time limit given when to appear at my in-law's for breakfast. Mr and Mrs Pothe realising our need to sleep, bade us goodnight. We thanked them for their offer of breakfast and their understanding that we would like to have breakfast together.

## Hameln, Tuesday, 11th October 1955

Awaking with daylight through the curtains and Engelbert out of bed, I guessed we both had slept well. A look at the clock made me get up 'pronto' military style with Engelbert just vacating the bathroom. With silence in the house, I assumed everybody was out at work. Not so, as Mrs Pothe, aware of us being awake wished us a 'good morning' as we were about to leave for our people. We were greeted as we had expected, "Good Morning long sleepers," Ehrentraut and I fell into each other's arms simply saying with one voice, "Is this how it will be for us now every day?" That really took some moments to sink in, how wonderful to be in love and be loved. Of course everybody had their breakfast. Ehrentraut was not to miss joining us with another cup of coffee, the meeting of our eyes indicating 'how wonderful to be together'. Engelbert offered his help, but was not required in the morning. He decided to go out and hoped to see Gretel. Before Ehrentraut and I went out to see to our documentations, I at last found the time for us to be alone in the sitting room and gave Ehrentraut that precious box with our rings. Opening the box carefully, at the same time fleetingly raising her eyes to me, she took the small ring and handed it to me, "Well, you better try it?" Clasping her arms around me, she whispered thank you, and put it back into the box saying "make sure you remember where you put them, we do not want to look for them on Saturday". Not wasting any more time we quickly said goodbye and were off to town. All is within easy walking distance and will suffice as exercise for our legs. Briefly, the officials at the offices were helpful and friendly, but asked why leave Germany? Then, reaching for our hand they wished us well. Satisfied and relieved that this important matter was settled, we did what Ehrentraut had waited and longed for, walking side by side and hand in hand, hoping to meet people she knew and to whom she could at last introduce me. One can imagine the pleasure it must have given Ehrentraut to prove that there really is a 'living' bridegroom. Of course I too felt proud and so pleased that at last we were together. To me Ehrentraut is a wonderful and beautiful woman who will make me happy.

There were a number of shops Ehrentraut wanted to visit with me, although she has a 'well-stocked' dowry, which caused me some surprise. Some were either bought on her own, or given as engagement presents. There are certain items which Ehrentraut would like to buy in Germany, but only with the approval of both of us. Having looked at it, and agreed on some and not on others we decided it best not to be late for Mum's lunch, and go back in the afternoon. After lunch Ehrentraut and I went out again to town to continue our 'expedition' to see, test and decide whether to buy any other useful or essential household items, keeping a careful eye on our limited finances. As in the morning there were again opportunities to meet friends and this time Ehrentraut took me to her shop and her colleagues. It was now my duty to thank them for their kind presents. Once outside, Ehrentraut was glad to assure me how happy she was to leave the shop behind.

Ehrentraut thought we did well and should make our way home. Walking through the beautiful and historic old town I suggested we ought to have a coffee. We had just passed one of the small coffee shops where my eye caught on display a four-inch-high layered cream gateau. I pointed it out to Ehrentraut who looked at it and smiled broadly expressing surprise to discover one of my weaknesses. Taking my arm happily, she led me into the cafe. Yes, I did enjoy it, and I must have it again sometime. "Don't worry, there will be more on our wedding day."

Making our way home, I broached the subject of our going to Bremen on the following day. The reason was to visit our Aunt Hedwig the nun, our Dad's sister who was sent to the US in 1924 as a hospital nurse. It is the same nun that I got in touch with whilst in the POW camp in Fort Bliss you may recall. There was no possibility of her going to visit our Dad in Poland, any more than our Dad getting out to see her. We felt we owed it to our parents since they too could not be at our wedding. Ehrentraut agreed, and would certainly come with us to meet Aunt Hedwig. I assured her that we would be allowed only a few hours to see her anyway, and that we would be back home before Dad came home from work.

Arriving home we showed our purchases to Mum who approved, knowing Ehrentraut had her own taste and would not go for anything too expensive or unnecessary. We would have to go and visit some of Ehrentraut's close relatives, especially her Grandma who was looking forward to seeing me again. Dad arrived from work, and like us was ready for supper. It was my pleasure to tell how our day went, and assured him we had not overspent, which pleased him. Ehrentraut and I spent some time after supper packing and sorting some of the purchases and gifts, most we would have to leave until after our wedding. I made myself useful taking some small bits and pieces up into the loft to make room. Well acquainted with a measuring tape we were able to draw up a plan of how to place the tables in the two rooms and at the same time considering what could be moved to the Bethke's next door for the two days. With Dad having to work in the morning, it was a convenient opportunity to have a glass of beer and then bedtime. Engelbert had returned from seeing Gretel and was in time to join us for a drink. Time for Ehrentraut and I to say goodnight.

**Hameln, Wednesday, 12th October 1955**

Three days to go now! Engelbert and I arrived at Muttel Krause's home in good time for breakfast. The morning embrace and kiss is still something so wonderful. We had agreed last night that Engelbert and I would be in good time for breakfast so that we could have it together. Ehrentraut had already made some sandwiches, so we could leave after breakfast as agreed. The route to Bremen was somewhat parallel northwards to Wildeshausen, and a good road. We arrived within our expected time in less than two hours. Engelbert, having lived in Bremen during his apprenticeship there, soon had us locate the convent. Engelbert led the way and rang the bell. We were welcomed by the duty Sister who led us to a meeting room. We introduced each other with Sister telling how excited Sister Godharda, our Aunt Hedwig, was to meet us. Within a minute this six foot tall nun appeared and embraced us with great joy in a mixture of English and German, which after forty years is no surprise. Aunt Hedwig took a very special liking to Ehrentraut. We had so much to talk about, not missing the correspondence we had when I was a POW in the States. Naturally she was most interested hearing Engelbert inform her about our parents, especially her brother our Dad. Aunt Hedwig was convinced that in a few years she would be allowed another visit and hoped by then our parents would be in the West. We were invited to have lunch in the guest parlour with Aunt Hedwig. After another hour or more we had to take our leave from Aunt Hedwig, Sister Godharda, and with great joy and thanksgiving we said our goodbye, and with Aunt Hedwig assuring both Ehrentraut and myself, that we would be in her special prayers, we took our leave.

We had again a good run and arrived back at Hameln in time for a late afternoon coffee. Shortly after, Dad arrived from work and wished to know how our visit went. Ehrentraut helped to prepare supper, after which the two of us went to pay Grandma the promised visit. Again and again, Ehrentraut's joy surfaced with my being at her side after our long wait, which filled me with great joy. Coming home, Engelbert and I sat down and wrote the promised letter to our parents about our visit to meet Aunt Hedwig. Undoubtedly it will make them so happy that we had visited her. The ritual glass of beer with Dad was the pleasant ending of our day. Ehrentraut pointed out that the following day would be for all of us a busy time in the house. There were a number of small but important items which also had to be seen to. Having never been involved in wedding preparations, I am only too pleased to be of any help if told where and what to do. We had had a good day, so we were thankful. I took my bride in my arms, told her how lucky I felt, and how I loved her. We said goodnight, with Ehrentraut and I praying for each other.

## Hameln, Thursday, 13th October 1955

Refreshed after a blissful sleep, Engelbert and I on our way out wished Mrs Pothe a good morning and hoped she would have a pleasant day. She replied in like manner adding it's going to be a busy day for us and wishing us well. It was an opportunity for us to assure her how happy and grateful we were for her kindness. Arriving at Ehrentraut's we were greeted with her usual smile, and an embrace and a kiss for me. Ehrentraut too had a restful sleep after our trip to see my aunt in Bremen. Dad and Annemarie were already at work, and Mum at her usual morning work cleaning the entrance hall and staircase of the house. I was fully aware of the burden Ehrentraut had borne in organising our wedding, yet calm and ever smiling with never a complaint. During breakfast Ehrentraut laid before us her well planned work for the day.

Engelbert and I had to move the furniture not required to the house of our neighbour, Mrs Bethke, who kindly had offered space. Some dusting, brushing, etc. was inevitable, I had lots of practice in Viewfield. We began setting up the tables in the sitting room, expanding them with the polished boards Dad had procured from his joiner friends. It was a system Ehrentraut had experimented with success when preparing for our engagement party in March, which I had to miss and she had to organise it all on her own. I must admit I felt guilty, but I was so far away.

Next, the bedroom now cleared, had to be set up. This would be where the younger generation would be seated with friends from outside the family. Tablecloths and provision of cutlery would come next. As dusk was falling we collected the promised number of chairs from the Parish Meeting Room. Annemarie and Dad had come home from work, which gave us the opportunity to have a coffee break. Dad and Annemarie thought we had done well so far. It was understood that I would wash the glassware, which Engelbert and I would set up in the morning. Dad gave the command to finish and have a nightcap. During the conversation we all agreed how well everything had gone and congratulated Ehrentraut and all the family. While the conversation continued I became aware of my thoughts absorbing the whole atmosphere of the day. How beautiful it seemed when all of us were involved, engaged in preparing for our wedding in such a familiar environment. How different from just walking into a hotel sitting down and then walking away afterwards. I mused on it before I fell asleep and remember it still.

## Hameln, Friday, 14th October 1955

My final day as a Bachelor! Not brilliant sunshine, but still a pleasant autumn day here in Hameln. The two of us, my brother Engelbert and I were ready to go over to Deister Str. 62, how many envelopes have I thus addressed? I pressed the bell twice, my personal signal. Soon the buzzer unlocked the door and we made our way up the stair, where as usual Ehrentraut met me with her perpetual smile and morning kiss.

Today we were at breakfast as a complete family with Dad and Annemarie present. One could assume that the thought had gone through all of us that some of us would leave the parental home shortly to start a new home, leaving those left behind facing the new situation. It is quite a thought if you're the mother! There was no lingering after breakfast with Ehrentraut ensuring that time was at a premium, with me interrupting by asking, "Have you got your wedding dress?" "Is it not a bit late to ask? My groom, have you checked your suit? You had better bring your shirt over after dinner so that I can give it an iron, it will be the first time to iron it for you, is it not lovely?" With surprising efficiency everybody had dispersed to their designated duties, Engelbert and me to set up the tables. Annemarie was busy at the decorations. Ehrentraut gave us the occasional visit and advice. There were always those inevitable minor matters which had not been considered before, but were always overcome with some head scratching, humorous remarks and sound advice! Ehrentraut and I had to dress and made our way to the one of our two important duties the Office of the Registrar for 10 a.m.

Our details checked by the Registrar, the important document read out and signed by us. A few kind words of congratulations and good wishes for our future, a handshake and we were married in the eyes of the State. On arrival at home we produced our documents and laid them safely aside.

Dad was busy seeing to the matter of drinks, with Heinz helping him. Dinner was quickly taken and I made for my shirt as ordered. At dinner time Ehrentraut reminded us about the 'Polterabend' in the evening, a German tradition when children and some friends of the bride bring damaged crockery and smash it in the entrance of the house, especially noisy on tiled floors. The noise is supposed to drive away evil spirits, always good fun if you're young! The bride and groom will then have to clear it up. The children might say a poem and will be rewarded with sweets, while the older friends will come up to have a drink and light snacks.

Ehrentraut and I still had to go to make sure everything was organised in the church, including the flowers. She had already checked with the organist and the banner bearers. The two ladies responsible for the cooking had arrived to start their preparation. Dad saw this as a reason to have a small apéritif for everyone, to wish each other success, which of course none of us refused. After a 'help yourself' supper we did our best to tidy-up, everything looked splendid and festive. Tears of happiness threatened as I took Ehrentraut in my arms. Ehrentraut opened the door in order that we could hear the noise of breaking porcelain from the entrance hall below. Once it had subsided Ehrentraut and I, with brush and shovel, made our way down to do the necessary, with everyone applauding us. Ehrentraut gave out their dues, while the older friends were invited to come up for their 'reward'. Soon it was time to have a look around and feel satisfied and happy. With my arms around Ehrentraut, I could not find words to say, neither to Ehrentraut nor to her parents and sister. I was sure everyone understood. One more evening praying for each other, and thereafter together. Ehrentraut kissed me and traced a cross on my forehead, "goodnight, may our angel care for us".

# Chapter 15

# Our Wedding day!

**Hameln, Saturday, 15th October 1955.**
**The Wedding of Ehrentraut Krause and Paul Lippok.**

Before falling asleep last night I had thought about whether in my excitement I would have a sound and refreshing sleep? I need not have worried. I woke up a few minutes before my travel clock was about to ring, and pushed the button to allow Engelbert to have a few more minutes sleep. It was to allow myself time to order my entangled thoughts of completely giving up all of myself to become part of someone else? Ehrentraut was to promise to share herself that we will start the promised lifelong bond. Wake up, silly boy, you've sorted those thoughts long ago. Had we not written about and talked of this day long enough?

"Wake up Engelbert, time to get dressed". I must remember to thank Ehrentraut for having ironed our white shirts last night. This is the day when at long last we would be declaring our commitment to each other before God and our loved ones, yes, I felt joyful. Mrs Pothe kindly offered us a light breakfast which we appreciated. At the Krause house they would be fully occupied with more important matters. It was time to go, one last check that nothing was forgotten and our suits were in order. Mr Pothe, our chauffeur for the day, drove us to the bride's house. The two of us making our way up that famous stair of a year ago, where I first met Ehrentraut in person, and she declining my offer of a kiss until I first met her parents.

It is common practice in Germany for the groom and best man to go to the bride's home in order that both parties leave the parents' house together for church. The bride will of course be dressed out of sight from groom and best man. Ehrentraut would be dressed at Mrs Bethke's next door, with Annemarie as bridesmaid to assist Ehrentraut. This was for Ehrentraut to be the most important day of her life. The moments when I was on my own allowed me to think what it must mean for any bride to loosen herself from her parental bond, in order to create one new such bond by joining herself to her about-to-be husband. A thought that created in me a most wonderful moment. This day was to be Ehrentraut's most important day, she whispered last night as we parted.

A hand shake with Mum and Dad, a look round the corner into the kitchen where amongst a hive of activity Engelbert tried to make himself useful but was quickly shown the door. Dad offered a small Schnapps but I politely declined and opted for fruit juice. Just then Annemarie entered with a smile wanting to tell me that Ehrentraut was ready and whispered in my ear, "Ehrentraut is calm and lovely", and there at last the moment when all of us faced the door, and in its frame, for a moment stood my bride Ehrentraut, beautifully dressed, glowing in her calm contentment. No kisses, it was not a moment for that. But I never forgot, her name flashed into my mind, Ehren for honour and traut for trust. For the two of us the ancient moment to kneel before our parents (mine in spirit) to receive their special blessing, a very emotional moment for us, my parents knew the hour and will also add their prayer.

Time to go down the stairs, our wedding was timed for 11a.m. With four flights of stairs and a six meter veil I was about to help, when Ehrentraut adapted in a blink of the eye and had the veil over her left arm, leaving her right arm for support on the handrail, thus we arrived at the entrance hall. Her sister Annemarie was carrying the bouquet. To our surprise, as the door opened a number of curious people are awaiting us on either side on the pavement, just to see the bride. But where is the car? Instead what is this? An authentic 'Landau' carriage pulled by two white horses, and a lady coachman. Ehrentraut, how did you think of that? What a wonderful surprise, I could not believe it. "Let me take the reins." "You'll do no such thing, help me into the coach and come in." With the bystanders applauding we were on our way. The coach attracted many people who waved to us happily.

'Arriving at church for the wedding'

'The solemn moment confirmed as Husband & Wife'

**'Banner bearers, husband and wife,
flower girls, and candle bearer'**

Arriving at the church, Annemarie with help from Engelbert, soon had the order of the Procession in place. In the lead were the four banner bearers. followed by young Klaus as candle bearer, my two young cousins the flower girls, then bride and groom, followed by the two train-bearers with bridesmaid and best man following. Especially ordered by Ehrentraut for me as a lover of organ music, there was a triumphal and joyful piece of organ music by the organist as we made our way to the altar. We had chosen Silesian hymns that we had sung in our youth, in our former Silesia, often with great gusto in defiance of Nazi suppression. It was a dignified marriage service led by Ehrentraut's parish priest Father Hövelman. In his inspiring sermon he did not omit to thank Ehrentraut for having given her valuable time to youth work in the parish. The blessing and exchange of our rings was the moving moment for both of us. We remembered my own parents, who had written to tell us they would be with us in thought, and in prayers during this hour, which was a consolation to know. The last hymn was sung and we followed the congregation to the step in front of the church door. There we waited while photographs were taken and hands shaken. It is traditional and for the groom's privilege to throw pennies {preferably larger coinage} to the waiting children, who seem to read wedding notices and make their way to the churches! On our way to the carriage we saw my youngest cousin and flower girl picking up the flowers that had been spread by the girls as customary between the carriage to church, believing they were meant to be taken home, how sweet. On our homeward journey we had ten minutes alone in the carriage to allow us to say a few words of earnest gladness that at last we are one, our long wait was worth it.

**'The dance under the bride's veil'**

Back home everyone relaxed and a companionable atmosphere was quickly established. It was the opportunity for those who had not met before to greet each other and there was much laughter. Engelbert and Annemarie's boyfriend, Heinz, made excellent waiters and eventually the invitation was given to take our seats. It was my privilege to say the grace. The aroma wafting through from the kitchen promised something exceptionally good. Between courses it was our pleasure to see our guests in the other room, Ehrentraut and I did this alternately. This was appreciated and we were happy to do so. It is amazing how such a gathering in the confines of a small home quickly creates a sense of close community. Joy was at the heart of our festivities. How radiant Ehrentraut appeared to me.

After an excellent dinner and equally outstanding variety of desserts - one of my weaknesses - appropriate praise was given to our lady cooks. In the growing convivial atmosphere relatives and strangers found common ground. Unfamiliarity quickly melted away, doubtless glasses being filled and refilled played their part. Eventually most felt the need to stretch their legs and soon various little groups formed. With all doors open and the corridor space, this too was found to be useful, and the whiff of a good cigar was by no means unpleasant. Many souvenir photographs were taken. Surrounded by such happiness, we found the time passed quickly.

The call came to take our places for coffee. The aroma of real coffee beans, which I had brought with me from Scotland was greatly appreciated, and the selection of gateaux and the variety of cakes, from cheesecake to poppy-seed cake, was mouth-watering. While more coffee was served the recitation of the Hochzeit Zeitung {Wedding newspaper} commenced. It had been composed by our friends, and Ehrentraut and I heard things about each other that were new to us or had been forgotten. The nodding of approval and the recollection of events caused much amusement. Occasionally Ehrentraut and I read it still at Christmas, and in the 60 years of our marriage we still wear our original wedding rings.

An unexpectedly heavy rain shower prevented a few guests from taking a short walk into the old town, and conversations continued animatedly until suppertime. Darkness demanded electric light to supplement the festive candles. Our cooks had presented a traditional German Abendbrot – supper, tables were laden with dishes of potato salad, a variety of sausages and dressings, bread, cheeses, and the choice of tea and beer. Room was found for some of Ehrentraut's close girl friends who joined us for supper. Thereafter we were entertained with several appropriate songs and guitar accompaniment, which

Ehrentraut had sung for many years with the youth group and most of us knew. It certainly helped to make it a particularly cosy family feast.

Time moved on as it always does and the final act was about to begin. With everyone watching, two of Ehrentraut's closest unmarried friends began to remove Ehrentraut's veil. It was then spread out and held high by the other young ladies. Tables were moved to make room and it was time for the traditional custom of bride and groom dancing under the veil, and gradually others who found room joined us.

It all had to end and we knew it. There is only one way traditionally for us Silesians to end an evening, we hold hands and sing the song which says it all, 'Kein schöner Land, no land more beautiful, our Silesia'. It was the time for me and on behalf of my 'Wife' Ehrentraut to thank Mum and Dad and all those who could walk home, those who had transport, those who stayed in hotels, etc. Finally it was also our time, a half hour journey by car, and the hotel locks up by 11.30 p.m. We thanked our parents and Annemarie, her Heinz and my brother Engelbert and "we will see you tomorrow to put the home back to its usual state." A special embrace and 'thank you' to Mum and Dad, and we were on our way. Before I started the car I put my arm round Ehrentraut and congratulated her and all I could say was "Now I can say Ehrentraut, we really are now together, no more letters saying 'with all my good wishes, or how I miss you'. No, we do not need to say goodbye, how wonderful". Time to go. We arrived at the hotel in time and were congratulated and given the time for breakfast.

Ehrentraut and I had long since decided to attend Sunday service at her beloved Youth Centre Church on Woldenberg. It will be her Auf Wiedersehen, but hopefully not forever. It would not have been like us, if we did not stand for a few moments entwined and give thanks for this day and the miracle of having found each other the way we did. Time to say in English "goodnight and God bless!"!"

# Chapter 16

# Our Honeymoon

**Sunday 16th October 1955**

The first day of our married life and how appropriate it being the first day of the week. About to go for breakfast I held Ehrentraut in an embrace. Almost in harmony we congratulated each other and gave thanks that our wedding celebration had satisfied our wishes and our hopes, Ehrentraut's sparkling brown eyes were proof of it all. After breakfast we thanked the hotel staff and paid the bill. We were ready to fulfil our intention by stopping at the Woldenberg Diocesan Youth Centre to say our special thanks at the Sunday morning service which meant so much to Ehrentraut during her premarital life. It could not have been anything other than a very emotional service and blessing for both of us. Congratulations followed from the staff, to whom Ehrentraut was well known. The invitation to call at any time was appreciated by both of us.

We arrived home, just after Mum and Dad had their 'forty winks', to a parental welcome. I made myself useful by setting up for coffee time. Annemarie's Heinz arrived, Gretel and Engelbert came shortly after. Time was spent looking at cards and any presents which had been brought in by the guests. Engelbert and myself spent time to dismantle our well-proven table arrangement to restore our rooms to normality. It all made for a cosy family gathering until Dad called for his and Mum's afternoon naptime herb liqueur. It was really time for bed for all of us, that is I persuaded Ehrentraut to take a half hour sleep, and I am glad she agreed. Engelbert and I spent the time to talk about our parents and the possibilities, and came to the conclusion that it will take its time and agreed to leave Engelbert to deal with it, who will probably achieve more than I could.

Everybody had a good rest and felt refreshed to prepare afternoon coffee which struck a chord with me. I actually felt everyone of us seemed to have succumbed to a mood of slow-down or just a feeling of satisfaction and time to relax. All of us few now savoured the satisfaction that all seemed to have enjoyed the day yesterday. After a lengthy coffee time, Ehrentraut and I made a start to gather some of the presents and put them in some order for packing, especially to take names and addresses of those who had given so we could reply from our 'home'. The rest of Sunday was spent in the circle of our family.

## Monday, 17th October 1955

Engelbert arrived in time for breakfast. Not much time was spent talking since our plan was for the three of us to leave next morning to visit our sister Ursula in Bavaria. Amazing how smoothly the reinstatement of the Krause household took place. A delay for afternoon coffee was accepted gracefully to await the arrival of the workers, Ehrentraut's sister Annemarie, and shortly after her Dad. An equally cosy evening was spent, although Ehrentraut's Mum and Dad were not too happy that we should visit my sister Ursula for two days. Understandably, they wanted to hold on to us for a few more days before we left for Scotland. I myself wanted for Ehrentraut to get to know our sister Ursula, who hoped to meet Ehrentraut. It would also be much appreciated by our parents to know that we did not forget our sister Ursula. We do not know when next we would come for a trip to Germany.

## Tuesday, 18th Wednesday 19th October 1955

Engelbert arrived in time and we were ready to go. With Ehrentraut now beside me and Engelbert in the back seat, we set off for Egglkofen in eastern Bavaria. Having arrived, Ursula welcomed us with tears of joy. It was a very pleasant meeting after two years with each of us feeling it would be a wonderful present for our parents, who would be extremely happy that we had made this first meeting of Ehrentraut with Ursula possible. Ursula led Ehrentraut and me to a widow whose daughter studied with Ursula, a small lady opened the door and made us most welcome. Engelbert too had been accommodated with a pleasant family. We attended evening prayer at the convent and wished each other a goodnight. Next morning we attended church and met with Ursula briefly. We would be able to see Ursula after dinner in the convent. With Engelbert the three of us had a look round the little Bavarian town. After dinner Ehrentraut had to tell Ursula all about our wedding day, which pleased Ursula much. We had to part in good spirits and Ursula was most appreciative to have got to know Ehrentraut and so was Ehrentraut. We had to say 'Auf Wiedersehen' but no doubt there will be other opportunities in future. With good wishes, a wave and a blessing we were on our way north. Engelbert suggested the next small town for us to go for an overnight stay. As we slowed down Engelbert spotted something and as we came to a halt Engelbert went in and soon returned saying here is room. I parked the car and we all fell asleep to be awakened in the morning by the cockerel!

## Thursday, 20th October 1955. Ursula's 27th birthday, happy birthday Ursula.

It was time for us to leave, with breakfast taken and overnight stay paid for, and we were off. After a good run we arrived at Deister Str. by one p.m. Mum was clearly relieved to see us safely returned. Ehrentraut quickly prepared afternoon coffee while I brought in our light luggage. We expected Dad to arrive from work, and Engelbert planned to see Gretel to say goodbye. He planned to go back to Düsseldorf by the evening train. The time had come to thank him for all he had done to help us to make it a splendid 'Fest.' Saying goodbye to him we promised to pray for his continuing effort to get our parents out of our old home in Silesia to join us in the west. Then time for bed, everybody was in need of a good sleep. We bade each other 'goodnight' and silence took over.

## Friday 21st October 1955

Good Morning, Dad off to work, Mum up and busy at her chores cleaning and brushing the staircase and the entrance hall of the house. We were up too and in time to say good morning to Annemarie who was about to leave for work. Ehrentraut actually made the first breakfast for the two of us and had fun at the thought. First thing we had to do was pack the trunk in order that we could have it ready to be brought to the shipping agents in the afternoon. It was easy to fill since there was no glass involved. That, we will take in the car. I am no 'apprentice' in that line, just bring me the stuff and Ehrentraut was soon surprised what could all fit into the trunk. Two hours was sufficient to fill and close the trunk. Clever Ehrentraut had taken a note of all that went in. When Dad comes home for lunch we will take the trunk down to the car. Then Ehrentraut and I will bring it to the shipping company in the afternoon, which we did. The shipping agents certainly knew what they were doing and assured us the trunk will arrive within ten days. Also after dinner we started collecting and sorting out all our things to make packing easier. It was now relatively simple to pack since it all went into our car. Ehrentraut had already done a lot of ground work to make it easy for us to pack everything as practically as possible.

"My goodness Ehrentraut what a lot you must have purchased already. Now adding all the useful gifts people brought to the wedding". Annemarie arrived from her work while we had to call at the office to ensure our papers were there and all correct, and so they were. Thank goodness for that. "You certainly did a lot of spade-work my Ehrentraut, my Love." A good collection of cardboard boxes are also to hand. Slowly we all notice that the first few cupboards and shelves are being robbed, i.e. becoming empty. I began to feel deeply humbled by my small contribution to bring into our home. By late afternoon a lot had been sorted and laid aside to be brought to the car. We can load most of it tomorrow. Annemarie came up with a wise suggestion namely to park the laden car at Heinz's house where it would be certainly safer. Heinz will be up later, Annemarie thought. At suppertime Ehrentraut thought it wise to go on Sunday afternoon to say our 'Auf Wiedersehen' to Oma, Uncle Paul and Aunt Lenchen. General approval, with that it was goodnight, and thanks to and for all. We did our duty and called at the office to check all the papers were correct, and after a good inspection we were handed back our papers and were wished a happy future, and would we visit Hameln again? Yes, indeed we would.

**Saturday, 22nd October 1955**

I woke up and noticed Ehrentraut was already busy making breakfast. Dad was up, everybody was up apart from me. I had a peaceful sleep without worrying about anything. Probably overtired. After breakfast Ehrentraut and I had a talk regarding what else should we take with us that will not be available in the UK, how about poppy seed for baking? Yes, I'll write it down with the others. It is the last shopping day. We need something for Ella and David, and what about Mrs Sellar? I have that already my husband, we can use my German Marks which I will not need any more. Ehrentraut has a list, we have to go, oh and something for Monday morning for the journey. We do not need anything expensive. There are plenty bottles of our presents we can take. Some can be left for Dad. With a moment empty of thoughts, I just realised how little I had to offer Ehrentraut as my contribution, apart from a sparsely furnished cottage. Foolish of me to have spent so much from my wages on cars. Too late for regrets. Hopefully, I may be given more chances, since I neither smoke nor drink. Stop dreaming, my good husband, time to come down to earth, we have to go to town to be back for dinner. "How pleasant Ehrentraut it is to walk beside you shopping. I could not have imagined, especially as my wife. I like it when we meet someone you know and you have to explain who I am. I look forward going shopping with you in Tain." Ehrentraut had it already planned to pop in at her shop to say 'goodbye' and both of us to thank them for their gift. That we did and soon it was time to make for home. We were repeatedly wished all the best on our way through town. We had our reply "Come and see us in Schottland". There is much to see in the Rat Catcher town which we will have to see every time we come to visit Mum and Dad. We arrived just in time for lunch. Being Saturday it was pleasant all of us together enjoying lunch. I could not resist remarking that however much we would like to welcome any visitors, please give us a year to bring our cottage to a civilised standard. After a truly family lunch, something pleasant to take to Schottland for all of us to remember. We all found somewhere to have an afternoon nap, which even I had to submit to this time on the sofa, too much excitement these days. I was up before the others which reminded me that I wanted to go down and check the car for oil, tyres, etc., to be ready for Monday morning. I arrived back up, for me on the fourth floor, all was ready for afternoon coffee with everybody together, even Annemarie's Heinz arrived in time.

No rest for those who want to build a home for themselves, there was still a good bit to do. If it was not for Ehrentraut having done the ground work, we'd have much more to do. Not exaggerating, but Ehrentraut's ability to organise and command, I marvel at her. Her work in the Youth Leadership is another proven skill. That caused me to wonder, just what might be possible with her at my side? I do have certain dreams as yet locked away. Time seems to quicken, Ehrentraut and I trying to get through the loft to check what is still ours or should be down in the flat. Anything for us placed in a special box. As we go from place to place we seem to have everything that should come with us. Anything that is not required on our journey, can go down to the car right away. Our aim was to have the evening for all of us together. And that was what we achieved after a light supper, just family sitting together with everyone having something to say. Recalling many interesting, happy, funny events, stories and experiences, many from the past. Did we miss the dancing? Not in the close circle of friends and loved ones. Will we ever meet in such a circle and atmosphere? The few small glasses of liqueur we have toasted to each other here at home made us realise it was time to wish each other goodnight.

## Sunday 23rd October 1955

It had been decided we would go to the ten o'clock Mass since that would be the main service when I could hear some good organ music. Also we would meet with many more relatives and friends of

Ehrentraut and family. For Ehrentraut and me attending this service, had a far greater impact on our soul than I could describe. We will leave it at that.

As Ehrentraut assumed after the service there was a large group of well-wishers who knew we would not see each other for some time. I have to admit, this was a moment when I myself had a flashing thought of would we not be happy here? Thank goodness it was just a flash, but it was there. At last the final handshake with a shout to Grandma we'll call in the afternoon. Home to prepare lunch, set up the table and I had a good talk with Dad. Now was the chance to explain what my plans are to bring the cottage up to date. The cottage itself is only six years old. Dad was somewhat inquisitive with my interest in doing certain joinery and masonry work myself. He could only express caution, and there was the call for lunch. "Well, Ehrentraut my treasure, who will cook next Sunday?"

We all rested half an hour or more and Ehrentraut and I got ready to say our goodbyes. Uncle Paul and Aunt Lehnchen, thanking him for the many times he repaired Ehrentraut's bicycle and other useful help so often. Then on to Grandma and Aunt Martha, telling them we will come and visit them again. Time to get back home and while there was time we began to fold and pack our Sunday clothes and put on what we will wear on our journey. We managed to pack some more before supper and I took so much down to the car. There is now very little left, as long as we do not forget in the morning the food we cannot get in Schottland. The call for supper and with Annemarie's friend Heinz our last meal tasted better than ever. The rest of the evening passed quickly and we were all ready to go to sleep. Yes, we will rise with Dad that will allow us to get off in good time.

## Monday 24th October 1955

There is no need to repeat what everyone does when you are about to go on a journey. We had breakfast with Dad and Mum, who will get on with her daily morning work. Annemarie is ready too. It was now time to say our goodbyes, no tears anywhere. Annemarie and Dad gone, I started to bring our last cases down, with Ehrentraut packing our food for the road. I climb the stairs for the last time, the 'stairs' I first climbed, the four storey staircase ten months ago, when first Ehrentraut and I looked into each other's eyes for real, no more on photographs only. Now, a warm hug from Mum and one more thanks for giving me her wonderful daughter Ehrentraut, I shall try to look after her as well as you did. And a final Auf Wiedersehen, see you in Schottland soon. I made my way down with the last case while Ehrentraut and Mum followed. In the opened door it was Ehrentraut's turn to say goodbye to her Mum who came down to see us off, a last wave and we were off, soon out of sight. Out of town I clasped Ehrentraut's hand asking "are you happy?" "Yes my husband!" I was very happy. We were off to the port of Hook of Holland.

We arrived punctually, with time to spare for unforeseen possibilities. Hoisting cars onto the ferry had started. After our lengthy correspondences, Ehrentraut and I kept looking at each other as I took her hand walking up the stair to board the ferry boat. As we stepped on to the deck, Ehrentraut expressed her thoughts while looking at me, "My dearest Paul how wonderful, I suppose we are on our 'love boat' that will bring us across the ocean to our own home, do you feel that way?" "Yes I do, but I also thought about finding our house a little cold when we get home?" I thought about our home not having modern central heating. "Then we will have to be closer together, won't we!" Yes, I had already learned that's the practical Ehrentraut. We found our cabin and both of us needed some sleep. Before I fell asleep my mind had already taken leave from Germany and Ehrentraut's home and thoughts were freely roaming about our cottage, and all the needs that are awaiting me, no now us.

We have crossed the sea in comfort, and now the drive to London where we deliver our hire car and change into our new Ford van. It is the first move to have transport, in order to get my material from the trades-shop for me to work with on our cottage, our home. With the late evening it was not too difficult for me to find my way to that garage to deliver the car and hopefully the new van was delivered for us to change our luggage from the car to the van. I was relieved when everything worked to plan. "Now Ehrentraut, the important thing is, although there is a heater in the van, you must have a blanket wrapped round you, please do that for me, as I believe I was born to care for you." Ehrentraut answered something sweet. Papers in order and we were off on the main road east and north to Scotland.

With Ehrentraut at my side now, it was a new and very pleasant experience. Within the hour Ehrentraut fell asleep, thank goodness, knowing she was wrapped up and warm. She must have slept for well over two hours when dawn broke. The journey gave us the opportunity for a whole day to talk uninterrupted, a mixture of the past, and especially what should be done for our first 'Home'. I was glad that Ehrentraut was able to fall asleep occasionally. It was my hope that after all the sleep she had lost these last two weeks, hopefully she would relax and catch up on sleep. In the early afternoon, about half way, I too had a good one hour's sleep.

After three breaks and sunset, and happy talk which we found so wonderful, we were nearing Inverness and then it's only one hour to Tain and home. "I can tell you where to go now, Paul." A left turn and we drove the last mile home to Viewfield. There in front was our cottage lit up by the head lights. I felt Ehrentraut's arm around my shoulder. A left turn and within a minute we knocked at my, now our adopted home, which I will exchange for our cottage. It was past suppertime and were greeted with joy by Ella and David who congratulated us and bid us take a seat. Ella prepared a cup of tea and her famous scones and our home made butter. Soon it was obvious to David and Ella that we were now really tired. I took our key and we said goodnight, and they will see us in the morning. I took the can of fuel for the oil stove to heat up the room. One other heater would warm up the bedroom. Unlocking the cold cottage without the flick of an electric light, I led Ehrentraut into the cold dark cottage with its cold sitting-cum-dining room and a cold bedroom. No, I did not carry Ehrentraut across the threshold for fear I might just trip over! Another time when it's light for sure! I first had to strike a match to light the table oil-lamp. My disappointment could not be hidden, otherwise Ehrentraut would not have put her arms round me saying "You said it is our cottage and home at Viewfield, so let us be and work as pioneers of old". It was not until next morning, when I got up that I really felt the pain of what sort of a home I had presented to Ehrentraut.

## Chapter 17

# Home at last ---
# our life together has begun

David had insisted the previous night that I rest after the long journey and that he would see to the morning milking. That allowed us a longer rest in the morning which we both made use of. I had to admit it was a long tiring drive home. On getting up I lit the heaters which actually warm the room relatively quickly. I had already been over to the farm to fetch the water. Ehrentraut began to prepare our first breakfast in our marriage and our own home. First I had to wash the newly bought dishes Ehrentraut had intended to use to cook the dinner. We had a good selection of food brought with us from Germany, it would help to make it more pleasant to change from German to Scottish provisions. Ehrentraut will have to get used to the soft British bread in place of the German rye bread. The aroma of cooking soon filled the room, and I reached for the camera to have a record of Ehrentraut having cooked her first meal for a family of two, wonderful! While I would clear up and wash the dishes, I had to insist Ehrentraut go for a rest. After a short rest I continued to bring all our goods from the car into the cottage. We will have ample time to place them around our new home. In due course Ehrentraut had awakened from a well-earned rest. It was my pleasure to make the coffee while Ehrentraut fished out the container where the left-over wedding cakes were, with which dear Mum had filled the box to the brim. This then was our first afternoon coffee time in our home, how wonderful as we looked into each other's eyes. For supper we had the loaf and rolls, as well as other goodies that Ella had bought for our arrival. For me it was milking time while I left Ehrentraut to potter around trying to find things that were needed. Ella reminded me that we were to come over for a chat after supper. On my way back to our cottage I had to fetch water from the well at the farm in two pails - almost a hundred yards each way. I had already purchased a closed water-container with a spout at its base. That will make it more comfortable to fill kettle and pans. There was a moment when Ehrentraut in the midst of what she was doing turned and flung her arms round me, "I'm happy Paul, let's be joyous, the Lord is good to us." Something strange for me, and over-powering for such a gesture.

For Ehrentraut it was a time to experience what our great grandparents had to do. As promised we both went to the farmhouse for a chat with Ella and David. We sat as usual in the warm kitchen. David for most of the time took part in the conversations. Ella made the tea and David asked for understanding that the long-promised completion of running water and electricity had not yet been done. Both were hoping that Ehrentraut will be happy here and would she come over if there was any need for something. Both were happy for Ehrentraut to use the house as I had. That was the kindest thing Ella could have said to Ehrentraut. Ella had already said that she would be happy to give Ehrentraut a lift to do her shopping and would go with Ehrentraut to pick mushrooms of which there are some ready. It was time for us to go, with Ehrentraut proudly saying "goodnight", and for me it will be the old routine. I had to light the oil stove in the bedroom to warm up the room, but it would not be left on overnight. The house had been empty for three months. As the evening before, we both watched for a few minutes the lighthouse lights flashing in our bedroom window, it fascinated Ehrentraut, and I was happy to join, folding my arms round her, and I began to wonder, will I be able to prove to her my worth?

Ehrentraut had no intention other than to fulfil her divine birth-right to be spouse and mother. True to her name, Ehren-honour, traut-trust, as many will discover in years to come. The iron and horsehair bed was not the 'Slumberland' of a German bed. Wednesday, was our first full working day. We had discussed and put in order our morning routines, which Ehrentraut was happy to follow. I would leave home at seven to do the milking and all that has to be done with it, in order that David would have the milk pails ready for the Mansfield crew and the eight o'clock start. David will discuss the order of the day with Jim the foreman and the others. I will then go for my breakfast. Walking to the cottage this first day with a pail of water in one hand, and two litres of milk in the other, I noticed the curtains had been drawn, and behind the glass, a hand was almost frantically waving. I was overcome with such a feeling of joy that I had not experienced before!

"I slept very well, no wonder, these last two weeks were tiring, oh Paul, is it going to be like this every day that I will see you coming from the farm, if I am up, with a pail of water in one hand and fresh milk in the other? I remember ten years ago when Mum crossed our small farmyard to bring the milk for us. Next day we had to flee in a hurry from the Russian front, leaving everything behind, never to return. It is good to be reminded, how good we have it here. I do not need a rich man, I am happy to build a home, with you at my side". These were the most encouraging words for me to hear from Ehrentraut. I have to snap out of my despondency and rebuild my confidence that I can do better. With Ehrentraut's encouragement, there should be no stopping us. "Ehrentraut, from tomorrow I will make my daily Scottish 'brose', a kind of porridge. Ehrentraut you make your normal 'Haferflocken' oat-flakes, the way we made it at home, try and find out which will suit you best. We are here as you already said, blissfully on our own, surrounded by nature. You do not have to get up for me, you need your rest after such a busy year. I can only hope it will not be too quiet for you, see you later."

My work is already laid out as usual at Viewfield or when and where an extra hand is needed. As more lambs put on weight they will go to the sales. More potatoes for the English are to be prepared and taken to the station to be sent wherever. As we go towards the end of November a pit of turnips will be prepared in case of a spate of frost later. Cattle will come inside near the end of November or early December. Threshing corn will also begin next month to bring in the straw for bedding the animals, and the corn to feed them. A certain amount of ploughing will be done, as long as the ground is in a condition to allow the tractors to operate without bogging down out of sight in the mud. Here ends my Viewfield farm report. Like many other trades, or life itself, it lives on in annual repetition.

As agreed, after lunch we drove down to the High Street to see the furniture shop. I was known to the owner and introduced Ehrentraut to him as my wife and the handshake of congratulation followed. Ehrentraut examined with a knowledgeable eye the bedroom suite and approved it as suitable for us. A deal was signed and delivery within the week. We drove home and turning into the farm road, I let Ehrentraut out to walk the twenty yards home, pleading to have an afternoon nap after all the hassle and work. I garaged the car and went off to my work. When I arrived home a pair of arms were flung round my neck, with a kiss and a voice saying "we have begun to build our home." Yes we did. Ehrentraut did go down to the town in the afternoon with Ella in the car to look into the mushroom hut to see if there was anything ready to pick. As soon as Ella opened the door, Ehrentraut apparently let out a soft yell at the number of mushrooms they had to pick. Ella had a bag for Ehrentraut to fill for herself. Then Ehrentraut and Ella picked the rest. Ella took a few, and the remainder were for the shop. Ella had arranged for Ehrentraut to go with her to show the grocer who buys them from us. She certainly enjoyed the time spent with Ella. What a welcome I received later from Ehrentraut, when I came home. She was truly excited to tell me about her picking our mushrooms, and calling with Ella at the shop. "Look this is the money we made for ourselves from the mushrooms, and guess what's for supper?" What a joy to come home and find my wife in such a happy form. Ehrentraut enjoyed accompanying Ella on her shopping trip, that way people will soon put matters together and will know, 'oh that is Paul's wife'! How pleasant to find my wife so happy on my coming home from work. It pleased me to hear Ehrentraut telling me all that in such a happy disposition. So one full day so far with breakfast, lunch and supper provided by my wife, Ehrentraut.

Two days later Ehrentraut called on Mrs Sellar for a cup of coffee before venturing to do some shopping with Trudi, as Mrs Sellar preferred to be addressed. Trudi introduced Ehrentraut to other shops she had not seen with Ella. Ehrentraut had insisted that she would walk the mile up to Viewfield with the small purchases, no need for me to pick her up. What a welcome as I entered the kitchen. "Paul, you never told me that all the people I met know you, they call me 'Mrs Paul', I'll be happy with that, and I will soon find my own way in town." Getting to know Ehrentraut, she will be determined to go on her own soon. As she said, "I can see and I can point, that is a good start, and I want to learn English to talk like Ella," who is happy to take Ehrentraut shopping in the car and bring her home instead of walking home with the messages.

Within the week, our bedroom suite was delivered. We had already chosen a carpet for the bedroom which now makes the room like a normal bedroom and relatively warmer. I should add there is a fireplace of course. That is what Ehrentraut had to get used to. I had already provided a draught-proofing timber frame cover to put before the fire place, it made such a difference. There are the occasional second hand auctions in town where bargains are to be had, of all sorts of good useful items. It was vital that I lit a fire in the living room where we will spend the most time. For the kitchen, I already have a small oil heater to make sure Ehrentraut has the necessary comfort. Taking a walk, she might see me in any of the fields, or working at sheep about the farm. Ehrentraut thought to assure me this would certainly prevent any threat of homesickness. Ella asked us to come over after supper any evening for a chat and let Ehrentraut learn to say a few words in English, which I knew Ehrentraut would love doing. Ehrentraut is certainly not word-shy and will try to speak without invitation in order to learn the language, regardless of mistakes. Her German shop assistant training was an incentive to talk. "My dearest Paul, with all the excitement to 'build' our home, how can we be homesick with so much of our own? See you for supper." That is Ehrentraut, I begin to understand her better, hearing her talk is like reading her many letters again. Thank goodness we both kept our letters safe for posterity.

What had been lacking at the cottage was an inside toilet and bathroom. A drawing of mine convinced David that I could build one with bricks and mortar, according to the local authority's satisfaction. As an attachment at the gable end of the cottage, the entrance was from a passage within the cottage. David was happy if I was willing and all the materials needed would naturally be paid by David. I had a free hand and with David's confidence the whole project was complete. Yes, I was proud when I told Ehrentraut I did it. A young farm worker of ours helped me in the evenings and Saturdays. My enthusiasm knew no barrier. I have on my previous visit to Germany purchased important tools for joinery and masonry, and very good books on both trades.

Our next priority was closing the open fire in the living-room, and replacing it with a free standing modern enamelled closed fire, to prevent the heat escaping up the chimney. David was happy to pay for the stove and any material required. By Christmas that too was in place and allowed us a comfortable happy first Christmas. These were the items I worried most to be in place. Ehrentraut could now leave the kitchen-sitting room door open, to allow some of the warm air from the sitting room enter into the kitchen. The heat from the new fire-stove exceeded our expectations.

Ehrentraut and I were both happy to have had all that for the time being to celebrate our first Christmas together as husband and wife, the core of a family. Yes, there was lots of baking going on with both of us having some experience. Christmas mail was criss-crossing the water, and there was a parcel or two going both ways. We had an excellent Christmas meal at Viewfield, cooked by Ella for the four of us, Ehrentraut, Ella, David and myself.

The most welcome Christmas present was the confirmation of the laying of the electric cable early in the new year, it will be an overhead cable into house and farm buildings. To our surprise three months later Viewfield farm and cottage had electric power and tap water. Celebrations, we certainly did, without going over the top. Ehrentraut with her happiness to have me work at the cottage for our benefit, gave me immense pleasure and encouragement for more. No longer was I doing things for myself. I hasten to add, it does not belittle the joy I felt to do things for David and Ella, who always showed their appreciation. So, what next? The enlargement of our woodshed. Having asked David, he had no objection to my enlarging the timber shed to whatever size I wanted. That was another appreciated kindness. Ehrentraut also had a brilliant idea, how about keeping a few chickens in it as well? The very idea. All I need is drive to town to the sawmill where they know me, and was offered off-cuts for a small sum. It was my new building project, and it paid off. Well, talk about 'pioneering', Ehrentraut, who never wanting to marry a farmer, now began to notice a small amount of money could be made with chickens. What followed soon was Ehrentraut letting me know she could manage the picking and selling of our mushrooms. It was Ella, who one day after shopping with Ehrentraut warned me, that I might well have married someone who will be the 'accountant' in the family. A continuation of her place of birth. Her Dad can be proud when they will surely visit us sometime soon. We are now half a year married, For the moment Ehrentraut felt she was not yet ready to learn to drive. I put it to her that once she could master the car she could drive down to the mushroom shed and leave the car there, do the shopping and three quarters of the journey she does not have to walk. It worked a treat. Our road was not classified at that time. It had the effect that Ehrentraut could without pressure learn to drive, reverse and operate the configuration of clutch, gears, and brakes. In time, she passed her test with satisfaction.

Well before the end of our first year I discovered Ehrentraut's true righteousness in all matters of life. The word 'lie' is not in her vocabulary. When she says "I love you" she means it. Ehrentraut was certainly setting out a high standard in our married life. It meant we had a guide-line set before our married life. I soon discovered I married a ready-made accountant. The result of that was her ability to establish within the year a personal rapport with the staff and Mr Fraser the Manager of the North of Scotland Bank, of which we became a customer. More, Ehrentraut simply threw herself into her destined role as wife and mother, and who always found flowers to grace our window-sills.

Within the year on July 24th 1956, by the grace of God her wish was granted, when she presented us with Andreas our first child and son. How happy we were. A real family had been established.

A carry-cot and a pram was now required, while there are still sunny and warm days to come. I was fully aware that I would be required to help wherever there was a need. Ella took walks over to the cottage to offer any help, at the same time inviting Ehrentraut to walk over to Ella as often as she liked. One could not get fresher and cleaner air than up here in Viewfield. Absolutely free from cars and any smoky air. It was my duty to inform our parents, brother and sisters, as well as our close friends. I really enjoyed writing that notification, was it wrong of me to feel proud? Of course there was the registration and the important Baptism. That was probably the hardest for my parents not to be able to just take a train to visit their first grandchild. However, one of Ehrentraut's best youth group friends Malve, who studied in Cambridge and was fluent in English, asked if it was alright for her to come over for a week? We answered saying yes, she was most welcome, and arrived not long after. Just a year in Scotland for Ehrentraut and we already had a visitor. I was delighted for Ehrentraut to have one of her best friends to come so soon to visit us. On the Sunday we took the car for an outing across the river and had afternoon coffee with our son Andreas on his best behaviour. A photograph shows Ehrentraut, her friend Malve and our Andreas in a most joyful disposition in brilliant sunshine. Malve could then report assuring my in-laws at home that we were not living at the end of the world. Malve has become the most frequent visitor from Germany to this day.

Our joy was complete when Ehrentraut's parents decided to follow our invitation to come and see their first grandchild in Scotland. Within six weeks, the three of us welcomed them at Inverness station. I was delighted for Ehrentraut to have her parents to see where we lived, and how a lovely place it is for children to grow up - these were actually Ehrentraut's words. It was good to have heard them say how pleasant was the air, the quietness, and what a view. For my mother-in-law it really was a wonderful relaxing time to spend with, and watch her elder daughter enjoying being the young mother. With Ehrentraut's parents now Grandma and Granddad {Opa} for the first time, I had great pleasure to take photographs with their first grandchild. Opa had ample opportunities to see Scottish farming at close hand. It surprised him how well grass, oats and barley grew, the barley mainly for whisky production. Granddad soon discovered just how many distilleries there were around us. Alas, there always is a time for leaving, but there was a promise of more visits to follow.

Other good news arrived with a letter from brother Engelbert. After five years of persistent badgering, Engelbert finally succeeded to bring our parents out from Poland! According to Engelbert, a small case filled with western cigarettes, several packs of German razor blades, and a few German hard currency Marks, and making good use of his limited Polish words, had the government official sign and hand Engelbert the important documents needed. The fact that only one person in the office dealt with Engelbert, was opportune. That's when the important papers were signed and Engelbert was at last free to bring our parents from our old homeland Silesia to West Germany. At his local town office Engelbert had already received the official residence permit for our parents, and the accommodation prepared for our parents to move into. Our sister Ursula, myself and Ehrentraut, owed Engelbert our deepest thanks.

In August 1957 the expected arrival of our second child was due at any day, and that it did on the 30$^{th}$. Within the week Ehrentraut presented us with another healthy son whom we baptised Marcus, {Roman emperor and Philosopher}, and it suited him. As Marcus began to crawl and run, it proved again how fortunate Viewfield was for boisterous boys to grow up. Once a day the post van and only the odd car, made them learn that care had still to be taken. By the time Marcus began to walk his best friend Andreas his elder brother, took him for a walk over to the farm to visit Ella, now of course Aunty Ella, who was never found short of sweets, biscuits or other goodies to come home with. Never forgotten was a peep at the animals in their stalls, and always accompanied by Ella. With the enlarged family our thoughts began to concentrate on a possible future. The question of a larger requirement for living-space was beginning to occupy our thoughts. It was natural that the onus was on me, something I could not burden on Ehrentraut. The no-longer secret desire of building our own house, was an ever recurring thought. Throughout 1958 in my spare time I had already drawn my own vision of a suitable home for us. There is a former German POW mason, who does work around our area. I had already met him and an interesting talk was worthwhile, at least it stimulated interest for a future meeting.

And then there we were in 1959, thirteen years in Scotland and working in Viewfield. After a reasonable winter, with little snow to sledge with our boys and Ehrentraut, I found time in the evenings to start attending to our and Ella's garden. All our spring time work was almost completed. This year, I had insisted to take on all the lambing work, and found David not resisting. It gave David time to see that the season's work was done. As usual there were some orphan lambs and a couple of breech births which I was able to put right without calling on the vet. It is always a satisfactory feeling with mother and lamb safe and well to run around within a day or two. At home at the end of May, we started to look forward and prepare for Ehrentraut's parents to visit us again, and admire their second grandchild. On the first of June I met my parents-in-law at the Inverness station in good spirits and happy that all went well on their journey. We arrived home to a great welcome with both boys too young to understand who the visitors were. I was feeling happy for Ehrentraut to welcome her parents once more. All of us were looking forward to a happy holiday time. Dad soon found his way around again and made himself useful in the cottage and the garden.

Within a few days after my in-laws' arrival, I returned from the field to attend to my evening jobs, milking, feeding, etc. As I turned into our yard and came off my bike I knew right away something was not right. Seeing Ella standing still against the shed door with no smile, I asked what's wrong while our two boys run around oblivious to what was going on. "I broke my leg, that is how it feels". "Come on, put your arm round my neck and shoulder, I can carry you, without putting your weight on your broken foot". I brought a comfortable chair from the sitting room, and the small stool to rest her leg. I then phoned the doctor and her brother Jack from down the town. I ran over to Ehrentraut to ask if she could come over to stay with Ella until the doctor came. I brought the boys over to Grandma to play with them.

David had arrived before the doctor and was glad I was at hand. I did all my evening jobs including the separator and all the cleaning and washing as normal. In time the doctor and ambulance arrived to take Ella to the hospital at Inverness. David would get his dinner at his brother Jack down in town. I will ensure he will have everything for his breakfast and supper. Having seen Ella off after giving me the necessary instructions, I told David I will be back later, which I did. At home in our cottage we had a cosy relaxing evening, hearing the latest how things are in Hameln the 'Rat Catcher town' which was of much interest for Ehrentraut. We do not need long evenings since we are all day close, and having our meals together. God willing we shall see everyone in the morning. I will be a bit earlier, to make sure David is alright and I will do Ella's work, the dishes and poultry feed and collecting the eggs, Ella insisting I take sufficient eggs for us in the cottage. In the morning I had everything ready for David to take the milk to the Mansfield crew and give me my orders for the day. David and I may stamp the 'V' sign on the sheep, 'V' for Viewfield, not victory.

We all hoped that all will go well with Ella and the doctor will ensure her foot will knit together to be as good as new. This situation was not new, since on a previous occasion Ella was happy that she could visit and stay with her sick sister without any worries with my being at home alone in Viewfield. The tidiness of Viewfield house is not in question, neither kitchen, dairy, hall or bathroom, neither windows nor washing, while Ella is in hospital. I have long learned from Ella to make wholemeal girdle scones which we always had for breakfast, so David was not deprived of them while Ella has been away.

On the following Saturday David drove north across the firth to attend the wedding of his niece, a daughter of his elder brother. Ella had insisted that he should go for her, Ella's sake. Ella was sure that I would make certain that David's dress would be respectable, and would not forget to polish his shoes, and I washed and polished his car the day before. On Saturday mid-morning I was at hand to help should David ask, yes his suit was in order. David did not wear a kilt. I waited to make sure he was ready to go, him knowing I would take the Land Rover to take a look that all was well around the farm. David started his car and I waved him off, and so did he. This being Saturday, I had so much more time to be with Grandma and Granddad and the children. It was a pleasant day for all of us. Granddad and the boys came over to the farm for the evening milking. With the two cows being out now in the paddock the boys had fun to drive the cows into their stalls. I wondered whether he missed his farm, but he said no. In the dairy room, the boys were fascinated seeing the milk come out of the two tubes. I could see Granddad enjoying seeing the children being interested. Having cleaned and washed everything, making sure all is in the right place, we locked the back door and left the key in the right place for David when he came home.

While the boys ran ahead home, Granddad and I followed the waft of a tasty supper. Welcomed by my wife Ehrentraut and Grandma, I changed out of my working clothes and washed my hands and those of our boys. The call came to take our seats and grace was said. We men and boys watched what was coming on the table, and it was very good. While the ladies cleared the table, Granddad tried to amuse the boys while I did the washing up. We had one whole hour to play with the children before it was bedtime for small children. Tired as they were they fell asleep in next to no time, while the elders had a good time talking about us here, and listening to hear how it is at home in Hameln, especially Grandma and Annemarie and her boyfriend Heinz. Ehrentraut suggested we should buy some cards to send them. It was time for us to raise a small glass and bid each other goodnight, and retired to a sound sleep. With it being Sunday in the morning, I could stretch my morning 'get up' to half an hour later, and all others even longer.

There is a German saying, so often proved true 'man proposes, God disposes'. I never thought I would be the one to whom it would come true. My alarm clock rang then set on silent, I got out of bed, dressed and made my way over to Viewfield to fetch the pail to get on with the milking. For the first time since we lived in the cottage, I found the back door locked. I knocked at the door first, then rang the bell. With no answer I assumed David had forgotten to unlock the door and not hearing well had not heard my knock or the bell. I knew he had arrived home from the wedding, since from our cottage we had seen David garaging his car before the sun had set the previous evening.

I did the obvious and went into the garden to look through the kitchen window and to knock on it. With no movement to be seen I went close to the glass and could not see David nor any breakfast dishes. That was when I began to think David might not be too well after the wedding, although I was sure he would not have drunk any alcohol. That was the moment when I knew I had to go in. The kitchen window was over three feet in height, with the lower half as a separate section, which I could lift up and keep in place supported with a piece of wood. My agility was tested since I had to negotiate myself over the sink. Standing up, I suddenly found the silence slightly uncomfortable with David not calling me.

I made my way up to David's bedroom and only the slightest turn towards his bed made me realise David had passed away in his sleep. I touched his face and hands, which had already cooled down, evident he passed in his sleep without pain, as he lay with his face serene and absolutely in peace, as if asleep. Automatically I said my short prayer over those who departed from us.

Since there was nothing anybody could do I decided to do the milking and attend to the chores that could be done within an hour. That would leave the house in peace until the evening attention. I then phoned David's brother Jack, he was shocked and thanked me for what I'd done so far. I took the milk pails down to Mansfield for Jim and Peter and brought the sad news. I then asked Jim if he would take a look round at the cattle in the field. I turned the Land Rover round and parked it at home and then made my way to see Ehrentraut, Mum, and Dad to tell them the reason I was late. Although we had been given some warning a while ago, it was still a surprise that it was so soon.

We all got ready to drive to Invergordon to attend Sunday service, that day we had a special reason. We met with our parishioner friends and many recognised and welcomed the grandparents. It was a lovely summer's day and the countryside looked enticing to have a run in the car in the afternoon. But first we had to provide a Sunday lunch at which I offered my help. The presence of Mum and Dad was a welcome blessing, especially with the boys being able to do and enjoy being with their Opa, Granddad. We needed a little time to face the shock of David's death. A good reason for us to take a run to the lighthouse which the boys love to see and run around. Home for afternoon coffee and time for me to go and see Ella in the hospital. She sat up as I walked in and stretched her arm to embrace me for a while. "Oh Paul, is that another reason why you were sent to us?" Ella wanted to know the details of this morning and was so happy to hear that David passed so peacefully without pains and in his own bed, when he could have so easily fallen and lay all night. Ella's ankle was mending well, but she was not yet ready to come home. I offered Ella the condolences of the few we met today especially our family. Ella wanted to know how the boys, Grandma and Granddad were, and how fortunate to be here at this time, when I would be needed more. Before leaving, Ella had a note of matters for me to see to. I wished her well and made my way home. I arrived safely to a cosy home and reported how Ella was and wished all well. I played with the boys until it was time for bed. We spent a pleasant evening and all were happy to hear that Ella took it all calmly and was looking forward to coming home when the doctor says so.

It was bedtime and we all hoped for a good night's rest, but I was not to escape a few moments' thought of the future for me. On Monday morning, I made my way across to do my daily routine. Unlocking the back door I first looked into the dining room where David lay at peace, and opened the window. A glance into the empty cool kitchen, it was what it would be like until Ella returned from hospital. The farm would function as usual and animals needed to be seen to. That applied to my daily routine, and on completion I had my breakfast. Jack called to pick up the milk for the Mansfield staff. As expected, Jack was happy for me to continue in the established routine, joining the others when and where needed.

The funeral took place on Wednesday late morning from Viewfield. A large number was expected and did so. It was a summer's day and a service was held outside for all to take part in. Ella asked for a chair to be placed outside to which I led her, and wanted me to stand beside her. Ehrentraut's Dad said it looked as if I was Ella's son. At the cemetery I was allocated a cord, which I appreciated.

Having laid David to rest, Ella was discharged from hospital and was looked after by her brother Jack and his wife at their home in town. We were invited to visit Ella anytime. Within a few days it was time to bring Mum and Dad to the station on their way back home, with our best wishes and until the next time. After two weeks Ella felt secure to come home. She knew I would see her in the morning and at other times during the day, and so of course did Ehrentraut. With Jack in charge normality took over and an amiable working together developed to everyone's satisfaction.

There was no question that I would go in the evening to see that the animals were settled and at the same time had a last cup of tea with Ella. It was on one such occasion when Ella mentioned that the family will soon have a meeting to discuss what is to be done regarding the farm and the best for Ella.

After ten years living and eating in the same house, there was never any doubt in David and Ella's mind regarding my confidentiality in discussions of privacy. Therefore it was no surprise Ella informed me of the solicitor's advice that considering Ella's age, it might be best to consider selling, taking into account no other member of the family was interested in taking on Viewfield and Mansfield. The solicitor's suggestion was not to hurry if there was no reason, considering the potential of the farm being located so close to town. The solicitor's suggestion was a three year time of waiting, during which a thorough evaluation would provide the necessary attraction to bid and buy. "Well Paul, I like the idea of a three year wait, to think about this. I wanted you to know in good time, I know you believe in providence, I want you and Ehrentraut to know I am with you on this." Such consideration was worth so much to me. The questions were, would I like to work on another farm, or would another owner even require or have me? At least we have a three year period in which to think about our future, with Ehrentraut and her willingness to save for our future, I already had a precious jewel.

After our evening meal and with the boys asleep, Ehrentraut and I sat down so I could tell her about my conversation with Ella. Jack would be manager and my 'position' at Viewfield would be as it had been for the previous ten years. Jack would depend on my knowledge and advise our foreman Jim at Mansfield. Ehrentraut was pleased and happy to hear what Ella had said. It is most likely that Ella might say something to Ehrentraut when she goes over in the morning to see what Ella might require. Ella had found a new entertainment when the boys knock and walk into the kitchen. I have since long discovered how 'youthful' Ella is enjoying taking the boys to feed the poultry and especially the young newly hatched chickens.

Ehrentraut guessed rightly that I would broach the subject of a larger home for us, preferably our own build. Ehrentraut recognised the need, but could not visualize the possibility. It was understood that we would confide our intention to Ella at the first opportunity. That I did next day at my evening call, assuring her that it would not affect my work at Viewfield. Ella understood and added her encouragement. Ehrentraut and I appreciated Ella's understanding and encouragement.

I had already trawled through the weekly County Journal and found the following advert 'For sale, cottage, kitchen and sitting-room with bedroom in attic.' Our conversation with Ehrentraut came to a close with me going to have a look at it the next day after work. It was time for me to go over to see all was well with Ella, and talking over a cup of tea I asked if there was anything I could do and wished Ella a goodnight. On my way home, I checked my animals and on arrival home, Ehrentraut was already asleep.

So, what happened was, during lunchtime I drove to make an appointment with Mr Cormack the solicitor acting for the sale of the cottage. I am known to Mr Cormack as he is also the solicitor for Viewfield, i.e. Ella Munro. I introduced myself and mentioned the reason for my call. To my surprise the secretary was to give me the key of the cottage and could I bring it back the next day. All I could say to myself was how pleasant a feeling to be trusted so much. I took time to call at the local architect, Mr Ross whom I'd never met before but I knew where his office was. Although it was lunchtime he afforded me time to ask if he could meet me to have a look at the cottage. Next day was fine and during my lunchtime was best. We met at the cottage and there was not much to look at, and as we looked at each other there was only one comment, "it needs gutting out, the only value are the roofing slates". Mr Ross asked when I could call. I said Saturday morning eleven o'clock, and that was when we next met. For the first hour we spent no time on the subject matter only each other's war experiences, and on my side my POW travels. Eventually we got on to the cottage and its possibilities. Mr Ross' suggestion was a Mansard roof construction, which means the second floor and roof construction will be in timber as one unit. When asked, Mr Ross was able to give us an approximate cost, to lay before the Bank for possible staged borrowing, since as the new construction progresses it will increase the value of the property. I got to know the local slater on repair work to our farm, and accepted his estimate to replace the old slates, an item we did not have to buy.

The most expensive cost was the timber construction of the two sides of the upper floor and the timber frame of the roof. On completion of the joinery construction my Polish friend and I fixed the new type of felt slates to the exterior second floor timber boarding. A substantial saving on a first class job according to the architect. The complete lining of the inside of the outer wall with plasterboard by my friend and myself provided additional insulation for the building. The painting of the complete building inside I managed to do evenings and Saturdays. The electrical and plumbing installations were executed by local firms. It was left for me to make the garden a pleasure when people walked by. It was the first and only Mansard-roofed house in town. What we have achieved is all new, on the ground floor a kitchen and a living room, a small utility cupboard and a toilet. On the upper floor two bedrooms and a complete bathroom. The house was a novelty in town and had people turn their heads. Ehrentraut could not believe what we have achieved.

Two and a half years have now elapsed and Ella and Jack thought it was time to sell the farm. An advertisement in the Farming Journal had sooner than expected produced a serious interest resulting in a sale. It was a family from further north that needed all the living space. It resulted in the pay-off of the Mansfield staff. Having met the interested buyers it was made clear to me that they would very much like me to stay on and continue to live in the cottage. I promised to reply within three days. My evening check-up and short talk with Ella reached the stage when Ella mentioned the question of a house to retire to. There was time to think about it, and I said goodnight.

My mind was beginning to be laden with a number of questions and thoughts regarding the new situation at Mansfield and Viewfield in particular. There was an idea I had often thought about but would like to discuss with Ehrentraut sooner than later, and that's what we did. I was not surprised but still pleased with both of us agreeing. We would suggest to Ella that until she finds the right place for a new home, why not move into our newly re-built house in town. I myself would begin with help, to build our new home on one of the two sites I was given on Moss Road and continue to work at Viewfield as offered. Briefly, our conversation with Ella resulted in an immediate approval on both sides. For Ella it was a welcome satisfactory solution until at a later stage she could think about building at one of her plots also in Moss Road. For us it was an equally satisfactory outcome. I would start our new home in evenings and Saturdays, but never on a Sunday.

Within the year in 1961 there was great joy in our home when Ehrentraut delivered a most beautiful new and also lady family member, baptised Bernadett. The boys cherished their new sister. To crown the occasion my parents with Engelbert's help arrived in Scotland in time for the Baptism of our daughter Bernadett. For us there was a double joy as it was the first opportunity for my parents to witness where we lived. Equally important was to meet my 'adopted' mother Ella. By good fortune our parents arrived before Ella was moving out of the farmhouse, thus allowing our parents the use of Viewfield's bedroom.

'Family Lippok in the Viewfield garden 1961 from l to r Andreas, Mum Ehrentraut holding Bernadett, and Marcus'

Ella's pleasure to have finally met my parents was evident. How sad that they had not met David. Our parents were extremely interested in my new homeland here, I had a feeling they had doubts of us ever moving back to Germany. That did not make them sad in any way. Our mother counted it as a special blessing to have come at that moment of time with the birth of Bernadett. Dad was happy that he could be of valuable help at the progress of our new bungalow. We all regretted the time when their holiday came to an end, and we all went to see them off at the station, and glad to hear of their safe arrival back in Germany.

**"Final milking on the farm!"**

Two months before Mr Harry Miller took over Viewfield as the new owner, Ella moved into the new house down in town. Our own men moved her furniture with the farm tractor to the house. We all thought it was rather poignant to have done it that way. We now had to get used to a new way to visit Ella. With our Primary school only five minutes from Ella's new house, our boys soon discovered it was great fun to rush to see Ella during their lunchtime, much to Aunty Ella's pleasure.

**'Last year at Viewfield Farm, Tain.
The Lippok Family and farming duties!'**

To avoid boredom the following is an abridged summary of my last year at Viewfield. All my spare time was still required to bring the construction of our new bungalow on Moss Road to a successful end. As the building became water-tight and floored, there was no time wasted in rainy weather to complete the inside of the house. I had already learned the use of a square and plumb. During my two weeks holiday I was kept busy supplying the mason with the material to coat the outside. I still had help to complete the partitioning of the rooms. Painting took some time, as I have learned from the local painter. Ehrentraut was always at hand with the children after school and on Saturdays to sweep the floor for us. The local roof slater, a one-man business was happy for me to be his labourer, {often accusing me of rushing him}. The last job for me was to prepare the drive for the laying of tar macadam.

In 1965 towards the end of the three years with the Miller family on the farm, I had given my three weeks' notice to end my employment at Viewfield. Within two weeks we moved into our new home to which we all gave thanks that we had made it. With Ella's rent for the house in town Ehrentraut was able to keep the Bank Manager happy.

Karl Steppat, also a former POW and German trained mason and self-employed, who had helped to build our new house, urged me to join him, as he had enough work for the two of us. Knowing what I could do at joinery work I would go with him as self-employed at maximum rate. Ehrentraut and I had a discussion and she was happy for me to go with Karl who was pleased, and a deal was agreed. It meant that I would not be able to visit Ella so often in the evenings. Ehrentraut, now living in town did visit Ella when shopping. Ella on the other hand, took the occasional walk to our new house.

Karl had several contracts on the west coast. The disadvantage was a three hour drive each way. Karl had already been working there for a year. The system was to accept accommodation to stay overnight, work longer hours and travel home earlier on the Friday evening, leaving the Saturday free to do what was needed at home. Primarily the contracts in the west were the refurbishment of older dwellings, in the main new dormer toilets, bathrooms, kitchens and enlargement of windows, etc. The fact that we were German-born seemed to please the folks, expecting German quality craftsmanship! The kindness of the people had to be experienced.

Three years on, Ella and I had a long discussion regarding her wish to have her own house, built on her own plot, Ella having taken walks up every week to pay a visit at the same time seeing how our house was being built had impressed her. It became noticeable how Ella watched how our house was being built. I always knew how important it is to let your client see the progress, I never called it spying, but rather on the contrary, it was my pleasure for the client to see that we never took any short-cuts.

That is the only way to achieve trust and a good reputation. Ella wanted me to draw a sketch plan, which when shown her on site thought it matched what she had in mind. I drew up a presentable and acceptable drawing for the local building department and began to apply for the necessary approval. To my surprise within two weeks it was approved and ready for submission for planning permission. I do admit to a sense of pride. Karl himself was happy to do the masonry work with my assistance. As the work progressed Karl took on a labourer as I began to concentrate on the timber and joinery work. It was the beginning of my self-employment in the building trade. I had now bought sufficient material and prompt payments to open accounts with our material suppliers which made it simpler for Ehrentraut's book keeping.

It caused some hilarity when I insisted to address Ella in public as Miss Munro. I did feel more comfortable doing that in public and at our place of work. At least once a week Ella would walk up to visit Ehrentraut, and a look at the progress of her new house. One particular day we asked her to have a look at the front of her house, and was pleasantly surprised at the effect and the beauty of the granite stone on the front of her house. I was rather pleased to have suggested it. I also suggested and with the approval of 'Miss Munro' we constructed the roof space with sufficient space for a possible upper-floor, should such a requirement be needed in future, an item that increased the value of the house immediately. Allowing for the drying out time, Ella was ready to move in to her new home. It was my pleasure to move Ella at last into her own new home. There was a moment when I considered how far I had come since first I set foot on Viewfield as a young stranger, and here I was admiring my third built house.

The suggestion to expand the business I dismissed, I had neither the 'know how' nor the means for such an expansion. To me small is beautiful, sometimes, and I cherished the time in the evenings and weekends with Ehrentraut, especially since time is so precious to us. Already new interests were coming into the house, perhaps meeting in the street, or at the site of a contract. With my new mason George Tonberg at my side I felt supported and could depend on his knowledge. As things were we could look forward to a reasonably fruitful future. Twenty years on, our firm had progressed as we had hoped with work for us and the few people we employed. Retirement was still fifteen years away.

Sadly, unexpectedly, Ella, 'Aunty Ella' to our children, died suddenly in the late afternoon a week before Christmas in her 83$^{rd}$ year in 1978. Only that same morning before noon we called to talk about her annual Christmas Eve meal she had always cooked for us as a family. Ehrentraut and the three children spoke to her only hours before. How poignant that, just as her brother David almost twenty years previously, I should be the one who first saw Ella in her eternal sleep. I well remember her words when she moved into her new home which I built, saying to me "if I get ten years out of my lovely new home, I'll be happy". She managed at least that and a bit more. Contemplating the past, I found it an extraordinary thought that it should have been I who came to Viewfield farm just a week after their father passed away. It meant something to me to have been a part of Viewfield farm while in the hands of the Munro family. I look upon it as being one very important part of my history and my story.

Building and refurbishing homes was our 'bread and butter', the means by which we survived and paid the wages. A recent appraisal of mine gave us sufficient orders in hand, a good projection for the next few years. A minor downturn in house construction did not at our stage cause us much worry because we hoped that repair work would continue, and so it did. There is no pleasure in having to be forced to pay off good staff.

Unexpectedly, a letter arrived offering me the opportunity to purchase a plot of land between the new Academy and the new Tain bypass, to be named Cameron Gardens. It included a copy of the local authority planning permission for private development, including single storey hall, or meeting room and a church, but no commercial property. With the out-of-town developments of a new aluminium smelter, oil-rig construction, etc., our Catholic community had increased and the cry for a new church in Tain grew in strength. It was that which interested me, as much as the possibility of a private housing development. An appointment with the writer of the letter confirmed its authenticity.

That same evening I called on our parish priest, Fr. Malaney, with my offer to sell a plot to build a church, presbytery and car park. Father Malaney assured me he would contact the Bishop that evening,

and later rung to tell me of the Bishop's del[ight?] [...]
know the cost.

Within the year I had a completed my o[wn plans?] [...] of the proposed development at Cameron G[ardens?] [...] approval. After a minor alteration, I had th[e final?] drawing. Having completed our contracts v[...] our own development. First, mark out the [...] out the plots and get on with the site work [...] site, without which you would not get far, [...] important, one large site hut and a small one. [...] plumbing, electrical and roof-tiling.

It took Ehrentraut and me only one evening to agree that the nearest plot to the church, would be our retirement home, with the garden gate leading us to the church car park. It came as a totally unexpected surprise that we never left the site, as one house followed another, without having to seek more tradesmen. It was no surprise when half way through, it was time for George to 'polish' his tools for the last time. We did celebrate George's final working day, and had an enjoyable party. I was fortunate to have found a first class mason. Our own two boys, Andreas and Marcus were always available during university holidays, earning valuable pocket money and learning about building houses. This came in useful when they had their own homes. Our daughter Bernadett was not lagging behind and soon found local hotels were looking for her.

Finally, as the last few years have passed it was my turn to prepare for retirement, from the building trade business certainly, but as for doing nothing in retirement, no chance! Now there were different things to be done, a new 'career'.

I wanted to thank God and Scotland for everything they had done for me and the family. I wanted to give back something meaningful to the community. So I decided to become a Deacon in the Catholic Church. After 3 years of study I was ordained in St. Joseph's in Invergordon on 17th April 1997 by Bishop Mario Conti surrounded by the family, including my brother Engelbert, sister Ursula, and friends. Even after 18 years and at the age of 89, I continue to serve when needed.

# Epilogue

As Time and Tide wait for no man, so our project moved towards completion. Each home having its own attractive style, the overall effect of the development was appreciated. It was an equally great moment for our parishioners when the new church was consecrated – the first Catholic Church in Tain since the Reformation. The ruin of the old pre-Reformation church is still to be seen near the shore of the firth.

In recognition of the people's kindness and affection in the town and beyond, we as a family adopted British Citizenship. Always shown friendship and kindness, we tried to support events in the town. Much appreciated was the invitation to join the local choral and operatic group under the leadership of Lydia and Forbes Jackson and many others.

Of precious value also was the education our children received as they made their way through primary school and Tain Royal Academy, all three, Andreas, Marcus and Bernadett attending Scottish Universities.

Let it be our tribute to a country with a heart!

# Acknowledgements and Thanks

For their constant encouragement, assistance and persistence with the script, I wish to thank Marjorie E. Taylor and John Banks. Without their help there would have been no 'Story'.

For their assistance with miscellaneous computer work, I wish to thank Gillean and Andreas, Bernadett, and Antonio Bruno.

For their creativity in the design of the front cover, Tain Royal Academy Art Department, with Annia, Fionn, and Duncan, also Head of Department Andrew Douglas and Assistant Deborah Marshall.

For the photographic work and outside back cover design, Gordon Photography Ltd., Tain.

Inside back cover sketch of Silesia, by the author.

'Sketch map of Silesia (by the author)'